Ten Million Steps

M. J. Eberhart

Ten Million Steps

Nimblewill Nomad's Epic Ten-Month
Trek from the Florida Keys to Québec

M. J. Eberhart

Published by Menasha Ridge Press
Printed in the United States of America
Distributed by Publishers Group West
First trade paperback edition

Cover design by Travis Bryant
Sketches by Lisa Harvey
Text design by Annie Long
Cover photograph by Larry Duffy
Author photograph by Larry Duffy
Indexing by Galen Schroeder

Library of Congress Cataloging-in-Publication Data

Eberhart, M. J.
        Ten million steps: Nimblewill Nomad's epic 10-month
trek from the Florida Keys to Québec/By M. J. Eberhart.—
1st trade paperback ed.
            p. cm.
        Includes index.
        ISBN-13: 978-0-89732-979-8 (alk. paper)
        ISBN-10: 0-89732-979-1 (alk. paper)
        1. Hiking—Appalachian Trail. 2. Hiking—East (U.S.).
3. Backpacking—Appalachian Trail. 4. Backpacking—East
(U.S.). 5. Eberhart, M. J.—Diaries. I. Title.

GV199.42.A68.E24 2007
796.510974—dc22

                                                    2006037845

Menasha Ridge Press
P.O. Box 43673
Birmingham, Alabama 35243
www.menasharidge.com

Table of Contents

Dedication

ONE OF THE THINGS I THOUGHT ABOUT a lot during the "Odyssey of '98" — and especially when the day or the circumstance chose not to go so great — was the folks who kept returning to the trail, the people who hiked multiple times, folks such as Ed Garvey, *Grandma* Gatewood, Warren Doyle, Jr., Earl Shaffer, Leonard Adkins, and Albie Pokrob. It's certainly not a new thing. In the early days there were folks who did similar tramping around, folks such as William Bartram, John Muir, Henry Thoreau, Myron Avery, Benton MacKaye, and Percival Baxter. My thoughts were always about where I fit into that strange and mysterious puzzle. After months of mulling and as my journey grew long and I grew weary, I simply began hoping and praying that I could finish: "Just let me get it done, dear Lord, and I promise this will be it." But, as I continue to work on this book I can feel the pull of the trail down deep inside, tugging at my heartstrings and gnawing at my gut — for there does persist such a gentle but constant voice, "Come back — come back to the trail." The urge is so strong, and it is such an instinctive urge. Now I know why those before me returned . . . and I know now that I will also return.

During the last 1,000 miles of the "Odyssey of '98" I suffered dearly with my pitiful feet. I literally walked them into the ground. Afterwards, I knew — should I ever desire to return to the trail, I knew — that my hiking days were over. But my feet have been fixed! The surgery has been amazingly successful. My feet feel great again . . . and they want to go! Oh yes, I'll be back out there again. Perhaps, as you read this, I'm back on the trail, for once it gets in your blood, it's there for good and you can't get rid of it, no matter what. It circulates and becomes part of your whole being—forever.

So, to all those who have ever ventured forth, who have ever shouldered a backpack, I dedicate this book. For all who have tried to put their story in writing, to tell of their adventure and the miracle of it, is this book dedicated. And to that one . . . that one weary soul who gained more understanding for the grand mystery of it all, and therein received more wisdom than all the rest of us—but who never whispered a word—is this book dedicated. And thank you, my dear friends, whose friendship I know and now cherish and who've made my miracle, the "Odyssey of '98," such an incredible part of the waning years of this old man's life—to you is this book dedicated. And to those of you dear friends, those whose names I do not know but who I know nonetheless, who are on that grand list in my heart, is this book dedicated. To all dear hearts of that cold, lonesome track, with that fire in your gut, and that faraway not-comin'-back glint in your eye, is this book dedicated. To all of you known to be kindred, many who have already climbed that grand treadway to the sky: The Muirs, the Thoreaus, the Bartrams, the Baxters, the MacKayes, the Averys, the Gatewoods, the Garveys, the Olsons, the Fletchers, the Rutstrums, the Shaffers, the Doyles, the Stoltzs, the Jenkinses, the Jardines, the Brills, the Deedses, the Marets, the Wadnesses, the Muesers, the Luxenbergs, the Selburgs, the Talones, the Hobsons, and the Soules . . . yes dear souls, to each and every one of you, to all so blessed with the bountiful riches of this clan, is this book dedicated.

As you read the account of all the great folks it has been my good fortune to meet along the trail, many with whom I have hiked, you must wonder as to their fate. And so I tell you it is my joy to remain in contact with many of them—near 1,000 in my database at this writing—but at the same time and alas, I must tell you that many dear friends have gone from me, friends that I will neither see nor hear from ever again. And so, to each and every one, to all of them, is this book dedicated.

Written and transcribed this first day of January in the year of our Lord, 2000.

LAND OF THE FREE

Here's to all hearts of that cold, lonesome track,
To the life of the wanderlust . . . free.
To all who have gone and have never come back,
Here's a tribute to you and to me.

With our feet in the dirt we're the grit of the earth,
Heads a-ridin' the heavens o'erhead.
And they won't find a nickel of value or worth,
When our fortunes are tallied and read.

But no richer clan has there ever been known,
Since the times of all ruin and wrack,
Than those of us lost to the dust outward blown,
Who have gone and have never come back.

[N. Nomad]

Foreword

By Larry Luxenberg, author of *Walking the Appalachian Trail*

THERE IS A WISDOM GAINED ONLY BY MILES. After months and miles on the trail, a hiker comes to understand certain things about himself and the trail. And those answers stay with a hiker for the rest of his life. There are two kinds of people: those who can understand the logic of a long-distance hike and those who cannot. The latter are far more numerous. But for those few adventurers, it can be a life-changing experience. Priorities come into focus and they are more likely to think "why" than "why not." They learn to accept adversity and to take pleasure in little things. When one has longed for a garbage can, a flush toilet, a full belly, and dry socks, he takes few wonders of the world for granted. Any man who walks the nearly 4,400 miles from Key West to Cap Gaspé must be comfortable with himself. Alone with his thoughts for months on end, there's no place to hide. *Nimblewill Nomad*, however, is a rare adventurer who connects with all kinds of people.

    When we chose *Nimblewill Nomad* as a speaker at the 1999 Appalachian Long Distance Hikers Association Gathering, we made only one mistake—we put him into too small a room. I stood and sat in the hall outside with several dozen others as *Nimblewill Nomad* began his account. "They say a picture is worth a thousand words. I don't have any pictures, so here's the thousand words." By the end of the talk, all of us felt we'd been along on a wonderful trip. Imagine a walk that begins in Key West, home to the legend of Hemingway and a cast of a thousand characters. Walking a thousand miles through Florida, seeing alligators close up in the swamp. Continuing on through the roads and mountains of Alabama along the Pinhoti Trail. And then, mid-adventure, hiking along the venerable Appalachian Trail. Then continuing on the new, beautiful, and wild International Appalachian Trail in Maine and Canada, a testament to Dick Anderson, who has pulled off the impossible in a remarkably short time. Finally, arriving at the breathtaking Cliffs of Forillon at the Gulf of St. Lawrence. It is a trip I will likely never take, but I thank *Nimblewill Nomad* for sharing it with me.

Few adventurers have been as ambitious as *Nimblewill Nomad* . . . ambitious in the sense that he's put one foot in front of the other longer than almost anyone who's ever laced on a pair of hiking boots. As the second person to hike the length of the eastern United States and on to Cap Gaspé, he's walked from alligator country to the home of the moose and caribou. Many times I've driven a quarter that length with my family and we find that exhausting. Even a flight that long is tiring. Walking 4,400 miles at a stretch—ten million steps—over eleven months is beyond the reckoning of even most long-distance hikers. At that length, the rhythms of a long-distance hike take over. Free from the fetters of everyday life, a person must listen to his own thoughts. And many find they like what they hear.

When I invited *Nimblewill Nomad* to stay at my home on his next trip, he told me, "I've always heard that it's better to give than to receive, but someone has to receive and I've learned to do it." The trail has had a large impact on *Nimblewill Nomad*'s life, and those lessons and his words have had an impact on me. As he finishes this book, *Nimblewill Nomad* plans to take to the trail again, this time to make the first southbound transit of the entire Appalachian Mountain chain and then some. The long-distance hiking community is a small, tightly knit group of no more than five to ten thousand people. Of these certainly no more than five hundred have done more than one long-distance trail—at least 2,000 miles. And of these hundreds, maybe a few dozen are truly hard core. In this book, *Nimblewill Nomad* poses the question of why go on a long-distance hike. I don't think anyone has given an entirely satisfactory answer. But having asked literally hundreds of hikers that question, the best I can do is this: Most people come to the trail because of the challenge and to spend a long time close to the wonders of nature. But they soon find they've found a home in the trail community. The bonds of friendship, the freewheeling lifestyle, and the alternation of great misery and the exhilaration of discoveries along the trail lead one to feel fully alive. No one captures that sense better than *Nimblewill Nomad,* one of the truly hard core. He has no pictures, but what I savor are the words. Happy hiking, my friends.

About the Author

BEST KNOWN BY HIS TRAIL NAME, *Nimblewill Nomad*, M. J. Eberhart, the son of a country doctor, grew up in a little village in the Ozark Highlands of Missouri. He's an Armed Forces veteran. After serving, he settled in as the senior practitioner in a busy three-doctor optometric practice in Florida. He's divorced, has two sons, Jay and Jon, and two dear granddaughters, Jillian Amber (Jay and Theresa) and Mia Simone (Jon and Terri). He now resides near his childhood home with his schoolmate and sweetheart, Dwinda.

Eb, as most off-trail friends know him, began hiking and back-packing in the early '80s. Always an avid outdoorsman, now retired, he's making up for lost time after being cooped up in examination rooms with no windows for nearly 30 years.

Preface
to the paperback edition

HIGH ON *Nimblewill Nomad*'s "ONE OF THESE DAYS" LIST — for many years — existed an ultra-long-distance backpacking trek. So inevitably, in January of 1998, deep in the Florida Everglades, the old *Nomad* shouldered his pack and headed north on a journey that would ultimately lead him across 16 states and 2 Canadian provinces, clear to the spectacular Cliffs of Forillon, Québec, o'er a grand amalgam of trails now known collectively as the Eastern Continental Trail.

That journey, "Odyssey '98," was daily recorded by *Nimblewill Nomad* in lyrical, narrative journal entries. They proved to be powerful, intensely honest, emotional human accounts. Over time, *Nomad* patiently polished and shaped them into the popular book *Ten Million Steps*. That epic limited-edition hardback, published by *Nimblewill* in 2000, has since become a classic in outdoor lore and epic adventure and is sought after and prized by collectors.

Now, through the cooperative effort of *Nimblewill Nomad* and Menasha Ridge Press, a highly respected publisher of many fun and interesting books (especially for folks who seek out and enjoy outdoor adventure), comes this first-edition paperback of *Ten Million Steps*. You'll find it a long, but exciting, spirit-filled journey — enjoy!

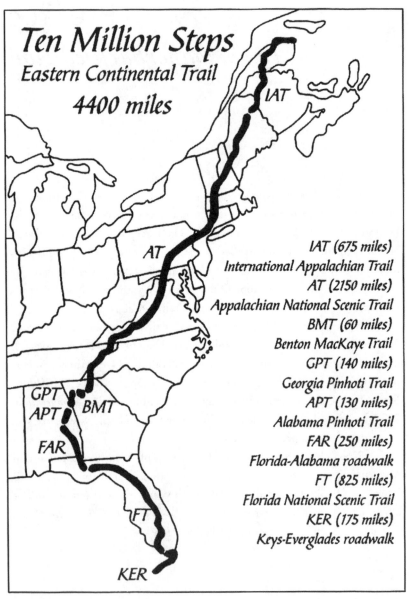

Ten Million Steps
Eastern Continental Trail
4400 miles

IAT

AT

GPT
APT   BMT

FAR

FT

KER

IAT (675 miles)
International Appalachian Trail
AT (2150 miles)
Appalachian National Scenic Trail
BMT (60 miles)
Benton MacKaye Trail
GPT (140 miles)
Georgia Pinhoti Trail
APT (130 miles)
Alabama Pinhoti Trail
FAR (250 miles)
Florida-Alabama roadwalk
FT (825 miles)
Florida National Scenic Trail
KER (175 miles)
Keys-Everglades roadwalk

Map courtesy of Jim Damico

Go to **www.nimblewillnomad.com** to see an updated map.

Ten Million Steps

M. J. Eberhart

Introduction

TEN MONTHS OF JOURNAL ENTRIES, NEAR 300 DAYS. "A bit much," you say? Yes, it probably is a bit much. But the design is to offer the reader just a glimmer into the staggering and incomprehensible length of this odyssey, the grand extent of it. For even though I've done it, I cannot believe it. Every day wasn't and certainly couldn't have been a blockbuster day. I could not have endured that. But the days of just hammering out the miles, just trudging them through, played a very big part in the mix and final texture of this story, of the length and incredible magnitude of it. I have attempted to be merciful to the reader on those occasions where there was little to say by simply not saying much. I've told friends this book is a compendium of short stories, 297 of them, all woven and bound neatly together by the threads of love—love for the trail, love for the grand and glorious bounty of natural wonders that God bestowed on those of us so blessed to live on this great continent called North America. And finally, the love-nurtured joy and good fortune to see, to truly see, life in a way only a trek of this magnitude could ever possibly offer up. And the strongest of all threads? Ah, that elusive search for peace, blessed peace . . . for the "Odyssey of '98" truly was a journey for the soul.

As I hiked north through Florida and Alabama, I thought the driving force that brought me to the trail and propelled me along was simply the wanderlust that dwells down deep in all of us, but as I journeyed north on the AT, and especially as I hiked alone again on the SIA/IAT into Canada, I knew that wanderlust had very little to do with it. The real reason? The answer is probably not that surprising. It's a journey that we all depart on at some point in our lives, quite often as in my case, in total desperation. And that journey? Well, folks, it was a journey in search for peace—true peace. For when I departed on the Florida National Scenic Trail on New Year's Day 1998, I was carrying an incredible burden—not the pack that weighed heavy on my back, but a burden so much more heavy on my heart and on my mind. It wasn't until I could truly look at myself, until I could overcome the anguish and revulsion of facing myself as a person; not till then could I see these burdens for what they were . . . and finally deal with them.

A hike the magnitude of trekking the Appalachian Trail, or indeed a distance over twice that on the Eastern Continental Trail challenges the individual on three separate planes. Each plane represents a specific journey, separate in itself, yet dependent and intricately and intimately interwoven with the other two. I have chosen to name these journeys collectively after three travelers from a far off place—from another time. They are the "Three Wise Men." Success as a long-distance hiker is measured by one's ability to excel in at least two of these three, the first two being required and the third elective. And these journeys? They are the "Physical Journey," the "Mental Journey", and the "Spiritual Journey." The Physical is the first and easiest to master, the Mental next, and the Spiritual is the last and most challenging. But, you ask, "Aren't these much the same as the journeys we all set out on and struggle with each and every day of our lives?" Ah! Indeed they are, but the truly successful long-distance backpacker takes each of these three incredible journeys to the wall . . . to their ultimate limits.

Fully eight out of ten who fail as long-distance hikers fail not because of the physical challenge, but as a result of the mental one. Isn't this indeed an interesting statistic? For wouldn't we all conclude that the physical demand of lugging a thirty- to fifty-pound pack over the mountains for thousands of miles—wouldn't we agree that this grueling ordeal would most certainly be the ultimate challenge? Oh, but it is not! The question really boils down to this: How many of us can honestly say that we have ever really dealt squarely with who and what we truly are as a person? When we start this analysis in this light, it can become very uncomfortable very fast! However, with all the diversions and distractions that surround us in the "real world," along with those that we so easily create from day to day, we are able to avoid these painful thought processes. But on the trail, mile after day after month, where these diversions do not exist, eventually all the masks, all the facades, all the little games we play get stripped away and we come face to face with . . . ourselves!

The third journey is the most rewarding of all. As we get to know the first of the Three Wise Men and can handle the seemingly endless miles of the daily grind that make up the Physical Journey, and as we open to ourselves and can truly deal with who and what we are as individuals, comfortably trekking along with the second of the Three Wise Men on our Mental Journey, then comes the opportunity to explore the incredible wonders of life all around and deep within. The Spiritual Journey begins by crossing a very high and narrow bridge, the search for which eludes most all of us all our lives. For not until we have mastered the Mental Journey can we possibly hope to find, much less take, that first step onto this narrow bridge. Of the few who have found this bridge, fewer have chosen to cross. For you see, suspended between the Mental Journey and the Spiritual Journey, there is this obstacle, a sky-bound span, which at first appears to lead to dizzying and impassable heights. This obstacle is called "The Bridge of Emotions" or simply the "Bridge."

To tackle this obstacle, should we choose to, involves our ability to fully extricate ourselves from that lofty ego-centered pedestal whereon we have become firmly ensconced, an established domain unto ourselves which we most assuredly believe was bestowed as a divine gift! We would first have come square up with this while struggling along on our Mental Journey. This task, wrestling with our ego, may take some time, but once it is accomplished,we're ready to take that first step onto the Bridge. And taking that first step was indeed an emotional experience for me—the most humbling in my life! For once on the Bridge, and thenceforth, do I now wear my heart on my sleeve, vulnerability inconceivable to most. But on the Bridge it's easy, perfectly natural. In the journey across the Bridge comes then one's ability to begin to master the virtues of patience, compassion, and understanding. Once across, we meet the third of the Three Wise Men, and here we are all together for that glorious and wonderful beginning of our Spiritual Journey. Opens now the wide and endless horizon only seen from this perspective. And this vantage? This vantage is called "Wisdom." Wisdom comes through faith and trust . . . through a "Trust." And this Trust is administered by God.

Onto the trail in the Everglades, I lugged a pack of incredible burdens. They were the burdens of anger, bitterness, contempt, despair, envy, fear, greed, hatred, jealousy, resentment, and vain pride. There's a word for most every letter in the alphabet to describe some form of burden. And I carried them all! But as I journeyed north with the second of the Three Wise Men, a change began to occur, a very subtle change, but a change nonetheless. For as I struggled along on my Mental Journey, lugging this incredible load, it became painfully evident to me that I had missed the mark on living, truly living, in my near 60 years on this earth—not a very comforting revelation! And as I began to unravel all of this, it was then I decided to change my life . . . and it was then I met the last of the Three Wise Men, and it was then that I set forth on my Spiritual Journey. From that moment on, I could sense that these burdens were slowly dissipating, leaving my mind and my heart—as if with each step (and it is estimated that there were ten million steps), these burdens were slowly but surely being drained from my body, down to the treadway beneath my feet and onto the path behind me. And that indeed is just as it happened, for there those burdens lie today and there those burdens will remain . . . forever!

Ah, yes. A desperate search for Peace. And how did old *Nomad* do on his journey with the Three Wise Men? Did he succeed, as did they, in their journey toward that perfect light? Well, please read along and, oh yes, if you would: When next you see the countenance of this old man, look in, and pray tell you see there the radiance of a man at Peace—at Peace with the world, at Peace with himself, and at Peace with God!

[N. Nomad]

Chapter 1
Florida National Scenic Trail

THURSDAY January 1, 1998
TRAIL DAY 1 ✦ TRAIL MILE 8
LOCATION US 41, Tamiami Trail, Oasis Ranger Station
Picnic Area, Florida

JON, MY YOUNGEST SON, HAS DRIVEN ME HERE to the southern Florida National Scenic Trail (FT) terminus at Loop Road, about 30 miles west of Miami. This trail certainly doesn't lure you in. We stand and look at it: six to ten inches of water over silt-covered porous limestone. The trail begins here just off the shoulder of the road. We talk about whether this is really what I want to do. Jon was one of only a handful of people who knew my plan to attempt an incredible journey all the way to Mt. Katahdin by foot, hoping, God willing, to be there sometime in late September or early October, a full nine to ten months on the trail. Here we linger and talk about it some more. Then finally, fighting tears, Jon and I hug and I step into it. Fifty yards later I stop for the last time, turn, and wave goodbye to Jon.

The next eight hours are impossible to describe. I've never hiked continually through anything even remotely like this. It would compare somewhat, I suppose, to going to the beach, wading out until you're up to somewhere between your knees and hips in it, thence to turn and thrash along with it—the only difference being the fact that no tall grass, brush, or invisible sharp-edged, leg-swallowing holes are there to contend with along the beach. This season has been the wettest South Florida has seen since 1940. The record was broken before the beginning of the fourth week in December. Last September, I was told, had been the wettest on record. El Niño was certainly making his mark. Nina Dupuy, FT 1 section leader, had told me the trail was impassable and that it was technically closed. FT 1 runs some 38 miles through the Everglades, beginning near the Miccosukee Indian Reservation in the Big Cypress National Preserve and proceeding basically north on a beeline to Alligator Alley. I did not know, but certainly I should have suspected, that I was entering some of the most difficult, nerve-racking, and dangerous treadway that I would encounter during the entire "Odyssey of '98."

New flagging leading to the nearly flooded old tramway dike saves me getting lost. I encounter a really scary section at one of the tramway cuts. There are no bridges at these cuts, and at this particular one, the tannic, coffee-colored water is blasting through with boiling, rolling force. There is no way around, just through! An old blowdown snag is lodged in the cut blocking my passage. As I grope to get through the tangle, I lose my balance. I have been taught and have read in most every book I've ever picked up on hiking and backpacking that the proper technique in negotiating turbulent water is to release your hip belt and sternum strap and loosen your ladder straps. This allows quick exit from your pack should you stumble or get swept down, time being of the essence for survival. This rule I dutifully follow before entering the turbulence. What is not addressed in this rule is how the hell you're supposed to *continue* surviving without your pack! As I grab for a limb on the old snag, it breaks and I lurch into the driving torrent. I am jerked and thrown violently and my pack is thrust away from me into the flush. It is fortunate that I had not cut the excess tail from my hip-belt strap, having forgotten that task in the last hectic minutes of preparation. As I lunge for it, I am able to clutch this trailing bit of pack stern as we both are swept swiftly along. With luck, I am able to grab other flood tangle and get stopped. My heart is pounding in my throat and my head is spinning. I have no idea how long I cling here heaving my nervously eaten breakfast, but it is a long time. Had I cinched my ladder and sternum straps and my hip belt snugly, this whole life-threatening ordeal would never have happened. Folks who camel full expedition loads on their backs, as most backpackers are inclined to do, may need to heed this rule. It does not, however, apply to me. So now I am immediately set full with anguish and frustration in realizing that I must reassess all the other rules I've ever learned.

Dragging mud, water, and grass step after step, mile after mile, totally saps me. I cannot recall not being able to maintain at least a two-mile-per-hour pace. Here, I'm hard-put to make just one. I hadn't considered this possible consequence in planning my itinerary for this first day, the intent being to hike the eight or so miles to Tamiami Trail and high ground at Oasis Ranger Station. Toward evening, as the shadows lengthen and the patchy, bleached blazes become increasingly more difficult to follow, and as the treadway keeps gradually but steadily submerging until I'm up to nearly my hips in it, I come to realize that there is no way I am going to get out of here before dark descends. I become terror-struck as the hot, humid, heavy air of the day drifts and gives way to the cold chill of the evening emerging from the shadows. I hear the sounds of the night beginning and I tremble with fear. I have lost the trail, what little there is of it, along with the occasional coin-sized remnants of blazing. I stumble through the cypress knees, the tangle and the brush. I am rushing now, pell-mell, totally exhausted. I know not in what direction or to where I am racing. As I pause, clinging to one of the gadzillion cypress trees, gasping for air, I realize that if I cannot quickly compose myself and get my wits about me, that this journey is going to be over before it ever begins. As my chest quits heaving and my heart quits drumming in my ears, I am able to slowly coax myself into analyzing my predicament with some degree of rational judgment. I know that Tamiami Trail runs east and west somewhere north of me and if I head in that general direction, I will eventually reach there. That is, if I don't end up going in clear over my head in a gator hole. I begin to tremble again. "Calm down, calm down, if you must stay out here all night it won't be all that bad," I try reassuring myself. As I hang my pack on a broken cypress limb, I realize this is the first time it's been off my back, save the tramway incident, since I shouldered it from Jon's tailgate. I get out my flashlight, my compass, and a Snickers bar for a much-needed boost of energy. The water bottle I'm carrying in my belt pouch is empty; so it is that I break one of my cardinal rules on my very first day. But has not one of my rules already forsaken me? So what the heck, I dunk my empty water bottle into the murky sink that surrounds me and drink my fill!

With much trepidation I hoist my pack, turn my flashlight on, and head out on compass bearing 360. The depth of the murk and slosh I'm pushing along climbs up and down my legs but stays below my belt as I stumble along in the dark. Nighttime in the swamp is very alien, eerie, and forbidding. Grotesque shadows cast by my little flashlight beam and the night sounds of the swamp conjure up images as horrifying as the boogeyman, who most surely lurked under my childhood bed. I grope from tree to tree to keep from going down as I trip over the submerged cypress knees. I know that a great distance yet remains to Tamiami Trail, yet it seems as though dark has become nearly eternal.

For the longest while, I think I am seeing things, but I finally realize that way out somewhere ahead blinking in and out and playing hide and seek through the endless maze of cypress trees—there's a faint light! At first its presence is fleeting. I can see it only momentarily, then it's gone. Even when I stop, I cannot keep its presence fixed. But it is there, and as it becomes more visible I abandon my compass bearing and head straight for it. It is yet another hour, as this elusive light seems to retreat with each unsteady step I take, until finally the night lights at Oasis, which have been my land beacon, guide me as I stumble onto the roadway at Tamiami Trail. I am totally exhausted, in a lather and covered with mud, but thankful to be out of it. I drag myself to the picnic benches over by the public telephone. It is 9:00 p.m.and there's no one here at Oasis Ranger Station. No cars have passed since I emerged from the bowels of the earth. I set up my little tent and try to dry myself off before rolling in.

So ends this incredible first day of a planned odyssey that I'm now unsure will ever come to pass. If what I've somehow managed to endure and survive today is any indication of what's ahead, what's really in store for me, I know I'll never be up to it. But I am too tired now, too exhausted to care, and I'm immediately in dreamland as I fall into deep, restful sleep.

"A journey of a thousand miles begins with the first step."

[Chinese Proverb]

FRIDAY January 2, 1998
TRAIL DAY 2 ✦ TRAIL MILE 20
LOCATION Lost Dog Prairie SE, Cabbage/Pine Hammock

I'M UP, OUT OF MY TENT, AND MOVING AROUND at first light, a little stiff but otherwise feeling good. I think my feet will become a problem before I'm out of the Everglades. From the time I stepped into it yesterday until I emerged here at Tamiami Trail, my feet were constantly submerged. The Swiss-cheese limestone and the cypress knees, invisible below the gumbo-like silt, make every step a new adventure. The doggies are definitely in for a pounding. I also have a hunch that having all of my clothing and everything in my pack totally soaked all the time may also take a little getting used to, and I haven't hit the rain yet!

There was very little traffic during the night, and only an occasional vehicle breaks the morning silence. A chain-link fence encloses a small drainage pond only a few feet from the little picnic area where I pitched. I glance over that way while whipping together a peanut-butter sandwich for breakfast and I quickly see the reason for the fence. Gators! They're no more than 20 feet away from where I bedded down. Over by the public telephone is a small pedestal with a trail register. I head over to sign in/out and see who's been through. What a wonderful and uplifting surprise to find a note at the bottom of the register page from Jon. He had gone west on Loop Road yesterday to where it loops back to Tamiami Trail and then came back east to stop at Oasis on his way to Miami. He knew I'd be coming through here! His note: "Good luck Pop! Love ya, Jon." The only other entries from the recent past were a couple of folks headed north for Seven-Mile Camp.

My itinerary shows this being a 16.4-mile day into Thirteen-Mile Camp. That distance would be a piece of cake almost anywhere else. But I know as I look at my map that there is no way to make this distance. A short jag to the left around the landing strip and I'm right back in it again. It doesn't take much slogging this morning until I'm totally exhausted. As I pass a little patch of dry ground between two pine trees, I pull off.

I've got a little homemade hobo "handy dandy" wood-burning cookstove, and I get it out, break off some dry palm fronds, and fire it up for some hot lunch. I figure I'd better have my warm meal now, as this may be the last high ground I see all day. Well, I think to myself, this odyssey isn't starting out quite the way I envisioned. During the next few minutes I've got enough excitement on my hands to last me the entire journey. With noodles cooking nicely on my little stove I move off a short distance to filter some water. When I return, my noodles aren't the only thing cooking. The little patch of grass around my stove is cooking and my pack, which I've laid right next to it, is also cooking! When nylon burns you've got a very hot and dangerous fire on your hands . . . literally on your hands. As I slap in desperation at the flames I get the melting, burning nylon all over me. I give my pack a kick into the water and manage to douse my hands at the same time. I stomp at the grass fire and in the process my stove, pot, noodles, and all go flying into the Everglades! As I watch my stove go down in flames on one side of the island, I turn to see my pack pop back up on the other side, belching black billows of smoke. I slog back over there and give it a stomp back under as it hisses and belches more black smoke at me. I then drag myself, coughing and gasping, back onto the charred patch of ground, collapse against the pine tree, and . . . cry.

I don't know how long I sit here with my head stuck between my knees, sobbing uncontrollably, but I know it's a good while longer than I hung on in the backwash of the flood throwing up yesterday. I finally manage to compose myself, but not before my eyes are nearly swollen shut. I begin the damage control check as I look at my hands. Miraculously, they're okay! Black carbon patches of nylon are vulcanized to my fingers and both my palms but there is no pain or redness. I go to where the noodles are bobbing in the water and retrieve my pot and stove. Back again to the other side of the island, I drag my pitifully charred and waterlogged (but still smoldering) pack back to the equally charred ground. I am soaked and covered with soot. I'm afraid to even look at this mess. I start sobbing again as I flip it over with my foot to see what's left of the other side.

I find the right shoulder pad completely gone and the ladder strap burned through, save a few threads. My sleeping bag stuff-sack is destroyed, and my sleeping bag is little more than a black, gooey char the consistency of Play-Doh. I don't need to unzip my pack to get in it anymore; there's a saucer-sized hole in the right top. A garbage bag wadded in the top of my pack has saved most of the contents. I've lost a pair of wool socks, and I'll no longer be able to be seen in public with my other pair of nylon pants. There's enough left of the burned ladder strap to hold the weight of the pack. I cut up what's left of the wool socks and manage to construct a halfway-functional shoulder pad. I pull out another garbage bag, shove what's left of my sleeping bag into it, shoulder the whole pitiful mess, point the compass back at 360, and head north.

I run into three army fellows near Barnes Strand in full (face) camo, and at Seven-Mile Camp (SMC) I meet Gary and his son and friend. Gary has been hiking into SMC for the past 20 years and claims he's never seen it this wet. I manage to get no farther today than the first northwest leg near Lost Dog Prairie. I'm lucky to find dry ground on the southern tip of a small pine island. The entire day, save a few hundred yards, has been in 12 to 18 inches of water and mud. What an unbelievable day. I am so thankful that I am able to go on.

> *"If you are ready to leave father and mother and brother and sister, and wife and child and friends, and never see them again . . . then you are ready for a walk."*
>
> [Henry David Thoreau]

SATURDAY January 3, 1998
TRAIL DAY 3 ✦ TRAIL MILE 32
LOCATION Old Truck Island

IT TOOK ME OVER AN HOUR LAST NIGHT, in the light of my campfire, to salvage what was left of my pitiful sleeping bag. It *was* a synthetic bag, which is basically all nylon. The bag's outer fabric and the filament comprising the loft were hopelessly stir-fried together. I used my pocketknife to try and strip away the countless lumps and webs of homogenized goo and petrified char. When I finally completed the bagectomy, I seriously considered throwing the whole sad mess into the fire to save it any further misery and embarrassment. But I needed the dear, battered veteran to keep me warm last night, as the temperature really plummeted once the sun went down. By covering my sleeping pad with my towel and my clothing, and by using the remains of my sleeping bag as a blanket, I was able to stay warm and I slept in reasonable comfort. My emergency pack repairs seem to be working fairly well, and by making do with what's left of my equipment, I'll be able to stay on the trail until it's more convenient to get to an outfitter.

I'm up at dawn this morning. Everything I have is soaking wet. I'm trying very hard, but I don't know if I'll get used to this! Cold, cold wet socks. Cold, cold wet boots! My feet are really shriveled up but otherwise they seem okay. I'm off to a clear sunny morning to continue the slog. With water everywhere, there is no treadway to be seen and I'm almost constantly off the trail. By zigging and zagging I am able to keep picking up the little specks of faded orange paint and the small tatters of bleached flagging. But I get lost many times and must turn and retrace my steps through the wake. Just north of an old sagging and rusted fenceline, I enter another really scary area. The water and mud keep getting deeper and deeper, and the cover is changing from dwarf cypress to the taller and much larger bald cypress. Once inside this dark, dungeon-like place, a lagoon opens, covered with broadleaf waterplants, a sure sign of deeper water. I'm already in up to my hips. Surely I must have missed a turn. Backtracking a short distance, I see a waving bleached remnant of flagging. I look and look in every direction, but the little strip of flagging is the last trailmarker I find. The patchy blazes have led me right into this God-forbidden place, and looking at the compass bearing I've been running, it appears I must go through.

So, with much doubt and hesitancy, I head on in. I'm immediately up to my waist in the murk and slime, and my pack is submerging. Having my pack in the water is very unnerving. There is an incredible jumble of submerged logs, brush, and cypress knees. I keep searching for another paint speck or a little strip of flagging, but there is none. Surely I am lost. I hear a loud splash on the far side of the lagoon. What should I do? I struggle to keep my wits about me. I look again at my compass. I've been running a pretty steady bearing just off north all morning, so I decide to stick with it. The water is holding at my hips and I'm getting through.

I must concentrate and take much precaution with each step to keep from going down, as the footing is treacherous. The eerie lagoon and the water plants finally give back to closely ganged cypress. There is no evidence of a path through here anywhere, and there still are no trail markings. Finally the bald cypress thins out and my pack begins lifting out of the murk as I emerge from the bog. I am feeling a little less anxious now, but I've been running totally on fear for the last two days and it's really starting to take a strain. Fear, it seems, has become my constant companion. I begin zigzagging again in an attempt to find the trail and as I look back . . . there it is! A small speck of orange paint. I heave a great sigh of relief. Thank you, Lord, I've made it through and I'm back on the trail!

The remainder of the day is uneventful, and I settle into enduring the monotony of the pulsing sounds of water as I push rhythmically into it. By evening, I arrive at a place that I have dubbed "Old Truck Island." The little island/oasis isn't ten yards across, but it's a mountain in the muck, towering over two feet. One hundred yards northeast of this little island lie the remains of an old truck, resting on its back in very ungraceful fashion as it attempts to endure the ravages of time. The old truck is noted in the trail mileage data and fixes my position at mile marker 32. In all this day I have covered just 12 miles. As the cool of the evening descends, the mosquitoes arrive in waves. These critters usually cause me little annoyance, but with my nerves totally uncoiled, I have no tolerance for them. I pitch my tent quickly and roll in. It is my plan to venture out later, get a small cooking fire going, and have a warm meal . . . but I never make it.

> *The "Odyssey" begins,*
> *There'll be no turning back.*
> *Lord, make a better man of me,*
> *Before I end this trek.*
>
> [N. Nomad]

I AM UP AT DAWN. The mosquitoes have launched a full squadron to descend on me as soon as I emerge from my little Slumberjack. It appears another fine day is shaping weather-wise. I break camp and head on north without breakfast to escape the relentless air attack. In a short while I find a small cabbage palm island and pull off to study my maps and trail data and to have some breakfast. The day is warming nicely and the mosquito air squadron has returned to base. I decide to try and make the remaining 6 miles to Alligator Alley plus the 11.5 miles to Kissimmee Billie Swamp Safari before dark.

I am in water to my knees all morning, dragging oatmeal-like silt and grass the whole way. The flagging and blazing are easier to follow and I am off-trail much less. I hit the fence at the I-75 rest stop around 1:00 p.m.—literally hit the fence. It is a chain-link barricade ten feet high. The gate, which provided passage before Alligator Alley became limited access, is gone, the hole wired shut. Old blazes still remain on the tree on the other side. The rest area is about 500 yards to the west, and the fence fortification appears to continue all the way around it with no way through. I head east along the fence and find an open gate that provides access to the woodsroad I was hiking earlier in the morning. I am able to pass through the fence onto the paved service road. Here I heave a long sigh of relief. I have successfully made it through FT 1. Nina Dupuy, I thank you, my dear friend. You and all the folks with the Big Cypress Chapter of the Florida Trail Association (FTA) have made a tremendous effort to get this trail through the Everglades. It just appears to me an impossible task.

I am tempted to take a break, get a pop and some snacks at the rest area, and make a few phone calls, but there are many miles ahead of me today, so I head for the break in the fence on the north side of the interstate. I will be hiking most of the remainder of the day across lands of the Seminole Indian Nation, only the second person to do so. The trail here is now opening up, thanks to Ken Carpenter and the folks with the Seminole

Chapter of the FTA. Rick *Vagabond* Guhsé was the first to hike this section only a few months ago, and he has provided maps and data to get me through. Steve Bowers with the Seminole Nation has granted me permission to cross the reservation. It seems my feet survived the endless submersion with little consequence, but to my dismay, as I follow the canal spoilbank road north, I haven't gone a mile with dry feet, dry socks, and dry shoes until I feel hot spots developing everywhere. I pull over and unload on an old blowdown beside the canal. It is here I meet one of nature's little delinquent troublemakers . . . sandspurs! I sit square on one, the experience of which, if duplicated and studied under laboratory conditions, would most assuredly unlock the secret to solving the Alzheimer's riddle, for this is definitely an experience that will never be forgotten! My laces are also full of the natty little spike balls. It's an impossible task to eject them without becoming totally impaled. These little nasties, I truly believe, are one of the most aggravating of nature's little bad guys.

My premonition about my feet has come to pass. The swamp water has basically melted my skin. As long as my feet remained in the cool water, friction was not a problem. But the tough skin and calluses that have developed over the years now just peel right off! Fortunately I have a pair of polypro liners, so I dust my feet good with medicated powder and put on the double socks. Another 5 miles and I am suffering again. I drop my pack and remove my shoes once more to find my feet covered with blisters. Now I almost wish to be back in the muck, but I know that I must adapt my feet to this dry, hot environment. So, I pop the blisters, adhesive-tape my toes, and duct-tape my heels and Achilles. I eliminate the liner socks and find that I do better with just the wool rags. It has been such a joy to be able to move out and do some truckin', which has no doubt exacerbated the blister problem. I must slow down to reduce the heat and friction.

This little-used woodsroad along the canal this afternoon must certainly be called either Gator Road or Turtle Road. Constantly and all along ahead of me is the repeated and resounding splash of the gators plunging and diving into the murky canal water, or the huge, basket-sized turtles tumbling from logs or their coquina-rock sundecks. I've seen some very big gators at Gatorland but nothing to compare to some of these guys. I'm sure you won't believe me when I tell you that the girth on some compare to a 55-gallon drum flattened out! Well, okay, I'm going to bring my camera along next time!

My shadow ventures out far ahead of me on Snake Road as I head east toward Kissimmee Billie Swamp Safari. As I enter the gift shop at Safari Village, a beautiful young Seminole girl greets me. I have been advised by *Vagabond* to make sure and tell the folks here right away that I am hiking the FT. Oh yes, was this certainly the right thing to do! For as I inquire about accommodations for the evening, the young lady tells me that I will be staying in one of the small, elevated, rustic, thatch-roofed huts called chickees. And in her words: "You can have it for . . . well, you can have it for . . . well . . . you can just have it!" And so, here at Kissimmee Billie Swamp Safari, in my first contact with anyone off the trail since leaving Loop Road, I meet my very first "trail angel." The first, as it turns out, of countless hundreds that it will become my pleasure to meet all along the trail all the way into Canada. This is one of the absolutely magical things about being on the trail! I am able to take a luxurious shower, have a delicious meal in the village restaurant, make a few phone calls, and get a much-welcome warm and dry night's sleep.

> *"Our doubts are traitors, and make us lose*
> *the good we oft might win by fearing to attempt."*
>
> [Shakespeare]

MONDAY January 5, 1998
TRAIL DAY 5 ✦ TRAIL MILE 68
LOCATION Second Pumping Station, C-1 Canal Road

IT IS FIRST LIGHT AND I AM SITTING ALONE under the large tribal chickee at Kissimmee Billie Swamp Safari. No one else is stirring yet and it is quiet. The moisture-laden air of the night has not yet yielded to the morning, its chill still present. I am thinking about these first three incredible days spent in the flood of the Everglades. I submerged at 12:30 p.m., Thursday, New Years Day, at Loop Road and did not really emerge again until Sunday afternoon at 1:00 p.m. at the fence at the I-75 rest stop. And the trail? The trail was not pleasant by any stretch. In fact, it was grueling. Fully 36 of the 38 miles were submerged. Had the trail been frozen, I could have skated most of it. The footing was treacherous, a combination of holes, ledges, voids, and cracks in the Swiss-cheese limestone, interspersed with roots, stumps, and cypress knees, all invisible, covered by 6 to 12 inches of silt the consistency of gumbo. Blazes and flagging were difficult to follow, nonexistent at times, requiring almost constant compass use. Orange, it would seem, would be a great color for blazing, but it really is not. What occurs, as the merciless tropic-like sun works intently and relentlessly, is rapid degradation of the blaze patches to little more than splotches resembling the millions of other chips of bronze-shaded bark on the longleaf pine. And the orange and red flagging? That should work great, wouldn't you think? But it does not. For the sun and the rain quickly bleach it slate gray to match the lichen attached to each of the gadzillion cypress trees. Only with luck and a breeze does the flutter of the tape show the way.

I was filled with elation on first spotting the rest area buildings at Alligator Alley, only to clutch with disbelief at the ten-foot-high chain link wall, like an animal in a huge cage, peering at civilization on the other side. What an incredibly agonizing moment as I pondered not being able to get through. I had just passed the trail register, a wooden box affair hanging loosely by a couple of nails from a pine tree. The lid was gone, the rusting spiral ring all that remained of the register book. No hikers had been that way for a long, long time.

I stoke up on a fine breakfast at the village restaurant, and upon returning to my chickee to do damage control to my poor war-torn doggies, I'm greeted by many Seminole, both young and old. None can believe from where I have come, the lands of the Miccosukee, their neighbors many miles to the south, and that I have walked through the Everglades to get here. They've never heard of such a thing. Most just turn to glance back occasionally in disbelief as they walk away! Before departing I go to see the two Florida panthers. They have been caged all their lives, yet they pace, as if looking for a way to the wilds and freedom just a pounce or two away. As I stand here looking at these strikingly handsome animals, I have a sense, from my recent experience, just how trapped they must feel behind bars. After stopping in the gift shop to thank everyone, I head back out on Snake Road.

Today is a roadwalk for many miles almost due east through Seminole Big Cypress Village and the wide and expansive countryside of the Seminole Indian Reservation. Their lands are professionally managed with large cattle ranches and endless expanses of citrus groves. I am in rain off and on for the first time today. Folks along the way are courteous and I am offered many rides. I was looking forward to seeing the beautiful new Seminole Museum, but it is closed on Mondays.

By early evening, I reach the C-1 canal and finally head north again. I make the mistake of hiking too long into the evening, for as the evening cool descends, I am attacked without warning by clouds of mosquitoes. I hurry on to the second pumping station, where there is a wide spot in the canal road, and pull off. I throw my pack down and feverishly work at getting my tent set up as I flail helplessly at the angry little spitfires. I quickly grab my pack and roll in, clothes and all. Looks like a peanut-butter-and-jelly sandwich night tonight! As I lie back to swat the mosquitoes swirling around my nostrils, I feel something on my leg . . . and then a hot jolt, as if someone had poked me with a flaming match. I get my flashlight out and look at the floor of my tent in disbelief and horror. The whole place is moving! In my haste to get my tent up I had haplessly tossed my pack into a bed of fire ants. They apparently were all over the bottom of my pack when I threw it in my tent, and now they're all over me! I thought sandspurs were nasty, but having these little demons all over me is like a living nightmare. At least with the sandspurs I had the option of sitting and pondering my next move. With this army of flamethrowers, I have to move! As I start to unzip my tent screen, I notice that it is literally a black mat of mosquitoes! Aww, I can't go out there, I'll be carried away. Two more hot pokers jab my leg and my back. I've got to stay in here and go after these guys. I start slapping and pounding at them with all my might. And then . . . my flashlight goes out. I bang and hammer at it in desperation, but it is dead from the hours of use in the Big Cypress Swamp. I have little branding irons stuck all over me now. All I can do is fight back as they come after me. The attack is relentless. It is 3:00 a.m. before I finally drift off in total exhaustion. The peanut butter and jelly will have to wait till morning.

> *"I will forget the happenings of the day that is gone, whether they were good or bad, and greet the new sun with confidence that this will be the best day of my life."*

[Og Mandino]

TUESDAY January 6, 1998
TRAIL DAY 6 ✦ TRAIL MILE 85
LOCATION Sugar Cane Field by CR 835 East of C-1 Canal

THE MOSQUITOES ARE STILL AROUND THIS MORNING as I roll out around 8:00 a.m. but there are fewer to contend with and they aren't as vicious. I make note of the fire-ant bed and give it plenty of room as I finally fix my peanut-butter-and-jelly sandwich and break camp. The hike today is a full day on the canal spoilbank road as I head north toward Clewiston. As I proceed, I quickly realize that this roadwalk has absolutely no redeeming value, other than the fact there are no vehicles whizzing by. I have entered the land of sugar cane, and for miles in all directions the tall green cane is all that I can see. Daydreaming, I walk straight up on a pygmy rattler, and he startles me out of my wits with a surprising lunge. I let him have his ground and pass well to the other side!

As I hike into the heat of the day, and with no shade anywhere along the canal bank, the sun is starting to work me over pretty good. I stop, put on my long-sleeved shirt, and get my towel out to cover my head. Then I beat a path down through the weeds to filter some water from the canal. I am hoping to be granted permission to cross U.S. Sugar Corporation lands today to avoid hiking on dangerous CR 835, but a call from a construction trailer just off the canal road brings the bad news that they are burning cane and I'll have to take to the road. I find a spot just off busy CR 835, in a cane field, to pitch for the evening. I prepare a warm meal and retreat to my tent just as the first scouts come to check me out. As I zip up my screen, the entire mosquito air force is descending. I still have to pulverize a fire ant or two as I try covering myself with my pathetic sleeping bag.

"Only those risking to go far will ever know how far they can go."

[Anonymous]

WEDNESDAY January 7, 1998
TRAIL DAY 7 ✦ TRAIL MILE 100
LOCATION Uncle Joe's Fish Camp, Hoover Dike

EMPTY SUGAR-CANE TRUCKS MAKE AN INCREDIBLE amount of racket. They're carrying large metal cages on the back of flatbed semi trailers, and these guys haul. CR 835 is rough and full of patches and has taken an incredible beating from the constant cane-truck pounding. This racket starts right after first light this morning, and I'm up and out with it. The roadbed is crowned up and very narrow, and in some places the shoulders are almost nonexistent. There has been much erosion all along and each step requires attention lest I turn an ankle or stumble in the ruts and washouts. I am walking facing oncoming traffic, and when no vehicles are approaching I sneak onto the edge of the road, where the going is much better. The traffic that I cannot see from behind is a full lane away and I pay little heed to what whizzes past me in the northbound lane. What I hadn't accounted for was the possibility of passing traffic coming up from behind. As an empty cane truck goes rattling past heading south, I start to move back up on the road edge. I assume all the racket behind me is from the southbound truck, but just as I'm taking my last step toward the roadway, it happens. A loaded cane truck is passing a slower vehicle from behind, and as I turn, I can see a flash out of the corner of my eye. At that same instant, I feel the percussion. To this day, I am unable to reconstruct what happened. The next thing I know I am lying in the weeds way down by the canal ditch and my pack is twisted around at an incredible angle. I lie there for what seems a very long time, afraid to move for fear of what I will discover. No one has stopped and I can hear the trucks roaring by. I reach down slowly, unbuckle my hip belt, and carefully roll out of my pack. So far, so good!

I finally manage to pull myself up. On closer inspection I find not a bruise or a mark on me anywhere. All the moving parts are working! Thank you, Lord! What a lesson learned . . . and what a way to learn it!

I am seven days on the trail, and with the exception of a few items that I've purchased in a little store while walking Snake Road through the Seminole Reservation and the two meals at Kissimmee Billie Swamp Safari, I have relied on what I have been carrying in my pack. So my provisions are getting pretty slim. There's a little grocery store on the south side of Clewiston and I head in for supplies. I am anxious to get to the Hoover Dike for my first look at Lake Okeechobee, but once there I am immediately disappointed to find that the view for the most part is blocked by a wall of Australian pine, which stretches to the horizon along the dike as I look to the north. I arrive at Uncle Joe's Fish Camp by late afternoon, pitch my tent on their neatly manicured lawn, and head for the bar . . . Michelob frosties, $1.25!

The hike in FT 2 through the Seminole Reservation was most enjoyable, but for the remaining near-45 miles north of there and into Clewiston, it was a matter of knocking it out. Ken, I know that you and all the folks with the Seminole Chapter FT are working very hard to get this section up and going. I sure hope you get it off CR 835 soon. I wish you all the best!

> *"Knowst thou the land where the lemon trees bloom,*
> *Where the gold orange glows in the deep thickets gloom,*
> *Where the wind ever soft from the blue heaven blows,*
> *And the groves are of laurel and myrtle and rose."*

[Johann Wolfgang von Goethe]

THURSDAY January 8, 1998
TRAIL DAY 8 ✦ TRAIL MILE 121
LOCATION Harney Pond Canal RV Park, Hoover Dike

I BREAK CAMP IN THE DIM SHADOWS OF EARLY DAWN. My tent is wet with dew, usually the sign of fair weather for the day . . . but not today. *Vagabond* and another great friend and FT thru-hiker who has helped me immensely in planning this odyssey, Joan Hobson, have told me that the place to go in Moore Haven is Wilma's Restaurant, right on the trail. So there I head, and indeed, once seated I am kindly served a tank-stokin' breakfast.

Then it's back on the Hoover Dike again to pound on north. The vantage from the dike, being at a considerable elevation above the surrounding countryside, provides a splendid view of all there is about, with the exception of the lake! Shortly, to the west and approaching rapidly from the horizon, I can see an ominous black wall. In moments, the huge curtain of water hanging and descending from it is upon me, and I am totally engulfed in its rage. Fortunately, for some reason there is no accompanying electricity, just driving sheets of water. There is no retreat, so I push on through it. I am instantly and totally soaked as the pounding rain strikes like millions of darts being hurled at me. I finally bail off the dike to the lee side to cower in the sandspur-laden grass. This anger continues for over half an hour. The rain is not only driving hard but it is very cold, and as I lie in the grass I feel the initial stages of hypothermia descending as my inactivity and the cold, driving rain cool my body. I manage to get my pack open and pull out my already wet tent and roll myself, pack and all, up in it. The storm continues as my body temperature improves. I finally manage to uncoil somewhat from the fetal position and get my pack around for a pillow. Here I remain rolled up in my tent, totally soaked but reasonably comfortable. As the exhaustion from fear overtakes me, I fall into deep sleep, to dream of the days of adventure that lie beyond the horizon.

I have not a clue how long the driving rain continues. I finally awake to find the storm gone, save for drizzle, and the sky is beginning to brighten from the west. I meet my second trail angel today. A lock-keeper hails me and hands me an ice-cold bottle of orange drink. By evening I manage to make it to the RV park on the north side of Harney Pond Canal. Here I pitch my tent under the palms behind their propane tanks. There is a new and very clean bathhouse and I'm able to get a warm shower. I hang and sprawl all my pitiful, wet gear in the little screened room adjacent to the showers and manage to work on my journal entries well into the evening. A couple of cool frosties (synonymous with dandy cold longnecks), some buffalo wings, and a double order of fries really bring the day back around!

> *"Reach high, for stars lie hidden in your soul.*
> *Dream deep, for every dream precedes the goal."*

[Ralph Vaull Starr]

FRIDAY January 9, 1998
TRAIL DAY 9 ✦ TRAIL MILE 138
LOCATION Kissimmee River Dike North of Okee-Tantie Recreation Area

---

A LONG DAY TODAY, BUT A SHORT ENTRY. Here I go again, back up on the Hoover Dike. Every year, a group of folks get together and hike clear around Lake Okeechobee on this thing. I have absolutely not a clue why, other than the fact there are some neat out-of-the-way places to party when you pull off in the evening. But you gotta be a better man than me to want to do much partying after a day up here getting whipped around by the wind and having your feet and brains fried by the unmerciful Florida sun! Please forgive me, Paul (Paul Cummings, FT 3 section leader); I'm sure all who hike the "Big O" have a grand old time. It just isn't my bag!

By early evening I've covered 17 miles and have reached Okee-Tantie Recreation Area at the Kissimmee River Bridge. This is a beautiful and very popular facility, which I find crowded with RVs and family-sized tents—kids whooping and running everywhere. It's really out of the thru-hiker's price range, with the fee running the same to roll out your sleeping bag under the stars or roll in—in your $300,000 mobile palace. I look the place over and then head for quieter, less-pricey real estate. It doesn't take me 15 minutes to find the perfect camping spot as I head on north on the Kissimmee River Dike. I pitch for the evening along a lovely canal where the bank apron has just been freshly mowed. Here it seems I've got the whole world to myself. I douse the fire from my poor, hot, blister-covered doggies by dunking them in the canal as I enjoy my evening meal.

"Because we live in a world that values activity and noise more than solitude and silence, we may not understand the life sounds deep inside us which could give directions to our lives."

[Paula Ripple]

SATURDAY January 10, 1998
TRAIL DAY 10 ✦ TRAIL MILE 156
LOCATION High Ground by Cattle-Watering Trough, Yates Marsh

AS A THRU-HIKER, I'LL BE THE FIRST TO COVER NEW GROUND today on the Florida Trail. Vagabond has prepared maps to assist me in getting through. Instead of continuing on the dike at the lock, the new trail goes north on Lochkeep Road to cross FL 70 and then onto Gache and Platt's Bluff Road. I'm in cattle country now. As I hike on this old Cracker sand road in the interior of Florida, I am also hiking back in time. I'm a sucker for nostalgia, and I really enjoy these kinds of places. Yates Marsh is mainly fine old cattle-grazing lands. I soon leave the sand road and enter the open fields. By late afternoon, I am near the campsite as marked on my map. I'm unable to make it all the way back to the designated campsite, as the hammock past an old cattle-watering trough is under water. I pitch by the water trough on higher ground and have a very attentive audience of about 40 of the locals (cows) circled around to hear my poetry recital.

Today was a pleasant hike and the roadwalk presented little traffic. I saw Indian rosewood trees and sandhill cranes along the Kissimmee River Dike. My feet are another matter. They are covered with open sores and are incredibly tender and painful. Before rolling in, I jot a little note of thanks to Doug McCoy and the Tropical Trekkers for their fine work on this new section of trail, seal it in a Ziploc bag, and tie it next to one of their bright new orange blazes in a nearby tree.

"The man is richer whose pleasures are the simplest."

[Henry David Thoreau]

SUNDAY January 11, 1998
TRAIL DAY 11　✦　TRAIL MILE 175
LOCATION Canal Bank, Hickory Hammock North

I'M UP AND OUT AT FIRST LIGHT. The cattle are over by the fence on the far side. There is no treadway on the new trail north through the fields and pastures, but the bright orange blazes are very easy to locate and follow. Soon I am in sight of Kissimmee River Lock S65D. I had stopped yesterday at Lock S65E and had a long chat with the lockkeep and some of the local fishermen. When I mentioned that I would be crossing the river tomorrow at Lock S65D, up came the lockkeep's eyebrows! "What time will you be crossing?" he asked. "As best I can figure, right after sunrise," was my reply. That's when the lockkeep informed me that the gate at the lock is kept locked and that the lady managing Lock S65D is not always the easiest person to get along with. He then opined that shortly after sunrise on Sunday morning might well be one of those times! I am standing now on a canal bank, which I can take generally north to the railroad grade and cross the river on the trestle . . . or I can cross the canal, follow the orange blazes, and get the lockkeep up at sunrise on this Sunday morning! With not a moment's hesitancy I head toward the railroad tracks!

In a short time I am standing on the east side of the trestle looking across. It surely is a long way to the other side. Trains passed at regular intervals all through the night and one had just passed again as I reached the grade about half an hour ago. I listen intently for the longest time, for whatever good that can possibly do. I have severe tinnitus and my hearing is most-near shot. I finally convince myself that I really can't hear a train coming and venture onto the narrow trestle. I am no sooner committed to this ordeal than I hear something. At least I think I do. Halfway across there is a small platform where I can step off. I hurry there in a fright and get off the tracks, just in time, it seems, to avoid the inevitable calamity. When I turn there is nothing, and I hear nothing save the gentle sound of the water lapping at the pilings below . . . way below, and my heart pounding in my ears. Then it dawns on me that if I get caught out here with a fast-moving train coming through, I'll get blown clear into the river! I hasten back onto the tracks and run pell-mell, pack lurching, to the far side.

I was told that new treadway was being cut on the Bassinger Tract, taking the trail from the shoulders of busy US 98. But I can find no evidence of any trail work here on the south end, so I take to US 98 for the roadwalk to Istokpoga Canal. Hickory Hammock is just that, a long and beautiful hammock of climax-growth oak and hickory, stately old knots. The trail to the ramshackle farmstead is the most beautiful section of trail so far. Here I finally meet another hiker on the FT. Steve Barbour from Yellow Gap, Tennessee, is out enjoying the day on this magnificent section of trail. After the old farm buildings, the treadway becomes overgrown and pretty much peters out. I manage to stay on trail to high ground near a drainage culvert and pitch for the evening. I snap some palm fronds and build a hasty fire to help ward off the cloud of hungry mosquitoes. My feet are stable—stable meaning they are no worse.

"[God] is always whispering to us, only we do not always hear,
because of the noise and distractions which life causes as it rushes on."

[Frederick Faber]

MONDAY January 12, 1998
TRAIL DAY 12 ✦ TRAIL MILE 188
LOCATION High Ground North of Hicks Slough Boardwalk

ON ARISING THIS MORNING I MUST DO IMMEDIATE BATTLE with the mosquitoes—I'll fix breakfast later. I'm out of here! I immediately begin churning through a quagmire along a new fenceline. The cattle have turned the entire area into 12 to 18 inches of rolling mud. That's the only way I can describe it. As I try moving through, the mud just seems to roll up and come along! This persists for over 2 miles, and progress is incredibly slow as I grope along the fence. I can see the trees along Bluff Hammock Road in the distance, where I'll pull up out of this mudbog, but it takes me over an hour and a half to get there!

Bluff Hammock Road is a pleasant roadwalk. The trail then follows along the Kissimmee River Dike to enter the Air Force Avon Park

Bombing Range. There is a stile to cross and a trail-register kiosk. No one has been this way in a long, long time. Here begins the Kissimmee River Section of the FT. And indeed it is a beautiful and secluded place. One majestic boulevard-like stand of oak could just as well be the grand promenade to Tara. And yet it is all Mother Nature's design! This is one of the best-maintained sections I've hiked so far. It was a pleasure talking and corresponding with Section Leader Jim Pace. These folks with the Heartland Chapter of FTA take great pride in their work, and it truly shows.

I talked briefly today with two fellows from The Nature Conservancy. They were on the bombing range doing a bird count. This organization is doing a remarkable job all over the globe. The success they have achieved in preserving habitat . . . even to include vast bioregions, while at the same time working hand in hand with local enterprise to maintain and create new jobs in those regions, to me, is a truly remarkable success story. I have found many sour-orange trees all along the trail this afternoon and have eaten my fill. Once I manage to get my pucker up they don't seem to taste all that bad! The trail today has taken me through a veritable wildlife haven. I have seen numerous deer and turkey, along with many snakes, an otter, and countless birds. I pull off to overnight at a lovely grassy spot just north of Hicks Slough. I find the mosquitoes much less troublesome, and despite the incredible mudbog earlier today, my feet are none the worse for wear!

"Faith is the bird that feels the light and sings when the dawn is still dark."

[Rabindranath Tagore]

TUESDAY January 13, 1998
TRAIL DAY 13 ✦ TRAIL MILE 207
LOCATION Trailhead parking area near River Ranch Resort

ALL ALONG THE TRAIL TODAY ARE SIGNS OF MAN'S LONG-PAST connection to the river. Many sour-orange trees, the remnants of long-forgotten groves; dwelling foundations crumbling into the earth; old pitcher-pump wells—some remarkably still working—and an interesting cattle-dipping vat. One is immediately set to pondering how effective that vat had been since the next landmark passed is Tick Island Slough! There's Fort Kissimmee (long since gone with the river trade), Ice Cream Slough (I guess they dreamed much as do we hikers), Rattlesnake Hammock (no doubt appropriately named), Orange Hammock (more sour oranges), and the mysterious little ghost village of KICCO (an acronym which I finally figure must stand for Kissimmee Island Cattle Company). And farther north are Wildcat Hammock, Sheep Hammock, and Buttermilk Slough.

The "Florida Trail Guide" describes the Kissimmee River Section as "one of the Florida Trail's most remote areas." Once there were many farms, groves and villages, thriving and bustling with commerce and activity. Today, long since abandoned and forgotten, their scant ruins and remains languish, to molder in the sun. And this old river? Ah! This grand old river just keeps rollin' along!

My pitiful feet. It is impossible to keep them dry. They have turned to raw, oozing mush, and I am wracked and tormented with constant pain.

"I gits weary and sick of tryin'
I'm tired of livin' and scared of dyin'
And Ol' Man River, he just keeps rollin' along."

[Jerome Kern, Paul Robeson]

WEDNESDAY January 14, 1998
TRAIL DAY 14 ✦ TRAIL MILE 224
LOCATION Godwin Hammock North

I'M BACK ON THE ROAD THIS MORNING. The trail goes right by Oasis Marina, where I again cross the Kissimmee River. I need provisions, so into the little mom 'n' pop store I go. It's 50 miles to FL 520, so I'll need supplies for about three days. In case you're wondering, there's certainly nothing magic or the least bit exotic about my trail diet. I've never gotten into the food-drop thing, but have simply relied on catch-as-catch-can as I trek along. A tad of coffee, a loaf of bread, a jar of peanut butter, a chunk of cheese, a can or two of sardines, a little rice or right-angle macaroni, and a few Snickers bars, whatever's available, goes far (no pun intended) in propelling me right on up the trail! And perchance these little crossroads-store proprietors have an ice-cream case . . . well, my friends, check out this smile, for it will quickly reveal that I am indeed in hiker heaven, blessed with another perfect day! Oh, and should this ration sound a bit unappetizing and a mite sparse to you, please consider that my weight usually varies less than five pounds on one of these extended jaunts. Most long-distance backpackers I've talked to lose upwards of 20 pounds!

The roadwalk on FL 60 this morning is no fun by any stretch. The 18-wheelers are coming at me heavy and hard. I count an average of five every minute barreling down on me southbound. The shoulder is narrow and rutted, and I must move along dangerously close to harm's way. Every ten seconds I brace and bow down against the shuddering blast of the desert-like, sand-driven gale. I have a soft spot in my heart for roadwalks and usually enjoy them immensely; however, this chopping and dicing today is sorely testing my level of joy for it. It takes me nearly three hours to cover the 5 miles on this brutal grinder. Finally, mercifully, the trail turns north to enter the Three/Prairie Lakes and Bull Creek Wildlife Management Areas (WMAs).

A Cracker road leads along for a short distance and then the trail pulls off to follow a fenceline. After no more than 200 yards, it becomes painfully evident what will be in store for the next 40 miles . . . mud and water, with plenty to go around! As I step off into it again, to my surprise comes immediate relief to my poor aching feet. The cool mud and water actually feel soothing, and I am able to make better time through this mire than was possible along the roadway. I am usually able to tolerate the worrisome presence of mosquitoes as long as I keep moving, but here, with my pace slackened, they form a veritable cloud-swirl all around me. Flailing and slogging along, I finally reach Godwin Hammock. I had envisioned a tranquil setting, peaceful and . . . dry. To my dismay, as I enter the Hammock, I find neither. The entire hammock is under water, save one small area in the scrub on the north end. I quickly pitch camp in the twilight caused by the waning hours and the storm of mosquitoes. I roll in and settle for a couple of cheese-and-peanut-butter sandwiches for my evening meal.

"Where you end up isn't the most important thing.
It's the road you take to get there."

[Tim Riley]

THURSDAY January 15, 1998
TRAIL DAY 15   ✦   TRAIL MILE 246
LOCATION Three/Prairie Lakes WMA Game Check Station,
US 441 and Williams Road

I AM OUT THIS MORNING IN THE DARK AND GLOOM. I have been in rain off and on the past 14 days, but it looks like today may well be the day I really slam into it. I find the trail through Fodderstack Slough and into Kettle Hammock nearly impossible to describe and nearly impossible to negotiate. What Mother Nature, through her prodding of El Niño, hasn't seen fit to churn under, the feral hogs and the hunters on quad-tracks have pretty much finished. The sky darks completely down, the wind comes up, and the rain sets in with chilling permanence around 11:00 a.m. I brace and trudge on into it, soaked to the bone.

By mid-afternoon, I reach the concrete tunnel under the Florida Turnpike and heave a sigh of relief as I pull in out of the hammering deluge . . . only to find the wind whipping through with such force to nearly pick me up, and in just moments, the chill of inactivity starts setting in. So reluctantly I push on through and right back out into it again. The trail is now following a well-crowned and graded road, but even here, much of the road is totally submerged and pure mush. In a short while I come across a pickup mired clear to the axles right in the middle of the road. The driver's door is open, and the water is lapping and pulsing in waves across the floorboards. While in the tunnel I had taken a look at my map and noted that the trail leaves the graded road shortly . . . to, as the trail guide describes, "cross through [a] wet area." A wet area, indeed! I have been in it up to my butt off and on today and this is the first mention of any "wet area." This seems a pretty good clue that it would probably be wise to steer clear of the place, so I stay on Williams Road and hoof it on toward US 441.

It is late afternoon now. The rain and wind have been relentless and are steadily gaining in intensity, and it is turning cold. I try increasing my pace, but I am nearly exhausted from churning through it all day, and I can feel the initial stages of hypothermia descending. What a relief to find the Game Check Station open and still manned at the Three/Prairie Lakes WMA entrance near US 441. Here I meet Paul and Doris Adams. Doris takes one look at me and runs for a towel and some dry clothes. In no time I am dry, warm, and comfortable. These kind folks hover over me, give me food, and provide a place to stay. What a blessing! Thank you, Lord, for these generous and giving trail angels! And thank you, Paul and Doris Adams!

> *"The rain keeps constantly raining,*
> *And the sky is cold and gray.*
> *And the wind in the trees keeps complaining,*
> *That [winter is here to stay.]"*

[William Wetmore Story]

FRIDAY January 16, 1998
TRAIL DAY 16 ✦ TRAIL MILE 256
LOCATION Crabgrass Creek Campsite

PAUL SAID THE HUNTERS USUALLY START EARLY, so he has to get up early. Sure enough, I hear him enter the check-station shed just before 6:00 a.m. He must have been up even earlier, for to my delight he greets me with a hot egg sandwich and a brimming cup of steaming hot coffee! Soon comes Doris and these kind folks then invite me into their cozy camper. They have offered the use of their phone so I can call Ron Julien, the FTA liaison with the Deseret folks. Ron has been working on getting permission for me to cross the Mormon property, and I was hoping on some word . . . but no luck. I then try calling Hood Goodrich, FT 6 section leader. Hood had updated my maps and provided information, not only on the Three/Prairie Lakes FT Section, but also on Bull Creek. This data was put together for me months ago as I prepared for my FT thru-hike. I was hoping for an update, but no luck here either. As hunters start coming, I bid these trail angels goodbye and head on up the road. Thanks, Paul and Doris!

I am soon on US 441. I have a 3 mile roadwalk this morning to get back to where the trail crosses north of here. The traffic is light, the roadwalk enjoyable. Soon it is decision-making time. Should I take the chance that permission has been granted me by the Mormon folks and go ahead and enter their lands here at Fontana Lane, or continue north on US 441, a fair distance to where a connector trail crosses the Broussard lands? Both provide access to Bull Creek WMA. I know I have permission to cross on the Broussard property. I decide to head on in and take my chances. I vividly remember the old saying, "Don't do as I do, do as I say!" So, as you read this, I know I am setting a very bad example . . . just don't do as I do!

The gate is secure, and on it a sign with these greetings: "No Trespassing, Tom and Tina." But this does not deter me, and over the gate I go to enter Fontana Lane . . . at least I *think* I'm entering Fontana Lane. I haven't gone a quarter mile until I see a vehicle approaching. My first reaction is to dive into the bushes and wait until the car passes, but I decide to stay on the little narrow road and take my medicine. I have been told the Mormons carry large-caliber center-fire magnum handguns. These folks are the largest single landowner in the state of Florida, with vast-reaching cattle and citrus holdings. Apparently they learned the hard way many years ago that the never-ending job of protecting their lands against trespassers and poachers was a job that they had to tend to themselves. So here I stand, thinking, "You dummy, you don't know if you're been granted permission. Why did you come in here? All the FT literature and all the kind FTA folks you have talked to cautioned you against this." The FTA walks a fine line with these private-land owners. It is through their kindness and civic-minded spirit that perfect strangers like me are permitted to tramp around on their property. It only makes sense that certain restrictions would be imposed. The Mormons have their restrictions. One is you're not supposed to be on their land during hunting season! Seems a reasonable restriction, wouldn't you say?

I am glued in my tracks. I couldn't move now if I wanted to. Visions of the inside of a cell at the local clink flash through my mind. The car stops. Down comes the window . . . and I meet Tom. He asks, "Are you supposed to be in here?" To my surprise, Tom is a kind-looking old gentleman with a pleasant countenance, not the gun-wielding, tobacco-spitting cowpoke my mind had wildly conjured up, and his voice is not threatening. I sigh a deep inner sigh of relief. I am less frightened. Stuttering, I manage to get out who I am and where I'm headed. And I tell him that I will turn and leave the Deseret. Tom then explains that I am on his land, not on Deseret; that their land is in the swamp on the other side of the fence and that I probably couldn't get through there any-way because of the high water. He sizes me up for a moment and then tells me to continue on his road east to the gate, where I can cross on rea-sonably dry land into Deseret. He says it is only a short walk from there to the fence at Bull Creek WMA, and that there is no one back there. He then bids me farewell as he drives away. My legs are rubber. I stand in perplexed amazement trying to get off the adrenaline-pumping and wildly slamming emotional roller coaster of these last few minutes. In just moments, Tom returns. Apparently he just went to his mailbox. Rolling his window down again as he passes, he waves to me and wishes me a safe journey! What a true trail angel! And what remarkable trail magic!

In a short time I am over the next gate and into Deseret. The woodsroad passes their beautiful hunting lodge, and as I bushwhack south, I soon find the familiar and welcome orange FT blazes. The trail crosses a stile into Bull Creek WMA, where I sign the trail register. From here, the trail continues in two directions, the East Loop Trail and West Loop Trail. I decide to take the East Loop Trail, as this is the much shorter route. I remember Joan Hobson telling me that this loop would probably be more difficult to negotiate and that I would certainly run into water. Was she ever right! The trail starts out pleasant enough, passing along a lovely sandy woodsroad through a tall sand-pine grove. But soon the trail reveals its true identity as the sand ridge gives way to an incredible bog. At Yoke Branch I really get into it. I thought I had gone through the ultimate bog in the Everglades, but the trail there pales in comparison to this incredible place.

It takes me well over two hours to go less than 2 miles. I push through a veritable tangle of brush and blowdowns along an old tramway, often submerging to my armpits in the water and slime. I stumble through the invisible obstacles of logs and stumps below as I push away or climb over the flotilla of brush and debris above. My pack becomes completely waterlogged from submersion, cutting into my shoulders as though weighing a ton. The rain comes again in a steady downpour, making this dark, forbidding-looking place even more ominous and scary. I try managing my fear and apprehension by exclaiming to myself, "*Nomad,* you're already soaked to the bone . . . So what if it's pouring!" I must take all precaution with each floating log as the slithering swamp folks have taken to these retreats, and I must keep my hands and other vulnerable anatomical parts from harm's way. Apparently there are bridges at each of the tramway cuts, but I'm unable to tell not only where the cuts are, but also where the bridges might be. Some I find by bumping into them with my legs. On these I can get down on all fours, keeping my head up out of the water, and crawl across. In other places where I most certainly am missing the bridges, I submerge to very scary depths before rising again.

I have at least been blessed with fair blazing and flagging through this place, and as the trail finally turns I begin emerging from the depths of it. In the next 100 yards or so the water drops from my hips to my knees, and in a short distance, as I am again churning through ankle-deep mud, I pass many canoes and johnboats chained and padlocked to the cypress! It is dusk as I near Crabgrass Creek Campsite, and I am thinking how difficult the task must be for Hood Goodrich and all the great folks with the Indian River Chapter of the FTA to maintain these last two trail sections. I have been a member of FTA for many years. The Indian River Chapter is my home chapter, and although it seems I know all its members personally from reading their great newsletter, I have never attended a single function. Thanks, Indian River Chapter, for helping to make this incredible journey possible!

What an absolutely bewildering and amazing day this has been. I had reckoned for excitement and adventure on this odyssey, but there is just no way I could have envisioned its coming with such profound intensity, nor could I have foreseen the physical and mental challenge that it would bring!

"All you need in this life is ignorance and confidence, and then success is sure."
[Mark Twain]

SATURDAY January 17, 1998
TRAIL DAY 17 ✦ TRAIL MILE 277
LOCATION Home of Jay and Theresa Eberhart, Port St. John

I'M BATTING A THOUSAND WITH THE MORMONS, so I decide to cross US 192 and head north on Levee 73. This eliminates a dangerous road-walk along this busy highway and is a shorter distance to CR 419, where I'll be hiking later this morning. I'll be able to cross over from the levee a little farther north. Anyway, this is the designated route for the FT. I haven't gone a mile along the levee when I hear ORVs in the distance. It's definitely time to blend in and I pull over in the tall weeds. In a moment, two hunters emerge on a high point on the levee and stop. From there they pan the area with their binoculars. Both are carrying large high-caliber rifles with scopes. It becomes apparent that these fellows are in no hurry. Even though they're over a quarter mile away, it's only a matter of time before one of them spots me, and I need to get moving. So before I can talk myself out of it, I stand up, get their attention, and head toward them. Arriving at their location, I am greeted cordially. Neither of them challenges me as to why I'm in here. In fact, both are intrigued by where I've been and where I'm headed. I keep the conversation short and head north, counting my blessings on the way. I don't know if circumstances over the past two days qualify me as living a "charmed life," but the description seems appropriate. I head over to CR 419 at my first opportunity!

This is a respectable roadwalk today, around 15 miles, but there is little traffic, the day is clear and cool, and there is no wind. Along the way I see sandhill crane, wood storks, great blue heron, cattle egrets, a covey of quail, and many cattle. At the Orange County line, it's decision-making time again. I can continue north on the county road to FL 520, or head east on the trail across the Mormon land about a mile to enter the southern end of the Tosohatchee Reserve. What to do? Oh yes, I head on east! The hike across the Mormon land is uneventful and I soon reach the fence at South Tosohatchee Campsite. From here, the trail is well marked to Taylor Creek. As I near the creek, I find the entire area flooded. Proceeding, I am quickly submerged in two and a half feet of water and mud. After 100 yards I can see a rope bridge. Here, the water is running very swiftly, and as I stumble in to near my hips, I can feel the force of the fast-rushing stream. I have never crossed a rope bridge before, and as I take a glance at this confusion, I quickly decide that I'm not interested. The Boy Scouts, I am told, built the bridge. I'm sure it's fine for their agile little bodies. I've got other plans. I grab the lower footrope and try fording the creek, but I don't get far with this grand idea until the bottom quickly goes where I don't want to go. Backing up, I realize I'm going to have to get up on this cobweb contraption.

The bridge consists of three ropes: a lower footrope and two handrail ropes, all three lashed together at five- to seven-foot intervals. The footrope is also tied off to surrounding trees with lateral stabilizers. Once on this bungee I seem to be doing quite well, until I get just this side of center. I'm not even over the fast-rushing current yet and the bridge is getting very shaky and unstable. Here there are no lateral stabilizers and the footrope definitely doesn't want me here! Every time I try putting my foot forward, I am violently pitched either right or left. This is scary! I finally find that by crouching, I am able to inch my way across. Before I reach the other side, my arms and legs are aching and my nerves are totally uncoiled, but I make it! There is another near quarter mile before I finally pull up out of the bog. From here the hike is pleasant to FL 520.

It is nearing dusk as I reach the highway, and most vehicles already have their lights on. I've got a roadwalk of about a mile to the St. Johns River and Lone Cabbage Fish Camp. There is much fast-moving traffic, but I make it in good order. The treadway north of here for most the entire Tosohatchee is gone. The St. Johns River floodplain is being restored. The mosquito- and flood-control dikes over which the FT passed have been pushed back under, the trail with them. To get around now involves a long and not-so-pleasant roadwalk. During the planning stages for this trek, my son Jay had recommended a canoe trip down the St. Johns (the St. Johns River runs north) instead of the roadwalk — and he has a canoe! That was a great idea, and that's what we'll do day after tomorrow. We'll leave Lone Cabbage Fish Camp at first light and head north on the St. Johns, a distance by river of some 20 miles, to Midway Fish Camp at FL 50. From there, a roadwalk west will put me back on the FT in the little town of Christmas.

On reaching the fish camp, I head for the pay phone to call my son. He lives about a half hour from here. So while I wait I have no difficulty putting away a hot dog and a couple of frosties. I also take time to think back over this day. I have now completed another section, FT 8, the section known as Deseret. It has been almost entirely a roadwalk. I previously talked and corresponded with Ron Julien, the FTA's liaison with Deseret, and also with FT 8 Section Leader Wiley Dykes, Sr. The trail through here is either on Mormon lands or is a roadwalk. Folks around have told me that, over the years, relations have been strained between the Mormons and those wishing to access or use their lands for one reason or another. My impression from talking with these two gentlemen is that the FTA has suffered as a result but is not party to it. I also believe that they are men of diplomacy and that there is a good line of communication between the Mormons and the FTA. I hope my passing has not created a problem for them. Thanks, Ron and Wiley! Jay soon arrives and we're off to his lovely new home. This has been a very fine day!

> *"Read nature, nature is a friend to truth."*
>
> [Edward Young]

SUNDAY January 18, 1998
TRAIL DAY 18 ✦ TRAIL MILE 277
LOCATION Winter Home, South Lake, Titusville

TODAY IS A DAY OF REST FROM THE TRAIL AND THE MILES. I'll be spending the day with my wife, Sharon; her sister Joyce and brother-in-law Ken, who are down from Michigan for the winter; and my younger son, Jon David. This is my first opportunity to see an outfitter since the near-trip-stopping fiasco on the second day. There is a wonderful outfitting store in north Orlando called Travel Country Outdoors (TCO). These kind folks have been much help over the years in assisting and getting me into the proper gear. Here I am friends with Mark McLusky, who is an expert in the backpack/tent/sleeping-bag area. Jon and I head for TCO first-thing. Everyone has a grand chuckle as I relate the story about my bag-burning incident. Looking back now, I realize how very fortunate I was to get through that day, and indeed all the days since, with no serious repercussions. I have an inner contentment and faith that the Lord will provide me safe passage and see me through to the end of this odyssey, and that is how I go day-to-day. Yet, human nature being what it is, there are always those moments of hesitation and doubt. The trauma caused by the fire and recovering from it was one of those moments.

Mark always has a laundry list of questions before making his recommendation on any particular item of gear. So it is with replacing my dear war veteran: the sleeping bag. Knowing that I'm headed for the southern Appalachians, and being the klutz that I am, I have pretty limited choices for my sleeping bag! He pushes away the rack of down bags right away. Down, being a natural insulator, is the very best (it seems nature's way is always the best); however, the drawback with down is that it loses its insulating ability when wet. And Mark knows that if it's possible for the old *Nomad* to get his bag wet, well, we look at the choices in synthetic bags. A synthetic bag will be a little more bulky when stuffed and won't have quite the equivalent insulation rating of a down bag, but it will keep me "warm-when-wet." There are many choices, and Mark patiently advises me as we work our way through the selection. I settle for a very fine three-season Mountain Hard Wear "Crazy Legs" design. The pack decision is easy. I simply replace my Kelty Redwing, a grand old workhorse. It really isn't an expedition pack, more in the weekend-warrior category, with less than 3,000 cubic inches of capacity, but it's lightweight and has an internal frame design, which I prefer for bushwhacking. So the little Redwing is the hands-down choice. I have lower-back trouble (who doesn't!) and can't carry a very heavy load with any hope of lasting long, so I must keep my total pack weight to a bare minimum. Thanks Mark and all at TCO!

My feet have really enjoyed this day off. They are trying to stabilize, but it is day-to-day and at times they are still very painful. I haven't spent a day with younger son Jon for a very long time . . . too long, and we have a very enjoyable time together.

*"The successful hikers are the ones who find goodness
and joy even in the difficult times, who see beyond the
misery to the beauty of nature and the comforts of trail
society. They're the ones who know that the rain turns
the forest into a magical wonderland and provides the
rainbow that caps the day."*

[Larry Luxenberg, GAME '80,
Walking the Appalachian Trail]

MONDAY January 19, 1998
TRAIL DAY 19 ✦ TRAIL MILE 294
LOCATION Home of Jay and Theresa Eberhart, Port St. John

AT 5:30 IN THE MORNING, JAY AND I ARE ON OUR WAY back to
Lone Cabbage Fish Camp at the St. Johns River. As we put in, here
comes one of Jay's good friends, Phil Sellers. Phil is pulling his Boston
Whaler. Jay thought it a good idea to have a "chase boat" in case we
needed assistance along the way. Obviously it had taken little coaxing to
get Phil to come with us on the river today; this morning he is full of
enthusiasm! We're in the water, everything loaded, gliding under the
bridge just after first light. It looks to be the makings of a perfect day.
The sky is bright with stars and there is a cool, gentle breeze to our back.
The St. Johns is very high, not at flood stage, but Phil barely has enough
room to squeeze his canopy under the bridge.

It is so calm and peaceful here. As the swift current and the gentle breeze carry us along, I take a moment to thank the Lord for this
blessing. What a joy it is to be with my son and his very good friend, to
be sharing the splendor of this new day. Then the sunrise comes to the
river, like a symphonic hallelujah. For as the sun and river awaken to yet
another day in their eternal lives, each of these ageless friends starts
anew. And indeed for each of them it is a new beginning, as it has been
for all the dawns throughout time. The river and the sun arise to new
life, all fresh and clean—the birth of another day! The voices of the
water birds and all the other river residents now join in the happy cho-
rus to greet this new beginning.

The most effort it seems we must exert this morning is the task of keeping the canoe to the current and headed downwind. By 10:00 a.m. we're well over half the distance to Midway Fish Camp. We have seen many beautiful things on the river this morning. One of the local residents, a very large and majestic bald eagle, came to greet us, then to tarry along with us on effortless wing above. My chest never fails to swell with pride when I see one of these grand symbols of our glorious free country, America, up there free on the wing! Though we can never experience the freedom as does that ruler of the sky, we are free indeed!

Phil has dallied nearby the whole morning, hastening ahead only to pull up and try his luck at casting, our only communication being the full-beaming smiles displayed as we pass from time to time! After we drift under the Beeline Bridge, lunch soon becomes the task at hand. We come ashore and haul the canoe up on one of the countless islands in the river. This one has a fine little cabin, complete with a screened porch and fully furnished with a table and chairs. Here we have our lunch in the most leisurely fashion. The view from this elevated vantage is grand—the full sweep of the river—and I relax and enjoy the company of my son and his (and now my) good friend.

The wind is picking up and seems to be swinging around ever-so-slowly from the west as we follow the lazy meander of the channel first east, then north, then west, and occasionally even south. We continue to make good time and must exert only the least bit of effort for the last 2 miles into Midway as the wind now comes at us from the west-northwest. We arrive at Midway Fish Camp at FL 50 well before 2:00 p.m. I remain to watch Phil's boat and the canoe as Jay and Phil hitch back to Lone Cabbage for the vehicles. This odyssey is setting in to be a most memorable experience!

I am the guest of my son and his wife again this evening and this night. And indeed the good times roll as we enjoy each other's company.

"All of the loveliest things that be, come simply, so it seems to me."

[Edna St. Vincent Millay]

TUESDAY January 20, 1998
TRIAL DAY 20 ✦ TRAIL MILE 307
LOCATION Mills Lake Park

THESE LAST TWO DAYS HAVE BEEN A MOST WELCOME BREAK from the trail. I have had time to spend with my family, time to get my gear straightened out, and time to rest my poor aching feet. Jay gets me up a little after 6:00 a.m., and in just moments I'm sitting at the table in front of a full-spread ham-and-eggs breakfast! Yesterday we enjoyed probably one of the best times together ever as father and son. The day on the river was good for both of us. On the way back to Midway Fish Camp this morning, we talk about many things, about the good times and the not-so-good times, all of which go to create and then either weld or destroy the relationship between a father and son. I was always so critical, always so hard on him as a child. Those days and those times that were not so good were of my own making and had nothing to do with him. He knows that now. Jay has always been the one who has made and kept the weld between us over all these years, and for that I am so thankful. I have two wonderful sons and I am so very proud of both of them. I think now, after these past few hours together, Jay understands that a little better. We tarry long here by the river, where we hauled the canoe out yesterday, content in each other's company, sharing the joy of just being together as pop and boy again. It is very hard to say goodbye, but it is time to go our ways—he to his wife and his work and I to the trail.

Another in the long line of numbers that make up the sections of the FT is now behind me. I have completed FT 9, the Tosohatchee section, without passing a single orange blaze. Doug Sphar is the section leader for FT 9, and while preparing for this trek I corresponded with him. The Tosohatchee is a pretty unsettled place as far as the FT is concerned, what with much of the thru-trail treadway being lost to flood-plain restoration. I became very frustrated and upset with Doug during the planning stages of this hike because of the problems here. But they are not of Doug's making, and I am ashamed now for some of the things I said in my letters to him. The day will soon come, I am sure, when the orange blazes will again lead the thru-hiker along the Tosohatchee, and when that day comes, it will be because of people like Doug Sphar. These are the folks who make up the army of volunteers that work so diligently and with such dedication. They're the ones who make this incredible trail experience possible for hikers like me. My apology, Doug . . . and thanks!

North of Christmas is Seminole Ranch WMA. Here the trail is groomed and well marked . . . and mostly out of the water! The rest of the day is a very pleasant roadwalk to Mills Lake Park in Chuluota, along Wheeler Road, Ft. Christmas Road, and Mills Lake Road. The park is a delightful spot, right on the lake. I'm given a campsite close to the bathhouse. I have plenty of hot water, a picnic table, and a grill, and there's a telephone less than 50 yards away! What do you want for five bucks? Oh, are my feet doing so much better now!

"Examine me, O Lord, and prove me; try my mind and my heart."

[Psalm 26]

WEDNESDAY January 21, 1998
TRAIL DAY 21 ✦ TRAIL MILE 327
LOCATION Powerline Easement near Rinehart Road

IN THE DELIGHTFUL NEW BOOK *From Here to There on the Florida Trail,* written for thru-hikers by thru-hikers, my dear friends Joan Hobson and Susan Roquemore talk about the little town of Chuluota. Their description reads, "Chuluota was a Florida 'Boom Time' community in the '20s." As I pass here today, it reminds me of the place where I was raised, a backroads community somehow passed over by time and progress. The trail goes right straight through the little burg. There's a post office, grocery store, bank, and fire station—my kind of trail town. I find now that I could have slept in a little longer this morning. I need to get some mail off to friends, but the post office doesn't open until 8:30 a.m. and it is now only 7:30 a.m. I decide not to burn an hour here and head on out. The trail follows an old railroad grade out of town, straight for the Little Econ (short for Econlockhatchee). I can remember when the rails and ties were torn up years ago from the tracks that went through my little hometown.

Personal watercraft are quite the rage here in Florida, and the Little Econ is the place to be on weekends. My son Jon has one that will flat move. It's quite an exhilarating sport. He and friend Duke had been up the Little Econ just a few weeks ago. The river was way out of its banks then, making it possible for Jon and Duke to run all around in the cypress. Jon said they jetted right over the center of the upper cables on the FT suspension bridge! So, as I head toward the river, I'm wondering what's in store for me. I'm prepared to get in it up to my butt again. However, much to my surprise, the treadway is not only out of the mud and water, but at the suspension bridge the river is nearly three feet below the deck. This makes the hike here this morning very pleasant.

By late morning there is more roadwalking. As the trail heads west through the central part of the state, it is never far from a large metropolitan area. Here I am hiking just north of Orlando. This section, FT 10, is also cared for by Wiley Dykes, Sr., and in a phone conversation with Wiley recently, he recommended that I try the new rails-to-trails section just being completed on the other side of the beltway toll road, so over I go. There is construction equipment and material all along. At the neat new concrete bridge just being completed over Howell Creek, I stop to chat with the construction workers and fix myself some lunch. These are all strong young fellows who relish lugging and throwing railroad ties around. They all have to hear my story when one of them finds out where I've come from and where I'm headed. And they all get a hoot out of this bearded old fellow sporting his very cool Adidas and Oakleys!

Well, I'm not one who gets real excited about all this rails-to-trails stuff, but it's a fine setup here today. As I hike along, I pull off for a short break and treat myself to a soda and an order of fries at the trailside McDonald's. By afternoon I'm in the Spring Hammock/ Soldier Creek area. Here's a lovely section of trail, but the treadway is beat down by folks on mountain bikes, and I most-near get run over as one fellow comes blasting around a cabbage palm like he's bent for hell. By early evening, I arrive at Longwood Fire Tower. The tower is on well-kept, spacious grounds, so I decide to polish my Yogi-ing skills and try talking the folks into letting me pitch for the night. But after checking a number of buildings and knocking on the door at the residence and finding no one about, I fill up my water bottle and head on up the trail.

It is now nearly dusk as I head north on a wide double powerline cut. I find a nice place in the grass, pull off the two-track service road, and start setting up for the evening. In just a few moments, a couple of young fellows come across the easement from a gate on the other side. They stop and we chat awhile. As usual, I must explain where I've come from and where I'm headed. I think it strange when one of the kids says, "I wouldn't camp here long if I were you," but I soon put it out of my mind. After I'm in my little tent and asleep for I don't know how long, here come voices and I am rousted. As a very bright light illuminates the interior of my tent, I hear, "Is someone in there?" I reply, "Yes, what do you want?" And then, "Come out of the tent, sir, this is the sheriff's department." I roll out, squinting my eyes to the bright light, to be greeted by two uniformed officers. They ask for my identification and if I am carrying any weapons. I am then informed that I'm trespassing on private land and that a warrant is being sworn out for my arrest. Aww, jeez! Now I understand what the kid was talking about! I try explaining that I am a member of the FTA and that the FT passes this powerline easement and that certainly it must be all right for me to be here. The officers will hear none of this, but one does suggest that if I pack up right away and move on, no more would probably come of it. I've never struck camp so fast before in my life, and I quickly put some distance between me and this unfortunate awakening! I stumble along in the dark for another mile or two and find a place to pitch where I won't be disturbed again.

What an evening this has turned out to be! But the night is cool and the stars still glisten just as brightly, as if nothing has happened. I am able to calm myself now as I lie back and stare up at the wonder of it all . . . to again delve into the mysteries of the universe.

> *For each star there's a number,*
> *As for each grain of sand.*
> *And for each day that's coming,*
> *As each . . . since time began.*

> [N. Nomad]

THURSDAY January 22, 1998
TRAIL DAY 22 ✦ TRAIL MILE 346
LOCATION Field near FL 44 Trailhead, Seminole Forest

I AM UP AND MOVING EARLY. This powerline is a weird place. There are houses all along both sides now, and the backyards of these homes extend into the powerline cut. So this morning I am walking, under these huge high-tension lines, right through people's backyards! I must step over their shrubbery and walk around all the little ornamental pieces of junk and other things that tend to accumulate. This is not a comfortable place to be and I can see people starting to stir as lights come on. So at the first opportunity I try to get out of here. I go for it where there are no dwellings, intending to avoid meeting Rover, and instead I'm greeted by a six-foot-high chain-link fence. Once I heave my pack over, I've got to get over. I've never climbed over a six-foot-high chain-link fence before. I do manage, but if you've never done this little exercise yourself, don't discount the consequence you may suffer in the process should you so choose . . . especially if you're near 60 years old! What I found out was this: There's a reason the link weave at the top of the fence is left open! I never really thought about it before. Anyhow, the delicate tangle I got myself into doesn't really make all that much difference. The word "terror," however, doesn't even come close to describing the gripping intensity of the moment!

Once I manage to beat through some brush and tangle, I'm out on one of the residential streets that feed to Rinehart Road. Once on Rinehart, I am able to head north again. There is heavy traffic, what with folks heading in to work, and after a half hour or so it's done a job on my nerves. I soon see a Kroger up ahead, and in I go for a few provisions . . . and free coffee! The trek along Rinehart Road, FL 46A, and Markham Road is not a fun roadwalk. I gave up on the rails-to-trails through here. This area is incredibly congested. I absolutely cannot understand how folks can live through this roar and confusion all their lives. I was hoping to hike the nature trail through the Lower Wekiva River State Preserve, but a sign at the gate reads, "Closed due to environmentally sensitive conditions." I finally figure this must mean that Mother Nature has a headache!

Once I get off the busy highway and into the Seminole State Forest, conditions improve dramatically. Here I find some of the most pleasant treadway hiked so far. Bill Taylor, FT 11 section leader, had told me there would be some very enjoyable hiking here, and his assessment is right on. The trail is well maintained and very well marked. I had planned to overnight at Sulphur Run Campsite, but arriving here, and even before the cool of the evening can bring on their misery in force, the mosquitoes are attacking me unmercifully. I usually can tolerate their annoyance, but these guys have all taken advanced fighter-pilot training. I reluctantly head on up the trail. Fortunately there is ample daylight to get me along until I am on higher ground and away from their incessant attack. And what good fortune awaits me as I find the most delightful spot to pitch for the evening: an expansive rolling meadow with interspersed longleaf pine and live oak. I pull in to one of these picture-postcard areas and set up for the evening . . . with not a single mosquito about!

Most of these days now involve hiking distances in excess of 15 miles, some as high as 20 or more. My body has adjusted to this daily demand remarkably well. And my feet? After all the crushing and mushing they have endured, after all the abuse, I believe that my feet are going to be okay!

> *"Escaped from a heap of uncordial kindness*
> *to the generous bosom of the woods."*
>
> [John Muir]

FRIDAY January 23, 1998
TRAIL DAY 23 ◆ TRAIL MILE 357
LOCATION Clearwater Lake Campground, Ocala National Forest

NO SOONER AM I ON THE ROAD THIS MORNING than the bucket brigade starts. I stop, get my tent fly out, and cover my pack. By the time I reach the register box at the beginning of Royal Trails, I am totally soaked. Roadwalks in the rain are usually no fun, and busy FL 44 is no exception. It's kind of like being at the airport or on the lake. The wind that invariably accompanies the onslaught is usually running either with the road coming straight at you or at your back, picking you up and hurling you into the next county. Stir then into this maelstrom the fact that there's no protection from passing vehicles. Added in now are these separate little monsoons. Semis bring on torrents more in the category of cyclones. At times it's prudent to just turn from the blast, go down on one knee, and wait.

At the trailhead register, I am pleased to find there've been some other hikers through this section recently. Most were southbounders lamenting their stories about getting lost. I sign the register and head on in. The rain finally lets up and the storm moves on through. I arrive at a gate and the blazing ends. I check the road in both directions but am unable to find the trail. In the process I find an old trail where blaze marks have been painted brown, indicating where the trail had been. I follow the brown blazes hoping to arrive soon at the new section. The trail here is overgrown and has not been used for a considerable time . . . and it goes on and on. Soon the brown blazes become difficult to follow, and at an intersecting two-track I become hopelessly lost. Out come the map and compass, and I "reckon" my way along. Through an ever-increasing labyrinth of mud and brush I arrive at one of the neatest old hunt camps I can recall in my memory; old campers and trailers and various sheds and shacks are here, along with plenty of high rails on which to hang and dress the deer. Here is Tracy Canal. On the map I can now figure my location and in what direction I must proceed to get back to Maggie Jones Road, the current trail location, but I've got to cross Tracy Canal. The canal looks a little scary, but at the spoilbank cut near the old hunt camp, I head on in. I find the bottom to be solid and the water only four feet deep by the far side. As I follow my compass bearing along old line cuts and two-tracks, I pass many deer stands. Some of these are grand affairs. Deer stands are usually pretty minimal, with generally no more than spikes to get up and a couple of boards nailed in the crotch of the tree, but here the stands are more like decks, some complete with railings and overhead canopies. Some are large enough to hold three or four hunters, with each able to scout a different direction. At Yankee Stadium, these would be the skyboxes!

The woodsroad I'm hiking now soon brings me to a large field and a fenceline. There's a gate across the way and I head for it. From here it's back to Maggie Jones Road and the fresh orange blazes. The trail soon heads back into the forest, past Pooh Bear Lake, La No Chee Boy Scout Camp, and then on to Clearwater Lake Campground. For some reason I had been dreading this Royal Trails Section FT 11N, but I have had a pure blast here today! Royal Trails is just that . . . royal trails! Thanks, Bill Taylor and all the great volunteers with the FTA Halifax/St. Johns Chapter!

Clearwater Lake Campground is a very fine facility, complete with bathhouse and seasonal resident caretaker. I get my tent set up in short order and head out for the little village of Paisley. I'm a trail-town boy, and this little place is truly classic. It has just what every hiker needs—no more, no less. There's a grocery store, a post office, and a mighty fine restaurant . . . and that's it! I arrive to find, to my dismay, that the post office closed just ten minutes ago. Dang! I've missed getting some post-cards off again. The Paisley Inn is a grand eating establishment and I manage to do the "Grand Order of Hiker Trash" very proud! This has turned out to be a memorable day.

> *"By now I have learned to listen to silence. To hear its choirs singing the song of ages, chanting the hymns of space, and disclosing the secrets of eternity."*
>
> [Kahlil Gibran]

SATURDAY January 24, 1998
TRAIL DAY 24 ✦ TRAIL MILE 374
LOCATION Buck Lake Campground, Ocala National Forest

ONE OF THE CALLS I MADE LAST NIGHT from the campground was to a good friend of mine in Rockledge, Florida, by the name of Jim *Thunder Chicken* Pitts. We raced off-road motorcycles together for years. One day I told him about the Appalachian Trail (AT) and that I had a little place at the base of Springer Mountain, where that grand old trail begins. From then on, at every race, he would pick my brain about this Appalachian Trail. Next thing I find out, he's decided to hike it! And in 1997, that is just what he did . . . a year before me! *Thunder Chicken* had expressed an interest in accompanying me here, but I'm unable to reach him. What a disappointment, for I was so looking forward to a grand time hiking with him for a few days in the Ocala . . . but alas, it was not to be.

As I head into the forest this morning, I meet the first backpackers on the FT. Tented just off the trail and just rolling out to greet the morning are Richard and Maria Nicholl from Boca Raton. They are on a shakedown cruise in preparation for this year's upcoming thru-hike of the AT. I wish them well as I tell them that I am headed for the AT and that I hope our paths will cross later this summer. As I continue into the forest, I am surprised to see the condition of the south forest area. There are quad-track ruts everywhere, with the trail bermed up at every curve. This really breaks my heart, because I enjoy off-roading just about as much as any one fellow can, and I've always been disheartened by the bum rap the sport has received from environmentalists and others—but here's a damn good reason why! The yahoos who have been ripping around in here have literally destroyed the treadway, which once consisted of soft pine needles, duff, and grass. Soon I also come by a pile of roof shingles and old tires lying near the trail! The forest wasn't like this in the '80s when I last hiked here.

The mess on and along the trail this morning puts me in kind of a funk, and I hike along most of the day with my own little storm cloud suspended above. It is late afternoon as I pull into Buck Lake Campground. This is a casual camping area, with sand roads, no resident manager, and no signs. I soon realize I've made a bad choice in pitching here for the night. It's Saturday and the weekend crowd is here in force. By midnight, they've got a signal fire going that lights the entire sky; the whole thing's off the ground, wheels up, with the roar and hoopla continuing well into early morning.

> *"A world that's super-civilized*
> *Is one of worry, want and woe;*
> *In leafy lore let me be wised*
> *And back to nature go."*
>
> [Robert W. Service, *My Trinity*]

SUNDAY January 25, 1998
TRAIL DAY 25 ✦ TRAIL MILE 389
LOCATION Hidden Pond, Ocala National Forest

AS I GREET THE MORN, IT IS QUIET AND PEACEFUL. The revelers and the grand flight have crashed. My little Campmor thermometer reads 35 degrees. I quickly move out and on my way to get the old jitney up to normal operating temperature. This part of the forest is in much better condition, more like I remember from the past. I see numerous Boy Scout packs and other day hikers today. It's pleasant seeing others on the trail for a change. Those I chance to chat with most all end up with a somewhat quizzical, hollow grin when I explain where I've come from and where I'm headed. That's usually also the end of the conversation!

The campsite that I have chosen for tonight is a much better choice than last. In fact, it is the nicest spot along the trail so far. Hidden Pond is a lovely little sink with a pure near-white sand bottom. I have the whole place to myself. I can't resist the lure of the little pool, and as soon as I have my pack off . . . off comes everything else and in I go! The air is cool but the water is warm, and I loll most nearly submerged for the longest time. There is plenty of wood from old blowdowns lying about and I get a fine cooking and warming fire going. I am able to work on my journal entries well into the evening as I enjoy a warm meal. This has been a grand day. I am pain-free, very content!

"Solitude is as necessary for society as silences for language and air for the lungs and food for the body."

[Thomas Merton, *No Man Is an Island*]

MONDAY January 26, 1998
TRAIL DAY 26 ✦ TRAIL MILE 410
LOCATION Trailside, North of CR 316

THIS IS THE DAY TO CROSS THE ISLANDS AND PRAIRIES. The trail reveals only occasional glimpses of Juniper Prairie, but Hopkins Prairie is bold, main stage, front and center! The trail skirts the edge of the prairie on a long sand lead that follows the eastern, then northern border. As the coves within the prairie basin undulate into the pine, the trail follows, touching all points on the compass, meandering the long, shoreline-like margin, first to and fro, then thither and yon. At the points where the piney woods project into the prairie do there open vistas most grand, extending great distances to the far wooded wall which becomes lifted, to then float on a mirage of vapor and haze. There are birds of all kinds and description, most of which I do not know. The prairie is alive with activity. And to the prairie from the surrounding wood come trails of another kind, laid down by the inhabitants around as they journey to the prairie from day to day. Here is one of the most delightful scenes to my eyes so far on the FT.

The islands? Well, the islands are an interesting matter. The FT guide may say that I am crossing the south side of Pat's Island, or the north border of Riverside Island, but there is no abrupt change in the landscape as with the prairies. In fact, I can seldom see even a subtle change as I pass onto an area noted in my guide as an "island." There may be very slight, almost undetectable changes in elevation or the least noticeable change in the plant community. Perhaps most apparent is the enormity of some of the southern and longleaf pine that reside on the islands proper, with the virtual open understory giving to the delightful pine-needle carpet. And there may tend to be a little softer give in the sand as the trail makes it way across, but these islands have neither docks nor boat slips!

Toward late afternoon I take to a side trail to head for Store 88. Here there's a bar, gas pumps, and a super-dandy BBQ! I fill up on everything but gas! Late in the evening now and crossing CR 316, I pull off in the scrub and pitch for the evening. This has been a great day, most rewarding, and as I pitch my little tent, I am immediately home again!

"When you have a backpack on, no matter where you are, you're home."

[Leonard *The Habitual Hiker* Adkins, GAME '82]

AS I AWAKEN THIS MORNING AND BUMP my upper tent wall, strange little dandruff-like crystals descend in a shower inside my tent! As I roll out and my little thermometer adjusts to the outside temperature, the mercury doesn't slow down until it reaches 30 degrees. The new and very plush Mountain Hard Wear sleeping bag that Mark has me in is working just great! The morning is bright and sunny and the day warms quickly, but as I near Lake DeLancy the sky darks over, and as the wind comes up there comes also a cold, driving rain. I am really getting hammered hard, but there is nowhere to pull out of it, and I must keep moving to keep my core temperature up. The storm finally passes and the day again turns mild.

I see countless scrub jays today. They're supposed to be on the endangered-species list. Ronnie, my very good friend in Live Oak, had so many coming to his feeder, he couldn't count them. One day he inquired to his neighbor about the nuisance the birds were causing, and his neighbor said, "Aww, those are scrub jays!" Don't you sort of wonder about this entire endangered-species hubbub sometimes? Like the spotted-owl ordeal. The lumbering industry was all but shut down in the Northwest because of the spotted owl. Remember? They said the spotted owl had to have the dark old-growth forests to survive. That area needed to be protected. It needed wilderness designation . . . and then somebody noticed a pair nesting in a Kmart storefront sign! On Springer Mountain, there's a plaque with these words engraved on it: "A Pathway for those who seek fellowship with the Wilderness." I have constantly chosen that path. This odyssey is for nine months. Few will enjoy more *fellowship with the wilderness* this year than this old man! The Juniper Prairie Wilderness is a fine place. There certainly needs to be a balance. I've seen areas virtually destroyed (for our lifetime) due to overuse and abuse. But I think this wilderness thing gets tugged a bit out of whack sometimes. I believe The Nature Conservancy is going about this the right way! While everybody is flying all over the place on this issue, these folks continue on their way, with cool heads putting ecosystem protection to work in a way that everyone can benefit. It is truly an amazing thing. I wish I could afford to bump my membership up to Ordway Associate, the conservancy's big-donor short list!

> *"Not one would mind, neither bird nor tree,*
> *If mankind perished utterly;*
> *And Spring herself when she woke at dawn*
> *Would scarcely know that we were gone."*

[Sara Teasdale, *There Will Come Soft Rains*]

WEDNESDAY January 28, 1998
TRAIL DAY 28 ✦ TRAIL MILE 447
LOCATION Near Old Starke Road, North of Rice Creek Sanctuary

I WAS DISAPPOINTED WHEN I FOUND the Rodman Recreation Area Campground under water. That was my planned destination yesterday, but as usual, things worked out for the better. For here on the spoilbank next to the canal has been a first-class overnight stay. I seem to always enjoy camping by the water (as long as I don't have to camp *in* the water!)

I departed the Ocala National Forest yesterday afternoon, and since then I have been thinking about my hike there and the way I'm feeling now about it. I've also given it a lot of thought again this morning as I head east along the canal. Mother always told me if I couldn't say something nice to try and keep quiet . . . but this is really bothering me. So I think I will write about the Ocala, for there is now within me a deep sense of sadness. In my memory are the hikes enjoyed here in the '80s. Back then the trail was well marked and groomed to the point of being near a walkway rather than a pathway. Where the treadway wasn't mowed, it was a wonderful blanket of oak leaves or pine needles. The campsites and facilities were in top-rate condition. There was no trash or unkempt conditions, no evidence of vandalism. That was the Ocala of the '80s.

I was in the Ocala National Forest for part of four days this trip. I didn't see one U.S. Forest Service vehicle or a single person with the USFS. That may be coincidental, but I've also noted that the FT no longer belongs to the hiker or backpacker. Folks with quad-tracks, motorcycles, and horses have found the Ocala National Forest to their liking, especially the Ocala Section of the FT. The trail through this beautiful area was once the crown jewel of the FT, but this is no longer true. I've heard few nice things ever said about quad-tracks or motorcycles, and seldom anything bad said about horses. But let me tell you this—if you want to tear up some trail treadway fast, you'd be hard put to do it any quicker or more thoroughly than with a couple of horses! The unauthorized use of the FT through the Ocala National Forest is evident for miles. The beautifully carpeted trail of the past has given way to berms and churned-up sand. Trailhead barriers are knocked down, signage is destroyed or molested, and there it is for all to see. It saddens me; it deeply saddens me.

The canal spoilbank is a pleasant hike. I am jolted back to where I am on the trail as I flush a covey of quail along the way. They scatter but don't go far. I don't think anybody much hunts quail down here. Snakes are hard on dogs, and you can't get through the scrub and palmetto, so the quail pretty much have their way. Dad would have gotten a "double" on that rise. I would have gotten some tail feathers . . . maybe!

I must cross one of the locks this morning to head north on the trail. As I approach the lock, I find the gate secured. No one is in sight, so I push my pack through a crack in the gates and wiggle through behind it. The lockkeeper is in his office (in the back of the building away from the lock, of course). We talk awhile, but he never does ask me how I got across the lock! Heading into the afternoon, the trail gets pretty soupy and I run into some slow, hard going through cut-over sections. I find a nice spot to camp just north of Rice Creek Sanctuary near Old Starke Road. A pretty much uneventful day for a change!

I think it not inappropriate to stop a moment here and make these comments: It is obvious Dick Wiseman took considerable pride in being Rice Creek FT 14 section leader. I sensed this from a phone conversation with his wife, just most recently his widow, who called me to respond to the letter that I had written to Dick just before he passed away. Dick left this section of the FT in fine shape. Volunteerism often receives little appreciation or thanks. My gratitude to you, Dick Wiseman, and to all the folks who worked untiringly by your side!

"Lord help me put away deceit
And live a life that's true —
And may there be integrity
In all I say and do."

[David Sper]

THURSDAY January 29, 1998
TRAIL DAY 29 ✦ TRAIL MILE 470
LOCATION Gold Head Branch State Park

WHEN I TRIED HIKING THIS SECTION BACK IN THE '80S, I got hopelessly lost and never did see Etonia Ravine. I have been looking forward to this day with much anticipation, for folks have told about the beauty that is here. It has been described as a place not like Florida: almost gorge-like, with deep sloping walls and the meandering Etonia running nearly clear as so many mountain streams much farther to the north. The trail is well marked now and I am soon at the ravine. Indeed, I am not disappointed in what I find. It is certainly an area in striking contrast to anything seen to the south, rugged and picturesque. The only indications that this is a semitropical setting are the cabbage palms and the palmettos. Here is evidence that the typical Florida terrain is beginning to yield ever so slowly to the rolling countryside that is more predominately northern.

This afternoon is spent on a not-unpleasant roadwalk into Gold Head Branch State Park, where yet another very striking ravine is cut deep into the earth. An interesting observation today: I pass a dog standing, looking at me from his driveway . . . and he does not bark! He is a sad-looking old fellow, though, and he just may not have a good bark left in him.

I arrive at the park by early evening and pitch in the primitive area. I am able to take water from the clear flowing stream nearby to prepare my evening meal. I have traveled over 80 miles in the last four days, and my bod and my feet are none the worse for wear. I think all the parts have finally toughed into this program!

"I think of nature as our compass, pointing the way to the creator."

[Ray Jardine, *Beyond Backpacking*]

FRIDAY January 30, 1998

TRAIL DAY 30 ✦ TRAIL MILE 486

LOCATION Bunkroom, Hampton Baptist Church, Hampton

I'M UP AND GOING RIGHT AWAY THIS MORNING . . . in the wrong direction! I head down a trail to the east and should be going west. I'd rather take a beating than double back on my trail. I'll even go the long way around just to avoid this sort of frustrating unpleasantness. But this morning I finally relent . . . turn around and start back. Forty-five minutes later I pass right by where I pitched for the night! This little exercise, so it turns out, is the harbinger of more to come. For, so it seems, this day is the day to get lost! I finally manage to find my way to the main gate and pay my camping fee. Then it's out the entrance and down toward Keystone Heights. I make it over the gate into Camp Blanding okay but then promptly head the wrong direction to Lake Lowry. Finally I get straightened out and am headed the right way toward the fence at Treat Road. I pick up the trail here for a short distance and then almost immediately make a wrong turn again. The trail goes north and I go east clear around Keystone Airport. I finally climb over a fence, enter a pasture, and make friends with a bunch of horses. It's over the fence again on the far side of the pasture, and I come out right behind the convenience store at the intersection of FL 100 and CR 18!

So in I go. This is a neat little store. They even have ice cream by the pint! I bypass the old freezer-burned Ben and Jerry's to find some good local stuff. Oh yes! This is turning out to be a great day. From here it's about 2 miles north to where the trail ties in with FL 100. But the decision was made early on while planning this hike not to go that way. I really believe that I can stay with the best at roadwalking, but the roadwalk up FL 100 into Starke and then on to Lake Butler is an absolutely insane place to be. I hiked some of that ten years ago. Thinking about it raises the hair on the back of my neck to this day! Instead, I've decided to try the old railroad grade out of Hampton. This old grade goes right into Lake Butler, and if I can "make the grade," that'll save getting beat to death by the traffic on FL 100. And Hampton's right up CR 18 from here! Now all I have to do is get across FL 100. Here I have completed FT 15. Paula Snellgrove is the section leader. Paula, no reflection on you or all the great volunteers who care for this neat section—it was just my day to get lost!

Hampton is a trail-town lover's delight! There's a little post office and a food store that sells pizza by the slice. A lot of neat old houses and churches, definitely off the beaten path. The main drag goes straight through. On the west end is Hampton Baptist Church, set back from the road with a sweeping lawn, lots of trees, a basketball court, the works. This looks like a great place to pitch for the evening. There's a hoop game going, so I head on over. Here I meet Rev. Charles Vickers. The scrimmage is breaking up, so we have a good chat. In a while I mention pitching for the evening. "Maybe back in the corner by the fence?" I ask. Without a blink he answers, "Sure, you're welcome to stay, but come with me a minute. You may decide you don't want to stay over there by the fence." I'm looking over that way expecting some kind of problem, but the only thing I see is a calf in a little wooden pen.

We're heading toward the church shop. The riding mower is blocking the door. Rev. Vickers says, "Come in here a minute and look at this." He moves the mower aside as we work around some other equipment and enter the shop. The shop is a pretty typical handyman setup, with a tool bench and all kinds of tools and such to keep a good-sized church facility running. Then he motions me toward another door over by the workbench. To this day, I still find it hard to believe, for here we enter one of the neatest little bunkrooms I have ever seen. A kitchenette, refrigerator, pantry complete with canned goods, cereal, rice, beans, all kinds of provisions. There's a bunk, a table and chairs, an electric heater, and, off a short side hall, a full bath! Now with a beaming smile, he says, "Wouldn't you rather stay in here tonight?" My mind is still playing catch-up what with counting my blessings over the pitch-in-the-yard deal he just gave me. "Oh yes!" I manage, "But I won't be able to pay you much." Sensing my hesitancy, he says, "It's here for you; there is no charge. If you would like to make a donation, the church would gladly accept that . . . and help yourself to the food." "Well, sure! I, well . . . sure!" He shows me how the shower works and, as he turns to leave, says, "I hope the calf doesn't keep you up. Sometimes he's a little noisy."

"Shall I find comfort, travel-sore and weak?
Of labour you shall find the sum.
Will there be beds for me and all who seek?
Yea, beds for all who come."

[Christina Georgina Rossetti, *Up-Hill*]

SATURDAY January 31, 1998
TRAIL DAY 31 ✦ TRAIL MILE 504
LOCATION Home of John Hamill, Lake Butler

I'M UP AT FIRST LIGHT. WHAT A GREAT NIGHT'S SLEEP! I tidy up the bunkroom, leave a note of thanks and a small donation for the church, and head toward the old railroad grade. Out of Hampton, I cross US 301, then head north on SW 66 Avenue for about a mile. The old grade is 75 yards to the east. A powerline cut leads there through an old broken-down gate. Looks like I'm in luck. The old grade is being used and is passable much as a good two-track. The rails and crossties had been removed long ago, and the gravel has been graded to eliminate the washboard. So as I enter and look down the old grade, I see an almost-level, straight, narrow gravel road. The hunters are keeping the grade beat down, and the section here has even been mowed. I find the treadway pleasant to hike all the way to Sampson City. The gravel on this section is approximately the consistency of crusher run, being of small aggregate and well packed. North of Sampson City, the treadway is more consistent with the typical railroad-grade fill, being comparable to #4's or #7's, much larger rock. A tougher hike, but a few more years and the duff (humus) will settle it in. There's a 1-mile roadwalk on CR 225 through Sampson City. Then, as the paved road ends, it's back to the well-used and -maintained old railroad grade. What good fortune I am having!

I don't know what to expect at New River. When railroad grades are closed and the rails and crossties removed, it isn't uncommon for the old trestle structures to also be removed. I had inquired of this at the convenience store in Hampton, but no one knew. To find out, I must do a 2-mile hike up the old railroad grade from the last place here where I can turn. As I approach the river and still from a distance, I can see the crossties on the trestle and I also see someone standing there—I presume a fisherman. I heave a sigh of relief, for had the trestle been torn down I would now have to backtrack the 2 miles or try swimming the river. A bad idea. I would then have to detour way north and still do a roadwalk along FL 100 the remainder of the way into Lake Butler. As I get closer, though, I am faced with the reality and sheer horror of it! For I stand here now, staring at the charred remains of this once-fine structure. The south one-quarter of the trestle nearest me has been burned almost completely away. It's a ghastly thing. The crossties are completely gone. Short segments of the main sill beams between the trestle piers are all that remain at the top level. There is no way to cross here, as there are large gaps in the burned-out sill beams. Some of the individual pilings that made up each pier are also burned mostly away. At the underpinning level, about halfway down each pier and some ten or more feet above the river, there are pier stabilizers. Two longitudinal beams interconnect each pier. As I look, it appears that at least one of these beams remains intact between each pier; however, most are burned away on one end and are hanging in space.

As I assess this whole eerie sight, I at least feel thankful for a bright, clear day. I can imagine the mood and appearance should I be gazing upon this in the fog and rain. It isn't difficult to visualize a ghost train careening into space, plunging to the raging river, to meet its final rest with wild screeching and grinding. I hail an old fellow on the trestle. He greets me with a wave of his arm. I shout to him that I want to try and cross. I describe the appearance on my end, and he shouts back that there appears to be at least one sagging beam as far as he can see. As I count the piers, I realize neither of us can see the very center. Trusting the center to be the same, I call to him that I am going to try crossing. He shouts that he will wait for me and try to help.

Just getting down to the first trestle is an ordeal, as I must climb and struggle through burned rubble and brush. The river is boiling and

rolling below as I first move above it, and I'm jolted by the first adrenaline pump that brings much hesitancy and doubt. I must remove my pack
to move about on the pier stabilizers. Moving across the first tie beam is
relatively easy, being that it is yet intact and bolted at both ends. I pass by
inching my pack ahead of me and holding it by the straps for stability. I
try to concentrate on my feet and block out the dizzying effect of the
rushing water below. Here at the second pier I must now move across the
lateral stabilizer, as the longitudinal beam leading to the next pier is on
the other side. This second beam is scary. The burned-off end is toward
me, and there is about a two-foot gap. As I swing my pack onto it, I see it
sag. I try holding onto the pier piling and my pack as I straddle the abyss.
As I put my weight onto the beam, it creaks and sags much more. Should
I commit myself to this or not? It is at this moment that I steel myself to
the task, whispering under my breath that I am going to cross this thing.
I swing onto it, grasping my pack for stability as the beam sags another
six inches . . . but it holds! I must now make my way uphill to the next
pier. This whole ordeal is so strange. These beams that once sustained
thrusts and forces of many tons as locomotives and loaded boxcars thun-
dered above are now being asked to just hold me and my pack, a combined weight of little more than 180 pounds!

　　　I now realize that the first beam, which was bolted at both ends,
and this last one, bolted on the far end, were the easy ones to cross, the
successful test of which has hopefully prepared me for what confronts
me now. For here I stand looking at the next beam that is bolted on my
end and burned off on the far end. With no way to test the ultimate
stability of this beam, I can only inch out on it, totally committing my
fate to it in the process. As I inch forward, shuffling my pack along and
clinging to it with white knuckles, the beam creaks and sags below me.
I stop. It stops sagging. I inch forward. It sags some more. Aww, what
have I gotten myself into! I really checked out the bolt holding this
beam to the pier before getting out here. But as I look back now, I can
see where it has pulled, ever-so-slightly, away from the pier. I try backing up, but I am unable to go uphill backwards, and the thought of trying to turn around out here absolutely terrifies me. Besides, I am

trembling and shaking so badly I'm sure I'll go right into the torrent if I try. I realize the fact of the matter: I am in this now, and there's no turning back. Something is definitely going to happen and I pray that it's good! I can't stay here much longer waiting and wondering what it is going to be. This ordeal is sapping both my energy and my resolve. So onward I inch. The beam sags no more, and I swing my pack and jump up in the same motion across the three-foot gap to the next pier. Thank you, Lord. Please let there be at least one beam between each remaining pier . . . I can't go back.

It turns out my prayer is answered, for there is indeed at least one beam still hanging between each pier. Many others are burned out on the far end, but the one I have just successfully crossed turns out to be the worst. It takes over half an hour to go these 150 feet of nightmarish "treadway." At any moment my pack and I could have been lost to the raging river below, but I have made it successfully. Once I reach the intact trestle, I thrust my pack above me as high as I can as the old fellow, hanging precariously over the edge from above, reaches and grabs one of my shoulder straps. I then scale this remaining trestle and pull myself to safety!

Here I meet Quentin Bloodsworth, a wiry and strong old gentleman in his 80s. Quentin lives on the river near here. I ask him why he had come down to this old burned-out trestle today. He couldn't think of a good reason, just that it had been a long time since he had been here. As we walk along now, enjoying each other's company, we both conclude that the Lord had our paths to cross!

From here, I have an easy and uneventful hike along the remaining distance of this old railroad grade into Lake Butler.

> *"Ten thousand precious gifts*
> *My daily thanks employ;*
> *Among them is a grateful heart*
> *To take those gifts with joy."*
>
> [Anonymous]

SHORTLY AFTER ARRIVING IN LAKE BUTLER LAST EVENING, I met John Hamill. John lives right across the street from the IGA. We seemed to hit it right off and he invited me to stay at his place for the night. John also fed me a grand supper of corned beef and cabbage, the whole thing topped off with ice cream for dessert! When I told John that he was a trail angel, he just got a quizzical look on his face.

John drives 150 miles round-trip to the shipyards in Jacksonville every day, been doing it for years. He's divorced; he has a little boy and child support. He showed me a photo of the lad. The picture is five years old, tattered and faded from constant handling. He never gets to see his son . . . just has the old picture to look at. I don't know what happened, didn't ask him. Got a glimpse into it, though. There's an old Harley shirt hanging on his wall. I asked him if he had a bike. He said he used to but his wife made him sell it. That's interesting. I've had a bunch of motorcycles in my time. Couldn't tell you how many. My wife even bought one for me once. His bike is gone and so is his wife. I'm still married. Go figure! John's in his 30s, still has some wildness in him; that glint's in his eye. But there is patience beyond his years there, too. It's apparent that he dearly misses his son. When I asked him why he continues to live in Lake Butler and drive to Jacksonville every day, his reply was, "My son lives here!" I sure hope I said the right thing. I told him to continue in his patience and his son will someday come to him.

Frank Orser, FT 16 Olustee section leader, will no doubt be disappointed with me. I blue-blazed a lot of his section. The ditches were full of water on CR 231 coming out of Lake Butler. A call to the Suwannee River Management District's 800 number at White Springs Gauging Station yesterday had the Suwannee at 78 feet, a foot above flood stage. Mr. Bloodsworth said the New River runs into the Santa Fe and the Santa Fe into the Suwannee. I figured all this water was waiting its turn, so I decided to roadwalk CR 231 to where the trail crosses at Swift Creek. This turned out to be a very smart move. I arrive here to find the trail totally submerged on both sides of the road, and there is evidence of 4WD activity on the south treadway where the trail comes out. Submerged treadway churned into a quagmire by 4WDs makes for treacherous hiking. I have already taken entirely too much risk with these conditions south of here. Each step is a crapshoot. Over 3,000 miles of the 3,500 still remain. There is much ahead and I don't want to "bust it" here! As I proceed north on CR 231, the clear-cut areas to the east look very bad. There has been much timbering activity and the whole place is flooded. There's a timber landing complete with Barco knuckle-boom crane just south of Holder Bay, but this operation is shut down. The trail looks better at FR 21 so I head in. This is not a good idea. The woodsroad and planted-pine section are both under as much as a foot of water in some areas. The trail above FR 29D proves particularly difficult. Motorcycle and quad-track ruts slow my pace to a deliberate grind. It's raining on me off and on every day now. There's just no place for all this water to go.

Considering the circumstances, the folks caretaking this section have done a remarkable job. They've mowed it, blazed it, and maintained it as best they can. My hat's off to you, Frank. Thanks! I really wish I could have hiked more of your section. The piney woods here are very lovely.

"All the shining angels second and accompany
the man who goes afoot, while all the dark spirits
are ever looking out for a chance to ride."

[John Burroughs]

MONDAY February 2, 1998
TRAIL DAY 33 ✦ TRAIL MILE 540
LOCATION Near West Tower, Osceola National Forest

I PITCHED LAST EVENING AT THE EDGE of a mature longleaf pine island near East Tower. The Olustee Battlefield Memorial is a very beautiful and well-kept park.

They are gearing up now for the annual reenactment of the Civil War battle that took place here. This is quite an affair and is celebrated with much fanfare. The museum is right by the trail and well worth the time. I've always enjoyed these sorts of places. While looking at the mannequins dressed in uniform, in scenes most like the midst of battle I am able to break the grip of captor time for a few moments and return to those days long past.

The little bit of treadway I attempt to follow today is hopelessly submerged. And I am not helping things in the least by churning along that path. I blue-blaze again along CR 250A all the way to CR 250. Here I decide to try the FT again . . . bad decision! It takes over three hours to hike 4 miles to a boardwalk area. And well as you might suspect, the reason for the boardwalk? Yes, this area is likely a problem even during the best of conditions, and these are certainly not the best of conditions! Another very scary ordeal now presents. There is fast-moving water even before I arrive at the boardwalk. The current is surging against my legs. The water is running relatively clear, however, and I can see the boardwalk even though it too is completely submerged. As I step up onto it, I slip and almost go down. So it's down on all fours I go to crawl along. The turbulence is banking water on one side of me and creating a wake on the other. Once across, I remain in the water and mud the entire afternoon. Finally, totally and demoralizingly exhausted, I pull up on the only dry patch of ground I can find, a spoilbank in a piney woods some distance yet from West Tower. Yes, even the piney woods are totally submerged!

I no sooner pitch camp and have supper prepared than the sky opens again. The rain and wind become torrential and continue throughout the night. With the combination of noise and bone-weary fatigue, I drift in and out of fretful sleep. Sometime during the night the high winds, which are attacking the mature pine in a rage, setting them to loud and mournful complaint, begin coming in ever-increasing waves, setting the grove to shuddering and vibrating. It is then that I begin hearing gunfire in the distance, like shotgun blasts. Bang! Bang! . . . Bang! As I lie awake now, with the wind whipping my little tent as if to carry me away, I think it strange that anyone should be out in this storm. It is pitch-black, the rain not coming down but being driven across, from side to side, in a fashion which would require one to cling to a tree. Then it dawns on me. These blasts I hear are trees snapping and being blown down! As the report frequency intensifies, the percussion from each blast also intensifies as the storm comes steadily closer. The hammering blasts become much louder. Bang! Bang! . . . BANG! I am struck full with terror. The winds are now passing with incredible force, the vibration and shudder working my eardrums much like ascending and descending mountains. Most surely I am in the presence of a tornado. I now dearly wish for a bunker nearby where I can crawl in and hide, but I must remain behind this wisp of nylon filament. I am not interested in the "wind's glad tidings" as was Muir!

I wince and cower as the raging storm makes its presence known. The deafening sound of trees snapping and crashing is full upon me. Then it happens . . . KABAM! I am nearly lifted from the ground by the report and percussion from a snag being blown down with crashing force directly by my tent. I want to run, to escape, but I know that I am now at the mercy of the storm and that I must not move. Lord, please have mercy on me!

"Yea, though I walk through the valley of the shadow of death,
I will fear no evil; for thou art with me; thy rod and thy staff they comfort me."

[Psalm 23]

TUESDAY February 3, 1998
TRAIL DAY 34 ✦ TRAIL MILE 559
LOCATION Suwannee River Motel, White Springs

THE STORM FINALLY PASSES, AND AT FIRST LIGHT I ROLL OUT. The pine snag, practically a foot in diameter, lies parallel with my tent no more than three feet away. Had I pitched my tent there or had I pitched at a slightly different angle, the tree would have fallen on me. I had placed my water bottle and cup outside. The bottle was nearly full, which prevented it from being blown away, and my cup also stayed put, perhaps because it now contained an inch of water!

As I finish the day and enter the little town of White Springs, I have completed another section of the FT. The numbers are really clicking off now. The Osceola National Forest is considered FT 17. Phil Niswander is not only the section leader here but is a USFS ranger for Osceola National Forest. Phil, you have a beautifully maintained section! Much more so than another national forest I have spoken about. You've kept the unauthorized use of the FT in the Osceola to practically zero! I had the pleasure of meeting and talking with a number of Forest Service personnel on my way through. I regret that I had to blue-blaze most of your section, but getting through would have been difficult if not impossible. Considering the conditions, I did try. I want you to know I did the best I could. I'll be back!

At White Springs I check into the neat and clean little mom 'n' pop Suwannee River Motel. Nice folks . . . cut me a hiker deal! From here it's over to Catfish's for a great meal. I make a number of phone calls, one to my dear friends Ron and Judy King, who now live near Live Oak. Ron invites me to stay tomorrow evening, and we make arrangements to meet along the trail late in the afternoon. Ron and Judy are both great cooks. Gonna be Garveyin' time!

> *"Nearness to Nature . . . keeps the spirit sensitive*
> *to impressions not commonly felt, and in touch with*
> *the unseen powers."*
>
> [Oliyesa, *The Soul of the Indian*]

WEDNESDAY February 4, 1998
TRAIL DAY 35 ✦ TRAIL MILE 581
LOCATION Home of Ron and Judy King, Live Oak

COMING INTO WHITE SPRINGS YESTERDAY EVENING and crossing the US 41 Suwannee River Bridge, I saw a few orange blazes on higher ground where the trail follows the river along and under the highway. Looking over the bridge railing then, I could see the blazes as they quickly disappeared beneath the Suwannee's flood. It sure looks like El Niño has taken a liking to this part of Florida and may well have moved in for the duration! So it is that I am sullen, and with much sadness do I review my maps this morning to see just which route I want to follow on this alternate roadwalk along the Suwannee River. Ed Wolcott, FT 18E Suwannee section leader, had told me months ago that if the Suwannee River was above 60 feet at the White Springs' Gauging Station that the FT, which follows the banks of the Suwannee, would be under. He also explained to me that should the river be near 60 feet, to make sure that it was dropping and not rising. This morning the Suwannee River is above 80 feet here at White Springs, and the flood has not yet staged! According to my calculations, that puts the FT under water as deep as 20 feet in some places.

On my way out of town this morning, I stop at the Stephen Foster State Folk Center. Here presents a grand setting with sweeping, rolling grounds right on the banks of this historic Suwannee River, made famous by Foster with his timeless work and beautiful song "Swanee River"! The center is constructed in true Southern-plantation style. Those responsible for this fine memorial and all associated with it these many years should be very proud. It certainly does Stephen Foster proud. I am sure he would approve. I do! I talk with the folks here, sign the guest book, and put a pretty good dent in their coffee before bidding them farewell and moving on.

All of the numbers which follow are certainly irrelevant, but I pen them here to set my path. This roadwalk is partial cause for the funk I'm in today. I first pick up CR 25A heading northwest out of town. Here I brace into the chilling wind and beginning drizzle coming straight at me. It is with much relief that I come abreast of the rear entrance to the Florida State Agriculture Inspection Station at I-75. With not a moment's hesitation, in I go to warm my trembling body. I am welcomed with the usual puzzled expressions as I explain this odyssey. The reward for my little engagement is more hot coffee and some energy-boosting candy. Shortly I arrive at CR 132 and then US 129. From here it's west on CR 158. The plan is to meet Ronnie at Mt. Pleasant Church around 4:00 p.m. I arrive in very good order at 3:30—not bad planning. Ronnie comes rolling up right at 4:00 p.m. I am greeted with a grand handshake coming at me on one hand . . . and a cold frosty from the other! What pure joy it is to see this longtime friend. I am sure that part of the funk hovering over me today, and which I'm finding I must fight off each day, is due to the loneliness that has beset me on this trek. And so it is that I am overjoyed to see this very dear friend!

We are soon at Ron's beautiful new home, where Judy now greets me. And, as I fully expected, no effort has been spared in making me feel welcome and at home. I am shown to my own room, complete with private bath . . . and for supper, some of the most mouthwatering pasta I've enjoyed in ages, prepared by both Ronnie and Judy. And the dessert? Ah, yes! The ice cream I had Ronnie stop to let me run and get on the way home. And finally, to crown this now absolutely perfect and memorable day, about 8:00 p.m. my younger son, Jon, arrives with his girlfriend, Terri. We all have such a grand time together again. What a most effective balm to soothe this old man's loneliness.

> *True friends are hard to find this day,*
> *Not like in times back when.*
> *So cherish I their love since they,*
> *Shan't pass this way . . . again.*

[N. Nomad]

THURSDAY February 5, 1998

TRAIL DAY 36 ✦ TRAIL MILE 581

LOCATION Home of Ron and Judy King, Live Oak

A DAY OFF, TIME WITH FAMILY AND FRIENDS —just what I needed. I can feel my energy level coming up, and the storm cloud that was starting to follow me everywhere is dissipating. I've had the opportunity to call and talk with two very dear friends whom I've come to know since planning the Florida Trail part of this odyssey. Both have hiked the entire Florida Trail, so each has provided invaluable information. I would not have made it this distance without their assistance. I have corresponded with *Vagabond* for a number of months, but last evening was the first time that I've spoken with him by phone. We had a grand time. Joan Hobson, the sweet lady whom I've dubbed as *Trail Angel*, has taken the time to sit down with me in her home and has spent hours answering questions and helping me with maps and trail data. We had a good long chat. Both of these friends are genuinely excited and full of enthusiasm about my success so far and have wished me continued good fortune. Thank you, my Florida Trail friends! I also had time to get postcards off to many of the section leaders all up and down the Florida Trail who have helped me prepare maps and data for their sections of my journey.

Garveying is the order of the day. Judy fixed me a whopping breakfast complete with sausage, eggs, biscuits, and gravy . . . and then another round, plus pots of steaming hot coffee. For supper this evening, to stave off starvation, it's steaks with all the trimmings! There are ten acres here on Ron's ranch, and we spend a leisurely good time walking his garden plot and then all around the fenceline to see the fine job he has done with his homestead. We enjoy another great evening together as we chat and catch up on old times.

> *"Cherish friendship in your breast —*
> *New is good, but old is best;*
> *Make new friends, but keep the old;*
> *Those are silver, these are gold."*

[Joseph Parry]

FRIDAY February 6, 1998
TRAIL DAY 37 ✦ TRAIL MILE 606
LOCATION Planted pine near Corinth Baptist Church

JUDY FIXES ME A HEAPING PLATE OF BISCUITS AND GRAVY to get me going this morning, packs a lunch for me to take along . . . and then sends me on my way with a good solid hug. Ron drives me back to Mt. Pleasant Church, where he'd picked me up Wednesday. This is a somber morning. It's no fun saying goodbye to dear old friends. Ronnie and I have known each other now more than 20 years. Our younger boys were also good friends. They grew up together. We went camping together. We ran everywhere together. We had many a cookout, and between the two of us we've probably helped finance the expansion projects for a couple of breweries. We've both moved away now from that quiet little residential street where we were next-door neighbors, and we seldom see each other these days. That seems so long ago now, like another lifetime. It's interesting how our individual paths in life can meet, run together for a while, then part again. We do try to stay in touch. Ron stands in the road as I shoulder my pack and slowly move away. In 50 yards or so I turn, and he is still standing there. Dang, this is tough. So long, Ronnie, my dear friend. I gotta go.

It's back to the roadwalk again today as I continue along the Suwannee River. The trail comes out from the river every once in a while, and we hike along together now and again. Near early afternoon I run across Y'all Come, one of the neatest little mom 'n' pop stores, near the entrance to Holton Wildlife Management Area. Milk and bread, ammo and bait—they've got a little bit of everything folks here along the Suwannee need. Oh, hey! And they've got an ice-cream chest! Look at this smile!

Ed Wolcott helped prepare my maps for the Suwannee River Section, but I got to use them very little. My appreciation to you just the same, Ed. I'm disappointed I didn't get to hike the Suwannee . . . I'll be back! I pull off the road at dusk and pitch in the planted pine near Corinth Baptist Church.

> *"Trail Angels can't know how much we appreciate*
> *the kind word, the friendly wave, the warm fire, a*
> *cold refreshment . . . a ride to the supermarket."*
>
> [Susan Roquemore/Joan Hobson,
> *From Here to There on the Florida Trail*]

SATURDAY February 7, 1998
TRAIL DAY 38 ✦ TRAIL MILE 625
LOCATION Planted pine near Pine Lake

TODAY IS A ROADWALK AGAIN AS THE FT CONTINUES ALONG the Suwannee River. As yesterday, the trail comes up from the river occasionally to join the road, and here for a while we go along together. By afternoon I arrive where the FT and Suwannee part ways. I regret missing your section, Carol Ann (Schiller, FT 19 section leader), but the trail was under. The Suwannee just wasn't meant to be. Maybe some other day! As the roadwalk leaves the river, I am moving to a little higher ground. No camping is permitted in the Gilman half of FT 20, but I cannot—hard to believe—find any water to prepare my evening meal, so into Gilman I go. Just west of Pine Lake, water is available from a culvert. I pull into the planted pine, well away from the woodsroad, and pitch my camp for the evening. Here, without bloodhounds, you could not find me, and when I depart in the morning you will find no sign where I have been.

"I've learned—of all the friends I've won
Dame Nature is the best,
And to her like a child I run
Craving her mother breast.
To comfort me in soul distress,
And in green glade to find
Far from the world's unloveliness . . .
Pure peace of mind."

[Robert W. Service, *The Learner*]

SUNDAY February 8, 1998
TRAIL DAY 39 ✦ TRAIL MILE 641
LOCATION First crossing, Econfina River

I FULLY EXPECTED GILMAN-FOLEY to be one of those thru-trail tie-together sections (as are many) linking one FT jewel and the next. Was I ever mistaken! This is one of the most pleasant and remote backwoods roadwalks on the trail! The blazes are bright and dependable, and I only dunk my feet once on Madison 5 just before Tower Road. I see not another soul here the whole time. Now I want to know how such a large tract of land like this can be so well managed, with excellent resource use, and be in private hands! You're supposed to need the government, with all its professionally trained experts, and all kinds of equipment to take proper care and get good use from a vast tract of land like this!

By God, it's nice to see the land respected and cared for. Here is fine silviculture on a grand scale, the crop being planted pine. It is evident that the caretakers and users of this land are all conscientious folks.

The small homemade road and hunt-camp signs aren't torn up and shot to hell. There is no junk or trash, no vandalism anywhere. The two-tracks and trails are not all ripped up by ORVs. How can this be with hunters around? Go look at some of our state- and federally managed lands to see the point I'm making. Start with what is professed to be the FT crown jewel, the Ocala.

I may be the only one to hike this entire section this year, but to the owners of this land who manage it so well and to Charlie Donahoe, FT 20 section leader who maintains the trail so well, please accept my gratitude and my thanks. This is a pleasant and enjoyable section to hike. Keep the pride in it! I camp at the road fork near Econfina River culverts, just like *Trail Angel* suggested.

> *"Behold how gracious and beneficent shines the roseate morn! Now the sun arises and fills the plains with light; his glories appear on the forest, encompassing the meadows, and gild the top of the terebinthine Pine."*
>
> [William Bartram, *The Travels of William Bartram*]

MONDAY February 9, 1998
TRAIL DAY 40 ✦ TRAIL MILE 658
LOCATION Second crossing, Econfina River

WELL, TODAY I'LL HIKE FROM THE ECONFINA RIVER to the Econfina River! Am I getting anywhere? A little after noon I am at US 221, the end of FT 20. On crossing the highway and entering FT 21, I quickly realize my good fortune in having a compass, a watch, good homemade maps, and the ability to use them. For here the blazes dim right out. What few there are, and there are very few, consist of little more than faded patches. I have no idea how long the trail has passed this way, but judging from the condition of the blaze remnants, it's been a long, long time. In addition to having my watch, maps, and compass, I have learned to judge reasonably well my rate of progress. The combination of these factors enables me to fix my position, by calculation, fairly accurately as I hike along. FT 21 is a veritable jigsaw puzzle of woodsroads leading in every conceivable direction. Without my compass and some basic idea of my location it would be impossible to stay on trail. A wrong turn most anywhere out here would lead me a "fur piece" from where I want to be!

To give you a little flavor for this, follow along for a while as I negotiate this maze as described in my data sheet. Here we go. "Road forks, watch blazes (there are no blazes)." At 0.2 miles, "Crossroads, trail turns (no blazes)." In 0.1 mile, "Intersection, trail turns (no blazes)." After 1.4 miles, "Road forks, watch blazes (no blazes)." In 0.6 miles, "Trail turns at crossroads (no blazes)." In 0.3 miles, my trail guide—and my watch and compass—tell me I should be crossing a wooden bridge. Eureka! There is a wooden bridge! In another 0.1 mile, the data sheet reads, "Crossroads, trail turns (and yet again, no blazes)." At this point, the guide suggests, "Use bypass route shown on map during high-water periods." Oh yes, I definitely want to take this turn, as the woodsroads I've been hiking to arrive here, where it's suggested I use the bypass route, have all been run through a blender! But in less than 0.1 mile I have a choice of going five, FIVE different directions! So looking at my compass once more, and based on where I think I should be in time, I choose one. Twenty minutes and 1 mile later, I finally see it—a faint blue blaze painted on a tree! So now after the last hour hiking nearly 3 miles, and after making seven route changes (make that seven coin tosses), I finally find confirmation that I am on trail, on the bypass route, and headed where I want to go! Stir in a dark, ominous day of cold wind and rain, along with an indescribable treadway of mix and mud, and you begin to feel the gravity of the portentous decisions I've had to make!

I have been hiking alone today, but on this bypass and from the woods now comes to join me along the road shoulder the largest set of bear tracks that I have ever seen in the wild. And as I look with amazement upon these hand-sized pits all along, and as the rain flushes them, I realize they are very, very fresh! I peer ahead into the rain and haze, fully expecting to see the dark hulking bruin that has just made them. But there is only the wind-driven rain and the roadway of soup disappearing into the murk. I soon arrive at the elevated (out of the mud) Econfina River Bridge. I had planned on pitching here for the evening, but it is here that the bear tracks leave the road, disappearing again into the bog. Putting the river between me and this fellow, a thought which now pops into my head as being a brilliant idea, I decide to cross the bridge and hike until dark in search of high ground where I might pull up out of it for the night. So on I slog into the darkening shadow. In a short distance I find an old overgrown spoilbank. The rain is giving me a break, and I decide this is it for today. After breaking off a number of dead lower pine branches and after a fair amount of whittling, I have a pile of dry tinder and kindling to set a fire. I soon have a fine cooking and warming fire going to drive the cold, damp gloom from the evening. As I enjoy the fire and my warm supper, I plumb my deep inner feelings about being on the trail. And I decide to stick with my opinion that there are no bad days on the trail, but in the process I also conclude that it won't take much to top this one!

> *"What have I learned by the toil of the trail?*
> *I know, and I know well.*
> *I have found once again the lore I had lost*
> *In the loud city's hell."*

[Hamlin Garland, *The Toil of the Trail*]

TUESDAY February 10, 1998
TRAIL DAY 41 ✦ Trail Mile 690
LOCATION St. Marks National Wildlife Refuge near US 98

I HAD GLANCED AT MY MAPS IN THE GLOW OF THE FIRE last evening, but I was too tired to concentrate. This morning, however, I must study them in detail as the maze of woodsroads continues, and the trail follows along. Upon further perusal I realize that it is decision-making time. The Suwannee is out of its banks and raging. On my way through White Springs the river had not yet crested, and there's been much additional rain since. The same conditions exist for the Alapaha, Withlacoochee, and Econfina rivers. Also recently, numerous bad storms have been reported west of here all the way into Alabama. The treadway conditions are bad to nonpassable and getting worse, if that's possible. So, what should I expect of the Aucilla River, along which the trail passes just ahead of me? The treadway has got to be under along the rises and sinks, making this section doubly treacherous as the trail rises and drops along the riverbank. I was looking forward to this section with much anticipation. I have never seen a river disappear to again surface and just as quickly go below the earth again. The rises and sinks of the Aucilla are reputed to be breathtaking. I had planned a day of less than 10 miles from where the FT comes to the river at Riverbend Campsite, and then from there to proceed most leisurely along the river to South Junction. I conclude, however, that to try and traverse Section FT 21W would be foolhardy. So, again with much dismay I realize, as has happened with the Suwannee on this journey, the Aucilla is not to be.

So the decision is made to head due west on an old improved tramway road instead of north from Fulford Bridge, where I had crossed the Econfina River last evening. Backtracking, I am soon at the bridge and heading west. I follow woodsroads until afternoon, first past Cabbage Grove Tower, then southeast to pick up the trail as it comes out of the rises and sinks near a limestone quarry. Along today I have had the opportunity to practice my navigation and location-plotting skills. So much for FT 21W. Sorry Vic and Carlene Danart, section leaders for FT 21W. I have been told you have a beautiful section! As I cross the Aucilla River Bridge on US 98, my suspicions are confirmed. The Aucilla River is out of its banks, and the secondary and tertiary channels are raging. An old-timer at the Spur/Aucilla River Store tells me I would never have made it through. I camp where a virtual river is flowing past an old three-point farm disc on the power-line cut heading into St. Marks. Rain has threatened all day, the wind brisk and cold, and as I search for firewood the rain begins again. I abandon the idea of an evening fire and a warm meal and quickly roll in. It's cheese sandwiches and Snickers for dessert tonight. The rain continues hard until dawn.

"And I go on my way rejoicing —
What's the use to complain or sigh?
Go the route, old scout, and be merry,
For tomorrow you may die."

[Unknown]

I NO SOONER BREAK CAMP, GARBAGE-BAG MY PACK, and get my rain jacket on than the sky opens again. The going for the first mile is slow and dangerous along an old spoil ditch. I am in water, mud, roots, and rocks clear above my knees almost the whole way as I become totally soaked again as usual. Once into the refuge, the treadway improves dramatically as it pulls out of it to follow the high, reasonably dry old Aucilla Trambed. Toward late morning the sky clears, the day turns mild, and I have a most enjoyable dike-hike into and around the gulf-shore salt marches. The vistas are breathtaking, a sweeping 180-degree panorama to the horizon from east to west across a sea of cordgrass. The marsh is alive with activity from the waters to the sky. Waterfowl abound. Here are gulls, terns, egrets, rails, and the little seaside sparrow. In and surrounding the saltwater and freshwater marshes are alligators, diamondback terrapin, snakes, mink, otter, raccoon, deer, and turkey. Today I see a fair representation of all these creatures, especially the alligator and the gull.

Reluctantly I pass the trail junction leading to Stony Bayou and Deep Creek, as it leads immediately into the murk, choosing instead to continue on the higher and drier blue-blaze Swamp Hammock Dike and along the old trambed. An interesting spot today, and appropriately named, is a campsite location known as Ring Dike. Here I find an attached extension to the meandering dike in the form of a huge perfectly circular ring, perhaps as large as five acres or more. In the fine FalconGuide titled *Hiking Florida*, writer Tim O'Keefe describes the St. Marks National Wildlife Refuge as "probably the best place in Northwest Florida for general bird watching. Founded in 1931 and one of the nation's oldest refuges, St. Marks encompasses 55,000 acres of land and another 31,500 acres of adjacent Apalachee Bay. It also includes a designated Wilderness Area of 18,000 acres." This is indeed a vast and unspoiled bioregion with the FT passing right through for a distance of 43 miles. Here is a well-kept secret. For here truly is the crown jewel of the Florida National Scenic Trail!

Late afternoon/early evening, I arrive at the ruins of Port Leon, a little port community on Apalachee Bay, devastated and abandoned after the hurricane of 1843. From here the trail turns sharply north on an old rail grade leading to the St. Marks River just across from the little town of St. Marks. I had considered swimming the river; however, once here and seeing its width and swift rushing current, better judgment prevails. I manage to hail Willie, a worker at Posie's Oyster House straight across, and soon Allen Hobbs from Allen's Shell Island Fish Camp comes to shuttle me over to Posie's.

Walter Beckam's Posie's Oyster House is a quaint old seafood establishment. Without a doubt, the fare of which one should partake here is the shrimp basket. It is a grand thing! After stuffing myself with shrimp and emptying their coffeepot, I head to Allen's for the evening. Allen greets me again, and I meet his wife, Ruthie. The accommodations are very fine, clean and neat. My tummy is full. I am warm and content. What began most iffy weatherwise has turned out to be a fine and most enjoyable hiking day!

> *"In the past year Florida has experienced flooding, drought, wildfires, tornadoes, and hurricanes, and that doesn't begin to tell you about our normal weather, which is wet, hot, cold, humid, windy, and perfectly wonderful."*
>
> [Susan Roquemore/Joan Hobson,
> *From Here to There on the Florida Trail*]

THURSDAY February 12, 1998
TRAIL DAY 43   ✦   TRAIL MILE 719
LOCATION Wakulla Field Campsite, St. Marks National Wildlife Refuge

---

THE ROOM IN THE LITTLE STRIP OF ROOMS where I spent the evening last was luxurious in comparison to my usual accommodations, complete with electric lights, offering precious time to work well into the night updating my journal entries.

So this morning I am out very late. It is nearly a mile from the fish camp back to the trail, and I get a ride right away from a kind old fellow as I hop onto his pickup tailgate. The trail north from St. Marks follows the old Tallahassee–St. Marks Railroad grade. This old grade has been converted to one of the nation's first rails-to-trails, and the treadway is shared for a short distance with the FT. It is a full-lane, fully paved affair. Here is some interesting history dating from near the time Tallahassee was chosen as the territorial capital in 1824, for only 11 years later and fully 10 years before Florida statehood, the Tallahassee Railroad Company was up and going. The old railroad, which was constructed originally of wooden rails, with railcars pulled by mules, continued across the St. Marks River to Port Leon. Over these tracks passed naval stores, products, stores for and from the logging and cotton industries across the South, and, later, Confederate troops and supplies. Many of the old telegraph poles, complete with pegs and insulators, have survived on the isolated Port Leon section.

I manage only a little over 9 miles today, tarrying at the canoe rental near the bridge over beautiful Wakulla Run. Toward evening, back in the St. Marks National Wildlife Refuge, I pull up at Wakulla Field Campsite. This campsite is in a lovely meadow, which as usual I have to myself. Water is nearby. (Water is always nearby!)

> *"The hiker has a unique opportunity to experience the perspective-altering impact inherent in the combination of solitude, time, immersion in the natural order and the beauty of the planet . . . This is about the beauty of another dimension."*
>
> [Jan D. Curran,
> *The Appalachian Trail—A Journey of Discovery*]

FRIDAY February 13, 1998
TRAIL DAY 44   ✦   TRAIL MILE 728
LOCATION Marsh Point at Oyster Bay,
St. Marks National Wildlife Refuge

THE RAIN BEGINS AGAIN BEFORE SUNRISE and continues heavy and steady throughout the morning and into the afternoon. I attempt to get out and break camp numerous times, but all attempts are foolish and futile. The rain keeps hammering hard, steady, and cold. Up until now I thought I had taken good protective measure in waterproofing my tent, not only the seams but also the tent fabric. For I had sprayed the entire tent and fly with Textron waterproofing and had sealed the seams with numerous dauber applications of seam sealer. But, alas, and perhaps due more to my neglect and poor care in handling the tent these many days, am I lying here now in a puddle of water. I am thankful for my little Thermarest, which keeps me mostly up and out of it. I am also thankful that Mark at Travel Country Outdoors had the foresight and good sense to put me into a synthetic sleeping bag, for I would be hopelessly and miserably cold now lying here in a waterlogged down bag. I continually mop with my towel, unzip my tent a bit, and wring out as much of the water as I can.

I'm finally able to break camp a little after 2:00 p.m. and get on my way. The wind picks up and the day becomes very cold, but the storm passes through. The sky clears to the west, and toward evening the wind dies down. I pitch at beautiful Marsh Point on the east shore of Oyster Bay, Gulf of Mexico, and experience a most memorable sunset. As the tide goes out, exposing the black floor of the saltwater marsh, I go down for water to prepare my evening meal. Taking a sip, I quickly understand the meaning of the famous quote:

> *"Water, water everywhere,*
> *Not any drop to drink."*

[Coleridge, *Rime of the Ancient Mariner*]

SATURDAY February 14, 1998
TRAIL DAY 45   ✦   TRAIL MILE 743
LOCATION Banks of the Sopchoppy River, Monkey Creek Bridge,
Apalachicola National Forest

TODAY I DEARLY WANT TO HIT A RESTAURANT for some grub and find a store for provisions. So I choose to take Carter Road west to the little town of Medart at US 98 instead of following the trail, which passes southwest of the village. This turns out to be a very bad decision, because I soon meet some very bad, BAD dogs! If barking and snarling dogs have a tendency to rattle you as they tear straight at you from their yards, perhaps the Florida Trail and the Eastern Continental Trail (ECT), each of which entails a fair amount of roadwalking, may not be your bag. I've found, however, that almost without exception, canines have a pretty predictable game plan. Even the most ferocious looking and meanest acting of the lot usually come to a screeching halt as you turn to challenge them, just when you think you're a goner, right at the edge of the road. From here they'll proceed to *dog* you, growling and snarling, to finally come onto the road after you from behind. Here, as you continue walking backwards, defending yourself, you're at least moving away from their territorial domain and in the right direction. They then quickly retreat, full of strut and pomp after their incredible display of heroism in successfully warding off yet another deadly threat to their absolute monarchy.

But today two mongrels are out in the road ahead of me and are charging, hell-bent, straight down the road at me! I know this is no welcoming committee and that some sort of action is in order, fast! For it appears now that instead of finding lunch soon, I am going to *be* lunch soon. I turn instinctively, making a mad dash for the ditch and the road-bank. Luckily, there is plenty of junk within easy reach, and I grab a four-foot piece of plastic pipe. I no sooner turn than they're right in front of me, two of the meanest Rottweilers I've ever seen, charging at me, baring their teeth from huge heads and jaws. Wielding the pipe stops their advance. I'm able to gain the center of the road again but here the dogs separate, one remaining to block my advance, the other circling my flank. This is not good. No matter which one I face, I have a vicious attack coming at me from behind. I must constantly pivot to defend myself. This isn't working; that last lunge at my legs came too close. I begin spinning around, swinging the pipe wildly. On the second revolution I catch the lead dog square in the jowls with the pipe. This lucky blow seems to gain me a little respect as this older dog, though still snarling like a mongrel from hell, keeps his distance. I continue moving forward, spinning and swinging the pipe as I go. I can see the ground coming at me time and again as I fight to remain upright, turning and swinging to keep these meat grinders away from me.

I become uncontrollably dizzy and disoriented but somehow manage to stay up and keep moving. The older dog finally retreats to join his mad accomplice behind, and I move away, backing up the road, crouching, holding and motioning with the pipe in both hands, like Sir Lancelot with his sword! Good Lord, what an ordeal!

I soon arrive at US 98, and my payoff is Register's BBQ right at the corner of Carter Road and US 98! Here I treat myself to half a BBQ chicken, huge helpings of potato salad and baked beans, two large pieces of Texas toast, and all the sweet iced tea I can possibly drink . . . but not before saying a very long, heartfelt, and most grateful prayer! US 98 goes right through Medart. Here I'm able to get some fresh oranges and some boiled peanuts at a fruit stand and, on down the road, all the provisions I could possibly need for the next few days at a Petro Station where US 98 and US 319 split. Oh yes, plus good local ice cream for dessert!

Dear old friend US 98, we have known each other over a great distance, but we must now part company. Seems we met way down in south Florida near Ft. Bassinger. Our paths first came together there, and we have been companions off and on for many a mile. You have been very kind to me with wide, smooth shoulders and friendly traffic. You'll head west now and I must turn north. So long, old buddy!

As I head for the trail crossing at US 319, a deputy sheriff pulls off the road and stops to question me. It was reported that I'd been seen in town. He wanted some ID. Then he asks, "What were you doing in Medart?" I tell him, "Not much, mainly just spending money, like at the BBQ, the fruit stand, and the convenience store . . . about 30 bucks in all." This seems to break the ice, and it's then I must answer all the usual questions that everyone else asks. I tell him about the fine welcome I received to his fair city by the dog committee at Carter Road. He tells me they've already been picked up once. I explain that's good to know but that it sure didn't help me much! As he turns to get back in his patrol car, I ask him if he'd mind doing me a favor on his way back through town. I ask him if he'd stop by his friend's place, the one who reported seeing me in Medart, and find out how much money he'd spent in Medart today!

Back on the trail now, I am leaving FT 22. The St. Marks is by far the most beautiful of all the sections hiked! I pitch at dusk on the banks of the Sopchoppy River just north of Monkey Creek Bridge. What a delightful spot, and what a very pleasant evening. There are lighter (pitch) pine stumps all around, and I'm able to pull up the heart from a few and get a delightful fire going. And its warm, glowing presence is so welcome, much as the warmth brought by the presence of a dear old friend. As I relax for the evening I'm thinking about the miraculous and safe path . . . the hand that led me past harm today and about the sad sarcasm I dealt the deputy this afternoon. He was just doing his job, but I now lament that I let it anger me so. I have been trying hard not to permit situations out of my control to affect me like that anymore. And I realize that I obviously need more patience as I search for such wisdom.

> *"Since His the sway of circumstance,*
> *I would not wince nor cry aloud.*
> *Under that rule which men call chance*
> *My head with joy is humbly bowed."*

[Dorthea Day]

SUNDAY February 15, 1998
TRAIL DAY 46　◆　TRAIL MILE 760
LOCATION Woodsroad between FR 314 and FL 375,
Apalachicola National Forest

I ENJOY A QUIET AND PEACEFUL NIGHT'S SLEEP with no rain for a change and am up and out this morning to a clear but cold day. Here the trail follows the Sopchoppy River along steep, undulating banks, indeed a most enjoyable and welcome change from the mud and the flood. If here is even the least indication of what I've missed along the Suwannee and Aucilla rivers, I feel much regret. Just before reaching the first cutoff to FR 329, I meet another hiker, Sherri *Mother Earth* Braddy, from Lutz, Florida. In the course of conversation I find that Sherri is not only very active in the FTA but that she is also good friends with Richard Graham, section leader of FT 23, the section through which I am now passing. Richard has been most helpful in providing current data not only for this section but for surrounding sections as well. I ask Sherri if she would mind giving Richard a call this evening to let him know that I have made it this far on my FT hike and that I have hopes of traversing most of the remainder of his section here in the Apalachicola National Forest by evening.

I reach the second cutoff to FR 329 by noon. Here I take a break and decide to protect my feet from the long stretch of cold, deep water which I must traverse just ahead of me in Bradwell Bay. Having just forded Monkey Creek, the water there being very cold, I feel I must prepare for the same conditions in the bay. In the hopes of providing some insulation for my ankles and feet, I pull a couple bread wrappers from my pack, punch holes in the bottom, slip them on over my wool socks, and loosely tie them off just above my ankles. With this arrangement I hope to create an envelope, much the same as with a wet suit, whereby the water exchange is reduced, in this case within my wool socks. I don't relish the idea of my feet going numb halfway through the bay. I have read and have been told much about this long, isolated, and submerged section of trail. But as I enter the bay I find it not at all noteworthy as to the degree of difficulty, nor for that matter even necessarily to my dislike, for I have cut my teeth on hundreds of miles of very similar, totally submerged treadway to the south.

I do encounter one problem area: a 200-yard section about halfway through that has the bottom literally blown out, creating a high-viscosity muck situation. There are many roots and cypress knees, making the going particularly slow and treacherous. The wrappers are working fine, however, and my feet are doing very well in the cold, numbing water. A lot of folks will go through the bay this year, but probably in groups of two or more, not alone like us nutso long-distance hikers. Three of Sherri's friends have gone through ahead of me today. Being alone under these high-risk conditions complicates things for the lone hiker. An injury, which under most other circumstances would be managed with relative ease, could prove catastrophic here in the bay. I finally decide to pull up out of the hiker-created muck slot, move to one side, and do much better.

It's clouding up again as I leave the bay, and before I can get to high ground the sky opens and the torrent begins anew. I finally make it to a crowned, grassy woodsroad between FR 314 and FL 375, but before I can get my tent set up in the deluge, my pack and everything in it are totally soaked. It's going to be peanut butter and jelly for supper — and a long, cold night tonight in my warm-when-wet (but not-when-waterlogged) sleeping bag.

> *"May your trails be dim, lonesome, stony, narrow, winding, and only slightly uphill."*
>
> [Edward Abbey]

MONDAY February 16, 1998
TRAIL DAY 47 ✦ TRAIL MILE 781
LOCATION The Beehives, FR 107, Apalachicola National Forest

I RISE AND AM GREETED BY A CLEAR BUT VERY COLD DAY. Climbing into wet hiking garb from shoes on up is not a pleasant way to start the morning. Even though it has become routine, nearly day in and day out, it is not a task one gets used to, if you know what I mean! For me, it is now shaping up as a very unpleasant ordeal. I am reaching my limit, growing very weary. I traversed Bradwell Bay yesterday in my running shoes. Thus, somehow I have managed to keep my boots and two pairs of wool socks reasonably dry. But I know better than to put them on. And this is the right decision. The section before Porter Lake Bridge I find to be a sad but typical 4WD, mud-choked, churned-up woodsroad.

In the past 46 days I have hiked nearly 800 miles of the Florida National Scenic Trail, much of it through submerged, nearly impassable treadway like this before me now. I stand here and look at it with a feeling of resignation and sadness, for I am just burned out on this kind of trail. The Good Lord has seen fit to keep me injury-free and out of harm's way. And that is a true blessing. Hiking these conditions is very unpleasant and the task is most dangerous, especially for the lone long-distance hiker who must try to maintain concentration hour after hour, day after day. We all have our limits, and I'm at mine with the mud and water.

To get a feel for this, take a day and go to the beach, wade in up to your knees, then turn and start churning through it. See how far you're happy walking like this. Throw in roots, brush, blowdowns, and bottomless bogs of mud multiplied by days and weeks, and you're ready for some other trail. So, at Porter Lake Campground, where the storm clouds are coming in and the rain is beginning again, I take my mud-bogging shoes off, go to the faucet, and wash the muck out of them for the last time. Here I put on what's left of my least soggy gear, garbage-bag my pack, don my rain jacket, and brace into it. As I head out yet again with my companion El Niño and into his seemingly endless torrent, I struggle with my conscience and inner feelings, for I have deep regret. Dear friends at FTA, I am on the road now and will remain on the road until I'm out of this nightmare. Please forgive me for passing by this trail, for I know you have built it with love and dedication. I could probably make it through if I really tried, but with conditions as they are I just cannot endure any more.

Ah! But what a great and unexpected surprise, for just as I become consumed by the hopelessly engulfing grip of total gloom and doom do I come upon this wonderful little section of trail between FL 375 and FH 13. The trail leaves the highway to climb a little sand ridge. I cannot resist, so in I go! Here the trail follows along the banks of the Ochlockonee River. The river is in a frightful flood, but the trail scampers along and above the rage, through ravines, along small bluffs—delightful ups and downs. I pass clear-running springs and northern hardwoods, and my feet remain dry! This is like hiking in the Appalachians! But alas, the sight of scrub palmetto quickly shakes me from this dream-like state, and I am back to the present, in the Panhandle, on the Florida National Scenic Trail. I sigh, for it will be weeks and weeks before I'm on this kind of trail for real.

I depart FT 23 late in the morning. To Richard Graham, and all who help maintain FT 23, my gratitude to you! I continue the remainder of the day along graded and crowned Forest Service roads. But even these built-up roadways are mostly a-sog and under water in many places. I trudge on. The storm settles into a steady, hypnotically monotonous drench to finally taper to a drizzle by early evening. The drear follows me as I work in the dim, monochromatic light of a dismal cast to pitch for the evening in a clearing near the beehives at FR 107. I am able to whittle some tinder, scrape the mushy bark from some kindling, and get a small, smoky cooking fire going. I no sooner have my meal of rice and gravy prepared than my companion who is ever near returns. El Niño comes again to stay for the night, bringing cold wind and rain interspersed with crescendos of flashing, thundering light, making sleep most fretful.

> *"Ye whose hearts are fresh and simple,*
> *Who have faith in God and Nature."*

[Longfellow, *The Song of Hiawatha*]

TUESDAY February 17, 1998
TRAIL DAY 48   ✦   TRAIL MILE 793
LOCATION Camel Lake Campground, Apalachicola National Forest

YET ANOTHER WAVE OF EL NIÑO PASSES THROUGH AT DAWN, and I rise to a clear and cool morning. During the night there has been at least another inch of rain. The elevated, graded, and crowned Forest Service roads like FR 107 are total soup and mush. Ditches are full and overflowing the roadway in many places. Apalachee West FT 24 is blue-blaze time, the right decision for sure. The FT follows near and weaves back and forth across the forest roads as I hike on west. Extensive, almost complete forest burn-over is present all the way to New River. Where I pass the FT treadway intersecting the road, the trail is completely under at nearly every crossing.

A word here about forest burn-over. Whether acts of nature, arson, or controlled burn, they make little difference to someone trying to get through. The extensive burn-over areas that I am passing today are all controlled burns, for I see rangers out with their little flame-throwers as I hike along. I break off and try a couple of these short loops that are out of the soup, and what I find is treadway that is hard to follow and at times totally obscure. All that remains is a narrow, brown, meandering ribbon set against the black carbon and char, the remaining treadway, a result of hikers who have pounded down the duff. Being compacted, the treadway is apparently more resistant to the incendiary attack than the surrounding loose humus. So where there appears a narrow brown line I find this most likely the trail. And why most likely? What about the blazes? Well, charred paint is black just like all the rest of the char, and where the burn-over has been most intense, the blazes have literally gone (you guessed it) to blazes! So if you're thinking about hiking Apalachee West in the near future, I'd wait a while . . . a long while.

If this dissertation on hiking through burn-over hasn't convinced you to let it go for another day, try this: Call up all your hiking buddies and tell them about a recent burn-over in your area. Then urge them to go along the very next weekend to hike through this blackened desolation before the rain has a chance to wash off the soot and char. This affords the grand opportunity to not only get totally covered with soot from head to toe, but to see everything nice and black to boot! See how many takers you get on that one! Needless to say, I got back on the service road and blue-blazed it on into Camel Lake Campground. El Niño hasn't caught up with me yet, and the day remains clear though windy and cold.

> *"Many potential hikers view the ultimate wilderness experience as sitting around a campfire cowboy-style eating stew and drinking black coffee from tin cups."*
>
> [Jan D. Curran, *The Appalachian Trail— A Journey of Discovery*]

WEDNESDAY February 18, 1998
TRAIL DAY 49 ✦ TRAIL MILE 810
LOCATION Planted pine by FL 12 north of Bristol

CAMEL LAKE CAMPGROUND IS A FINE FACILITY. The caretaker graciously provided me a large grassy area complete with water faucet, fire ring, and picnic table. I managed to get in early enough, and with the aid of the wind, late-afternoon sun, and a good fire, I was finally able to dry out some of my gear. Sleeping in a dry bag was a new experience!

I blue-blaze the remainder of the distance to FL 12 by hiking FR 105 which is the main road leading to the campground. This supposedly all-weather road is even 4WD territory, a churned-up track of axle-deep sand and mud. Once on FL 12 and heading north toward Bristol, I see in a short distance the familiar orange FT blazes where the trail emerges from the johnboat-passable treadway. I pause here for a moment to fix in my mind the last of the blazes that I will see on what is considered the thru-trail. For although Torreya State Park has an orange-blazed loop trail that is part of the Florida Trail System, the park is not considered part of the continuous trail.

I reach Bristol a little after lunch, just in time to enjoy the fine buffet at Apalachicola Restaurant. Then I head for the Apalachicola National Forest Ranger District Headquarters to see Ronnie Traylor. Ronnie is not only with the USFS but is also FT 24 section leader. I am disappointed that he is away, but I leave him a note thanking him for the great partnership and cooperation shared by the FTA and the USFS. From here it's a beeline to the laundromat to shake some of the crud from my fine hiking wardrobe, then a few provisions from the market, and I head north toward Torreya State Park. I find a fine pine-needle-carpeted spot in the planted pine north of town. The shrieking call of the coyote drifts in as the cool of the evening descends, but I am quickly asleep and the sound, which continues at intervals, is far, far away.

> *"Endurance is the crowning quality, and patience*
> *all the passion of great hearts."*
> [James Russell Lowell]

THURSDAY February 19, 1998
TRAIL DAY 50 ✦ TRAIL MILE 825
LOCATION Torreya State Park

TODAY IS A ROADWALK ALONG PAVED SECONDARY ROADS as I head north to Torreya State Park. The day remains clear, with a mild breeze to my back. The sun soon warms things nicely. What a beautiful day to be alive! The road I am hiking is little-traveled, rolling along, undulating through the remote north-Florida countryside. To the west is a vast area of land extending to the reaches of the Apalachicola River, and here as I pass, it ranges along with me for miles. This land is now known as The Apalachicola Bluffs and Ravines Preserve, more than 6,000 acres of pine and sandhill uplands, river bluffs, spring-fed creeks, and steeps and ravines that belong to . . . me. Yes, to me! For I am a member of The Nature Conservancy, and this land belongs to the Conservancy. Here we have undertaken the massive project of restoring the preserve's native longleaf pine/wiregrass habitat. It is a beautiful thing. This is just one small project among countless Conservancy projects. What a great organization, what glorious and far-reaching goals. I'm proud to be a Conservancy member and to be part of this advocacy, this grand vision.

As I enter Torreya State Park today, I am again walking into Florida history. For it was here in 1828, when Florida became a U.S. territory, that the first government road crossed the Apalachicola, providing passage for settlers and commerce to this strange and wonderful new land, to the far reaches of the Panhandle. The 7-mile loop trail, which follows the river bluffs and ravines, is not only part of the Florida Trail System but is also designated as a National Recreation Trail. It is a delightful hike on what has turned out to be an unusually clear, warm, and glorious day!

This isn't the end of the FT, but it is the end for me. The FT heads west for a very long roadwalk, and I head north for Alabama. I look forward with much anticipation to the adventures ahead, but I know I'll often think back and miss the reassuring guidance of the bright orange Florida Trail blazes! My itinerary was set to do this 825 miles and 25 sections in 52 days. I had allowed generous time for the Suwannee River and Aucilla River sections, but I ended up blue-blazing both to blaze past them. It is difficult to believe that after having El Niño as my near-constant companion, I have actually arrived here two days ahead of schedule.

Another screwup this evening. The public telephone is about a quarter-mile from the campground. While I call home from here, the sky opens again. I seek cover from the deluge under the ROPS canopy on one of the park tractors. I am thinking how fortunate I am to have my tent pitched and my camp all set, but as the rain continues to hammer the metal shield above me, I retrace my mental steps of a few moments ago. Yes, my tent is pitched and my camp all set . . . except that I've left my tent wide open! When I'm finally able, I return to find my sleeping bag totally soaked. Ditto for my pack and everything in it! The park has a first-class recreation hall with probably a dozen or more tables, complete with a wood-burning stove. I'm the only one in the park tonight, so I move in, stoke up the woodstove, and spread and hang everything all over the place. I'm up until 2:30 a.m. drying and shuffling my meager belongings. I finally fall asleep on the couch. The great folks who manage Torreya profess to be laid-back. A lucky thing for me! When I'm discovered here in the morning, my junk hanging helter-skelter and scattered everywhere, they aren't the least bit upset! But all things always for the better, for this gives me the opportunity to meet and talk with Paul Rice, ranger and manager of Torreya. Thanks for your kindness and hospitality, Paul; this is a remarkable place you have!

And now a final word about the Florida National Scenic Trail. And that is . . . my thanks to you, FTA! You're a great organization. I'm proud to be a member. And to you, volunteers all, who have given and continue to give unselfishly and generously of your time and talent, who have breathed life into Jim Kern's dream, my deep, heartfelt gratitude! These last 50 days spent hiking this remarkable FT are destined to become a milestone, a grand memory in this old man's life. They have made me a stronger, a much better, and a more tolerant person. I know that for a fact. These changes are prayers answered. And all of this has been made possible because of your untiring effort and dedication. God bless you all!

> *There's a Trail, this grand ol' Florida,*
> *Here my journ' to seek true worth.*
> *'Cross shifting sand, failed mortal plan,*
> *'To'rd peace, sheer joy . . . rebirth!*

[N. Nomad]

Chapter 2
The Grand Connection

SECTION 1: Florida/Alabama Roadwalk

FRIDAY February 20, 1998
TRAIL DAY 51/1 ✦ TRAIL MILE 845/20
LOCATION Ball Field Announcer's Score Box, Sneads

THE ROADWALK INTO CHATTAHOOCHEE IS LITERALLY A BREEZE, for I have a gentle breeze to my back, and the weather is again fair. There is very little traffic, but I'm offered many rides. I also meet lots of friendly dogs along the way, with none wanting to take my leg off for a change. I'm in by early afternoon and head for the Home Place Café for a grand fried-chicken dinner.

The roadwalk out of here is no fun. I'm on busy US 90 and must cross the new Apalachicola River Bridge. There's a fully paved emergency lane, and I keep tight against the concrete sidewall, but the trucks and heavy traffic are really barreling at me and I get a good sandblasting. The bridge continues for what seems better than a mile. Then I'm finally able to pull well off and walk in the grass. Just west of the bridge, I pass the Apalachee Correctional Institution. Facilities like this used to be called prisons. Here, convicts (now called inmates) are housed to the tune of nearly 50 bucks a day. I'm thinking that with this luxury, I could be pounding out 50-mile days and still be averaging the good old budget standard of a dollar a mile! But I decide that my 15 miles, 15 bucks per day—and my freedom—are a much better deal. By late evening I

enter the little village of Sneads. Here I head to the supermarket for a few provisions.

There's a ball-field complex right next door, and I head over in search of a quiet corner to pitch for the night. There is no shrubbery or any cover to be found, just the dugouts, the score boxes, the usual backstops, and chain-link all around. I check out the dugouts. They're all dark, dank, and dirty. For some reason I decide to take a look at one of the score boxes. There must be half a dozen or more standing high on stilts, perhaps 12 feet off the ground. Each is secured with a chain-link gate, and each has a ladder leading to a trapdoor in the floor. To my surprise, the first gate I check is unlocked and the trapdoor is wide open, so up and in I go. This place is neat! It is equipped with benches and a long built-in table along the full shuttered wall facing the field. There are fluorescent lights, and the place is clean. The first order of business is to close the shutters to hold in the warmth of the day. By dropping the trapdoor, I have more than enough room to roll out my sleeping bag. There may be no armoire, no vault to store my valuables, no concierge desk nearby, nor an Yvon Goetz to prepare his famous Mediterranean cuisine for my exquisite dining this evening, but this is definitely and truly a Hiker Trash Ritz-Carlton penthouse!

> *"And one summer-morn forsook his friends,*
> *And went to learn the gypsy-lore,*
> *And roamed the world with that wild brotherhood,*
> *And came, as most men deem'd to little good . . ."*
>
> [James Michener, *The Drifters*]

SATURDAY February 21, 1998
TRAIL DAY 52/2 ✦ TRAIL MILE 863/38
LOCATION Planted pine by CR 271 south of Hornsville

ON MY WAY OUT OF SNEADS THIS MORNING, I stop at a little mom 'n' pop restaurant hooked to the side of a gas station and am served a fine tank-topping breakfast. What a beautiful, warm morning as I head north for a roadwalk on CR 271. The road crosses many little inlets and streams leading to Lake Seminole, then finally follows the shoreline for miles. Boaters are out fishing along the shore, and many greet me as I hike along. One laments that all would be better if the fish were a-bitin'. When I suggest that he has already caught a perfect day, all in the boat raise a cheer to that!

What a glorious spring-like morning. This is the first day in a long while that I have really felt the comforting warmth of the sun. I am thinking about the book *Walking with Spring*, written by Earl Shaffer in 1981. Earl was the first to thru-hike the AT after its official dedication in 1937. He did it in 1945, just after returning home from the war. The book is aptly named, for it was on his thru-hike that Earl literally walked with spring. For you see, as one hikes north from Springer Mountain, an interesting coincidence occurs—that being the simultaneously changing tilt of the sun to the earth, which moves spring north with you! And if you can hike at the rate of 15 to 20 miles per day, you remain on that very day that you met spring . . . until spring slowly accelerates to bid you farewell and leave you behind somewhere in Virginia.

My walk with spring has already begun, because I have seen my first azaleas blooming in a neatly kept farmyard south of Bristol, Florida. Redbuds and azaleas are in full bloom along the streets in Chattahoochee, and by the roadway this morning in the woods I see the beautiful white bloom of the wild pear. So, Earl, I'll be hiking with spring, but much earlier and for a considerably longer time. There are two distinctions, the Good Lord willin', I hope to make as I hike along this year: One, that I'll be the only person to walk near the entire breadth of the eastern North American continent, and two, that I'll have enjoyed spring longer than anyone else in America!

By evening I have made it to just south of Hornsville, and I pitch in the planted pine by the road. This day and this roadwalk have been delightful!

> *"Content with birds and trees and flowers*
> *In mellow age I find*
> *'Mid monastery's holy hours*
> *God's Peace of Mind."*

[Robert W. Service, *Tranquillity*]

SUNDAY February 22, 1998
TRAIL DAY 53/3 ✦ TRAIL MILE 876/51
LOCATION Planted pine by AL 75 south of Gordon, Alabama

I AM GREETED BY A COLD, VERY DREARY MORNING. By the time I reach the Alabama line, I'm in the middle of a hard-pounding electrical storm. I cross from Florida into Alabama at 10:00 a.m. this day. Florida will be the longest state to hike by far, nearly 900 miles. One down, 15 to go! Reflecting now, I find it most fitting to be leaving Florida in the driving rain! El Niño does not heed this line that man has drawn, and so it is that we continue on together. I will truly not miss the water, mud, and muck. It remains to be seen if anyone else succeeds with much of the FT this year. The Good Lord has seen fit to provide me safe passage, and for that I am truly thankful.

The rain comes harder, and I am not only soaked but becoming very chilled. So I pull into Chattahoochee State Park. The park is open but there is no one around. As I slog clear to the river and back, I find no place to get out of it, save the office's front porch, so I pitch right there on the wooden floor with my tent pegs stuck in the floor cracks. I can't get into my tent and sleeping bag fast enough, as I am shivering uncontrollably from the familiar descending stages of hypothermia. As soon as the reflex tremors subside, I fall into a very deep sleep which lasts for well over two hours.

As I look out, the sky is clearing somewhat and the storm seems to be moving on. So I pack up and head on north to pitch in the planted pine near a lovely field just off CR 75. The rain continues off and on all night. I have picked up a piece of plastic that can be lashed over my tent. This keeps the deluge from coming straight through.

> *"The real voyage of discovery consists not in
> seeking new landscapes but in having new eyes."*
>
> [Marcel Proust, *The Power of Travel*]

MONDAY February 23, 1998
TRAIL DAY 54/4　✦　TRAIL MILE 896/71
LOCATION Planted pine by AL 95 north of Columbia

I PICKED UP AN HOUR WHEN I CROSSED the Chattahoochee River, so now I'm on the eastern edge of the Central time zone. It's almost like being on daylight saving time, for now I have daylight, as far as the hours go, much later into the evening. This time setup I much prefer. Another gloomy, rainy day is shaping up as I stop for breakfast at a little black-run café in Gordon. I'm a Southern boy, and I like my grits. And here I'm served some of the finest grits I've had staring back at me in a long time. I go for the biscuits, gravy, sausage, and eggs too! Everybody wants to hear my story about where I've come from and where I'm headed. The grits and the coffee keep coming, and I can hardly waddle out of the place.

Chirp trees are starting to bloom now. Don't know about chirp trees? They're swamp (red) maple. When the seedlings fall, pick a dry one up. Break off the end bulb and place the reed crosswise on your tongue, back about an inch with the feather-edge forward. Then touch your tongue lightly against your palate and say "Shhhhh." With a little practice, you'll be able to "chirp" all of the wonderful nostalgic old Stephen Foster songs! So off I go "chirping" along today, entertaining myself through the gloom and the rain. It's a Huckleberry Finn day all the way! I hit a sub shop in Columbia for supper, then move on to pitch in the planted pine just north of town on CR 95.

*"Happiness ain't a thing in itself—it's only a contrast
with something that ain't pleasant."*

[Mark Twain]

TUESDAY February 24, 1998
TRAIL DAY 55/5　✦　TRAIL MILE 911/86
LOCATION Piney woods by AL 95 near Abbie Creek

THE DAY DAWNS CLEAR AND COLD, and I quickly crank the old jitney, getting it rolling along and up to normal operating temperature. Yes indeedy, it's going to be a fine day. My plans were to cut over to CR 97 and head on north, hard by the Chattahoochee River, but the going along AL 95 has been most pleasant and I decide to continue on its friendly path into Haleburg, population 106. As I make my entrance, the burg's most prominent citizens, the neighborhood dogs, quickly hail me. I am treated with courtesy and kindness, but everyone in town soon knows that someone has arrived! As I pass through, the wind picks up from the north, so I jiggle and tug the throttle a bit and lean into it for the remainder of the day.

I'm always ready for a little diversion, some excitement if you will, and my share comes full measure today. As I'm happily chugging north, totally enwrapped in my usual little daydream cocoon, I am soon graced by the presence of two big, BIG, Black Angus bulls, one on either side of the road. It's immediately apparent they're having a turf problem. Judging by the respective holes they've dug and are standing in, this display of taurus might didn't begin just a few moments ago. Assessing the situation, I'm not at all pleased with what I see, for the only thing physically separating these rhino-sized mammoths (and me near in the middle) is a thin, almost invisible filament-sized strand of electric wire running along both fencelines. I abruptly halt some distance from them.

They continue facing off, each as close to the wire as possible. First the bull to my right thrashes and stomps angrily, followed in perfect queue by the bull to my left, each kicking and throwing dirt like some out-of-control backhoe. The larger of the two has worked up a full frenzy, throwing dirt everywhere, much of it landing on his back and on the top of his head! I'm really not the least bit anxious to go parading right through the middle of this thunder party, for I can feel the ground shake and tremor even as I hold my distance. As I continue standing here, trying to explain to myself in a most convincing manner that there is this whole road width through which I can walk, I become puzzled and taken by the road's incredibly narrow appearance! And as I ponder proceeding, the possibility of needing a quick path of retreat finally strikes me. It's then I realize that there isn't a thing, save a power pole, anywhere close to hide behind. By enduring the insignificant electric jolt for just a second, these fearsome hulks could charge full-tilt through the wire and into the roadway! Then what would they do, indeed what would *I* do? Aww, jeez! This is really scary. This is surely more excitement than this old man has ever hoped for or could possibly want!

For the last four days I've been diligently rolling along this highway on my odyssey, and the logging trucks have been diligently rolling along to the mill. Over this short course of time we've become like old friends. There's "Haulin' Heavy," "Dixie Red," "Road Runner," "Rebel," and many others. From each I get that delightful, wanderlust-tugging airhorn blast as they pass me by . . . WOONK . . . WOONK . . . WONK, WONK. Ya gotta smile and feel that tingle clean up your spine!

Well, these fellows pass here many times each day, and here comes one now. He quickly sees my dilemma. I hear the SKOINK . . . SKOOINK of his airbrakes as he slows to let me jump the running board, and in just seconds I'm past and out of harm's way! Thanks, Dixie Red!

Near dusk, as the wind settles down for the evening, I settle down too, just off AL 95 near Abbie Creek. What a remarkable, adventure-filled day! This one sure will remain in this old man's memory for a long, *long* time. Folks, you gotta believe me, there's more to this hiking and backpacking thing . . . there's more to it than just climbing mountains!

> *"A truly wise person kneels at the feet of all creatures*
> *and is not afraid to endure the mockery of others."*
>
> [Mechtild of Magdeburg, 1265]

WEDNESDAY February 25, 1998
TRAIL DAY 56/6 ✦ TRAIL MILE 936/111
LOCATION Piney woods by CR 95 at Chester Chapel Church

I'VE DEFINITELY BEEN HEADING FOR HIGHER GROUND—no big hills, just a gradual steady pull the last few days. You wouldn't even notice it rolling along in an automobile, but it's there, and I can definitely feel its gentle tug as I hike along. I suppose I should start remarking about some of these little communities that I'm passing. I don't have a clue where the folks come up with some of these names. Up just ahead this morning is the little country crossroads of Screamer. Ha! See what I mean? "Say, fella, where y'all from?" "Uhh, well, I be from Screamer, how about you?" "Oh, I'm from Smut Eye, over by The Bottle!"

The pleasant roadwalk continues. Traffic is definitely not a problem. The logging trucks that have been running fairly steady give me all the room they can, swinging into the other lane if there's no oncoming traffic. The road finally claims the ridge here at Screamer, and from this vantage I can see across Lake Eufaula to the east, all the way into Georgia. This roadwalk isn't anything like I had anticipated. It has been most pleasant, and I am enjoying it very much. I even pass two well-built beaver dams today. I stop for water at Chester Chapel Church and then pitch in the piney woods across the road. A most pleasant, uneventful day.

"Heaven is under our feet as well as over our heads."
[Henry David Thoreau]

THURSDAY February 26, 1998
TRAIL DAY 57/7 ✦ TRAIL MILE 949/124
LOCATION Terrace Motel, Eufaula

WHAT A BEAUTIFULLY CLEAR, WARM DAY—perfect hiking weather! I stop for coffee at White Oak and then head for US 431. There's about 7 miles of this major highway to hike to reach Eufaula, but the shoulders are wide and the traffic is moderate. Most drivers are very courteous, honking or waving at me as they pass. I arrive in Eufaula by noon and head straight for Pierces for dinner. The fare served up this noon is them good ol' pig knuckles and greens—*Umm*-um!

This town has seen few if any hikers, I'm sure, but I'm able to get a good Hiker Trash deal at the Terrace Motel. I haven't had a shower, save what Ma Nature has seen fit to provide, since Torreya, and my hiking garb is just the least bit soiled. The hot shower feels soooo good! I wash my clothes in the tub and string them to dry on my makeshift line in front of the television. Supper is at Captain D's. I like the extra cracklings they serve free in a little paper side basket. All you need do is ask!

As I head back to the motel after supper and just at sunset, El Niño has finally caught up with me. As I hasten along, the gray, rolling clouds descend, thunder rattling and crashing. I duck into my room just as the bucket brigade begins in earnest. What a joy to have secure shelter and to be out of it for a change! The storm continues, pulsating throughout the night with lightning illuminating the room like so many flashbulbs. But I am warm and dry, so smug and snug in a luxurious bed with linen and a pillow! I dearly needed this short hiking day. This is "give the dog a bone" day, and I feel only a tinge of guilt about the extravagance lavished upon myself and the gleeful manner in which I have indulged. This has been a most, *most* welcome time for rest and recuperation, and even in the presence of El Niño's anger I sleep soundly, his attention-seeking, carnival-like sideshow clamor so much a dream!

> *"A carelessness of life and beauty marks the glutton, the*
> *idler and the fool in their deadly path across history."*
>
> [John Masefield]

FRIDAY February 27, 1998
TRIAL DAY 58/8   ✦   TRAIL MILE 966/141
LOCATION Piney woods by US 431 near Comers Pond

LEAVING EUFAULA ON A BLUSTERY, OVERCAST DAY, I pass many beautiful homes, some antebellum. All are impeccably restored and painstakingly maintained. Here is the Old South in the grandest and finest tradition. I can close my eyes and see the beautiful belles in hoops and bustles poised on the grand porticos and along the colonnade. Some of these remarkable old homes are mansions in the truest sense, all listed on the National Register of Historic Places. As I proceed along North Eufaula Avenue, I first pass the Holleman-Foy home. This beautiful structure is adorned with the most striking semicircular porch roof, supported by tall Corinthian columns. Beneath this and above the grand entrance is a recessed, arched balcony giving the appearance of a stately rotunda. Just two blocks north, I pass the Shorter Mansion, constructed in 1884, a stunning example of Neoclassical Revival architecture. It has such a spectacular presence, graced on the fore and both sides by 17 Corinthian columns. And just next door is the Foy-Beasley home. The exterior of this glorious old structure still proudly shows its original brick veneer, a remarkable square tower, dentil molding, and a most notable porte-cochere. There are many other grand old homes gracing both North Eufaula Avenue and the adjoining streets as I pass. More than 700 structures within the city are on the National Historic Register. Just in the next block is the Drewry-Mitchell-Moorer home. This is a lovely Italianate structure with broad verandas on three sides, supported by elaborately carved columns.

The traffic on US 431, as it turns out, is not nearly as bad as I had anticipated. In fact, the sojourners here are most friendly and accommodating. Thus, in my memory will this visit remain. Indeed, in my memory will this roadwalk remain, a journey with the kind and friendly people of Alabama. Slowly but surely I am coming to realize that this entire Florida/Alabama roadwalk is shaping up to be, and most assuredly will be, a memorable and grand affair!

I stop today at two black-run community stores. At the first I meet proprietor Harold Purifoy. Harold becomes intrigued as he sets his mind to the possibility of a 3,400-mile hike. He keeps shaking his head. He cannot comprehend that I have actually walked from Miami to his store. He wrestles most uncomfortably with the fact that I have indeed walked this distance . . . to now stand here before him! As he cogitates, I pull up a stool. We then proceed to have a most relaxed and enjoyable conversation. Soon comes an old fellow, a Vietnam vet. He goes to the cooler, grabs a cold one, and pops it right on the spot. (Dang, Harold, I hope this doesn't get you in trouble.) He then joins in the conversation. Of course, by now I've gone to the ice-cream chest and helped myself to a pint of the local best! As I plunk down a couple of bucks, Harold will have nothing to do with it. I linger, and Harold and I talk for the longest time.

The old vet has long since departed the store as I shoulder my pack to go. It is then that I discover this kind old gent has left behind a five-dollar bill . . . right there on my sleeping-bag stuff sack! At the second store I am greeted with kindness and the grandest Southern hospitality . . . and given a free energy-boosting trove of confections! Three trail angels in the span of less than three hours! Folks, please keep in mind that this white boy has seen only one other white boy in the span of the last three hours!

I have been looking with great anticipation toward the first of the grand and majestic white pine, but I suspect I'll have to venture much farther north before seeing one. But I believe, I truly do believe, that I have seen the last of the scrub palmetto and the cabbage palm.

There's a subject to which I have been giving much thought. Since meeting so many kind folks on this roadwalk, I think it certainly must not be coincidence the interesting repetition and narrow spectrum of questions I am constantly asked. There are basically two standard questions. The first: "Hey, old feller, where ya headed?" I've started hitting them straight out with it . . . KA-BAM! "Maine!" The almost-universal exclamatory response: "MAINE!" Then their eyes kind of glass over and I get a blank stare . . . far away, for a moment or two! Then they manage to stutter out, "Th-, Th-, That's a long ways." End of conversation! This odyssey worth it just to see this happen over and over again. It's a gut-bustin' hoot!

The second: "Aren't you afraid of snakes and bears?" I say, "Hell, yes, I'm afraid of 'em, the same as you and everybody else! I don't want to stumble into a pit of vipers or have a not-so-gentle Ben cuff me around any more than you do. But truth be known, you'll probably see as many snakes passin' through your backyard as I'm gonna see on this whole odyssey. And as for bears? If you're lucky enough to see one in the wild — and "lucky" is the correct word, for it's a joy to see these animals — I'll tell you this: Out here on the trail, if I see a bear, I'll be lucky to get a glimpse of his butt! Should I want to see the whole bear, head and butt, I'll have to go to the zoo, same as you. Bears in the woods are no problem!"

I pitch in the piney woods off US 431 near Comers Pond, past the water tower. For some reason or other, El Niño has failed to find me today!

"You only live once, but if you work it right, once is enough."

[Joe E. Lewis]

SATURDAY February 28, 1998
TRAIL DAY 59/9 ✦ TRAIL MILE 984/159
LOCATION Piney woods by CR 169 near Uchee Creek

THE DAY DAWNS COLD—40 DEGREES—BUT VERY CLEAR. I get the old jitney cranking and am out at 7:00 a.m. There is much more traffic today on US 431. This will probably be one of my toughest roadwalk days. I no sooner get rolling good (it takes me a while to get rolling good!) than I come to this neat crossroads country store at Pittsview. Here is an interesting old rusty-tin-roofed mom 'n' pop gas-pumpin' café. Looks like breakfast time to me, since so far this morning I've experienced the repeated grand joy found only in a peanut-butter sandwich! As I head in I give a nod to a couple of questionable-looking characters pumping gas. The greasy spoon is way in the back, and I no sooner get my order in for the full spread of bacon, eggs, biscuits, and grits (the works) and sit down with a tin of coffee than one of the fellows from out front comes to my table. I nod again as he approaches. Next thing I know, he's square in front of me and I'm hearing, "You wouldn't by chance be the *Nimblewill Nomad*, would you?" Jeez! I come right up out of my chair! What to hell is this? I'm in the Alabama backwoods, 400 miles from noplace . . . and this guy walks right up and asks if I'm the *Nimblewill Nomad*! Damn, now I know how Bocephus feels. I gotta get some bigger shades!

Here I meet Patrick Jackson. Soon comes his friend Ed Talone. Turns out they've just completed some section hiking on the FT and are headed home the roundabout way to Pat's place in Tennessee and Ed's place in Maryland. They had seen my scribbling in a couple of trailhead registers while on the Florida Trail, and when they saw me this morning they put two and two together! We stand chuckling and shaking our heads. Then we sit down, continuing to chuckle and shake our heads! We look at each other in total disbelief, finding this whole screwy thing incredibly hard to believe. We're probably the only three people on the whole continent who have given the FT a go this year, and here we sit in the back room of a little lean-to nobody has ever heard of . . . in the Bama boonies. Public Enemy #1 on the run couldn't hope to get lost any better than this! Dang, folks, I know you don't want to hear this and it's gonna make you cringe . . . but can you think of a better example of "It's a small world"?

We have a grand time "bench hiking" for the better part of an hour, talking and enjoying each other's company. In the course of conversation, I mention that I would sure like to know how to get hold of Ed Garvey. Right there on the spot, Ed Talone rattled off Garvey's home phone number in Falls Church, Virginia. He knows it by heart, says he (Ed and Ed) talk on a regular basis. I'm flabbergasted, can't believe it. I grope in my pack for a pad and pencil as he recites the number for the fourth time! We linger, not wanting to break the spell of this incredibly enjoyable coincidence, but unfortunately, as in all good things . . .

There's a grand, modern, and well-illuminated store/café near the junction of AL 169 and CR 22 north of Seale. The rain has joined me again, so I head in for a break and for supper. The special posted on the marquee says "Catfish Dinner." That's all the encouragement I need. The catfish is great, and the kind folks let me loiter around the rest of the afternoon as I jot notes in my journal about this amazing day!

The rain relents as evening approaches, and I'm able to hoof it on up the road to pitch in the piney woods by CR 169 near Uchee Creek.

> *"I want to travel the common road*
> *With the great crowd surging by,*
> *Where there's many a laugh and many a load,*
> *And many a smile and sigh."*

[Silas H. Perkins, *The Common Road*]

SUNDAY March 1, 1998
TRAIL DAY 60/10 ✦ TRAIL MILE 999/174
LOCATION Lakeshore by CR 169, south of Opelika

THE FOLKS IN FLORIDA HAVE NO LONG-DISTANCE-HIKERS' association, but the time has come. So, henceforth, from this day forth and forever there will be the "Wanderlust Society." In addition to others who will soon step forward and be recognized as charter members, the founders are Joan *Trail Angel* Hobson, Frederick *Vagabond* Guhsé, John *Daruma* Brinda, and Eb *Nimblewill Nomad* Eberhart. As of February 28, 1998, two new inductees have been added to the Wanderlust roster. They are Patrick *Garcia* Jackson and Ed *Tric* (for "Trail Icon") Talone. This brings the membership of the society to a grand total of six so far. There are only three requirements for membership: You must be an FTA member and profess to be a Florida Trail long-distance hiker; you must have a bona fide trail name—that's all we will accept—and you must take the Pledge of the Wanderlust, which appears at the end of this journal entry. That's it!

There is very little traffic on CR 169, making for a most enjoyable roadwalk today. I stop for breakfast at a little mom 'n' pop (and daughter) BBQ place in Crawford, then later I pull up on the road shoulder for lunch. It's funny watching motorists rubberneck as they drive by! Come to think of it, I suppose it is a little unusual to see someone lounging by the side of the road eating a sandwich. I pitch for the evening on the grassy shore of a lovely little lake about 11 miles south of Opelika. Picturesque countryside, a wonderful hike today!

Pledge of the Wanderlust

There's a trail way up yonder I'm preparin' to hike,
It has no beginning or end.
But awaitin' that journey, Ol' FT and I'll be . . .
A-chasin' rainbows 'round the next bend.

[N. Nomad]

MONDAY March 2, 1998
TRAIL DAY 61/11 ✦ TRAIL MILE 1,008/183
LOCATION Motel 6, I-85/US 280, Opelika

ONE OF THE NOT-SO-MUCH-FUN CONDITIONS I find associated with getting old is decreased circulation. I dearly suffer from this in my fingers and hands, so when the temperature starts dropping, everything I try picking up also starts dropping! Ice is about as I roll out this morning, and before I manage to break camp and get going, my fingers pretty much quit working.

I've noticed over the past few days a steadily increasing stream of pickups and trailers with "hogs" heading south for Daytona Bike Week. "Hardly Ableson" owners affectionately call their motorcycles "hogs." You can see what I not-so-affectionately call them. I'm sure the American-made machines of today are well built and dependable, but I could never keep "Springer," my old '47 Harley, running. It seemed I was in a crouch beside it much more than I was astride and riding it!

I've been trying to reach Marty Dominy at every opportunity since Eufaula, with no success. Dialing the right phone number would probably have helped! Marty is president of the Benton MacKaye Trail Association, and he's also one of the founding members of the Georgia Pinhoti Trail Association. Marty is the driving force in new trail building in the southern Appalachians. He will be sending me marked-up topos and other maps to guide me along the proposed Georgia Pinhoti route. Here in Opelika, the end of my trek for today, I finally reach Marty by calling the right number. I am relieved to know that the maps will be waiting when I arrive at Goodwater, a little village near the southern end of the Appalachians. What faces me up ahead, before I reach the Appalachian Trail, is a fair amount of bushwhacking. When the Georgia segment of the Pinhoti Trail is completed, however, it will connect the Alabama Pinhoti Trail with the Benton MacKaye Trail, which links up with the Appalachian Trail near Springer Mountain!

This whole glorious idea—opening the southern Appalachians and in the process providing the hiker and backpacker the opportunity to gain a broader perspective and a deeper appreciation for these grand old Appalachians and what they are truly about—was the dream of one R. Michael Leonard. I quote from an article written by Mr. Leonard in this winter's issue of the beautiful *Outdoor Alabama* magazine: "In early 1985, *Alabama Conservation Magazine* (the former name of *Outdoor Alabama*) published an article I wrote entitled, 'It's About Time for a Plan to Connect Alabama's Mountains to the Famous Appalachian Trail.' The article set out a plan for correcting the fifty-year-old oversight of having the Appalachian Trail system end in north Georgia instead of in east central Alabama where the Appalachian Mountain range actually ends."

Little did Mr. Leonard know, I suspect, that during this same time another man, Richard Anderson, was dreaming the same dream about the northern Appalachian Range. For it was in June of 1994 that *Le Sentier International des Appalaches*/International Appalachian Trail, an international nonprofit organization, was officially formed and charged with the goal and task of completing a trail from Mt. Katahdin, the northern terminus of the Appalachian Trail, through northern Maine to the far reaches of Canada, where the Appalachian Mountains plunge to the sea at the spectacular Cliffs of Forillon, Cap Gaspé, Québec! (I have added this as I edit my final manuscript, for I feel it is timely and appropriate. Indeed, I did not know about this grand SIA/IAT until approaching ATC headquarters in Harpers Ferry some 1,400 miles and four months on up the trail.)

Today is a short mileage day—just as well, as the day remains very cold, the wind is kicking, and yet another storm seems to be brewing. I stop at Motel 6 near I-85 and US 280 to lavish myself once again with a warm room, a bed . . . and another luxurious hot shower—my reward for reaching the four-digit mark in trail miles! I go for the evening's full spread at Shoney's.

> *"Always will I take another step. If that is of no avail I will take another, and yet another. In truth, one step at a time is not too difficult."*

> [Og Mandino]

TUESDAY March 3, 1998

TRAIL DAY 62/12   ✦   TRAIL MILE 1,028/203

LOCATION Wildlife clearing, piney woods by US 280 near Camp Hill

---

THE RAIN HOLDS, BUT THE DAY IS CUTTING COLD. The wind continues hard as it has the full day past, pushing me back relentlessly as it rumbles through with its refrigerated freight from the north. This is an angry wind and I can feel its bitterness clear to my core. Oh, the ides of March are yet 12 days ahead. I dearly pray this is not a grand rehearsal!

I stagger along today as the nor'wester continues to buffet me. Maintaining my balance becomes even more of a chore, for I have my hands in my pockets to keep them from turning any darker blue. I can see a Kroger ahead, and I pull right in and head for the deli. Here the lady presents the most sympathetic expression as she sees the forlorn old *Nomad* approaching. She turns, and before I know it she's got a sausage biscuit and a steaming cup of coffee sitting on the top of the case, even before I have a chance to greet her! She says, "Here, mister, you need this! It's on the house." As I linger to answer her questions and give her my pitch about this odyssey, she refills my Styrofoam cup and hands me a jelly roll!

Back on the road and fighting into it, and just before noon, a pickup pulls beside in the wrong lane from behind. The driver quickly rolls his window down, hands me a familiar-looking package, and before speeding away just as quickly says, "Bet you can use that!" Oh yes! A hot, hot double cheeseburger! I holler back, waving at him, "Thanks, THANKS." But he doesn't hear me. I've always savored chomping into a juicy, thick double cheeseburger, but as I stand here on this windy highway this morning, I can't remember ever thinking about how warm and great one feels in your hands!

Now in the little town of Waverly, I head for the post office. Here I ask the postmistress if she can tell me the hours of service for Goodwater. She jots the hours down for me and then, just to make sure, she gives them a call. Looks like I'm in luck. I hope to get into Goodwater, still about 45 miles north of here, sometime Friday. The post office is open until 4:30 p.m. during the week, and just in case I miss it, I still have a shot at getting my mail Saturday morning from 9:30 until 11:30. I have supper at a little mom 'n' pop general store in Waverly and pitch for the evening in a lush little wildlife clearing just off US 280.

"The measure of a man's life is the well spending of it, and not the length."

[Plutarch]

I TAKE THE SIDE ROAD FROM US 280 INTO the little community of Camp Hill. I have another grand full-course breakfast at a little black-run store. From here I follow the back streets through Camp Hill to the railroad tracks. The exhaust fumes from the heavy diesel trucks and buses are starting to work me over pretty good, and each time I hear the crackle and cackle of my now-falsetto-like voice, I think back to the bumbling, acne-faced puberty phase of my not-so-nimble childhood. So a change to a less hacking-prone atmosphere is definitely in order, if for no other reason than to get my mind off the unpleasant memories that now accompany my funny voice, memories from those ill-fated days of utter failure at girl conquering. The suave ladies' man I most certainly was not!

The hike on the railroad grade goes fine through Dadeville and into near Jackson Gap. It's a most welcome break being away from the constant rumble, drone, and fumes of US 280. Now I know I'm climbing. I've jumped up on one of the rails, and with the aid of a couple of sticks I'm soon throttled up to full locomotion. Filled with glee and now in this little repetitive-motion trance, I fail to notice a side spur up ahead. Parked there is this Norfolk Southern Railway service vehicle. We've all seen these contraptions, the truck up on the tracks with the neat little steel railroad wheels front and rear. I've always wondered what it would be like to actually ride in one, to be tooling down the tracks, no need to hold the steering wheel or even pay any attention to where you're headed, for that matter!

Oh yes, I forgot to mention, here also are two Norfolk Southern Railroad employees. Uh-oh! Well, I'm greeted cordially enough, in a manner I consider to be most diplomatic. We exchange the time of day, and they both want to hear my pitch. I can see they don't really want to be angry with me, but at the same time there is this unsettled air of formality. And so now with much restraint is it explained to me that I am trespassing on private property, just as 20 or 30 signs they know I have passed have also explained! Their tact seems even more amazing as they relate the grim story of the two teens who recently jumped to their deaths in the rocks below the Tallapoosa River Trestle, trying to outrun the train. That trestle is just a few miles ahead. Short of having me arrested, turning me around and making me walk back the way I came would surely have given them some satisfaction, but instead, and no doubt due to kindness, they suggest I continue on to the next rail crossing and move back over to US 280. What fumes?

I pitch on a small flat blowdown ledge on the side of a very steep hill near Peckerwood. I listen, and sure enough, in just a moment I hear it again. It's a donkey. Yes, a donkey . . . and yes, the name of the place is *Peckerwood*! The rain is back. So I listen to the donkey, the rain, and then the trucks, the *donkey* . . . the rain, and th — ZZZZ

> *"Not till each loom is silent,*
> *And the shuttles cease to fly,*
> *Shall God reveal the pattern*
> *And explain the reason why."*

[Unknown]

THURSDAY March 5, 1998
TRAIL DAY 64/14   ◆   TRAIL MILE 1,056/231
LOCATION Empty trailer behind carpet store, US 280, Alexander City

THIS DAY IS NOT STARTING OUT SO GREAT. It is raining steadily, and this rain has that no-nonsense kind of permanence about it . . . and it is very cold. Making and breaking camp are the two most vulnerable times of the day for me. I've never learned how to effectively cope with them during bad weather. There's usually a trick to everything. The more you practice, the easier it gets. But in the rain, and with one of these little lightweight dink tents like mine, there's just no way that I've been able to figure to get everything set up or repacked without a major soaking. So I start this day not only soaked, but cold and soaked. Looking on the brighter side, however, a wet pack is heavy and lugging this thing will help me warm up faster!

Just across the Tallapoosa River there's a convenience store complete with a grill. I've really been chugging but still haven't warmed up, so in I head to get out of it. When folks around southern Alabama see someone backpacking their byways, it's obviously a novelty to them. Here this morning, a fellow comes over to my booth right away. He says he's seen me on the road and asks two or three of the usual questions — the ones that have the T-shirt answers — and I smile, inviting him to join me. Come to find the old fellow knows all about the Talladega National Forest, so I also get in a few questions. The rain has shifted from steady to steady with pounding waves, so after finishing my breakfast I linger, and we both keep downing the coffee. The rain finally settles back to light and steady, and the sky actually brightens a little, so I bid the old fellow good day and head back out.

I am actually able to make it into Alexander City between the waves of rain. But as I pass a strip center, the wind picks up and another wave starts coming through, so I head for the covered walkway and flop down on one of the bus benches. While I sit here now for only a moment trying to decide if I want to hit the grocery store for a few provisions, up pulls this little Honda. Down goes the window a crack and I hear a wee voice: "Come here a minute, mister." I get back up and take the few steps . . . to stare down into the widest, whitest eyes of the littlest kid I've ever seen, the most petite black child with this bright and glorious expression of alarm! Our mutual stare is finally broken as the mother instructs her daughter, "Give da man da money, child!" Up and out the window thrusts this little hand with a wad of bills. I look in disbelief — a five and three ones. I'm thinking, "Don't refuse this kindness." I manage to reach for them, "My . . . My goodness ma'am, thank you, thank you so much!" As I stoop down to look across, the lady says, "I saw you walking the road south of here for the last two days. I wish there was more I could do to help you." I don't know what to say. I turn, stand a moment, then shoulder my pack and head out across the parking lot.

I don't walk 20 paces when I hear steps behind me. I turn to see the black lady running toward me, so I stop. Heaving a sigh, she says, "Mister, give me back that money!" I'm shaking my head, "Yes, ma'am. Oh . . . yes ma'am." I reach in my pocket and hand her back the wad of bills. She says, "Here, take this 10!" Then turning, she says again, "Mister, I wish there was more I could do for you." I'm taken aback again by this incredible show of kindness, but manage, "Well, ma'am, there are a couple more things you can do for me. First, would you please tell me your name?" She stops, "My name is Angela." With not much composure I say, "Well, Angela, have you ever been away from home, away from your family and friends for a long time, long enough to really get to feeling sad and lonely . . . when all you really needed to fix everything back right was a good old solid hug?" Well, folks, stop reading here for just a moment, sit back in your chair, close your eyes, and try to visualize this picture. Here's this grizzly old white guy, the only white guy probably in three counties, scroungy soaked clothes, filthy backpack, beard, mangy wet hair . . . and a very professionally dressed young black girl, standing in the middle of this shopping-center parking lot in Alexander City, Alabama, in the pouring rain, hugging each other! Who says there are no miracles anymore!

As Angela returns to her daughter waiting on the walkway, I raise my voice so she can hear: "Angela, I want to take this money right now and get a hot meal, where's a good place?" She shouts back, "Two blocks up the street, Ella's Country Kitchen." I wave goodbye to Angela and her little daughter and head for Ella's. Only moments later, as I enter the restaurant and drop my pack, guess who's standing there right in front of the serving line . . . oh yes, it's Angela! She says, "Take a tray and get whatever you want." I manage to blurt, "Angela, you've already given me money to buy this meal." She then explains, "These are my friends; they run this place. They want to help you!" The black waitress who brings my drink, then some extra rolls later, comments on how good it is to see someone really enjoying his meal. We strike up a conversation, and as the dinner crowd begins thinning out, I ask her to sit down and relax for a minute. She is taken as I explain how I have been befriended today and how the Lord has so generously provided for me. I ask her if she knows Psalm 23. She then takes my hand and begins . . . and we recite together, "The Lord is my Shepherd, I shall not want. . . ." Who says no one really cares about their fellow man anymore!

Back out on US 280, with the rain changing from steady and cold to hard, steady, and cold, I manage to find an old empty house trailer with the door hanging open behind a carpet store. The floor in the back bedroom is sloping hard to the west, but it is clean and dry. Here I make my bed for the night. It rains hard, pounding in waves till morning, rocking the old trailer.

"He maketh me to lie down in green pastures,
He leadeth me beside still waters. He restoreth my soul."

[Psalm 23]

FRIDAY March 6, 1998
TRAIL DAY 65/15 ✦ TRAIL MILE 1,065/240
LOCATION Covered walkway, Goodwater Baptist Church, Goodwater

I MANAGE TO GET ON THE ROAD BY 7:00 A.M. The sky is making a halfhearted effort to clear, but halfhearted isn't going to get it done. The forecast is for rain through Sunday and continuing cold. What a memorable and joyful milestone I reach this morning. For now on a high ridge south of Goodwater on CR 85, I get my first glimpse of the mountains to the north . . . the grand and majestic Appalachians, where I'll be spending the next six or seven months in time and near 2,500 miles in distance. The reality that I am here after walking the flatlands for so long is a reality hard to accept.

I pull into Goodwater before lunch and head straight for the post office. I really hit the jackpot. Here is a package with many needed items and a beautiful card from my wife, Sharon. There's a pile of cards and letters from both my sons and from many very dear friends. Springer Mountain and my home at the base of Springer are the next objectives in the many objectives which lie ahead in this odyssey. I box up some items I no longer need from my pack, read the cards and letters one last time, then box them up to mail on ahead and home. Here also is the package from Marty Dominy I've been awaiting with much anticipation, with all the finely detailed hand-drawn maps for the northern section of the Alabama Pinhoti and all of the completed roadwalk and bushwhack sections of the Georgia Pinhoti. These maps will get me across the (until now) uncharted no-man's-land between northeast Alabama and Springer Mountain, the southern terminus of the grand old Appalachian Trail.

I enjoy a fine supper at Mike's restaurant, where I meet police officer Joe Davidson. Joe explains that there are no motels or boarding houses in Goodwater but that he'll try finding me a place for the night. Goodwater is a dandy little trail town. One really nice aspect I've found with many of these little off-the-beaten-path communities through which I have passed is the survival of their old downtown districts. Here in Goodwater exist few, if any, places we know in modern jargon as "outskirts." Most of the two-story and false-front stores in the old downtown are still occupied, doing business, and in fairly good condition for their age. I like communities with these intact old business districts for a number of reasons, not the least being the ease with which I hark back to the little town where I lived as a child. The simple design of it all is driven by the fact that years ago folks walked from their homes to the grocery store, to the post office, and to work. Consequently these little burgs weren't spread out in 40 different directions. Reverting to shank's mare, we backpackers unavoidably journey back in time, not only as we trek across the near-ageless backbone of these mountains, but also during the roadwalks o'er the byways and through the villages along the way. Little communities like Goodwater, which time has passed over, are back there in time too, remaining in step with us. This enjoyable aspect of hiking can only be experienced and understood by one who hoists and shoulders a pack for the long journey!

Joe has no luck finding me a room for the night, but in the course of conversation I get the impression that I won't be hassled if I find a dry place to get out of it . . . for yet again the hard, steady rain is setting in. Looking around I find a number of places that I can enter. But I don't want to push my luck, so I finally decide to bed down under the walkway awning at the Goodwater Baptist Church. The rain continues all night, but luckily there is no wind, as here I have found no room to pitch my tent.

"The hills are our symbol of eternity. There they stand, the evidence of things seen, as everlasting and unchangeable as anything man may know."

[Maurice Brooks, *The Appalachians*]

SATURDAY March 7, 1998
TRAIL DAY 66/16 ◆ TRAIL MILE 1,068/243
LOCATION Pavilion, Hatchet Creek Presbyterian Church

I AM UP AT 6:00 A.M. AND MOVE AWAY from the church before any-one comes by. The day appears to be clearing and not as cold. My first stop this morning is the Piggly Wiggly for a few provisions. I figure my next resupply will be in Heflin, so I need provisions for about four days. I check the post office one more time. No more mail, but I'm not disap-pointed as this has been the best mail drop by far. I head over to Mike's, but the restaurant isn't open yet. There's activity at the gas station/food store nearby, so I try there for some breakfast. Here I meet Randy, a truck driver, and his mom, who works the grill. Randy, who is ahead of me in line, asks his mom to put a couple more sausage biscuits and a cof-fee on his tab for "The Hiker." Next thing I know I'm enjoying a fine breakfast, compliments of Randy and the house!

As I make one more pass down the main drag, an old black man approaches in bib overalls, one bib strap loose and dangling. As I nod and pass, he says, "Mister, could you stop a minute?" I smile and pull up as he fumbles in one of his floppy bib pockets. Momentarily, his bony, wrinkled old hand outstretched, he motions me to take three wadded-up one-dollar bills! He says, "Here, I want you to take these." He stands with the most puzzled and perplexed look on his deep-rutted face, most like, "What am I doing giving this white man my money?" Again, as on Thursday in Alexander City, I must resist the temptation to refuse this incredible expression of kindness. As I accept the money and thank the old man, he raises more erect to stand with much beaming pride and with such a bright countenance, most like Angela's child.

On my way north out of town now on CR 7, I think back to my feelings while crossing the state line into Alabama. For it was with much doubt, hesitancy, and trepidity that I embarked on this leg of my odyssey. I knew I would be hiking through near-totally black communi-ties for many days, and truthfully, I was scared. But now I am so ashamed. Since that day there has been not one moment of fear or anxi-ety, save the situation on the railroad tracks, which was my own doing.

I have never been in the presence of more gentle people, young or old, nor have I ever been treated with such kindness and compassion by total strangers . . . never, ever before that I can recall in my memory!

The uphill pull is serious and steady now. As I climb, a wide valley opens into view. There are mountains all around, picturesque mountains. The rain begins again in a manner leaving little doubt as to its intent. The higher peaks are soon engulfed in the cold, swirling clouds. Hatchet Creek, just to the west of the road, is running wild out of its banks and all over the bottomlands. Thunder in the distance demands more of my attention as it approaches. I can see the lightning as the storm becomes more intense, heading straight at me. I no sooner reach Hatchet Creek Presbyterian Church than the deluge comes in buckets. I seek shelter under the old pavilion behind the church. Soon the storm totally engulfs the church with the most violent thunder and lightning, the rain crashing against the old roof as if from a waterfall.

It has now just turned afternoon, but this may well be it for today. I am wet and cold, and the wind is whipping the storm into a swirling mist all around and within the pavilion. Now that I have stopped walking, I am getting very cold. So I hoop and tie off my tent on one of the long wooden tables and call it a day. In my bag and in my tent, I am soon warm, feeling reasonably secure. The storm continues driving the rain in a rage, most-near a cataclysm, slamming it against the old pavilion. I am sure this is not the worst blast this old structure has had to endure, but it's getting a good shaking today. It is a huge post-and-beam affair. Without exaggeration I would say it is as big as a good-sized barn. The old roof is near a 10/12 pitch covered with cedar shakes, and around three sides are built lean-tos with a 6/12 pitch. The whole structure is totally rustic, not a brushmark of paint anywhere, weathered to that glorious driftwood shade of gray. And here it stands in proud but uncomplementary contrast to the beautiful, pristine, pure white of the sanctuary right next. I am visited just after dark by a deputy sheriff making his rounds. He asks for some identification, the usual questions. Seems sure I'm going to get sent back out in the storm, but as we talk I can tell he has made up his mind not to run me off. Finally, he says he can't see any sense in sending me back out in it. I quickly agree! The rain and wind continue very hard all night, but I remain warm and secure under the roof of the old pavilion.

"A wild weird clime . . . out of space—out of time."

[Edgar Allan Poe]

SUNDAY March 8, 1998
TRAIL DAY 67/17 ✦ TRAIL MILE 1,075/250
LOCATION Hatchet Creek Trading Post

AS I ROLL OUT THIS MORNING, THE SKY IS DARK, completely over-cast, and a steady light rain greets me as I leave the church. The pull con-tinues. I keep climbing and climbing. The road soon enters to open into yet another wide, beautiful farm valley. I see spring daffodils blooming for the first time in the fields all along, their bright yellow blooms and wide, green bracts adding happy dabs of color here and there in contrast to the near-monochromatic grays and browns of winter. The serviceberry, or shadbush, is starting to brighten the gray woods with its showy white blooms. I soon hear thunder behind me. The storm is coming at me once more, closing fast as I cross AL 148. In less than half an hour, thunder and lightning are all around me again. I soon come to Hatchet Creek Trading Post, an old house, aged brownish-gray with such a proud appearance, crowned and adorned by the most remarkable rusty metal roof. As I climb the porch steps, the storm begins unleashing its fury again.

The door is open, and as I look in I am greeted and invited to enter. Here I meet Tom *Mountain Man* Hess, proprietor of Hatchet Creek Trading Post. In just a moment I also meet Paul *Tall Paul* Wright, a young fellow who also lives here. Tom has a most inviting fire glowing in the fire-place, and I need not the least bit more encouragement as he motions to a chair and offers me a cup of coffee! As I linger and we talk, he becomes intrigued by the notion that I am bound for Maine over the ridges and through the valleys of these majestic old Appalachians, and that I have in fact walked from the Everglades to where I now sit. So it is that *Mountain Man* invites me to stay for supper and to spend the night. The electric storm is chugging through in full locomotion, the rain pounding hard in waves again. As I glance with the most tentative expression toward the rain rattling the window, I tell him, "My momma didn't raise no dummy," and with an ear-to-ear grin I promptly accept his kind invitation!

The supper Paul prepares can best be described as a feast! During the course of the afternoon and into the evening, I manage to down the better part of a gallon of coffee, the last cup carefully seasoned with a tablespoon of "Bama's smoothest and finest." After supper, we relax again by the fireplace, and *Mountain Man* tells me much about his life. We then go from room to room as he shows me many bright paintings and other forms of art he has created. In mentioning that there are so many things to see, I learn that each creation represents at least one day of the four years he spent in Talladega Prison! Until now he hasn't mentioned that part of his life, but I quickly learn, and it seems *Mountain Man* found and brought out some of the treasure from the Superstition Mountains. A no-no! He now shows me numerous paintings of the Superstitions, all in a primitive but balanced and pleasing style. He also shows me much other handiwork: medicine pouches, jewelry, belts, purses, pipes. You name it, all created by *Mountain Man* and all in the same primitive but appealing form. Now he pulls out this big wooden box. It is full of all kinds of gadgets, tools, brushes, and many other things needed to create his works of art, ingeniously made from all sorts of things one might find around a prison!

As we relax by the fire again, I ask *Mountain Man*, "What else haven't you told me about your life?" Oh yes, there's more! Seems as though *Mountain Man* has also gained pretty fair notoriety for his ability to grow large, LARGE quantities of marijuana. Also a fairly serious and punishable offense . . . and for which he also eventually got caught! He seems to have no regret, though. In fact, as we continue along this path, he says, "Ha! I got off light with only four years!" I quickly figure this guy out, though. *Mountain Man* wants to give you the impression and would have you believe that here is one mean hombre . . . definitely Public Enemy #1! It's really quite comical hearing him try to spin this, because it's so plainly evident that he has not, nor could he ever, truly hurt anyone. What's so hilarious is that he doesn't have a mean bone in his entire body, and he can't hide that fact! His gentle nature and peaceful countenance give it away. In a while *Mountain Man* gets up and leaves the room to return in a moment with some gifts for me. He had seen me admiring a finely designed and constructed medicine pouch, put together without a single stitch, and also a finely embossed leather bracelet. Both of these fine works he now hands to me, each a bit of a calendar, each a day in his life in prison. I tell him how very proud I am to have them and that it humbles me that he would give me such objects of obvious sentimental value.

I learned a lot this day from Tom *Mountain Man* Hess, but one thing he just would not reveal to me is how he has trained a Dominique (dominicker) hen to fly up, sit on the back of a chair in the corner of the front porch, and crap in a bucket! I turn in around 9:00 p.m. and sleep very soundly, with only the slightest recollection of hearing the wind whistling through the cracks in the old house or the rain snaring its tat-a-tat on the rusty tin roof.

"These are a mountain man's mountains — wide, tall, and awesome."

[Thomas Connelly, *Discovering the Appalachians*]

SECTION 2: Alabama Pinhoti Trail

MONDAY March 9, 1998
TRAIL DAY 68/1 ✦ TRAIL MILE 1,089/14
LOCATION Near Adams Gap, Cheaha Wilderness,
Talladega National Forest

TOM SENDS ME OFF WITH A BREAKFAST OF FRESH (very local) eggs cooked in his old cast-iron skillet right over the fireplace embers. What a most memorable time I've had at Hatchet Creek Trading Post. I know I'll return to spend time here again. The day greets me with its gray overcast sky, and rain is most certainly just behind the curtain. And indeed another encore begins just as I turn onto AL 77 to head for Porter Gap. Tom has given me a poncho and I quickly cover my pack with it. The rain stays with me, but not in the torrential fits that I've had to endure in recent days.

I arrive at Porter Gap before noon, and the rain, which has accompanied me for most all this walk through southern Alabama, arrives with me. The roadwalk over the past few days has introduced me to the beginning of the Appalachian Mountain Range, but here at Porter Gap, the southern terminus of the Pinhoti Trail, I am at the true beginning of a marvelous network of trails which will soon traverse this entire grand and glorious Appalachian Mountain Range. The Alabama Pinhoti is the start of it and follows the Talladega National Forest to the northeast, ending some 120 miles from here by trail at the Alabama/Georgia state line.

As I turn onto the Pinhoti I have ended my journey to the west. From here I head north and east. The courtship with this trail lasts for about 20 minutes, and then it's up, up, up as I crest the first ridge before descending into Chandler Gap. Here it is no longer raining, the precipitation having turned to snow! The snow showers continue intermittently all day and into the evening. And the flakes are still falling, turning the forest a wonderland of white, as I pitch for the night near Adams Gap. I am very fortunate to have the gloves that *Mountain Man* insisted I take, for it is getting biting cold. I don't attempt a fire but instead set up and roll in as fast as I can to get warm. It's peanut butter and jelly for supper tonight. I am in the lee, the ridge forming a natural windbreak, but the wind whips the tent most of the night just the same, as the snow continues.

"All that is gold does not glitter,
Not all who wander are lost;
The old that is strong does not wither,
Deep roots are not reached by frost."

[J. R. R. Tolkien]

TUESDAY March 10, 1998
TRAIL DAY 69/2 ✦ TRAIL MILE 1,103/28
LOCATION Heated restroom at chapel, Cheaha State Park,
Talladega National Forest

IT IS 24 DEGREES AS I ROLL OUT THIS MORNING. There is snow on my tent and all around. Tending to my "morning duty" is very unpleasant under these circumstances. I am very cold and my fingers feel like so many sticks before I manage to break camp and shoulder my pack. As I get going again, the snow also gets going again, but I warm up quickly enough as the Pinhoti lets me have it. I'm definitely traversing internal-packframe territory, and my snug sternum strap is coming in handy! This section approaching Cheaha State Park through the Cheaha Wilderness is as demanding as anything I've previously encountered on the AT, and I've hiked that grand old trail all the way into Pennsylvania. I immediately encounter much side-slabbing on very steep terrain that has benefited from little recent Pulaski work. This off-camber hiking quickly mushes out my ankles. Leaving the side-slab, the treadway now traverses large, steep boulder fields flanked on both sides by smaller rock gardens. The boulder fields require much scrambling and slow my pace to a crawl. Upon entering the Cheaha Wilderness, blazing which had been excellent starts playing hide and seek. With no treadway to follow through the boulders and rocks and few blazes, I'm off the trail more than on. Here is a whole new experience for me. The rocks and boulders present incredibly unstable treadway, being covered with snow, which covers last fall's leaves. My poor doggies are really starting to bark! The ascents and descents are not the endurance tests that I'll face farther north, but they are abrupt and steep.

The mountains here in Alabama are rugged and beautiful beyond anything I had expected. I will need a few more days than planned to hike this rugged terrain! The mountainsides are forested in beautiful longleaf pine, while the ridgelines are predominately hardwood, making for spectacular open vistas. There are views and lookouts all along. Oh, it is such a pleasure to be back among mountain laurel and rhododendron again, but my search for the elusive white pine continues.

I arrive at Cheaha State Park Lodge toward evening and head for the restaurant. Though I am a stellar example of the un-finest Hiker Trash, upon entering a first-class eating establishment with exquisite table settings complemented by the finest linen, I am greeted graciously by the hostess and then the waitress, each with a welcome smile. I dine in the most luxurious and eloquent atmosphere on the finest cuisine, and the view out and across the mountains, which are now being bathed in the scarlet hues of sunset, makes for a magic memory moment in this brief flicker of time. As I near the final course, here comes now Ranger Tim Whitehead. His wife, who works in the gift shop down by the main gate, had told him of my arrival. He comes to offer assistance as he explains that temperatures are predicted to drop into the teens tonight. The lodge is being renovated and no rooms are available for the evening. He kindly suggests an alternative to the frozen snow-covered ground and the cold shelter up the trail. He takes me in his truck to the park chapel up the way and unlocks the clean, spacious, warm, and lighted men's room for me! I am most content, my tummy is full, and I am snug as a bug . . . life is good! Now isn't this roughing it!

> *"Give me the luxuries of life and I will willingly do*
> *without the necessities."*
>
> [Frank Lloyd Wright]

WEDNESDAY March 11, 1998
TRAIL DAY 70/3 ✦ TRAIL MILE 1,118/43
LOCATION Base of waterfalls, north of Morgan Lake,
Talladega National Forest

TIM PICKS ME UP THIS MORNING AND DELIVERS ME to a trail that leads to Blue Mountain Shelter. He had told me of another hiker who was also heading north on the Pinhoti, and here at Blue Mountain Shelter I find his tent, pack, and other belongings, but he is nowhere around. I leave a note of introduction and my tentative hiking schedule, hoping that we may have an opportunity to meet and hike some together. I have been alone on the trail now for 70 days, and it tends to get lonely out here at times. I could sure use some company for a while.

The day starts clear and very cold, but by afternoon, and from the constant exertion demanded by the trail, both the day and I warm up nicely. My hike is interrupted as I reach Hillabee Creek. The creek is of fair width and depth, and there is no bridge . . . wading time, so it appears. I drop my pack and change to my off-road running shoes to make the ford. On the other side I quickly dry my feet and get my warm wool socks and boots back on. Here, as I lie back basking on a large rock that is being bathed and warmed by the sun, and as I look around, half observing, half daydreaming, I make a very strange and perplexing observation. We have all seen tree stumps in the woods, and I am looking at a tree stump. But after a couple of takes, shifting from the daydream mode to the observing mode, I realize that this tree stump is different from any that I have ever seen before, for this stump is not at ground level . . . but somewhere between 10 and 12 feet up! My gaze is fixed on it now. What is this? Why did someone cut this tree off 10 feet up? And as I look closer I wonder how someone cut this tree off 10 feet up! Here is a very narrow trail. No vehicles could possibly get in here, and there are no telltale spike splinters left by pole climbers, but the top of the tree is gone! I finally give up trying to figure this one out.

I pitch for the evening some distance north of Morgan Lake at the base of a beautiful twin waterfall, probably one of the tributaries to

Hillabee Creek. In short order I get a very comfortable warming and cooking fire going.

"Hiking for days [and weeks and months] by one's self can be very lonely."

[Jan D. Curran,
The Appalachian Trail—A Journey of Discovery]

THURSDAY March 12, 1998
TRAIL DAY 71/4 ✦ TRAIL MILE 1,132/57
LOCATION Private hallway, Heflin Police Station

ARE TEMPERATURES SUPPOSED TO GO BELOW FREEZING in Alabama in March? Okay, well how about down to 14 degrees? That is the chilling news my little Campmor thermometer greets me with this morning! I am very reluctant to roll out, but I do stick my nose out, then tuck it right back in to go back on "snooze" for another half hour . . . But finally the moment of truth, for here I am, and here it is, so here we go! Brrrr! I tug my long johns on, then it's up and over with the sweatshirt given me down in Florida by trail angels Paul and Doris Adams. My wool socks are already on, but my boots have decided to be the wrong size. I finally manage to break camp and get chugging.

Today I meet the first backpackers on the trail since the Boy Scouts in Florida! Coleman and Tina are both really loaded down with winter gear. They are doing the Pinhoti in sections and are out giving it another go. We have a long, enjoyable talk. Seems I can't shut up! What a delight seeing someone else out here and at a time I would never have predicted. I have managed to postpone my "morning duty" until reaching Spears Store near Five Points. I really believe steaming hot coffee never *felt* or tasted so good!

I decide to set my sights on Heflin today and I go at it in earnest, but I no sooner get up the trail from Five Points than I get lost. I finally manage to stumble on north and down from Horseblock Mountain to US 78. Here I try hitching a ride into Heflin but have no luck as the traffic is flying, so I end up walking the 3 miles to town. I head straight for the drugstore to restock my coated aspirin, then on to the little downtown mom 'n' pop for supper. To keep from getting hassled in these little villages, I have found it best to go straight to the police station and introduce myself. This is to thwart the calls when they start coming in . . . and they *will* come in. It always helps to keep the local constabulary from getting all riled. The police chief here is Billy Hugh Lambert. After a short conversation with Chief Lambert, I am invited to spend the night in the hall leading to the public bathroom. Well, now, this may not sound like much, but let me tell you . . . this is Hiker Trash five-star! The hallway is like a room, complete with plush carpet. There is a door separating the hall from the front area, which I am permitted to keep closed and locked, and the place is warm as toast. Oh, and right off this room (hall) I have my own private bath!

I stash my pack and head the short distance—this is the typical Southern-style downtown—to the local Piggly Wiggly. Then it's right back to my little private room! It's really turning cold. Chief Lambert said it would be down in the teens again tonight. But I'm warm and snug (with my own security guard) as I spread out to lounge in sheer luxury and spend the remainder of the evening catching up on my journal entries.

> *"Too much of a good thing can be wonderful!"*
>
> [Mae West]

FRIDAY March 13, 1998
TRAIL DAY 72/5 ✦ TRAIL MILE 1,140/65
LOCATION Lower Shoal Shelter, Choccolocco WMA,
Talladega National Forest

AFTER WRITING A SHORT THANK-YOU NOTE to Chief Lambert and handing it to the duty officer, I head down to Jack's for breakfast. Here I load up on two eggs, bacon, cheese biscuits and gravy, and about half a gallon of coffee . . . for three bucks. I'm up and nearly out the door when one of the counter gals comes over to ask if I am "the Long-Distance Hiker"! She gives me a phone number and a message to call the HoJo down by I-20. The call, she says, came in a little while ago from another hiker. Must be the fellow Tim had told me about and the one whose gear I'd seen at Blue Mountain Shelter. Craston Roberts, a fellow I had been chatting with in the adjacent booth, overhears this conversation and invites me out to his truck to use his cell phone. He says, "Figure out which room and I'll drive you down!" In a moment I'm talking to Keith Pskowski and he gives me his room number at HoJo's. On the way down, I'm thinking this guy had to hike I-20 for nearly 4 miles to reach this interchange, for he said he had walked there. I'm thinking, "What sort of fellow am I going to meet here?"

In moments Craston drops me off at room number 34. I bang and bang on the door. Finally it opens and I am greeted by the other nutso. Keith said that he would be ready to go when I got here, but as I look, there are piles of clothing and a staggering collection of other paraphernalia strewn from the bed, cascading onto the floor, clear to the vanity counter and beyond. What am I getting into here? By the time Keith gets all his things shoved into his old rickety gargantuan pack, it is time for lunch! I keep telling him, "We gotta go, Keith . . . we gotta go!" He's finally ready and we head over to Taco Bell. The lunch crowd is now here and it takes forever to get served. I'm really getting antsy about this whole thing. Finally, we sit down to eat and, as luck would have it, I strike up a conversation with a couple of fellows who are working on a microwave tower at the trailhead near Cleburne. They offer us a ride, which is a lifesaver, but it's still 2:00 p.m. before we're back on the trail.

We manage only 8 miles today, ending up at Lower Shoal Shelter. This is not good. Quite often I am unsuccessful, but I make a concerted, unflagging effort to keep my daily mileage around 15 . . . or better if possible. So far, for the entire 72 days, I am averaging just slightly under 16 miles per day, and I am most pleased with that number. I have packed enough provisions for five days but could stretch them to last seven if push comes to shove. My plans are to get on through the Alabama Pinhoti, out of the Talladega National Forest, across Indian and Flagpole mountains, through the bushwhack at the state line, and on into Georgia at Cave Spring. I know this is doable, but we gotta get rolling. I should be another 7 miles up the trail tonight. Keith did reasonably well today, but he is carrying entirely too much weight.

The shelter here this evening is like an old friend, for it is identical to one that I have slept in many times. And that is the old shelter that used to be located just above the spring on Springer Mountain. That shelter was long ago flown out by the Army Rangers and now resides to serve its retiring years on the approach trail from Amicalola Falls.

"The woods are lovely, dark and deep,
But I have promises to keep,
And miles to go before I sleep,
And miles to go before I sleep."

[Robert Frost]

SATURDAY March 14, 1998
TRAIL DAY 73/6 ✦ TRAIL MILE 1,149/74
LOCATION Laurel Trail Shelter, Choccolocco WMA,
Talladega National Forest

WE ARE WAY TOO LATE GETTING OUT AND GOING this morning. There is more traffic on the trail today than in the past many months. We meet a group of Scouts and talk with one of their leaders, Mike Smith. Here we learn the origin of the unusual but most pleasing name for one of the nearby side trails. It is called the Chinabee Silent Trail, named in honor of those who constructed it: students at the nearby Alabama School for the Deaf. Bushwhacking around Sweetwater Lake we meet Jay Hudson. Jay is a director of the Alabama Trails Association. There is much to discuss, and as we talk we also spend the next 30 minutes trying to keep from sliding into the lake. The lake is way above its normal level, taking the trail under, and we have to bushwhack over blowdowns and through brush nearly the entire perimeter. No doubt this is good practice for what lies ahead near the Georgia line.

We manage only slightly over 8 miles again today to pull up at Laurel Trail Shelter. This is a fine shelter with water nearby and plenty of firewood. Just before dark, Jay and his son, Troy, come in, and the four of us enjoy the evening together roasting marshmallows. I am dismayed that this has been another short mileage day, but considering our late start, dallying and talking and then bushwhacking around the lake, we did quite well.

"But our lakes are bordered by the forests, and one is
every day called upon to worship God in such a temple."

[James Fenimore Cooper, *The Pathfinder*]

SUNDAY March 15, 1998
TRAIL DAY 74/7 ✦ TRAIL MILE 1,164/89
LOCATION Headwaters, Dry Creek, Dugger Mountain,
Talladega National Forest

WE'RE OUT LATE AGAIN THIS MORNING. Keith takes off like a shot. I fall in step 20 paces behind. This is great; we're really truckin'. In three hours we've covered nearly 9 miles. Soon, there is this beautiful old log church at Shoal Creek, and we take a break to enjoy the peace and solitude that just seem to prevail in the shadow of these serene old time capsules. There is a social pavilion in the rear and lingering here is a very simple task.

Keith has come up with a couple of flat tires by now, so I take the point. Today I blunder into the biggest covey of quail flushed so far on this entire odyssey—around 16 birds. I'm hiking along totally contained in my little daydream cocoon, oblivious to little more than my rhythmic tramping, when World War III breaks out right at my feet. In all these years I've never been able to maintain even a minuscule of composure when these little minefields explode. I don't believe there is anything man has ever devised that will accelerate any faster then these feathered fellows, save a shotgun volley. And even that won't keep up with them, at least not one launched from any blunderbuss I've ever shouldered. I don't know which is worse, just walking up on a covey and flushing them or waiting as you creep forward, dog frozen and locked on point, awaiting, to finally shudder when the birds erupt from the ground. Dad was a marvelous flash of motion and precision at that instant, seldom failing to get a double. I always froze, to nearly collapse in a spent puddle of adrenaline. And this harvest of nature's bounty? There is just absolutely no better fare to grace any table . . . even to *set before a king.* An old iron skillet, a little fat, and some cracker meal, and you've got the makings of a feast rivaling the finest that Chef Palladin could ever serve up.

We pitch camp in a lovely cove with its fast-rushing stream and plenty of firewood. The evening is delightfully warm, as has been the day . . . the first day I've been able to go without thermal undies for quite a while. Keith is totally spent. This is only his tenth day out and he is packing entirely too much. Much like a mule. Ah, there it is, Pack Mule! Keith, from now on you will be known as *Pack Mule*, or just plain old *Mule*!

> *"[The Pinhoti] . . . trail stretches from Dugger Mountain on the north to the hospitable community of Friendship on the south. In between lies some of the most beautiful, least-trodden backpacking country in the southeast."*
>
> [Scott Deaver]

MONDAY March 16, 1998
TRAIL DAY 75/8 ✦ TRAIL MILE 1,177/102
LOCATION Trailside, north of CR 94 near Borden Springs,
Talladega National Forest

FIRST THING THIS MORNING WE HAVE A HARD PULL up Dugger Mountain, the second-highest point in Alabama. This is a tough climb to the rugged, rocky ridgeline. Nowhere in Alabama will you find the Appalachians rising much above 2,000 feet. Cheaha is the highest at 2,405. "That isn't much of a mountain," you say. And that may well be true, but let me tell you this. You will be hard put to find, throughout the individual mountain groups anywhere along the Appalachian chain, any to compare with these in respect to ruggedness, remoteness, flora and fauna diversity, and sheer beauty. (I know because as I edit this, I've hiked the whole range.) "How can that be?" Do this little exercise. Get your trail profile maps out. Go to the one that shows Clingmans Dome, the highest point on the Appalachian Trail. Now look at the contour changes encountered for a few miles in either direction. Okay, now go to most any trail-contour profile for the Pinhoti Trail in the Talladega

National Forest and look at a few miles of this rascal! For now will come a marvelous revelation, an enlightenment if you will! Let me ask you this: What difference does it make, as far as the hiking experience is concerned, at what elevation these gyrations occur? Sure, you're not going to get a nosebleed climbing up and down in the Cheaha Wilderness . . . but neither will you in the Great Smoky Mountains National Park!

Coming off Dugger, we pass Terrapin Watershed Lake. This lake, Choccolocco Lake, Coleman Lake, and Sweetwater Lake all have high earthen reservoir embankments to impound water during periods of heavy rain, so the areas near the dams aren't particularly attractive due to apparent low water levels. But the shorelines of these lakes undulate against the rugged, picturesque mountain shoulders, creating picture-book settings, the view from the dams being totally unobstructed and panoramic. We pitch just north of CR 94 near a happy little stream. The evening fire is a poor fire but I manage to get a hot meal prepared. *Pack Mule*'s pack has got to weigh at least 50 pounds. I have not a clue what all he's got squirreled away in there . . . but it isn't food. *Mule* is out of food, so I share my "porridge" with him. Rain seems to want to join us all evening and into the night, but shy an invitation, it holds off.

> *"Its highest peak stands a half-mile shorter than the foot of the Colorado Rockies; its deepest gorge could be stacked 20 deep inside the Grand Canyon. Superlatives of scenery and natural history have rarely described the state whose name partly stems from an archaic word for brush . . . Alabama is the nation's fourth-richest kingdom of plant and animal species; in species per square mile, only Florida can match it . . . Only two years ago, a near barren patch of rock—within 50 miles of the state's largest city—presented eight undescribed species of flowering plants."*
>
> [William Stolzenburg]

WELL, LOOKS LIKE IT'S COMING TODAY, INVITATION or not . . . the rain. The forecast is for rain—pretty sure bet! So it is, as I break camp and head on up Augusta Mine Ridge, the rain begins. As I climb, the rain really starts pounding, the wind driving a bitter cold. At Ferguson Memorial on top of Augusta Mine, I am exposed to its full rage. The wind, rain, and cold become nearly unbearable. I have packed out ahead of *Mule* and now I'm concerned about the worsening conditions behind me, so I move to the side of the trail and crouch in the lee against the wall of a small rock overhang. Here under the ledge, I rig my poncho. *Mule* pulls in ten minutes later, shivering uncontrollably and soaked to the bone. We tie his tent fly to my poncho to enclose a small area beneath the ledge. The wind is now driving the rain at full gale force as it roars, howling and shuddering around and above us. Our makeshift shelter is being ripped and attacked as the storm increases in intensity. We are both soaked, and the cold sets its grip as we huddle together. The sky has turned dark as night and the temperature continues to drop, turning the rain to sleet. I find some dry sticks and leaves lodged in the cracks and crannies between the rocks around us and am able to get a small fire going, aided by a chip of fire starter that I have been toting along. We remain huddled over this little bit of glimmer unable to move for more than three hours as the storm continues to tear at our makeshift shelter. By now it is 3:00 p.m.

We can't remain here much longer. We have got to get down off this mountain and find a place to pitch in the lee before dark. Surely this storm will show mercy and permit us to break from its grip. Finally, the wind seems to tire, and as it backs down a bit, we make a run for it. We're able to get down into a little cove in the lee and pitch our tents. I even manage to get a pathetic little fire going again to prepare supper and to dry our bodies a little before rolling in. This day has been a wild and scary ordeal that will be remembered for a very, very long time! Thank you, Lord, for seeing me through this one!

> *"There is a line by us unseen;*
> *That crosses every path;*
> *The hidden boundary between*
> *God's patience and his wrath."*

[J. Addison Alexander]

WEDNESDAY March 18, 1998
TRAIL DAY 77/10   ✦   TRAIL MILE 1,185/110
LOCATION Lamont Motel, Piedmont

WE FINISH THE REMAINING 2 MILES of the official Alabama Pinhoti Trail at US 278 by 10:30 a.m.

The forecast is for thunderstorms and continued cold wind. We've got that in spades. *Mule* wants to hitch a ride into Piedmont, get provisions, and stay overnight there. I want to head on north. I figure I'm at least a day behind already. *Mule* offers to treat me to supper and put me up in his room, so reluctantly I go for the deal. We try hitching for over an hour with no luck, then end up walking 4 miles to the nearest gas station. Here we get a ride to Piedmont with Buck Jennings, the station owner. We have a fine meal at Ranch House, and *Mule* gets the provisions he needs to get into Cave Spring, Georgia. I thoroughly expect the next couple of weeks, from here on into Springer Mountain, to be a problem weatherwise, but resolve to just take it a day at a time and hope for the best.

"There are some who can live without wild things, and some who cannot."

[Aldo Leopold]

WE'RE GREETED BY FOG AND MIST as we leave Lamont Motel. There's no luck hitching again, so we're faced with another more-than-3-mile roadwalk back to Spring Garden Station. We've hiked nearly 8 miles now in the last two days, not an inch of which has been on the trail. I should be leaving Cave Spring, Georgia, by now, and it's at least another day to the state line. At the station we're in luck. The Rhinehart brothers, Robert and Jeff, give us a ride back to the trailhead parking lot on US 278. It's now late morning as we head east on the highway for a short roadwalk to continue the Pinhoti Trail north over Davis Mountain. Neither of us sees the trail junction. We climb US 278 all the way to the next gap before I finally realize what has happened. So now we backtrack the half mile as I try not to get steamed. We've now managed to hike almost 10 miles but only a half mile of actual trail!

The hike over Davis Mountain is very enjoyable. As we make the ford at Hurricane Creek, I can hear an ORV in the distance. It comes to near where we're crossing and stops. *Mule* wades right through as I pull up to change to my running shoes. Salem Church Road is right across the creek, and as I come along behind *Mule,* he's at the road talking to two men who have just returned to their vehicle on the ORV. Here I meet Bill Burks and Mike Hinson with the Alabama Department of Conservation's State Lands Division. They're both working on the Forever Wild program, which has been successful with recent land acquisitions for the Pinhoti Trail, making it possible to continue the trail to the Georgia state line. As I'm drying my feet and putting my boots back on, I learn from Bill and Mike that in 1992, 84 percent of the voters in Alabama passed the Alabama Forever Wild Land Trust Program. Through a constitutional amendment, this enabled funding of up to $15 million per year through the year 2000 for setting aside wildlife areas. *Mule* and I will be the first hikers passing through this section. Some of the trail is completed, but tomorrow we'll be bushwhacking where the trail is not yet constructed. I'm given a copy of their department's great magazine, *Outdoor Alabama,* in which Mike Leonard's fine article appears. They are excited to see us, for tomorrow R. Michael Leonard's dream will become a reality—The Appalachian Trail Connection—as *Mule* and I hike on into Georgia . . . and into Alabama hiking history! What a remarkable coincidence meeting these gentlemen. What far-sightedness and what a grand program. Thanks, people of Alabama!

We make it to the end of the newly constructed trail on Indian Mountain, and here, just below the last Pulaski cut, we pitch for the evening by a clear, cold-running spring. Tomorrow we'll be sighting over a compass and following Marty Dominy's redlined topo maps.

"Alabama to me is the biggest biodiversity story of North America today . . .
This is the 20th century environmental story."

[Paul Hartfield, Endangered Species Biologist, USFS]

FRIDAY March 20, 1998
TRAIL DAY 79/12 ✦ TRAIL MILE 1,204/129
LOCATION Cave Spring, Georgia

FORTUNATELY FOR US, WE ARE IN A PROTECTED RAVINE and we've both pitched in old blowdown holes, for during the night one of the most intense electrical storms that I have ever witnessed crashed and reverberated through the mountains, passing directly overhead. The lightning frequency was such that one could literally read by it. As to the thunder, there was no silence, just a steady and continuous roll as wave after stampeding wave herded through. The wind followed, pulsing in like fashion, bringing bucket brigades of rain slamming against my little shelter. The madness of it seemed to continue for hours, though I am sure the time was much less.

We both roll out at first light. The storm has moved off to the east and across the mountain, and the sky is clearing above us. Departing trail's end, but before bushwhacking on over Indian and Flagpole mountains, I stop to leave a note for the Alabama Trails Association trail builders thanking them for their dedication and work and for this fine trail.

The wind remains, but the weather is clear for this first bit of bushwhacking. Once on Flagpole Mountain, there's a trail coming up from a cove below and we pass an old hunt camp. Here we stop to rest awhile and to enjoy the splendid view into Georgia. The route as marked by Marty takes us over the top and along the ridges and saddles. The area is rocky and thick with brush, but the rugged jumble at the higher vantages provides breathtaking vistas, the finest so far since the bluffs at Cheaha. This indeed will be a grand finale to a most grand trail, the Alabama Pinhoti Trail. Take her right over the top, boys; that's what Myron Avery would have done!

I track back and forth for ten minutes or better, trying to find a survey cut or some other evidence indicating where the state line crosses. But there is none, so I estimate as best I can where I believe it to be, and *Mule* and I linger and have a grand time building a rock cairn. We spend maybe 20 minutes, but it takes us an hour and 20 minutes, for this is also the line between the Eastern and Central time zones . . . so we lose an hour.

We reach Cave Spring by 2:30 p.m., get our mail, and have a good hot meal. Here we find out about the storm of last night. It seems the storm continued southeast into Georgia, leaving a path of destruction and 14 fatalities along the way. In Murrayville, where the kind lady who has been transcribing my journal entries teaches computer classes, the storm did incredible damage. When she arrived at school this morning, she found that her classroom was completely gone, the school destroyed! The fact that the storm passed in the middle of the night when no one was at school prevented an unthinkable disaster.

Mule is just not up to this bushwhacking and there is much bushwhacking ahead if I'm to stay on the planned route for the Georgia Pinhoti. Much of the trail north of here in the Armuchee Range and through the rugged Cohutta Mountains to the east is yet to be completed. We'll work up a roadwalk so he can reach the Appalachian Trail at Springer Mountain by a better route.

> *"Do not go where the path may lead, go instead where*
> *the is no path and leave a trail."*
> [Ralph Waldo Emerson]

SECTION 3: Georgia Pinhoti Trail

SATURDAY March 21, 1998
TRAIL DAY 80/1 ✦ TRAIL MILE 1,229/25
LOCATION Planted pine by GA 100 north of Holland

CAVE SPRING IS A GREAT LITTLE TRAIL TOWN with Todd's
Restaurant, Gray Horse Restaurant, pizza and ice-cream parlors, a post
office, and motels. *Mule* and I have breakfast at Gray Horse, then I head
for Holland. I hate to part company with *Mule*, but he isn't prepared
equipment-wise, and his physical limitations present serious problems
when trying to bushwhack cross-country. He had a bout with encephali-
tis at age 13 that left him with severe visual limitations. He has also sustained head injuries which have left him with less-than-normal motor
function and he must take Dilantin to control grand mal seizures. I feel
he will be able to handle the AT, but bushwhacking over rough terrain is
not for him. I hope to hike with him much more this summer.

Today has been a most pleasant roadwalk, a grand 25-mile day. I
reach Holland around 5:00 p.m. Here is a typical little crossroads community with the usual gas station/limited-food store. I pick up a few
odds and ends for my pack, then head on north to pitch in the planted
pine north of Holland.

"The right to be left alone is indeed the beginning of all freedom."
[Justice William O. Douglas]

SUNDAY March 22, 1998
TRAIL DAY 81/2 ✦ TRAIL MILE 1,248/44
LOCATION Gated FSR just below CR 224, near Hammond Gap

I FINISH THE SHORT ROADWALK FROM HOLLAND to Taylor Ridge to
arrive a little before 10:00 a.m. There is a fine new trailhead here complete with parking. The newly constructed treadway leaves the parking

area to claim the ridgeline for a very pleasant hike, which provides wide open views from both sides. The trail passes through the eastern extent of Sloppy Floyd State Park, and I can see the large, serene lake just below to the west. At Mack White Gap, where my old friend US 27 passes, the treadway ends and the bushwhacking begins anew. The cross-country going is no problem here as the proposed trail follows the ridgeline for some distance along game trails, old treadway with faded flagging, and woodsroads and service roads. I pass a new microwave tower, complete with a service road leading down to Chapel Hill Church Road. Here I become confused for a moment as none of this is shown on my map . . . so I mark the approximate location and continue on.

I am making remarkably good time today, considering that about half the day has involved bushwhacking. I get on the wrong ridge spur a couple of times, but with my compass and topo map I can quickly tell I am going the wrong direction and manage to turn and make corrections. I pitch by a small branch next to a gated Forest Service road (FSR) just below CR 224 near Hammond Gap. It has been a windy but pleasant day. There seems to be a gradual but noticeable change in the weather, but I must not get my hopes up too high.

> *"Come, heart where hill is heaped upon hill:*
> *For there the mystical brotherhood*
> *Of sun and moon and hollow and wood*
> *And river and stream work out their will."*

[William Butler Yeats]

MONDAY March 23, 1998
TRAIL DAY 82/3 ✦ TRAIL MILE 1,261/57
LOCATION Keown Falls Picnic Area

I STAY ON NARROWS PICNIC ROAD TO FR 325, then bushwhack straight up Strawberry Mountain. At the ridge I find a delightful new service road all in fresh-sown grass. This I take up the ridge past a large clear-cut area to the north. From here a recently constructed horse trail leads on northeast for a short distance. Then it's bushwhacking time again.

The bushwhacks are getting more difficult, and I haven't beaten my way through the blowdowns and brush far until I realize I'm going the wrong direction. Two clues: The compass is pointing the wrong way and there's a "No Hunting" sign on the tree just ahead. So I turn around and beat my way back. Hunters are in the woods in full camo, and I have seen and talked with some of them today. Spring turkey season seems to be very popular here, for it seems that for each hunter I chance to meet I count additionally probably five or six vehicles parked along the service roads.

I soon come to West Armuchee Creek crossing, a picturesque spot. There is no bridge, just a concrete slab where vehicles ford. I remove my boots and begin wading across. I quickly realize this is a big mistake, one I'm sure many others will make what with concrete being kind to one's feet. To my dismay, and as I am committed to this, I find the concrete dangerously slippery from moss slime. The creek is of good size, with a fair volume of moving water, the velocity of which is creating a force to be reckoned with. I slip and am almost swept down. This is becoming treacherous. I can hardly maintain my footing on the ice-slick surface. By inching my way I manage to gain the far bank. The depth gauge shows a mere foot of water, which seems insignificant, but when footing is reduced to near zero, it doesn't take much to get pushed around. The water drops from the ford to a rocky pool, and I certainly did not want to go in there head first. Putting my off-road running shoes on, which is certainly what I should have done, might have helped to some extent, but I have my doubts.

Crossing Subligna/Villanow Road and bushwhacking along a blowdown-filled old road grade, then following some old, old flagging, I reach East Armuchee Creek. Here is a formidable stream, more near the size of a small river. The only crossing I am able to find is near a large tree with blue paint rings. Here I change to my off-road running shoes and hunt for a sturdy pole. As I enter the turbulence, I am immediately confronted with rapids moving at a rate to create substantial hydraulic force. My footing is hindered by large rocks, many of which are over a foot in diameter and very slippery. Taking my time and groping along I am able to ford without incident, but the experience definitely makes my adrenaline pump!

Confronting me now is the rim swamp for the better part of 100 yards. This is muck, briars, brambles, and brush, an almost impenetrable bushwhack. The Florida titi swamps have nothing on these Georgia river-rim swamps. Maintaining a passable treadway through here is going to present a fine challenge! Finally through this maze, it's a bushwhack straight up John's Mountain, over 500 feet in vertical elevation gain in less than a quarter mile! On reaching the top I have a short bushwhack along the ridge. Proceeding, I soon find the white blazes of the well-maintained Keown Falls loop trail. Glory be, arriving here just as planned is a joy! Steps are constructed, leading down beside the falls, providing a most enjoyable experience. I pitch for the evening in the picnic area near the park entrance. I no sooner get my camp secure than the rain begins again.

> *"The bubbling brook doth leap when I come by,*
> *because my feet find measure with its call."*
>
> [Jones Very, *Nature*]

TUESDAY March 24, 1998
TRAIL DAY 83/4 ✦ TRAIL MILE 1,273/69
LOCATION FSR 207A, Middle Mountain

THE RAIN HAS STOPPED, BUT THE SKY REMAINS OVERCAST and threatening. I'd just as soon stay in on this cold, wet, and dreary morning, but indeed "I have miles to go before I sleep," so I roll out and shoulder my heavy, wet gear and head out to greet another lonely day on the trail. When it is mild and the birds are singing, I am not nearly as alone. But the birds are not singing this morning, and mild is not the word for this day. It has been a wonderful diversion seeing and talking with the hunters, but most have had to muster effort to remain kind and tolerant. After all, they're in the woods for peace and quiet, too—and maybe a turkey—but certainly not for a disheveled, yapping backpacker. I journey on alone toward Horn Mountain.

Upon reaching S1264, I discover recent Forest Service–controlled burnover along the entire east side. The cross-county bushwhack, which starts here, heads east right through this nightmarish setting. I want no part of it and head north on S1264! Turning at FR 233 I proceed southeast on this way-out roundabout, crossing Furnace Creek. Here I pick up an old woodsroad and head north. In a short distance the two-track peters out, deteriorating into heavy briars, blowdowns, and brush. After struggling through it awhile, I turn away to face the near-vertical wall that is the west face of Horn Mountain. Here the terrain is open but nearly straight up. There's no need hurrying this sort of ladderless ascent. There is no pace, save slow and steady, every sapling, root, and tree being nature's handrail. Approximately 150 to 200 feet from the ridgeline, I hit beautiful, newly cut treadway! I guess if I had gone a little farther up FR 233, past Furnace Creek, I would have happened upon it there, avoiding all this crazy bushwhacking I've just been through. I bet it comes up through the burnover from Pilcher Pond.

Heavy horse traffic is already shredding the side-slab berms on Horn. The treadway has been completed to the parking lot at Snake Creek Gap. Heading for Mill Creek Mountain out of Snake Creek, I see the first new plastic-diamond Pinhoti Trail blaze tacked to a tree. What a delight to find the trail completed all the way to the ridgeline on Mill Creek Mountain. From here, however, it is cross-country again until I connect to the FSR below Middle Mountain. In the brush now and stumbling and fighting through, thinking I must certainly be the first and only human to ever pass this way, I come upon this huge rock cairn! I look at it and walk around it in total disbelief. Surely there must have been a time when this had some significance, but as I stand here today gawking at it in awe, I have not a clue! I pitch on Middle Mountain FSR in the warmth of a most comforting evening sun.

> *"It is not so much for its beauty that the forest makes a*
> *claim upon men's hearts, as for that subtle something,*
> *that quality of air, that emanation from old trees, that*
> *so wonderfully changes and renews a weary spirit."*
>
> [Robert Louis Stevenson]

I AM UP AND OUT TO A GRAND MORNING. Unquestionably, the weather is changing, slowly, but it's changing. The storms are still coming through, but not with the regularity or the intensity with which I have been getting slammed. Today, I'll be hiking over familiar terrain on Middle and Hurricane mountains, for I have not only hiked here in the past, I have also helped construct some of this trail. The Georgia Pinhoti Trail Association, of which I am a member, is a small organization, but the goal that has been set is a grand one indeed. For on the shoulders of this group rests the responsibility of closing the gap in connecting the southern Appalachians to Springer Mountain by trail. This will be the final link in the chain of links needed to fulfill Mike Leonard's dream of a trail to the end of the Appalachian Range.

The trail from here to Dug Gap near Dalton is almost complete save a short section along Rocky Face Mountain. The hike along these long, level ridges provides views in all directions; indeed, the trail leads in all directions, following this interesting geologic arrangement. On Rocky Face I pass another very strange rockwork. Here is a fire ring the likes of which I have never seen before. It's really more a monument than a fire ring if that is possible. It is not only a remarkable structure in size, but it is complete with promenade-type walkways all around, each lined with rocks collected from all over the mountain and brought here to this place. Someone or some group has spent an incredible amount of time hauling and stacking these rocks! I take the full tour before heading on.

I get into Dalton by 3:00 p.m. My first stop is Wendy's for a Coke and a Frosty (the soft-ice-cream variety). Dalton is a large city with much traffic and confusion.

I dearly love trail towns, but not ten all at once! My nerves are pretty much in a jangle before I get through. Surely there must be a motel out here someplace, for I am not only on a busy state highway, but this is also US 76. Pulling into the pumps at the next station and talking with the attendant, I find that I am out of luck. A fellow in a pickup stops and offers me a ride. I decline, but as he insists on hauling me along, I find that he's going to Chatsworth, where there is a fine motel. And he offers not only to drop me off there this evening but to pick me up first thing in the morning and deposit me right back here to this very spot. Okay, now that's a deal! So it is that I meet Steve Griggs, a fellow member of the Hiker Trash clan. As we motor along toward Chatsworth, I'm thinking how strange it seems, covering the ground so quickly. In minutes we have gone farther than I can hike in a whole day. Hikers certainly live in another time zone.

I'll head for Ramhurst to begin bushwhacking the rugged Cohuttas tomorrow. And I'll be carrying a very heavy pack, for I have taken on provisions to last me seven days, hopefully getting me to Springer Mountain . . . and home!

> *"Oft when the white still dawn lifted the skies*
> *and pushed the hills apart*
> *I've felt it like a glory in my heart."*
>
> [Edwin Markham, *Joy of the Morning*]

THURSDAY March 26, 1998
TRAIL DAY 85/6   ✦   TRAIL MILE 1,309/105
LOCATION By Rock Creek near Dennis, Cohuttas,
Chattahoochee National Forest

WHAT A FINE TIME HERE IN CHATSWORTH. The innkeeper provided a room being worked on . . . at no charge! I've found a very successful Yogi-ing technique as far as motels are concerned. I explain to the innkeeper that I need no linen, bedding, or towels, that I have all of these things with me and that I desire only a warm shower and a place to write. I also explain that the room will be left exactly as found with no need to bother maid service. And finally . . . that surely this could be provided at a special rate! I was able to call my family and many friends and to get caught up on my journal entries, have a grand shower, wash some clothes, and get a very good night's sleep. Steve is right here at 6:30 a.m., and we're on our way back to Dalton. Thanks, Steve, for stopping last evening and for all your kindness and help!

This is an event-filled day as I hike across the lush Great Valley from the Armuchee Mountains to the rugged Cohuttas. This is a road-walk past many lovely farms, and though I am on backroads with very little traffic, I am offered many rides by the kind Georgia folks. The road rolls up and around through the countryside past old houses with porches all around, horse farms, and sod farms, with beautiful Fort Mountain as a backdrop, setting a scene most grand, serene, and peaceful. I have been very concerned about my ability to make it through the Cohutta bushwhack. I talked with Marty Dominy at great length about this last night. He suggested I stay on the roads, but that is just not an option. Today I fret and worry myself about it again as I hike toward the tall and grand Cohuttas just ahead. The Armuchee bushwhack wasn't a piece of cake by any stretch, but it was easy enough to stay on the trail, for once up on the ridgeline, getting lost pretty much meant falling off. Looking at the topo for the Cohuttas, however, scares me. Here the mountains go every direction. Ridges drop into ravines, and these wind to be diverted by ridges and spurs from other mountains. Gaps and saddles interconnect in a maze. The topo is black with lines, indicating very steep and rugged terrain. And through this all goes the bushwhack o'er what one day will become the Georgia Pinhoti Trail.

This has been a warm and sunny day; what a joy! East of Ramhurst, near Dennis, I break from the roadwalk to enter the forest and start the bushwhack near Rock Creek. I promptly get lost, beating around in a side-hill pine thicket full of brush and greenbriers. I end up with brown, prickly pine needles down my neck and in everything, including my boots. I finally manage to beat my way off the ridge to follow the creek along and to climb where it tumbles from the mountain. I pitch for the evening by a most picturesque, pristine spot just above Rock Creek. The creek is full of gladness as it sings its happy song. In the soothing sound of its restful lullaby, I soon fall asleep.

> *"Sweet are the little brooks that run*
> *O'er pebbles glancing in the sun,*
> *Singing in soothing tones."*

[Thomas Hood, *Town and Country*]

TRAIL ANGELS: WHAT A WONDERFUL SUBJECT. I must tell you about two I encountered yesterday. Steve, the fellow who stopped to give me a ride and listen to my story about this odyssey and who lives in Ellijay, was the first. Even he, a long-distance backpacker, got a little glassy-eyed when I answered his questions about where I'm going and where I've been. He just kept saying, "That's awesome! That's awesome!" The next were the fine folks who gave me some biscuits at the gas station/mom 'n' pop deli a mile or so past the Conasauga Bridge. Would you believe five biscuits? Three ham and two sausage . . . and these weren't leftovers. It was just past 8:00 a.m. and people were buying breakfast biscuits! The sweet old lady said, "This'll help you get over those mountains." Doggone, I didn't get their names, but I've sure marked that place on my map! *Five biscuits*! I ate three yesterday; the other two I downed this morning.

As I've mentioned, I've been most apprehensive about the cross-country coming up on this north end of the Georgia Pinhoti. Looking at the topo lines on the map this morning makes my head spin! These mountains are massive. Spurs creating deep ravines go everywhere. The mountains lie at every compass position and the ridgelines are indistinct and hard to follow, often being no more than a spur from one knob hitting a spur from another. Not like the cross-country in the Armuchees to the west before crossing the Great Valley. Taylor Ridge was straight and almost level. Ditto for Strawberry, John's, Horn, Mill Creek, Middle, Hurricane, and Rocky Face mountains. All I basically had to do was get up on those ridges and truck! My nervousness and fear were reflected in my voice when I talked with Marty. "Marty," I said, "I don't think my map and compass skills or my climbing ability are up to what's ahead in the Cohuttas. It's not like the Armuchee Ridges." In his slow, matter-of-fact South Georgia drawl he said, "Some of the going will be painfully slow, especially with a backpack." I invited him to come up and go with me, which certainly wasn't fair to him. He's gone way out of his way to help me already. Preparing all of these maps had to take hours. They are incredibly detailed and very accurate.

The first section really threw me for a loop. I expected the cross-country to be tough but not quite so much up and down and through impenetrable thickets. But as I push on this morning, two things are becoming clear above all in my mind. First, even though this cross-country is scary and incredibly difficult (my back is sore from the pack being pushed and shoved, even with the sternum strap as tight as I can get it), I really haven't gotten lost! I know where I am every minute! I'm reading the topos and following my compass just fine! And second, I am seeing some unbelievably beautiful country, the very first Georgia Pinhoti thru-hiker to see these places. So these last few days before I reach Springer and the AT are going to be magic and exciting days. I'll follow the maps Marty has prepared for me. I'll probably blunder and get lost, but these will be the kind of days memories are made of! I've been on the trail 86 days. I've prepared myself. I believe I can handle this!

I get on through Rock Creek just fine. It's slow, hard hiking, just like Marty said it would be, but I'm enjoying the mountains in a way that is totally different than that enjoyment when following a beaten path. Here there is a different attitude, a different state of mind. The adrenaline is pumping; it is the mystery, the unknown, the doubt, and the challenge of it all. The air is charged, and I am vibrant and totally alive! A short FSR roadwalk and it's cross-country time again. Up one of the tributaries to Rock Creek (a misnomer — it should be called Boulder Creek). This terrain is indescribably rugged, making for tough climbing. There are many blowdowns, much brush. I am able to get my sleeping pad (Thermarest) off the outside bottom of my pack and inside this morning, so this allows me to move my sleeping bag from the top of my pack to the bottom. Not getting it hung up in everything I'm trying to get over, under, and through helps immensely! One of my comments while lamenting to Marty was, "It looks like you're running me straight up a waterfall." Well, would you believe four? Four dandies in less than half a mile! Folks, this place is rugged! What incredible sights, the falls, the lush vegetation all around. There is not the least hint of a path — no game trails, nothing! The map is black from the topo lines running together. I am able to climb through, around, and over them okay. This Georgia Pinhoti is going to be a remarkable trail!

Oh yes, here they are! Today I see them for the first time. I've been looking and waiting so long, each day with more and more anticipation. And here they are at last, beautiful and majestic, the unmistakable, stately white pine! I am in the mountains now for sure, no doubt about it! The white pine confirm that fact. Eighty-six days of hiking and I am here at last in these most-grand mountains. I'm home! I reach half-mile-high elevations today for the first time. As I hike on, my map and compass tell me that I should be nearing a service road again, and here it is without a hitch, just as Marty has marked. I pitch just inside the Forest Service line in a lovely sheltered cove with a clear brook, about 2 miles south of GA 52. Gathering rocks, I build a great fireplace, then level a spot to tent for the night. I'll leave this fireplace standing here. Others will want to stay here also when the finished trail passes by. This evening I am a member of the Georgia Pinhoti Trail crew building a campsite!

> *"Going to the mountains is going home."*
>
> [John Muir]

SATURDAY March 28, 1998
TRAIL DAY 87/8 ✦ TRAIL MILE 1,329/125
LOCATION Old blowdown hole, Bear Creek Trail by Parks Ridge,
Chattahoochee National Forest

I DIDN'T REALIZE JUST HOW LOVELY A CAMPSITE I picked last night, for I enjoyed a beautiful sunset over Fort Mountain to the west and could clearly see the lights of Dalton, across the Great Valley, a two-day hike away. Just before falling asleep I could see the lights from vehicles coming over Fort Mountain on GA 52, and I could also hear the faint whistle of train horns from Dalton.

I arise to another beautiful day, sunny and warm. Oh, if this weather will just hold one more day, as I must constantly refer to my maps. A rainy day would be a real problem. Cross-country bushwhacking is difficult even under ideal conditions. Today is another day of slow, hard going. Trail construction over Turkey Mountain to Holly Creek Gap is going to be a very tough proposition! The corridor is narrow through here, driving the trail down from the ridgeline into the steep ravines which run back on themselves.

Well, today is the day to get lost! I know I'm not where I should be right away when I see a spring box and black plastic pipe going down the creek, providing gravity-fed water to a home below. I stay on course, not wanting to climb back up the ravine, rehearsing my lines as I descend in case I am met by the landowner. I come out right in his back-yard. Luckily, no one is home and there's no dog! I get across his field and almost to the road at Mulberry Gap before the neighbor's dog starts yipping. I was one small ravine south of where I should have been, prob-ably off compass and map course no more than 100 yards or so!

I really have trouble getting down to Holly Creek Gap. The Forest Service has constructed a full two-lane-wide grassy road leading north just past Double Top, so I jump on it figuring it has to go out to the gap. Wrong! It slabs around Double Top and goes back south. I find this out by hiking all the way down and around as my compass needle keeps swinging the wrong direction. But here I see the first large and most stately hemlock. The ridge and saddle leading northeast off this grassy road are obscured by the recent construction, and I hunt and backtrack up and down for over an hour before I get back on track. Ha! Then the old narrow trail off Double Top forks. Yup, I take the wrong one. I finally make it to Holly Creek Gap, but the day is pretty much shot.

I have managed only 10 miles today, pretty much in line with what I've allowed but still somewhat disappointing. I'm anxious to see those white-diamond blazes on the Benton MacKaye Trail, but I know at the same time I'll most likely feel a bit of sadness as the truly adven-turous part of this odyssey will be over.

> *"It is because they have so much to give and give it so lavishly to those who enter them that we learn to love the mountains and go back to them again and again."*
>
> [Sir Francis Youngblood]

SUNDAY March 29, 1998
TRAIL DAY 88/9 ✦ TRAIL MILE 1,341/137
LOCATION Cove by Halloway Gap, south of Dyer Gap,
Benton MacKaye Trail

I AM UP EARLY AND OUT AT 7:30 A.M. I'm very excited about today, for if I go the right direction I will reach the Benton MacKaye Trail. Here, I'll be only 64 miles from Springer Mountain. As I get rolling—more tripping, stumbling, falling, and then rolling—I am able to follow my compass and topo maps fairly well. But it seems this is going to be bumble, bump, and bruise day! I've already managed to do two headers. One pitched me clean off the mountain into the puckers, and the other was a face-plant right in the dirt. Though I was shaken up, damage control reports I'm none the worse for wear! Oh yes! And now I am managing to get lost; nothing drastic, just time-consuming, frustrating little ordeals as I turn . . . to burn and finally return.

Marty's detailing for the proposed trail location is superb. Indeed the Georgia Pinhoti Trail, when completed, will thread its way through these precipitous slopes just as it should. However, the problem is the maps are not always correct, especially as to the actual woodsroad locations, and the cross-country today is some of the most challenging and technically demanding with which I've had to deal. It's interesting, for it seems the degree of bushwhacking difficulty has gradually and systematically increased from novice to near-expert right along with my ability to cope, calculate, and navigate with it, much as if a tactical-training course had been designed and prepared to teach me all levels of cross-country travel!

The Cohutta Wildlife Management Area comprises some incredibly rugged terrain. It's Sunday, but never do I see a soul in the Mountaintown area. There is finely constructed treadway here for hikers and mountain bikers, laid down in classic fashion. But it is a very tough and rugged trail. Mountaintown and Crenshaw creeks are formidable streams and the trail crosses them repeatedly. The area is pleasant to the eye but unpleasant to my (water-soaked) feet. There is bear sign all through here: trails, scat, and hair, but alas, no bruins are about.

The Georgia Pinhoti Trail is going to be a diverse and most delightful five-star trail when completed. It will have a little of all the grand things an outstanding trail should have: easy sections; challenging sections; roadwalks; peaceful stretches providing quiet solitude; breathtaking scenery including waterfalls; an unparalleled composite of flora and fauna, vistas, and majestic trees (the southernmost groves of hemlock and white pine on the continent); splendid campsites; babbling brooks; and Cave Spring—a really neat trail town! Oh yes, and mountains—above all, incredibly rugged, picturesque mountains! I finally reach the Benton MacKaye Trail (BMT) at 3:00 p.m.

Please humor this old man's chest-puffing now for just a moment, for it has been said, "If ya done it, it ain't a-braggin'." I feel proud and humbled to be the first to experience all that these combined Pinhoti trails have to offer. I may not be the first to hike the entire Alabama Pinhoti from where the grand Appalachians begin near Porter Gap to the Alabama/Georgia state line, but I suspect I am. I know I'm the first to hike the entire Georgia Pinhoti from the state line through the Armuchees to the BMT here in the Cohuttas. Both of these hikes have been "thru" hikes, done and combined as one thru-hike. So I know I also have the distinction of being the first to hike the entire Pinhoti Trail—a distance, according to my calculations, of some 260 miles, the Alabama segment being a little over 125 miles and the Georgia segment nearly 140 miles.

I would like to thank all the great folks with the Alabama Trails Association, the Georgia Pinhoti Trail Association, the Forest Service people, and all other personnel involved and associated at the federal, state, and local levels who, through love and dedication for their chosen work, so diligently and professionally caretake these treasures of ours. And to Marty, especially to you, Marty Dominy, my dear friend, for your help in making the Pinhoti Trail such a pleasant and rewarding experience. It is destined to become one of the most memorable parts of this odyssey. And finally, above all, I thank the Good Lord for the determination, stamina, good health, and safe passage so lavished upon me.

I pitch near a lovely mountain brook by the BMT. This has been another beautiful, rewarding, and memorable day. Now on to Springer

Mountain and the bushwhack home for a much-needed rest before adventuring on north!

> *"If you would measure the quiet majesty, the beauty,*
> *the sanctity of the woods, do it with a two-foot rule . . .*
> *to be part of the great sanctuary — walk."*

[Unknown]

SECTION 4: Benton MacKaye Trail

MONDAY March 30, 1998

TRAIL DAY 89/1 ✦ TRAIL MILE 1,355/14

LOCATION Home of Leroy and Kathy Rice, Cherrylog

WHAT ANOTHER WONDERFUL DAY! Hiking in this kind of weather is grand. Spring is indeed my companion again. As she greets me once more, and to brighten her debut, she adds gaiety to the occasion. For now I find dainty little wildflowers in profusion, like so much garland, gracing the trail all along. Small, fragile stars are they in yellow, blue, and violet. The trees are starting to bud and so are the blackberries. The white bloom of the serviceberry is lighting up the gray wood, pushing the somber monochrome of winter to the wings. Ah, and the dogwood! The dogwood cannot be far behind. And to add sweet music, the grouse are drumming everywhere.

I'm having much difficulty adjusting to marked trail again. I've become accustomed to seeing no blazes, to the need for being constantly tuned to compass bearings and contour changes. My map and compass were my guide, telling me where to head, which way to (literally) blaze the trail. Now I need no focus, no concentration . . . for there is the path, like the yellow brick road! What effort does it take to stay on a path so beaten down, the task presented being no more than to spot the bright white blazes painted on nearly every tree? If I want to know my location now, I simply take my map and compass and look back to see where I've been! This passive exercise requires no alertness. There is no need for skills that have been honed to proud fineness, no need for keenness of senses, no awareness required here! What has replaced this constant drama, the excitement and the unknown of it, is nothing more than a resigned reenactment of someone else's trailblazing creativity — someone who passed this way many years ago. Here's a whole different rhythm, for now all that needs to be done is simply fill in the dots! Have I become just a blunt-headed pencil, drawing so many lines?

The hiking here is like what I'll be dealing with on the Appalachian Trail (AT): lots of ups and downs and side-slabbing going every direction. When I tell folks I've hiked over 1,000 miles from the Everglades, the comment is, "It isn't that far to south Florida." I say, "Maybe not as the crow flies or even as the highways go, but the trail drifts along more like the butterfly, in every direction and with frequent regularity."

I am saddened to see the BMT so badly damaged by ORV (quad-track) use. The section south of Halloway Gap looks more like a road than a trail with the buildup of berms and ruts, and I see nothing being done to stop it. Perhaps ORVs are permitted here, as there are no signs as at other gaps. It would be strange, however, for motorized use to be permitted on a trail named in honor of Benton MacKaye. That would be anathema to all he professed and believed. Ask anyone in the Forest Service about Benton MacKaye and they will proudly tell you that of all his titles, of all the hats he wore, he was first, last, and foremost a forester!

The trail through the Sisson development is delightful. A shelter, a covered bridge, a chapel, decks, and walkways right on the trail. Someone here must be a hiker! A friend of mine lives in Cherrylog, just down from where the trail crosses the railroad tracks, so I take a detour and head there along the old grade. Leroy Rice has worked in logging most all his life. I've never seen anyone handle a chainsaw with the sheer skill and finesse this man possesses. He has taught me much of this technique, not the least of which is the proper method of sharpening a chain—in the woods, on the ground, bogged in mud. Some of you folks will remember the old galvanized washtubs. Well, Leroy has these things chock-full of used-up and worn-out saw chains! When I saw this incredible display one day, I asked him, "Leroy, why in the world have you saved all this junk? The chains are shot; they're worn out!" With a sigh, he lamented, "I just never could bring myself to toss 'em out!" So, there they are. What an incredible history book for all to read! Bad arthritis took him away from log bucking a few years ago, and he now works at a lumberyard in Jasper. So here I sit on his porch this afternoon, catching up on my journal entries, waiting for him to get home from work.

Well, I expect you can tell that Leroy is my very good friend.

And indeed he is . . . for today he's good for a hot tub of water and a much-needed bath, and a few tall frosties! I am dearly looking forward to another trip to the Pink Pig BBQ, but, alas, Leroy says they're closed on Mondays. Instead, he and Kathy and I load in his pickup and head for Blue Ridge for a fine steak dinner at Circle "J." Oh yes, there's plenty of good old soft ice cream, too! Thanks, dear friends, for your kindness and hospitality. These "don't know you're coming" kind of friends are the very best by far!

> *"Pour, pour of the wine of the heart, O Nature!*
> *By cups of field and of sky,*
> *By the brimming soul of every creature —*
> *Joy-mad dear Mother, am I."*

[David Atwood Wasson, *Joy-month*]

TUESDAY March 31, 1998
TRAIL DAY 90/2 ◆ TRAIL MILE 1,373/32
LOCATION Ravine with small spring near Tipton Mountain

WE'RE UP AT DAWN, AND AS LEROY HEADS TO WORK he drops me off at Sisson, saving me the mile hike back up the railroad grade. I've got a tough pull right off the bat this morning from Weaver Creek Road to the top of Rocky Mountain, over 1,400 feet in 3.5 miles. I fully expected my legs and my wind to be in top condition by now, having hiked over 1,300 miles. But I'm just not ready for the strenuous demands of these long, rugged uphills. The fact that I'll be 60 years old this fall is going to be my excuse.

What started out to be a nice day is quickly turning very gray. My friend in West Virginia would say, "It's a-darkin' over." By 10:30 a.m. steady drizzle comes, and it appears there'll be more company soon. As I pass a long row of summer cabins down Stanley Creek, the deluge begins. I can see the screen door ajar on the back porch of one of these little retreats across the way, so I head over to get out of it. I am fortunate to be out of this downpour. As I settle back on the porch floor with my head on my bedroll, the sound of the creek and the steady rain on the tin roof send me away on a two-hour nap. When I awake, the sky is clearing and I'm able to resume my hike past many lovely summer homes and mountain cabins along Stanley Creek.

The Toccoa River is crossed the first time by passing over the old iron box-frame Shallowford Bridge. This well-maintained bridge brings back childhood memories of similar bridges that were very common at river crossings near my home in the Ozark Hills of Missouri. I can remember how all of them would shake, rattle, and make a joyful sound when vehicles passed. I used to ride my bicycle down to the old Rockhouse Bridge to play around and listen to the cars and trucks go by. The bridge is gone now, replaced by a concrete slab that will never shake and rattle. So here I find myself standing, waiting around again, much as in bygone days, hoping for a vehicle to pass so I can once again listen to and reminisce about that shake, that rattle, and that joyful sound. Oh, and I'm in luck, for here comes an old pickup now. I close my eyes as it passes. And as the old bridge shakes and rattles, there's that unmistakable joyful sound! For just this moment, it is once again the endless days of summer and I'm a barefoot boy . . . playing on the old Rockhouse Bridge. As I head on up the road, another vehicle crosses, and that delightful faraway sound from another place and time echoes true once more. Continuing on my way, and with tears in my eyes now, I'm thinking, "Isn't progress sometimes such a sad thing?"

There's another good pull from Dial Road up Brawley Mountain, over 1,000 feet in a little over 2 miles. Recent tornadoes, probably spawned by the same storm that killed folks in Hall County, have ripped the tops out of trees and made a most incredible tangle of brush everywhere. Nature can be so quirky, making breathtakingly beautiful offerings in one spot and ghastly, dismal displays in another. I have to pitch camp tonight in the latter. The ground is uprooted, brush all around, ruts, gullies, and mud everywhere. Miraculously, however, right in the middle of all this staggering destruction is this small, clear running spring. So here I stay for the night. No sooner do I get supper cooked and my tent up than the deluge starts again. It rains hard all night.

*"Everybody needs beauty as well as bread, places to play
in and places to pray in, where nature may heal and
cheer and give strength to body and soul."*

[John Muir]

WEDNESDAY April 1, 1998
TRAIL DAY 91/3 ✦ TRAIL MILE 1,388/47
LOCATION Hemlock, Toccoa River Suspension Bridge

MUD IS EVERYWHERE. What a glorious mess! Light brown camo will
be the color of the day—tent, pack, and me! Although I'm on the BMT,
it's bushwhacking time again. Nature has really worked the trail over
with brush, blowdown, and mud-choked ruts. Here, the expression "this
is slick" carries a less-modern connotation. Easy does it. With patience—
and much flexibility—I manage my way through, around, and over the
worst of it. Fate and the Good Lord spared me this devastation as
the storm passed over me on Indian Mountain last month.

Hiking seems to be getting easier on the legs. They're coming up
to the task and the uphills aren't whipping me nearly as badly . . . but
come early afternoon, I have the 1,000-foot climb from Skeenah Gap up
Rhodes Mountain in less than 2 miles. I've managed to eat my way
through most of the provisions lugged out of Dalton a week ago, so my
pack isn't nearly as cumbersome. As I turn from Payne Gap toward
Skeenah Gap, I pass the northernmost point on this leg of the journey,
almost reaching North Carolina. Heading almost due south now, I'm
bound for Springer Mountain and home! I'm so anxious to see the AT,
Springer, and my little place in the Nimblewill again.

The second crossing of the Toccoa River is at the remarkable and
picturesque hiker suspension bridge. The roaring river, stately hemlock,
and this man-made structure reside in pure complement! Man and Ma
Nature seldom engage to work such side-by-side harmonious repose.
The BMT certainly has much to offer those who venture along its path.
I pitch for the evening at the delightful campsite beneath the hemlock,
near the bridge on the banks of the roaring Toccoa. There's plenty of

drift for a campfire, and as twilight withdraws, my fire creates light, which casts the most dignified glow o'er this whole scene. Quiet contentment and restful sleep are a wonderful combination!

> *"No outdoorsman attains freedom as completely as the*
> *backpacker. . . . you can walk with the wind, stand with*
> *the trees, or pause with the silence."*
>
> [Bill Riviere, *Backcountry Camping*]

THURSDAY April 2, 1998
TRAIL DAY 92/4 ✦ TRAIL MILE 1,402/61
LOCATION Springer Mountain,
Southern Terminus, Appalachian Trail

TODAY IS ANOTHER DAY OF GREAT EXCITEMENT. As I approach Long Creek Falls, where the Benton MacKaye joins the Appalachian Trail, I hear voices. As I near, I see hikers heading north, laden with gargantuan packs, bound for Mt. Katahdin, Maine. I wait for them to pass, for I want to savor this moment alone as I stand looking at this first familiar white rectangular blaze. The fifth leg of this odyssey has ended, and in a moment I will set foot on the grand old Appalachian Trail. It has taken 92 days and nearly 1,400 trail miles to arrive at this point, but I am here. Through miles of lonely, mud-filled trail, through relentless rain, through snow and cold, through the shove from the winds of countless 18-wheelers along countless miles of highway, I now stand where I can see that familiar white blaze; and I stand in humbleness and thanks as I look . . . the AT, I am here at last. I am tying it all together, the trail I hope will someday become known as the ECT, the Eastern Continental Trail, a continuous footpath stretching near the entire breadth of the eastern North American continent.

As I turn south and head toward Springer Mountain, the trail is no longer mine alone. Over the past 91 days, I have seen three Scout packs and three other backpackers, including *Mule*. Now there's a steady stream heading north on the AT bound for Katahdin. In less than an hour I meet no fewer than a dozen northbounders. There is Bryan,

Flatlander, Cowboy, Mt. Muz, and *Panhandle Patty.* I meet Chris, *Yertle,* (and I yack and yack), *Patches, Squish-Squash,* and *Red.* I ask *Mt. Muz,* an old fellow about my age, to stop a minute, but looking over his shoulder as he keeps pounding on, he says, "Can't stop now, got a long ways to go!" Ah yes, dear friend, indeed you have!

What a wonderful, pleasant surprise, for just before arriving at Cross-Trails, who comes gliding along but none other than Dave *Skookum* Irving and his dog, Baxter. They're back for another season as the ridge runners for the Georgia section of the AT. I met *Skookum* during one of my many trips up Springer Mountain last year. We linger and have much to discuss. Late in the evening I arrive and pitch on the summit of Springer Mountain. As the shadows lengthen and evening wanes, the sky is set ablaze with one of the most colorful sunsets I've ever witnessed over these timeless Appalachians. What a glorious, rewarding day!

> *"Paradise is the here and now, the actual, tangible, dogmatically real Earth on which we stand. Yes, God Bless America."*
>
> [Edward Abbey]

FRIDAY April 3, 1998
TRAIL DAY 93/5 ✦ TRAIL MILE 1,402
LOCATION Springer Mountain,
Southern Terminus, Appalachian Trail

I'M UP AT 5:30 A.M., FULL OF EXCITEMENT, anxious to get started on the six-hour cross-county bushwhack off Springer Mountain, down Lance Creek ravine to Bull Mountain (horsey-bike) Trail, and home! But Mother Nature has other plans. Thunder is rumbling nearby—that ominous, hollow sound of mountain thunder, and I see almost constant lightning. The wind starts up and comes driving through. I'm crouched by my tent, feverishly stuffing my sleeping bag, trying with all effort to break camp, get my raingear on, and get off the summit before this next blast hits. But with the wind comes cold, driving rain, and it's all I can do to get my bag back out and roll right back in behind it before getting soaked. The full fury of the storm slams the summit. I spread-eagle in my tent to keep the wind from ripping it from the ground. The storm seems incessant, and my arms and legs ache and are near spasm as I fight against the lifting force of the storm.

El Niño has followed me, dogged me all the way to Springer Mountain, and now in total glee does he keep me pinned to the ground, causing me to shudder in uncontrollable fright. Finally the initial blast passes, and as I lie here frustrated and fretting, I'm thinking, "Let's just go for it; you're gonna get soaked and half frozen, but it's only six more hours and then you're home." In no rush to respond to this impulsive urge, and as the morning passes, more rational judgment prevails. For I realize there is no way to make it down in this weather. The bushwhack starts in the first saddle below on the blue-blaze to Amicalola Falls State Park. Bailing off there, the drop is precipitous, most-near straight down through rocks and briars and brush for three-quarters of a mile. It's a tough nut under ideal conditions, and these are far from ideal. So here I stay, so close to home . . . but not today.

With age comes patience, a grand virtue indeed. I am finally able to emerge again around 4:00 p.m., the wind still kicking. The break in the storm gives me a chance to get some water, prepare a hot meal, and make a much-needed dash to the privy. Unfortunately, though, there is not enough time to bushwhack off the mountain before dark. So here I stay again another night as the wind and rain continue.

Time's such a 'plexing medium,
It's off and then it's on.
At times there seems so much of it,
Yet when you turn, it's gone.

[N. Nomad]

SATURDAY April 4, 1998
TRAIL DAY 94/6 ✦ TRAIL MILE 1,402
LOCATION My home at Nimblewill Creek, near Springer Mountain

SOMEHOW, EVEN WITH ALL THE ANTICIPATION AND EXCITEMENT, I have managed to sleep the night, for I do not rise until 7:30 a.m. The rain has stopped, but the wind continues. The summit is shrouded in heavy moisture-laden clouds that continue roaring through, and the temperature is 34 degrees. Of the seven days' provisions (stretched to nine) toted from Dalton, I have a little rice and a small helping of macaroni left. I have to get off the mountain today. The wind chill for 35 degrees and 30-mile-per-hour wind is 5 degrees, and I believe it. The wind is very cold, much colder it seems than the 14-degree morning in the snow on Cheaha Mountain. My hands and fingers are ignoring my signals, and I have difficulty packing my wet tent and fly.

Fortunately, the bushwhack this morning is down the lee side of the mountain away from the wind. Once into the descent, conditions improve considerably. I am soon out of the cloud-swirl, and the rocks, brush, and blowdowns present little difficulty. The rain threatens all morning but for some reason holds, and I am able to get off the mountain to the warmth and comfort of my little place at Nimblewill Creek. Here, friends and family share my joy. Ah, a warm shower, good food, and my own bed! I'll rest here a week or so, get my affairs in order for the remainder of the year, and then I'll bushwhack Springer again to continue this odyssey as I journey on north o'er the Appalachian Trail to Baxter Peak, Maine.

"So Thou shouldst kneel at morning dawn
That God may give thy daily care,
Assured that He no load too great
Will make thee bear. "

[Anna Temple Whitney]

Chapter 3
Appalachian National Scenic Trail

MONDAY April 20, 1998
TRAIL DAY 94/0 ✦ TRAIL MILE 1,402/0
LOCATION Springer Mountain, Southern Terminus, Appalachian Trail

I HAVE FOUND IT ALMOST IMPOSSIBLE to get all the things done that need to be done in the "real world," things that inevitably must go on in my absence for the next five or six months. It's already 2:30 p.m. as I work feverishly, getting my little place here at the Nimblewill straightened up and mothballed so I can depart. I should have been out of here at least an hour ago. The bushwhack to the summit of Springer Mountain takes at least six hours, with the last three-quarter-mile leg being the most difficult—nearly straight up. I don't want to be tackling that in the dark.

I finally have my pack on and I'm out the door. I guess it's normal to have misgivings, especially when faced with a challenge the magnitude of thru-hiking the Appalachian National Scenic Trail (AT). This is something I have been looking forward to and planning for years. I have faith that the Good Lord will provide me safe and successful passage, but I have feelings of doubt and fear nonetheless. The fact that I've been on the trail 94 days and have logged over 1,400 miles in the process is no guarantee, no assurance, that I will make it any farther. The longest segment of this incredible "Odyssey of '98" lies ahead: the AT. I've read many an account and many friends have told me about this grand affair—what a far-reaching adventure it will be. The AT stretches for over 2,100 miles, from Springer Mountain above me here in Georgia, through countless mountains and valleys, across 14 states, to the "Greatest Mountain" in Maine: Mt. Katahdin.

I've descended now to Nimblewill Creek, where my good friend and fellow backpacker Robert Seaton waits to greet me and send me off. I linger and we talk. I know he would like to come with me. I know I would like him to journey along. One of these days we'll get to do some backpacking together I'm sure. We bid farewell and I'm off for Springer Mountain and that far horizon that lies out there—that mysterious beyond that beckons the wanderlust in all of us.

The hike and bushwhack from my little place to Springer Mountain covers over 9 miles. In that distance I will climb in excess of 2,000 feet—nearly half a mile. First I have a short bushwhack followed by a walk along paved roads and woodsroads. From here I head up the horsey-bike trail around Bull Mountain and up Lance Creek watershed. First I pass a cove, then the upper ravine, then along by the creek to the springhead near the summit of Springer Mountain. Then comes the final ascent straight up the mountain to the blue-blazed approach trail from Amicalola Falls State Park.

There are many different ways to gain notoriety, some which are planned, some which simply happen. It's hard to believe there would be much notoriety in how one arrives at Springer Mountain, but if you mention the name Robie Hensley, you will realize fame can indeed come in strange and unusual ways. For Robie is best known for how he reached Springer to begin his Appalachian Trail thru-hike. He para-chuted onto the summit! There was no problem tagging Robie with his trail name. He immediately became known as *Jumpstart*! And so it is that I am probably the first to walk from home to the summit of Springer Mountain to begin an Appalachian Trail thru-hike. But you're not likely to read about *Walkstart* in the evening paper! I arrive and pitch on the summit of Springer Mountain just as the sun is setting.

> *"This day be bread and peace my lot;*
> *All else beneath the sun,*
> *Thou knowst if best bestowed or not,*
> *And let thy will be done."*

[Alexander Pope, *The Universal Prayer*]

I STAND HERE NOW BY THE OLD PLAQUE on the summit of Springer Mountain, my heart in my throat, my mind in the mist. I have stood here countless times before . . . but my presence here now, this moment, is somehow different. For all of the intrepid who have stood here, each has a story to tell. For from this very spot does there begin a marvelous and incredible adventure that many have described as "the journey of a lifetime." But for me, the old *Nomad*, from this point does there continue an odyssey that began many days and many miles to the south. So the feelings and emotions that are flooding over me must be a jumble compared to those experienced by others who have passed this way.

Five sections of the Eastern Continental Trail (ECT) have been completed: 825 miles of the Florida National Scenic Trail, 250 miles of the Florida/Alabama Roadwalk, 125 miles of the Alabama Pinhoti Trail, 140 miles of the Georgia Pinhoti Trail, and 60 miles of the Benton MacKaye Trail. As I look at the first white blaze leading north, marking the Appalachian National Scenic Trail, knowing that over 2,100 miles remain, emotions flood over me. For by the Grace of God am I here at this shrine. Tears of sadness, tears of joy, and tears of pride well in my eyes. Emotions I've never before experienced and cannot fully describe overwhelm me. My obituary could have been written at least three times since beginning this journey on New Year's Day. But the Good Lord has seen fit to open a path for me, and I have had safe passage.

I am literally living Psalm 23. For I did lie down in green pastures, I have walked beside still waters, and my soul, indeed, is being restored. For it is that the path o'er which I trek is directing me toward the paths of righteousness. Slowly my countenance is beginning to reflect that of a man at peace . . . at peace with himself, at peace with the world, and at peace with the Lord. The anger, the hatred, the resentment, the envy, the vain pride, all of which have consumed me over the last many years, a burden carried heavy on my mind and in my heart onto the trail in the Everglades, a burden every bit as heavy as the physical burden of the pack on my back, is slowly going out of my body, down to the trail beneath my feet, and onto the path behind me. In a moment I will take that first step north—into the unknown, to continue toward the paths of righteousness, for His name's sake. Surely goodness and mercy shall follow me.

Within the swirling mist passing over this summit do spirits also reside and pass, for I feel their presence. And of these do I remember William Bartram, John Muir, Henry David Thoreau, Benton MacKaye, Myron Avery, Percival Baxter, Walter Greene, Healon Taylor, George Outerbridge, Orville Crowder, George Miller, Emma Gatewood, and Murray Chism. God willing, I will reach Mt. Katahdin, and then, too, will there be a place here for my spirit to dwell someday.

A scant 3 miles north from Springer Mountain by trail is found one of the most awe-inspiring places along the entire Appalachian Range. Here exists a most proud community. Its residents make up the oldest virgin stand of hemlock in the eastern United States. As I descend the cove at Stover Creek, I sense there are grand sky-hinged cathedral doors opening before me, as if I am entering Nature's very own place of worship. I stand now among majestic, towering monarchs, ancient, almost everlasting, their places taken here long before this land was a civilized nation, magnificent still. How could they possibly have endured the ravages of time and survived the encroachment of man! Their presence is humbling, overpowering. I stand and gaze in silence and awe. Three of us with our arms outreaching could not encircle the girth of these giant statesmen. It is impossible to adequately describe these proud towers to you—you must come and rest your eyes on them. For you too will not believe! Here is a true legacy of the forest primeval, this small swatch that man has somehow passed over, to remain, and to be cradled in the bosom of Nature . . . by time.

It seems El Niño has chosen to continue this journey with me. I arrive at Gooch Gap Shelter in hail. There were many hard pulls today, and I am very tired. A fire is going and I prepare a warm meal. And so ends my remarkable first day on the Appalachian Trail. Sleep comes soon!

"Poems are made by fools like me,
But only God can make a tree."

[Joyce Kilmer]

WEDNESDAY April 22, 1998
TRAIL DAY 96/2 ✦ TRAIL MILE 1,433/31
LOCATION Neels Gap, US 19, Goose Creek Cabins

WE HAD AN INTERNATIONAL GATHERING at the shelter last night: Frank *Sneakers* Clarkeston from Detroit, Michigan; Eric *Pure* Joy from Marietta, Georgia; and Eric *Voyager* Schmidt from Woodstock, Ontario, Canada. The rain pounded most of the night. What a blessing to be in a shelter and out of it for a change! This morning the rain has backed off, but the sky remains gray and threatening. The four of us enjoy hiking together into Woody Gap. What a fine experience having company on the trail. But at Woody Gap I bid farewell to these new friends. for it is my desire to reach Neels Gap by nightfall.

It is noon now and the sun is trying to burn away the higher-elevation mush. Down below, the valleys and mountainsides are adrift in white, streaming clouds, the sun occasionally dodging through, creating brilliant contrast and relief across the fresh light-green fabric of spring. The shadows from the traveling banners visit to linger and dance in the pockets and coves all along. But alas, the sun will have no luck with the gray swirl as it descends again, bringing an ever-darkening blanket of gray-black clouds. First the summits are embraced and encircled round-about, then the saddles and spurs, and finally the ravines below. I hike on and into it through the mist, then through the rain, then into the driving cold wind . . . and, finally, through the sleet! So it seems the weather and I have gone full circle. Let's see: searing sun burning my arms, face, and neck in south Florida; cold, relentless rain in central and northern Florida and into Alabama—ditto for subfreezing temperatures; snow and freezing rain in the Cheaha wilderness; and the incredible rain, wind, and lightning on Flagpole Mountain near the Alabama/Georgia state line— the storm that spawned the tornadoes that devastated Hall County,

Georgia. Yesterday there was hail and today sleet! Oh, did I forget to mention the month and a half of flooding?

As the rain and sleet continue, the treadway deteriorates. The hundreds and hundreds of backpackers who have tramped through before me have widened and deepened the trail to a highway-wide quagmire in many spots, making progress slow and difficult, reminiscent of many a day in Florida. But with age comes patience, a true virtue. I know this trail will get better by and by. Everybody is still hammering on this thing . . . but that will change soon. The attrition rate for those bound for the "Greatest Mountain" is between 80 and 90 percent. That is a staggering statistic, a number to put fear in the heart and doubt in the mind of the most seasoned intrepid. The Appalachian Trail tends to take its toll, and in that regard it doesn't seem as patient as me. But I believe that I'll be there, God willing, when the snows descend on Baxter.

I reach Walasi-Yi, Neels Gap, at 3:00 p.m. and am greeted with a grand smile by Dorothy Hansen. Dorothy makes the call and I wait for the free shuttle to Goose Creek Cabins. Goose Creek is a neat place with kind and gracious hosts.

> *The trail leaves Springer Mountain,*
> *Six lanes wide, deep-trodden.*
> *But narrower it will become,*
> *Before I reach Katahdin.*

> [N. Nomad]

THURSDAY April 23, 1998
TRAIL DAY 97/3 ✦ TRAIL MILE 1,450/49
LOCATION Blue Mountain Shelter

PERMIT ME JUST ANOTHER WORD ABOUT THE BAILEYS, the good folks who run Goose Creek Cabins. Keith is out of town, so Claude, his father, now has the job of driving the shuttle to and from Neels Gap. Claude also drove 20 miles round trip to Blairsville for pizza and subs for all of us staying at the Cabins last evening—no charge for delivery! I meet two other thru-hikers as Claude delivers us back to the Gap—

Mary *Mary-Go-Round* Blewitt from Connecticut and Dave Chambers from Indiana. Had a great time at your place, Claude, thanks!

Back at Walasi-Yi Center I go in again for a few minutes to gab a little more with Dorothy before heading on north. I remember a comment in one of *Wingfoot's* earlier editions of *The Thru-Hiker's Handbook* where he mentioned that the Hansens, Jeff and Dorothy, put in long, hard days, especially Dorothy, who also had to care for their two small children. We chuckle as Dorothy mentions that the 13-year-old now helps at the Center and can run the cash register! Looks like I'm northbound thru-hiker #992 to sign in at Walasi, heading for Katahdin!

The sun is trying to play its bright, warm glow as I look from Cowrock Mountain. Before descending to Tesnatee Gap, I witness the sun now and again striking the Cliffs of Raven, transforming the stark gray vertical walls of granite, iced now from endless rain into brilliant shimmering jewels, as if so many reflections from a crystal palace. Ah, the constant, ever-changing magic, collectively known as the wonders of nature, revealed to those of us who have chosen to pass this way on this grand Appalachian National *Scenic* Trail!

As I stand here now in Tesnatee Gap, I am at the spot where it is believed John Muir passed on his 1,000-mile walk to the sea. Might I pause and ask you something? Permit me, please. Do you find it perhaps strange, as do I, this time capsule in which we are enclosed, as if so many passengers traveling along? For indeed, we are most definitely slaves and servants to our captor time, a medium most brilliant of our minds have been unable to understand or fathom. So it is now that I extend my hand in greeting to that intrepid of many decades past, for both of us have made our journey here. But alas, as I wait . . . the greeting is not returned. I will depart this place in a moment and my presence here will become, as did Muir's presence here, just another of the countless entries in the logbook of time.

I arrive at Blue Mountain Shelter in a driving sleet storm.

> *"Climb the mountains and get their good tidings.*
> *Nature's peace will flow into you as sunshine flows into*
> *trees. The winds will blow their own freshness into you,*

>   *and the storms their energy, while cares will drop like*
>   *autumn leaves."*
>
>   [John Muir]

WE HAD ANOTHER INTERNATIONAL CROWD at the shelter last night:
Chick Mitten with her Australian Shepherd, Ilsa; *Cheerio* Kid from
Montreal, Canada; Robert and Benjamin from Columbus, Ohio; Alex
from Kansas City, Missouri; and *EZ1* from Shelby, North Carolina. A bit
more about Lee Barry, this gentleman who goes by the trail name *EZ1*.
Lee will celebrate his 75th birthday here on the trail this coming Sunday.
He's been hiking for 25 years, belongs to the Carolina Mountain Club,
and is twice a 2,000-miler, not including a thru-hike in 1996 at age 73! I
am talking with him here on the trail as we hike along this morning. Folks,
this *EZ1* makes the trail look EZ! This is a marvelous thing, a proud and
energetic man still going strong at the age of 75 and having a blast! Here's
to you, Lee, and as the kid from Montreal would say, "Cheerio!"

As I descend into Unicoi Gap, I am thinking about the three *original* AT plaques cast in bronze in 1938. They show a hiker, pack shouldered and on the trail, the likeness of Warner Hall, the second Georgia
Appalachian Trail Club president. On these plaques are engraved the
famous lines coined by members of GATC and believed to have gained
the joyful approval of Benton MacKaye: "A pathway for those who seek
fellowship with the wilderness." One of these plaques marks the southern AT terminus on the summit of Springer Mountain. It is embedded in
the granite monolith at the overlook vista. The second rests at the trail
junction in Neels Gap, across from Walasi-Yi, right beside the busy road
shoulder of US 19, where thousands pass each day. And the third is
fixed to a boulder here beside GA 75 at Unicoi Gap. If you haven't seen
one of these beautiful historical AT monuments, by all means, go! I
would urge you to visit Springer Mountain to see the one there and

at the same time enjoy one of the most beautiful vistas anywhere in the southern Appalachians. Having seen all three of these beautiful bronze memorials in the span of the last four days goes far to restore my faith in humankind. For to me it seems that for all three of these plaques to have survived without being stolen or molested is most-near a miracle. Count the years they have graced this trail . . . yes, it's been 60 years! This year these beautiful memorials celebrate their 60th anniversary!

It is a delight to have such a simple and useful wildflower guide as has been published in the 1998 edition of *The Thru-Hiker's Handbook*. Finally I have a way to identify these fragile, mysterious little wonders of nature! From Blue Mountain to Powell Mountain the following spring wildflowers, many in profusion, grace the trail today: bluet, toadshade trillium, common blue violet, crested dwarf iris, toothwort, great chickweed, bloodroot, pearly everlasting, daisy fleabane, wood anemone, dandelion, and large flowered bellwort. As if this show bordering the trail is not enough, bright green garlands of grass dress the pathway, almost uninterrupted, and in their way, say "Follow us!" And follow I do, down and through the spectacular "Swag of the Blue Ridge." As I observe the patience of Mother Nature, I too can learn to practice patience in order to enjoy all that she reveals to me.

The day is sunny, bright, and warm, the kind of day I've waited and longed for and patience has brought. There could not have been a more perfect day to hike the "Swag." I've looked forward to visiting and passing here again with high anticipation, and I literally skip on through as if on the "yellow brick road." How soon we forget. For it wasn't that many years ago a battle raged, a virtual tug-of-war. It involved a proposal brought by road builders to lay down a road right over the Swag. Thanks to the Good Lord and the ATC and its staunch supporters and allies, those who opposed this road plan prevailed. If any of you reading this were involved in that valiant, successful effort, you have my deepest and most heartfelt thanks! Earl, it looks like this beautiful showy maiden — the "Spring of '98" — is going to delight us all on this the 50th anniversary of your first AT thru-hike — your first "walk with spring."

> *"Flowers were blooming everywhere. Sometimes one patch extended for miles, so thick they couldn't be avoided, even on the footpath."*
>
> [Earl Shaffer, *Walking with Spring*]

SATURDAY April 25, 1998
TRAIL DAY 99/5 ✦ TRAIL MILE 1,482/80
LOCATION Wateroak Gap, North Carolina

PROFESSIONALISM ALWAYS SHINES THROUGH. When you've got your act together and know what you're doing, it makes all the difference in the world. And that describes the Blueberry Patch on US 76 near Hiawassee. Gary *Trail Chef '91* Poteat and his petite wife, Lennie, run this delightful little hiker hostel. Found here are first-class accommodations, great pizza, and fine prayer-led breakfasts: food for both body and soul. And the word apparently got out early as over one-third of the hiker "Class of '98" has stayed here so far. These are kind, God-fearing folks. Thanks, Gary and Lennie, for your friendship and hospitality.

I met two more members of the Class of '98 here last night, *The Fence*, from south Florida, and *Phoenix* (like the one that rose from ashes), who just had a liver transplant. I manage a ride back to the trail with *Free*, who has stopped by the Patch, thus saving Gary the shuttle, which otherwise would have been graciously provided.

I have a couple of hard pulls coming out of Dick's Creek Gap first thing this morning. It reminds me of Ramrock Mountain last Wednesday. During that long, demanding climb, I had just stopped for a moment to catch my breath when *Voyager*, the gentleman from Canada who since has become my good friend, passed by, cursing the ever-increasing difficulty of climbing these rugged mountains. I later talked to *Voyager* about how I once, too, had that same reaction to the difficult conditions the trail often dishes out—and how something I once heard Warren Doyle, Jr., say turned it all around for me. Succinct and penetrating as an arrow, Warren said, "The trail is not here for you; you are here for the trail." Being mindful of this little "trail proverb" for just a short while brought about in me a total change in attitude, a whole other mindset about the trail. So now, as a result of this inspiring revelation, with each mountain I must climb I say to myself, "When I reach this summit, I will be a better person, I will be a stronger person; this mountain I am climbing will teach me tolerance, patience, and a deeper appreciation and understanding of the meaning of the word 'humility.' " And so, indeed, with this attitude are coming all of these virtues to penetrate the very core of my being. Thank you, Warren, for the revelation, and thank you, Lord, for your grace!

So as I near Bly Gap, I have mixed emotions. I am indeed a better person, that I know. It is a result of climbing these Georgia mountains! But at the same time I am leaving the beautiful Blue Ridge, my home. As I enter Bly Gap, and to my amazement and joy, do I find it still here—the old kneeling oak . . . still alive. It's been 15 years since I was here last, since I set eyes upon this remarkable tree. But it is as if yesterday, for the old oak thrives in such a grand and glorious fashion. As the family of man has its physically challenged—members with less-than-perfect physical abilities and features—so, too, does the tree family. This old oak is so unusual it is the subject for many a photographer and painter. I doubt few who pass this way do not recognize and know it. I have found that if one observes this old knot casually, it looks entirely grotesque. It appears beaten down, broken, and defeated. But how many of our own do we know with this sort of disability who are fighters, survivors—vibrant and vital, living life to the fullest! And so, too, this old oak!

Upon closer observation, I see a strange transformation occur right before my eyes. For I see now a radiance and beauty which must surely come from deep within. No longer do I see the beaten down and broken. I see instead tenacity, strength, courage, inner dignity, and humble pride. These virtues, these traits, have made it a survivor with the unshakable will to live, to grow and flourish another year. I know that soon it will bud and be beautiful, full of life, and green again—and many more will come to photograph and to paint this beaten-down and broken old knot of an oak. And all will marvel in disbelief at such a grotesque thing so wrought by nature. Ah, but dear old oak, though we appear beaten down and defeated, do we not know each other? Thanks for letting me truly see you, and through your inspiration take a moment to look deeper within myself, to see myself from this new perspective, and to see us both for what we really are . . . survivors!

I am blessed with yet another day of perfect weather, and this being Saturday, many are out enjoying the AT, either for the day or packing in to their favorite spot for the weekend. I suspect that for each of the relatively few of us who are thru-hiking the AT this year, there are a thousand more up and down the trail, out for a shorter stay. Such is the case for the young couple I chance to meet as I near Wateroak Gap. These two are most surely the epitome of the weekend folks, at their favorite spot on the trail, camp set up, each rocking gently in their own hammock without a care in the world, reading their favorite books! "Locals" they are, so with evening descending I inquire as to perhaps another spot so delightful nearby where I might pitch for the night. With glad smiles, I am promptly directed to a piped spring and a small level spot near the gap, just off the trail! Oh, and I promised I wouldn't tell! A gorgeous sunset, campfire, supper . . . day!

> *"There is no simpler lesson in courage and tenacity than a strong oak."*
> [Clyde Ormond, *Complete Book of Outdoor Lore*]

SUNDAY April 26, 1998
TRAIL DAY 100/6   ✦   TRAIL MILE 1,506/104
LOCATION Wallace Gap, Old US 64, Rainbow Springs Campground

LOOKS LIKE TODAY IS GOING TO BE ANOTHER CLEAR and glorious day, a perfect day to celebrate one's 75th birthday . . . Happy Birthday, *EZ1*! The trail has been very muddy, but conditions are improving. A few more days without rain will help considerably. As I descend into Deep Gap I can look across to Standing Indian Mountain. This is a big mountain! Oh, I'm going to be a much better person in just a little while! This old warrior is standing tall indeed, approaching the first climb above 5,000 feet. And a proud warrior he is this morning—dressed in full ceremonial regalia, complete with a war bonnet of clouds. As I reach the summit and stand atop his white crown of quartz, I have total command of the high ground and the wide and expansive skies hereabouts.

And for a brief moment do I share the heaven-reaching dominance this old Indian has claimed his own for near eternity.

As I hike along today, 100 days into the "Odyssey of '98," my thoughts turn to that AT thru-hike in 1948, this year being the 50th anniversary, and to Earl Shaffer, known on the trail as *Crazy One*, who set out on that trek, now known as "The Lone Expedition." Our hikes are separated by 50 years in this mysterious capsule of time, but the similarities of our two hikes cannot be separated. For we share a common understanding of the days, weeks, and months, which began in peaceful, enjoyable solitude but which slowly through time gave way to the loneliness that prevailed. For to walk alone, for days and weeks and months, with no one beside you and no one to talk to, becomes a truly lonely affair.

As was the solitary adventure for *Crazy One* during "The Lone Expedition," so, too, the long, lonely trail for the *Nomad* during the "Odyssey of '98," from the Everglades in south Florida to the literal trail of hikers at Springer Mountain. The paths over which we passed were often obscure and at times nonexistent, with instinct and compass leading the search for any faint sign that the trail might be beneath our feet, signs that often belonged more appropriately in the locker of the lost and found.

> *"The Lone Expedition" adrift in the clouds.*
> *The "Odyssey" lost in the glade.*
> *Half a century apart, the intrepid move on,*
> *Joined through time by spring's gay parade.*

[N. Nomad]

MONDAY April 27, 1998
TRAIL DAY 101/7 ✦ TRAIL MILE 1,513/111
LOCATION Siler Bald Shelter

WHAT A NEAT OLD BUNKHOUSE AT RAINBOW SPRINGS Campground, all rough-cut butted boards, door too, with bread wrappers and newspapers stuffed in the cracks. I had the place to myself, so I fired up the old woodstove, read, and caught up on my journals.

I came in last night in the rain and it doesn't look too hot this morning, the forecast being for rain again today. So it looks like I'm in for another slamming. Days and weeks like this in the mist and rain, hiking along in a near-hypnotic state caused by constant rhythmic striding, give one lots of time to think. In fact, it becomes a process impossible to suppress. The day-to-day static, confusion, preoccupation, and racket in our normal lives prevent us from ever really delving into deep thought, but out here in the seclusion and quiet it becomes easy and natural. And so it is as I hike along today, my feet in the mud and my mind in the mist, that my thoughts turn to yesteryear. Now it seems as though, as a cloud lifts before my mind's eye, there is revealed a door which swings open wide. Oh, and what a view, for here is a room full of all kinds of things from the past! And as I gaze with wonder and glee into this beautiful chamber . . . comes a flood of wonderful memories. Ah, for isn't it true, just as we've been told, that we really do remember the good times!

And so I have noticed from time to time, as my senses become keenly attuned when it is quiet and these thought processes are in motion, when I see something, hear something, smell something, or touch something, that I am suddenly transported back to those wonderful days. My first encounter with this experience occurred while passing through a beautiful grove of cedar, their aromatic, fresh, and most delightful fragrance pervading. Suddenly I was eight years old again, hatchet in hand, my father by my side, crunching through the snow, searching for that perfect cedar for our beautiful Yule tree!

As I near Siler Bald Shelter, the sky looks more and more ominous, and though it is only 2:00 p.m. I decide, since the next shelter is 12 miles ahead, to pull up at Siler. And is this ever the right decision, for in only moments the rain comes hard and steady. What a luxury to be out of it, not to be faced with getting soaked, making and breaking camp in its presence. Warm and dry is such a better choice!

"I thought as I sat there this was the quiet we knew in
our distant past, when it was part of our minds and
spirits. We have not forgotten and never will, though the
scream and roar of jet engines, the grinding vibrations

of cities, and the constant bombardment of electronic noise may seem to have blunted our senses forever. We can live with such clamor, it is true, but we pay a price and do so at our peril. The loss of quiet in our lives is one of the great tragedies of civilization, and to have known even for a moment the silence of the wilderness is one of our most precious memories."

[Sigurd Olson]

TUESDAY April 28, 1998
TRAIL DAY 102/8 ✦ TRAIL MILE 1,530/128
LOCATION Wesser Bald Shelter

I SPENT AN ENJOYABLE EVENING LAST WITH JON LEUSCHEL, a Citadel graduate and river guide for Appalachian Rivers Raft Company at Wesser; Dan *U-Turn* Glenn from Osierfield, Georgia; and Allison *Allison Wonderland* Fuleky from Ann Arbor, Michigan.

It's cloudy this morning, with a light mist off and on, but I sense a good day in the making. At about 5 miles out, the AT treadway is shared as the Bartram Trail joins and comes along for a little over 1 mile. This trail is named in honor of William Bartram, a mid-18th-century botanist from Philadelphia. He had a wanderlust, traveling far and wide, and is probably best known for his canoe adventures to the upper reaches of the St. Johns River in Florida. In the early stages of this odyssey, my son, Jay, and I traveled that same river, as did Bartram over 250 years ago. William and his father, John, were renowned botanists of that era. John established the first U.S. botanical gardens in Philadelphia. Quite remarkably, these gardens exist and flourish to this day. Through my family genealogy, a voluminous book that has been published and is periodically updated, I know that my ancestors lived in Philadelphia during the mid-1700s and would have known not only the Bartrams, but would have been acquaintances with and probably would have bartered with Benjamin Franklin!

Younger Bartram's colleagues in Europe, Linnæus being one, constantly marveled as they opened packages from Bartram filled with buds, leaves, and flowers from plants they had never seen before pressed between the pages of books—all discovered, named, and cataloged by Bartram. He indeed traveled extensively, for besides the many exotic Florida plants that he named and cataloged, he also journeyed to these mountains, discovering and naming many of the beautiful plants that are such a joy to see along the AT.

The daily entries from Bartram's travel journal were published in a book entitled *The Travels of William Bartram.* His writings were in classic style for the time, being composed in a delightful, lilting, poetic prose! It is available in paperback and I highly recommend it. If you like John Muir's style, you will be delighted with the writings of Bartram, whom, it appears, Muir read and studied extensively.

I was right on with my prediction for a good day, for I am awarded sweeping, panoramic views today from Wayah (pronounced "War-ya") and Wesser Balds. Even with the ever-present blue haze over these timeless mountains, it is possible to see into Georgia to the south and Tennessee to the north.

I had the pleasure of meeting Bob McCormick popping along the trail today. Bob is a spry 72-year-old man from Melbourne, Florida. He is a member of the Florida Trial Association, Indian River Chapter, also my home FTA chapter. We shared a most enjoyable time talking trail.

> *"On approaching these shades, between the stately columns of the superb forest trees, presented to view, rushing from rocky precipices under the shade of the pensile hills, the unparalleled cascade of Falling Creek."*
>
> [William Bartram,
> Western North Carolina, 1775]

WEDNESDAY April 29, 1998
TRAIL DAY 103/9 ✦ TRAIL MILE 1,536/134
LOCATION Wesser, US 19, Appalachian Rivers Raft Company

THE TRAIL-CONTOUR MAP SHOWS A ROLLER COASTER downhill from Wesser Bald Shelter across Jumpup Lookout all the way to Wesser.

Sections of this descent are over precipitous ledges and outcroppings with breathtaking vistas. Seen below is the dramatic demarcation line marking the upward advancing reaches of spring. Here Jon, *U-Turn*, and I pause to stare in wonder. For below us, undulating along the mountainside, lies the battle line between Old Man Winter and Fair Maiden Spring, a line separating the dark green valleys and coves, lower spurs and ridges, ravines and gaps, where the lighter green of her advancing troops leaps the budding trees to ever climb, freeing the bare, still-gray forest, captive to the clutches of winter here at these higher elevations. From the level in Nature's hand is this battlefront line scribed, being surprisingly abrupt and evident.

Every time I see this rule about climate/vegetation regions and the influence elevation has on them, I tell myself I'm going to remember it this time, but it seems I never do. However, if memory serves me halfway, I believe the general rule for vegetation types and seasonal occurrences is approximately this: For every 1,000-foot increase in elevation, the conditions are equivalent to being 200 miles farther north. I have read with interest about the presence of certain species of conifer in the Great Smoky Mountains National Park and the more northern climatic conditions normally associated with them—a fascinating variant, as if they've been displaced from a region hundreds and hundreds of miles to the north, yet their grand communities thrive nonetheless. So it is that this Fair Maiden, "Spring of '98," is not only moving north . . . but moving up and onto these displaced elevation islands, bypassed, so it seems, in her haste, as together we travel on.

Jon, *U-Turn*, and I arrive at the Nantahala River in Wesser at 11:00 a.m. Here we head for Rivers End Restaurant to load up on the famous Wesser Burger. *U-Turn* orders the Wesser Burger/Chili Burger combo, a gargantuan open-faced platter heaped high with bun, hamburger, and mounds of chili. I have not a clue how this skinny little rail-of-a-friend manages to get on the outside of this . . . yet somehow he does. But after being audience to his mournful moaning and groaning, then to later witness his most dramatic and highly acclaimed passing-out ceremony, I'm sure glad that better judgment prevailed on my part!

The guests of gracious host Jon, the river-raft guide—now and henceforth to be known on the trail as *Class Five*—we lounge and rest in the grand bunk room at Appalachian Rivers Raft Company Outpost. Oh, the wonders of a luxurious hot shower and a warm, soft bed. The rain comes hard and stays all night. What a remarkable day this has been. Thank you, Lord, for your bountiful blessing!

> *"Let us remember to give thanks for air still clean enough to get us to the top of the hill, water still pure enough to drink (with a little iodine), and friends still friendly enough to share their ice cream at the end of the day."*
>
> [Dan *U-Turn* Glenn, GAME '98]

THURSDAY April 30, 1998
TRAIL DAY 104/10 ✦ TRAIL MILE 1,543/141
LOCATION Sassafras Gap Shelter

IT'S BEEN RAINING HARD ALL MORNING, so we get out late. *Class Five* treats *U-Turn* and me to breakfast, then drives us down to where the trail leaves Wesser. Here we linger and linger. *Class Five*, thanks for all your kindness and generosity. Hope to see you on the trail again. *U-Turn* and I cross the railroad tracks and head toward Wright Gap at 1:00 p.m.

Climbing from the Nantahala River, I pause at a beautiful stone monument upon which is affixed a plaque in memory of Wade A. Sutton, a North Carolina Forest Service ranger who lost his life while fighting a forest fire near here. Standing now reading these few short words about this man's life gives me pause to reflect. I have found it so easy to take for granted these grand mountains and broad forests. These are national treasures that belong to all of us. People dedicate their lives to the protection and care of these priceless resources. So, too, this Appalachian National Scenic Trail, this footpath through time. For it is no less a national treasure that can also be taken for granted. Lest we forget, it is this remarkable footpath that provides us access to and passage through these verdant mountains. So, to the thousands of men and

women who have dedicated their lives—and to those who this day dedicate their lives—to the task of managing all of these vast national treasures,—and to individuals such as Wade A. Sutton, who have made the
ultimate sacrifice,—permit me to extend my deepest gratitude.

There are two tough pulls from Wesser today: the climb from
Wright Gap and the ascent to Swim Bald. So comes to mind now a subject I would like to discuss. Contour maps are such grand, impressive
documents. Oh, what fun to pore over them and study them. Beautiful
contour maps have been created and painstakingly prepared for the AT,
showing all the ups and downs for the entire trail. I have talked about
them briefly in other entries. I carry none with me; however, I very
much enjoy taking a glance over the shoulders of other hikers while
they've got theirs out. The reason I mention this has to do with an observation, one which I've made over the past ten days. During this period I
have observed that by looking at a particular spike as shown on the trail-
contour grid, then fixing that image in my mind—that impressive little
spike being stored here in the muscles between my ears—then compar-
ing the actual degree of difficulty involved as explained to me by the
muscles in my back and in my legs . . . I have found, surprisingly, that
there is no relationship between the two whatsoever; they simply don't
jibe! For it is that a climb which shows on the map to be formidable
turns out to be so much a cruise, while yet another which is totally over-
looked because of its apparent ease more often than not turns out to be
the real hump-buster! On more than one occasion have I watched with
amusement as hiking companions pull their contour maps back out
while exclaiming, "Where to h—did this one come from!"

And so it is that the old *Nimblewill Nomad* has arrived at the most
scientific solution thus to deal with this whole perplexing dilemma. For
you see, there now has been devised a method to quiet all of this confusion . . . a rating system if you will, based on what the muscles in our
backs and our legs tell us we are dealing with . . . disregarding as totally
irrelevant what the muscles between our ears have picked up from our
gazing the contour maps! And the scientific basis for this grand rating
system? Ah, dear folks, this is flawless, for the system is based entirely on
the finite amount of atomic energy that is stored within the confines of the

lowly little Snickers bar! Simple systems are always the best, and this is a
very simple system based on an ascending scale of difficulty, with the
least difficult with which we'll trouble ourselves being rated as a three-
Snickers pull and the most difficult nearing a ten-Snickers pull. Initially
now, I simply beg your patience and indulgence, as this revolutionary
new system is inaugurated. For most assuredly you will come to trust,
respect, and appreciate the uncanny accuracy of *Nomad*'s judgment!

U-Turn and I spend a very entertaining evening at Sassafras Gap
Shelter with section hikers Bob *Smilin' Bob* Nelson and Pete *Broken-
Spoke* Fornof, both from Edwardsville, Illinois.

> *"Make no little plans: They have no magic to stir men's blood."*
> [Burnham]

FRIDAY May 1, 1998
TRAIL DAY 105/11 ✦ TRAIL MILE 1,565/163
LOCATION Fontana Dam, NC 28, Fontana Inn

THE SUN TEASES US THIS MORNING after hard-pounding rain all
night, but the gray, swirling mist so common to these high, lofty places
will have none of it and soon the eerie cloud curtain descends to darken
our path, thence to accompany us along.

From my hike through here in the early 1980s, I can remember
the section from Wesser, across the Stecoahs, to Fontana as being one of
the most difficult. There were many, many uninterrupted five-Snickers
pulls. The climb from Wright Gap and Grassy Gap, over Swim Bald and
Cheoah Bald, these are all still here, but as for all the rest of the knobs in
the Stecoahs, where the trail went up and over—their ruggedness has
since been tamed by sideslabbing or switchbacking. Looking close as I
pass the short, deep gaps, I can see where the old trail went straight up,
that treadway concealed now by piled-up brush and years of over-
growth. So the old knee-numbing, ankle-mushing, back-bowing,
reserve-tank-sapping pulls are pretty much gone. Though the hike
through here is still technically difficult, this section has been tamed con-

siderably. I guess this saddens me a little as I think about it, because more than likely Myron Avery laid out that old treadway originally, for Avery was noted for taking the trail up and over, straight up . . . always!

I ran into toe-stubbing territory yesterday afternoon. I assumed it was due to late-day fatigue, but here we go right away again this morning—toe-stubbing territory. Aww! There's another one. Pitches me right out there. I've gotta run to catch up with myself. I'm sure not going to see any bear making this kind of racket!

As we descend to Fontana Dam, spring is all around. The dogwoods are about to the end of their near-exclusive show. In some small coves here, and blooming very early, are the flame azaleas and the pinxter flower (purple honeysuckle). Other spring wildflowers that I pass are nodding trillium, white trillium, rue anemone, false Solomon's seal, spring beauty, and pink lady's slipper. We manage to get off the trail just before the rain returns.

I catch up with *Pack Mule* today at Fontana Dam Shelter. Though I was glad to get on my own way back in Cave Spring, Georgia, it's great to see him again. *Pack Mule, U-Turn,* and I get the shuttle into the village of Fontana Dam and Fontana Inn. Here we share a room, make an effort to get presentable, then head straight for the all-you-can-eat (AYCE) buffet at the Peppercorn Restaurant.

It's been a long, hard, but memorable day!

> *"Remote for detachment.*
> *Narrow for chosen company.*
> *Winding for leisure.*
> *Lonely for contemplation.*
> *The trail leads not merely north and south*
> *But upward to the body, mind and soul of man."*

[Harold Allen]

AS THE TRAIL GOES, FONTANA INN IS A SOLID FIVE-STAR facility
with a hot tub, sauna, phone in the room . . . warm and dry, no less!
There is a large and well-maintained shelter on the trail just above the
dam affectionately known by Hiker Trash as the Fontana Hilton. We
arrived last evening, however, to find the facility filled to the rafters, so
heading for town and the Fontana Inn was certainly the right decision.
Splitting the cost of a room three ways made for a very affordable and
luxurious stay. At the "Hiker Hilton," I was able to meet many thru-hikers
whose entries I've been reading all along in the shelter registers. Among
the intrepids here last evening were *Trumpet Call, Grym, P.O.D. (Path of
Destruction), Yogi* and *Boo Boo* (brothers), *In-Between, Dogfish, Moon Doggie,
Hobo Rob, Gypsy,* and *Mighty Mouse.*

After a fine breakfast in the most leisurely and decadent fashion,
we pack out and head for the village store and post office. I buy a few provisions and mail some cards and letters. Fontana Dam is a popular mail
drop and the place is buzzing this morning, hikers lined up at the counter
and milling around on the covered walkway outside, food boxes open and
packages scattered and stacked along the railing and all around. Here I
meet David *Spirit of '48* Donaldson. His trail moniker was chosen to commemorate Earl Shaffer's thru-hike, the first known or recorded 50 years
ago. Thousands and thousands have since made this seemingly endless
journey since Earl proved in 1948 that it could actually be done, and *Spirit
of '48* is one of well over 1,000 of us who will attempt it again this year.

U-Turn has decided to hang a little longer here at Fontana, so
Mule and I get the shuttle and head back up to the dam. By now it's
nearly 1:30 p.m. We won't get far today but head on out anyway.
Crossing the dam, we lean into it against Shuckstack. It rained all night
and into the morning, but it's beginning to fair-up. On the ascent we
soon overtake and pass *Moon Doggie* (a smoker). The hike to Russell
Field Shelter is relatively short, but getting out late from Fontana puts
us in late at Russell, near 7:00 p.m. Down at the dam we entered the

Great Smoky Mountains National Park. This national park is one of our most popular, a source of pride for all Americans. Annual visitation figures run consistently in the ten million range. So I'm not surprised, especially with this being a weekend, to find the shelter filled to capacity. Appropriately named, Russell Field does indeed have a small grassy field, and thru-hikers are permitted to pitch around the meadow if the shelter is full. *Mule* and I find a most comfortable spot and are just setting camp when *U-Turn* and *In-Between* come cruising in from Fontana.

Folks, aren't these trail names a pure hoot! And here's a good example . . . *Tween*. For you see, *In-Between* has been blessed with this novel and happy little name by fellow hikers who've noticed the mud in between her toes as she hikes along from day to day in her customary foot attire . . . sandals! We've also been hiking off and on with Sam, who is here this evening, lounging comfortably by the fire with his nose in a book, as usual. I'm still working on Sam's trail name. *Bookworm* just doesn't fit . . . There's something else here. I'll figure it out soon.

The evening is passed in pleasant conversation with some fellows who are out on a short section-hike. One offers me free grabs from his trove of goodies. He'll be leaving the Smokies tomorrow and doesn't want to lug the stuff any farther. I go for the Pop-Tarts, coffee, pepperoni, lemonade mix, and a Moon-Pie. Yes, the guy lets me take his Moon-Pie! Made a complete hog of myself. I'll be toting a load till I down this grub! Aww, but gee-whiz folks, no self-respecting member of the Hiker Trash Clan could ever, ever pass up a treasure trove such as this.

The day did indeed turn warm and beautiful, a fine afternoon for hiking back and forth, first from North Carolina into Tennessee and then back again into North Carolina, following the AT as it meanders along this grand high ridge in the Great Smoky Mountains National Park.

> *"As I wander these mountain paths and relish their*
> *grand vistas, I found myself in a quandary. When I*
> *was in Tennessee, I said: This is exactly what I've been*
> *seeking; but when I crossed over into North Carolina I*
> *found it equally rewarding and cried with vigor: This*
> *has got to be it. I can see it now. Soon I shall have to*
> *choose between them."*
>
> [James Michener]

SUNDAY May 3, 1998
TRAIL DAY 107/13   ✦   TRAIL MILE 1,595/193
LOCATION Double Spring Gap Shelter

THIS IS MY FIRST FULL DAY IN THE Great Smoky Mountains National Park. As I get rolling this morning, the sun teases and plays with me for the better part of 15 minutes—then the dark, gray-swirling mist engulfs me once more. At these high elevations, I am literally in the clouds. Shortly comes the cold rain, lasting the entire day, first in gentle greeting, then at times in hard-pelting waves mixed with sleet and hail. Many of the pulls and pushes range in the four- to four-and-a-half-Snickers category. Thus now I bring forth and debut *Nomad*'s new trail-profile rating system. The grid spikes I describe here are Rocky Top, Thunderhead, and Derrick Knob. There are also many three- and three-and-a-half-Snickers pulls today, the trail being basically up or down. I find the treadway rough and rugged, choked with mud, the bottom literally blown out in many places. The incessant rain is making progress slow and treacherous.

Some sections of the trail here in the park are shared with the horsey-back folks. Where there has also been heavy horse traffic, the dreadful treadway deterioration is ever evident. Equine tend to cut and groove the treadway narrow and deep compared to the wider eroding effect of excessive human use. These very narrow, deep grooves, some only a foot or so wide—and just as deep—make it difficult, if not impossible, to stay the track. The purpose for this note in passing and to make my point . . . It is my opinion that horses and humans on the same trail just don't mix!

The rain-filled cloud-swirl breaks and lifts occasionally, providing spectacular views o'er this majestic, seemingly heaven-bound path. Toward evening and in the cold mist, I reach Double Spring Gap Shelter. Here I spend the night in this very-leaky-but-welcome den with *Turtle* and *Bear, Goback,* Sam, *100# Stormcloud, Joyful Girl,* and *Monkey Boy.* We share a most enjoyable evening of conversation, neither heavy nor heady. As I managed along this afternoon, I noticed skid marks in the downhill mud, some extending for great distances, perhaps 8 to 12 feet. In the course of conversation this evening, I find out how *Monkey Boy* is capable of performing uninterrupted, almost vertical, downhill mud slaloms. Says he, "It's kinda like riding a skateboard." Okey-dokey! The steady rain softly serenades us most all night.

In the next number of days, as we hike along and as the opportunity presents, I will be profiling some of the remarkably friendly folks that it's been my pleasure and good fortune to meet out here on the AT, folks that are now my very good friends. For the most part, they're younger people whom I would find occasion to give only a nod if met on the street or in public places, folks with whom I would have but passing concern . . . and for that matter, their response and take on me being likely the same. In the "real world," we would have no common bond, no shared interests, very little—if anything—to discuss for long. However, here on the trail, the age and generation gap, cultural differences, and the influence of career and educational backgrounds, have little play in the mix. One glaring variant, which is immediately evident, is our usual difference in age, for I am old enough to be father or, for that matter, grandfather, to many of these younger hikers. But I've found it such an interesting puzzlement. By simply setting foot on the trail, I immediately become attuned with them, their interests, their lives, as if we're almost instantly bound together by some mysterious, invisible sort of glue! I am totally mystified by it. Is it the wanderlust that dwells deep within each of us coming forth, or perhaps the love for the outdoors, for wilderness, for nature, and the sheer joy that stirs right down to our heart and soul; is that what's mixing and binding us together? Whatever it is, it is very real, a force that cannot be denied, the result being a happy, joy-filled, and very tightly knit family!

This newborn community, a subculture if you will, is continually forming, much as the links in a continuous chain are formed, as the folks leaving Springer Mountain mingle, take trail names, and move north toward Mt. Katahdin. A community for such a short time that it would seem to be as fleeting as the passing mist, but within this short time frame and within this family are created bonds and friendships that last a lifetime. I hope you will revel and take joy, as am I, in getting to know these fellow intrepids, who along with the old *Nomad*, and this ragtag family, journey on.

*"At night, when the lights go on, there seems to be a
great hole in North America—a dark place, fifty-five
miles long and by almost twenty miles broad, where the
glare of civilization does not shine up at the sky. Man
has imposed this area of darkness, as he has imposed
the lights around it, by his own will. He has set aside
this vast area of mountain and wood and falling water
in the valleys, to preserve his own sanity, to refresh his
body and his mind."*

[Nicholas Harman, *The Magnificent Continent*]

MONDAY May 4, 1998
TRAIL DAY 108/14   ✦   TRAIL MILE 1,609/207
LOCATION Icewater Spring Shelter

THE SUN MAKES A SHOW AGAIN THIS MORNING for about 20 minutes, then the gray, swirling mist engulfs me once again, embracing the mountain peaks and slopes all about. The treadway today seems not the least bit forgiving, but the relentless rain mostly proceeds along by another way, giving some blessed relief.

Spring beauties form a blanket of white and green rising and descending to embrace the trail from the slopes and intimate little glades all around, creating the perfect pathway for the finest formal bridal procession. Trout lilies add just a touch of yellow, while the ubiquitous common violet graces the very trail fringe, adding its formal gesture to greet the grand procession. I literally skip along as I weave my way through this gala of pureness. You could not bedeck a hall for the most grand occasion with any more beauty or fineness than that which nature has decorated these ridges and coves, for here is the ultimate creation of beauty in the most tender and exquisite form. Today is not a hike on the AT, but rather a remarkable journey through fairyland.

The mist-filled clouds seem ever-present over Clingmans Dome, as if it is their permanent residence. Of the many visits I've made to Clingmans, only one has ever provided me the panorama for which the dome is famous. I'm standing now at the side trail to the summit, the highest point on the AT, deciding whether to move on or take the tour to the tower. Here, the eerie presence of the old balsam monarchs, embraced by the chilling swirl, their bark shed, crowns gone, reduced to naked snags by the balsam woolly aphid, forms the most ruthless and macabre scene. Here were once such beautiful old sentinels, standing tall, so proud, so strong. As I close my eyes, I can see them still. But now they can only stand, bowing in such a sad and pitiful way, testimony to the ravages of nature and of time, for there has been no favor. But as I look down now into the mass of moldering old hulks lying defeated all around, I see the next generation of fir, lush and green, springing forth anew with bold vigor, determined to withstand the destructive atmospheric acidity and the seemingly harmless little insects that destroyed all but precious few of their ancestors.

I have been witness to and have gazed upon nature's full spectrum of talent today, her most exquisite tender touch, contrasted by her seemingly unconscionable, ruthless wrath. I find that I cannot comprehend the least bit of this. Indeed it has been both a spiritual and humbling experience.

I arrive at Icewater Spring Shelter around 3:00 p.m., just as the rain begins anew . . . with focused vengeance. But I hurry in to escape its anger. Somehow today we have taken mostly separate paths to arrive at this evening's destination. At 4:00 p.m. *100# Stormcloud* comes in, soaked to the bone; at 5:00 p.m., ditto for Sam; and at 7:00 p.m., incredibly, after hiking all day in 40-degree bone-chilling rain, ankle-deep mud, and feet-numbing rock, *In-Between* arrives, clad in her sandals!

The shelter, though dark and dank, proves a true blessing, for the rain stays, driving cold and hard all night. High Snickers ratings today—four-plus for Clingmans, Mt. Love, and Mt. Collins, and there were more than a few threes.

"However much you knock at nature's door, she will
never answer you in comprehensible words."

[Ivan Turgenev]

TUESDAY May 5, 1998
TRAIL DAY 109/15 ✦ TRAIL MILE 1,622/220
LOCATION Tri-corner Knob Shelter

I DO MANAGE TO GET OUT AND GOING THIS MORNING, but it's already 9:00 a.m. The sun and wind finally emerge victorious in their battle to burn and sweep the ethereal-like mist from Charlie's Bunion. And here I stand now to get a glimpse of the far-off day. For as the skies around and the ravines and stark spires and walls of granite below are revealed to me, I begin reeling as if hanging to the rail of a pitching ship. I must move back away from the precipice, crouch, and clutch the rock around me until my head quits spinning. If you've ever clung to the railing at a circle-vision theater . . . then you know the feeling. It's most-near the same reaction as the last time I stood at this spot some 15 years ago. I will just say this, once you've gazed over this hulking precipice at this mind-slamming vista and felt the surge of emotion and raw fear that being here evokes, you will never, ever forget it! I simply cannot adequately describe this place to you. Not until you come here, stand here, and gaze out at these crags and upon this place can you ever possibly understand.

The Sawteeth. What an appropriate name! Bare, veined rock, leaning, weatherbeaten, splintered spires, ever reaching toward the heavens. These sheer rock faces are all that remain from what must have been an incredible inferno that raged and swept clean these high places decades ago. Now, only scant, scattered evergreen, clutching and clinging to the walls and towers of granite, manage somehow to exist and survive. As I stare down and past the shards of the Sawteeth, the warm, welcome sun is lifting the remaining shroud of mist from the coves and ravines below. Revealed now is the ever-climbing line of spring, true to each spur and ridge, weaving its gentle pastel-green lifeline, as if fine stitches to silk, separating the lush, dark greenness of the fully-leafed forest below from the gray, forbidding harsh clutches of winter above. There is only the contrasting serviceberry indicating any life in these mile-high reaches.

A blessed clear day is forming. I did not complain, but took what joy and happiness there was to be found in the rains of the yesterdays, my

patience rewarded now with these grand vistas, this grand day . . . and
the high of these high places. Oh, how we take all that is around us, and
indeed, our very existence, as ordinary and commonplace, looking every
day for that one grand miracle—when every day and everything we see
and do are true miracles. Unquestionably one of the most brilliant minds
of our time, perhaps of the ages, Albert Einstein, said, "There are only
two ways to live your life. One is as though nothing is a miracle. The
other is as though everything is a miracle. As for me, I choose the latter."
As to God's mysterious miracles, consider the mist that I have described
this morning. A wall of vapor, engulfing, permeating all, limiting my visi-
bility, from miles and miles to no more than the distance of my arms outstretched, this wall created by a gadzillion moisture particles, infinite—a
number not described by any number we know or can conceive in our
mind, much as the sands of all the seas. And yet I have watched the gentle warmth of the sun, and the winds, and in just moments it is all taken
away and it is gone! What is such as this, if not a miracle? So, too, I consider this beautiful day and all that it brings me here on this path in the
sky, along this Appalachian Trail . . . it is all a miracle.

> *"For look! Within my hollow hand,*
> *While round the earth careens,*
> *I hold a single grain of sand*
> *And wonder what it means."*

[Robert W. Service, *A Grain of Sand*]

WEDNESDAY May 6, 1998
TRAIL DAY 110/16 ✦ TRAIL MILE 1,637/236
LOCATION Davenport Gap, NC 32,
Mountain Moma's Kuntry Store & Bunkhouse

I AM HEADING OUT OF GREAT SMOKY MOUNTAINS National Park
today. I have mixed feelings about leaving. I have tried to describe the
splendor and majesty of the park, an awe-inspiring place to see and visit,
one of the most popular of all our national parks. And therein lies the rub,
for the park is literally being loved to death, the sheer number degrading

the hiking experience. The treadway in many places has the bottom literally blown out, which has made progress slow and treacherous.

The history of the park, like most any story, has two sides — one
usually good, one usually not so good. And so it is with Great Smoky
Mountains National Park. The park is unquestionably one of the crown
jewels in our national parks system. Acquiring the land, protecting the
resources for all generations, was farsighted, and it was right. Yet in a
wonderful hardbound book titled *Reflections of Cataloochee Valley and Its
Vanished People from the Great Smoky Mountains*, written by Hattie Caldwell
Davis, are the sad stories told, the consequences of creating the park. For
in this book are the heartbreaking stories of families that were uprooted
and moved from their land. A few brief passages from this book reveal
the disbelief and suffering during that time:

> *"In the 1830's the Cataloochee Valley was opened up to
> development. Terms of the purchase from the U.S. gov-
> ernment specified that the land must be settled, so the
> call sent out for families willing to 'prove' the land.
> Many answered that call. They came to make the
> wilderness into a place called home. After 100 years the
> community was informed that the beautiful land that
> surrounded them was to be shared by all. The govern-
> ment has decided to form GSM, with Cataloochee
> Valley at its heart — the families had to leave."*

Folks likened the forced exodus to the infamous Trail of Tears, when
the Cherokee were driven from their lands and relocated to Oklahoma.

> *"The Rev. Pat Davis was preaching at the Palmer's
> Chapel in 1928, and announced that the government
> would buy all the land in the area to establish GSM,
> saying 'you will be here no more.' The people could not
> believe this, but, the preacher had said it, so it must be
> true. They expressed their utter amazement, then fell
> into depression and anger. First, there was a lot of talk-
> ing and then worry. Some started to cry. Some were*

*sitting on the porch, on the steps and in the grass. They
were so sad, saying, 'Where will we go, what will we do.
We can't bear to give up our homes, our land and our
good neighbors. . . . Oh Lord, what in the world will we
do? We can't leave here.' "*

Signs of these old homesteads exist to this day all through these
lush, high ridges and valleys. An old wagon path here, a row of stately old
boxwood there. The carefully placed rocks forming an old spring box,
sour apple trees, a cluster of clover or dandelions, little time capsules
from the past, all that remain of another time. The pioneers have long
since passed, driven from their land, but I find this not an unhappy place,
for that brave, independent frontier spirit that brought them to these
beautifully rugged places remains and has not been driven from the land.
Indeed it is here, adding to the radiance and beauty and I feel it as I pass.

As I descend into Davenport Gap I am thinking about the hard
three- and four-Snickers pulls over the last two days: Charlie's Bunion,
Mt. Sequoyah, Mt. Chapman, Mt. Guyot, Cosby Knob, Mt. Cammerer.
This has been a tough, hard hike. At this lower elevation, I find to my
delight the beautiful flame azaleas beginning to bloom. These lush and
radiantly blooming plants were discovered and named by William
Bartram. I no sooner reach the road than a whiz-bang new Ford pickup
truck pulls off and I'm offered a ride down to Mountain Moma's by none
other than Edsel Ford. Oh, and would you believe that Edsel has a brother
named Henry? Folks, there's just no way I could make this stuff up!

*"The epithet 'fiery' I annex to this most celebrated
species of azalea, as being expressive of the appearance
of its flowers, which are in general of color of the finest
red-lead, orange and bright gold . . . The clusters of the
blossoms cover the shrubs in such incredible profusion
on the hillsides that suddenly opening to view from dark
shades, we are alarmed with apprehension of the hills
being set of fire."*

[William Bartram]

THURSDAY May 7, 1998
TRAIL DAY 111/17 ✦ TRAIL MILE 1,653/252
LOCATION Max Patch Summit

FIFTEEN YEARS AGO, ON A RAINY SUMMER'S DAY, and as fate would have it, I became the first backpacker coming through from Springer Mountain to stand in total awe on the summit of Max Patch. The excitement of that memorable day was recorded in an article published in the March/April 1986 issue of *Appalachian Trailway News* (now *Journeys, The Magazine of the Appalachian Trail Conservancy*).

Returning again to this magnificent summit has been a very emotional experience. Thousands have come since I was first here, but none could possibly have felt the intensity of the moment, then or now, as I relive that memory. That article, as published, will be my journal entry for today:

> *"It rained off and on all night, and sleep was fretful at Groundhog Creek Shelter. I was up at daybreak. While putting on my wet pants, wet socks, and wet boots, my blisters reminded me of the miserable mistakes I had made in planning this journey. I was 250 miles and 16 days out of Springer Mountain, Georgia, with only one pair of wool socks and boots that lacked a tongue web. It had rained almost every day, and the wet trail was really taking its toll on my feet.*
>
> *"As I left the shelter, it began raining again and my spirits really dropped. There had been heavy horse traffic through this section, and I was having difficulty keeping my footing through the mud and rocks. As the rain became more intense, the trail deteriorated, and the thought crossed my mind—for the first time since leaving Springer—that I might not make it, that I might have to give up and quit. Burkes Garden, Virginia, my planned destination, was still more than 300 miles ahead. As on other occasions, I prayed for the weather to break and for the trail to dry. But I knew*

that on days when the clouds would break and the sun would come out, the trail often stayed wet, due to the heavy canopy above. It seemed hopeless as I slogged, soaked to the bone, through the mud and rain.

"I had fought off depression for the past two days. To lift my spirits, I sang and made up silly poems, like:

When it's dismal and dreary,
When you feel there's no hope,
When your heart's filled with naught but regret.
May your thoughts all be heady,
Your pack feather-light,
And the trail six lanes wide when it's wet!

"But, there was no singing, no catchy poem to lift me up, just the swirling gray, dismal, dreary, damnable rain. My pack was wet and heavy and cut deep into my shoulders, and I could no longer fight off the pain and depression engulfing me. As the trail seemed to close around me, I prayed I could just make it to Hot Springs.

"Looking back now, I realize that I had reached my mental 'low' for the journey. Little did I know that I had not only 'passed through the valley' but, in the short span of less than two hours, would be swept to the highest 'high' I was to experience for the entire 32-day trip! As I entered the open at Max Patch Road, the rain stopped, and it looked like the clouds were going to break. I gazed toward the sky and a feeling of renewed strength and hope came over me. To the right across the road men were working, and even though my trail guide read, 'Trail continues N (to left) on road 3.8 miles to Lemon Gap,' I crossed the road to see what was going on and for a little welcome conversation. It was here I met Arch Nichols, Carolina Mountain Club trails supervisor. Arch and fellow Carolina Club members Dwight Allen, Perry Rudnick, Ed Dunn, and Jack

Trump were busy setting posts at the edge of the road. They continued working as they enthusiastically talked about the new Max Patch section. As I listened, I became caught up in their enthusiasm.

"In a few short moments I learned that Max Patch was a towering, 4,600-foot-high grassy bald, part of a 392-acre Forest Service acquisition purchased to protect and enhance the Appalachian Trail for the enjoyment of all. I learned that the view from the summit of Max Patch provided a panorama of some of the highest ranges in the eastern United States. And, I also learned that through the cooperative effort of the Carolina Mountain Club, the AT Conference, the U. S. Forest Service, the Konnarock crew, a chapter of the Sierra Club, a Boy Scout troop, and the Appalachian Long Distance Hiker's Association, the 6.2-mile relocation work on Max Patch was almost completed.

"I was swept up with their enthusiasm completely and I wanted to hike this new section. I asked if the new trail was blazed and was told that it was marked only with orange flags and orange, red, and blue ribbons. Without further question, the five of them began mulling whether the new section was marked well enough for someone unfamiliar with it to follow without getting lost. After a few minutes of discussion about how to get across a road and where to get over two or three fences (the stiles were not yet made), Dwight Allen looked at me and said, 'You know, if you get through there by yourself, you'll be the first hiker to traverse this new section, the first to reap the rewards of our efforts over the past 14 months.'

"That did it! They asked me if I wanted to try. After a few more minutes of directions and instructions, I was off! The new trail dropped off Max Patch road and back into the woods on a newly graded path, crossed *a graded road and climbed into an open field. The sky was clearing now, and I could see the graded and widely mowed trail above me, leading to the summit of Max Patch. As I climbed, I realized that my feet were still as wet as before, but they didn't hurt anymore. My pack had become feather-light and I could feel my spirit soaring up the mountain ahead of me. I was living that silly poem, line by line, written only two days previous, as I went from the depths of depression to the heights of exhilaration.*

"As I reached the U.S. Geological Survey marker on the summit, I felt 'higher' than any kite could fly over the beautiful meadows of Max Patch. The clouds would break momentarily here, then there. The views were spectacular: what a truly beautiful place! And now, for all AT hikers to enjoy."

> *The Maker's countenance 'round,*
> *Seen from these mountains high.*
> *Fills us with peace . . . Profound!*
> *Until the day we die.*

[N. Nomad]

FRIDAY May 8, 1998
TRAIL DAY 112/18   ✦   TRAIL MILE 1,673/271
LOCATION Hot Springs, Sunnybank Inn

AS I BREAK CAMP AND PREPARE TO MOVE ON, I pause to gaze, to try and comprehend the mystery of such a place. These are rugged, timeless mountains, their legions stretching to the horizon in all directions. Why does all this exist—what does it all mean? Perhaps, someday I will know the answer. For now I must be content to feel the Master's presence and to know that all is right.

Each day reveals new wildflowers to identify. The variety and abundance of these bright, cheerful spring children offers both delight and astonishment. To pause at every turn in the trail would not suffice to fully appreciate their glorious presence! Along with others already seen, and generally in great abundance, are the birdsfoot violet, mayapple, yellow violet, and trout lily.

The hike into Hot Springs is long but enjoyable. These downhills give me the opportunity to practice perfecting "*Nomad*'s Neutral," a downhill hiking technique that relieves stress on the toes, shins, knees, and hips, permitting, in the process, progress at the rate of near 4 miles per hour. I arrive at Hot Springs just before 3:00 p.m. It's time to hurry for mail, then head for Elmer's Sunnybank Inn, a lovely old bed-and-breakfast. Here at the old Victorian mansion, I am greeted at the kitchen door by Elmer Hall, much in the same fashion as Elmer greeted me at this very spot 15 years ago. Elmer has been the proprietor and host here at the Inn, catering to thru-hikers for over 20 years. I am treated to a wonderful supper and a bed for royalty! This has been a very satisfying day.

> "*Someday He'll make it plain to me,*
> *Someday when I His face shall see;*
> *Someday from tears I shall be free,*
> *For someday I shall understand.*"

[Linda Shivers Leech]

SATURDAY May 9, 1998
TRAIL DAY 113/19 ✦ TRAIL MILE 1,673/271
LOCATION Hot Springs, Sunnybank Inn

I'VE DECIDED TO SPEND A COUPLE OF DAYS HERE in Hot Springs for a much-needed rest. Elmer has a wonderful library full of hiking/wilderness-related books. I have a very enjoyable time entertaining myself as I spend the day reading two great ones. First is David Brill's *As Far as the Eye Can See*, and the other is Ed Garvey's latest book, *Appalachian Hiker III: The New Appalachian Trail*. I'm also able to catch up on my journal entries. I'm meeting many folks hiking the AT and am delighted to run into Tim *Long Distance Man* Anderson from Winchester, Virginia. Tim is a friend of my good friend *Thunder Chicken*, from Rockledge, Florida, who thru-hiked the AT last year.

"Being taken by its narrowness for chosen company is indeed one delightful aspect of the AT. One easily recognizes those whom the trail has chosen. One senses kindred spirit. Some folk say the chosen are a special breed; I mean if you enjoy, if you can really get in to going up mountains where you can stand up straight and bite the ground or can thrill in downhill descent where a person wants hobnails in the seat of his pants; I mean you be a special breed! Mountain wilderness lovers are chosen company."

[Bruce Otto, GAME '74]

SUNDAY May 10, 1998
TRAIL DAY 114/20 ✦ TRAIL MILE 1,673/271
LOCATION Hot Springs, French Broad Hostel

HOT SPRINGS HAS A WAY OF MAKING YOU WANT TO LINGER. So I will stay the day and another night. Elmer is fully reserved for the evening, but he tells me he'll make room. I know that a place will be found, but at the same time I feel that to stay would be taking advantage of Elmer's soft spot for smelly, dirty hikers, so I move on to the French Broad Hostel. Here I relax for the day and work some more on my journal entries.

"Little did I dream more than fifty years ago when I sat down with two men in the New Jersey Highlands and outlined to them my idea of a footway through the Appalachians that such plans would be translated into the institution that has now come to pass. I did little more than suggest the notion: I set the match to the fuse and set the chain reaction that has come about."

[Benton MacKaye,
ATC Meeting, Boone, North Carolina, 1975]

THIS IS GOING TO BE A GRAND DAY, WARM and partly cloudy, perfect for hiking. The ruggedness of these mountains through which I've been hiking most assuredly discouraged early settlement, save the most determined of the pioneers. Only scant and scattered remains give hint of their presence long ago. But now the hills have become gentler, the treadway and the lands traversed more friendly. Hiking along now, the trail winds from below an old impoundment. Gaining the headwall, I am greeted by a placid, picturesque lake embraced by grassy fields and lush meadows all around. As I look across these gently rolling pastures, I can visualize where old log dwellings and outbuildings might have stood. Ah, but there are no shadows now from those settlements of frontier times, nor from the brave who cleared these lands. All are gone, all long forgotten. This is such a quiet and peaceful place. But alas, shortly the trail passes over US 25/70 and I am jolted by the noise and grind as 18-wheelers rumble below, jake-braking the downhill grade.

The trail soon presents another four-Snickers pull up Rich Mountain, thence to descend into Hurricane Gap. Here is the Rex Pulform Memorial, erected in memory of Dorothy Hansen's father, who died here attempting to thru-hike the AT in 1983. As I stand before this marker, memories flood over me . . . fond memories of my father and how he loved the forest woodlands, for he passed away in similar fashion. Dad had just completed loading his old, rickety 1964 Ford pickup with hickory and oak firewood when he sat down on the running board to rest—and the Good Lord took him then to his final rest. I suspect Dorothy's thoughts were much as mine during that heartbreaking time, a whirling confusion of sorrow and gladness—sorrow in suffering our loss, but gladness in knowing our fathers were where they loved to be.

I soon reach Spring Mountain Shelter, one of the old round-log structures. If this classic little shelter is not an original, it certainly dates back many years. And here it remains, providing comfort and safety to countless AT hikers. I want to get a few more miles in today, so I push on to the next small gap, where a fine campsite and a small spring are located. I build a delightful evening campfire, prepare my hot meal, then relax awhile before rolling in to quickly drift into restful sleep.

"Sometimes when you're in the middle of business and life as usual, you think, 'What's it all about?' You're born, you live, you die. . . . But when you're out there, you know why you're there, and you feel grateful."

[Dorothy Hansen, GAME '79]

TUESDAY May 12, 1998
TRAIL DAY 116/22   ✦   TRAIL MILE 1,705/303
LOCATION Flint Mountain Shelter

I'M OUT AND GOING THIS MORNING ABOUT 8:30 A.M. as I hustle along toward State Line Gas Station at Devil Fork Gap. Here I hope to get a pint of ice cream and a resupply on Snickers bars. But alas, they're closed on Tuesday. Old places like these are fascinating, not built in any fashion nor for that matter with much any thought to looks or design. I sit down on the old gas-pump island and lean against one of the rickety, rusty old pumps. No gas here, just weeds. I linger and work on my journal entries as I look the place over and take it all in. I suppose "seedy" best describes the sights before me. It is certainly not unpleasant, however, more just a hodgepodge, how structures that are needed get built. Adorning the grand old facade is a rusty Coca-Cola sign; broken windows are simply boarded up. The front door is secured with double-hasp/padlocks, more to hold the door up than to keep folks out. Inside the dingy window near the door is posted a cracked and faded flier, "Upper Paint Creek Church, happy to announce Pastor Jerry Boles, starting a Revival on May 14 at 7:00 p.m." Doesn't say what year. Cigarettes are the reason the old store has survived. Staring into the dreary darkness, I can see racks and racks of cigarettes . . . I guess they'll be back to rotate the stock tomorrow.

Now in gentle and more rolling terrain, I'm not far from the daily din—the whirring sound of a lawnmower, the rasping buzz of a chain saw, the grinding whine of 18-wheelers—all remind me that this tread-way is no longer a quiet, secluded footpath. But over the last few days I have been hearing many more songbirds, their happy, cheerful voices giving me a smiling face and a lighter heart.

Well, so much for the gentler mountains—no sooner said than I'm faced with the ascent out of Allen Gap, for the better part of 6 miles, all the way to Camp Creek Bald firetower, which proves to be a hard, nearly uninterrupted four-Snickers pull. I soon arrive at Blackstack Cliffs, a rugged and beautiful sight to see. The cliffs are home to nesting peregrine falcons. This section quickly turns to rough, muddy, boulder-strewn treadway. It's hard to believe that the top of a mountain could be a bog—but here it is for the better part of a mile! Much of the trail along this high ridgeline passes within the Pisgah National Forest before crossing into the Cherokee National Forest in Tennessee.

It's time to rest and take in the sun, so I stop for a welcome lunch break at Jerry Cabin Shelter. My puppies enjoy the break and an airing before being rewarded with some dry socks. This place is really Sam's Cabin, honoring Sam Waddle, the shelter caretaker for the past 26 years. The "cabin" will soon have all the modern conveniences, being pre-wired as it is for electric lights and telephone. Hopefully, someday, Sam will get around to hooking things up!

> *"When the Lord led Moses out of the desert, He took His servant to the top of a mountain and showed the Promised Land spread out below. The mountain was Pisgah. Moses never entered the land of his people, but he came down from Pisgah and died content."*
>
> [Nicholas Harman, *The Magnificent Continent*]

WEDNESDAY May 13, 1998
TRAIL DAY 117/23 ✦ TRAIL MILE 1,724/322
LOCATION Campsite north of Bald Mountain Shelter

WHAT A GRAND AND SOCIABLE EVENING last at Flint Mountain Shelter. I arrived just behind *100# Stormcloud* to meet *Tumbleweed*, and then *Tween* and *U-Turn* came in just before dark. We had a very fine cooking and warming fire.

It looks to be another clear, cool, glorious hiking day as I cross NC 212 to enter a lively meadow. A couple of stiles help the trail in, then out. There must be 100 different ways to build a stile—these have steps straight up and over. Above the meadow, I reach a small, old, family cemetery plot on the edge of the mountain spur. One grave gets my attention, that of a Dorothy Hensley, May 2, 1865–April 30, 1965. Testimony to the longevity of these mountain folks, Dorothy lived to within two days of her 100th birthday!

And just above the family gravesite, at the upper reaches of this lovely little cove and beside the clear mountain brook, molders the remains of an old settler's homestead. The log cabin is pitifully broken down, the earth reclaiming its remains. But the old weatherworn logs seem to be waiting, hoping to be put to use once again. Above the cabin, the trail climbs a high-reaching ravine, then passes the tumbled remains of three old log outbuildings, sliding and decaying into the rocks . . . a spot so steep, as Otto would say, "a man could might nigh stand straight up and bite the dirt." And as I ascend into still higher reaches, I find a cool, shaded waterfall.

Today I am not far from the trappings of civilization, but it is not unpleasant. The treadway follows an old fenceline along the ridge for miles, zigging first into Tennessee, then zagging back into North Carolina. The old woven barbs of wire which once bound the line have long since gone to dust, but the old locust posts stand straight and tall, solid and seemingly invincible, much as ranks of infantry, standing ready to spring to action at the first call, patient, ever faithful. As we struggle with our meager packweight over these rocky ridges and knobs, I can't help but consider what must have seemed endless back-breaking toil to the settlers who cleared and set these fencelines. First a path had to be opened, then trees found, felled, bucked, and split into posts. Then the near-impossible task of prying holes between the rocks to set the posts . . . post after gap, after mile! Certainly we hikers move along effortlessly, as if on wings, in comparison to the progress of those pioneers!

As I descend a wide, high meadow, the trail now passes beautiful flowing communities of wildflowers not before observed. I am able to identify false Solomon seal, pure clusters of little white flowers, and in the meadow all about, golden ragwort, a bright and cheerful yellow-gold flower standing, waving tall in the gentle breeze. It is all so peaceful, so serene. All that I see and marvel hereabouts, "toil not, neither do they spin," but reside in pure peace and harmony. Oh, the bountiful, gracious love of the creator of it all!

There's a five-Snickers pull up the approach and final ascent to Big Bald. Sweating and bone-weary, I pull myself the last few steps to the summit—to find a small child skipping about, only yards from her parents' BMW! The car is parked square on the highest ground, right on the summit. Will someone who can make some sense of this please explain it to me? The evening is most pleasant. I am still not used to the luxury of company on the trail or during the evening. What a pleasure sharing an off-camber campsite with *100# Stormcloud*. Great campfire, wonderful conversation!

> *"Along the eastern line of Tennessee,*
> *High in a gap with vistas either way,*
> *The old log cabin fascinates me,*
> *While passing by one sunlit April day.*
> *One end is tumbledown. The chimney stands*
> *Half sundered from the once snug-fitting wall*
> *Long since neglected of its builder's hands,*
> *An aura of decay pervading all.*
> *Who built this lofty home along the Trail*
> *So long ago and chose the site so well?*
> *If these old logs could speak what rustic tale*
> *Of plans and hopes and toil would they tell?*
> *Reluctantly, I leave for here there seems*
> *To be fulfillment of somebody's dreams."*

[Earl Shaffer]

THURSDAY May 14, 1998
TRAIL DAY 118/24 ✦ TRAIL MILE 1,740/338
LOCATION Uncle Johnny's Nolichucky Hostel, Erwin, Tennessee

THE TRAIL IS MOSTLY DOWNHILL TODAY INTO ERWIN. Time to get *Nomad*'s Neutral working again. I've been hiking with *Tulie* and her shep, Tenaya, since Spivey Gap. *Skookum* and his shep, Baxter, meet us part way up Temple Hill as we are descending to the Nolichucky River. Skookum greets us with a big smile and ice-cold, fresh strawberries. What a fitting way to celebrate the halfway point of this "Odyssey of '98."

We reach Uncle Johnny's great new Nolichucky Hostel on Chestoa Pike around 3:00 p.m. I get to the phone right away to call my friend Pat *Garcia* Jackson who lives here in Erwin, hoping to get a ride north to Damascus for Trail Days this weekend, but, alas, I am told Pat "left out" this morning. However, as this odyssey goes, I've been offered a ride up and back with *Skookum*!

This has been another memorable hiking day. I pitch in the cool, lush grass behind the hostel along with many thru-hiker friends: *U-Turn, Tween,* Sam, *T-Bone Walker, Long Distance Man, Fletch, Joliet Joe, Joyful Girl,* Dave, and *Innkeeper.* Johnny had the grill going for burgers. Beer is permitted on the premises in cups—great bunch, great evening!

> *"There's a race of men that don't fit in,*
> *A race that can't stand still.*
> *So, they break the hearts of kith and kin,*
> *And they roam the world at will.*
> *They range the field and they rove the flood,*
> *And they climb the mountain's crest.*
> *Theirs is the curse of the gypsy blood,*
> *And they don't know how to rest."*
>
> [Robert W. Service]

FRIDAY May 15, 1998
TRAIL DAY 119/25 ✦ TRAIL MILE 1,740/338
LOCATION Tent City, Front Street near Laurel Creek,
Damascus, Virginia

TENTING OUT LAST NIGHT ON THE LUSH, green lawn behind Nolichucky Hostel was the right thing to do, as those who chose the bunkhouse found it a little too warm. I slept cool and comfortable with the fly rolled back on my little Slumberjack.

As I work on my journal entries here at Nolichucky Hostel, two groups of thru-hikers load up and head for Trail Days in Damascus. About 11 a.m., one load departs in an old VW bus, the back end squatting and the old air-cooled engine wheezing. I hope they make it okay! My ride to Damascus will be with *Skookum* and *Tulie* and their dogs, Baxter and Tenaya. They arrive about 3:00 and we load up—three people, three packs, and two dogs in his little Ford!

We're faced with a couple of tough pulls through the mountains, but what a welcome break, sitting back and letting the little Ford do the work! We arrive in Damascus about 6:00 p.m. I dearly love trail towns, and Damascus is probably the ultimate in trail towns. The folks here profess to have the friendliest stopover along the AT, and to my knowledge that statement has never been questioned or challenged. Damascus, indeed, is a hiker-friendly place.

I head right for Tent City down by the river. Here is a grassy expanse, most nearly a lawn, but the size of a meadow, stretching all along Laurel Creek. The entire area is completely filled with tents for the better part of a quarter mile. The waves of brilliance throw my color vision into overload as I attempt to fix some mental order to this confusion. The large dome tents like Eureka and North Face seem to be popular with the couples, many being here just for the weekend. The thru-hikers' preference is evident—smaller tents, with the Clip Flashlights brand standing out predominantly. I probably have the smallest and lightest one-man tent in the meadow, the little Slumberjack. But, it has served me well so far these past 119 days. Although I am now on my second one, the folks at Slumberjack have provided for me and have kept me going.

The atmosphere here is not "carnival," that description having a certain detractive connotation, but there is certainly plenty of excitement and revelry all around. The vendors and manufacturers have their booths and tables set up all along the way. Every conceivable kind of item or product even remotely associated with hiking and the trail experience is on display and for sale. Over in one corner, near Mountain Smith, two fellows have their large commercial-style sewing machine set up with piles of packs and other gear lying in a heap, awaiting repair. And food: even the insatiable appetite of the thru-hiker can surely be satisfied here!

The meadow by the river, the expanse that it is with hundreds of tents, is not the only camping area within the city of Damascus. The Methodist Hostel, known as "The Place," a lovely two-story residence converted years ago, first to accommodate bicyclists on the Transcontinental Bike Trail and now to host AT thru-hikers, is filled and the lawn and yard jammed with tents clear around. Up by the community swimming pool, just off the Virginia Creeper Trail, and in a lovely place called "The Island," countless more tents are set up, row after row.

Ah, folks, this is it! It's Friday night in Damascus, the excitement and fun just beginning. The "Class of '98" is here, along with the classes of countless years past, each with their reunion—members greeting each other, mingling and sharing the joy of being together again. "Trail Days"—the wheels are up, the flaps are in, and this thing is flying! Ya gotta be here; you just gotta be here!

PROFILES '98

THIS IS THE FIRST IN WHAT I HOPE YOU WILL FIND to be a delightful series of profiles. Each will tell a little about the kind and friendly people I have met during the "Odyssey of '98."

I got to know David *Skookum* Irving on the summit of Springer Mountain last fall. Dave is a happy lad with an infectious excitement about the AT. He is 24 years old and single, and hails from Salisbury, New Hampshire. He has a degree in wildlife ecology with a minor in conservation biology from the University of Maine at Orono. He is currently employed by the Georgia Appalachian Trail Club, The Appalachian Trail

Conference, and the U.S. Forest Service as the ridge runner for the 72 miles of AT in Georgia, along with some 20-plus miles of side trails. Dave logged over 2,000 miles while fulfilling this responsibility in 1997. What a joy seeing Dave back again in this same capacity for 1998! He is not only the current expert on the Georgia section of the AT, but he also knows the entire AT well, having thru-hiked as a member of the "Class of '96."

Dave's reflections on the trail: "A lot of little things that made the big thing great. My sister, Susan *August*, age 15, hiked with me for a third of the way. She helped me escape the Virginia blues. I met a lot of good people, both on and off the trail. The daily news gives us such a bad impression of everything. It's good to know that people are still nice. Dave's future plans: "Goals? Have fun! Been thinking about it . . . Thought maybe I'd figure it out on my thru-hike. That didn't happen. Then I thought maybe I'd figure it out last year as ridge runner. That didn't happen. Maybe I'll figure it out some time in the next decade or so!" A final quote: "Alaska would be a good place to end up. I like it in northern New England. I've never experienced the West, Northwest, Southwest—lots of places to check out, lots of places to go!"

Tell me this young chap isn't full of wanderlust to the soul . . . like Muir and Bartram. It's always a highlight of the day when I meet *Skookum* and his pal Baxter on the trail. I hope our paths cross again, my friend!

> *Nature's splendor, the great outdoors,*
> *God's glorious wonders to see.*
> *No finer place to enjoy this peace,*
> *Than along the old AT.*
> *A life akin to the mist on the wind,*
> *This, the wanderlust's way.*
> *As he roams about to his heart's delight,*
> *A calling he must obey.*
>
> [N. Nomad]

SATURDAY May 16, 1998
TRAIL DAY 120/26　✦　TRAIL MILE 1,740/338
LOCATION Tent City, Front Street near Laurel Creek, Damascus

A SIT-IN JAM SESSION, MOSTLY GUITARS, continued by the bonfire
right next to my tent until 2:00 a.m. After that, I managed to sleep fine. I
awake with a ravenous appetite, so I skip breakfast and head straight for
the BBQ chicken dinner at Damascus V.F.D. Oh yes, was this the right
choice!

What a grand day to rest and visit again with a number of trail
friends. One is a young man that I had met leaving Springer, bound for
Katahdin. Here in Damascus he walks up to me and asks if I remember
giving him his trail name. He's from Hawaii, and *Hawaiian Hoofer* just
seemed natural . . . and it stuck. We have a grand time "bench hiking" as
we talk about his experiences since leaving Springer. I also catch up
again with *Garcia*. I'd met him while on the roadwalk through Alabama.
And oh, so many other great friends: *Tween, U-Turn, Yogi* and *Boo Boo,*
Sam, now *Chaser* (his tent got caught up in the wind on Max Patch, and
he chased it down the mountain — as it got away), *Chris, Selky, Saint,
Hobo Rob, Pack Mule,* and many others.

I relax most of the day while taking in all the Trail Days sights
and activities. I really enjoy attending most all the Appalachian Long
Distance Hikers Association (ALDHA) meetings and programs at the
Methodist church. Warren Doyle, Jr.'s famous, inspirational, and hys-
terically funny presentations are held here. One never tires of listening
to the accounts, yarns, and "lies" so eloquently woven by this raconteur
extraordinary. I also attend as many other great slide shows and presentations as is possible in so short a time. Later in the day, I have the
notable privilege and pleasure of meeting and shaking hands with Ed
Garvey, Warren Doyle, Jr., Bill O'Brien, Larry Luxenberg, and Sam
Waddle. Everyone is disappointed that Earl Shaffer is not here this year.
But Earl, as it seems, is a bit preoccupied as he thru-hikes the AT once
again on the 50th anniversary of his legendary first thru-hike, accomplished in 1948 . . . this time at the age of 79!

Back at The Place, I sit and chat with friends. *Selky* is busy doing some sewing. As I watch her needle flying with fine precision, a little idea lightbulb flashes on in my head. It is time to polish my Yogi-ing a tad. I'm the only hiker in town still hiking in long pants; everybody has switched to shorts weeks ago. My problem? I have no shorts. So it is that I appeal to *Selky* to cut the legs off my pants and hem them into shorts. "No problem!" she says. So I hunt around for a pair of scissors to accomplish the legectomy. In no time, the task is done, pant legs cut off and my new shorts hemmed and ready to go. Thanks, *Selky*!

In the evening, and to cap a perfect day, I head to Quincey's for calzones and pizza with *U-Turn* and *Tween*. Later I spend time with good friend Jim *Thunder Chicken* Pitts from Rockledge, Florida, who thru-hiked the AT last year, and also with his good friend *Poppasan*, a 64-year-old retired Navy fighter pilot who also thru-hiked the AT in 1997.

Well, the huge bonfire is roaring again, and what they've got going here tonight is whooping and dancing to bongos! The raucous goings-on continue until after 2:00 a.m. again, but I manage again to sleep soundly into the morning.

"When I die, bury me well,
Six foot under the Appalachian Trail.
Lay my pack frame upon my chest,
And tell Ed Garvey I did my best!"

[Unknown West Virginia Poet]

SUNDAY May 17, 1998
TRAIL DAY 121/27 ✦ TRAIL MILE 1,743/338
LOCATION Home of Chuck and Lenore Parham,
Mars Hill, North Carolina

I HAVEN'T MENTIONED THE PROBLEM WITH MY TOOTH. The reason I haven't talked about my tooth problem is because I have been blessed with perfect teeth all my life. I've never had the least trouble, though I've listened to countless friends relate their woes about their dental pains. I have not a filling in my head . . . and to this day do I proudly possess a single remaining baby tooth at the age of near 60! So I guess denial is a natural reaction to this whole ordeal. But my toothache is not going to be ignored this day. My jaw is hurting and I must get some relief. Along the midway yesterday I had the pleasure of meeting a wonderful lady, Elizabeth McKee. Elizabeth is the mayor of Damascus. Getting her aside, I asked if she would be kind enough to refer me to a local dentist, with my pain and all, the day being a Saturday and the dentists all out. She said, "You won't be finding any dentist today" and that my best bet would be to head over to the drugstore and get myself some Anbesol. That I did. But I still couldn't bring myself to face the reality of it, so I just shoved the bottle in my pocket, telling myself in the process that all would be fine real soon. But real soon has passed and all is not fine. So, this morning, I pull the little bottle back out and slather the stuff across my gums. Oh, glory be, what a relief,. The stuff helps immediately and immensely. I suspect this molar is going to have to come out pretty soon.

I have been invited to visit and spend the evening with dear friends Chuck and Lenore Parham in Mars Hill, North Carolina. Chuck was a colleague for years. We hit it right off and have been great friends. He's retired now and living the good life up here in the mountains. It is intriguing how this odyssey continues to thread its way. I have been offered a ride out of Damascus with *Thunder Chicken*—all the way, it seems, to Mars Hill, as his path home passes nearby. So I am delivered straight to the Parham's front door. Thanks, *Thunder Chicken*. Didn't we have a grand time at Trail Days! I'm no sooner greeted by Chuck and Lenore than Chuck cranks up the grill. Dining in the most genteel and lavish fashion in trail lingo is called Garveying, for Ed is well known far and about for enjoying the finest full-course cuisine right on the trail. Oh, did I ever Garvey out! Indeed, I did the clan proud!

> *"If I had my life to live over, I'd try to make more mistakes. I would relax, I would limber up, I would be sillier than I have been on this trip. I would be less hygienic, take more chances; take more trips. I would climb more mountains, swim more rivers and watch more sunsets. I would eat more ice cream and less beans. If I had it to do over again, I would go places and do things and travel*

lighter. If I had my life to live over, I would start bare-footed earlier in the spring and stay that way later in the fall. I would play hooky more. I wouldn't make such good grades, except by accident. I would ride on more merry-go-rounds—I would pick more daisies!"

[A Friar, Atonement Friars, Graymoor]

MONDAY May 18, 1998
TRAIL DAY 122/28 ✦ TRAIL MILE 1,757/355
LOCATION Cherry Gap Shelter

MARS HILL IS ABOUT 15 MILES SOUTH OF RUFUS SAMS GAP on US 23, so we cross the AT by road, where I passed five days ago by trail, as Chuck and Lenore deliver me back to Nolichucky Hostel at Erwin. We say farewell and I'm off toward Damascus again, this time by the AT. Thanks, Chuck and Lenore, for your kindness and hospitality.

The first day back on the trail after a couple of days off is always tough, especially when you're out late. There has been an absolute explosion of bugs and insects since the latter part of last week. There are crickets, grasshoppers, flies of every color and size, ticks, gnats, spiders—and butterflies, beautiful butterflies! At the lower elevations coming out of Erwin, I see the lovely, early-blooming Catawba (red) rhododendron, also mountain laurel, flame azalea, purple honeysuckle, and the more rare yellow azalea. I dearly need to get in a full hiking day, so I stick with it until after 7:00 p.m. There were some tough pulls today—four Snickers to reach both Beauty Spot and Unaka.

Dusk arrives as I arrive at Cherry Gap Shelter. A great cooking fire is going, so I'm able to prepare a nourishing hot meal—a real blessing. I soon drift into a deep and restful sleep.

"The spring wildflowers are something to see and walk among. We saw acre-size fields of trillium, mayapple, bloodroot, bluets, violets and buttercups. . . . Fields upon fields of ferns rise out of the forest floor in the shade of newly leafed trees."

[James and Hertha Flack]

TUESDAY May 19, 1998
TRAIL DAY 123/29 ✦ TRAIL MILE 1,771/369
LOCATION Roan High Knob Shelter

I HAD THE PLEASURE OF HIKING SOME YESTERDAY WITH *Little Sippi,* *Grym, P.O.D, Otherwise, Half-Pint, Starburst, Tulie* and Tenaya, and *Skookum* and Baxter. Today I'll be with *Second Chance, Holly Hobbie, Scrabble, Bald Eagle, Alfredo, Long Distance Man,* and *Quarter-Pounder.* A day-hiker/trail angel hangs with me all the way up Roan. Once on the summit, he asks me to wait a few minutes near the parking area while he goes to his car for an ice-cold Coca-Cola. What a surprising and refreshing treat . . . I simply can't remember a Coke tasting so good!

As I sit here sipping and savoring my cold Coke, before me is the most splendid scene. Roan is famous for the Catawba (red) rhododendron, considered by many to be among the most beautiful sights in nature. Near Roan High Bluff are found the remains of the former Cloudland Hotel. The Tennessee/North Carolina state line ran right through the center of the majestic ballroom. Cloudland was a thriving resort during the late 1800s and early 1900s. A few steps and part of the old ballroom floor are all that remain. If one were to take a notion, however, I suppose it would still be possible to Tennessee Waltz your partner clear into North Carolina across the old ballroom floor! My Coke and I take the stroll.

I had two difficult ascents today, one being the hardest so far— first, a four-Snickers pull up and over Little Rock Knob, and second, still in my memory from 15 years ago, the ascent up and onto Roan High Bluff, a steep, hard five-plus-Snickers pull. Both of these have all the attributes of a higher degree—that being represented by the Four R's: ruts, rocks, roots, and rough! I am blessed with two more absolutely beautiful days of hiking, complete with panoramic vistas: yesterday from Beauty Spot, and today, seemingly the top of the world, the view from Roan Massif.

I arrive at Roan High Knob Shelter around 4:00 p.m. and quickly get a fine cooking fire going for my evening meal and some hot coffee. The water source here is a lovely little seep coming from the rocks under a red spruce about 50 yards below the cabin/shelter, a wonderfully preserved old log structure once used as a fire warden's cabin. Roan High Shelter is the highest shelter on the AT, standing at 6,285 feet.

In a while, some section hikers arrive, followed by *Alfredo, Quarter-Pounder, Long Distance Man,* and finally *Hollie Hobbie.* After preparing our evening meal, we rebuild the fire for warmth, as the chill at this high elevation comes in right along with sunset. What an enjoyable and most pleasant evening of lighthearted conversation and jollity. I pitch my tent on a bed of evergreen needles under the red spruce and roll in for a warm and most restful night.

> *"Strange that so few ever come to the woods to see how*
> *the pine lives and grows and spires, lifting its evergreen*
> *arms to the light, to see its perfect success, but most are*
> *content to behold it in the shape of many broad boards,*
> *brought to market and deem that its true success!"*

> [Henry David Thoreau]

WEDNESDAY May 20, 1998
TRAIL DAY 124/30 ✦ TRAIL MILE 1,791/389
LOCATION Campsite past Campbell Hollow Road

I MANAGE TO GET OUT FROM ROAN HIGH KNOB SHELTER about 8:30 a.m. to be greeted by yet another beautiful, clear, sunny day. From the shelter, the trail descends along an old woodsroad practically all the way to Carvers Gap. The treadway appears to be descending a dry creek bed, for by simply adding rushing water it would appear as a mountain brook. But alas, where there was once earth and duff now remain only rocks, the final and most unpleasant result of erosion caused by the army of hikers who have trod this path. One only need stop and look where the trail bails off the old roadbed to descend down the mountain to see the sad reality of it. For at this juncture an interesting comparison can be made between where the old woodsroad continues, complete with earth, duff, and a narrow, grassy pathway, and the incredible erosion of the turning treadway. Here the trail is beaten down to hip-deep bare rock, testimony to the cumulative effect — the ravages, if you will — of the constant beating and pounding we who love the trail deliver and that this old trail has endured over the decades.

Oh, what a perfect day to ascend the Balds and to look out from their lofty heights. Though it has been 15 years, I remember all of this as if yesterday. It is all so vivid, the sights and sounds from Round Bald, especially the sounds of that day so long ago. That day was also clear and beautiful, much like this day. I remember lying back on these rocks, at this very spot, enjoying the warm sun, relaxing, half daydreaming, half in slumber. And then from far off it came, drifting across the highlands from above and descending all around, the unmistakably clear, melodic ring of a banjo. Oh, the happy sound it was, so crisp, so pure, so clear. The music seemed to be like the air, as if broadcast across the skies, lifted from a glorious amphitheater. From the lower slopes all around reverberated the chime of nostalgic, old banjo bluegrass—"Rocky Top," "Arkansas Traveler," "Reuben," "Cripple Creek," "Cherokee," "Foggy Mountain Breakdown." For most of an hour this recital to the Roan Highlands continued, the notes so perfect, so clear as to bring joyful glee to the ear and to the heart, touching my very being to the depths of my soul. Oh, the sense of sound, it is such an incredible sense.

And then it ended as abruptly as it began, leaving a perfect stillness and a perfect clearness. I stand here now, looking at the very spot atop the boulder where I lay. I recline again, close my eyes, and I am transported back to that time so long ago and I hear those pure, clear notes ring perfect in my memory. This place is ageless, never changing, and my memory doesn't fail those precious fixed moments in time. Now, as then, I linger for one last look from this heavenly highland before traveling ever onward. As I hike the path off Round Bald, my mind constructs an idyllic little cabin, nestled peacefully in a lush, green cove just below. And on the porch swing, a young man picks away to his heart's content as the possessor of his heart rests content in the cool shade of the old sycamore by the well. I used to sit each evening in the comfort and security of our little home in a manner most content, to listen as my young son Jon practiced and perfected those very bluegrass banjo songs. But alas, time sweeps us along and we must go, and all that was is no more.

The sideslabbing along the trail today is so typical of the AT treadway in the Southern Appalachians. It appears as though the tree trunks are literally holding the trail up on the side of the mountain. For the trail drapes around these trees as does garland on the boughs of a Christmas tree, the trail looping and lifting from one tree trunk to the next, much as the garland loops o'er the boughs in similar fashion. As I drape my way along this trail-garland, I wonder if it has occurred to the trail maintenance folks that if they would just take hold of one end of this thing and give it a good hard tug, they could pull all of this slack on through. Just think, all of this perfectly good treadway that could then be put to use elsewhere!

As we tread the pathway along the AT, we are literally treading on history, for the route of the Overmountain Men intersects the AT. I stand now in the Pisgah National Forest at the Overmountain National Historic Trail monument, on which is inscribed,

> *"September 25, 1780, down yonder at Sycamore Shoals they gathered, 1,000 men from the militias of Virginia, North Carolina, and what is now Tennessee, joined forces to resist the British. They provided their own horses, rations, and guns. They rode up this mountain as the weather turned bitter. Through this gap they trudged without benefit of supplies, surgeons, or chaplains. The Overmountain Men continued the 170 miles to Kings Mountain. There they defeated the British-led Loyalists in bloody battle. They won a significant victory in the Revolutionary War."*

On the top of Hump Mountain is (was) a beautiful bronze plaque in memory of Stanley A. Murray, who led a fundraising campaign years ago to purchase the "humps." He was ATC Chairman at the time and hiked this very trail with Ed Garvey when Ed passed this way on his thru-hike in 1970. Mr. Murray died in 1990. As a result of this man's unflagging dedication and effort, the trail was moved onto Houston Ridge and to the Balds and Highlands of Roan. The memorial was beautiful, but is no more because, sadly, it has been vandalized — battered and bent as a result of the fury and rage vented by someone who wielded a very large rock with incredible might. I absolutely cannot comprehend this senseless, wanton destruction. It is indeed a sad scene.

The Southern Balds are treeless summits below treeline, a baffling mystery to investigators. Balds such as Roan Massif, Hump, Jane, Pump, Beauty Spot, and Max Patch are all examples. Some believe Native Americans cleared the Balds; others blame overgrazing, too much wind, lightning. Still others point to UFOs! I like *Wingfoot*'s explanation, for his may be the most plausible. He says, "Perhaps the baldness is hereditary!"

On Doll Flats I meet Tom, the Coke-toting trail angel from yesterday. He's section-hiking south today and guess what? Trail angel true-to-form, he offers me another ice-cold Coca-Cola — said it would be waiting for me at US 19 E. Sure enough, when I reach the highway, there's Tom with the Coke. It's amazing how nice these things go down on a hot day! It was also my pleasure to meet and hike some with his friend Richard. Richard was good for a bag of trail mix! It's always good to see trail angels.

The trail today reminds me of the old truism: "What goes up must come down." The AT corollary to that being: "What comes down must go up." The pull out of Carvers Gap and the one from US 19 E both earned a rating of four Snickers!

Passing Campbell Hollow Road, I pitch in a small camping area complete with a fire ring, and I get a respectable fire going to prepare supper. It has been a clear, glorious, fun-filled hiking day!

> *"Out on the blue horizon,*
> *Under an aerial sky,*
> *With aspect always sylvan,*
> *The days go strolling by."*
>
> [Earl Shaffer]

THURSDAY May 21, 1998
TRAIL DAY 125/31 ✦ TRAIL MILE 1,805/403
LOCATION Dennis Cove, Kincorra Hostel

THERE CAME A SHORT THUNDERSTORM DURING THE NIGHT, but I slept soundly on both sides of it. I break camp and am on the trail by 8:30 a.m. The sky clears before noon, making for a very nice hiking day. Slowly but surely, the hiking days are getting longer, warmer, and generally drier! What a blessing to have warm hands and warm feet!

I arrive at Kincorra Hostel around 3:00 p.m. to meet Bob Peoples, the owner. This facility comes highly recommended by *Thunder Chicken,* who has since become good friends with Bob. The hostel is a newer log structure attached to the older log main dwelling, which dates to the time of the Civil War. The stay here is most comfortable. I wash some clothes, even do a little cooking. As he showed *Thunder Chicken* last year, Bob showed *Fletch* and me how to identify, dig, and prepare ramps (Nature's combo of onions and garlic!) while sharing a most humorous story about how *Thunder Chicken* dug up some ramps, brushed them off, then popped the whole bundle of little breath-fresheners in his mouth . . . with Bob standing by wide-eyed in total astonishment! The area behind Bob's house where the ramps grow is now known as the *Thunder Chicken* Memorial Ramp Patch!

Bob drives some of us to Hampton for provisions and a stop at Down Home Lakeside Restaurant for their famous wagon wheel hamburger. It's a 20-ounce monster on five combined large burger buns, a massive thing filling an entire large carryout container. This giant also comes with another large container of potatoes, an impossible amount of food to consume, but I did try. Bad idea. Nightmares? Oh yes!

> *"Awoke drenched with mountain mist, which made a grand show as it moved away before the hot sun. Crossed a wide, cool stream. There is nothing more eloquent in Nature than a mountain stream — its banks are luxuriantly peopled with rare and lovely flowers and overarching trees, making one of Nature's coolest and most*

*hospitable places. Every tree, every flower, every ripple
and body of this lovely stream seems solemnly to feel the
presence of the great Creator. Lingered in this sanctuary
a long time thanking the Lord with all my heart for his
goodness in allowing me to enter."*

[John Muir]

FRIDAY May 22, 1998
TRAIL DAY 126/32 ✦ TRAIL MILE 1,822/420
LOCATION Vandeventer Shelter

WATAUGA DAM IS A VERY LARGE EARTHEN (rock) impoundment that
has created a lake with a remarkably long and circuitous shoreline. This
result of man's intrusion into the grand scheme of things runs for miles
and can be seen for the better part of two hiking days. So today's hike
will no doubt prove to be excitement-filled, what with Laurel Fork
Gorge, the falls, the flats, and the bluff-walk above Watauga Lake.

The trail north out of Kincorra enters Laurel Fork Gorge as it
descends gradually to follow along an old narrow-gauge railroad bed. To
accomplish the construction for a railroad through this precipitous
gorge was, I am sure, considered an incredible accomplishment. The
main trestle that spanned the gorge is long-since gone, but must have
been a pretty impressive sight indeed. In latter-day Disneyland lingo,
I'm sure a trip across that trestle atop a rocking-and-rolling railcar
would surely have been considered an "E-ticket" ride!

On my hike through here 15 years ago, the AT followed the railroad grade all the way to Laurel Fork Shelter, bypassing Laurel Fork
Falls. To reach the falls, one had to descend the wall of the gorge by a
blue-blazed loop trail. I chose at that time to continue on, as looking
down the blue-blaze into the gorge appeared a formidable, time- and
energy-consuming side trip—a decision I've regretted ever since. For
since then, one of the questions always asked by others when we discuss
the AT has been, "What did you think of Laurel Fork Falls?" Many folks
have since tried to describe these beautiful falls. So now I will close this

loop, literally, as I descend the neatly placed boulders that form the steps (now the AT treadway) down into the gorge . . . and to Laurel Fork Falls.

As I turn at the very depths of the gorge to face the falls, the sun casts its perfect radiance in exact alignment through the gorge, to lift and bounce prismatic light from the millions of water droplets propelled into space above the upper, main cascading cataract. I must don my Oakleys to reduce the brilliance. And as I try adjusting to this visual impact, the crashing bombardment caused by the tumult creates such a trembling roar that I must brace against its crescendo of overwhelming sound. My senses of sight and of sound are in total overload—kicks in now the emotional shudder that leaves one in paralyzed, captivated awe. As I manage to lift my eyes from the visual clutches of the falls, to peer more heavenward— above the falls—now comes into focus the overhanging precipices, boul- dered ledges, and cliffs towering into the open blue! The majesty of this, the impact, the might and power in such grand excitement and profusion create a scene never before experienced in my memory.

Does this even begin to describe what I am now trying to com- prehend? I tell you, it does not! For just as with that mysterious swirl of emotions experienced as I stood to gawk and peer from the summit of Max Patch do such raw and vibrating emotions descend on me now— you must come here, you must stand amidst this cacophony and bril- liance to really understand. You, too, must someday come to the falls in Laurel Fork Gorge.

As I lean into the four-Snickers pull up Pond Flats, I'm thinking about all the great thru-hikers that I found pleasure staying with at Kincorra: *Fletch, Joliet Joe, Hawaii, Weatherman* and *Boyscout, Pianobloke, Wanderer, Grateful Granddad* and *Yodi, Wylie Coyote, Buddha Boy, Dutchie, T- Bone Walker, Redness Rushing, Innkeeper,* and *Redneck Rye.* The home fries, leftovers from last evening, I prepared along with three eggs, compli- ments of *Weatherman*—aided by a little bacon fat from the mason jar on the counter and in the best-cured old cast-iron frying pan I've ever seen. I split this grand creation with *Joliet Joe* and we both had our fill.

What a delight reaching the lovely park and beach at Watauga Lake. I drop my pack and jump right in! The warm sun feels so good as I "drip-dry" while fixing a light lunch. The place is packed to overflowing and I am lucky to have found this little picnic table here on the end. Kids are playing and laughing, but I find it not the least bit distracting as they scamper about . . . and as I lounge on the lush lawn. Watauga Lake is set against a tall, lush mountain backdrop. Ah, what a beautiful, peaceful place!

I'm faced right away with another steady four-Snickers pull to Vandeventer Shelter. The climb is more than worth it as the views from the remarkably uniform bluff and ridgeline are many and varied, first back and down into Watauga Valley and then the beautiful meandering lake. The high-pitched whine from motorboats way off and down the distant lake can be heard most all afternoon from this high-mountain vantage.

As I journey on, the sun bids bye and the day soon turns to steady rain; so I hasten my arrival at the shelter. I am able to get a warming and cooking fire going under the shelter eaves. The rain, never slacking, decides to stay, setting in hard to finally become the evening sentinel, standing guard throughout the night. Over these past 125 days, I have learned to get by with few trappings, few of the worldly things if you will, and I have been more content with the independence of such a lifestyle perhaps than during any other period in my entire life. Living in this manner has been so vibrant. Offered me and joyfully received have been bountiful, loving gifts of pure invigorating vitality—being close to the grit and grind has brought me closer to His face, through His grace! But oh, isn't the luxury offered up by these cozy shelters along this grand old AT so very comforting to find at the end of a long, tiring day! It is but sheer indulgence to accept their warm and inviting hospitality. Lest I become softened to these ways, must I now keep in mind the wise words of two of my very dear friends:

"He who needs nothing has everything."
[Ron King]

"A man is rich in proportion to the number of things
which he can afford to let alone."
[Henry David Thoreau]

SATURDAY May 23, 1998
TRAIL DAY 127/33 ✦ TRAIL MILE 1,837/435
LOCATION Double Springs Shelter, Holston Mountain Trail

A VERY UNCANNY AND UNSETTLING THING HAPPENED this morning . . . and apparently if here, one could witness this each and every morning. At precisely 5:30 a.m., I was rudely and abruptly awakened by the shrill, hyper call of a whippoorwill. He was so close I could hear him sucking wind between each escalating and succeeding blast as he cranked his siren up to full tilt. Indeed, he would now be a poor-will if I could have gotten my hands on him, but alas, before I could get one eye partway open and before I could gather my wits, he had accomplished his task and vanished. *U-Turn* also reported encountering the scoundrel at precisely the same time during his stay here. Later I learn that the spirit of a dearly departed hiker comes to the fire ring in front of the shelter at precisely 5:30 a.m. every morning, alighting in the form of a whippoorwill, to greet the intrepids who are unfortunate enough to have spent the night!

After nature's little alarm clock, to which I halfheartedly saluted the day, and now influenced by both the dreary rain and the not-terribly-pleasant feeling of standing before the Grindstaff grave again (I passed here many years ago), this day is weaving a fairly formidable funk. For it is that I look upon old "Uncle Nick" 's grave with pensive melancholy and heart-struck sadness. Here is an interesting, perhaps one-of-a-kind headstone marking the grave of a most interesting and one-of-a-kind man. Nick's grave is marked by his old stone fireplace and chimney, all that remain of the cabin where he lived by himself for 46 years. You see, Nick was a hermit. The story goes that Nick, following the wanderlust in his heart and of his youth, was driven to venture west to seek his fortune. It is reported that while there he was robbed of all his earthly possessions, and as a result became much the loner, withdrawing from society, never again to place the least bit of trust in all of humankind. He returned to this very place to become one of the South's most famous hermits; his only friend, a rattlesnake that frequented the cabin. Nick is buried here close by his fireplace hearth, near where he most surely sat alone for decades in the glow from the only warmth that he ever knew or trusted on this earth. The firebox is now filled with his headstone. I wonder how many have ever really stopped to think or contemplate this sad, depressing association and the irony of it.

My memory is vivid—standing here 15 years ago trying to fathom the least bit of this, to make any sense of it. I remember trying to understand how any man could become so embittered by all of life as to isolate himself from family, friends, and indeed from all of society, to live the remaining days of his entire existence in self-imposed exile. I stand here now once more, reading these cold words chiseled into the cold gray stone, "Lived alone, suffered alone, died alone." Who has ever read these words, indeed who among us with the least of compassion could read these words and not feel the slightest bit of a lump in his throat, the least bit of a tear in her eye?

In a moment, Nick, I will turn to leave your grave yet again, but this time I want you to know that departing from this place will be kindred, your kindred. I'm a little late, but I'm here. And before I go, there's something else I want you to know—I want you to know, Nick, that now I understand; I truly do understand. I want you to know that I know who you were and what you were as a man. It has taken a long while, but I have come to realize that there is nothing wrong, there is nothing to be ashamed of, for a man to be so full of love and full of trust that in his mind it would be impossible for even the least of it to ever be destroyed or taken away. I also know now that a man is nonetheless a man to live with that fullness of heart and to wear that vulnerability on his sleeve for all to see.

We both stood one day, shattered, destroyed, at the end of our bright horizons, past the darkest reaches of hell-on-earth imaginable. I know the path that led you here Nick, for I, too, was on that path. But I have chosen another path now, and though I am here at this same place as you, I will make it on by, for the path on which I now journey is the path toward peace . . . true peace in my life. For along this path is being cast aside all the bitterness that you and I have brought here, all the hopelessness, all the forlorn despair. Nick, I dearly wish we could continue now, along this path . . . together. This has been such a sad day. Ah, but this also has been a most joyful day.

"If you'll go with me to the mountains,
And sleep on the leaf carpeted floors,
And enjoy the bigness of nature,
And the beauty of all out-of-doors.
You will find your troubles all fading,
And feel the Creator was not man.
That made lovely mountains and forests,
Which only a supreme power can.
When we trust in the power above,
And with the realm of nature hold fast,
We will have a jewel of great price,
To brighten our lives till the last.
For the love of nature is healing,
If we will only give it a try.
And our reward will be forthcoming,
If we go deeper than what meets the eye.

[Emma *Grandma* Gatewood, GAME '55]

SATURDAY May 24, 1998
TRAIL DAY 128/34 ✦ TRAIL MILE 1,856/454
LOCATION The Place, Damascus

THE WEATHER HAS CLEARED NICELY and I have another lovely hiking day. There's a short pull over McQueens Knob, then it's downhill, full bore all the way to Damascus. *Nomad*'s Neutral is kickin' today! Where do you head when you get to Damascus? Oh yes, Quincey's! Calzones and sweet tea, that's the ticket.

PROFILES '98

Amanda *In-Between* Schaffer, age 23, is from Hayward (Frisco Bay), California. *Tween*, as she is affectionately known, is an enthusiastic and energetic young lady. She is a fourth-generation Californian, raised in Castro Valley, a graduate of Castro Valley High. *Tween* has attended

Humboldt State University in Redwood, where she has studied sociol-
ogy and community development.

The common thread linking us all here on the AT is the wanderlust within us. *Tween* has been blessed with a very generous portion,
indeed! She has long been drawn to the wilds, having spent three summers in Alaska working on a cable-run ferryboat on the Kenai River.

Says *Tween*, "I had been dreaming about the AT after being told
about it by friends in Massachusetts. We hiked on Stratton Mountain,
and I knew then that the AT was where I wanted to be. I sold my car and
headed for Springer Mountain!"

An interesting distinction: *Tween* is hiking in Chaco sandals!
Impossible, you say? Well, she hanged one toe up a bit, but she's getting
along just fine. She plans to clip-clop it all the way to Maine!

After the AT, *Tween* plans to return and complete her education in
community development, directed toward psychiatric rehabilitation. She
feels the understanding she is gaining about the AT "family" and her
knowledge of the outdoors will benefit her as she pursues her career goals.

To Phyllis and Fred, *Tween's* parents—you can be proud, for you
have raised a wonderful daughter! Being a lady in the woods has proven
no challenge for *Tween*. Being in her company is both a pleasure and a joy.

"The air is like a butterfly
With frail blue wings.
The happy earth looks at the sky
And sings."

[Joyce Kilmer]

MONDAY May 25, 1998
TRAIL DAY 129/35 ✦ TRAIL MILE 1,856/453
LOCATION The Place, Damascus

THIS IS MEMORIAL DAY, SO THE POST OFFICE IS CLOSED. Just as
well, I need the rest and at least one full day, perhaps two, to get caught
up on my journal entries. Hiking is hard, writing is hard . . . hiking and
writing is real hard.

It is just most-nigh impossible to tote enough food on the trail to properly provide for the energy demand to propel even the most efficient backpacker along. I hear and keep reading 5,000 calories a day. That's not a high number, in my opinion. It takes a lot of energy to hike these mountains, and the farther you hike day to day and the more you tote, the more it takes. I don't know the most lightweight, compact foods or the equivalent weights thereof required to consistently provide 5,000 calories a day. Finicky figuring and I don't mix, but I suspect whatever it would take is way more than I want to carry, especially when packing for five to seven days, which is not an unusually long period of time considering the trails I've been on and will be hiking. It seems to me the point of diminishing return can be reached, perhaps even exceeded, real fast. It's kind of like what Warren Doyle, Jr., says, "In your avoidance of discomfort, you may become more uncomfortable." I liken it to "The House That Jack Built," the house being the pack on our back. Another analogy would also fit very well: "the straw that broke the camel's back."

So what to do? Well, follow along and you'll quickly see my solution . . . you may even like it, for it involves a very simple skill, one that must first be fully perfected and mastered before ever applying for membership in the least of the Hiker Trash Fratority (*frat*ernity-sor*ority*). It's called "piggin' out." You've heard of it. Come, I'll show you. We're going to make up the deficit for last week, then work on getting at least two days ahead. We're bound for CJs and breakfast! Biscuits, sausage gravy, bacon and eggs, home fries, the works . . . and watch me put in my order for the second round when they call me for pick-up. Wait, we're not done . . . oh no! Now it's back to Quincey's for supper and a grand time with plenty of friends and plenty of pizza, calzone, stromboli, oh . . . and a few tall frosties to wash it all down and settle it in just right! Staying over another night? Catch me in the morning for breakfast at CJs!

Damascus, you folks are great! This is such an interesting little town. Brushing up on your history a little, I've learned that Damascus reached its heyday back in the early half of the 1900s. The dreamers had a grand vision to create another Damascus of old, the steel city of America. The plan seemed reasonable enough, what with the iron ore, manganese, plenty of water, and the coalfields nearby. But those dreams never materialized. Damascus had its glory-day anyway, though, during the grand logging boom from 1910 to 1930. Today Damascus is probably best known far and wide for its arms-open policy to hikers, for the little burg is known everywhere as *the* trail town. Damascus is indeed one of the friendliest little burgs along the entire trail. *Nomad* loves trail towns, and Damascus is on *Nomad*'s five-star list!

> *You squirrel in the food,*
> *'N load your pack.*
> *To tote it along*
> *O'er the boundless track.*
> *The more you haul,*
> *The more you eat.*
> *To get the juice*
> *To'rd your screamin' feet.*
> *But the more you tote,*
> *The worse you wilt.*
> *To finally toss "The House*
> *(Off your back)*
> *That Jack Built!"*

[N. Nomad]

TUESDAY May 26, 1998
TRAIL DAY 130/36 ✦ TRAIL MILE 1,856/453
LOCATION The Place, Damascus

TODAY I'M ABLE TO GET MY MAIL, MY CARDS and letters from friends and family, and the bottles of vitamins, coated aspirin, Osteo Bi-Flex, and other goodies sent from Nimblewill Creek by my very good friend Frank. Thoughtful as always, Frank has sent along a 500-unit Sam's calling card . . . Thanks, Frank! I've been in and out of Mt. Rogers Outfitters a dozen times and I finally pick up a couple of items. This little store, right downtown in one of the old streetfront establishments, is well stocked. Great outfitter, great folks. Thanks, Damascus Dave!

The trail really takes its toll on those heading north from Springer. Many who quit do so right here in Damascus. *Fletch* and *Tumbleweed Walt* both went to the clinic today. Both were diagnosed with *Giardia lamblia.* It is reported through the grapevine that *FreeMan* is heading in with the same symptoms. We figure they got into some bad water down in Great Smoky Mountains National Park. That was about a week or so ago, and the boars had definitely been rooting in some of the springs. I don't filter or otherwise treat my water and I gathered water from those very same springs, but I am immune to giardia, having built up resistance to the cysts over the many years I've been in the woods. *Fletch* is a strong, strapping young kid, but when he came stumbling into The Place Sunday evening, he looked like death warmed over. The lad was totally emaciated, in a fever, and near delirious. There is no over-the-counter medication that will kill this bug. You've got to see the doc. *Fletch* will rest here a few days, get his strength back, and continue on. *Tumbleweed Walt*, a most kind and gentle gent, and being toward the back of the train like the old *Nomad* (age), his sap clear gone, will leave the trail here to return to his home in Dallas.

And so it is with so many who are set with that grand vision, that dream of thru-hiking the AT. All have pounded it out the best they can; they've given it their all, every fiber of their being to accomplish that goal, that dream. But somehow it seems, for the overwhelming majority, that extra bit of something, that elusive ingredient that it takes, just isn't there. So leaving the trail here along with *Tumbleweed Walt* are *Otherwise, Second Chance, Saint,* and many others. Dear friends, I will miss you. Please know that your leaving is not a sign of failure, but rather your accomplishments should be celebrated triumphantly now as a remarkable success in your lives. For each of us who've dared there are thousands who want to go but will never make the sacrifice, never take the risk, for fear of failure. They are the failures. We are the winners, for we alone have risked it all on just one roll. We're out here giving it all we've got . . . our best shot. Go in peace, and God bless!

The Place, the hostel here in Damascus, is the property of and is maintained and managed by the Damascus Methodist Church. It is an old two-story residence, little changed since I first stayed here 15 years ago. The church is—as it seems are all the folks and all the institutions here in Damascus—a true friend to hikers, opening their main sanctuary of worship for the purpose of lectures and slide and other presentations during Trail Days . . . and managing the hostel for our use and convenience, relying all the while on nothing more that donations placed in a wooden box on the dining-room wall. It does my heart good to see the respect that hikers have for this fine and traditional institution, the support given. My deep appreciation and gratitude is extended to the congregation of the Damascus Methodist Church . . . Thanks!

As I lie here in my bunk this evening, the rain pounding on the old roof, and before I drift to restful, contented sleep, aware in my mind and do I know that I must leave (this) The Place tomorrow. Many dear friends—this incredible ragtag trail family that we are—take shelter here with me this night.

We are such a dynamic and vibrant family. I know most all of them so well. We have spent peaceful days in each other's company hiking this grand old AT and have sought shelter and lounged under the same roof many a night. I take joy in their company and am saddened when they or I must go. Some it will be my pleasure to rejoin on up the trail; many I will never see again. Here with me tonight are *U-Turn, Joliet Joe, Jingle,* Greg, *Long Distance Man, Alfredo, Redneck Rye,* Kevin, *Weatherman* and *Boyscout, Fletch, Walrus* and *Roots,* Nathan, *Hootie,* Brian, *Birch, Flint, Skitz, Desperado, Saint, Tumbleweed Walt, Shelter Monkey, Hawaii, Hollie Hobbie, Buddha Boy, Dutchie, Slim, Minstrel, Lion Tamer, Lightweight, SG, Gideon, Wildflower, Shrn Love, Redness Rushing,* Wanda, *Trail Gimp, Geronimo, Deacon, Ozone, Tony-V,* and the church helper and volunteer, *Trashman.*

> *"Now hollow fires burn out to black,*
> *And lights are guttering low:*
> *Square your shoulders, lift your pack,*
> *And leave your friends and go."*

[A. E. Housman]

WEDNESDAY May 27, 1998
TRAIL DAY 131/37 ✦ TRAIL MILE 1,869/467
LOCATION Virginia Creeper Trail

I SORT OUT A WEEK'S SUPPLY OF COATED ASPIRIN and my supple-
ments and repack the rest to "bounce box" ahead to my good friends
Alex and Carol Chamberlain in Burkes Garden. I have managed to
catch up on my journal entries and these I mail to Debbie, who tran-
scribes for me in Dahlonega. I'm finally able to get back on the trail and
out of Damascus at 4:30 p.m. It's oh-so-easy to linger in these grand trail
towns and oh-so-hard to leave!

The two hikers I chanced to meet at the little mom 'n' pop greasy
spoon in Alabama, *Tric* and *Garcia,* both highly recommended I stay on
the Creeper out of Damascus. *Tric* drew me a map showing me how the
Creeper went along and how to get back to the AT at the other end. I've
carried this little pencil sketch with me ever since. *Garcia* said I would
miss nothing noteworthy by bypassing the AT through here. To the con-
trary, by staying on the Creeper to hike up through Whitetop Laurel
Gorge, I would be provided some most memorable and breathtaking
scenery . . . so stay on the Creeper I do.

The Virginia Creeper Trail is one of the finest examples of "Rails-
to-Trails" in the U.S. It runs from Abingdon through Damascus to
Whitetop Station, a distance of 34 miles. Whitetop Station was once the
highest passenger-rail station east of the Rockies, standing at nearly
3,600 feet. This railbed was put to good use again in the latter part of the
last decade. It was in 1987 that the Virginia Creeper Rails-to-Trails trail
was dedicated by Congress as a National Recreation Trail. As the trail
enters Whitetop Laurel Gorge just out of Damascus, this old narrow-
gauge railbed begins a two- to three-percent climb that continues the
entire distance of the gorge. In many places, the grade has been literally
blasted from the sheer vertical rock walls that form the gorge. The
nearly continuous creek-crossing trestlework is an engineering marvel;
the old trestles are still intact, still standing in such proud fashion. I quit
counting them at 25! When the old steam locomotives were still chugging up through the gorge, this train ride was considered by railroad

buffs to be one of the most scenic in eastern North America. The designated AT route follows this old railbed for a short distance through Feathercamp Crossing and Creek Junction. Whitetop Laurel Creek is the only stream between the New River in Virginia and the Watauga River in Tennessee to cut through Iron Mountain. This beautiful stream is a steady, continuous cascade of rapids and falls for near the entire distance of the gorge, the accessibility to which provides prime fishing for the native brook trout and the imported rainbow and brown.

It was at the main 500-foot-long trestle that I met Del Loyless a decade and a half ago. We had a most enjoyable time hiking the gorge as we literally gorged ourselves (no pun intended) on huge thumb-sized blackberries. Come to find out Del's daughter and son-in-law are my good friends! I recently saw a letter to the editor in *Appalachian Trailway News* written by Del. Hope you're doing well, my good friend!

In one of the high coves, and along the Creeper on trail not shared by the AT, the old railbed leads not only forward, but back . . . to go back in time past fields and meadows and old log cabins, none restored as we would perceive in our mind's eye, but continually cared for over the countless decades by tireless, constant love and attention. Here also are old log sheds and outbuildings, and tumbledown, rusted old plows, harvesters, and other ancient farming implements, and machinery put out to pasture . . . all sitting quietly now, their work long since completed. Ah, do I hark back to a simpler, and most surely in my mind . . . a better time. Oh, how could you not want to see all of this for yourself? But you can! For the thought occurred to me, why not rent a bike, get a shuttle, and put in at Whitetop Station, from there to coast and glide back down through the wonders of this glorious gorge, through its delightful and inspiring time capsule . . . all the way to Damascus!

I find a soft, grassy spot beside the Creeper to pitch for the night, here to listen to the peaceful lullaby played by the cascading waters tumbling down Whitetop Laurel Creek . . . for only a very short time.

"De railroad bridges
A sad song in de air.

Ever' time de trains pass
I want to go somewhere."
[Langston Hughes,
Homesick Blues]

THURSDAY May 28, 1998
TRAIL DAY 132/38 ✦ TRAIL MILE 1,888/486
LOCATION Grayson Highlands State Park, Wise Shelter

HIKING FOR A WHILE UP THE CREEPER THIS MORNING and by a side road, I see an old fellow sitting on his porch swing, so I venture over to make sure I've got my directions figured for getting back to the AT. "Sure," he says. "Take Walnut Mountain Road up to that 58, then left to the gummint trail. You can't hardly miss it." I couldn't believe my ears; the old fellow called the AT the government trail! I remember Earl Shaffer mentioned this in his book, *Walking with Spring,* how the mountain folks referred to the trail as "the government trail." That was 50 years ago, and I'm hearing it here today!

I'm soon back on the AT, to be greeted right off with a long four-Snickers pull up to Buzzard Rock, thence to Whitetop Mountain, the second highest peak in Virginia. Here are alpine-like meadows and, all around, wide expanses providing grand and picturesque views to the horizon. Whitetop is considered to be a true Appalachian bald with resident red spruce, a glacial remnant of 20,000 years ago. Here is a whole new forest scene, Fraser fir and spruce at the crown. And below, the northern hardwood, birch, beech, and sugar maple, all much more common to New England and Canada. As I enter this zone above 4,000 feet, which includes Whitetop Mountain, Mt. Rogers, Wilburn Ridge, and Grayson Highlands State Park, I am in what is considered The High Country Crest Zone. The Crest Zone is renowned for its scenic quality, a combination of fir/spruce stands, northern hardwood forests, rocky pinnacles, and mountain meadows . . . the whole landscape often likened to "a bit of Montana dropped on the rooftop of Virginia."

I'm in early at Wise Shelter and get a fine warming and cooking fire going first thing. Oh, this grand handwarmer feels so good!

*"We passed away the remaining part of the day in
observing the beauties of the place. As I was wandering
about embosomed in the woods and mountains, I could
not but reflect what an insignificant creature I appeared,
among these magnificent works of the Divine Creator."*

[Francis Baily, 1796]

FRIDAY May 29, 1998
TRAIL DAY 133/39 ✦ TRAIL MILE 1,908/506
LOCATION Trimpi Shelter

WHAT A REMARKABLE TRAIL—THIS AT TODAY. All my senses are
flooded anew with overwhelming experiences, from the touch of the
treadway beneath my feet, to the aromatic fragrance of the conifers, to
the sound of the gentle wind through their boughs, and finally to this
absolutely stunning landscape. Each bald, each open highland area offers
something different to behold. The closely woven grass may be unusually
lush, the distant outcroppings and jutting pinnacles of volcanic rhyolite
more dramatic and striking, or the alpine conifers and hardwoods more
bold. The trail this morning leads me through constantly varying mixes
. . . constantly dazzling my already reeling senses. The highlands—
they're everything I remember them to be—so amazingly diverse. It all
seems so new and strange, sights not seen to the south or below these
sky-high elevations . . . and to be here on such a bright, sun-drenched
day. The Lord lifts up his countenance upon me and gives me peace.

Oh look, here are my little friends again! The first time I've seen
them in many a day, beds of just-blooming bluets, when I thought for
sure these little children were all through with their joyful scampering
about for this year. But here they are again, as fresh and as new as the
breeze that now arrives to set them dancing, as if they're happy to see me,
too! I have seen many other wildflowers in the last few days that I have
not yet mentioned: buttercup, squawroot, yellow stargrass, fire pink, wild
lily-of-the-valley, sweet white violet, clintonia, and white baneberry. Just
when I'm convinced the show is over, there's more to behold anew!

I have some tough, hard pulls today, in the three- or four-Snickers range. Somehow, I know not how, I have injured my left knee and lower leg tackling the highland rocks. I've heard folks tell about the sheer pain and discomfort suffered with shin splints. Now I'm getting a dose of what it's all about. So the pull up Stone, up Pine and Iron mountains, and the climb up to High Point have proven particularly arduous and difficult today, most-near agonizing.

I have estimated the remaining distance to Trimpi Shelter perfectly: 1,000 yards. Approaching camp, I like to find a couple of nice solid old blowdown limbs to drag along, because it's certain there won't be anything worth trying to burn anywhere nearby. But I don't like dragging and lugging these lifeless bodies any farther than I have to. One thousand yards—that's the outside limit. Trimpi shelter has a fireplace, yes, a fireplace! This is a grand affair. I remembered this fine arrangement from my last journey through, so I've lugged a good load of firewood along this evening. In moments I have a delightful, warming fire going. What a most pleasant and cozy little den. As the shadows lengthen, the gentle light from the crackling fire casts its warm glow full within the little shelter. Soon comes family . . . *Redneck Rye, Weatherman* and *Boyscout, Buddha Boy,* and *Dutchie.* Oh, this is grand! *Redneck Rye* will be seeing his folks tomorrow afternoon at Mt. Rogers National Recreation Area Headquarters. He's apparently given them ample instruction, for they will be bringing coolers chock full of food and refreshments, and guess what? We're all invited! Looks like a fine day shaping up. Hope I can hobble fast enough to get there.

> *"Nature never did betray the heart that loved her."*
> [Wordsworth, *Tintern Abbey*]

SATURDAY May 30, 1998
TRAIL DAY 134/40 ✦ TRAIL MILE 1,919/517
LOCATION Mt. Rogers National Recreation Area Headquarters,
Partnership Shelter

I MANAGE ONLY 11 VERY DIFFICULT, PAINFUL MILES TODAY. The downhills are excruciating. I have had to set a slow and most deliberate pace. Everyone passes me. But I make it in time to share in the grand "tailgate party." Good food, great folks. Thanks, *Redneck Rye*!

Partnership Shelter, what a place! I must tell you about Partnership Shelter, for this dwelling is an architectural work of art, pure and simple. It's all whiz-bang brand new, constructed from milled logs. It's a two-story affair with spacious sleeping quarters below and a full loft with windows above. The shelter is reached by terraced steps, no less, with mulched landscaping and walkways all around. There's a fire pit and a dandy new picnic table. Behind the shelter and on the rear wall is a laundry tub with piped-in hot and cold running water, and here's the kicker . . . this is going to be hard to believe, but it's a fact: built-in and integral to the shelter is a spacious shower stall, complete with hot water, paved floor, and benches! And it can't be 150 yards by a level gravel path to Mt. Rogers NRA Headquarters, here to find flush toilets—his and hers with sinks and mirrors, along with telephone, pop machine, and snacks! Remember what *Nessmuk* said? "I go to the woods to smooth it, not to rough it . . ." Tell me if this isn't about as smooth as it gets! Members of the family here tonight to help celebrate the up-and-running, fully operational new shelter and to join in the unofficial dedication are *Turtle, Pirate, Red Wolf,* Nathan, *Teaberry* and *Double Cup,* Kevin, *Jingle, Hootie,* and *Desperado.*

We share a fun-filled and exciting evening. Pizza is ordered up from the pay phone and delivered right to our table, along with jugs of pop. My tummy is full and I am with great friends. I've doubled up on my coated aspirin and the leg pain is easing off. I'm going to sleep just fine.

"For all the happiness mankind can gain
Is not in pleasure, but in rest from pain.
[Dryden]

MOTHER NATURE HAS ROLLED OUT HER RED CARPET for me today . . . literally. I am going to suppress my pain and concentrate on this glorious gift, for it will become the ultimate gift to treasure forever, the reward for my unrelenting and unflagging faithfulness. For is there now such a bountiful offering being placed before me and heaped upon me. All along this morning is the treadway fit for the finest formal bridal procession, more splendid even, if that is possible, than that path previously trod, that having been festooned with the dainty and most feminine of Mother Nature's own, her spring beauties. That well may have been the first amorous advance of Fair Maiden Spring, a most-loving gesture perhaps, of her affection for me. And did I not blunder straight through, with only the least and most pitiful acknowledgment?

How cold, and in what uncaring fashion did I spurn her presence and gentle advance. The path before me now is unquestionably set for our grand union, for it is adorned with a carpet of scarlet Catawba rhododendron petals placed with such care and in such fashion as if the only task of countless angel fairies . . . and the old *Nomad* is here again, totally enamored and infatuated, in the presence of Fair Maiden Spring. I have been her most faithful suitor, courting her from the moment she first set foot on the pathway with me far to the south and many, many months ago. I have been her constant companion, and she, mine. We have had such a grand courtship, and here today will she accept and take my hand as her most faithful and adoring follower. With Father Time attending as the Lord's minister, and in the presence of all Mother Nature's own is this communion and ceremony held. Indeed do we now dwell most-near the House of the Lord.

Also to remain in my memory today, two numerous man-made structures—fence stiles and bog puncheons. I even pass one stile where no fence is seen for miles! As for the puncheons, these are boards, split trees, or ties placed in low areas to aid passage and reduce erosion.

There are many puncheons today, with the grand old venerable railroad crosstie working remarkably well.

I dearly want to get into Burkes Garden, so I hike the last mile in the dark to reach Knot Maul Branch Shelter—25 miles for the day. Remarkably, my knee and shin seem no worse. The day's hike, however, is slow—long and deliberate. I arrive at Knot Maul to find Kevin, and we enjoy a most pleasant evening together. As I make my place to rest, the rain begins anew, soon sending me away into the most deep and contented sleep.

"See! The mountains kiss high heaven,
And the waves clasp one another;
No sister flower would be forgiven
If it disdained its brother;
And the sunlight clasps the earth,
And the moonbeams kiss the sea:—
What are all these kissings worth,
If thou kiss not me?"

[Shelley]

MONDAY June 1, 1998
TRAIL DAY 136/42 ✦ TRAIL MILE 1,960/558
LOCATION VA 623, Home of Alex and Carol Chamberlain,
Burkes Garden

KEVIN FIXES COFFEE FOR BOTH OF US, then he's out and gone. The sky is dark and overcast, but the rain has ceased sometime during the night. I'm stiff but moving and manage to get on my way. After two long four-Snickers pulls yesterday, over Little Brushy and then up Big Walker Mountain, today should be relatively easy. The clouds and haze have burned away as I enter the open fields along Chestnut Ridge. Here opens a long, gradually sloping, high bluegrass meadow. A short way along I come to an oasis-like spring-fed pond built in a small cut beside the meadow. Sour-apple trees bear witness to an old homestead long since gone and forgotten.

Chestnut Knob Shelter is an improved old rock building with four sides, a paved floor, snug door, and tight, weatherproof windows. This old building was once most likely a homestead or bunkhouse for high-meadow laborers. It now sports a new roof, and the fireplace has been blocked off. The renovation is fine work—but somehow I much preferred the way it was 15 years ago. The fireplace was functional then, and the mantel looked like it belonged; the low shed-of-a-roof made it seem much more inviting. The old outbuildings and machinery have long since been removed, but remaining as testimony, a hint to the long-ago use of this high-meadow stead, is an old rusty six-volt-generator housing, still being put to use as a door-closing weight.

To the side of the cabin, at the edge of the meadow, I can peer down into Burkes Garden for the first time. Standing here taking in the view of this lush high valley I am reminded of similar views from the ridgetops overlooking the beautiful Shenandoah and from above the rich Amish farmlands of Pennsylvania. Looking across Burkes Garden, walled in by mountains all around, it becomes evident that it has been aptly named, "God's Thumbprint."

As I enter Walker Gap and ascend Garden Mountain I am literally walking on the edge of the bowl—the upper rim of Burkes Garden. Overlooks are few, but the rocky overhangs and jutting ledges up which one may scamper offer breathtaking panoramas into the patchwork of farms below. Behind me stands Big Walker Mountain, a seemingly endless ridge merging with the far-off haze, unbroken in both directions.

As I near the high rocks, there is another splendid overlook just above VA 623, the "back door" to the Garden. As I approach the precipice I hear voices. Here I meet four young men, one a direct descendent of the original settlers in this area. They have come up from their homes near Marion to enjoy this perfect afternoon atop Garden Mountain. I linger to enjoy their company as the sun begins casting shadows behind the ridge. Fitch, one of the young fellows, then offers me a ride down and into Burkes Garden, directly by the Chamberlains' front door!

From a recent telephone conversation with Alex Chamberlain, I know that he and his wife will not be home, having gone to visit their daughter and family for the week, but they insisted I stop for a rest just the same and make myself at home, which I promptly do! Theirs is a modest home, built probably sometime during the first half of this century. It is well kept, warm and cozy, a necessity up here at 3,500 feet. I have counted 23 windows in this delightful dwelling, each offering a slightly varied but unobstructed view of the mountains and the peaceful, pastoral valley all around. Here I will linger for healing and a much-needed rest until Wednesday.

> *"Beyond the last horizon's rim,*
> *Beyond adventure's farthest quest,*
> *Somewhere they rise, serene and dim,*
> *The happy, happy hills of rest."*

[A. B. Paine]

TUESDAY June 2, 1998
TRAIL DAY 137/43 ✦ TRAIL MILE 1,960/558
LOCATION VA 623, Home of Alex and Carol Chamberlain,
Burkes Garden

REST COMES EASY IN A RESTFUL PLACE! I took a luxurious hot bath last evening, prepared a warm supper on a kitchen range, and enjoyed ice-cold orange juice from the refrigerator.

I'll spend the day catching up on my journal entries as I sit on the sun porch at Alex and Carol's, with the windows open and the gentle, cool breeze that brings to me the fresh clean scent of newly mown bluegrass. Looking out the sun porch windows, I watch Black Angus quietly grazing, their dark frames in bold contrast to the bright sheen of the bluegrass pasture—and beyond, set against the mountain up the meadow a ways, the old log homestead . . .

> *Leaning, yet to time defiant,*
> *Seems it never had a care.*
> *Carols cabin up the meadow,*
> *Like a loved one standing there.*
> *Oh, what glad and joyful memories,*

Pray it speak to me this day.
Those to whom it offered shelter,
Since to pass and go their way.
Likened mist cast o'er the Garden,
Soon now lifted by the sun;
There are those who'll come to linger,
Passing by here one-by-one.
Bringing memories cherished, ever;
To return unto her care.
Carols cabin up the meadow,
Like a loved one standing there.

[N. Nomad]

WEDNESDAY June 3, 1998
TRAIL DAY 138/44 ✦ TRAIL MILE 1,963/561
LOCATION Jenkins Shelter

LAST NIGHT WAS A MOST RESTFUL NIGHT at the Chamberlain home. I've eaten about everything in their refrigerator and cupboard, ditto for the refrigerator downstairs! I've spent the morning and half the afternoon trying to get out and back up the mountain. Washed and dried clothes and packed up my sleeping bag for Alex and Carol to send back home for me. My bounce box awaited my arrival, and I now take out a week's supply of vitamins/meds and close it back up to bounce along to my next mail drop in Daleville. I've also borrowed a blanket and towel from Carol to take with me—they said "make yourself at home," and have I ever!

The weather has been looking real troublesome this afternoon, and sure enough, just as I'm preparing to head back out, the wind comes strong, the sky "darks over," and the thunder, lightning, and hard rain come stampeding across the garden. I drop my pack and sit back patiently to wait it out. As I relax again on the sun porch I see one of the most incredible acts of nature that I've witnessed, ever! Lightning has been mostly cloud-to-cloud, but as chance would have it, I am looking out the side window, and just at this instant a blinding bolt of lightning strikes the ground in the pasture not more than 100 feet away. The brilliance of it seems to last forever and the report, which sounds like a thousand shotgun blasts, comes right along with it. The ozone is so heavy I can nearly cut it. My heart is up in my throat and the hair on my arms is standing straight up! Even with the pounding rain, dark, gray-black smoke swirls and drifts from the strike site for minutes. If this storm is looking for some attention, it sure has mine.

The torrent soon passes, clearing out across the garden almost as quickly as it came, and I am able to head back up the mountain before evening. I dearly regret that the timing has been such that I've missed seeing my good friends of many years.

> *"Friendships that have stood the test —*
> *Time and change — are surely best;*
> *Brow may wrinkle, hair grow gray,*
> *Friendship never knows decay."*

[Joseph Parry]

THURSDAY June 4, 1998
TRAIL DAY 139/45 ✦ TRAIL MILE 1,978/576
LOCATION Helveys Mill Shelter

THE DAY-AND-A-HALF REST AT THE CHAMBERLAINS' has done little if anything to alleviate the knee and shin splint discomfort that seems no worse but is no better, and to make matters worse I manage to take a hard, jolting header at the third-to-last crossing at Little Wolf Creek. At each of the crossings, large rocks have been placed to provide stepping stones, the creek being somewhat deep and of fair width. I have been hiking in hard rain on and off today, and the rocks are wet and slippery. While jumping from one to the next, I slip, and down I go headfirst into the cold creek, pack and all. It happens so fast that I'm barely able to get my hands out to prevent a total face-plant, but I still manage to whack my head and chin pretty hard. As I pull myself up, my body and pack totally soaked, I feel a sharp, hot pain in my right side. My left hand also feels funny. Holding it up, palm facing me and staring at it in disbelief, do I see my thumb facing west, index, second and ring finger are facing north . . . but my little finger is facing east! Comes now a gut-wrenching feeling, knowing full well what I must do and knowing best not to ponder long. Closing my eyes and gritting my teeth, I grip the finger with my right hand, giving it a mighty, arching jerk! A loud "pop" ensues, and as I glimpse with one eye I see the finger properly set back in its joint. Oh, thank you, Lord!

I drag myself from the creek and dry off as best I can with my wet towel. I manage to splint-tape my little finger to my ring finger, not an easy task with my wedding band in the way, but I'm not about to remove the ring, it having been right there since 1959. Assessing the damage, I conclude I've taken on both a sore chin and noggin, a banged-up knee (the same one that's already sore), a dislocated finger, and probably three or four cracked ribs. Ho boy! It's time to "suck it up" and prepare myself for some difficult days.

Mine is a deep, inner contentment, a constant feeling and reinforcement that the Lord will lead me on a path toward timely completion of this odyssey—but I know and have just been informed again by a calm, gentle inner voice that I must be prepared to meet adversity. How I wind this path now that I am facing and must deal with adversity will test my faith and provide deeper meaning and understanding of what life has taught over these many years.

> *From the constant grind of this old AT,*
> *Comes the grist to try a man's soul.*
> *But from the Lord's mill*
> *Grind the strength and the will,*
> *To carry me on to my goal.*
>
> [N. Nomad]

FRIDAY June 5, 1998
TRAIL DAY 140/46 ✦ TRAIL MILE 1,994/592
LOCATION VA 606, Trent Store and Campground

THIS IS A TOUGH, PAINFUL, 16-MILE DAY, COLD AND RAINY. The mind is compelling a body rebelling! My knee and ribs are very troublesome. I'm having much difficulty breathing, what with the cracked ribs, but then again, I'm not moving all that fast so I don't have to breathe too hard. We all know what pain is, so I'll keep this short. Trent Store is a neat place. Fine pizza. I move over to their campground for a hot shower, picnic tables, and clover under my tent.

> *"Five hundred miles behind us lie,*
> *As many more ahead,*
> *Through mud and mire on mountain high,*
> *Our weary feet must tread."*

[Hamlin Garland, *Line Up, Brave Boys*]

SATURDAY June 6, 1998
TRAIL DAY 141/47 ✦ TRAIL MILE 2,007/605
LOCATION Sugar Run Gap, Sugar Run Road, Woodshole Hostel

ANOTHER TOUGH, "GRIND-IT-OUT" DAY. The mountain laurel is now in almost full bloom, trying to cheer me along. I am very glad to get down the gravel road to Tillies!

PROFILES '98

Tulie *Tulie* Kaschub is 25, single, and lives in Maine. To further her education, she plans to attend Colorado State University in Fort Collins, Colorado, where she intends to study English and creative writing. "Writing, especially writing children's books, would be a great career," says *Tulie*.

"I hiked a lot with my family in Maine when I was little. There were a lot of trails close by my home. I remember seeing the white blazes of the Appalachian Trail and the people hiking by . . . looking and smelling the way I do now! That intrigued me 15 years ago. It left quite an impression on me, so here I am!"

Tulie's hiking companion is a shepherd/lab named Tenaya. Tenaya was the last Indian Chief of the Yosemite Valley. They hope to reach Katahdin the first or second week in October.

> *"Who can tell, when he sets forth to wander, whither he*
> *may be driven by the uncertain currents of existence; or*
> *when he may return; or whether it may ever be his lot to*
> *revisit the scenes of his childhood?*
>
> [Washington Irving, *The Voyage*]

SUNDAY June 7, 1998
TRAIL DAY 142/48 ✦ TRAIL MILE 2,022/620
LOCATION Spring and Campsite north of VA 641

MOST OF THE FOLKS I'VE BEEN HIKING WITH have elected to go into Pearisburg today. I remember from my last trip through here that much time was spent walking to get around Pearisburg. There are great folks in this trail town, and the Holy Family Hospice is a grand place indeed, but with the way I've been hobbling and the pitiful mileage I've been working and hammering to grind out—going with them is really not an option. I've got to stay to the task and keep heading north.

I do manage to treat myself though, as I stop at Wades Market just off the trail for fried chicken, ice cream, and some provisions. I've heard there may not be water at Rice Creek Shelter, or for the next stretch into Pine Swamp Branch Shelter, so I pull up at the trailside spring/campsite just up the ridge and call it a day. I manage to get a good cooking and warming fire going and am glad for the success of this day. I am finding no relief from the painful knee/rib condition, but I have managed to stay of good cheer.

An earthbound mystery . . .
The strangest thing;
Backpack up, the closer we
To sprouting wing.

[N. Nomad]

MONDAY June 8, 1998
TRAIL DAY 143/49 ✦ TRAIL MILE 2,037/635
LOCATION Pine Swamp Branch Shelter

THE DAY IS BRIGHT AND SUNNY WITH GREAT VIEWS from Symms Gap Meadow, a great hiking day. I am trying to keep a good attitude, but alas, lots of rocks and rough treadway late in the day leave me pain-wracked, wobbly, and exhausted. I am ready to reach the shelter and log this day's entry.

The Pine Swamp Branch Shelter is a "Trimpi" design with an internal fireplace built into the rear rock wall. I really like this layout with the internal fireplace. I get a good cooking and heating fire going but spend little time before rolling in. I am having difficulty finding a comfortable sleeping position because of the rib discomfort.

PROFILES '98

MELISSA MAE *Selky* Sumpter, age 22, is from Hemet, California. She is a graduate of Hemet High and is currently a student at the University of California at Santa Cruz. Her major is community studies with a focus on children's outdoor education.

Selky is interested in crafts, especially sewing, quilting, beading, and weaving. Her passion is the great out-of-doors. She especially enjoys swimming, running, bird watching, sailing, rock climbing and, above all, hiking and backpacking.

Selky was drawn to the AT through reading about this grand old trail, especially the writings of the Watermans and their book *Backwoods Ethics*. "From reading this book, the AT experience sounded like something I would enjoy. I didn't know anything about the East Coast but I had the time and the 59 bucks for a Greyhound ticket, so why not? I saw this opportunity as a great way to spend time outdoors learning about the mountains and the trail. Once I was on the trail I became part of the AT family, and that has made it easy to continue on. The love and friendship I am experiencing is amazing."

We'll all remember *Selky* as the cute kid in cat-eye glasses with that bright, shiny-faced smile. Says *Selky*, "I'm the blonde-dreaded girl hiking in a skirt, but otherwise I'm looking and feeling just like everyone else—dirty, stinky, tired, and wet!"

Selky, it is a joy knowing you and calling you friend. The hiking shorts you crafted for me are working just great! I know you'll be standing on Katahdin come fall. It would be great to be there with you.

> *"People and creatures and worrisome miles,*
> *Storm camps and pinnacles . . . How will it end?*
> *Somehow the joys seem to balance the trials,*
> *Found in the future around the next bend."*

[Earl Shaffer]

TUESDAY June 9, 1998
TRAIL DAY 144/50 ✦ TRAIL MILE 2,049/647
LOCATION War Spur Shelter

I'M FACED WITH LOTS OF ROCKS AND LOTS OF RAIN and a tough, hard, four-Snickers pull up over Wind Rock. The knee is stable—no change in the constant pain level, but the downhills are really difficult and trying with the shin splints. I hate to admit, but I must admit, as many of my friends on the trail have admitted . . . the Virginia blues are here:

> *The Ginny blues they git ya,*
> *Make ye grumble, make ye groan.*
> *But life be much more toler'ble,*
> *To find yer not alone.*

[N. Nomad]

WEDNESDAY June 10, 1998
TRAIL DAY 145/51 ✦ TRAIL MILE 2,068/666
LOCATION Niday Shelter

I MUST DEAL WITH A NUMBER OF THREE-AND-A-HALF-SNICKERS pulls today, ups and downs. I manage much better than anticipated. The pink and white of the mountain laurel is a delight to behold. It seems there's always something exciting along the trail, something to attract my attention, pique my interest. Pulling into the shelter for the evening I meet a southbounder, *Sister Smiles*, and her dog, Sky. She's from Orlando, Florida. *Sister Smiles* hiked from Baxter Peak to Waynesboro last year, and she's back on the trail this year to complete her hike from Rockfish Gap to Springer Mountain. Turns out she's a part-time employee at the outfitters in Altamonte Springs where I purchased most of my gear at the beginning of this journey—small world for sure! *Sister Smiles* says, "Say 'hi' to Mark and all at Travel Country Outdoors!"

I've been hiking the past few days with a very nice young man from Albuquerque, New Mexico, Greg Barnes. I've stuck him with the trail name *Dusty*. I don't know why, but the name just seems to fit. I'll bet it's dusty around Albuquerque! I know barns are dusty. I usually get out a little ahead of him but limping along as I've been, he soon catches me. I know he's kind of keeping an eye on me to see how I'm getting along, and he lets me know where he's headed in the evening. His cheerful company has uplifted me, a real delight!

"To the edge of the wood I am drawn, I am drawn."

[Sidney Lanier]

THURSDAY June 11, 1998
TRAIL DAY 146/52 ✦ TRAIL MILE 2,083/681
LOCATION Backyard of Catawba Valley General Store, VA 624

A LITTLE PATIENCE, AND IN ONLY A LITTLE WHILE, I am blessed again with a very enjoyable hiking day, much less pain, much less strain. The trail soon leads up Brushy Mountain to the Audie Leon Murphy

Memorial, a very simple but most dignified granite stone piece on the highest point of the mountain. How befitting a location to honor the combat soldier who fought repeatedly and so fiercely, successfully capturing and securing the high ground time and again. Audie is a true American hero . . . my kind of hero, for this man was America's most decorated World War II veteran. He received every decoration for valor this country had to offer—24 decorations, including the Medal of Honor, Legion of Merit, Distinguished Service Cross, and three Purple Hearts. A poll was taken recently wherein one of the questions asked was, "What does Memorial Day mean to you?" Sadly, many answered with "It means I don't have to go to work."

The AT no longer passes Dragons Tooth to continue down the mountain spur, but Dragons Tooth is reached now by a blue-blazed trail, with the AT bailing off the side of the mountain through precipitous rocks. Fearing I would be tempted, as I was 15 years ago, to climb out to the very point of the inclining precipice that is Dragons Tooth, thus scaring the wits out of myself, I continued down the AT. Dragons Tooth can now be seen from the trail below, presenting a most impressive angle of view up and into space.

Coming down off Rawies Rest I'm calculating how much time it's going to take me to get from VA 624 to VA 311. I want to be there in time to hitch the mile into Catawba, Virginia, to go for the AYCE special (BBQ pork) at the Home Place. Hiking along in a daze and as I approach VA 624, lo and behold, here's a blue cooler setting right in the middle of the trail! Peering in, I find a trove of treasures the likes of which might adorn the finest treasure chest—pop, water, sandwiches, and a large Tupperware container full of the tastiest brownies I've ever sunk my teeth into. All under ice! I'm thinking to myself, as I help myself, "Now here's no ordinary trail angel." Turns out it's the doings of *Southpaw*, GAHF (Georgia to Harpers Ferry hike) '95. Inscribed on the cooler lid is "If you started in Georgia at Springer Mountain you have hiked 681 miles. Take a load off and enjoy some trail magic! Get your fill, good luck, and thanks for letting me be part of your journey. Jeff Williams."

While sitting on the cooler having my second pop and second brownie—oh yes, Hiker Trash sure don't pass this stuff up—I hear a car door slam below and up the trail comes *Southpaw* himself. Seems he not only lugs this cooler up here each day, chock-full of all kinds of delightful treats, but he returns to check and keep it filled during the day (good thing). He not only offers me a ride to Home Place but suggests letting him introduce me to the Sauls, for I will probably be offered a spot to pitch my tent in their backyard right behind the General Store . . . which he points out is right across the street from the restaurant. The offer also includes picking me back up in the morning and delivering me right back here to VA 624. Now here's a man who knows how to make an offer that can't be refused! I've seen some trail angels, and have been the beneficiary of some mighty fine trail magic these past 146 days, but *Southpaw* is strictly pro.

At Catawba Valley General Store, Southpaw introduces me to Marie and Billie Saul, who immediately and most graciously offer me free tent space on their lush lawn. Glancing over to *Southpaw* I get that one-brow-up "what did I tell you" nod! At the Home Place Restaurant I have supper with *Dusty, Fletch,* and *Jak.* The Sauls are kind, hospitable folks, their accommodations most grand. Thanks, friends, and thanks, *Southpaw*! I am so stuffed I can hardly move. I roll in for a very enjoyable night in the clover behind the general store.

> *"With mountains of green all around me*
> *And mountains of white up above*
> *And mountains of blue down the skyline,*
> *I follow the trail that I love."*

[Charles Badger Clark]

FRIDAY June 12, 1998
TRAIL DAY 147/53 ✦ TRAIL MILE 2,100/698
LOCATION Lamberts Meadow Shelter

THE MORNING STARTS OUT "IFFY" BUT CLEARS nicely for a slow but enjoyable hike to McAfee Knob. This section of trail is heavily traveled and all the soil and duff have long since disappeared, leaving a continuous trail of rocks. The knob offers a breathtaking view down into the valley. This overlook is one of the most photographed spots on the entire Appalachian Trail, for here projects a cliff-hung precipice, shaped much like the head of an eagle, jutting into space. From a side vantage and standing on top of the eagle's beak, it is possible to have your picture taken with sky most-near all around you . . . even beneath you! I have this remarkable overlook all to myself.

I don't know why the Tinker Cliffs area is not more popular. Perhaps the difficulty in getting up here is a factor, but in my book, the cliffs are much more impressive than the knob, what with the trail literally tracking the very edge of the cliffs for the better part of half a mile. Picture this if you will and you'll see what I mean—here to my right as I head north the trail is populated with beautiful blooming mountain laurel, crowding the treadway toward the precipice, and on my left, only occasional winged population as the trail edge drops uninterrupted for hundreds of feet. Here is not the place to be daydreaming!

I am tired, my energy spent, but at the same time this has been a day well spent. I have little problem getting a fine cooking and warming fire going at Lamberts Meadow Shelter.

> *"Without weariness there can be no real appreciation of rest, without the ancient responses to the harsh simplicities of the kind of environment that shaped mankind, a man cannot know the urges within him."*
>
> [Sigurd Olson]

SATURDAY June 13, 1998
TRAIL DAY 148/54 ✦ TRAIL MILE 2,109/707
LOCATION US 220, Daleville, Best Western Coachman Inn

I'M UP AND OUT EARLY AHEAD OF *Dusty*. He gives me a head-start every morning so he can check on me as he comes by. He soon catches and passes me on his way to Daleville. I also meet and hike some with Bud and Vicky Hogan, section hikers who are heading north. The morning is very fine with great views from both sides of the ridgeline. Down below I see a high dam and reservoir on one side and the lush, fertile valley on the other. I arrive at the Best Western before 1:00 p.m., and *Dusty* and I head straight for Pizza Hut!

PROFILES '98

D AN *U-Turn* Glenn is a single 24-year-old from Osierfield, Georgia. He attended Irwin County High School in Ocilla, Georgia, and is a graduate of the University of Georgia, with degrees in English and journalism. His plans—after his AT thru-hike—are to pursue a career in writing, especially about rural living and sustained agriculture.

Dan's hobbies include photography, photo developing, reading, and playing Ultimate Frisbee.

Dan says, "I'm hiking the AT as a spiritual, a mental, and a physical challenge, as a process of moving from childhood to adulthood—a right-of-passage to develop the characteristics and qualities I may use to shape the rest of my life."

Dan is planning to move back to Athens, Georgia, and work as a bartender/chef at one of the finer restaurants while doing some writing for one of the local alternative publications, and hopefully, some successful freelance work for a magazine or two.

"My goal is to pursue my bliss while developing and nurturing a moral foundation which brings happiness to my life and the lives of others with whom I interact. I wish to envision and create a living community that is self-sustaining and harmonious with the natural order of life, focused upon growth and the ability to adapt to an ever-changing planet. I believe that improved family relations and more enlightened educational standards can empower humanity to overcome the forces that threaten our welfare and very existence: greed, fear, and narrow-mindedness."

I simply cannot pass on this. I've got to tell you how Dan came by his trail name. Here's how the whole funny thing came about . . . It seems Dan departed Cross-Trails parking lot near Springer Mountain and from his very first step he was headed the wrong way. He took off north following the white AT blazes instead of south to Springer, where the AT begins. Somewhere, perhaps after the second mile or so, he apparently realized that something wasn't quite right and he got to thinking about how he was supposed to be climbing Springer Mountain. But he kept on going anyway until it finally dawned on him that he was going downhill, and that he had been going downhill for a long time! Realizing his plight, he was presented with two choices. One, to hike the entire trail to Mt. Katahdin in Maine, a distance of some 2,150 miles, having missed the first three-quarters of a mile, or make a U-turn and go back! Well, I guess from his trail handle you can figure what he did! Way to go, *U-Turn*! Aww, but what a great kid!

He's way out ahead of most of us in dealing with all that life dishes out, for Dan has no problem seeing the humor in this and having a good laugh on himself about it. Dan, it's surely a blast knowing you and hiking with you, my good friend!

> *"Walking the entire Appalachian Trail is not recreation. It is an education and a job . . . [It] is not 'going on a hike.' It is a challenging task—a journey with deeper ramifications."*
>
> [Warren Doyle, Jr.]

SUNDAY June 14, 1998
TRAIL DAY 149/55   ✦   TRAIL MILE 2,109/707
LOCATION US 220, Daleville, Best Western Coachman Inn

LAST NIGHT *Dusty* AND I SPLIT A ROOM WITH *Skitz* and *Quest* (Nathan) making our stay at this fine motel very economical. *Skitz* is up and out about 8:00. *Dusty* and *Quest* decide to rest another day. Oh yes, me too! I'm able to catch up on journal entries and make a number of phone calls. In the evening, *Dusty, Quest, Flint, Birch, Joliet Joe,* and I head for the AYCE multi-bar right across the street at Western Sizzlin. It's *Dusty*'s 26th birthday and time to celebrate.

PROFILES '98

Joseph Eugene *Joliet Joe* Nemensky is a single 32-year-old from Romeoville, Illinois, near Joliet. *JJ*, as I call him, is a graduate of

Romeoville High School and Western and Eastern Illinois universities with degrees in computational mathematics and mathematics with teacher certification. He is currently employed as a systems administrator with Electronic Data Service (EDS).

His interests include archaeology, paleontology, anthropology, physics, flying (has his license), music (guitar and drums), reading, medicine (homeopathic, naturopathic), computers (fractal designs), the science of recycling, bike riding, and hiking . . . Whew!

Joe says we'll probably remember him as just being there . . . the "average Joe." But that is not how I will remember him. He's a great conversationalist, knowledgeable in a remarkably diverse array of subjects and topics. Joe has fun being with people and is fun to be with.

Joe says, "One interest that brought me here is to learn to be more self-sufficient. I have a need to rely less on other people and more on my own abilities. So I wanted to come out here and find out what I have inside me—to be in tune with my body—and for the peace of mind that comes when mind and body are in sync."

Future plans include bicycling across the United States, sailing down to Australia, going on a dig with the Smithsonian, volunteering for Peace Corps work, and building his own home. The biggest future plan is to retire, and at only 32 he's now into the seventh year of a ten-year plan!

"I want to live life, experience it, and have fun. I tried to listen to my dad when I wasn't being too stubborn. I've tried to work smarter, not harder. I hope the future holds great things for me because I have high expectations."

> *"But just buckle in with a bit of a grin,*
> *Just take off your coat and go to it;*
> *Just start to sing as you tackle the thing*
> *That cannot be done, and you'll do it."*

[Edgar A. Guest]

I ENDED UP IN A ROOM-SPLIT AGAIN LAST NIGHT WITH *Dusty, Quest,* and *Joliet Joe.* Another day of R&R was such a luxury! The breakfast this morning at Coachman Inn is a real fine spread. Motel continental breakfast deals usually consist of little more than a dried-up donut or Danish and a pot of warm coffee in the lobby, but not here at Coachman Inn. These folks have a room with tables and a fine, help-yourself break- fast consisting of hot coffee, tea, milk, orange and apple juice, and a vari- ety of cereals, fresh fruit, and just about everything that can possibly fit into a toaster or microwave—filled me up, and that's saying something!

Around noon our good hiking friend *T-Bone Walker* comes by sporting his wheels to pick us up. He lives nearby in Roanoke and has also taken a couple of days off. *Joliet Joe, Flint, Birch,* and I pile in and we head to the post office and then to Super Wal-Mart, where *Joliet Joe* buys a Walkman and I pick up another mini-recorder to replace the one I dunked one too many times.

We finally get back on the trail about 4:30 p.m. after picking up a few provisions. *Joliet Joe* and I manage to make it to the great Fullhardt Knob Shelter. This shelter is right on top of the ridge . . . and there really is water from a spigot behind the shelter! Here is a neat cistern setup with water diverted from the shelter roof via a slick gutter/downspout system!

> *"The tops of the mountains are among the unfinished parts of the globe. Wither, it is a slight insult to the Gods to climb and pry into their secrets and try their effect on our humanity."*
>
> [Henry David Thoreau]

TUESDAY June 16, 1998
TRAIL DAY 151/57   ✦   TRAIL MILE 2,127/725
LOCATION Bobblets Gap Shelter

A COUPLE OF DAYS OFF SHOULD HAVE HELPED MY KNEE and shin splints, but I found a tough time of it yesterday, for the short pull up to Fullhardt Knob has left my knee and ankle stiff, swollen, and sore. I hope to make the 13 miles into Bobblets Gap Shelter. I'll be happy with that. *Joliet Joe* and I are late getting out and before we get going *Roo* arrives from Coachman Inn. *Rx,* his hiking partner, has gotten off the trail, but *Roo* is continuing on.

Today we meet the Blue Ridge Parkway and for the next 100 miles into Rockfish Gap the trail crosses the parkway many times, sharing the same ridgeline as we go. At the Montvale Overlook we see *Roo* again. Here he also decides to get off the trail. Flagging a passing motorist, he loads his pack in the trunk and is gone!

I manage to make the three-plus-Snickers pulls up Taylors Mountain and Harveys Knob without too much difficulty, but the downhills are a dear lesson in pain tolerance. Toward evening my knee seems to settle down and I make it into Bobblets Gap Shelter okay. I meet *Wolfhound* here and spend an enjoyable evening with him and *Joliet Joe.*

> *"The silence of the forest, the peace of the early morning wind moving through the branches of the trees, the solitude and isolation of the house of God: These are good because it is in silence, and not in commotion, in solitude, and not in crowds, that God best likes to reveal himself intimately to man."*
>
> [Thomas Merton]

I HAVE BEEN LOOKING FORWARD WITH CHILDISH ANTICIPATION for days to standing again at the Peaks of Otter overlook, because I truly believe this vantage to be one of the most magnificent anywhere. These majestic peaks are commanding indeed, with two of the most prominent being formed from Sharptop and Flattop mountains. They give such a remarkably glad and exciting impression of extending—as if reaching upward all the while one continues to gaze—toward a sky that presents to be so heavenly blue, even more so than any such scene in my memory. This morning is there before me pure ether, not a cloud, not a wisp of mist or haze, thus it seems are these peaks draw nigh unto me. The little sign before me here however tells me their grand and striking presence is more than 6 miles distant. No one knows for certain how this mystic storyland came by its name. Perhaps it's from the Cherokee word *ottari*, meaning "high places." Early settlers might have named the peaks after Scotland's Ben Otter Mountain, which resembles Sharptop. And then again the name may have derived from the abundance of otter that inhabited the nearby rivers and streams long ago. Ah, but indeed, it is all the better for the mystery of it!

It is in times of perfect stillness and calm, as is the ethereal-like vastness before me this morning, that far-off sounds can sometimes be ever-so-faintly heard—melodic sounds, neither cheerful nor sad, but more pensively melancholy, sounds that call from afar, not only in distance but seemingly also from back in time, as if from some other day long past, stirring the fire, the wanderlust deep within, to the core of one's very soul. For a brief, fleeting moment this morning I hear the Pipes, drifting on the still silence across the vast expanse and o'er the distant peaks. The voyagers of the Far North heard these mysterious and beckoning sounds over a century ago. Sounds likened to the "Pipes of Pan," spoken about with near reverence by Sigurd Olson in his delightful books *Wilderness Days* and *Open Horizons*. The old men of the great north woods surely heard these sounds and were attuned to their far-off call. To read of this mystery provokes such grand imaginings, thoughts that leave one in pure puzzlement and disbelief. "That night I thought I heard them too . . . Wilderness music? Imagination? I may never know . . . but for a moment the Pipes had sounded . . . and a sense of the old fantasy of long ago was mine. While I stood there I was one with all adventurers, all explorers, and those who had ever looked into the unknown, part of a forgotten world of glory and romance, where things cannot be seen unless there is belief." Could the Pipes be no more than the wind in the hardwood and the pine, or the joyful tunes echoed and reverberated across the distant stillness from the waterfalls and cascading brooks? Who's to say? Perhaps down through the ages we've all just been hearing things . . . but then again, perhaps not.

I enjoy a most pleasant evening at the spacious, three-decker Bryant Ridge Shelter. Trail angel *Jackleg* brings in a two-gallon container of chocolate trail magic! I am ashamed to report that those of us here this evening, all members of that grand Hiker Trash Fratority, are guilty of casting disrepute and total disgrace upon our grand name. For, though each of us tries, using all talent, all training, all diligence . . . in the end, *Jackleg* is left to tote a fair portion of that delightful cream-for-the-Gods back out! The knee is definitely improving, but the shin splints are incredibly painful.

Far o'er the Peaks of Otter,
Across the Meadows of Dan.
Hark! From afar they beckon . . .
The mysterious Pipes of Pan.

[N. Nomad]

THURSDAY June 18, 1998
TRAIL DAY 153/59 ✦ TRAIL MILE 2,162/760
LOCATION Matts Creek Shelter

THE DAY STARTS RIGHT OUT WITH A FOUR-SNICKERS pull up Floyd followed by a dandy full five Snickers up Apple Orchard Mountain.

I manage to survive the "guillotine", two close vertical rock walls with a large boulder lodged near the top. The trail goes right under the boulder, which is wedged precariously above, the whole natural phenomenon resembling a guillotine. Should this thing ever come crashing down on an unwary hiker however, decapitation will certainly be the least obvious of the terminal complications. There is a noticeable briskness to my pace as I pass.

Breaking off Hickory Stand I get an immediate and spectacular view down onto the James. The impact of the abrupt change from relative darkness within the woods canopy to the blinding brightness of open space is a visual jolt. Add then, as if needed, is there emphasis from the auditory impact created by the hissing blast from an F-15 passing so tightly tucked to the mountain that I can near touch him. For that split second, and as the pilot uses the mountain terminus as a pylon, we are looking directly at each other! I have got to blink and re-shutter the frame . . . and it is then that I can see through his canopy, right into the cockpit! As I sit to regain a modicum of composure and enjoy the panorama, I'm thinking, now wasn't that an interesting occurrence, the most spectacular form of speed, and the most ancient form of travel simultaneously enjoying the same view all around and below for thousands of feet! Folks, life is never dull on the AT—maybe a little trying at times, but never dull!

Matts Creek Shelter is a great spot. The little brook has a couple of natural and invigorating pools just below the footbridge, right by the shelter. I quickly manage a fine fire, then head for the natural tub. The remainder of the evening is enjoyed most casually then in the company of *Joliet Joe, Florida Guy,* and *Wolfhound.*

> *Friendship and frolic, pain and fear,*
> *In the wilderness, footloose and free.*
> *Stir them all up and brimfill your cup,*
> *For a "trip" on the ol' AT.*

[N. Nomad]

FRIDAY June 19, 1998
TRAIL DAY 154/60   ✦   TRAIL MILE 2,176/774
LOCATION Punch Bowl Shelter

I NEED A FEW PROVISIONS AND COULD SURE USE a nourishing hot breakfast, so on crossing the James River I stick out my thumb toward Glasgow. In just a few moments and just as the rain begins, and as luck would have it, I get a ride. Tossing my pack in the back seat and moving right up front, I'm greeted by this grand smiling old gentleman. He says, "I'm John Taylor. I stopped to pick you up because I recognized you from the other day." I look with some puzzlement, and then, "Oh yes! I remember you. You were running the loppers with the trail maintenance crew near the parkway!" John lives in Boonsboro and is a member of the Natural Bridge Trail Club. They maintain about 90 miles of the AT south of the Tye River. As we head toward Glasgow, John tells me all about the damage done along and to the treadway by last February's ice storm, the blowdowns alone making the trail totally impassable. He relates with an expression of pride how it took more than 2,000 man-hours during February and March to get the trail back open.

John had been planning a short day hike and was headed that way before stopping to pick me up. The rain changes his plans, so we enjoy a relaxing breakfast together. John waits as I get a few provisions, then he drives me back to the trailhead. So it is that the first time I see John he has on his trail maintenance hat, and now today it's his trail angel hat. John, I hope you're able to get your hiking hat on soon. Thanks, friend! And thank you, all of you who labor so hard and with such commitment and dedication to keeping the trail open for all of us to use and enjoy!

Up from the James, the storm is moving across the mountain. Just as well as I'm faced right away with a solid five-Snickers pull up and over the combined Fullers Rocks, Little Rocky Row, and Big Rocky Row. These ascents are not at all unpleasant however, as my knee is much stronger now, my ribs not griping nearly as badly, and my shin splints much more tolerable. At Little Rocky Row there is another breathtaking panorama down onto the James. Here the James River is a wide, expansive river with countless rapids that create miles and miles of whitewater . . . disappearing into the haze on the horizon. The river is in constant motion, as the sun now at perfect angle reflects the pure white glistening light from the watery turmoil. But so strange the sight, for not a whisper of all this violence can be heard over this lofty precipice. I stand and gaze into the silence, at this pure majesty, at the expansive beauty and at the awesome power below.

> *Gazing in wonder down on the James,*
> *From Little Rocky Row.*
> *The manes of a million galloping steeds,*
> *Blaze white in the noonday glow.*
> *Such splendor and beauty viewed from above,*
> *From above, 'tis a gift to me.*
> *A sign of our Maker's steadfast love,*
> *Through time . . . till eternity.*

[N. Nomad]

SATURDAY June 20, 1998
TRAIL DAY 155/61 ✦ TRAIL MILE 2,193/791
LOCATION USFS 48, Hog Camp Gap Meadow Campsite

OH WHAT KIND AND BENEFICENT TRAIL ANGELS! Last night to Punch Bowl Shelter came Ed and Mary Ann Williams, bringing much food and cool refreshments for *Joliet Joe* and me to enjoy! And did they not revel and share in that pleasure with *JJ* and me!

I am faced soon today with yet another five-Snickers pull, the second in two days, up and over Bald Knob. This section of Virginia is rough, rugged country with seemingly endless near-vertical rocky tread-way. But, ruggedness makes for raw beauty at its finest, and the view out o'er these granite walls, knobs, sky-high temples, and lush green valleys below afforded me here on Bald Knob brings an abrupt halt to my forward progress. I am dizzy from the demanding ascent and now do I become more spin-headed as I turn and turn and yet turn again, trying to take it all in, and as Benton MacKaye would most assuredly say, " . . . to see what we truly see."

The meadow at Hog Camp Gap is a setting straight from a picture book! I pitch in the shade of an old sour-apple tree. And to provide such luxury as nature is often known to do all around there is a soft green carpet of clover to welcome my tired aching feet. The water source is a spring below the upper meadow a short distance via a winding path. I must tell you about this idyllic little spot, this little pocket in time where I am greeted by the most joyful voices. For here, within this hospitable little glen springs forth the happiest brook I have ever met. And from where it makes its presence flow the finest, cool-clear waters it has been my fortune to lift to my parched lips. The spring is at the verge of an intimate forest-bordered meadow, walled in a grove against the rugged mountainside and resting in the shadowed carpet of lush green grass. Here, from within this cove emerges this glad little fellow, to run, meandering, into and through the narrow meadow, skipping and jumping o'er the moss-covered pebbles and rocks that set it to murmuring in lilting, melodic tones beckoning in the most mysteriously pleasing way, much as do the Pipes. There is no landscape architect with such talent or skill, nor any sum one could possibly pay such a person might he or she exist, to create the likes of this . . . save the Divine Architect and Creator of it all!

Ed Williams had told me about this very special place last evening at Punch Bowl Shelter. And lo and behold, who comes up the meadow just before sunset? It's Ed and Mary Ann Williams with more great food and cool refreshments. Thanks again, dear friends, for your kindness and for sharing your knowledge of these majestic mountains. It's my good fortune to have met you both!

> *Up from the peaceful meadow,*
> *Here drift the Pipes of Pan.*
> *In peaceful medley mellow,*
> *Unlike the din of man.*
> *Unto me now in calm repose,*
> *They hearken days of yore.*
> *Dear family, friends and all of those,*

Who've passed to Heaven's door.
And so my prayer; a path this day,
From harm and travails be.
Then lead me safely to'rd Thy way,
Till pure the light I see.

[N. Nomad]

SUNDAY June 21, 1998
TRAIL DAY 156/62 ✦ TRAIL MILE 2,207/805
LOCATION The Priest Shelter

SUNDAYS ARE GREAT DAYS TO BE OUT HIKING, especially if they're pleasant, for that's when you see the most day hikers, it seems. Today is such a Sunday and folks are on the trail in numbers. I meet *Wahoo* and *Mountain Laurie* and *Penny Wise* and *Pound Foolish*. This latter young, bright-eyed, shiny-faced couple stop me and ask my name. When I tell them I'm the *Nomad*, Penny Wise asks, "Are you the *Nimblewill Nomad*?" Oh my, what a surprise! Time to don the bigger shades again, it appears! They'd become familiar with my hike and knew about me from the Internet. So young folks, should you read this journal entry, I would encourage you to move to the next level of trail names. You've done— I'm sure, as all of us who will admit have done—the penny wise/pound foolish "thing" with all the hiking gear! You're past that point now. You're out here enjoying this grand and glorious scheme that is nature's cornucopia of treasure. So to me, and from this day forth, you'll always be known as *Footloose* and *Fancy Free*! Great meeting you, and good luck!

I arrive to find family and spend a great evening at the Priest Shelter with *U-Turn*, the *Soft-Shoe Banditos* (*Flint* and *Birch*), *Hopalong*, *Wolfhound*, *Florida Guy*, and a great bunch of Scouts and their leaders.

"Again the freshness and the odors,
Again Virginia's summer sky, pellucid blue and silver,
Again the forenoon purple of the hills,
Again the deathless grass, so noiseless, soft and green."

[Walt Whitman]

MONDAY June 22, 1998
TRAIL DAY 157/63 ✦ TRAIL MILE 2,232/830
LOCATION Campsite near Humpback Rocks

OH, WHAT A JOY TO HAVE A NEAR PAIN-FREE DAY OF HIKING AGAIN.
I am able to get in a 24-mile day with only minor rib, knee, and shin splint
discomfort. I'm almost back up to speed—I would say near 90 percent. I
know that the caring concern and prayers from all my friends both at
home and here on the trail have played a most important role in this miraculous recovery. I was told that I could not continue with the knee, rib, and
shin splint problems I was suffering . . . but I did continue. And I have also
been told that a dear friend here on the trail has said, "I very much want to
finish this journey, but I want *Nomad* to finish, too. Should it be that only
one of us will make it, I would *will* that it be *Nomad.*" This having been said
by a young man who has dedicated nearly two months of his life to the
trail and has hiked more than 800 miles. This humbles me greatly and
brings deep and emotional meaning to the word "friend!"

I relax for the evening in the late-day glow from a crimson sunset
o'er the heavens . . . and o'er the bluffs atop Humpback Rocks. As I
lounge, content in the warmth of this waning day, do I realize that spring
is nearly gone and summer has arrived. There are a few lingering mountain laurel yet blooming at these higher elevations and yesterday did I
see the most beautiful red columbine still flourishing. But oh my dear
sweet maiden, "Spring of '98," have you aged so quickly. Ah, but have
you also aged so gracefully! Soon you will be no more and I will be left
with but a memory of your loving presence and your glad and most joyful company. Have we not had such a frolicking grand time together!

> *"For me, Virginia is memorable because it is beautiful in*
> *landscape and in ways of life. There is an atmosphere of*
> *repose and maturity, a grace that comes only with age."*
>
> [Pearl S. Buck]

I ARRIVE AT HUMPBACK ROCKS PARKING AREA about 8:00 a.m. This place holds many memories for me, as it was from here that I hiked south to Burkes Garden 15 years ago with my former brother-in-law. The following year, my older son, Jay, and I departed from this very same spot to hike north together through the Shenandoahs to Harpers Ferry. I linger here for the longest while with these most pleasant memories.

I reach Rockfish Gap a little after 11:00 and head straight for HoJo's and breakfast. Then it's up to the inn at Afton for my mail. What an interesting coincidence to be picked up instantly as I stick out my thumb to hitch into Waynesboro. I hear a familiar voice as I hurry toward the truck, "Come on, *Nomad*!" As I look into the truck cab the driver says, "Come on, *Nomad*, get in!" Oh my, it's *Wahoo;* he has recognized me standing along the road! Our paths crossed a couple of days ago on the trail. *Wahoo* waits for me at Graham's Shoe Service while I drop off my boots with Dave Young for much-needed repair; then he takes me straight to the Loft Springs Camping Area across from the YMCA. Thanks, *Wahoo*! Was this ever a lucky break. The YMCA here is a top-notch facility, and after I set camp in their park, a grand little spring-neighbored meadow just for thru-hikers, I head for the showers — where a towel and soap and plenty of hot water are provided!

U-Turn, Flint, Birch, Fletch, Dusty, and I get a taxi to Western Sizzlin for the AYCE "works." I don't think I've ever eaten so much at one time in my entire life. This grand evening of dining starts out innocent enough in a sociable, dignified, and most genteel manner, but in only a short while does it degenerate into a disgusting, vulgar pig-out. Braggadocio challenges and counterchallenges fly full-circle around the banquet table. Bets are bantered about as to who can pack in the most grub. The event no sooner begins than the waitress is kept busy bringing stack after stack of clean plates. The whole thing quickly becomes an undignified and most uncivilized affair. As the royal banquet continues I am confident no one at the table can possibly pack grub the likes of the old *Nomad*, but alas, I'm quickly made out the piker. The feast continues for nearly two hours without interruption, the only break coming when the soft-ice-cream machine gets blitzed and then fails.

During this most welcome respite and as all respectfully bow to acknowledge *Fletch*, the "King of Pig," he is asked to reveal his secret. In the most humble fashion does he point out that he has finished only the first course and that all are invited to remain to witness the continuation of his royal feast. Reluctantly, and only because we are family, does he agree to divulge the secret to his remarkable and uncanny ability to get on the outside of heaping plates of food. He asks that we observe his most graceful posture, that being a semi-reclined position with a hard lean to the right. He then asks if we might recall seeing the old painting of King Arthur and his Court, the one showing the full assemblage feasting with zest and gusto at that historic and famous "Round Table," and can we think what might appear unusual about that picture. All nod the affirmative to the recollection but none can recall the least unusual thing about it. *Fletch* then suggests that if we visualize the scene for just a moment do we not recall that all there are sitting way back and leaning hard to the right just as he is now sitting way back and leaning hard to the right? "Sit way back and lean hard to the right," he says. So we all sit way back and lean hard to the right! Holding this King Arthur's Round Table pose for only moments does then each of us, one by one, heave the most pleasant sigh of relief! "Ah," says he, "Now you know the secret." *Fletch* then politely excuses himself while picking up a clean plate, and as we all groan in total disbelief, he returns to the food bar for yet another heaping plateful.

The Loft Springs Camping Area next to South River is a lovely spot, and even with much mournful groaning from adjacent tents, I manage to sleep very soundly.

"The mission of the YMCA is to build strong communities, strong families and strong youth through programs that promote Christian principles and values. . . ." It's a joy to see this institution surviving and thriving.

YMCA HOUSE RULES

1. Speak for yourself, not for anybody else.

2. Listen to others, then they'll listen to you.

3. Avoid put-downs . . . who needs 'em?

4. Take charge of yourself; you are responsible for you.

5. Show respect; every person is important.

WEDNESDAY June 24, 1998

TRAIL DAY 159/65 ✦ TRAIL MILE 2,239/837

LOCATION Loft Springs Camping Area, Rockfish Gap, Waynesboro

I AM NOT INTERESTED IN NOR DO I NEED ANY BREAKFAST this morning—hard to believe, but true! I am greeted by a beautiful, sunny, warm morning. Here in the meadow I survey all the tents around. Camped with me are *U-Turn, Dusty, Quest,* the *Soft Shoe Banditos (Flint* and *Birch), Lightweight, Fletch, Redneck Rye, French Phry, Weatherman* and *Boyscout, Yertle, G. I. Jane, Hojo, Indy, Easy Go, Bump, Oasis, Mitch, Blue Eyes, Jeffe, Hopalong, Joliet Joe,* and *Phoenix,* all "seasoned" thru-hikers, all bound and destined for Katahdin.

What a pleasant coincidence this morning, for camped here also are Richard and Maria Nicholl from Florida. They came in and camped just down from me. I first met them at Clearwater Lake, the southern entrance to the Ocala National Forest. They were camping as I passed by on the Florida Trail. They were doing a shake-down hike for their planned AT thru-hike. I recall mentioning at the time that I hoped our trails would cross and that we would meet again somewhere on up the trail this summer . . . and here they are! This young couple is now hiking by the trail names *Running Ribcage* and *Rosie,* but I think I'll always remember them as, ah-hmmm, *Lucky Boy* and *Pretty Girl!*

A second very pleasant coincidence occurred this afternoon at the spacious, beautiful Waynesboro Public Library. I got a chance to chat for a while with Warren Doyle, Jr. He is the support crew for a young man by the name of Sam, trail name *Poet Warrior,* who is attempting to break David Horton's record AT thru-trek of 52 days. Here at Waynesboro,

Sam is 19 days out of Springer! He is hiking, not running, more than 20 hours a day. According to Warren, he seems to be doing okay but may be suffering from *perceived* sleep deprivation! *Trail Dog,* who had been running the trail in an attempt to break Horton's record, is reported to be off the trail in Vermont. Here at Waynesboro, Sam is 88 hours ahead of Horton's time to here . . . but it's still a long way to Katahdin!

> *Folks, this ain't no stroll in the park,*
> *And sure 'tis not a picknickin' lark.*
> *'Cause gettin' out hikin' this ol' AT,*
> *There's a price to pay, believe you me!*
>
> [N. Nomad]

THURSDAY June 25, 1998
TRAIL DAY 160/66 ✦ TRAIL MILE 2,246/844
LOCATION Calf Mountain Shelter

WELL, IT'S TIME TO "GET OUT OF DODGE." Two days in any trail town is long enough, and these two days are up today at high noon. I've got to break camp, go to the library for a couple of hours, get some provisions, hit an ATM and the post office, then get some lunch, and I'm on my way. *U-Turn* suggests we hit the AYCE buffet at the Chinese restaurant next to Kroger. What a great idea! *U-Turn, Redneck Rye, Joliet Joe, Fletch, Flint, Birch,* and I stuff ourselves again. What a variety and we load it all . . . everything from frog legs to watermelon. There's not much of anything left when we get up from the table!

Nearing the post office, an old gentleman, probably in his late 70s, pulls up to the curb on the wrong side of the street and asks if we need a ride back up the mountain. I tell him we sure do, but that there's a slight problem—we have about an hour's worth of errands to run yet. He says, "Fine, here's my phone number and my name; call me when you're ready and I'll come back and pick you up." As I reach for the piece of paper I can't believe it, but manage to stutter, "Sure, mister, sure, thanks!" Now, how's that for trail angel hospitality? Waynesboro is a great trail town with some mighty fine people.

In about an hour we're ready to go, so I give the old gent a call and in only moments he's "Johnny on the spot." I've noticed recently that things are tending to happen in runs—rainy days, fair days, trail angels with trail magic popping up . . . and the run now, it seems, is on coincidences. John Taylor (who had seen me before) picked me up, *Wahoo* (who had seen me before) picked me up, and then the young couple (who had seen me before) months ago in Florida. But folks, this coincidence I'm about to relate to you is an absolute charmer. There's no way I can make this stuff up! Let me set the stage for this one by quoting an excerpt from Earl Shaffer's classic book, *Walking with Spring,* an exciting account of his AT thru-hike 50 years ago:

> *"A government car stopped and the driver looked over at me hunchbacked under my dripping poncho and rain hat, then offered a ride. My refusal brought a quiet question: 'What's the story?' He was an . . . engineer on the parkway project and a personal friend of Ross Hersey, Editor of* The News Virginian *in Waynesboro. He said that Ross was very keen about such things and would surely be happy to see me. Since Waynesboro has been designated as a mailing point, I said, 'I would think about it.' He said he would call Mr. Hersey in the meantime. . . . In the morning I hid my pack in the blueberry bushes near the parkway beyond Rockfish Gap, then hitched a ride to town. The girl at the post office handed me some letters, the first received on the trip, then said, 'Mr. Hersey called and said to come right over.' Says I to myself: 'Why not?' Mr. Hersey acted something like a kid on a picnic. . . . the resulting article and picture appeared the following day on the front page of* The News Virginian."*

Well, folks, I suspect you've guessed it by now . . . the kind old gentlemen driving us back up to Rockfish Gap. Yup! None other than Ross Hersey, the editor of *The News Virginian* 50 years ago! Okay, you're thinking, "So what?" So what! Folks, there are 20,000 people living in Waynesboro, Virginia, now, and this thing with Earl and Ross happened 50 years ago! And to add even more interest and spice, it is my hope that Earl and Ross can get together again soon, for it is now fairly common knowledge that Earl Shaffer is on the trail again, thru-hiking the AT again on this the 50th anniversary of his first thru-hike back in 1948. As I understand, he's only about five days south of Waynesboro as I write this! What a wonderful coincidence. Thanks, Ross, for stopping and giving us a ride . . . and even though not a word of this has been spoken, we know who you are! Thanks for giving us the opportunity to peek into this exciting little fragment of trail history.

It has cooled off nicely from what was becoming a scorcher afternoon. We check in at the Shenandoah National Park office and then head on out for the 7-mile hike to Calf Mountain Shelter. The shelter is packed with tents all around, but no problem. A very enjoyable evening is had by all, including *Joliet Joe, Flint, Birch, U-Turn, Redneck Rye, Weatherman* and *Boyscout, Fletch, Bump, Cloudwalker, Purple Puerto Rican,* and Pete MacAdams, the PATC Ridgerunner.

> *"The charms of the Shenandoah,*
> *Are its foaming waterfalls;*
> *Its legends and its vistas,*
> *And its geologic walls."*

[Earl Shaffer]

FRIDAY June 26, 1998
TRAIL DAY 161/67 ✦ TRAIL MILE 2,266/864
LOCATION Loft Mountain Campground

I'M UP AT 6:00 A.M. AND ON THE TRAIL A LITTLE BEFORE 7:00. I want to get in 20 miles today, as the treadway here in the park is much friendlier to feet and body. There are some ups and downs, but nothing like the treadway just south of here along the Blue Ridge Parkway. Twenty-mile days can be relatively easy if one can carve out a 10x12. This kind of 10x12 is not a large beam you are having hewn at your local mill for your fireplace mantel, but rather this 10x12 refers to getting in 10 miles by noon. One then has all afternoon to knock out the other 10, making the day much more enjoyable and the hike so much easier.

I don't get far this morning before there's plenty of excitement, for I have just made the acquaintance of a not-so-happy bunch of yellow jackets. They're nesting in the ground right by the trail and they get pretty darn mad when I come tramping through. I'm able to outrun all but one of the little flying hypodermic needles. He catches and drills me right in the calf. I realize now however that he did me a favor, for it was with his assistance that I moved smartly on up the trail and away from the rest of his little vespid cousins. So much for the daydreaming mode I was just sliding into!

Here in Shenandoah National Park the trail shares the same ridge with Skyline Drive for most of its distance, crossing it frequently, usually at scenic overlooks. The first such crossing this morning presents wide, sweeping views across the ridges, to the horizon. Discussed on this over-look's information marker is Shenandoah's patchwork forest:

> *"Pine trees climb the slope, to crown the mountain crest. In the drainage below, other pines huddle among hardwood neighbors. These pines illustrate the patchy, quilt-like nature of Shenandoah's forests, with each patch offering a clue to the forest's past. Many forest sites were once cleared for tilling, grazing, and home sites. Natural and human-caused fires opened other areas. . . . whenever you notice a forest difference you can suspect an underlying cause: A former homestead, a fire, a climate or soil difference."*

Looking down, as I am this morning, into this patchy mosaic and not having this information, would I be presented with a quandary, indeed! I arrive at Loft Mountain Campground where I'm invited to pitch right at the campground host's campsite. I have the picnic table and grill to myself. I set my little tent right on the manicured grass. This has been a very fine hiking day, and I am pleased with meeting my goal.

Other than the momentary discomfort from the yellow jacket sting, this has been a glorious, pain-free day!

> *You can keep your wine and your bourbon and your beer.*
> *Hang onto your scotch and gin and other forms of cheer.*
> *Don't offer me your sody pop, your coffee or your tea,*
> *Fer I am high on Shenandoah's pure sweet majesty.*

[N. Nomad]

SATURDAY June 27, 1998
TRAIL DAY 162/68 ✦ TRAIL MILE 2,292/890
LOCATION Lewis Mountain Campground

I'M OUT EARLY FOR A 26-MILE DAY INTO Lewis Mountain Campground. Sure glad I'm hitting this section early and in the cool of the morning, because the gypsy moths have managed to defoliate thousands of acres of the Shenandoah National Park, leaving an open canopy along the trail for miles. In the afternoon sun this trail would be a real scorcher. Standing deadwood trees, known as snags, are everywhere. Looking down into the coves and ravines from most any vista, the stark gray vertical slashes, which are the snags, add a coarse and eerie weaving to the otherwise lush green landscape. It is truly hard to believe that little "wiggly worms" could cause such incredible widespread destruction, but in their countless armies they are a force to be reckoned with. The Forest Service has introduced a form of fungus, which apparently destroys the gypsy moth larva, and their count is down significantly. But don't we all hope and pray that there won't be some unforeseen side effect from the introduction of the fungus?

I arrived at Pinefield Hut around 9:30 a.m. to find *Fletch* still breaking camp. He shows me the profile for our planned day's hike. It appears there are a number of three-and-a-half-Snickers pulls ahead, but I wouldn't bet on it. The old Snickers rating system seems to be much more reliable. There's just no use fretting about all of this until I get there! There's also a lot more to this whole degree of difficulty thing, much of which has to do with the actual treadway conditions. Here in the Shenandoah the treadway is so much kinder to a hiker's feet. There is more duff and not so many rocks, a pleasant surprise, since the trail here gets heavy use.

Mother Nature's most amazing life form south of here was the incredible variety and array of wildflowers. Here in the Shenandoah do the fauna reign! Don't try counting the deer, for you will quickly lose count, they are so friendly and tame and so numerous. It is a pleasure to see them up close, as they peer at you with obvious curiosity. Yesterday, at Mondo Campground, one came up to me as I was sitting in a shady spot having lunch. He was happy with a little of my bread, which he took from my hand. This morning I see squirrels, numerous bunny hoppers, and chipmunks. A wide variety of birds are abundant here also, and I am awakened now shortly after dawn each morning by the joyful, melodic songs of these songbirds.

There's a large population of black bear in the park, and I've heard numerous stories of bear sightings from my hiking friends, but I've not had the good fortune of seeing one yet and more than likely will not. My older son, Jay, pointed out the only bear I've ever seen in the wild. He saw numerous black bears when we hiked the Shenandoah together years ago. He would say, "There's one, Dad, over there in the laurel. Can't you hear him?" Ah, and therein lies the rub. You would expect an old fellow like me nearing his 60th birthday not to have the keenest hearing in the world, but I have suffered from serious hearing impairment for many, many years. It all started when I was in the Coast Guard stationed on the icebreaker Mackinaw (WAGB-83) commissioned out of Cheboygan, Michigan. Our job was to break the ice and keep the shipping lanes open so ore carriers could run out of Lake Superior. I was an engineman and my station was in the engine room on a little narrow catwalk between two huge Fairbanks-Morse opposed-piston engines. Air was forced into these huge engines by blowers the size of washing machines. And when we were breaking and plowing ice these engines were revving, the blowers literally screaming. No one thought of wearing hearing protection back in those days, and as a result of months of exposure to these high-pitched and high-decibel sounds, I've since suffered with a condition called tinnitus, an incessant and annoying ringing in my ears. So those with keen hearing will probably be keener on bear. I'll just keep an eye out so I don't trip over one along the way!

The pulls up and over Little Roundtop and Hightop mountains aren't a big deal, and I arrive at Lewis Mountain Campground in time to enjoy orange juice and ice cream at the camp store. I have a grand evening sharing a campsite with *Wolfhound, Flint, Birch,* and *U-Turn.* There is wind and rain most of the night, but I sleep comfortably in my little Slumberjack.

> *"Something lost behind the ranges,*
> *Something hidden, go and find it.*
> *Go and look behind the ranges,*
> *Something lost behind the ranges,*
> *Lost and waiting for you. Go."*
>
> [Kipling]

SUNDAY June 28, 1998
TRAIL DAY 163/69 ✦ TRAIL MILE 2,309/907
LOCATION Skyland Lodge

THE RAIN LETS UP AND I'M ABLE TO BREAK CAMP by 7:30 a.m., then to move off into the cloudy mist. I figured on finding *Fletch* at Bearfence Mountain Hut but have no luck. I suspect he's moved on ahead. I arrive at Big Meadows Lodge just in time for a fine lunch with *Cloudwalker. Flint, Birch,* and *U-Turn* come in shortly and we hike out together for a little while. I'm old enough to be a grandpa to these young fellows, and with a full stomach trying to digest, I don't stay with them long. These "power hikers" have incredibly long, smooth strides, and to maintain the pace they keep I literally have to jog, so I slow to my pace to enjoy my hike on into Skyland. There are numerous overlooks today, but the rain prevails and I am in the clouds. Skyland is appropriately named. I meet *Stagecoach* this afternoon. He'll become a 2,000-miler when he reaches Rockfish Gap. Congratulations, *Stagecoach*!

Shenandoah National Park has a history not unlike Great Smoky Mountains National Park as relating to the vast area taken by the government in order to create the park. The following is a quote from *Shenandoah National Park Interpretive Guide,* written by John A. Conners:

> *"By 1936 the year SNP was dedicated, only 432 families . . . were known to have been living in the park area. When the state government moved in to claim the land that became SNP, most mountain folk appreciated the opportunity to sell their land and relocate. Many bought land elsewhere or took advantage of government loan aid to move into one of the seven settlement communities located not far outside the park boundary. A few individuals became wards of the Virginia Welfare Department and 13 were allowed to remain and live their lives inside the park because of 'hardship or meritorious service.' The last inhabitant, Annie Shenk, died in January, 1979."*

And a final, interesting quote from *Shenandoah, The Story Behind the Scenery,* by Hugh Crandall and Reed Engle:

> *"Shenandoah is many things to many people. For some it is their heritage, the green lichens slowly growing on the ancient grave stones tell of their past. For others, it is a chance to escape the heat and humidity of the city and picnic happily in a shelter erected by the men of the CCC. The more rigorous and adventurous find peace and strength in walking isolated trails and sleeping under the stars. And for many it is simply a Sunday drive, a view from an overlook, the wonder of placid deer grazing on a road shoulder, or familiar sites revisited. Shenandoah National Park has become part of the collective consciousness and memories of generations who have shared in her riches."*

I arrive at Skyland Lodge around 4:00 p.m. to share a room with *Wolfhound, Flint, Birch,* and *U-Turn.* I enjoy a great meal at the lodge restaurant and relax later in the pub in the company of *Mitten Chic, Moe,*

Yorkie (from Yorkshire, England), and *Redneck Rye*. I am saddened to hear that *Redneck Rye* is leaving the trail. We have hiked together off and on over the recent weeks and have become such good friends. I will never forget the "tailgate banquet," compliments of *Redneck Rye* and his parents at Mt. Rogers Visitors Center. He has extended me much kindness. I will truly miss you, son!

> *This pack* o' young hounds can burn the trail,*
> *They've been taught to bear the torch.*
> *While this old dog, tucked in tail,*
> *Watches quietly from the porch.*

[N. Nomad]

**Skitz, Fletch, Hopalong, U-Turn, Flint*, and *Birch*,
all 4-mile-per-hour "power hikers"

MONDAY June 29, 1998
TRAIL DAY 164/70 ✦ TRAIL MILE 2,327/925
LOCATION Range View Cabin

I SAT IN SKYLAND'S LOBBY LAST NIGHT until about midnight reading and catching up on my journal entries. Just as I was preparing to return to my room, the sky opened up. Came then a hard steady thunderstorm that persisted for more than two hours. I had to remain in the lobby until 2:30 a.m. since I hadn't sense to carry my raingear, my room being a ten-minute walk away.

So this morning I'm not in any hurry to get up or get out. Just as well, what the heck . . . I go for breakfast at the lodge, and with this being the peak tourist season, I am not only fortunate to have gotten a room last night, but also a table for breakfast this morning. I've had a grand time here at Skyland!

By noon the skies have cleared and at Stony Man Mountain Overlook I am awarded one of the most remarkable views to be seen or enjoyed anywhere along the ridge, down into the lush, green Shenandoah Valley. The soft-settled haze aligns the distant ranges, creating relief as if to display so many towering sentinels standing in rows to the horizon. The result is a creation of perfect order, each ridge, gap, spur, and ravine made important by its presence. And now this heavenly majesty provides such a grand backdrop for the colorful puzzle of mosaic that is the landscape across this rich, historic valley below. The roads, farms, fields, and streams all offer their undivided attention, combining to present a precious moment in time, a moment to be enjoyed only by me and the hawks free-sailing the thermals above.

I have been hiking this morning with a delightful gentleman from England: Brian Nicholls, trail name *Yorkie*, for Yorkshire. My chest swells with pride as Yorkie comes to stand here on Stony Man with me. We talk about this glorious spot and the remarkable abundance of natural beauty that is America. It never ceases to amaze me—the people from other countries who have studied our history and know so much about our country. *Yorkie* says, "I have read much about your Civil War and have always wanted to see the Shenandoah. I am not disappointed." And there is yet another great view from Marys Rock . . . 360 degrees . . . and the day has turned perfect! As the "Pack O' Young Hounds" passes us, I tell *Yorkie* how I must break into a jog to keep up with them, not a good idea with a pack on. *Yorkie* is moving along well so I suggest he hike out with them. He looks at me with that shiny and polished Englishman's smile and says, "I'll give it a go!" Last I see, he's right with them as they disappear up the ridge.

At Thornton Gap is Panorama Wayside, a fine restaurant and gift shop. It's only a stone's throw off the trail, so everyone goes in. Great burgers, fries, and wild blackberry milkshakes! We see *Fletch* and *T-Bone Walker*'s packs outside against the building. We decide they are slack-packing as they are nowhere in sight. Sooo, when they shoulder their packs in a while they may or may not notice how much heavier they are, as some select rocks will be moving north with them!

At Elkwallow Wayside parking area I meet Mark and his sister Ann. They have come to the U.S. from South Africa to see the Shenandoah and to do some backpacking. When they find that I have come for a few provisions, the Wayside being closed, they offer me food from their supplies. I am given an apple, a banana, a can of lasagna, fresh sausage links, and a liter of apple juice. This has got to be some kind of record for trail angels from farthest away! I enjoy a very good supper, compliments of Mark and Ann, cooked in the quaint old fireplace on the porch at Range View Cabin.

> *"The wonder of the world, the beauty and the power.*
> *The shapes of things, their colors, lights and shades.*
> *These I saw. Look ye, also, while life lasts!"*

[Epitaph, Tombstone in England]

TUESDAY June 30, 1998
TRAIL DAY 165/71 ✦ TRAIL MILE 2,346/944
LOCATION US 522, Front Royal, Front Royal Motel

I'M OUT FROM THE LITTLE ROCK PORCH AT Range View Cabin at 7:00 a.m. as the wind kicks up, boosting me along. But the looks and makings are for another beautiful day. As I hike today, the trail weaves back and back again over Skyline Drive as the braid forms its crisscross between the motorway and the treadway. Hearing the constant drone and grind from the automobiles and motorcycles is neither annoying nor distracting, but I believe that I am near ready for a change to a more serene path. I'm faced with some three-and-a-half- to four-Snickers pulls along and over the Hogbacks, Marshalls, and Compton Peak. *Bump* and *Redbeard* come by and hike with me for a while.

My feet have been, and I guess will remain, a day-to-day concern. Early on in this odyssey I suffered the not-so-pleasant experience of shedding the nails off both my feet, the final result of the constant soaking and pounding dealt by the Florida swamps. I have since suffered blisters, sore toes and pads, and other assorted foot aches and pains. Now I'm in the process of losing the nails (which have tried growing back!) off my great toes and both second toes again. So I can occupy my concern now with these ailments; the sore knee, cracked ribs, dislocated finger, shin splints, and tender noggin having become secondary discomforts.

I finish this 19-mile day at 3:00 p.m. and hitch a ride into Front Royal to share a room with *Wolfhound* and *Yorkie*. *Yorkie* leaves the trail tomorrow after completing his planned hike through this mystical paradise, the glorious Shenandoah. A good friend for such a short time. Keep in touch, *Yorkie*!

> *"At this discovery, the stars were so overjoyed that again each of them took the brightest jewel from his crown and cast it into the long winding river. There all of these same jewels still lie and sparkle and ever since that day the river . . . and the valley, too—has been called Shenandoah."*
>
> [The Legend of Shenandoah]

WEDNESDAY July 1, 1998
TRAIL DAY 166/72 ✦ TRAIL MILE 2,367/965
LOCATION US 50, Ashby Gap, Winchester, Super 8 Motel

I MADE ARRANGEMENTS LAST NIGHT FOR THE INNKEEPER to shuttle me back to the trail this morning. *Yorkie* and *Wolfhound* want some pictures, so they follow me out to the truck. As the innkeeper snaps us, we put on the best faces possible at 7:30 a.m. I say goodbye to *Yorkie* and *Wolfhound* and manage to get back on the trail by 8:00 a.m.

On my way this morning, I cruise in to see the Jim and Molly Denton Shelter. I've heard much about this spot. And, oh, what a place! This is a hiker's fairyland. If we could ever have a gingerbread house, the Jim and Molly Denton Shelter would be it. The shelter is complete with windows, a large deck, and benches, and there's a covered pavilion complete with BBQ pit right next to it. And get this—the whole compound is tied together with herringbone pavers! *Redbeard* and *Bump* are in residence, and I can hear their happy chatter long before arriving. I linger and we have a grand time.

The Potomac Appalachian Trail Club, chartered years ago by Myron Avery, is the keystone Appalachian Trail Conference chapter. What a history and what a grand tradition. You folks do a super job, thanks!

There are plenty of ups and downs and more than enough rocks today. I again hike for a while with *Redbeard*, thence to hitch a ride into

Winchester with a fellow who drives all the way to Washington, D.C. to work every day. He's on the road 20 hours a week. Jeez, sure didn't take long to get jolted back into the real world again! The fellow's a union plumber working on a parking garage. Even with the great pay, this is as close as he feels he can afford to live. He gets home around 7:00 p.m. — to start the whole grueling, grinding daily ordeal all over again at 4:00 a.m. As he calmly relates all this to me, I'm thinking, "This is insane!" But he seems to be perfectly content and happy! I recall the occasional drive I've taken around the perimeter of Atlanta, where perchance I get tangled in the rush hour traffic, all eight lanes moving slowly or not at all, the commuters, their hands glued to their steering wheels staring into space as if in some kind of hypnotic trance . . . and I wonder, "How in God's name can these folks stand this day in and day out?"

I splurge, lavishing myself with my own private room at Super 8 Motel. I take a long, soothing warm bath, then hit the AYCE Chinese buffet across the way. Tim Anderson (*Long Distance Man*), a good friend of *Thunder Chicken* and now also my good friend, had extended an invitation to me while at Roan High Knob Shelter. Tim said, "Give my wife, Ruth, a call and stay at our place when you pass by Winchester." But, once reaching Winchester and standing with pay phone in hand, I thought about how a dirty, stinky, ratty-looking thru-hiker such as I could dearly strain the very best of Southern hospitality. So better judgment prevailed as I reluctantly hung up the receiver. Thanks, Tim! True, sincere, Southern hospitality at its best. I dearly hope our paths meet again on up this trail.

> *"The simplicity in all things is the secret of the wilderness and one of its most valuable lessons. It is what we leave behind that is important. I think the matter of simplicity goes further than just food, equipment, and unnecessary gadgets; it goes into the matter of thoughts and objectives as well. When in the wilds we must not carry our problems with us, or the joy is lost."*
>
> [Sigurd Olson]

THURSDAY July 2, 1998
TRAIL DAY 167/73   ✦   TRAIL MILE 2,388/986
LOCATION Blackburn Trail Center

RIGHT NEXT TO THE MOTEL IS A HARDEE'S, and I head there in the dark at 4:45 a.m. for coffee, eggs, and biscuits. They're open all night for the truckers who are already running hard and steady this morning. I'm able to hitch a ride back to Ashby Gap with a young fellow who also drives all the way to D.C. every day. He, too, seems content and happy! This whole thing is so baffling, yet as we travel east there's a constant and steady stream of vehicles heading for the capital in the dark this morning. It seems inevitable, I suppose, that we will all be heading toward the bosom of that grand provider of all things to all people eventually—that all-knowing, all-loving, all-providing federal bureaucracy that is Washington, D.C. I hope that getting back to the trail this morning is as close as I'll ever have to go.

I'm back on the trail by 6:15 a.m., and I prepare myself for difficult and slow going today. I have been told that the trail that lies ahead and into Blackburn Trail Center is a series of rugged and constant ups and downs with total vertical elevation change in excess of 5,000 feet. Here is a fine example of the peaceful, smug, and secure feeling one can get lulled into by perusing the profile maps, for on the maps these contours appear most benign! Oh, but do they conceal the truth of the matter, for I am getting an incredible workout! This section proves to be one of the most technically challenging so far. Tough ups and downs through rocks and roots . . . and more rocks and roots! Coupled with the heat and humidity, I really have my hands full.

The opportunity for a much-needed break presents, and I head up the short side trail to Bears Den Hostel. Here I lounge and take lunch at the picnic table on the clover-carpeted lawn. What a welcome and very needed respite. The hostel is an old castle-like granite structure now under total restoration by the Appalachian Trail Conference. I meet Dave Appel and am given the grand tour. My son and I stayed here years ago, and we found it in serious disrepair then. This proud old structure will be in its glory once more when this restoration is completed. What a pleasure to see this work being done. ATC, don't you folks ever rest!

The treadway becomes even more challenging as the day wears on. Negotiating Devils Racecourse, an incredible jumble of rocks, requires jumping and leaping from boulder to boulder, demanding every bit of strength, balance, and concentration that I can muster. Four miles still remain to reach Blackburn Trail Center, and I can feel the stress and tension from the day's constant exertion and pounding having its effect and taking its toll on my knees. My balance is becoming a serious problem due to the heat, exertion, and fatigue. I recall being told by *Poppasan* and *Thunder Chicken,* who thru-hiked the AT last year, that the time would come that I would relent and resort to using hiking sticks. I never disputed these words of wisdom, but at the same time I held the opinion that if I didn't want to use sticks I wouldn't have to. Today, and as a result of the past few hours hiking through this incredible jumble, I have made a reassessment and have arrived at a different opinion. Realistic, oh yes! Fatalistic, *oooh* yes!

So now it appears the time has arrived to start "stickin' it." And what an incredible coincidence, for as I'm cogitating getting some sticks presents now the perfect opportunity: at this very moment am I hiking through a young poplar stand with hundreds and hundreds of tall, straight, closely crowded saplings! So, I pull up, drop my pack, and, finding two identical poplars perfect for trekking poles, spend the next hour on my knees with my dull pocket knife whittling out a pair of walking companions . . . much-needed bodyguards that will no doubt accompany me the remainder of this odyssey.

I arrive at Blackburn Trail Center around 4:00 p.m. and make myself at home on the screened-in porch. The Center is a quaint old hostel owned and operated by the Potomac Appalachian Trail Club (PATC). These facilities, located at the verge, the very upper reaches of a cove, consist of an old hand-hewn log cabin complete with screened porches on three sides, porch swing, tables and benches, a small bunkhouse with privy, a garage with bunks in the studio above with privy, the neatest "Barney Oldfield" solar shower (which will scald your tail), and a spacious, level, manicured lawn complete with enough picnic tables for the community Fourth of July cookout. The resident caretakers, Laura Poole and Morgan Lane, GAME (Georgia to Maine thru-hike) '95, greet me with a smile . . . and a cold frosty! In return for their kindness and hospitality, and with the aid of my "Little Dandy" cookstove, I manage to burn a big hole in one of their fine picnic tables! All is forgiven, however, and I relax to enjoy a very pleasant evening with these kind folks and with *Redbeard, Easy Rider, Farther, Old Fhart,* and *Turtle.*

> *"Each part of the Appalachian Trail presented a new kind of challenge. Sometimes the trail felt like a stern taskmaster saying, 'Well, you've dealt with the steep ups and downs, now I'll throw in a little rain and see if you can take that. Okay, so, you handled the rain; let's try 95 degrees and 90 percent humidity. Thought that was tough? How about some mosquitoes and gnats? Hmmm, now I'll add ticks and deer flies. You still here? Well, let's add a dose of rocks and throw in some hand-over-hand climbing. Rest? No, you can rest when it's over.' "*

[Jean Deeds, *There Are Mountains to Climb*]

FRIDAY July 3, 1998
TRAIL DAY 168/74 ✦ TRAIL MILE 2,400/998
LOCATION Harpers Ferry, West Virginia, Hilltop House Hotel

THE 13 MILES INTO HARPERS FERRY IS A CRUISE, mostly downhill, a couple of little blips with *Nomad*'s neutral kickin' and I'm in! It's a jolt coming to U.S. 340 and the bridge over the Shenandoah River. The traffic is roaring along. And down below, the Fourth of July weekend fun is underway with swimming, tubing, canoeing, and kayaking. The Shenandoah is a rocky, rolling river here. Looks like rollicking fun!

A blue-blazed side trail leads a short distance to the Appalachian Trail Conference Headquarters on Washington Street. I am very excited and full with anticipation as I arrive at the center, for here is the psychological halfway point on the AT. My reward is a grand smile and a cheerful greeting from John *Peter Pan* Tatara, GAME '94 and GAME '97. John is a member of the Georgia Appalachian Trail Club, volunteering time here at the center. Before I can greet him, John says, "I know you; we've met before. You're the *Nomad,* and you're hiking from Florida."

Indeed we had met a couple of weeks ago on the trail, where at that time John was swinging a Pulaski with a work crew doing trail relocation. He said, "I'm here giving back to the trail after hiking and enjoying the trail for two years."

Also volunteering time here is Dave Appel, age 74, from Wisconsin. I met Dave yesterday back at Bears Den. Dave is hiking sections of the trail south from Harpers Ferry. Dave relates that this particular section of trail brings many memories as he hikes it again, for his family maintained trail here in the late 1930s. Dave is also helping on the renovation of Bears Den Hostel, getting the old windows in tip-top condition again. Many years ago, when my son and I entered the front door here at AT headquarters we were greeted with a "Hello!" and that grand smile from Jean Cashen. It's so good to see the tradition continuing. Thanks, John and Dave, for your kindness and your hospitality!

I was supposed to meet family at Harpers Ferry National Historical Park headquarters. They made a two-hour trip here from Maryland to pick me up for the weekend, but since I was last here the park headquarters have been moved from downtown. I didn't realize this and I waited for them at the wrong place. I will try to see them when this odyssey is over. While waiting I passed the time talking with *Skitz*. He's getting ready to do the 4/40/24 (four states, 40 miles in 24 hours). While *Skitz* and I lounge on the lawn by the old park headquarters, *Joliet Joe* comes in. We decide to share a room at Hilltop House Hotel. We're able to get a room and have a grand evening meal. Then we "Garvey out" in the finest Hiker Trash Fratority fashion as we dine in luxury, enjoying the stupendous scene of the Potomac below.

> *"The passage of the Potomac through the Blue Ridge is perhaps one of the most stupendous scenes in nature. You stand on a very high point of land, on your right comes up the Shenandoah, having ranged along the mountain a hundred miles to seek a vent. On your left approaches the Potomac in quest of a passage also. In the moment of their junction they rush together against the mountain, rend it asunder, and pass off to the sea."*
>
> [Thomas Jefferson]

SATURDAY July 4, 1998

TRAIL DAY 169/75   ✦   TRAIL MILE 2,400/998

LOCATION Harpers Ferry, Hilltop House Hotel

THIS WILL BE A WELL-EARNED DAY OF REST AND RELAXATION. I
head over to ATC headquarters to do a little research and study . . . yes
the building is open on Saturday, the Fourth of July. These folks
absolutely never rest! While reading, I hear the front door open and, as
I look up, in comes *Wolfhound*. I invite him to stay with *Joliet Joe* and me
at Hilltop. He says he doesn't mind pitching on the floor and would help
split the room cost. We've had to change rooms at the hotel and when *JJ*,
Wolfhound, and I open the door, we can't believe what we see. Oh yes,
three beds. As *Wolfhound* would say, "Life is good!" We head right down
to Garvey up the AYCE lunch buffet in the grand old hotel dining room.

"He who rides and keeps the beaten track studies the fences chiefly."

[Henry David Thoreau]

SUNDAY July 5, 1998

TRAIL DAY 170/76   ✦   TRAIL MILE 2,400/998

LOCATION Harpers Ferry, Hilltop House Hotel

THIS IS ANOTHER DAY TO KEEP MY FEET UP and try to rest my knees.
The breakfast buffet here at the hotel is a fine spread. By arriving late, it
is possible for one to overlap into the dinner buffet! I spend most of the
day reading and studying again at the Conference Center.

There has been much attrition since Springer Mountain. The first
heavy dropout occurred at Hot Springs and the second at Damascus. I
was #992 to sign in at Walasi-Yi, and here at ATC headquarters I am
#397. Historically, another big dropout occurs here at Harpers Ferry, and
it's sure understandable considering the difficulty of the treadway just to
the south. The trail is slowly and steadily taking its toll.

"Would you tell me please, which way I ought to go from here?"
"That depends a good deal on where you want to go," said the cat.

"I don't much care where," said Alice.
"Then it doesn't matter which way you go," said the cat!

[Lewis Carroll, *Alice in Wonderland*]

MONDAY July 6, 1998
TRAIL DAY 171/77 ✦ TRAIL MILE 2,410/1,008
LOCATION Crampton Gap, Gathland State Park, Maryland

I'M UP AT 6:00 A.M. IN ORDER TO CATCH THE BUS to Charles Town
and the Super Wal-Mart. I need to get some medication to aid these old
bones and joints as they endure the pounding dished out by the AT. I
have been taking combination tabs of glucosamine HCL 250 mg and
Chondroitin sulfate 200 mg. This nutritional OTC medication, com-
monly known as Osteo Bi-Flex, helps to maintain healthy, mobile joints
and cartilage and aids in connective-tissue building and repair. I am also
taking a multivitamin along with coated aspirin. I feel I am getting considerable beneficial effect from these medications. In addition, now that
the heat of summer is upon me I am constantly perspiring, which is
depleting my electrolytes. I have ordered Succeed Electrolytic caps,
developed by Karl King, from Ultrafit. They should be waiting at my
next mail drop in Duncannon. In the shelters, eyebrows always raise as
my young thru-hiker friends watch me open my meds bag and pop all
this stuff. I just tell them what my grandfather used to say to me, "We
get too soon olt and too late schmardt."

Many good friends have come in since I arrived here at Harpers
Ferry Saturday morning: *Fletch* is now here as are *Easy Rider, Weatherman*
and *Boyscout, Buddha Boy, Dutchie, Yertle, Saint,* and *Tulie.*

When I return to Hilltop House Hotel to get my pack, *Joliet Joe*
and *Wolfhound* have already departed. The personnel here at the Hilltop
House Hotel have been most gracious, from the desk clerks, waitresses,
housekeepers, and the chef and all who help on the food line, all dedicated to making the guests stay an enjoyable and memorable one. My
stay certainly was, and it will remain in my memory. Thanks, folks!

At the post office I receive a package from Slumberjack. They've
sent me new aluminum tent hoops to replace the fiberglass ones I've

been having problems with. I was so looking forward to getting a package from home, sent days ago, priority mail. But it is not here. Upon returning to the ATC center, John Tatara informs me that a local resident just called and said they have my package and would bring it right over. I'm thinking, "What's going on here?" Sure enough, in just a few minutes the door to the center opens and a young man and his mother enter. John directs them to me and the young man comes over and hands me my priority mail package. He says, "My name is M. J. Eberhart, and this package was delivered to me by mistake." My mouth gapes open and I look at the youngster in total disbelief, then I look at his mother. She looks at me most quizzically . . . and while shrugging says, "This is my son. His name is M. J. Eberhart." Somehow I manage, "Pleased to meet you M. J. Eberhart, I'm M. J. Eberhart!" Folks please believe me, there's just no way that I can make this kind of stuff up!

While here at Harpers Ferry, I've had the pleasure of meeting most of the staff at ATC: the volunteers, John Tatara and Dave Appel; and the professional staff, Dave Startzell, Brian King, Laurie Potteiger, and Kisha. I was able to sit down with Dave for a few minutes and talk about the progress being made in the final stages of land acquisition to protect the AT corridor. We also talked for a few minutes about what I anticipate will be the up-and-coming popularity of the Appalachian Mountains Trail (AMT) and the Eastern Continental Trail (ECT). I am but one of hundreds and hundreds who pass through the ATC center on a regular basis, bur I was certainly made to feel at home. Thanks, John, the Daves, Kisha, Laurie, and Brian! I'm disappointed not to personally meet Sue Ellen Weinkopf, whom I have corresponded with and talked with on numerous occasions, but, alas, she is out today, so I've left a note for her.

Back to the post office to get my "bounce box" off and mail a few postcards. Now comes in a huge van with two canoes lashed on top, and piling out are *Flint, Birch, U-Turn,* and *Shelter Monkey*. They have just completed their 60-mile canoe trip from Front Royal to Harpers Ferry on the beautiful Shenandoah! They all yak at once, totally giddy with excitement about their adventure.

I finally manage to get back on the AT a little before 5:00 p.m., cross the hiker bridge over the Potomac, then onto the historic C&O

Towpath, finally to climb Weverton. This has been such a grand week-end and a most interesting and memorable day. It's good to be back on the trail as I arrive in the dark at Gathland State Park. I know that *Fletch* will be coming through soon doing the 4/40/24. I roll out my pad and blanket on one of the picnic tables under the pavilion and quickly fall into deep restful sleep, not hearing him pass.

> *"In about forty miles the Appala*tchin *Trail*
> *becomes the Appala*shun *Trail."*
>
> [ATC toilet wall]

TUESDAY July 7, 1998
TRAIL DAY 172/78 ✦ TRAIL MILE 2,431/1,029
LOCATION Hemlock Hill Shelter

I'M OUT ABOUT 7:30 A.M. ON A BEAUTIFUL MORNING to arrive shortly at Crampton Gap Shelter. I want to look in the shelter register to see who's been through recently so I head on over. As I stand here now reading these words for the second time, I'm wishing I'd kept right on going, for on this last page and in this most recent entry is there revealed the bitter reality, for written here is harsh testament to the attrition this trail has taken. I knew that many more friends would leave the trail at Harpers Ferry, but now I am faced with it, I must look at it straight on, for I know and realize now there are many dear friends I will never see again. And so it appears from this entry that I am not the only one who has departed Harpers Ferry with a heavy heart and a similar burden of sadness. I read the following entry again, written from the heart by a thru-hiker named *Ender*, as I brush tears from my eyes and from the page,

"Feels good to be back on the trail, but sad to be leaving friends. So many people are pulling off the trail; a lot of people I've gotten to know out here and who I feel honored to call friends. I am sad to see my friends leaving, maybe to be never seen again, I hope not. But who knows what roads they will take, what paths may lead them where? I hope those paths will lead back to me, at least for a short while. It would be a shame, a sin, to never see these friends again. So, I will look forward to the day when I may see my friends again. Until that day when our trails may cross again — I will miss them."

Let's just push on, *Ender*, and try not to think about it anymore this day.

I arrive about lunchtime at the Washington Monument. The citizens of nearby Boonsboro erected it in 1827. It stands at 30 feet in height and from this vantage can be seen lands surveyed by Washington and Fairfax. The towns of Harpers Ferry and Winchester are visible. Also seen from atop the monument is the Antietam National Cemetery at Sharpsburg where Lee and McClellan fought. The architecture it seems is not the most appealing. One hiker, as the story goes, stopped to stare at it, then turning is purported to have said, "What a crock." Folks, it is shaped kind of funny!

There's some really rough, rocky going this afternoon near Annapolis Rocks and along Black Rock Cliffs. I have heard much about them, and today I have the pleasure of hiking for a while with the Allen family from Festus, Missouri, better known on the trail as simply *The Family*. They are a mother and her five children and they are thru-hiking the AT! What a great and fun group. The mom is Suzy *Suches '75*, and the kids are Sara *Rosey*, Martha *The Artist*, Jesse *Sport*, Annie *Appy Anne*, and Casey *4x4*. I manage to get into Hemlock Hill Shelter around 7:00 p.m. to spend an enjoyable evening with *Birch* and *Caterpillar* and his daughter. Rain begins about 8:00 p.m. and continues intermittently throughout the night.

> *"The mountains of Maryland, even quite near, are*
> *blue — the color of clouds and of memory."*
>
> [Paula M. Strain, *The Blue Hills of Maryland*]

WEDNESDAY July 8, 1998
TRAIL DAY 173/79   ✦   TRAIL MILE 2,448/1,046
LOCATION Tumbling Run Shelters, Pennsylvania

MY WASTE-MANAGEMENT SYSTEM AWAKENS ME ABOUT 6:00 A.M. After a brief duty cycle I return to kill time the good old-fashioned way . . .

three more hours of sleep. For this morning it is pounding hard, the whole scene casting a no-nonsense appearance of dreary permanence. The downpour finally relents and the day manages to "fair-up" a little . . . and I finally manage to get out and on my way again. I am afforded the luxury now of burning two or three hours from day to day while still managing respectable mileage, as daylight is lingering much longer. Up here on the ridge—which is where the trail usually leads—the twilight hours extend remarkably far into what is usually nocturnal domain. The fog and rain finally manage to rebound, shutting the brightness down . . . and a muddly kind of funk comes with it as my mind returns to the thought of never seeing so many friends (certainly the smarter ones) ever again. To brighten my spirit I try to be mindful of the ever-positive attitude of Warren Doyle, Jr., who under such circumstances would surely be skipping along singing, "Ho! Ha! Who cares? This is the song of the trail!" At least there are no flies or gnats! How's that, Warren?

I arrive at Pen Mar State Park around 2:00 p.m. after an extended and very difficult up-and-down, mud-and-rock scramble . . . just in time to catch *Birch* leaving on a grub run with the park ranger. I manage to get my order in for a foot-long combo sub and jumbo Coke! *Fletch* is also here at the park pavilion . . . not looking too hot again. He did manage the 4/40/24, but he did it last night in the pitch black, in the mud and rocks and rain. The four states are Virginia, West Virginia, Maryland, and Pennsylvania. The distance is 40 miles, beginning at the last stretch of trail in Virginia and ending here at Pen Mar at the Mason-Dixon Line, where the Appala*tchin* Trail becomes the Appala*shun* Trail. *Fletch* is in a funk too, for it seems the duration of his incredible jaunt exceeded the 24-hour limit by 45 minutes. This is so incredible! How on God's green earth did he get through that maze and mush in a pitch-black downpour? I'm just trying, with all my energy and determination, and with good fortune and the Grace of God, to get these miles behind me, and these young kids are out here making games of it! We talk for quite a while, while waiting for *Birch* to return. *Fletch* continues to be hard on himself, for in his mind the whole ordeal during the last 24 hours (and 45 minutes) has been a total failure. I finally say, "Look, *Fletch*, you've heard of leap year, right? That's where Father Time throws in an extra day. Okay, well, I've just had a conference with both Mother Nature and Father Time, and after hearing the circumstances of your situation, they've both agreed—and just for you—that yesterday was leap day, there being an extra hour!" This cheers him up as we both have a good laugh and he seems to feel a little better. *Birch* returns and we all have a grand (Garveying in the woods) feast, out of the cold murk, right on the stage apron.

It's 4:00 p.m. before I finally reach the Mason-Dixon Line. Eight states behind me, eight more to go. Alas, but do I know that this state line pretty much marks the end of sweet tea, biscuits and gravy, grits, good old corn fritters, BBQ, and hush puppies, but I've still got my GORP and glue stew! The treadway finally settles into flat terrain, many roads, and barking dogs. *Birch* and I had talked about staying at Deer Lick Shelters, but a large church group occupies both so I read the shelter journal and push on. Hiking through ahead of me today are *Weatherman*, *Joliet Joe*, and *Wolfhound*. *Boyscout* was one of those getting off at Harpers Ferry. Saying goodbye to *Weatherman* and all of us, she hopped a commuter back to NYC and was gone. Gonna miss you, dear friend! I soon pass the picturesque old log shelters of Antietam, built years ago on a flat spit of land next to a clear-rushing brook. In a short while I arrive at Tumbling Run Shelters. Here are two log lean-tos, a privy, a lovely spring, picnic tables, clotheslines, a water gauge, and a thermometer. There's no one around, so I have my pick. *Birch* comes in shortly and we spend a relaxing, enjoyable evening together . . . capping off a great hiking day!

PROFILES '98

WHITCOMB WICK *Fletch* FAIRBANKS IV is 24 and single, and hails from Marco Island, Florida, and more recently, Dublin, Georgia. He attended high school in Saratoga Springs, New York, and Laley, Florida. *Fletch* is a graduate of Georgia Southern University with a degree in natural and cultural resource management. His pregraduate employment included working winters in south Florida at a beachside hotel, restaurant, fitness center, and gift shop. His postgraduate plans were to return to hotel work, but after his first resume, first job application, and first interview, he landed his first job! He was hired by Boy Scouts of America in Macon, Georgia. With the Scouts he served as district director for eight Georgia counties. The position involved recruiting, speaking engagements, program management and, oh yes—fund-raising. *Fletch* beams with pride as he relates one successful event that raised $17,000 in one night! He had hiking the AT in the back of his mind all along as something he dearly wanted to do, but, alas, with the new job the trail would have to wait.

His interest and hobbies include reading, golf, fishing, inline skating, and any and all outdoor sports. "In the spring of '97 and as I settled into my new job I knew that my plans were to be on the AT at that time, but I really liked my work and I wanted to hold onto the job for at least three years. When the spring of '98 rolled around, it became unbearable. I knew I needed to get this trail thing out of my system once and for all . . . before settling down and dedicating myself to a career. So on February 22, 1998, I took that fateful step . . . I walked into my boss's office and explained that they needed to start looking for someone to take my place." Ah, and here that fateful step has led him today, for he is living his dream!

Fletch's future plans: "I could go back with BSA, but I'd like to get into the sales field, such as a rep for a pharmaceutical company or perhaps one of these outdoor firms. The trail experience could help me get a job like that. I like sales because it is incentive driven—the harder you work, the better you do. I've been thinking, while here on the trail, just how important work is to me. Everyone should be, and indeed everyone needs to be, an active part of society. For the next 20 to 25 years in my life I'm looking forward to working extremely hard."

Fletch, you're a positive and upbeat young man. Your vitality and the ethics and moral standards that I see in you, which I thought were lost to the young in our society today, are characteristics I am finding to be a most common thread throughout this family of young folks here on the trail. How refreshing to see this over and over again. You and all of our friends out here laboring in this journey have gone far in restoring my faith in the future of this great country of ours. There actually are young people around today who can still think and act and do for themselves. What a joy to see! You're a self-starter, *Fletch*, a go-getter. I predict a very successful future for you. Never lose your magnetic smile and your positive attitude. It's truly a blessing to call you and to be called . . . friend. See you on Katahdin!

> *"The sunrise was a precious time for me as I watched*
> *the sun slowly rise over the horizon; and felt God's*
> *awesome peace descend upon the mountains."*
> [Kenneth Wadness, *Sojourn in the Wilderness*]

THURSDAY July 9, 1998
TRAIL DAY 174/80 ✦ TRAIL MILE 2,468/1,066
LOCATION Birch Run Shelters

I GET OUT A LITTLE AFTER 9:00 A.M. to be greeted by the makings for a great day. *Birch* will be going into the village of South Mountain for a mail drop, so I probably won't see him again until this evening. *Hopalong* is ahead of me, having already passed through Deer Lick Shelters early this morning. The trail into Caledonia State Park is over smooth, flat, treadway, and I make very good time. Once in the park I find *Hopalong* sitting at one of the picnic tables reading a book. Not far is a swimming pool, complete with a concession stand, so we head for the food. Great burger and fries plus another order of fries, then to polish it all off comes lemonade and a huge bowl of the most incredible Hershey Dairy Moose Track ice cream. I absolutely cannot understand how any self-respecting member of the Hiker Trash Fratority would ever shell out the incredible bucks for a pint of that other brand when these local dairies are scooping up this kind of stuff.

While here at the concession stand, up comes a thru-hiker—*Two Showers*. She holds up an object and asks if we might know to whom it belongs. I can't believe my eyes! I clutch my chest, look at *Two Showers*, then clutch my chest again . . . indeed it is gone, and she has it, dangling there from her fingers—my medicine pouch given me by *Mountain Man* clear down in Hatchet Creek, Alabama. I didn't even know it had fallen from my neck. *Two Showers* says she picked it up right in the middle of the trail. What a miracle to have it returned to me, and what a joy not to have suffered the loss, even for one moment! The pouch itself now means much to me, but of even more value, sentimental though it might be, within the pouch have I placed a priceless touchstone, a bridge to the past, to all of nature, if you will, and to my grandfather who I loved dearly. Fifty years ago we found it together, in a freshly plowed field where we would often while away hours searching together for Indian artifacts. This, a perfect point, the smallest and most beautifully shaped I've ever seen—flawless! Less than an inch in length and a quarter-inch wide, near as thin as a wafer, perfectly barbed and tapered, delicately crafted thousands of years ago from pure gray-white flint found only along the Osage in Missouri. I have seen many fine Indian-artifact collections and have a respectable collection of arrow points, spear points, fulcrum points, scrapers, and drills myself, but I have never seen another point so small and perfectly shaped as this. And here, after having lost it, is it now handed back to me. Oh, I am so blessed to have it returned. This is a miracle! I must not risk losing this precious link with the past ever again. *Two Showers,* thank you, oh dear friend, thank you so much!

I've had a few days now to get into the swing of using my poplar-sapling hiking sticks. I absolutely don't know how I managed so long without them. They have proven invaluable. The relief to the knee-and-foot pounding alone is nothing short of miraculous. The knee pain I had been suffering—to the point of becoming increasingly troublesome and chronic—has improved markedly. I now am confident I'll be over the problem soon. Without the use of sticks, I had to concentrate almost constantly on balance and foot placement. But with the sticks, which provide consistent two- and three-point contact, foot placement—precise and perfect foot placement—becomes a simple and almost effortless task. Without the sticks, I had been stubbing my toes so often and so hard that I was knocking my shoe soles loose. Re-laminating the front soles amounted to the major repair needed in Waynesboro. With the sticks I'm now getting that extra fraction of an inch lift with each stride, just enough to clear 90 percent of the obstacles I'd been stumbling over. Without the sticks I was suffering pooling and swelling in my hands from constantly swinging and slinging them by my side. With the sticks I have had 100 percent relief from this annoyance, and I can now feel development and strength returning to my shoulders, arms, and upper body. Without the sticks, foot tracking tended to stagger left and right of the trail's centerline as I moved along. With the sticks, and by pushing with each forward stride, progress is stepped up and foot tracking tends to follow closer (and more efficiently) to the treadway centerline. There are many other benefits, such as better downhill control and a ready device to poke rattlesnakes off the trail, but these are the main ones. Yes, I like my sticks a lot . . . you won't catch me without them the remainder of this odyssey!

I arrive at Birch Run Shelters around 7:00 p.m. to find *Birch* and *Hopalong* already here. We get a cooking and warming (yes—warming) fire going. I borrow some hydrocortisone cream from a group camped down in the lower meadow. We were all hit hard by yellow jackets today, and *Hopalong* has a mean-looking poison ivy rash on his ankles. Oooh, does that cream ever feel good! *Fletch* comes in just before dark.

> *"I never imagined that existence could be so simple, so uncluttered, so Spartan, so free of baggage, so sublimely gratifying. I have reduced the weight of my pack to 35 pounds and yet I can't think of a single thing I really need that I can't find, either within myself or within my pack."*
>
> [David Brill, *As Far as the Eye Can See*]

FRIDAY July 10, 1998
TRAIL DAY 175/81 ✦ TRAIL MILE 2,494/1,092
LOCATION Alec Kennedy Shelter

I'M OUT EARLY, BEFORE 7:00 A.M., as I want to reach Pine Grove Furnace State Park by noon. The store at the park is home to the thruhikers "Half-Gallon Club." All you need do to join is eat a half gallon of your favorite ice cream as fast as you can. When *Fletch, Hopalong,* and *Birch* arrive we go at it. I'm able to down a half gallon of Hershey Dairy peanut butter in 24 minutes but am easily beaten out by *Fletch* who downed his butter pecan in 21 minutes!

I see and talk again (after I'm able to move my tongue and lips again) with good trail friends *Skitz* (who downed his ice cream yesterday in 14 minutes), *Weatherman, Moose, Buddha Boy* (who's getting off the trail), and *Old Goat.*

We've been faced with but a few difficult ascents since leaving Virginia. In West Virginia, Maryland, and now Pennsylvania, there have been only a handful of anywhere-near-respectable pulls, most being in or below the three-Snickers category. Here in Pennsylvania the treadway is just very rough, filled with miles of loosely piled and jutting rocks. When I try explaining this to folks—how difficult this sort of treadway can be—I simply make this analogy: "Have you ever seen brick masons building a house or an office building, and below the scaffolding where they're working there's this pile of rubble made up of broken block and brick? Well, just imagine mile after mile and day after day of piles of this stuff . . . that's the trail." I hit more rubble this afternoon, and progress again becomes slow and deliberate. It's almost dark as I arrive at Alec Kennedy Shelter. Finding the shelter full, I pitch in a small clearing near the stream. During the night I put on every stitch of clothing I have as the mercury drops to 44 degrees.

A few days back I alluded to the inevitable impending loss of nails from both great toes and second toes . . . again. The nails on my second toes have grown back, and those on my great toes have almost grown back since losing them after emerging from 50 days in the swamps of Florida. Why I'm having this problem again this late in the game beats me, but the entire intact nail on my right second toe comes completely off this evening, leaving an indented horseshoe-shaped area where it used to be! This will sure make for some tenderness for the next few days. It seems like there's always something. I'm tending to become weary now at times . . . but I'm still here.

"If you'll pick 'em up, O Lord, I'll put 'em down."

[Anonymous, *Prayer of a Tired Hiker*]

THE "CUMBERLAND VALLEY ROADWALK" is history, the trail having been removed from the secondary county roads and busy US 11 some ten years now. No more Bonnie *The Ice Cream Lady* Shipe, or tenting in the Messer yard. The trail now zigzags through hay and wheat fields and along the lower valley ridges. This relocation has added a delightful new trail town for all to enjoy. As trail towns go, Boiling Springs, Pennsylvania, is classic: a small, quaint setting, more rural than urban, with historic, neat old homes, churches, shops, and businesses, and a beautiful, spring-fed lake complete with Canadian geese. This trail town has it in spades! And there is an ATC regional office here, where hikers are welcome to use the porch to congregate. The trail now crosses the Pennsylvania Turnpike over a secondary-road overpass, ditto for I-81, and is completely off US 11, crossing it via a great new pedestrian bridge. Guess I'm set in my ways, but the nostalgic old roadwalk? I found that much more to my liking.

Just before entering Boiling Springs, near the railroad crossing and sitting beside the trail, I am greeted by a young hiker with the largest food-drop box that I believe I've ever seen. I stop to find out what gives, and it is here where I meet *Pan. Pan* is the last remaining of a foursome that departed Springer Mountain months ago with high hopes and grand dreams of thru-hiking the AT. They were known as the *Fabulous Four.* Making up the foursome were *Pan*, her younger sister, her older brother and her brother-in-law. As we sit together now, and with tear-filled eyes, *Pan* relates her story to me. It seems their odyssey started out so well, with such wonder and anticipation. But once the grand excitement of hiking together wore off and as the day-to-day grind of it all descended upon them, they became discouraged and disheartened. *Pan*, who was the slowest and weakest of the group, often delayed their progress. Finally, sensing the mounting impatience and frustration, she did the only thing she knew to do—she urged them to go on ahead and leave her to plod along alone. So it was that they all decided to go their separate ways, to enjoy their separate days on up the trail, leaving *Pan* to bring up the rear. Well, so it seems, and as her family all hastened north ahead of her, that one by one each of them gave it up, got off the trail and went home . . . all that is, except *Pan*. And here she sits today, more than 1,100 miles north of Springer Mountain, all alone. And here, this day does this not-so-happy story also end, for this is *Pan*'s last day on the Appalachian Trail. Today, she, too, will be leaving the trail, going home. So here she sits now with this huge box of food, sent with so much love-filled anticipation to Boiling Springs . . . for the *Fabulous Four*. With the saddest expression and as she looks over to me now, *Pan* says, "Please take some of this food, *Nomad*, I won't be needing any of it anymore."

In Boiling Springs today congregate many thru-hiking trail friends: *Two Showers, Joliet Joe, Pan, Wild Gess* and *Mountain Laurel, Jelly Bean* and *Cuppa-Joe* (his daughter), *Turtle, Yo-Yo, Fletch, Bump, Birch, Moose, Hopalong, Skitz, Little Mac,* and *Flutterby*. A grand lunch seems the thing to do, so *Pan, Two Showers, Joliet Joe,* and I head to Anile's Italian Restaurant for pizza. My poplar-sapling hiking sticks usually draw a fair amount of attention, and as we're enjoying our pizza the topic turns to the subject of trekking poles. We talk about how much easier it is to hike with poles, and I relate my recent learning experience using the poplar saplings and how they're already wearing shorter . . . and how it would be great to someday own a fine pair of well-built professional trekkers.

Back now at the ATC regional office and as I shoulder my pack and prepare to leave, *Pan* comes to me and holds out her beautiful Leki Super Makalu Trekking Poles. "*Nomad*, I want you to have these, please take them." I look at her in astonishment. I am totally flabbergasted. I don't know what to say. In a moment, I manage, "*Pan*, I can't take your poles. Oh, thank you so much, but I can't take your poles. You need them." Continuing to hold the poles out to me, *Pan* says, "I won't be needing them any longer. I really want you to have them. Please take them." I persist, "*Pan*, please, I just can't take your beautiful hiking poles." Reaching now for my old saplings, she says, "Okay, then trade me, you take these and give me yours." Sensing now her never-take-no insistence, I relent. Accepting her wonderful generosity and with tears in my eyes, I reply, "Okay *Pan*, okay, it's a deal. I'll trade." As I turn to go, *Pan* gives me a big hug. "Just one more thing, *Nomad,* " she says, "Send me a picture of you and my poles by the old sign on Katahdin." And so I will, *Pan,* and so I will. What a remarkable example of the unity, the bonds, the incredible and unexplainable ties, and the from-the-heart caring that is this thru-hiker community. I have known *Pan* for less than three hours . . . I'd have to look back in my notepad to even remember her name.

Ascending to Darlington Shelter I'm afforded a grand view across the entire breadth and a great width of this beautiful, rolling, lush-green Cumberland Valley. I arrive to share Darlington Shelter with *Joliet Joe* and *Wild Gess* and *Mountain Laurel.* The cooking-turned-warming fire feels very good. Nice old shelter. Water way, way down. What an incredible, emotional day.

> *Come look o'er this Eden, the Cumberland.*
> *Come walk through this valley of time.*
> *On a crisp, clear Sunday morning,*
> *Hear the peal of the church bells chime.*
> *Through the waving fields of golden grain,*
> *Past the springs of Conodoguinet.*
> *The trail, the boroughs and quaint old farms;*
> *'Tis a journey you won't forget.*
>
> [N. Nomad]

SUNDAY July 12, 1998
TRAIL DAY 177/83 ✦ TRAIL MILE 2,523/1,121
LOCATION Duncannon, The Doyle Hotel

IT'S ONLY 11 MILES TO DUNCANNON, and I would like to be there by late morning, so I'm up and out shortly after dawn. There is much rough and rocky treadway along the ridge, but the view from Hawk Rock down onto the beautiful Susquehanna River and the little town of Duncannon is picture perfect, making the hike most rewarding. I am able to literally glide over the rocks and boulders with the Leki trekking poles. My old saplings bounced, quivered, and skipped off of everything, but these puppies stick no matter where I jam them. I arrive and check in at the Doyle Hotel at 11:00 a.m. It's been a blue-perfect hiking morning.

I have lunch at the Doyle and lounge most of the day with my feet up. I manage to work on my journal entries, do some laundry, and make a few calls. In the evening I go for pizza at Sorrento's Italian Restaurant, and I'm in the sack by 9.

> *"When the thought first occurred that the Lord might want me to hike the trail, I put it out of my mind, When the idea kept coming back I told God He had the wrong Bill Irwin, I'm the blind guy, remember?"*
>
> [Bill Irwin, *Blind Courage*]

MONDAY July 13, 1998
TRAIL DAY 178/84 ✦ TRAIL MILE 2,541/1,139
LOCATION PA 325, Clarks Valley Campsite

I SLEPT GREAT LAST NIGHT HERE AT THE OLD DOYLE in room #112, third floor, same room I stayed in 15 years ago. I do believe the dresser, chair, and bed are the same. And I wouldn't be a bit surprised if the little concave mattress and old gray pillow are the same ones, too! I'm up and down to the bar at 7:30 a.m. for a fine breakfast. I notice the outside door to the bar still sticks badly, just like it did 15 years ago. About the only thing I can tell that's changed around here is that the ceiling is gone now out of the upstairs bathroom. I know that every day this old relic continues to stand increases the odds that it won't be here in the morning, but I really like the old palace and I'm willing to take that chance. I bet *Crazy One* would've stayed here had he passed this way in 1948. The trail crossed the Susquehanna downriver at Harrisburg back then. But it's passed through here now for many a year, and this section, plus much of the trail north of here, was relocated because of Earl's effort.

My pack straps have really been creeping the last few weeks, and the problem is getting worse and worse, to the point of becoming downright annoying. I contacted the folks at Kelty a while back, and they said

I needed some new buckles. They're waiting for me general delivery here at the post office this morning, along with lots of mail from family and friends . . . also waiting patiently, my old friend, the bounce box. I pick up a few items at the drug store, head over to the convenience store, and then it's back to the Doyle to get what I need from my bounce box, then to get it sealed and ready to bounce on to Bear Mountain, New York.

I get my pack organized and check out of the grand old Doyle a little after 11:00 a.m. Back at the post office to mail my bounce box and some postcards, I see *Skitz*, *Birch*, and *Hopalong* getting their mail drops. I don't envy *Skitz*. He's got a new pair of boots to break in. I manage to get out of Duncannon a little after noon. Duncannon is a neat trail town, and I feel a little smug for not getting stuck here as I head across the Juniata Bridge.

The trail crosses the Susquehanna on the Clarks Ferry Bridge, then it's over the railroad tracks for the first respectable pull in quite a while, up and onto Peters Mountain. Even with liberal switchbacks I still give it three Snickers. As I climb I'm looking at how people have been cutting the switchbacks all along, creating washouts and much erosion. The problem with switchbacks seems to be that somebody's always cutting them, hand-over-hand straight up, or butt-slidin' straight down, don't matter; somebody's always cutting 'em! Once I gain Peters Mountain to arrive at Table Rock I'm afforded a grand and sweeping view of the Juniata and the Susquehanna. Both are emerging from the far mountain haze to tumble along to where they finally merge here just below. It's been a tough climb to gain the view here from Table Rock, but it's been well worth it!

From Table Rock on, and for the remainder of this day, my thoughts are about my last hike up Peters Mountain many years ago with my dear sister, Salle Anne. We were visiting family just over Peters Mountain in the beautiful little mountain village of Elizabethville. I can remember the summers we would spend there with our grandparents. They've since gone to their final rest, high on a hill, as has our mother . . . across the valley here and most-near in the shadow of Peters Mountain. It is a bittersweet hike today as I tread this path again—alone.

Well, I cut the last switchback, skid-tumbled, and fell,
And got wracked like I knowed that I would.
But in 4,000 miles I saved 94 feet,
And that really made me feel good.

[N. Nomad, *Now Cut That Out!*]

TUESDAY July 14, 1998
TRAIL DAY 179/85 ✦ TRAIL MILE 2,566/1,164
LOCATION William Penn Shelter

THE EVENING LAST WAS VERY ENJOYABLE as I relaxed with *Flutterby,*
Little Mac, and *Truly Blessed. Truly Blessed* is up early this morning to greet
her brother, who has come to visit. I break camp and am on my way
before 8:00 a.m.

On Stony Mountain, where the Horse-Shoe Trail begins, thence
from here to lead to Valley Forge, I see *Moose* again. We tarry as he talks
about how Horse-Shoe Trail was the first he'd hiked many years ago as
a Scout. *Moose* is from Lancaster, Pennsylvania. I enjoy sharing his joy as
he recalls, with that faraway glint of reminiscence, those fond memories.
Moose takes a picture of the bronze plaque marking the trail's beginning,
and after a brief and final glance over our packs, we move on north on
the AT.

The old AT coasts along pretty good today, mostly flat terrain.
But on the ridgeline, and as it narrows, come the rocks and boulders.
That doesn't stop the trail, and through this helter-skelter we go! The
likes of it will surely slow you down, wear you down, and if you don't
concentrate every second it will finally take you down!

I reach William Penn Shelter around 6:00 p.m. *Two Showers*
comes in shortly after. With the shelter down the dark side of the mountain, I've decided to pitch on the ridge near the trail to enjoy the
evening breeze, the view, and the morning sunrise. As I relax here this
evening in quiet repose, gazing out across this lush, fertile valley and
countryside, settled now centuries ago, I think of those brave and

adventurous settlers. I am one of those adventurers, just as surely as I am one of their descendants. What a proud heritage, what a remarkable ancestry. My parents, grandparents, great-grandparents, and all of theirs were born and raised near this place. I am an eighth generation descendent of the Enders family, who immigrated to the New World in the 1700s. There is a quaint little village, Enders, Pennsylvania, nearby in a quiet, picturesque high valley up from Harrisburg. In a shady, five-acre grove by the rolling countryside near Enders is found the family picnic grounds, complete with croquet lawn, horseshoe pits, and covered and enclosed pavilions. Here each August, family members come from most every state and many foreign countries to attend the family reunion. It's such a grand affair with much fine celebration and fun . . . and much-too-much good food!

> *The ribs of Pennsyltucky*
> *Form backbones straight and rough.*
> *And here the trekker's lucky*
> *To make it through this stuff.*

> [N. Nomad]

WEDNESDAY July 15, 1998
TRAIL DAY 180/86 ✦ TRAIL MILE 2,593/1,191
LOCATION Port Clinton, Port Clinton Hotel

I MANAGE TO GET UP AT DAWN and back on the trail shortly after 6:00 a.m. I'll be doing 27 miles today over rough rock-and-boulder-strewn treadway. I'm anxious to get on through Pennsylvania and get this continuous rocky trail behind me. There's about 70 miles of this mentally taxing and difficult going remaining. I stop at the 501 Shelter, arriving around 8:00 a.m., to find *Joliet Joe, Plush, Weary Pilgrim,* and *Lollipop. Townsman* and *Wolfhound* have just gone out. About noon I find *Wolfhound* relaxing along the trail and we discuss sharing a room at the Port Clinton Hotel.

There's not much water along the trail up here on these ridges, so I must conserve. But it's a mild, overcast day, and my strength and stamina remain high. I've been taking the electrolyte caps Succeed, which help me maintain a more-constant energy level. Negotiating the rocks and boulders for hours on end becomes both physically demanding and mentally taxing. I have a few bumps and bruises, but the feet seem to be holding up pretty well. I'm wearing a sturdy three-pound boot with Vibram lug soles and steel shanks. They're called Danner Lights, made by Danner out in Oregon. I've had them resoled and the soles re-laminated once, but they're working very well. This is an absolute and certain blessing, as many, if not most, thru-hikers are starting to have boot problems.

There's poison ivy everywhere in the rocks and boulders, so I have my gaiters hiked up as far as they will go. The ivy presents no problem for me, but avoiding it is prudent. Neighbors used to have me come over, dig the vines up, then rip them down from their trees.

I reach Port Clinton by 5:00 p.m., and shortly thereafter I arrive at the Port Clinton Hotel. After spending 11 long and stressful hours in the rocks and boulders, I reward myself for a successful injury-free day by hoisting a couple of tall Yuengling frosties. Yuengling is America's oldest brewery, famous for its fine premium beer. Ahhh, yes, this is fine. "Here's to ya, Yuengling! And here's to you, too, *Nomad*, ya done good today!" The Port Clinton Hotel is clean, neat, and well maintained, a modest but most proud establishment hosted by its proud owners, Billie Ann Russell and Paul Engle. *Wolfhound* makes it to join me, and we share a room. After getting cleaned up as best as we can, we head down for supper and a few more tall ones. I'll sleep well tonight!

> *The rocks of ol' Blue Mountain*
> *Strike brutal and relentless.*
> *Lord on your help we're countin'*
> *'Cause . . . we are near defenseless.*

[N. Nomad]

I HAD A MEMORABLE STAY AT THE VERY FINE OLD Port Clinton Hotel. Billie Ann is an innkeeper and bartender par excellence, and Paul is a great cook. So the stay, the meals, and the hospitality were really grand. These folks truly care about and cater to hikers. And what a wonderful family gathering here last evening. Some good old friends and some new faces. Coming and going were *Kodiac, Soul Sharer, Townsman, Walkabout, Caretaker,* and *Wolfhound.* Billie Ann insists on getting her picture with me by their front door. I stand with my pack on and ready to go, she and Paul follow me out, and Paul snaps a picture of Billie Ann and me while we both stand with tears running down our faces. Folks, don't ask me to explain this. I know, I know, I only met these folks yesterday. Believe me, I don't understand it, either! Thanks, dear friends, for your kindness and for caring.

The trail down into Port Clinton was a slider, no switchbacks, just straight down, so, too, for the climb back out . . . a strong three-Snickers pull. I pass three old boxed, swift-flowing springs today. A tin of cold, clear water from one of these springs and a little lemonade mix and you couldn't prepare a better refreshment for a tired, thirsty, hiker . . . and the springs' names just add to their appeal: Pocahontas, Minnehaha, and Gold Spring! Of course, those who must care for us and feel we need constant direction, lest we perish, have posted these beautiful springs: "Water source not tested for potability, boil or treat all water." If this water is going to make us sick, God help us if we must drink the water from New York City, Boston, or Philly!

"Now this is what we believe. The mother of us all is earth, the father is the sun, the grandfather is the creator, who bathed us with his mind and gave life to all things. The brother is the beasts and the trees. The sister is that with wings. We are the children of earth and do it no harm in any way, nor do we offend the sun by

not greeting it at dawn. We praise our grandfather for
his creation. We share the same breath together, the
locusts, the trees, the birds, the man."

[Nancy Wood, Taos Indian]

FRIDAY July 17, 1998
TRAIL DAY 182/88 ✦ TRAIL MILE 2,636/1,234
LOCATION Palmerton, Palmerton Hotel

I FINALLY CATCH UP WITH MY GOOD FRIEND *100# Stormcloud*. He was
at Allentown Hiking Club Shelter when I arrived, and we shared a most
enjoyable evening talking trail. We hiked the Smokies and most of
Tennessee together. I got off and went to Trail Days in Damascus and
Stormy stayed the trail getting ahead of me. It's taken me more than two
months to catch up and finally see him again. He's still lugging a helluva
load, but he and his pack have both slimmed down. Stormy got tagged
right off the bat with his trail name . . . had to do with the incredible load
he lugged off Springer and the accompanying storm cloud that seemed
to hover above him. I also enjoyed the evening with *Ender, D and D Rose,*
Canucklehead, Ringbearer, King Cheese, and *Walkabout.*

The hike today offers one of the most exciting boulder scrambles
ever, along the ridge at Bear Rocks—boulders the size of boxcars with
smaller boulders (automobile size) lodged helter-skelter in between! It's
hop, skip, and jump time, a great adrenaline pump. Then it's back to the
tedium and monotony of miles of rocks and slow, hard going. Along the
way today I meet and hike some with *Rascal, Frank'n Pops, Nomad*
(another *Nomad*), *Hippie, Tim,* and *Puck.* I'm meeting all these new folks
as I catch and pass them.

As luck would have it and as I stick my thumb out at PA 248, I'm
given a ride right away clear to the front door at the Palmerton Hotel. I
can't believe it, but I'm in at 2:30 p.m. The main floor in most of these old
hotels is mainly bar. And the Palmerton Hotel has a fine bar. Checking in
and cleaning up a bit, I'm right back down to belly up for a couple more
premium Yuengling frosties! *100# Stormcloud, Ringbearer, Bump* (yup, *Bump*

is back again), and *Canucklehead* make it in about 4:00 p.m. They were unable to get a ride and had to walk the 2 miles into town. *Stormy* moves in to split the room with me and *Canuckle*, *Ringbearer*, and *Bump* head for the police station where they'll spend the night in the basement—yup, free lodging for thru-hikers in the police-station basement! Palmerton is another neat, friendly trail town.

> *"In town, stay at the hostel, the church, the hospice, the monastery, the fire house, the community center, the fraternity house, the mountain inn, the boarding house, the hotel, the motel or the home of a former Georgia-to-Mainer. (Don't forget the police station.)"*
>
> [Darrell *The Philosopher* Maret, GAME '80]

SATURDAY July 18, 1998
TRAIL DAY 183/89 ✦ TRAIL MILE 2,657/1,255
LOCATION PA 33, Wind Gap, Gateway Motel

THERE'S A FINE LITTLE MOM 'N' POP RIGHT ACROSS the street from the hotel where we all congregate for a hiker kind of breakfast. Last evening I'd called Dr. Howard Cyr. Doc Cyr is a retired Palmerton dentist, a local trail angel who offers free shuttles. He said he'd be glad to give us a ride. He'd also recommended this café, and he's right here curbside at 8:00 a.m. to shuttle us back to the trail at Lehigh River Bridge. Thanks for the lift, Doc!

We all begin the climb from the valley at 8:30 a.m. And what an incredible climb it is, near straight up over sheer ledges, rock faces, and boulders. At times the blazes seem to go straight up. I finally get my mind better set and can handle the ascent much easier by convincing myself, as I stare up at the rocks jutting into space, that if the trail crew made it up there with a paintbrush and a bucket of paint, surely I can get up there with my pack. This silly little mental game pays off, and I make it up just fine! Once on the ridge the environs turn almost alpine, with rocks and stunted, wind-whipped conifers. And what far-sweeping views into the lush, green Lehigh Valley and the mountain ranges beyond. And what a joy to be blessed again with perfect weather, clear and cool, with a light, refreshing breeze, which the kind hawks rest their outstretched wings on, to glide and soar for hours.

There is much more incredibly rocky, rough, and rugged tread-way today. I hear many complaints of bruised feet and ankle pain. But my feet, ankles, and knees do fine as I cruise right through, my new poles letting me glide across the rocks. This is definitely hard work, and I sweat profusely nearly all day long. The electrolyte capsules have proven to be a great help, and I'm handling the heat okay.

Hiking along and alone through the rocks, and in a daze-like trance, a mental state that I have found not only unavoidable but at times very welcome, I come upon a large eastern diamondback rattlesnake — right on the trail. Whoa! It's time to shake it off and haul 'er down! Gaining my composure from this rude interruption, it becomes apparent that this fellow is in no hurry to relinquish his fine spot in the sun. It's time for a break anyway, so I decide to relax on a boulder next to him and enjoy his company. What a gorgeous serpent. His skin just glistens in the rays of the bright sun, radiating all the remarkably rich and colorful shades of royalty, much as the luminance reflected from the undulating movement of oil on water. He finally tires of my company and decides to move on. A gentle tap from my pole on his large pitted and arrow-pointed head discourages him and brings him to coil, rattle, and hiss at me. "It's okay. Don't get upset now," I say. "I just want you to stick around awhile so the others can see your most impressive size and alluring beauty." Settling back down and while we continue in each other's company, soon come *Ringbearer, Stormy,* and *Canucklehead.* All must get his picture, for they, too, are impressed by the serpent's size and strikingly beautiful color. As snakes go, three feet is not a great length, but rattlesnakes can be incredibly large . . . and very short. This fellow is pushing three feet, is as big around as the business end of a baseball bat, and is sporting 13 rattles. I finally usher him off the trail and into the woods where he and other unwary hikers can both be out of harm's way.

We arrive at Wind Gap around 4:00 p.m. to hike the short distance to Gateway Motel. I manage to Yogi a hiker deal out of Pete, the proprietor, and, as if in choreographed unison, we all sigh and drop our packs. *Stormy* and I split a room and *Canucklehead, Ringbearer,* and *Bump* pile into another. Part of the special deal . . . Pete agrees to fetch a case of premium Yuengling right away and then drive us into Wind Gap later for supper. The longneck Yuenglings, as usual, are most refreshing—in a way only tired hikers would know, with plenty left over for Pete. And the stromboli at Sal's Pizza? Ah, simply out of this world. Thanks, Pete!

> *"The woods are made for the hunters of dreams,*
> *the brooks for the fishers of song."*
>
> [Sam Walter Foss]

SUNDAY July 19, 1998
TRAIL DAY 184/90 ✦ TRAIL MILE 2,672/1,270
LOCATION PA 611, Delaware Water Gap,
Presbyterian Church of the Mountain Hostel

Stormy AND I MANAGE TO GET OUT AT 8:30 A.M. to be greeted to another perfect hiking day. There are only 15 more miles of Pennsylvania rocks, and we're into New Jersey! These long, straight Pennsylvania mountains are not only tough going but dry. Up here on the ridge there is no water, so what a pleasant surprise at Fox Gap to meet *Fanny Pack,* GAME '95. *Fanny Pack* is thru-hiker-turned-trail-angel of the highest order. As *Stormy* and I approach, we are greeted by the biggest smile, larger, if that is possible, than the huge cooler *Fanny Pack* has lugged to the trail. And what is this magic? Oh yes, cold pop, donuts, and the finest of the finest of all trail magic: PBJs . . . good old peanut-butter-and-jelly sandwiches! We enjoy the break, the good food and refreshments, and the lively and exhilarating trail talk with *Fanny Pack.* This is Christmas in July . . . thanks, *Fanny Pack*!

Our thirst quenched, *Stormy* and I continue on to marvel in disbelief at the remarkable views down into the Delaware Water Gap, first from Lookout Rock thence from Council Rock. The angular granite strata on the mountainous wall across the gap is such an unusual and interesting sight. As I gaze, in the most impressive and near-realistic fashion this rugged mass of rock appears to lift and slide away right before my eyes. I must blink and then try to fix a reference to convince myself that what I see is indeed no more than a very fascinating optical illusion.

Stormy and I reach the Delaware Water Gap around 3:30 p.m., and as he waits for his sister to pick him up for a much deserved day or two rest at her place in the Poconos, I check into the hostel. What a joy seeing so many friends. I haven't crossed paths with *Long Distance Man* since way back in the Smokies. Here also are *Easy Rider, Frank 'n Pops, Thirty Seconds, Son Ray, Wood Butcher, Sunburn, Model-T,* and *Walkabout. Fanny Pack* also comes by for a while. In the evening and with tears welling up in me and a lump in my throat, I bid farewell to *100# Stormcloud.* Mayhaps I'll see him again, but not likely.

Model-T and I spend the remainder of the evening lounging on our bunks talking about many things. We first met on Springer Mountain in early April. He was standing at the first AT white blaze preparing to depart on his third AT thru-hike at age 62, and I was just arriving from my long and lonely journey from Florida. We hit it right off, but it's taken nearly three months now for our paths to finally cross again.

> *"The Delaware Water Gap lies within a couple of hours' driving of almost 30 million people in the great cities of New Jersey, Pennsylvania, and even New York, itself. It seems some sort of miracle that it should have remained so unspoiled."*
>
> [Nicholas Harman, *The Magnificent Continent*]

MONDAY July 20, 1998
TRAIL DAY 185/91 ✦ TRAIL MILE 2,697/1,295
LOCATION Brink Road Shelter, New Jersey

A QUICK TRIP TO THE POST OFFICE, and I'm back on the trail by 9:00 a.m. It's a long walk across the bridge over the Delaware River to New Jersey, and there's heavy truck traffic pushing hard through the Gap on I-80. But I'm thinking as I get buffeted along, *"Nomad,* you really are making progress. You started almost seven months ago with I-4 way

down in Florida, and now you've worked your way up to I-80 clear up
here in New Jersey . . . that's a lot of I's!"

The terrain is changing in New Jersey, but the rocks are still
here. Instead of Pennsylvania rocks, now they're New Jersey rocks. I
reach Sunfish Pond around 9:30 a.m., the first glacial pond the trail
passes. Yes, the terrain is definitely changing . . . this is a calendar-picture
setting! There's a tough pull over the rocks up Rattlesnake Mountain. I
am very glad to get to the shelter. This has been an incredibly rugged 25-
mile day.

PROFILES '98

ROBERT CLAYTON *100# Stormcloud* PETERMAN is 44, divorced with no
children, and hails from Hummelstown, Pennsylvania. *Stormy* is a graduate of Bishop McDivitt High School in Harrisburg, Pennsylvania. He
has a BS degree from the U.S. Naval Academy and an MA from
Georgetown University. He is a retired commissioned officer, U.S.
Navy, 22 years. *Stormy* was a Navy Seal and the first Commanding
Officer of Seal Team 8, a highly respected team that's still going strong.

"I was in Lebanon from July '83 to July '84. If you remember
your history, you will recall that the American Embassy there was
bombed in June of 1983. So I arrived during one major incident and was
there during another. For on January 1, 1984, and by the grace of God, I
avoided becoming the first American hostage in Lebanon. My guardian
angel protected me! In 1990 I helped Americans and many others from
other countries escape from Liberia by negotiating with the rebels that
were holding these people. On one expedition our team managed to bring
out the Spanish Ambassador, the Papal Nuncio, and the Swiss Chargé
d'Affaires along with their entourage, a total of 103 people.

"I am most proud of being a Boy Scout/Eagle Scout. Back when
I was about 14, we were on a Boy Scout trip in the Pine Grove
Furnace/Caledonia area. Here I met my first AT thru-hiker. Listening to
his stories and tales about the trail, I decided right then and there, 'One
of these days I'm going to do that — I'm going to hike the Appalachian

Trail.' So here I am, finally, after 30 years, after retiring as a Commander in the U.S. Navy, and before getting involved in anything else . . . I'm finally hiking the AT."

Stormy's future plans? "Two of my many options are: one, to study Chinese Oriental medicine, and two, to expand a family security business overseas. I really want to travel, visit, and see other countries."

"I look at the trail as a microcosm of life. You start at Springer Mountain and your final goal is Mt. Katahdin, and on the trail, as in life, you go through many challenges, many trials to get there. You learn things that will help you throughout life. Too many people are looking for that shortcut to success, the easy way, rather than setting their goals and taking the steps, one step at a time to get there. This approach, one step at a time, is the true path to success. This approach makes the accomplishment that much more worthwhile."

As you can see from the profiles so far, it is simply amazing, the vast spectrum that makes up this thru-hiker family . . . the folks who have come to hike the AT. Rob certainly has been one of the most interesting to know, to talk with, and to now consider a true friend. It is a joy that our paths have met, but it is with sadness now that I realize our paths must separate. I hope and pray that time and destiny will treat us kindly and that our paths may come together again. Until then, Godspeed, my dear friend!

> *"We never know how high we are*
> *Till we are called to rise;*
> *And then, if we are true to plan,*
> *Our statures touch the skies."*
>
> [Emily Dickinson]

TUESDAY July 21, 1998
TRAIL DAY 186/92 ✦ TRAIL MILE 2,716/1,314
LOCATION High Point Shelter

THESE ARE ABSOLUTELY PERFECT DAYS FOR HIKING: clear skies, cool breezes. Summertime is the hiker's true friend. It is upon us, and we must enjoy it. But, try as I may, today will not be one of those joyful summer days.

The pathway of broken brick has not ended here in New Jersey. The brickyard goes on, and the trail goes directly through it . . . on and on, mile after treacherous mile. I must deliberate intently with every step, exercising total concentration hour after hour. One miscue and it's all over, instantly, wrecking not only my day but my hike for good. So I plod along, head down, oblivious to all that is around me. And with the fatigue, which cannot be avoided, progress becomes so slow, so agonizingly slow, more of a staggering on than a hiking on, over, around and through the jumble and maze of never-ending rock.

Another grand challenge from day to day now is finding water. I have had to resort to taking water where I find it, even from puddles and tracks and other uninviting places. Not only is getting thirsty no fun, but it's also an invitation to a variety of very nasty things. But I have learned an important lesson here on the trail, and that lesson is about patience, not patience as we know it in ordinary life, but patience to a higher magnitude, to a higher degree. Having this form of patience now do I know that in a while the treadway will smooth out and water will again become abundant. So with a heightened resolve do I now trudge on . . . exercising patience!

I arrive at High Point Shelter at a surprisingly decent hour, to spend the evening with *Buzzy*.

PROFILES '98

J. R. *Model-T* TATE IS 62, MARRIED (Judith), with four children and six grandchildren. He's from Woodlawn, Tennessee. *Model-T* graduated from Springfield High, Springfield, and from Western Kentucky University, Bowling Green. He is a retired USMC Lieutenant Colonel.

Model-T enjoys gardening, fishing, backpacking, and loafing. But a loafer he is not, for he is now on his third journey thru-hiking the AT, the first being in 1990 and the second in 1994. *Model-T* professes to be a master Yogi-er. Says he, "You should see the old *Model-T* in action!"

And why hike the AT . . . three times? According to *Model-T,* "The first time it was the challenge—to be that one in ten. After that it was the call of the trail—that strong, undeniable pull. There was also a need for renewal—spiritual, mental, and physical—that I seem to require every few years—just to shrug off those bloated trappings of civilization, of modern-day living. I get that renewal from the rigors of hiking the AT." Pausing now, with that far-away glint, he says, "I got my eye on some trails out west!"

On completion of this third thru-hike, *Model-T* plans to write a book about his adventures (and misadventures) along the AT and make a video presentation about this 1998 hike. *Model-T* likens the human body to a sponge. What an interesting analogy. Says *Model-T,* "The human body is a sponge—it soaks up all the drippings of civilization, to the point where nothing else can be sucked up. When the body and mind get to that point, something needs to be done to squeeze it, to get it back to manageable levels, otherwise everything becomes distorted, over-loaded, overstimulated . . . even insane. There are many ways to wring the sponge—such as exercise, proper diet, a shrink. I've found my sponge can be squeezed by shouldering a backpack and taking to the woods and the trail . . . the longer, the better."

And, finally, a little of what this USMC veteran has gleaned from life: According to *Model-T,* "There's no such thing as a 'free lunch,' that is, unless you're a great Yogi-er! Even then it's quid pro quo, for the giver expects to be remembered through trail stories and in the ways one recalls experiences on the trail. So if you're a couch vagrant, expect to pay for it somewhere down the pike. If you use people, if you take more than you give, if you hog more than your share (like shelter space), it will all come back like a big crow to roost on your head—you'll have bird poop to remind you of your transgressions."

Folks, are you starting to get just a taste of the true flavor of this, for the joy that comes through the stimulation and intrigue offered by the day-to-day challenge, for the shared excitement and friendship of the remarkable people met along the way, for the memorable experience that just being out here brings, and finally . . . for what hiking this grand old AT is all about?

"When I was just a lad, my dad brought me up here one Sunday afternoon, and pointing to a sign on a tree said, 'That sign marks a solitary foot trail that runs all the way from Georgia to Maine.' I was just so intrigued by it, that there could be such a thing. I never got over it. I'm still not over it."

[Sam Waddle, Caretaker, Jerry Cabin]

WEDNESDAY July 22, 1998
TRAIL DAY 187/93 ✦ TRAIL MILE 2,736/1,334
LOCATION NJ 94, Vernon, Firemans Pavilion

I WAS DISAPPOINTED YESTERDAY TO ARRIVE at Culvers Gap to find Worthington's Bakery closed. It was no fun having to hike back into the woods with no pastries, pies, cinnamon rolls, or coffee. They take Tuesdays off. Today, after hiking the half mile down Lott Road, I am looking forward to a good meal at the Side Road Kitchen in Unionville. Yup, closed on Wednesdays! But, as luck would have it, just across the street is Horler's General Store. They're open, so I beat a path right in. Well now, this is fine. A well-stocked store, complete with deli and a picnic table to enjoy such delights in their spacious backyard. Okay, this'll work! I order a sub, and just as I'm picking up chips, pop, and ice cream, I glance up to notice another hiker across the aisle. The face looks familiar but I can't quite place him, yet I have a strong feeling we've met somewhere before.

So now with joy, will I relate to you another wonderful coincidence—more rather—a matter of destiny. For it seems that, for some strange reason, was I drawn this day into Unionville, New York, 93 days and more than 1,300 trail miles north of Springer Mountain, Georgia. I've got plenty of food in my pack and seldom do I walk off-trail this far for much of any reason, choosing rather to continue on north and on course toward Katahdin. So today, there is something else about this diversion to Unionville, some purpose other than a break for a pop and a submarine sandwich.

As the clerk wraps my sub he tells me I'm welcome to enjoy my meal at the picnic table behind the store where the other hiker has gone. So approaching the table with my bag of food, I find the old fellow sitting there reading the paper. He glances up, then continues reading as I sit down across from him. "What's your name, pop?" I say. As he looks back up I know immediately who he is. He replies in a soft, gentle voice, "*Just An Echo.*" I say, "You know we've met before, don't you?" Again in a low, yet penetrating voice he replies, "Yes, on Springer Mountain. You're the *Nimblewill Nomad.*"

And so it goes, for when I arrived from Alabama at the beginning of April, *Just An Echo* was at the Springer Mountain Shelter preparing to depart on the AT. We talked for quite a while on that cold and rainy day. When I came on the trail a couple of weeks later I began seeing his brief but thought-provoking entries in the shelter registers. They were all short sentences, written in a very light, small hand, barely, but with some effort, always legible. His entries roamed the spectrum, always brief, always succinct, like hammer set to nail—wham! His short comments were about the very most important things in life: honesty, integrity, friendship. truthfulness, love, patience, tolerance, an ear to listen, and on and on. Prime example: "Speak the truth, then let it be." Signed, *Just An Echo.*

What an incredibly appropriate trail name—*Just An Echo.* For what he penned in register after register spoke of the echo deep within all of us—that still, small voice that when heeded propels us along the paths of goodness and righteousness. And so, I popped into shelter after shelter, looking into register after register, hoping to find another of his entries and to keep track of his progress. Nearing the Smokies I came within two days of catching him. I very much wanted to talk with him again and to thank him for the inspiration I had gained and the enjoyment I had derived from his writings. But, alas, his entries stopped abruptly and he just seemed to vanish. Many thru-hikers I met along the trail for the next few weeks knew of him but none had seen him recently, nor could any of them tell me what may have happened to him.

And so, now you know and understand what a wonderful day this is for me. We sit and talk for a very long time about many things.

And in the course of conversation, as if it should be a surprise at all to me, *Just An Echo* explains, "What I wrote in those registers was for one purpose and one purpose only, and that purpose was to constantly remind me of the truly important matters in life."

Just An Echo, you're a remarkable inspiration. You speak softly yet with such assured conviction. You listen with patience and sincere interest and understanding. Your countenance radiates the unmistakable peace that only glows with such brightness when a man is truly at peace with himself and with his fellow man and with God. I now know that *Just An Echo* is working on becoming a 2,000 miler for the second time. Today, through this section, he's southbound and our paths meet again, here at the picnic table behind Horler's General Store in Unionville, New York, such a brief flicker out of boundless time. It seems such an incredible coincidence, but then again, I wonder. Godspeed, *Just An Echo*, and God bless!

I'm having increasing difficulty with my jaw. It has become unbearably painful, and I can no longer chew on my right side. The poison in my system is really sapping my strength, and I've been pooping out fast at the least demand and exertion. Something has got to be done. So arriving in Vernon early I beat it to the dentist's office. He takes x-rays and says he can't help me and that I need to see an oral surgeon. I was afraid of this. I tell him to set me up. He gives me the name of a surgeon in Monroe, New York, and he also gives me a script for penicillin, which I promptly fill. I'm determined to follow through, so I plan on rising early and hitching into Monroe.

I have the pleasure today of hiking some, then spending the evening at the pavilion with *Long Distance Man*, *Enlightened Rogue*, *Son Ray*, *Woodbutcher*, and *Buzzy*.

> *"The virtuous man is happy in this world, and he is*
> *happy in the next; he is happy in both. He is happy*
> *when he thinks of the good he has done; he is still more*
> *happy when going on the good path."*
>
> [Buddha, *The Dhammapada*]

THURSDAY July 23, 1998
TRAIL DAY 188/94 ✦ TRAIL MILE 2,753/1,351
LOCATION Eastern Pinnacles, New York

I CALL THE SURGEON'S OFFICE FIRST THING THIS MORNING. The answering service says he'll be in. The cook at the local mom 'n' pop restaurant says he knows exactly where the surgeon's office is located, and he takes a moment and writes down specific directions to the doctor's office in the 800 building.

So after breakfast I hitch out, getting a ride right away, right to the 800 building, arriving at 9:30 a.m. As I look, the doctor's name isn't on the office directory, but I figure that isn't unusual and I thank my hitch for the ride. Entering the building and looking for the information desk, I am informed by a passing nurse that the oral surgeon's office that I'm looking for is in the 800 building in Monroe and that I'm in the 800 building in Goshen, over 10 miles from where I need to be. So much for the helpful handwritten directions!

So back out to the street I go to hitch a ride to the 800 building in Monroe. I stand here for over two hours as thousands of vehicles pass, not one driver paying me even the least of a nod. Finally, an old fellow in a beat-up pickup with his dog right up front stops. I toss my pack on top the pile of trash in the sagging old bed and climb in with the two of them. The kind old gent takes me straight to the doctor's office even though it's about 5 miles out of his way. He says, "If I drop you off here where I turn, you'll still be standing right here when I come by in the morning!" I'm thinking, as we wobble and lurch along to Monroe, how this kind old gent doesn't fit in at all with this New York bunch, but I'm sure he already knows that. Arriving finally at Monroe I thank the old fellow for the ride. Climbing the stairs at the 800 building that lead to the surgeon's office I find his door locked. It's now a little after noon. Yup! Their office closes at noon on Thursday.

I have a devil of a time getting back to the trail where I came off yesterday, but I finally manage a ride. Thanking the young lady I cross the road and enter a field. I'm finally back on the trail at 3:30 p.m. I'm

learning slowly but surely to roll with the punches, go with the circumstances as they come along, not an easy trick for this old dog to learn. A
lot of things happen, sometimes day-to-day, that we just can't control or
perhaps ever even understand, and this day has been chock full of them.
Thinking this whole day over, I conclude that for some reason I just
wasn't supposed to get my jaw operated on.

I manage to make it to The Pinnacles and pitch on a bed of needles under a tall, slender fir. As I drift off I set my mind to letting the
penicillin do its thing and worry about getting my jaw fixed later.

> *"Thou great First Cause, least understood,*
> *Who all my sense confined*
> *To know but this, that thou art good,*
> *And that myself am blind."*

[Alexander Pope]

FRIDAY July 24, 1998
TRAIL DAY 189/95 ✦ TRAIL MILE 2,773/1,371
LOCATION William Brien Memorial Shelter

I'M OUT EARLY, HIKING INTO ANOTHER CLEAR, COOL DAY. I catch
up with *Son Ray* and *Woodbutcher* at Mombasha High Point. Sun Ray
gets his compass out, and we try locating the New York City skyline.
Through a low gap on the far-most ridge at approximately 160 degrees,
we all agree that we can see two mirage-like spires appearing and disappearing as they float and dance on the horizon.

Descending from Mombasha High Point, we decide to do the
roadwalk down West Mombasha Road to Pappy's Deli. This is the right
decision! Great subs, potato salad, chips, and, oh yes, Hershey Dairy ice
cream by the pint! Uncapping our Sprite, *Son Ray* and I both hit it big . . .
another 20-ounce Sprite, free! Also here at the deli are *Just Playin' Jane*,
Coke, and *Buzzy*.

A car is parked where the trail intersects the Orange Turnpike.
As I cross, the driver comes forth and offers me a lift down to the spring.
The section through here is very dry, but I have adequate water so I

politely thank him just the same. However, I suggest he wait for *Just Playin' Jane,* who should be coming through shortly.

Just across the New York State Thruway I see another car parked just off the road with some hikers gathered around the open trunk. They motion me over. Here, trail angel Johnson is handing out ice-cold Mountain Dew, apples, and Snickers bars! *Free Spirit, Confucius,* and *Lars* are already enjoying the trail magic.

I am dealt many tiring, rocky ups and downs today. The penicillin is definitely helping, but my jaw hurts terribly and my energy is running low. I arrive none too soon at the shelter. It is dusk, no one else is about, so it looks like I'll have this amazing rock-structure shelter to myself.

> *"My only regret is that I started late in life*
> *(in my later fifties) to plumb the depths, riches*
> *and peace which a walk into nature provides."*
>
> [Fr. Fred Alvarez, S.A., Graymoor]

SATURDAY July 25, 1998
TRAIL DAY 190/96 ✦ TRAIL MILE 2,789/1,387
LOCATION Old West Point Road, Graymoor Monastery

THE TREADWAY NOW IS CERTAINLY NO CAKEWALK, but the rocks have settled down. Today there are a number of three- to three-and-a-half-Snickers pulls with some leading to really breathtaking vistas into the wide, lush New York valleys below. Hopefully I'll be able to chalk up some miles now as I look with more anticipation with each passing day to reaching the mountains of New England.

I've been hiking off and on the past few days with *Twilight,* an energetic and delightfully talkative young lady who has discovered a hidden talent while here on the trail. She has a most gentle and pleasant vibrato voice and has composed the lyrics and melody to a beautiful song about the Appalachian Trail and her months spent here. She performed this lovely melody at the talent contest at Trail Days in Damascus and walked away a winner with a new $300 backpack.

I have a mail drop waiting at Bear Mountain, New York, so I hike out early this morning to cover the 8 miles before the post office closes at 11:15 a.m. I make it just in time. Then it's over to the Bear Mountain Inn Cafeteria for a slice of pizza and a tall glass of Mountain Dew. I first considered dining at the Wildflower Restaurant on the second floor, but perusing their menu I found it a little rich for my blood, so I settled for the pizza and moved on. Bear Mountain State Park is packed, every picnic table and patch of grass by the lake is taken. The trail goes right down the lakeside path, the very first treadway built in 1922–23. Here was truly the beginning of the Appalachian Trail. Within the Trailside Museum and Wildlife Center, constructed in 1927 at the urging of Benton MacKaye, is the nation's oldest nature trail. And indeed it was here the term "nature trail" was coined and first used. Thru-hikers are permitted through the turnstiles at no cost (I wonder how they can tell) to hike the trailside museum and zoo. As I study the cages and all the signs, plants, and other features, it dawns on me that now is my chance to finally see a bear on the trail. But, alas, the bruins have retreated to the darks of their inner dens and are not to be seen. Here near the Hudson River, which I will cross in just a while, is the lowest point on the AT, a mere 124 feet above sea level.

Twilight, Buzzy, and I arrive at Graymoor, home of the Franciscan Friars of the Atonement (at-one-ment) a little after 3:00 p.m. We are promptly greeted by Father Fred, who shows us to our private rooms in the old friary. The monastery is a quiet and spiritual place. Excerpts, written by the Reverend Peter Taran, S.A., Director, Graymoor Christian Unity Center and quoted from the Putnam Reporter Dispatch describe this place that is Graymoor much better than can I: "Today, [we] are bombarded by levels of noise, distractions, and pressures unknown by previous generations. Our lives are pulling us outwardly in every direction. In our modern technological age, there is little time for slowing down, little space to just be. So how do we renew ourselves, find a haven, get away from it all? Places do exist where one can take a respite from the world . . . slow down, have a space apart, get in touch with and look for the spirit in our lives. The Graymoor Christian Unity Center is one of them." The registry entry by *Easy Rider,* a strong, young thru-hiker I have gotten to know, sums it up pretty well, "The comforts provided here go far beyond a meal, a bed, and a shower. I feel refreshed in body and in spirit. Be sure to look around while you are here. Just like on the trail, there are many 'treasures' to be discovered . . . if you only look." After the evening meal Father Fred gives us the tour and shows us the grounds. And from the upper garden, this quiet and serene summit, is there such a remarkable view across the Hudson—all the way to the shimmering spires of Gotham City, the grand skyline of New York.

From this spiritual summit at Graymoor,
O'er the Hudson far away.
See the bright-lit twilight skyline,
The towering spires by day.
What is the meaning of all of this
Majestic earthly show?
Only our Savior, the Son of God
And the Friars at Graymoor know.

[N. Nomad]

SUNDAY July 26, 1998
TRAIL DAY 191/97 ✦ TRAIL MILE 2,807/1,405
LOCATION Hortontown Road, RPH Shelter

TODAY MY JOURNAL ENTRY CONTAINS THE TEXT of an open letter to Father Fred. I have known this man for less than half a day, and yet I know that a bond has been formed that will last the remainder of our lives:

"Father Fred, the time spent with you, our evening walk to the summit, your prayer for me, have given me renewed strength and an inner peace and contentment. I now have an unshakable confidence, like a rock, that the Lord will provide for my continued safe passage as I near the end of this incredible odyssey. I have been living and will continue to live Psalm 23, day by day with an intensity few could appreciate, for the Lord has not failed to provide my wants. The key to knowing and appreciating this comes from the ability to separate true need from want. One hundred and ninety-one days on the trail has helped me make that distinction, for now my wants and needs are basically the same and I am thankful for the unfailing fulfillment of them.

"I did lie down in green pastures and I have walked with the Lord beside still waters. One must experience this to truly understand the meaning. Your quote at the end of this day's entry gives us a glimpse, for from this comes the beginning of the restoration of the soul. When I suffered the knee pain and the excruciating shin splints to the point of tears; when I fell in Little Wolf Creek on that dreary, cold rainy day and hit my head, cracked my ribs, and dislocated my finger, I had reached my mental and physical low. It was then that I doubted the Lord, that I felt a terrible feeling of loss, and that I suffered the fear of being forsaken. But, a near-still and hushed inner voice quickly and quietly calmed me, 'There will be adversity, which you will endure and overcome.' Now I truly understand, 'Though I walk through the valley . . . thy rod and thy staff they comfort me.' Without fail, a table has been prepared before me, my cup indeed runneth over. Goodness and mercy have followed me—from all of the places I've been to all of the kind and generous folks I've met. I now enjoy an inner peace and contentment in knowing that goodness and mercy will follow me for all the days of my life, and I know without question that I will dwell in the house of the Lord forever.

"Thank you, Father Fred, for being such a caring and gracious host, not only to me but also to all the intrepids whose paths meet yours at Graymoor."

I will close now with one of his spiritually inspiring quotes:

> *"All of nature blends and fits together and is good. Scientists call it the ecosystem. Religiously, we refer to it as God's wonderful creation . . . The greatest good which nature offers us is when God speaks through it, not vocally, but in the depths of our soul, and tells us that it all comes from him."*

> [Fr. Fred Alvarez, S.A.]

MONDAY July 27, 1998
TRAIL DAY 192/98 ✦ TRAIL MILE 2,833/1,431
LOCATION Wiley Shelter

WHAT A GREAT BREAKFAST AT GRAYMOOR. Platters of scrambled eggs, bacon, and country fries, along with plenty of coffee and orange juice. And this entire, glorious feast prepared just for *Buzzy, Twilight,* and me! Father Fred joins us, and after breakfast I ask him to say another prayer for my continued safe passage. Then we bid farewell.

The following is a quote from *The Story of Hikers in Graymoor:* "It was in the summer of 1972 that the first Appalachian Hiker literally stumbled into the Graymoor Friary and asked the Superior if he could stay overnight. The request was granted and, of course, notice of it went up and down the trail with lightning speed. In short time, numbers of hikers were lodging at Graymoor. The year 1998 marks our 26th year of lodging the hikers at Graymoor. We are happy to have you."

The pleasure and joy of it is all ours! Thanks again, Father Fred.

The trail now skirts, passes, and winds around and through populated areas to end (for this day) at Wiley Shelter. There are many roads to cross, and the people up here literally fly their cars. The Taconic State Parkway could just as well be an Indy 500 training track, for getting across this road is a hair-raising experience. You'll be wishing your mommy were here to hold your hand for this one!

I have been really trying to improve my hiking technique, as to foot placement, stride, and overall efficiency, and I've made considerable progress, especially with the benefit of the Leki Trekking Poles. Roots, however, continue to give me much trouble, and today it seems is the day to finally have my grand run-in with these uncoiled and unyielding little snakes. For this day do I finally perform an absolutely classic "flying W." During a particularly steep downhill, and while partially in *"Nomad's* Neutral,"* I hang my toe on a root and out into space I go, fully propelled, to finally land back on earth, spread-eagle with my pack shoving full force, providing the traction needed to finally dig me in and bring me to a not-so-graceful screeching and grinding halt. The term "flying W" comes from my old motorcycle-racing days and describes the silhouette appearance one presents while doing the spectacular over-the-handlebars crash and burn! I am able somehow, however, with agility never before possessed, to pick myself up, dust myself off, and start all over again . . . none the worse for wear!

Relos certainly offer variety to the hiking experience, and I have the pleasure of hiking one today. Fresh new trail has treadway not anything like the old "3 R's," of the usual track — roots, rocks, and ruts. The new sections are more like what Earl Shaffer must have hiked for his entire journey in 1948 before the mass of human plows started packing the trail and beating it to a pulp.

I have the pleasure today of hiking some with *Buzzy, Twilight, Landscape* (with her dog, Kip), *Flow Easy* (with his dog, Linville), *Woodpecker,* and *Sightseer.* I also have the distinct pleasure of meeting *Bullfrog,* who thru-hiked the trail last year, and *Kuviac,* who just became a 2,000-miler, having climbed Katahdin yesterday. They've parked where the trail crosses NY 22, giving back some trail magic . . . yours truly being the happy recipient!

I arrive at Wiley Shelter at dusk, just in time to meet and talk for a while with Bob Wooden, the shelter caretaker who's come up to check things out. And I spend an enjoyable evening with Mark and his son, Mark, age eight, and his daughter, Jessica, age ten. Mark insists I use his stove to prepare my evening meal, the offer which I decline only half-heartedly and, as he insists, quickly accept.

> *"I learned a very important lesson on that journey . . .*
> *I need people, I can't make it in this world alone*
> *and I don't want to try."*
>
> [Cindy Ross, *Journey on the Crest*]

TUESDAY July 28, 1998
TRAIL DAY 193/99 ✦ TRAIL MILE 2,856/1,454
LOCATION Silver Hill Campsite, Connecticut

I'VE PUT ANOTHER STATE BEHIND ME TODAY. I cross the New York/Connecticut state line early this morning to beat a path to the

Country Mart just off the trail. On the way, the road passes through an old covered bridge. Covered bridges have always fascinated me, and I have read and studied much about them, the different methods of truss construction, and about the craftsmen who built them. Unfortunately, like the thousands who depart Springer for Katahdin and never make it, there were once more than 11,000 covered bridges all over this great country, and most have not made it, for their numbers have now dwindled to a little over 800. This particular old bridge on Bulls Bridge Road is of sound, strong construction, and its longevity is testimony to the fine craftsmanship common in that day. The truss design is Town Lattice, patented by Ithiel Town in 1820. This truss design has a most pleasing appearance, much like the latticed rose trellis, familiar and so appealing. Inside this old bridge is revealed the secret to its longevity and survival, for superimposed internally over the Town Truss is an arch-shaped truss designed and patented by Theodore Burr in 1804. This Burr Truss adds an incredible amount of additional structural integrity and support to the bridge suspension and is protected remarkably well by the roof above. In Nimblewill Creek Community, at the base of Springer Mountain where I live, the roads are private and include a bridge across Nimblewill Creek, a spring-fed trout stream. Don't be surprised if in the near future the homeowner's association decides to turn this structure into a covered bridge!

I arrive early at Silver Hill Campsite and spend the evening with a very happy and energetic young lad. And does this young fellow have one of the most fascinating, funny, and most creative trail names I've ever heard.

And, indeed, as you are reading these accounts along you are reading some very, very funny trail names! And, so now it is finally time to discuss this most interesting and very fascinating subject—trail names. It seems these days that most everyone on the trail has a trail name. Quite often that's the only name you'll know them by, never finding out their given name. The trail has its own culture. It's a society in its own. That's why friendships made on the trail are very special friendships. On the trail there are no doctors, truck drivers, school teachers, students. All things in the "real world" get distilled out on the trail and everyone is just trail family.

There are two basic methods that one may come by in getting a trail name. And to keep things on the lighter side, which is what trail life is truly all about, these methods are "the easy way" and "the funny way!" The easy way is to choose a trail name before someone else finds one for you, which is usually done the funny way, as the funny way usually relates to something one has done that's either funny, foolish, or just plain stupid!

I'll give you a few examples. Two very good friends of mine were given their names as a result of getting lost on the AT. The parallel to this would be likened to not finding the centerline on Interstate 95. Dan started out going the wrong way on the AT his very first day. He was never able to live it down. *U-Turn* has stuck with him all the way. Ha, this second guy's name is Dan, too. Never thought about that. Dans apparently have a problem getting lost. This poor fellow must now live with *Go-Back* for the remainder of his hike. But this third one, folks, you're just not going to believe this one, and again, please believe me, there is just no way I can be making this stuff up. This poor, unfortunate fellow apparently has a serious and debilitating social problem. For it is, since we're family on the AT, we're together most all the time . . . even at night in the shelters. And, well, see if you can figure out the trail name for the young fellow who is keeping me company here this evening.

If I told you his name was a multipart name and I revealed to you that the first part was Ivan, could you figure out the rest? Don't be disheartened. Nobody else has ever been able to figure out this little riddle either. Everybody comes up with Ivan the Great, Ivan the Horrible, and so on. But this poor chap apparently has a problem with BO. I don't know, there's no shelter here and we're tenting out, maybe just as well. Anyway, the trail name they've stuck this poor kid with? *Ivan Odor*!

Well, I decided early on to choose my own trail name. It comes from where I live and basically my lifestyle. I live in the Nimblewill at the base of Springer Mountain, and I guess you can see where the other half comes from!

Silver Hill is a lush little glen, once a shelter site, but the shelter burned in 1991 due to a faulty fireplace and has never been rebuilt. The great campsite remains however, complete with a covered cooking pavilion, privy, swing (with a view), a large deck with benches, and another picnic table . . . and an old pitcher-pump-topped well punched straight down through the crown of solid rock, the coolest and sweetest well water I've ever tasted. What a most serene firefly/starlit evening. I linger for hours in total contentment.

> *Stars delight, fireflies bright,*
> *Dim shadows from the moon.*
> *Comes now dawn to capture night,*
> *And ends the spell . . . too soon.*
>
> [N. Nomad]

WEDNESDAY July 29, 1998

TRAIL DAY 194/100   ✦   TRAIL MILE 2,868/1,466

LOCATION Belter Campsite

THE LITTLE MEADOW AND THE PLEASANT OVERLOOK here at Silver Hill create such a peaceful, serene spot. I linger until mid-afternoon enjoying the beauty and solitude, sitting at the picnic table, catching up on my journal entries.

At Old Sharon Road, and just as a gentle rain begins, I meet trail angel *Washboard*. He had started at Springer on March 15 but got off at Waynesboro suffering from injuries sustained during a bad fall. He had planned on continuing after recovering from that misfortune, only to contract Lyme disease. So, instead of hiking the AT, he's out mixing a little trail joy with some trail magic. Thanks, *Washboard*, for the Coke, the apple, and some most enjoyable conversation. I dearly hope your fortunes change soon and that you'll be back on the trail again. I have donned my cheapy poncho, but the rain soon ends and the day turns sunny and warm. Even though starting late, this day is turning into another grand and glorious hiking day. At Pine Swamp Brook Lean-to I go in for a moment to check the shelter register. Here I meet *Thog, Master of Stix,* Mark and dog Rebel, and southbounders *Greenleaf, The Duke of Hazzard,* and *Crawdad.*

I am confronted with a most annoying hassle as soon as I pull into Belter Campsite, the mosquitoes viciously attacking. I can usually tolerate this nuisance, but these fellows are pure mean. It seems as though they are even pushing me around. I pitch camp, prepare a hasty supper, then roll in to finally evade their relentless attack. The night turns a bit on the chilly side, but I manage to sleep well. I can see that I'll need my sleeping bag back soon and it's not yet August!

White Blazes Lead Me On (Chorus)

Oh, white blazes lead me on, lead me on,
Oh, white blazes you're my guide.
Oh, white blazes, south to north I am bound,
My heart, my mind, my soul you've opened wide.

[Lyrics and music, Debbie *Twilight* Smith]

THURSDAY July 30, 1998
TRAIL DAY 195/101 ✦ TRAIL MILE 2,888/1,486
LOCATION Bear Rock Stream Campsite

THIS MORNING STARTS IN AN INTERESTING and most novel manner. I awake at first light, get my flashlight out, and check the time. My watch says 7:30 a.m. Whoa! I know the days are getting noticeably shorter, but this is startling! I hurriedly break camp the best I can in the dim morning light and manage to get on the trail by 8:00 a.m. Once off the mountain I beat a path to the Village Coffee Shop and Restaurant for breakfast. Aww, now what's this . . . they're closed on Thursdays? No, the sign says they're open Thursdays at 6:30 a.m. I can't figure this out. The southbounders raved about the great breakfast they had here just yesterday. But here I stand, my watch reading 9:00 a.m. and the place is closed. I loiter around out front in a dither, and it's then I notice a light on in the kitchen. So I saunter around the side of the building, and I can see someone in there working. What in the devil is going on here? I go to the open side window and get the lady's attention. "Why aren't y'all open today?" I say. She looks a little annoyed as she says, "We'll be open at 6:30 just like we're supposed to be!" Oops, now I see what's wrong. The day is coming along on time just fine . . . it's me that's all mixed up. No wonder it's still so dark and nobody is moving around. My one-dollar watch, purchased at the pawnshop in Live Oak, Florida, has finally gone on the fritz! Somehow it's managed to gain two and one-half hours. So at 6:30 a.m. and right on time the Village Coffee Shop and Restaurant opens for business this Thursday morning, and I head right in. Before breakfast is over, the display window on my watch goes completely blank. I really can't complain . . . don't need a watch to tell me it's time for a new dollar watch!

I take the blue-blazed Mohawk trail across the tracks, and I'm back on the AT by 8:00 a.m. In a short while today I meet and talk with AMC Ridgerunners *Flyin' Scotsman* and *Walking Stomach*. I also have the pleasure of hiking some with *Blue Moon* and *Townsman*. The views, coupled with the luscious, sweet lowbush blueberries taken in from Bear Mountain complement each other very nicely! I arrive at Bear Rock Stream Campsite around 5:00 p.m. to meet *Lake* and *AT-2* with dog Sheba. What a pleasant surprise as *Easy Rider* comes rolling in just before dark after a 33-mile day.

> *"Man is not himself only. He is all that he sees, all that flows to him from a thousand sources. He is the land, the lift of its mountain lines, the reach of its valleys."*
>
> [Mary Austin]

FRIDAY July 31, 1998
TRAIL DAY 196/102 ✦ TRAIL MILE 2,907/1,505
LOCATION Great Barrington, East Mountain Retreat Center

THE CLIMB UP RACE MOUNTAIN THIS MORNING brings the immediate reward of great views into the lush Massachusetts valley below. I enjoy hiking some with *Lake*, Sheba, and *AT-2*. *Easy Rider* and I will be hiking together on into Canada (I've decided to hike on into Canada— more on this later). It is exciting contemplating having company on the remainder of this odyssey.

Southbounders over the past few days have talked about a new hostel that has just opened. It is reached by a faint blue-blazed trail just south of the Tom Leonard Lean-to. I decide to give it a try, and I'm so glad I did. It is an interfaith retreat facility for seekers rooted in a faith tradition, now open to thru-hikers. Reverend Lois F. Rose is the center director. The buildings are near new and quite nice. Bunks are twin beds with mattresses and linen. There is a full, modern kitchen, two full baths, washer and dryer, and a very nice library. Reverend Rose is a delightful host. I would highly recommend the East Mountain Retreat Center.

The evening is spent in grand fashion enjoying the company of friends *Jingle, Desperado,* and *Easy Rider.* The last we were together was at Partnership Shelter. Also here, and is it my pleasure to meet *Professor, Peace Pipe,* and their friend *Snoop,* who thru-hiked last year.

> *"What joy awaits you, when the breeze hath found*
> *you out among the trees, and calls you forth again!"*
>
> [Wordsworth]

SATURDAY August 1, 1998
TRAIL DAY 197/103 ✦ TRAIL MILE 2,927/1,525
LOCATION Upper Goose Pond Cabin, Massachusetts

Snoop IS VERY KIND TO GIVE US A RIDE into Great Barrington. I want to stop at the outfitters for some socks and a new water bottle belt pouch, but they don't open until 10:00 a.m., another hour, so I head to the grocery store, get a few provisions, and we're soon headed back to East Mountain Retreat.

I'm able to get on the trail by 10:00 a.m. At the MA 23 road crossing, I meet Hank and Bob, who are waiting for their wives to pick them up. They're completing a section hike and have plenty of food left over that they would like to share with me. I end up with lots of good freeze-dried stuff that takes a lot of fuel to prepare. Since it doesn't matter to me how much fuel it takes to prepare a meal, I gladly accept their offer.

While on the subject of hard-to-cook foods, with interest have I noted the ease with which I can always find uncooked rice. Seems it doesn't take folks long to figure out they're going to need a five-gallon can of gas if they want to prepare this stuff on their little gasoline stoves, so the hiker boxes all along are usually full of resealable bags of rice. I've pretty much made it a rule now not to buy any rice, but to simply load up at the hostels and other locations where hiker boxes are in play. Hiker boxes? These boxes, usually cardboard and around a couple of feet square, are found at hostels, post offices, and other locations frequented by hikers. They contain useful items, equipment, food, etc., not wanted at the time. The idea is to take something from the box that you can use and leave something you don't want. The problem is, everybody pretty much wants to get rid of the same stuff . . . and everybody's looking for Snickers bars and chocolate pudding! But seldom do I peruse a hiker box and not find something to my liking, usually rice.

And how do I get by so well on foods that others neither want nor have the means to cook? Well, the secret is my little homemade wood-burning cookstove, which weighs only seven ounces (fuel not included but always readily available).

The small, dead lower limbs of the pine, hemlock, spruce, fir, rho-dodendron, and mountain laurel work great and will usually burn hot even when wet. *Nomad*'s "Little Dandy" stove folds down flat and can be assembled and disassembled in just a minute. It is made from light gauge sheet metal and consists of a floor and three sides. The top and one end (into which the fuel is fed) are open. The cook pot sits on the serrated top. It's a neat little creation, one of those "tab A into slot B" contraptions. (See stove pattern at **www.nimblewillnomad.com.**) It really works great . . . so if my rice isn't cooked I don't need to dig out another bomb canis-ter that I've been lugging up and down the mountains. I just add another stick or two and in moments my dinner is ready! Anyway, thanks, Hank and Bob. I'd never shell out the bucks for these gourmet delights, but I can sure cook them and I'll most definitely enjoy them.

In just a while I cut through a farmer's field just past the Shaker Campsite and pick up the old AT, which passes all the lovely summer homes along the shore of Goose Pond. Upon reaching the outfall from Upper Goose Pond into Goose Pond, I give a shout toward Upper Goose Pond Cabin. I immediately hail *Snoop* and *Professor* and *Peace Pipe*, who jump in the cabin canoe and come around the point to get me straight away.

At the dock, and before I even head for the cabin, I drop my pack and jump in for a cool, refreshing swim in Upper Goose Pond. Relaxed and reinvigorated, I enjoy a most memorable evening with *Easy Rider* and many new and old friends at Upper Goose Pond Cabin: Nancy (the cabin caretaker), *Professor* and *Peace Pipe, Snoop, Ivan Odor, Bagman, Jingle, Desperado,* and *Thog.*

> *"Sky so bright it makes you wonder*
> *If it's heaven shining through;*
> *Earth so smiling way out yonder,*
> *Sun so bright it dazzles you."*

[Robert W. Service]

SUNDAY August 2, 1998
TRAIL DAY 198/104 ✦ TRAIL MILE 2,947/1,545
LOCATION Tom Levardi's yard, Dalton

PANCAKES, PANCAKES, AND MORE PANCAKES seem the order for breakfast, made in the quaint old kitchen at Upper Goose Pond, compliments of Nancy. There's no power to the old cabin, so propane fires the whole operation, stove, lights, the works. I won't hit the trail hungry today, as I sure have my fill of pancakes . . . a few more than three, topped with dollops of strawberry jelly, all washed down with cup after cup of great camp coffee. Before I get cranking this morning, I'd like to digress a moment to talk a little about my peregrinations yesterday. There are those who would quickly condemn what I did, in that I strayed from the designated AT treadway to go my own way and to follow a path other than that marked by the familiar white AT blazes. It's known here on the trail as blue-blazing. And there are other terms, other trail jargon that describe how we all move along in our quest to reach Baxter Peak. I'll discuss a few.

BLUE-BLAZING is a manner of hiking where one follows a route other than the white-blazed AT. There are many trails marked with blue blazes that lead to and from the AT. Some go to shelters, some to water sources, and some to roads, parking areas, and other trails, thus the term blue-blazing.

PURISM, or WHITE-BLAZING, describes hiking in a manner where all the white blazes on the AT are passed. If there is a blue-blazed trail into a shelter, for example, and another one back out, the purist will return by the same route to avoid missing any white blazes.

ULTRA PURISM is also white-blazing and describes a form of hiking wherein not only all of the white blazes are passed but where no deviation from the designated treadway occurs. The difference between the purist and ultrapurist, by example: In negotiating a blowdown (a tree across the trail), the purist will take the path beat down around the blowdown, just like the rest of us, and keep on truckin', but the ultra-purist will walk up to the blowdown, touching the treadway beneath. Once around the obstacle, the ultrapurist will return the short distance back down the trail to touch the spot beneath the blowdown, thence to continue uninterrupted on the exact, official AT treadway.

TRADITIONALISM is a term coined by *100# Stormcloud* and describes blue-blazing in the truest sense. For this is a form of hiking wherein one walks the entire distance from Springer to Katahdin, but where the path varies away from the official AT treadway from time to time, the routes to and from shelters being one example. These excursions away from the designated path may or may not be shortcuts. My hikes along the Virginia Creeper and past the beautiful summer homes at Goose Pond are classic examples of blue-blazing in its most traditional sense. One of these excursions involved a shorter distance, the other considerably more. Probably most of us thru-hiking the AT will fit into this category to one degree or another.

YELLOW-BLAZING describes hiking in a manner where a part or parts of the AT are skipped by using some form of transportation other than walking, either by hitch-hiking, taking a bus, hopping a train, or some other way. Some of my good friends thru-hiking the AT had a grand time taking a side excursion to continue by canoe down the beautiful Shenandoah River. Oh, and then there's *Bump*. You'll read more about *Bump* shortly.

SLACK-PACKING describes hiking without a backpack. This is done when a ride is available along the route, the opportunity often presents at hostels. Using this method, the hiker can stay two nights at the hostel. For the second night's stay the hiker is driven to a point where a road crosses further up the trail, say 12 miles north, thence to hike back south to the hostel without a pack. Then the next morning the hiker is driven back to that same point to continue on.

So, all of us fit into one or perhaps a combination of these categories. One of my very good friends, *Bump*, is a make-no-apologies yellow-blazer. He's a great guy, lots of fun to be with. I have dubbed him the "Will Rogers of the trail." *Bump* is a war buff, and anytime a battlefield or anything historic or even remotely related to a skirmish is nearby, good old *Bump* blue or yellow-blazes right on over. I don't know of a single soul out here on the trail having more fun than *Bump*. It's obvious to all that he's having a blast. It's been a pleasure seeing him now and again, sometimes at the most unlikely places. I'll end this day's journal entry with a little ditty written by Tony *Ringbearer* Falcone, who's obviously become a bit frustrated with *Bump*'s antics!

There are a couple of good pulls today up and over Becket and Bald Top mountains. *Easy Rider* and I enjoy a great visit with Roy and Marilyn *Cookie Lady* Wiley. Their lovely, well-kept farm is just off the trail at Washington Mountain Road. Water is available at their home, and you're likely to be treated to fresh-baked cookies! Blueberries are in now and Roy invites *Easy Rider* and me to help ourselves to the luscious high-bush blueberries in his grove. Roy has 1,200 well-kept bushes. We eat our fill—what a great treat. Thanks, Roy and *Cookie Lady*!

Easy Rider and I arrive at Tom Levardi's beautiful home in Dalton around 6:00 p.m. Here we're greeted most graciously by Tom. "Would you like a little ice cream?" he says. "Sure would," we reply. Over his shoulder, and as he heads for the back door, he says, "Okay, have a seat at the picnic table, and I'll be right back." *Desperado*, who had arrived before us and is now sitting at the table says, "Wait till you see this, you're in for quite a treat." Moments later Tom emerges from his back door with a most impressive offering in the most formal butler-like manner, tray in hand, adorned with huge silver chalices (I don't know how else to adequately describe these things) filled to the glistening brim with ice cream, topped with whipped cream, the whole concoction coated with colored candies . . . and to the side, cheese Danish!

Dalton, Massachusetts, is a neat, well-kept little burg, as it seems are all the quaint little villages throughout New England. Tree-lined streets, cockeyed sidewalks, beautifully kept lawns, all gracing and embracing grand old porch-fronted two-story homes. What memories come flooding back — childhood memories from times long past when Mom and Dad would take sis and me back east to visit family. It was always such a joy seeing my grandparents again. They lived in a little town much like Dalton on a street just like Tom's little street . . . like a thousand little streets in a thousand little towns, all built over a century ago throughout these grand old mountains. I enjoy the evening talking with Tom and many friends. Later a few of us visit a local pub to lift some cold ones, and for the night I share Tom's yard with *Soren, Bagman, Good Times, Planting Flowers, Jingle, Desperado,* and *Easy Rider.*

> *"Now that strange fellow* Bump's *a merry ol' soul.*
> *Havin' fun 'long the trail, not hikin's his goal.*
> *Just when you think you've passed that old cuss,*
> *He'll stick out his thumb, hop a train or a bus.*
> *When you come into town the first one you'll see,*
> *Is that merry ol'* Bump *as content as can be.*
> *He'll say with a smile and he'll say with a grin,*
> *'I've been hangin' for hours, where the devil you been?'*
> *Yellow-blazin' is one thing, what* Bump *does . . . another!*
> *Come out and be with us, try hikin' it, brother!"*

[Tony *Ringbearer* Falcone, GAME '98]

MONDAY August 3, 1998
TRAIL DAY 199/105 ✦ TRAIL MILE 2,967/1,565
LOCATION Wilbur Clearing Lean-to

TOM IS A HIKER, AND AS IS THE GENERAL TENDENCY with hikers to get up early, Tom is up with us this morning, so we invite him along for breakfast. He suggests Buff and Dell right down the street. The food is fine, but again, as it goes with hikers . . . all know there just won't be enough to eat, so everyone but Tom orders two breakfast specials right off the bat!

This is going to be a cruisin' good day, I can just tell. We have a five-Snickers pull up to Bascom Lodge. On the summit of Mt. Greylock are views, it seems, to the end of the world. *Easy Rider* and I stop for a bowl of soup at the lodge then gawk at the beautiful mosaic tile artwork in the tower Rotunda before hiking on out to Wilbur Shelter and a memorable 20-mile day. We see some other hikers today: *Berwin,* a southbounder who departed Katahdin on June 4 and *Mother Nature* and *Father Time,* having the time of their lives on this grand old AT. Also, what a joy today to see *Innkeeper* again. This is the first our paths have crossed since Damascus.

> *"The whole visible world is only an imperceptible atom in the ample bosom of nature. No idea approaches it. We may enlarge our conceptions beyond all imaginable space; we only produce atoms in comparison with the reality of things. It is an infinite sphere, the centre of which is everywhere, the circumference nowhere. In short, it is the greatest sensible mark of the almighty power of God, that imagination loses itself in that thought."*

> [Blaise Pascal, 1623–1662]

TUESDAY August 4, 1998
TRAIL DAY 200/106   ✦   TRAIL MILE 2,990/1,588
LOCATION Melville Nauheim Shelter, Vermont

THE EVENING LAST WAS COOL, NO BUGS AT WILBUR! We relaxed with *Good Times* and *Voyager,* and *Shutterbug.* Another fine hiking day is shaping up as we're off to a good start. Three miles out at North Adams, *Easy Rider* and I head west at the light and soon find the Garage Sub Station. They're open for breakfast, so we head in. This little place used to be a gas station; now it's a sub station. The bay doors are still here! One rolls up to open a screened area and the other is fixed with a standard entrance door built right in. The grease racks have been removed. The breakfast is fine and the price is right . . . and there's a hiker register.

The three-Snickers pull up to Eph's Lookout is well worth it. We bag another state as we leave Massachusetts and enter Vermont. This line and this spot are historic, for here is the beginning of the Long Trail. An old weathered sign attached to a leaning maple states, "A footpath in the Wilderness, the Long Trail, a scenic hiking trail that starts here and follows the Green Mountain Range for approximately 263 miles north to the Canadian border. The AT follows the Long Trail for approximately 97 miles, then at Sherburne Pass turns east." Of the two trails, the AT is certainly the longest and most well known, so it is interesting to see stated that the AT follows the Long Trail. But it is a fact that though the AT has been around for over 60 years, the Long Trail has been in existence since 1909!

Easy Rider and I hike some today with *Nothing Ordinary* and have a long talk with southbounder *Amino Acid*. We spend the evening at Melville Nauheim Shelter with three women section hikers and *Wanderlust*, a southbounder. One of the women has sprawled her pack, sleeping bag, and a grand array of other assorted gadgets and gear over the entire upper sleeping area, enough room to accommodate three thru-hikers. I roll out my pad and sleeping bag on the narrow, dirt-covered first landing, just under the eaves and just out of the intermittent drizzle, which comes to visit during the night. I chuckle as I prepare my little spot, thinking about what *Model-T* said: " If you hog more than your share (like shelter space), it will all come back like a big crow to roost on your head — you'll have bird poop to remind you of your transgressions."

> *"For a moment of night we have a glimpse of ourselves and of our world islanded in its stream of stars — pilgrims of mortality, voyaging between horizons across eternal seas of space and time."*
>
> [Henry Beston]

WEDNESDAY August 5, 1998
TRAIL DAY 201/107 ✦ TRAIL MILE 3,011/1,609
LOCATION Home of *Easy Rider*'s sister, Kelly Stand Road

THE TREADWAY TURNS INTO A GRINDER TODAY. Many elevation changes make for a bumpy ride through countless rocks and bogs. The terrain has really been changing. The Green Mountains are certainly

different than the Berkshires, different than anything we've seen so far.
Slow, steady progress over the last few months has brought us ever
north, the conifers gradually but surely dominating. The hardwoods are
still present, but the fir and spruce abound, thus the visual and olfactory
senses are daily receiving a major jolt—ah, but all is for the better. These
lush, verdant mountains are the most brilliant shade of green, a scene so
striking and captivating, the redolent fresh scent of the woods, seeming
as though someone must surely be hiking just ahead, spraying the air
with pine-scented freshener. We are afforded a "360" o'er these majestic
Green Mountains from the Glastenbury Mountain Tower, an old fire
tower still safe to climb and enjoy. We linger long in silence and awe.
Easy Rider and I stop in for a rest at Story Spring Shelter. Here we meet
and talk with southbounders *Technical Difficulties* from Atlanta and *Oobee*
and *Choobee* from Montreal.

      We arrive at Arlington–West Wardsboro (Kelly Stand) Road just
as planned and are soon met and greeted by *Easy Rider*'s girlfriend, Nikki,
and his brother-in-law, Rudy. *Easy Rider* hadn't expected to see Nikki, so
it is most amusing watching him giggle, giddy with delight! Now folks,
there are brothers-in-law and then there are brothers-in-law, if you know
what I mean, but I'll tell you this, if you've got to have a brother-in-law,
Rudy is definitely the kind you want. He's a math professor—but he isn't
the math-professor type—that just being what he teaches at Vermont
Academy in Saxton's River, Vermont. Rudy's married to *Easy Rider*'s sister, Erika, who is in the third trimester of pregnancy . . . that vibrant and
glowing period of pregnancy. They've just moved into one of the dormi-
tory apartments on the academy campus—the job of "Dorm Parents"
being one of their additional responsibilities. They've managed to make it
a homey place already. I sure make myself at home, their warm hospitality naturally making it so. *Easy Rider* and I have looked forward all day
with great anticipation and excitement to this evening, having been told
that Erika will be preparing the lasagna of all lasagnas for us. And wow,
what a payoff. The biggest gravity-defying platter of lasagna I think I've
ever seen . . . so big that two bottomless-pit thru-hikers end up groaning
and waddling away from it . . . neither able, even collectively, to meet the
challenge Erika has placed before us. Oh my, and talking about putting a

hurtin' on, who could possibly resist saucer-sized out-of-the-oven chocolate-chip cookies with ice cream for dessert? Great seeing you Nikki, and thanks, Rudy and Erika. Your kindness, generosity, and down-home hospitality will remain in my memory!

> *There's a mystic shade of green . . .*
> *Sets the rainbow's show to want,*
> *Seen across these verdant mountains*
> *From the Long Trail in Vermont.*

[N. Nomad]

THURSDAY August 6, 1998
TRAIL DAY 202/108 ✦ TRAIL MILE 3,028/1,626
LOCATION VT 11 and 30, Manchester Center,
Zion Episcopal Church Hostel

RIGHT OFF THE BAT WE'RE DEALT A TOUGH FOUR-SNICKERS PULL up Stratton Mountain to the tower and the caretaker's cabin. From the tower are we provided distance-defying vistas south to Mt. Greylock and north to Killington and Pico Peaks and beyond. It's another blue-magic day as we gaze in wonder o'er these grand, verdant-magic mountains that are the Green Mountains of Vermont—all around and fading to the distant horizon, thence from there does there come a silent beckoning from over the horizon. As if in a sanctuary of worship now, for indeed we are in God's cathedral on high, and in a sense of reverence, not wanting to break the spell of peaceful silence, do I whisper to *Easy Rider*, "We're definitely amongst 'em now!"

Coming off Stratton, the treadway pretty much becomes a cruise. The view from the trail across Stratton pond is everything I've read and have been told it would be—a jigsaw puzzle picture-perfect spot! Where I'm from, ponds and lakes are at the bottom of the mountain. Up here they are on the mountain, sometimes near the very summit, reached only after a strenuous climb. These mountains are all so strange and new to me. All of this is definitely going to take some getting used to! *Easy Rider* and I get a quick hitch into Manchester Center,

right to the hostel. The rain, threatening most of the afternoon, finally
sets in as we arrive.

> *"Long distance hiking is not a vacation, its too long for*
> *that. It's not recreation, too much toil and pain*
> *involved. It is, we decide, a way of life, a very simplified*
> *Spartan way of living . . . life on the move . . . heavy*
> *packs, sweating brow; they make you appreciate warm*
> *sunshine, companionship, cool water. The best way to*
> *appreciate these things that are precious and important*
> *in life is to take them away."*

[Cindy Ross, *Journey on the Crest*]

FRIDAY August 7, 1998
TRAIL DAY 203/109   ✦   TRAIL MILE 3,044/1,642
LOCATION Big Branch Shelter

THE NARROW LINE OF INTREPID HIKERS MOVING SLOWLY but
surely north on the AT, though seemingly strung out, forms one of the
tightest "family circles" you could ever imagine. I've spoken about this
enjoyable and fascinating social relationship on previous occasions.
Again last night at Zion the family (new and old alike) got together,
sleeping bags on the main hall floor all around, the central attraction
being the TV. Present were *Easy Rider, Firecracker, Jarhead, No Sox, Brother,
Loaves 'n Fishes, Abol, Fargo, Squirrel, Just Chris, Spiff, Rhubarb, Hoosier
Daddy, Fisher Cat, Ginko, Sundance, LSD, Boscoe, Violet, Sole to Soul, Mountain
Man, Czech'n It Out, Firefly, Crow, Snoar A Saurus, Wonder Girl, Raisin,* and
Tough-Hikin Tim. I've never been much for TV, so I head for the kitchen
where I meet Hugh and Jeanne. They are members of the Green
Mountain Club and are the caretakers for Stratton Mountain, and at
present call the incredibly neat, snug little cabin atop Stratton their
home. I walked all around and marveled at this little cabin while on
Stratton yesterday, and now I've had the pleasure of meeting the folks
who stay there. We spend a grand evening talking. From Hugh and
Jeanne do I learn that on the summit of Stratton Mountain in 1909,

James P. Taylor, founder of the Long Trail and GMC, got the inspiration for creating a hiking trail spanning the entire breadth of Vermont. Also, atop Stratton Mountain in 1921 after construction of the Long Trail had begun, Benton MacKaye conceived the idea for a continuous footpath from Maine to Georgia, now known as the AT.

Rain has set in steady and it continues throughout the night and into the morning. Everyone is sticking at Zion as *Easy Rider* and I move out quietly, off into the dark, gray drizzle. We head first for the post office and, hopefully, my mail drop. I hit the jackpot again with many fine letters and cards . . . and my bounce box. I add and subtract from my bounce box, then bounce it on. Back on the trail and as the day tries to "fair up" we head right into a four-Snickers pull up Bromley Mountain. The lower fog and clouds are clearing out now and the view from the tower on Bromley provides a fine show. There is a ski lift to the very summit of Bromley with a large map showing the different runs. This skiing thing is all new to me and I get a chuckle out of some of the names: Havoc, Avalanche, Pabst Peril, Pabst Panic, Corkscrew, Mighty Might, the Glade, and how about this one . . . The Lord's Prayer!

The day finally turns quite fair as the rain and clouds clear out. *Easy Rider* and I both agree that we are probably through the worst of the heat and the bugs. We spend a very pleasant time together hiking on to Big Branch Shelter. Here we enjoy the evening with Rick, Sara, and Bryce, all thru-hiking the Long Trail.

> *"An' as it blowed an' blowed*
> *I often looked up at the sky*
> *An' assed meself the question,*
> *What is the stars, what is the stars?"*

[Sean O'Casey]

WE'RE OUT INTO CLEAR SKIES BUT MUDDY TREADWAY. However, I sense this is going to be an incredible day nonetheless. And to the wonder and mystery of it all do we reach Little Rock Pond, another famous landmark along the trail, to stare, as in dream-like disbelief, at the beauty before us. This indeed is a place of unparalleled grandeur. Ah, but this one I will leave to the mystery of it, for all to wonder what it can be. You simply must come and see. Special places such as this now have resident caretakers to protect these priceless treasures that are America. In residence here are Rick and his sister Ann. They have a "stand-up-and-dance-in" tent set on a large, generous platform, along with a remarkable assortment of civilized amenities. We linger and talk. Folks just cannot believe how long I've been on the trail or from whence I have come. It's simply becoming prudent to avoid talking about it.

Well, the coincidences keep rollin' in—this one involving *Easy Rider*. Through a mutual friend, he knows that one of his third and fourth grade classmates is also on the trail. They were childhood chums. They haven't seen each other now for nearly 20 years. Yup! After a tentative exchange with a southbounder, *Easy Rider* tells me later, "After I saw his face up close and heard his voice, I knew it was him." What a joy watching and listening to *Easy Rider* and *Dahl-E-Lama* play catch-up after nearly two decades . . . in the remote wilds of Vermont!

We reach VT 103 around 3:30 p.m. and hitch a ride to The Inn at Long Trail. Here *Easy Rider* calls our good hiking friend *Jingle*, who has invited us to stay the night at Killington. What a great surprise, as *Jingle* arrives to pick us up, to see *Hootie* along for the ride. We had hiked together further south, but it's been weeks and weeks since our paths have crossed, so I'd pretty much figured that was it for *Hootie*. But as fate would have it, here we are exchanging happy greetings once more. With a big smile, *Jingle* says, "I thought this might surprise you!"

We have been told that the place here at Killington is a condo, but it's really a very lavish and spacious home. This lovely abode is skiing headquarters for *Jingle*'s sister Anne, her boyfriend, and their friends. There are ski slopes everywhere on Killington and Pico and this grand place is right in the middle of it, so winter is the big time up here. But summers are cool and beautiful here also . . . I wouldn't be a bit surprised to find that every season here is beautiful. Anne and *Jingle* prepare a feast for us: pork roast, mashed potatoes and gravy, fresh corn-on-the-cob, broccoli, and a great tossed salad. This banquet is followed up with nothing less than strawberry shortcake!

Staying the evening and enjoying this luxury along with yours truly were Anne, *Jingle, Hootie, Easy Rider,* and *Desperado.* Tonight I'm sleeping in a real bed with a mattress, pillows, and linen! Oh, what a luxurious night's sleep, then to be greeted as I arise by the aroma of freshly brewed coffee, followed up by a full breakfast spread. Thanks, Anne and *Jingle,* for your kindness, friendship, and hospitality!

> *"May the road rise to meet you.*
> *May the wind be always at your back.*
> *May the sun shine warm upon your face,*
> *The rain fall soft upon your fields and,*
> *Until we meet again . . .*
> *May God hold you in the palm of his hand."*

[An Irish Blessing]

SUNDAY August 9, 1998
TRAIL DAY 205/111 ✦ TRAIL MILE 3,077/1,675
LOCATION US 4, Sherburne Pass, The Inn at Long Trail

AFTER SAYING FAREWELL TO ANNE AND *Desperado, Jingle* and *Hootie* drive *Easy Rider* and me back to the trailhead at VT 103. Just as we're exchanging sad goodbyes with *Jingle* and *Hootie,* what perfect timing—for a pleasant uplift—on the trail and crossing the road comes *Innkeeper!* I hadn't expected to see him again. We had exchanged tearful goodbyes miles south, but now we'll get to hike together again! What unexpected blessings come with each passing day.

This day is steady, hard hiking into the haze and the clouds. We're dealing now with the first five-Snickers pull for quite a while, up to Killington Peak. The AT comes short of the peak by two-tenths of a mile, which is virtually straight up through the rocks. *Thunder Chicken* and *Poppasan* had both written in my handbook: "Go to the top—plan on it." So up we go. And what a spectacle. It's like standing on the tiptop of a projectile! Just below, I can see the ski lifts and the ski run paths. The haze has cleared now and the "360" seems endless, to the horizon all around. Just standing here makes me dizzy and I must take care as I spin, panning from one breathtaking scene to the next. From this summit, where the state was first christened "Verd-Mont" (French for "Green Mountain"), it is possible to see south to the ocean and north into Canada. Southbounders have been telling me that it just keeps getting better and the recent experiences are making a believer out of me!

I arrive early evening . . . again, back at The Inn at Long Trail, to split a room with *Easy Rider* and *Innkeeper.*

> *The trail goes up and over,*
> *Seldom does it lead us down.*
> *And at most treadway junctions,*
> *There's an easy way around.*
> *Now Warren* has been known to ask . . .*
> *"Which path will you choose?"*
> *The answer? One small clue to life,*
> *Who'll win and who will lose.*

[N. Nomad]

*Warren Doyle, Jr.

MONDAY August 10, 1998
TRAIL DAY 206/112 ✦ TRAIL MILE 3,077/1,675
LOCATION US 4, Sherburne Pass,
the Inn at Long Trail

AFTER BREAKFAST *Easy Rider* and *Innkeeper* are out and gone. I'll be taking a day off to rest and see my son, Jon, who with his girlfriend, Terri, has flown into Boston to take a break between college terms and to come and be with me! I am sore afraid . . . what their reaction will be when they see me again. I'm not emaciated, but I'm pretty much muscle and bone and haven't trimmed my beard or cut my hair since Jon dropped me off at Loop Road way down in Florida back on New Year's Day. So I feel most apprehensive about their reaction when we meet again. But not the least are they taken, neither aback nor hesitant, as I'm greeted with a big hug from both of them! We spend a great day together, beginning with lunch and a brew at the Long Trail Brewery. In the evening we drive into Rutland for pizza. Even with this short time together, Jon and I have one of the best father/son, from-the-heart talks we've had in years.

But always, as it seems, the time must come and they must go. Meeting is always such joy, but parting can be such a very sad and emotional time. They're grown kids now, adults . . . aww, why can't we face that fact and just let them go? They have their own lives, their own friends. But aren't they always our children, our little kids . . . forever! The upstairs room where I'm staying faces the parking lot and the highway below. I stand now, looking out the window, seeing only a veiled blur as I brush away tears . . . watching them pull from the parking lot and drive away. "Goodbye, Jon; goodbye, Terri," I whisper. Oh, this trail can be so lonely at times. I feel such despair, such hopeless emptiness as I catch the last glimpse of their car disappearing down the mountain. Don't we always hope and pray for the best, then have such doubt and lost heart? I guess it's just human nature to feel so sad and forlorn when being separated from loved ones . . . then only to fear constantly for their safety. I find the anxiety of it nearly impossible to suppress. In only the worst nightmare could I possibly imagine the experience, the heartbreak and agonizing sorrow of losing a child.

And so, now I will tell you the heart-wrenching story of a child and the beautiful family that lost their child. This is the story of Jacob *Gatorboy* Cram, 12/6/74 to 8/20/97. For as it turned, this story is about just one day, and so short were the days of Jacob's life on this earth. Until that fateful day in August of 1997, Richard and Elizabeth Cram knew their loving son to be a strong, energetic young man of 22, having the time of his life—in the prime of his life—hiking the Appalachian Trail. But on that day did their son Jacob lay dead atop Mt. Lincoln, the victim of a life-snuffing brain tumor. Oh, how we take each day for granted, how we become so complacent, how we complain so much and find so much fault. And yet how dear life is, how fragile, how fleeting. What a lesson, how precious each day, how blessed we are to have our family, our loved ones, whether near or far . . . each and every day.

I met Jacob's wonderful and loving parents, Richard and Elizabeth Cram, here at the Inn at Long Trail. I sat and listened with tear-filled eyes as they, also in tears, talked about their son Jacob, recalling with such heart-wrenching emotion the memories of their son as they continued turning the cold pages of an album containing pictures that Jacob had taken on his journey. From the photos, I could see that *Gatorboy* and *Thunder Chicken* were good friends during the time they hiked together last year. The Crams are here now, having returned for a small memorial service for Jacob that was held this past Saturday on the mountain. During that service some of Jacob's ashes were spread . . . over the path where he last trod.

With kind permission from the Crams, I will close this bitter-sweet day with a note and card that contains a verse, sent to Jacob's sister from his good friend Dirk.

> *"Life is too short to let even one day,*
> *To be frenzied or frazzled or frittered away.*
> *Life is too short not to take time to do,*
> *The things that will hold the most meaning for you.*
> *So, let yourself float like a leaf on a stream*
> *Relax with your memories and let yourself dream.*
> *Throw out your list that's impossibly long,*
> *And dance a few steps to a favorite song.*
> *Turn off the news and go find someone real,*
> *Who'll listen and talk and affirm what you feel.*
> *Life is too short and flies by if you let it,*
> *So, choose what you want every day, and go get it."*

Vanessa,

I think Jake embodies the essence of this card. He serves as an inspiration to us all, I will never forget his verve for life . . . don't you forget it either. —Love, Dirk

TUESDAY August 11, 1998
TRAIL DAY 207/113 ✦ TRAIL MILE 3,085/1,683
LOCATION Stony Brook Shelter

I SPLIT A ROOM LAST NIGHT WITH *Bagman* and we had breakfast together. I worked on my journal entries until 3:00 p.m.

Soon I will be seeing no more Long Trail hikers as the AT and Long Trail split just north of Sherburne Pass, the LT going on north and the AT turning east toward New Hampshire. Getting out late makes for a very short trail day, but I'm able to make it to Stony Brook Shelter to spend the evening with *Bagman, Good Times, Chief Frodo, Dr. Daisy G., Firecracker, Jarhead, Konoa,* and southbounders Aaron and *Sleepy.*

PROFILES '98

JEFF *Innkeeper* VENUTI, IS 24, SINGLE, and from Tewksbury, Massachusetts. Jeff is a graduate of Tewksbury High School and has a master's degree in electrical engineering from Cornell University. He is employed by Analog Devices, Wilmington, Massachusetts, a company that designs, manufactures, and markets integrated transistor circuits. Jeff designs the circuits for wireless communications devices, such as cell phones and pagers . . . the "little chips that go inside those things you use to call people, with no wires attached. Funny, because I've never even used a cell phone, but I know how they work and I know how to design the parts that go inside!"

Jeff has been given a six-month leave of absence to hike the AT, an agreement made with Analog. "At the time I interviewed, both the people I talked with slapped their foreheads, exclaiming, 'Oh no, not this again!' It turned out the last person they had recruited also wanted to hike the AT. Since they needed someone to start right away, the leave of absence was a promise down the line. But they came through and here I am on the trail. Analog is a great company. They've given me the time to achieve one of my personal goals." In addition to electronics, Jeff is also interested in backpacking, "I've always been an avid backpacker since Boy Scouts."

Jeff will certainly be easy to remember for a number of reasons. One, for spending eight nights and seven days at the "Fontana Hilton" shelter while mending a sore, injured ankle. Thus the well-deserved trail name *Innkeeper*! Oh, this is a good one. "I drank a lot of olive oil received in a mail drop. I didn't want to take it with me and I didn't want to waste it! I thought, hmm, all these great fat calories, why don't I just drink it. That was a big mistake, I promptly threw it right back up!" And a final distinction, "People have been somewhat surprised with how much I can eat, even other thru-hikers. I tend to be able to put down the food."

When Jeff's AT odyssey is through, he will return to his professional career with Analog Devices. "I really like the job I have. I find it quite rewarding. There are great opportunities with this company."

Jeff concluded his remarks with "I've always had a profound respect for the wilderness and I love backpacking, and the two go hand in hand. Hiking the AT is a personal challenge. I've never done anything that requires this amount of motivation and perseverance. It will be a tremendous reward when completed. I've spent a lot of time getting rid of things that I don't need and concentrating on only that which I do need. And, I think I am a happier person for it. I believe greatly in rational thought and I've put a lot of effort in trying to be a completely rational person."

Jeff, you are already a success in all of these things. You are a man with wisdom well beyond your years. Folks will no doubt look back to the beginning of this profile to make sure of your age, thinking it must certainly be a typo. It's been my good fortune knowing you, hiking with you, and having you as a friend. I hope our paths meet again soon.

> *"There are no words that can tell of the hidden spirit of the wilderness, that can reveal its mystery, its melancholy, and its charm."*
>
> [Theodore Roosevelt]

WEDNESDAY August 12, 1998
TRAIL DAY 208/114 ✦ TRAIL MILE 3,106/1,704
LOCATION Thistle Hill Shelter

ON THE WAY DOWN TO RICK AND TINA'S GENERAL STORE for breakfast this morning I pass this old barn with a sign painted on it. Now we've all seen these old barns with signs painted on them: "See Rock City," "Chew Mail Pouch Tobacco," "Meramec Caverns," and on and on. But this sign really gets my attention. It reads, "Leslie, Marry Me!" in big faded and weathered letters. As I pull abreast of the old barn on the left, to the right of the road is this lovely picture-book-perfect little bungalow, complete with a kiddie play center. I'm thinking, "Could be!" What mystery, what suspense (remember I'm near 60 now, so to me this is suspense). At the General Store, Tina quickly solves the mystery. Leslie said yes! Well now, don't you just love happy endings? I sure do! This day is going just great, and I get a fine meal at the store, too.

On the trail today I see and talk with *Spirit* and *Grateful,* then spend an enjoyable evening with *Cool Breeze, Mad Max Mel, Crying Violet,* and *Tweetie.*

"When you are close to nature you can listen to the voice of God."

[Herman Hesse]

THURSDAY August 13, 1998
TRAIL DAY 209/115 ✦ TRAIL MILE 3,129/1,727
LOCATION Mink Brook, New Hampshire

Desperado CAME ALONG AND WE HIKED TOGETHER into Hanover. It was great to see *Innkeeper* again while having pizza at C&A Pizzeria. He showed us to Tabard Hall, a Dartmouth fraternity house where hikers are welcome to stay. It's great to see *Selky* here again and to finally meet *Bush Baby.*

I stop on the way out of Hanover for a few provisions at the co-op, then head on up the mountain. Crossing the Connecticut River at

Hanover puts another state behind me as I move into New Hampshire. The day is long and steady, a good mileage day. The nights are cooling nicely now and it's already in the 50s when I roll in.

There is no land discovered,
That can't be found anew.
So travel on intrepid,
Into the hazy blue
And as you seek your fortune,
And near your life-long quest.
There'll still be countless peaks to climb,
Before your final rest.

[N. Nomad]

FRIDAY August 14, 1998
TRAIL DAY 210/116 ✦ TRAIL MILE 3,149/1,747
LOCATION Hexacuba Shelter

I USUALLY WAKE AROUND FIRST LIGHT, but I rolled in very tired last night so don't rouse this morning until 8:30 a.m. I thought my watch was playing tricks again but I've just slept in. I never have been the quickest to break camp, so I'm not on the trail until 9:30 a.m., really not good when trying to do a decent mileage day. I am dealt some hard, tough pulls today as the terrain is really becoming rugged and much more alpine-like. I still manage a 20-mile day, but I arrive in the near dark at this interesting old hex-shaped shelter. I'm able to get a good fire going in my "Little Dandy" wood burner to prepare a warm supper. I share the shelter with southbounders *Hard Core, Jayrod,* and *Fade Out.*

"In the country it is as if every tree said to me, 'Holy! Holy!'
Who can ever express the ecstasy of the woods?"

[Ludwig van Beethoven]

SATURDAY August 15, 1998
TRAIL DAY 211/117 ✦ TRAIL MILE 3,173/1,771
LOCATION NH 112, Kinsman Notch, North Woodstock,
Cascade Lodge Bed and Breakfast

I'VE BEEN TOLD THE GOING WILL SLOW DOWN considerably now that the elevation changes will become much more extreme and abrupt. I'm out and moving by 7:30 a.m. My goal for today is to reach Kinsman Notch, a 24-mile day, with the formidable Mt. Moosilauke, a near-5,000-foot peak right at the end of the day. I've also been told the Snickers rating system I've developed will be put to the test in the Whites and Presidents. And indeed, it appears this is going to be true. Mt. Moosilauke has already reached into the upper digits of the rating system, coming in somewhere between six and seven on the old Snickers scale. It is evident that I will need to add more Snickers to the pack as I add more Snickers to the pulls.

Folks have tried to describe what lies ahead, with little success. After confronting Moosilauke today I understand why! The majesty of these mountains, their beauty revealed, is the reward for the effort and time spent in scaling them. It has been estimated that although 80 percent of the hike is behind us, 50 percent of the work yet remains! I arrive at Kinsman Notch at 7:00 p.m., my energy very near spent. I am able to thumb a ride right away into North Woodstock and Cascade Lodge.

"By maple orchards, belts of pine
And larches climbing darkly
The mountain slopes, and over all,
The great peaks rising starkly."

[John Greenleaf Whittier]

SUNDAY August 16, 1998
TRAIL DAY 212/118 ✦ TRAIL MILE 3,173/1,771
LOCATION NH 112, Kinsman Notch, North Woodstock,
Cascade Lodge Bed and Breakfast

I'M TAKING A DAY OFF FOR A MUCH-NEEDED REST. *Easy Rider*, whom I have been hiking with and who will be accompanying me into Canada, got off here Friday to attend his grandmother's birthday party. We have decided not to get back on the trail until tomorrow, so he and his mother will be picking me up here in the morning to take us back to the trailhead at NH 112.

Relaxing another day here at the Cascade Lodge is a pleasure. The owners, Bill and Betty Robinson, cater to and enjoy having hikers. The place is well kept and very comfortable. Frosties and food on the porch are no problem. I am having a great time visiting with Kevin, *Gnatcatcher*, *Boomerang*, *Screamin' Ankle*, *Lorax*, *Thorin*, *Mo'*, *Ol' Crawdad*, *Yahoola*, *Stoneman*, *L. W.*, *Red Bz's* (Mike and Bronson) *Abandoneer*, and Eric.

I have been invited to dinner with *Grym* and *POD*. We had met at the "Fontana Hilton" and hiked together off and on throughout the southern Appalachians. They're working here now in North Woodstock, and as soon as *POD* gets off work we head out. *Grym* treats me to a steak dinner with all the trimmings! It was a wonderful evening with the best of "trail family."

> *"Not many people really get to chase their dreams. Not many people get to do something no one else has done."*
>
> [David Horton]

MONDAY August 17, 1998
TRAIL DAY 213/119 ✦ TRAIL MILE 3,192/1,790
LOCATION Liberty Spring Tentsite

Easy Rider AND HIS MOTHER, ELAINE DRESSER, pick me up at Cascade Lodge at 8:00 a.m. and we're off to the trailhead at NH 112. Elaine is very enthusiastic about our planned adventure on into Canada, which pleases me greatly. Her son is a strong, consistent hiker with four-season hiking experience, especially in winter alpine hiking, and her pride and confidence show.

The White Mountains of New Hampshire are nothing at all like the Appalachian Mountains south of here. They are incredibly tall, rugged, and steep, with a good portion of the treadway in the alpine zone near or above 4,000 feet. The climbs begin abruptly, go almost straight up and never seem to end. The Snickers rating system pulls will be consistently at or above five here in the Whites. The climbs up South and North Kinsman and Mt. Wolf are all rated at least six Snickers or better. We've encountered nothing even close to these pulls south of here and here are three in one day!

By the time *Easy Rider* and I drop into Franconia Notch, then climb back up to Liberty Spring, we're ready to call it a day. *Frenchie* slack-packed this section, from NH 112 into Franconia Notch, and *Rider* and I both enjoyed his company. He had many interesting stories to tell. We arrive at the tent sites at dusk and are fortunate to get the last tent platform. Just as I get my little tent set up and *Rider* has his tarp strung, the rain begins. This exhausting but enjoyable day owes us nothing!

> *"The land of the great woods, lakes, mountains and rushing rivers is still mysterious enough to please any-one who has eyes to see and can understand."*
>
> [Norman Collie]

TUESDAY August 18, 1998
TRAIL DAY 214/120 ✦ TRAIL MILE 3,209/1,807
LOCATION Zealand Falls Hut

THE RAIN HAS CONTINUED INTO MORNING as we break camp, but we're able to get out reasonably early into the gray swirl. Views today from Mt. Lafayette, Mt. Garfield, and Mt. Guyot are nonexistent, but we do not complain for we have been so blessed with incredibly good weather. A Canadian front, which has brought cold rain, is forecast to blow this dank weather on out this evening, giving us cloudless, haze-free skies for the remainder of our hike through the Presidential Range.

The hike today, both long and hard, brings us only 17 miles. It is near dusk as *Easy Rider* and I arrive, tired and weary, at Zealand Falls Hut. But the storm is breaking now and the view down the mountain from the porch here at Zealand, the first for the day, is another of God's mystifying wonders, making for life-long memories. The ditty closing today's journal entry, having been inspired by such absolute grandeur, gives testimony to the splendor and majesty of it all.

The huts throughout the Whites are operated by the Appalachian Mountain Club. The young folks who manage these huts, prepare and serve the great meals, and otherwise care and provide for the needs of their hiker guests are some of the friendliest and happiest guys and gals you'll meet anywhere. *Rider* and I are the only thru-hikers at Zealand this evening (a full house otherwise) and we are greeted with interest and enthusiasm by Anthony Greco, Lila, Jarad, and Dawn, a volunteer. Anthony is in his third season and is now Hut Master here at Zealand.

The AMC's policy for thru-hikers, an indication of their genuine soft-spot-in-the-heart for us, is to permit a limited number to enjoy the comforts, meals, and lodging at the huts in return for work. *Rider* and I help in the kitchen for a while this evening and we'll do some cleaning up for a short time in the morning, but believe you me, the balance in this deal sways well in the thru-hiker's favor! Totally content, our stomachs full to capacity, we retire and sleep soundly in the warmth and comfort, above the clouds, at little Zealand Falls Hut.

We're at the hut on Zealand
And from this vantage watch,
The wind blow out the storm clouds
Down in Carrigan Notch.
The sun is dancing 'long the ridge
In splashing yellow hue,
This show? A restless beckoning,
A'callin' me and you.

[N. Nomad]

WEDNESDAY August 19, 1998
TRAIL DAY 215/121 ✦ TRAIL MILE 3,228/1,826
LOCATION Lakes of the Clouds Hut

THE PRESIDENTIALS — WE'RE REALLY IN THE THICK of them now. The ascents and descents have become near vertical, near endless. The first encounter this morning involves a ricocheting plunge down into Crawford Notch. We no more recoup from this pell-mell off-load than we're hurtled against it as the treadway recoils to literally block us with boulders and rock, forcing the most desperate struggle up and over Mt. Webster, Mt. Jackson, Mt. Pierce, and Mt. Franklin. Here it would it be beneficial if we could simply distill the Snickers bars and go straight to IV. This treadway contains a boundless and awesome might, radiating it seems, in a manner to grip us in such a strange way, forcing us to pit our limits of strength, energy, and resolve against it. This is most surely the path built by Thor and trod by Atlas. For from here, on a pathway we mere mortals attempt to follow, could this mystical god of might have supported all the heavens on his shoulders, much as Zeus commanded.

Easy Rider and I are glad to see the Lakes of the Clouds Hut below as we descend the trail from Mt. Franklin. It is late evening, near dusk, and the large crowd at the hut (another full house) is being served supper. Today we've encountered heavy traffic, so we're not surprised to see the hut filled to capacity. We wait patiently for the dining hall to clear, for we've been invited to dine later with the hut "croo." For a small fee, which includes victuals, are we then permitted to roll out our sleeping bags on the dining room tables just before lights out at 9:30 p.m.

> *"Upon the next bright peak I saw thee kneel,*
> *And heard thy voice upon the billowy blast;*
> *But, climbing, only reached the shrine to feel*
> *The shadow of a Presence which had passed."*
>
> [Henry Timrod, *Elusive Nature*]

THURSDAY August 20, 1998
TRAIL DAY 216/122 ✦ TRAIL MILE 3,243/1,841
LOCATION NH 16, Pinkham Notch, Nikki's folks' retreat in Jackson, NH

Easy Rider AND I HIKE OUT FROM LAKES OF THE CLOUDS HUT at 6:30 a.m. I'm thinking as we depart that I will long remember the warm hospitality we've received from the really great young folks that make up the hut "croo." You just couldn't find more kind and friendly hosts! Thanks, Karen Baglini, Hut Master, and you too, Steve, Traci, Adrienne, and John! The air is crisp and clear this morning, and as I climb I soon find that before me this day will be some of the most amazing hiking that I've done . . . ever. The treadway is demanding and indescribably difficult to negotiate, long near-vertical ascents and descents through rock and boulders and up and over ledges, with sheer drop-offs. But, once the peaks are reached, the ridges above tree line gained, the unusual alpine landscape inspires the senses, the views overwhelming!

By 7:30 a.m. we're standing on Mt. Washington. The summit is ours, for there's no one up the auto road yet, and the old cog railway steam locomotives are still getting their boilers fired up as the coal smoke rises from great distances down. In a while *Gnatcatcher* comes and we greet each other with huge ear-to-ear grins. With only a slight haze and no clouds, the view in all directions is grand. It seems that we are on the top of the world. Mt. Washington is notorious for having some of the foulest, most unpredictable weather in the world, but here this morning we are favored with a gentle, cool breeze. The AT goes on to climb a little bump, an elevated rocky projection above the otherwise flat expanse of numerous buildings, towers, and other summit ornaments scattered around. Up this last little pop the AT is superimposed on Crawford Path, the oldest mountain-hiking trail in America, constructed and first put in use in 1819. I add now to the continuity of it as my name is etched in time along with the millions of others who have passed this way. On the wall inside the welcome center is a list of those who have perished on this mountain. At last count they numbered 125. Beside this list of names is this simple but poignant inscription, "This can be a dangerous place. No one on this list planned to die here." Also at the summit, the highest point in New Hampshire, is this very moving and most befitting memorial, honoring those members of the 10th Mountain Division from New Hampshire, mountaineers who made the supreme sacrifice in WWII.

> *"Throughout his life he set one goal,*
> *To reach on high a mountain's soul.*
> *His climbing days now over . . . past,*
> *He scaled the peak which death had cast.*
> *On top the summit all aglow,*
> *He stands in God's great light — and so,*
> *He could no lesser life have known,*
> *Than of the one he lived, full blown!*
> *The mountain of the great beyond,*
> *Still beckons with an ice-axe wand.*
> *And mountain men no matter where,*
> *Must meet the challenge that is there.*
> *He was a member of our clan,*
> *A 10th Division mountain man."*

On a sign near one of the summit vantages is written, "The Appalachian Mountains are among the oldest on earth, reaching back more than 500 million years into time. The present chain, which stretches from the Gaspé to Georgia, once may have been higher than the Alps or the Rocky Mountains. Weather and erosion have sculpted them and left them as they are today." Actually, the Appalachians begin in south-central Alabama and stretch over 3,000 miles by trail north to the Gaspé peninsula in Québec Province, Canada, where they plunge dramatically to the sea at the Cliffs of Forillon, the Gulf of St. Lawrence. Some even claim these old mountains submerge beneath the sea, only to reemerge again in Europe!

In the course of hiking most-near the breadth of the Eastern North American continent, the old *Nomad* will hike the entire length of these magnificent Appalachians. Soon, connecting trails will be completed making it possible for others to do the same. In the South, all but a few miles of the Pinhoti Trail through the beautiful Talladega National Forest in Alabama are completed. In western Georgia, connector trails will link the

Alabama Pinhoti to the AT on Springer Mountain. These are the Georgia Pinhoti Trail, which is still under construction, and the Benton MacKaye Trail, Georgia section, which is completed. In the north, under construction in Maine, and for the most part completed in Canada, is *Le Sentier International des Appalaches*/International Appalachian Trail. This trail, when completed, will connect to the AT in Baxter State Park, Maine, making it possible to hike to the northern end of the Appalachian Range in Canada. I predict that thousands who have hiked or who plan to hike the Appalachians will no longer be satisfied with only that section traversed by the AT, but will soon want to experience much more!

As we leave Mt. Washington and begin our descent we enter what is known as the Madison Loop, a treacherously rocky but most magnificent stretch of treadway entirely above tree line. The clear-cool breeze holds, and the 360s are spectacular. And as for this seemingly boundless mountain expanse, I can truly say, "We are amongst them." On our way down to Pinkham Notch and arriving at Madison Springs Hut, we hear voices from within, "*Nomad, Easy Rider!*" What a perfect day this is now, for what a surprise to arrive and find good friends *Wolfhound* and *Farther.* We haven't seen either of them for weeks and weeks, having said our goodbyes way back down the trail, never expecting to meet again . . . and here we are together once more! They're slack-packing the Presidentials (a smart move) out of Marianne and Bruno's Hiker's Paradise in Gorham. We linger for the longest time while sharing the enjoyment of seeing each other again!

As we near Pinkham Notch, scampering up the trail directly toward us are two of the happiest and most gangly looking black labs. I hear *Easy Rider* call out with excitement, "Albert, Mattie" just as he is literally jumped on, overrun, and then totally smothered by the two grown pups. *Rider* was wondering if they'd recognize and remember him after all these months on the trail. Well, *Easy Rider,* wonder no more! Both the pups knew the skinny little fellow with the full red beard. But I don't think he recognized them right away! Coming along a few paces behind is *Easy Rider*'s girlfriend, Nikki. She's brought the pups out to scamper along as she hiked part way to meet us. Nikki's folks have a new home on the mountain above Jackson and I've been invited to tag along as their guest. In just a short while we reach Pinkham Notch, load up, and are on our way to Jackson. After a few cold ones, a delicious dinner prepared by Nikki, plus the exhilaration of one of the most remarkable hiking days in my life, I'm ready to hit the hay!

> *"Bids me dream and bids me linger—*
> *Joy and beauty are its goal;*
> *On the path that leads to nowhere*
> *I have sometimes found my soul."*

[Corinne Roosevelt Robinson]

FRIDAY August 21, 1998
TRAIL DAY 217/123 ✦ TRAIL MILE 3,264/1,862
LOCATION US 2, Gorham, Nikki's folks' retreat in Jackson

WE ARE UP EARLY, AND AFTER A GREAT BREAKFAST prepared by Nikki, she has us back to Pinkham Notch and on the trail by 8:30 a.m. We have a long, hard day with many six- and seven-Snickers pulls over the Wildcats, Carter Dome, Middle Carter, and Mt. Moriah. Nikki and the pups come in to meet and greet us again from US 2 near Gorham. She had met *Lorax* as she was climbing Mt. Moriah and has invited him to come along for the evening. *Easy Rider* somehow survives a rerun of yesterday's knockdown greeting from the pups. This has been another memorable day, countless breathtaking vistas, but oh-so tiring!

> *"I meant to do my work today,*
> *But a brown bird sang in the apple tree,*
> *And a butterfly flittered across the field,*
> *And all the leaves were calling me.*
> *And the wind went sighing over the land,*
> *Tossing the grasses to and fro,*
> *And a rainbow held out its shining hand,*
> *So what could I do, but laugh and go?"*

[Richard Le Gallienne]

WE'VE DECIDED TO TAKE THE MORNING OFF, run some errands, and get a few provisions. One of the much-needed stops is at the Limmer Boot Shop in Intervale, a short trip from Jackson. Here I meet Carl Limmer and the gentleman who fits their stock boots, Ken Smith. I dearly need some new boots since my Danner Lights, fine boots in their own right, are really coming apart. In all due respect, the Danners were well worn and had already been resoled once before beginning the Odyssey of '98. They just have no more miles left in them. *Easy Rider* wears a stock pair of Limmers and I like the way they're constructed. Ken takes a look at my feet, asks me a couple of questions, then disappears into the back. Moments later he emerges with a shiny new pair of Limmers and I pull them on over a new pair of rag wool socks. Ken checks the fit and I wear them around the shop for a while, and that's it!

While I'm giving the boots a walkabout, in come two young fellows, Doug Connelly and Chris Davis, both members of the AMC Technical Field Crew (professional trail builders). Doug is in to get some boots and to invite the Limmer folks to the work crew's year-end bash to be held this very evening at an old cabin just across the Androscoggin River. Upon finding out that *Lorax*, *Easy Rider*, and I are all thru-hikers, we're also invited to attend! Since the decision is pretty much a no-brainer—oh yes, we're going to the party—the day is quickly shaping to be a no-hike day. This is all well and good, as another day's rest is certainly welcome. The plan now is to have Nikki drop us off at US 2, hike the short distance across the river, hitch on in to the party, then pitch somewhere in the woods nearby after the bash is over. This works great and we arrive at the old cabin around 7:30 p.m. to be promptly greeted by Doug and 16 other 1998-season crewmembers.

The AMC/TFC work year runs from mid-May to mid-August. Their job is to tackle the really heavy stuff that can't be handled by the volunteer crews. This backbreaking work mostly entails moving, stacking, and building the incredible rock steps and water bars that help us get up and over these rugged mountains. Their axe work in removing huge blowdowns from the treadway is a sight to behold. All this work, almost without exception, takes place on slopes and inclines that make standing upright, let alone doing heavy, physically demanding work, next to impossible. And yet, somehow, they get it done—steps straight up the mountain, built from rocks and boulders weighing many hundreds of pounds. It's absolutely baffling to look up at their masterwork. When I reach one of these remarkable places I just stop, to look and shake my head in amazement!

So now here we are, enjoying their hospitality and sharing in their joy and the pride that comes with another successful trail-building season. We meet some very kind, enthusiastic young folks, lift a few with them in celebration, put away some great grub, and watch a very entertaining slide show highlighting their year's accomplishments. Thanks, Doug, for inviting us to be part of your special celebration. And most of all, thanks to all of you for making the Appalachian Trail the greatest trail in the world!

Present at the party is—oh yes—Ken Smith! Ken is going through Jackson and offers us a ride back to Nikki's . . . which we promptly accept! So now it's off for another very enjoyable and relaxing night's rest in a real bed.

In five-hundred million years
These mountains will be smaller.
Just as five-hundred million past
They were a wee bit taller.
The race of man may race away,
So, we'll not know for certain.
But chances are these mounts'll stand
To see the final curtain.

[N. Nomad]

SUNDAY August 23, 1998
TRAIL DAY 219/125   ✦   TRAIL MILE 3,282/1,880
LOCATION Carlo Col Shelter, Maine

NIKKI SHUTTLES US BACK ACROSS THE ANDROSCOGGIN and drops us off with a goodbye . . . one more time! We're off to climb into a steady drizzle, which continues until mid-afternoon. While we're resting and taking a lunch break at Gentian Pond Shelter, in comes *Desperado*! He has been pounding out the miles to catch up with us. We hike the rest of the day as a foursome; what an enjoyable change of pace. Two other thru-hikers we have the pleasure meeting today are *Mac 'n' Cheese* and southbounder *Gots-to-Go*.

We arrive at Carlo Col Shelter in good order. I crank up my "Little Dandy" woodstove and prepare a warm evening meal. The shelter is crowded, but we're all able to squeeze in for the night. The rain comes hard at times, but I sleep very soundly.

> *"I long for wildness; woods where the wood thrush*
> *forever sings. Where the hours are early morning ones*
> *and there is dew on the grass, and the day is forever*
> *unproved. A New Hampshire everlasting and unfallen."*

[Henry David Thoreau]

MONDAY August 24, 1998
TRAIL DAY 220/126   ✦   TRAIL MILE 3,296/1,894
LOCATION ME 26, Grafton Notch, *Easy Rider*'s folks' place in Bethel

WELL, TODAY IS THE DAY TO DO "THE NOTCH"—the Mahoosuc Notch, that is. The Notch, which is just across the New Hampshire/Maine border, runs for the better part of a mile and entails some of the most technically difficult rock scrambling found anywhere on the AT. Boxcar-size boulders are lodged at incredible angles, heaped in a seemingly impenetrable maze one against and upon the other in a frightful jumble, often in piles, making the going very slow and at times very scary. We have all oft-heard the old axiom "time is of the essence," but here the opposite becomes the truism and is much more realistic. Here indeed "the essence is of time." For it is that mysterious medium of the ages, the medium of time, that has created and formed this natural wonder, and it is time in great quantity that must be consumed in the task of traversing this most remarkable place. I keep repeating to myself, as did Dan the grand old backpacker repeat to himself in Lynne Whelden's adventure documentary *27 Days*, "Don't bust it, Dan; don't bust it, [*Nomad*]!" This short yet seemingly endless mile will remain in my memory as one of the most exciting times during the "Odyssey of '98." Leaping, scampering, and wriggling through this remarkable place has been a truly whacking adrenaline pump! As I emerge from the Notch, my legs so much rubber, my body ceases to respond, as if it is little more than a pile of frameless mush. I collapse in a heap as the trail turns to ascend Mahoosuc Arm. Here I rest as I try to gain some composure and to fix the jumble in my mind caused by this last hour through the incredible jumble of boulders and rock. Yet remaining is the unbelievably demanding eight-Snickers pull up Mahoosuc Arm to Old Speck.

Back with *Easy Rider* and *Lorax* now and near consumed with anxiety and anticipation do I find great relief in arriving at Grafton Notch, here to be greeted by Nikki and the pups! We wait and wait for over an hour, anxious for *Desperado* to arrive from the mountain, but he does not come. I had been hit hard by wind, then pelted by driving rain-turned-to-sleet as I climbed Old Speck. So we assume that *Desperado* has pulled up at Speck Pond Shelter to get out of it. We finally depart, leaving a note for him at the trailhead. No sooner do we arrive in Bethel than Nikki turns to make the trip once more to Grafton Notch in hopes of finding *Desperado*. But she returns with no good news.

The little town of Bethel is a stereotypical quaint New England village, each street lined with beautiful, well-kept old two-story homes. The Dresser residence is grand indeed, in keeping with tradition and with the pride that folks all around seem to take in maintaining these beautiful old structures. It is the love within that shows through and is so immediately evident. The warmth, enduring care, and devotion dedicated to keeping these old places is reflected in the radiant beauty of their grand presence, offering a most joyful and welcome sight to see. *Lorax* and I are greeted warmly by the Dressers, Dutch and Elaine, and Derek's younger brother, Chuck, along with the Dressers' good friends Eric and Lucia. Elaine has prepared a wonderful meal for us and we hurry to get reasonably presentable before joining them at the supper table. The Dressers are very happy and full of joy to have their son home again. This evening has been such a very happy time and I feel blessed to have been included and made part of this grand celebration. With a clean body, full stomach, and a fresh bed, I quickly fall into restful sleep, to dream of that "greatest mountain," Katahdin.

> *"From the crest of old Speck Mountain,*
> *On the wild Mahoosuc west.*
> *To the summit of Katahdin,*
> *And the ending of the quest."*

[Shaffer]

TUESDAY August 25, 1998
TRAIL DAY 221/127 ✦ TRAIL MILE 3,296/1,894
LOCATION ME 26, Grafton Notch, *Easy Rider*'s folk's place in Bethel

---

THIS IS GOING TO BE A MUCH-WELCOME DAY OF REST—time to relax and get caught up on my journal entries. And what a mighty fine start for this day with blueberry pancakes topped with fresh blueberry sauce prepared by Elaine! *Easy Rider* then cranks up his Harley (now you know how he came by his trail name), and he and Nikki cruise back up to Grafton Notch to look for *Desperado*. And what great timing, for just as they arrive, *Desperado* is emerging from the mountain! He'd pulled into Speck Pond Shelter just as we had hoped, to avoid the thunderstorm and sleet that was crossing over Old Speck yesterday afternoon. *Easy Rider* and Nikki then return, get the car, and go back out for *Desperado*. So, it turns out, we're all back together again!

For lunch it's a short walk to Skidder's Deli for subs. Then on the way home we stop at the market for a few things. Nikki, *Easy Rider*, and *Lorax* get all the fixin's for burritos for the evening meal. They also pick up the ingredients for brownies. My contribution? Oh yes, the ice cream and chocolate to top off the brownies! Life on the trail is great. Life off the trail—ah, absolutely superb!

PROFILES '98

MATT *Lorax* POMRANING, AGE 23, IS SINGLE and from New Cumberland, Pennsylvania. He graduated from Camp Hill High School and has a degree in elementary education with certification from Shippensburg University.

His hobbies include hiking, cooking, *scherenschnitte* (German paper-cutting), rugby, and working with children.

"I never really hiked much before. When I was a Boy Scout there was this kid that said he wanted to hike the AT. That sparked my interest, so I started reading about it. I couldn't hike during high school or college, but when I found I could graduate from college a semester early and leave in time to hike the AT, that's what I did. When I was younger I made a list of all the things I wanted to do in my life, and hiking the AT was one of the things at the top. After the trail I hope to get a teaching position eventually, probably away from where I'm living now, travel, have a family."

"Personally, I wish there were more places in the world, like life here on the trail, where everyone could trust each other, where all were willing to help each other out, do things for each other. This journey is giving me faith in people again. It's always been a dream of mine to work with little kids. I hope to be remembered as someone who brought something good."

For those of you who may not remember (including me), the Lorax was one of the delightful little characters created by Dr. Seuss. The Lorax was the saver of trees. The choice this young man has made for his trail name gives insight into his personality, his sensitivity, and his vitality for life, which is immediately evident to those of us who've had the good fortune to meet and to know Matt. A more upbeat and positive person you will not find. What a great background he's developing, what a fresh and grand resource to draw from to teach our children. Matt, life will be better for all who know you . . . Go for it, *Lorax*, my dear young friend!

> *"Each kindly act is an acorn dropped*
> *In God's productive soil;*
> *You may not know, but the tree shall grow*
> *With shelter for those who toil."*

[Ella Wheeler Wilcox]

WEDNESDAY August 26, 1998
TRAIL DAY 222/128 ✦ TRAIL MILE 3,312/1,910
LOCATION Hall Mountain Lean-to

ELAINE, DUTCH, AND I ARE UP EARLY. Nikki has already had the dogs out for a run. Dutch brews the coffee and Nikki gets me set up to make pancakes, a new experience for me. I find that following the directions on the box works great, but I beat the batter a little too hard and the pancakes turn out pretty rubbery. Elaine's great blueberry sauce thankfully saves the day for me!

I sure hate to leave this great little town of Bethel, Nikki, and the Dressers, but the time has come to hit the trail. We get loaded, Elaine drives us back to Grafton Notch, and we're on the trail a little after 9:00 a.m. Thanks, Dutch, Elaine, Chuck, and Nikki. I had a memorable time.

The going is slow and difficult with long, tough pulls over the Baldpates and Wyman Mountain, especially so for me as I'm trying to break in my new boots. Ken had taken them back with him after he dropped us off from the AMC party to stretch the toe area out a little. We had decided to do this to reduce the break-in time and to make what could have been a difficult, uncomfortable process much easier. To get the boots back to me in time, Ken made a special trip to Bethel to deliver the boots personally! I couldn't believe it when Dutch told me Monday that my boots were already there. And just to make sure that I started out right, Ken had filled both boots, toe to top, with Snickers bars! Thanks, Ken, and thanks, Limmer.

> *"One final paragraph of advice: Do not burn yourself*
> *out. Be as I am, a reluctant enthusiast, a part-time*

crusader, a half-hearted fanatic. Save the other half of yourself and your lives for pleasure and adventure. It is not enough to fight for the land, it is even more important to enjoy it while you can, while its still here, so, get out there and hunt and fish and mess around with your friends. Ramble out yonder and explore the forests. Encounter the griz, climb the mountains, bag the peaks, run the rivers, breathe deep of that yet sweet and lucid air. Sit quietly for a while and contemplate the precious stillness; that lovely, mysterious, awesome space. Enjoy yourselves. Keep your brain in your head and your head firmly attached to your body; the body active and alive and I promise you this much. I promise you this one sweet victory over our enemies—over those desk-bound people with their hearts in a safe deposit box and their eyes hypnotized to desk calculators. I promise you this—we'll outlive the bastards."

[Edward Abbey]

THURSDAY August 27, 1998
TRAIL DAY 223/129 ✦ TRAIL MILE 3,325/1,923
LOCATION Bemis Mountain Lean-to

THE TRAIL TODAY PROVES TO BE some of the most difficult going so far. The first day back after a layover is always difficult, this one especially so. We manage scant few miles. The vertical ascents and descents over Moody, Old Blue, and Bemis West are all seven Snickers or better. I arrive late and very tired at Bemis Mountain Lean-to to spend the evening with *Easy Rider, Lorax, Loon, Flatlander,* and *Redman.*

*"To see a world in a grain of sand and heaven in a wildflower.
Hold infinity in the palm of your hand and eternity in an hour."*
[William Blake]

FRIDAY August 28, 1998
TRAIL DAY 224/130 ✦ TRAIL MILE 3,344/1,942
LOCATION Piazza Rock Lean-to

TODAY I HEAR THE FIRST SHRILL, ALLURING CALL of the loon rever-
berating and echoing across Moxie Pond. Even from afar it is an eerie,
piercing sound. Indeed it is a call in the truest sense, the ancient, everlasting and unchanging call of the North Woods. This singular sound, perhaps more than any other sound we have ever heard or could ever hear,
stirs in us a sense of restlessness to the bottom of our very soul, a sound
that beckons all who hear to venture forth toward that great unknown,
that pristine and unspoiled wilderness just over the horizon. Oh, but so
elusive do we find this destination and the journey in search of it, for we
are uncontrollably drawn, ever onward toward that mysterious and
boundless expanse that lies beyond. The call of the loon is a lure, a call to
awaken the wanderlust — that basic, instinctive desire that each of us possesses deep within. It is the call to return again to our primal home, to the
bosom of nature, and there, finally, to be free . . . truly free.

Today we see some trail family members whom we haven't seen for
many a week: *Turtle* and *Bear* and also *Florida Guy.* They're hiking south
from Katahdin now after flip-flopping to avoid severe weather here later.

Upon reaching ME 4, we meet *Spring Chicken*, GAME '91. He's
been doing some trail maintenance and is just finishing up, so he gives us
a ride into Rangeley. There are two good reasons for going into Rangeley.
One, we need to pick up some provisions . . . and the other? Well, read
on! Rangeley is a neat, well-kept little burg thriving on vacationers from
the large, coastal metropolitan areas. While here, *Easy Rider* and I head
over to the Red Onion for a pizza and a pitcher. Here we meet *Junebug*,
another flip-flopper. He is really moving, covering many miles per day,
and carrying an ultralight pack. This fellow is what most would label a
gearhead. His pack is mesh and weighs only 7 ounces, utilizing his
Ridgerest sleeping pad to form the pack frame! He's fully loaded at 12
pounds (without food or water), the lightest setup I've seen so far. With
comparable gear, my pack weighs in at around 23 pounds, almost double
Junebug's pack weight. Compared to most however, my Kelty Redwing

weekend pack is small and very lightweight, less than 3 pounds. Most lightweight backpackers also use a down bag, but it seems I'm never able to keep anything dry, so I lug along a synthetic bag, paying the price for the "warm-when-wet" benefit in bulk and weight. A wet down bag is a real bummer and I absolutely would not wish this evil method of torture on anyone! Many have commented about my meager pack and how little weight I'm toting . . . but compared to *Junebug,* I'm a piker.

Down in North Woodstock a while back, I'd spent some time at Frog Rock Café, a local café/pub where my very good hiking friend *Grym* was working at the time. Here I relaxed, taking an extra and much-needed day off while *Easy Rider* attended his grandmother's surprise birthday party. Consequently, while lifting a few at Frog Rock I made the acquaintance of Greydon, Frog Rock owner and bartender. During the course of conversation he asked if I'd be going into Rangeley. I told him I hadn't planned that far ahead. That's when he says, "Well, in case you do, give this card to Randy." Turns out they're partners, also operating a Frog Rock Café here in Rangeley. On his card Greydon had written, "Randy, buy this man a beer!" Well, I'll tell you, right then and there I decided that I'd be making a stop in Rangeley! So, here we are, *Easy Rider* and me, bellied up to the bar at the Frog Rock Café in Rangeley. The bartender comes over; sure enough it's Randy. "What'll it be?" he says. That's when I pull Greydon's card right out. Well now, I want you to know that I haven't seen a bartender smile like this in years. Yup! Randy draws us both a free one. Great fellows, great establishments! Thanks, Greydon and Randy, we had a hoot!

It is dark when we reach the new lean-to at Piazza Rock. Had the shelter not been occupied with light illuminating the skylights we would have missed the place entirely. Once down the blue-blaze and stumbling into the shelter, we meet Donnabeth Stewart from New York. Come to find out her goal is not to hike the AT but to climb all the 4,000-footers in the Northeast. She says there's 113 all told, of which she has done about half. They're in New York, New Hampshire, Vermont, and Maine. *Easy Rider* and I really enjoy the short bit of evening remaining, listening to Donnabeth tell about her adventures.

> *"The Appalachian Trail exerts a primal pull beyond*
> *the merely recreational! . . . perhaps it beckons to the*
> *pioneer spirit buried in us, the desire to strike out for*
> *parts unknown . . . perhaps it's the romantic notion of*
> *discovering a bit of America by walking across the*
> *country and stumbling upon traces of early settlers . . .*
> *or maybe it's the sheer distance, scope and accessibility . . .*
> *regardless, for many hikers, the storied Appalachian*
> *Trail promises adventure and the opportunity to expe-*
> *rience a legend."*

[Elizabeth Lee, *Appalachian Adventure*]

SATURDAY August 29, 1998
TRAIL DAY 225/131 ✦ TRAIL MILE 3,361/1,959
LOCATION Spaulding Mountain Lean-to

WE HEAD OUT INTO A COOL, GRAY MORNING to be confronted with a very long, hard day. We're in serious Snickers territory now, over Saddleback, The Horn, Saddleback Junior, Oberton, Lone, a chunk of Mt. Abraham, and the starting pull up Spaulding. We arrive at Spaulding Mountain Lean-to totally bushed, only to be greeted by a young, giggling, chatty bunch of coeds from Tufts out on an orientation hike.

We have the pleasure this evening in meeting a very nice young man from Providence, Rhode Island, Andrew Ryan, who goes by the trail name *Groovin' Moose.* Andy is doing what has become known as "yo-yo-ing." This sashay is done by the more adventuresome who haven't had enough of the AT when they reach Katahdin, so they just turn around and head back south toward Springer Mountain, their journey now only half completed, hoping to be over the Balds and the higher elevations in the Smokies before the snow flies. Ryan departed Springer on March 19 and climbed Katahdin on August 16. So here today he's into his 13th day on his southbound odyssey.

"The Appalachian Trail. Those are magic words to anybody who has ever so much as spent a night in the woods."

[Paul Hemphill, *Me and the Boy*]

SUNDAY August 30, 1998
TRAIL DAY 226/132 ✦ TRAIL MILE 3,375/1,973
LOCATION ME 27, White Wolf Motel, Stratton

WE GET OUT ABOUT 7:30 A.M. TO COMPLETE the pull up Spaulding Mountain. A bronze plaque affixed to a boulder at the summit just off the trail catches my eye. I've always been interested in the colorful and sometimes rocky (no pun intended) history of the AT. This plaque commemorates a joyful occasion.

"In honor of the Men of the Civilian Conservation Corps who, from 1935 to 1939, contributed greatly to the completion of the Appalachian Trail in Maine, and who, on August 14, 1937, near this spot completed the final link of the entire 2,054-mile trail."

We're faced with another day of tough pulls over Spaulding, Sugarloaf, and the Crockers. As I reach ME 27 I find *Easy Rider* sitting by the trail. He's been waiting here for me for an hour. My feet are really tender and sore and I will lose my right big toenail, which has just about grown back, yet again. I'm also suffering some nasty blisters on the back of both of my heels. Breaking in these new boots is proving to be quite a chore. They're a stiff, rugged boot, but I'm getting there.

We manage a ride into Stratton right away, right to the White Wolf Motel. No sooner do we flop than it's food order-up time, room service no less! *Easy Rider* goes for the pizza, and I get their famous "Wolf Burger."

I simply cannot remember a hot shower feeling so luxurious! After supper I soak my feet in a five-gallon bucket of warm Epsom salts solution. There's no trouble dropping off tonight, to dream of the Mahoosucs and their mystic and mysterious high-held ponds.

> *"Weird phantom shapes of mist are rising on the pond, figures that seem to tread out a ghostly measure with bowed heads and trailing garments before they vanish into the darkness. Perhaps 'tis the ephemeral life of the human race that nature stages nightly on the dark water."*
>
> [Pauline Green, *Vacation Days* 1926]

MONDAY August 31, 1998
TRAIL DAY 227/133 ✦ TRAIL MILE 3,390/1,988
LOCATION Little Bigelow Lean-to

WE'RE UP AT 7:00 A.M. AND HIT THE STRATTON INN for a great breakfast. I'm at the post office just as they open to get my bounce box while *Easy Rider* does the laundry. I have a good talk this morning with Dick Anderson, president of the International Appalachian Trail. He will be sending maps to my next mail drop in Monson, Maine, which will help us through northern Maine and on into Canada.

Limmer makes a special "boot grease," which I am now bouncing along in my bounce box, so *Easy Rider* and I are able to seal our boots. By the time we get provisions, get packed, and are ready to go it's almost noon. We get an easy hitch back to the trailhead and are headed into the Bigelows by noon for a long 15-mile day, as there are some six-plus-Snickers pulls over South Horn, Bigelow Mountain, Avery Peak, and Little Bigelow.

Of all the ranges I've seen so far, over all the Appalachians from Alabama to Maine, I truly believe the Bigelows to be, hands down, the most magnificent! It is easy to see why so many of the old-time mountain trekkers, like Walter Green, Healon Taylor, Arthur Perkins, Percival Baxter, and Myron Avery, so loved the Bigelows. Bigelow Mountain, a massive sharp-top peak standing at 4,088 feet, is now named Avery Peak in honor of Myron Avery, a fitting and well-deserved tribute to the man. On a huge boulder atop Avery is affixed a bronze memorial which reads,

"Myron Haliburton Avery
1899–1952
Whose foresight, leadership and diligence
made possible the Appalachian
Trail, this 2000 mile footpath from
Maine to Georgia."

Avery was born in Lubec, Maine. He was a Navy man, a veteran of two world wars, and was awarded The Legion of Merit. He was a graduate of Harvard Law School and practiced admiralty law with the Arthur Perkins firm in Hartford.

Perkins was the first Appalachian Trail Conference chair and enlisted Avery, with his boundless energy and enthusiasm, to assist in the trail-building project. Avery was the founding president of the Potomac Appalachian Trail Club, to this day the bulwark of ATC chapters, and he was the driving force in organizing many of the ATC clubs from Maine clear to Georgia. At age 31, Avery became chair of the ATC, a position he held until his death in 1952. Pushing his famous measuring wheel over miles of trail he had personally laid out, Avery was the first to hike the entire Appalachian Trail.

At Horns Pond Lean-to, the two new log structures are a sight to behold. They are, without a doubt, two of the most beautiful shelters along the AT, their design most professional, their workmanship impeccable. And the two old lean-tos have been left standing, their longevity a tribute to their fine workmanship. Here at the Pond we meet Rob, the caretaker, and thru-hikers *Thor, Gray Cloud, Raising Wind, Baltimore,* and *Iron Pan.*

Arriving late at Little Bigelow Lean-to we are greeted by yet another giggling gaggle of Tufts preppies. And here tonight we also meet thru-hikers *Stickman* and *Mousetrap.* The Tufts group shares their pizza with us, which they've made in an open frying pan . . . not bad, not bad at all!

I stand on Little Bigelow
In all its majesty.
While all around, vast wilderness
Is all that I can see.
Once lived a man who loved this more
Than anyone I know.
Tears cloud my view of Avery Peak
From Little Bigelow.

[N. Nomad]

TUESDAY September 1, 1998
TRAIL DAY 228/134 ✦ TRAIL MILE 3,407/2,005
LOCATION Pierce Pond Lean-to

WE HAVE LEFT THE BIGELOWS BEHIND but are able to look back on them from numerous vantages today. They are magnificent from every perspective, bold and majestic beyond description, with wildness all around. *Easy Rider* and I have been hiking together for many days, and as my pace slows to accustom my feet to my new boots, I have slowed him down. Standing here now, shuffling the dirt and looking pensively and dejectedly into space, we reach the decision for him to hike on without me. And so I stand watching, with feelings of anguish and sorrow as he fades to the trail and passes the far bend beyond . . . but it is the right thing.

Hiking with constant foot pain is a struggle. My toothache is also back with a vengeance, coursing its poison through my system, causing my endurance and energy level to steadily drop. Heavy traffic has taken its toll on the trail in Maine. The treadway is literally a "beaten path" with miles of exposed rocks, roots, and bottomless bogs. Total concentration is necessary every step of the way. My head stays down, and each step, each foot placement, is a deliberate matter. If I wish to look up, to see the beauty and the remarkable landscape and vistas around, I must first stop, otherwise I risk the dire consequence of tripping and falling . . . and "bustin' it." This AT has been an adventure of a lifetime, but I am ready for some other trail as I near the completion of this stretch of the "Odyssey of '98."

The Bigelows of western Maine
Are something to behold,
'Twill take a chapter in my book,
A story yet untold.
I'll write about the mountains, lush
With birch and fir and spruce,
You'll read about the porcupine,
The beaver and the moose.
I'll write so vivid you will hear,
The calling of the loon.
Across the silent, high-held ponds,
Pure diamonds in the moon.
You'll understand why Percival*
And Myron** loved this place.
I'll paint in words —a picture,
Of its majesty and grace.
And when you go to close the book,
And put it on the shelf.
Beware! 'Twill haunt you till you've seen,
The Bigelows, yourself.

[N. Nomad]

*Percival Proctor Baxter
**Myron Haliburton Avery

WEDNESDAY September 2, 1998
TRAIL DAY 229/135 ✦ TRAIL MILE 3,426/2,024
LOCATION Bald Mountain Brook Lean-to

IN JUST A SHORT DISTANCE FROM PIERCE POND LEAN-TO goes off a blue-blazed side trail to Harrison's Pierce Pond Camps. This trail leads to an old log lodge owned and managed by Tim and Fran Harrison. As I approach this remarkable place, o'er the wooden walkway constructed in such an interesting fashion all along, I am immediately taken by the lodge's most-pleasing and natural presence. Here is an old log structure with more "character" than any I believe I've ever seen. The walls of this old place were built up many years ago from site-cut fir and spruce, stacked in a manner according to how the logs came, with not-so-much-care be they straight nor so neat—to age and lean—and to age and lean some more. And here this stately old place stands in such proud fashion, posing before me now with a stature that only time in years could possibly create. A shed porch of aged, knotty-bent posts and planking goes full around. As I casually stroll the porch do I hear the happy song of the little brook and is there immediately such a stunning and breathtaking view down and onto the cascading and tumbling outfall from Pierce Pond. Here among the lush-green fir and spruce, backdrop sentinels that frame this spellbinding scene, do I find cause to tarry, to sit and rest . . . and look.

It is here that *Stickman, Mousetrap,* and I await the call to breakfast, a full-spread massive, fruit-filled, pancake-stacked affair, prepared with obvious pride by Tim and Fran Harrison. The Harrisons—kind and generous in their offering—are obviously not in this endeavor for what it might provide for them, the purpose being more, it seems, for the time-honored tradition, a dedication, an expression if you will, of their caring and friendship they've extended and continue to extended to thru-hikers. What a way to begin this day! It will be long remembered. Thank you, Tim and Fran. For all who yearn for the wilds, who seek true freedom, you are our example. In the grand education of life, you both possess the ultimate doctorate!

Before us now lies the last remaining obstacle in our quest for Katahdin, the roaring, raging Kennebec. A hiker perished here years ago and many have been swept away, trying to ford this river. Consequently, the PATC and ATC, in joint effort and support, have been providing free ferry service for many years. The gentleman who operates the service, quite professionally and with contagious enthusiasm might I add, is Steve Longley, now in his 12th year. On a sign near the crossing is posted,

> *"The Kennebec River is the most formidable, unbridged crossing along the entire 2100 mile AT. The Kennebec is approximately 70 yards wide with a swift, powerful*

current under the best of circumstances. However, as a
result of releases of water from the hydro facilities
upstream, the depth and current of the river surge
quickly and unpredictably. You cannot cross faster
than the water level rises. DO NOT ATTEMPT TO
FORD THE RIVER. Please use the ferry service."

I quickly decide to heed this advice . . . and take the ferry! I arrived late at Bald Mountain Brook Lean-to, to be greeted by another group of preppies. They seem to be making less commotion and racket and most are tenting out, so there's room in the shelter for *Mousetrap* and me. We enjoy the evening with *Late Start,* a flip-flopper from Pennsylvania. The preppies have a fine fire and a good bed of coals going, so I'm able to prepare a hot pot of rice, flavored with canned herring and gravy. I've doubled up on my coated aspirin and the pain in my jaw has eased some. Later I make the mistake of downing three strong cups of coffee, which, along with the now-giggling guests, jitters me for more than two hours. However, in a while the hard, pounding rain on the metal shelter roof works its soothing magic to cast its spell and I finally drift into contented sleep.

"Amid the wide waves of green wood there are spots of
autumnal yellow, and the atmosphere, too, has the
dawning of autumn in colors and sounds. The soft
light of morning falls upon ripening forests of oak and
elm, walnut and hickory, and all Nature is thoughtful
and calm."

[John Muir]

THURSDAY September 3, 1998
TRAIL DAY 230/136 ✦ TRAIL MILE 3,445/2,043
LOCATION ME 15, Monson, home of Sydney *The Pie Lady* Pratt

TODAY PROVES TO BE AGONIZING AND SLOW. I'm enduring the foot pain but I've had to reduce my pace considerably. The struggle is wearing on me, causing loss of concentration as I stumble through the roots and rocks. The toothache is now excruciating, almost unbearable, sapping me of much-needed strength and stamina. My body is sluggish, my arms and legs rebel at every step, and my pack feels like it's full of rocks. The pain in my feet and the poison in my system are driving me to tears. I fell hard yesterday, totally dislocating another finger, which I've reset and taped off. Pain shoots up my arm with each thrust of my hiking pole. I am down, but not out. Please, dear Lord, this must change.

I have staggered and dragged myself 19 miles today to reach Pleasant Road. I had hoped to hitch a ride from here into Monson. To my dismay, Pleasant Road turns out to be a dead-end gravel road leading to seasonal homes on Lake Hebron. During the 2-mile walk to town I see one vehicle—going the other way. When I finally reach Monson I am very tired. I need a quiet place where I can rest, recuperate, and write. Southbounders and other thru-hikers over the past few days have told me that *The Pie Lady*'s place would probably be my best bet, so that's where I head. Entering this grand old home I am greeted by Sydney *The Pie Lady* Pratt. I'm in luck as she shows me to a private room in the rear of her lovely home. This is perfect, just what I've dreamed of finding. Please, Sydney, my dear friend, don't be upset with me, for I must tell folks that you would accept hardly any compensation for this beautiful private room.

Mousetrap and *Stickman* (who wisely tented out last night) have already arrived here hours ahead of me and are in a room upstairs. It is a joy to see them both again. I feel much better after a long, soothing hot shower and a short nap, so I head over to Shaws to see who's there. Relaxing in the grand lounge upstairs I find *Easy Rider, Lone Wolf,* and *Tinman,* all good fiends and fellow northbounders. After exchanging greetings with these fellow trail family members I notice someone else sitting on the couch . . . with a newspaper held up concealing his face. Someone I know, perhaps? Who could it be? Everyone is chuckling and smiling now. Finally, I hear a giggle and then a laugh from behind the newspaper, a dead giveaway! You've probably already guessed. He just keeps popping up—yup! The Will Rogers of the Trail, good ol' *Bump*! What a pleasant, unexpected surprise. Ah, this day is turning out just fine, after all.

In the evening, *Stickman, Mousetrap,* and I go for a great pizza at Sal's Diner. Then back in my snug little room I'm out as soon as my head hits the pillow.

> *"The trail knows neither prejudice nor discrimination. Don't expect any favors from the trail. The trail is inherently hard. Everything has to be earned. The trail is a trial."*
>
> [Warren Doyle, Jr.]

FRIDAY September 4, 1998
TRAIL DAY 231/137 ✦ TRAIL MILE 3,445/2,043
LOCATION ME 15, Monson, home of Sydney *The Pie Lady* Pratt

AS IT TURNS OUT, I'VE HAD A VERY RESTLESS AND FRETFUL NIGHT. Sometimes, when you're overly tired and fatigued, as I'm sure you've found, it's almost impossible to sleep. I have really been popping down "Vitamin I" (ibuprofen) the last number of days, but the toothache is even worse this morning, if that is possible. The right side of my face is badly swollen, from my cheek, past my jaw and clear down into my neck. Even opening my mouth is painful and I've had a tough time eating the bountiful breakfast Sydney placed before me, if you can believe that, given the ravenous way I usually eat.

After breakfast I hurry to the post office. Awaiting are letters and cards from home and friends, and the maps from Dick Anderson to help us north into Canada, just as promised. I rush back to Shaws to share this good news and to review the maps with *Easy Rider.* But to my dismay I find circumstances are now such that *Easy Rider* will not be accompanying me on north from Katahdin. This proves a terrible disappointment to both of us. We've developed such a great friendship and have become the best of hiking companions, having hiked together so well over such a difficult and long distance. I must tell you now, and I am not ashamed to tell you now, that *Easy Rider* and I hug much as would father and son during final farewell. *Easy Rider,* my dear friend, it has been such a joy knowing you and all your wonderful family. Godspeed to you and Nikki—there's a wonderful, exciting future before you!

I know that something must be done about this terrible toothache. I have put off the inevitable way too long, so I appeal to Sydney for help. When she sees how I am suffering, she drops everything to come to my assistance. I'll conclude today with my entry in her 1998 guest register.

> *"When you first meet Sydney, you may encounter a bit of a crust, not unlike the crust on her delectable pies, but don't be fooled. For, as you chip a little at this enamel, beneath you'll find a sensitive, caring person . . . a gal with a heart of gold. She runs a business, yes. But I know now that the business is truly secondary to her sincere dedication to, and love for all us hikers—for, try as she might, she cannot hide that. I'm here today and gone tomorrow, but it's as if I'm her family. She befriended me, cared about me, showed deep compassion when I told her of my pain. She dropped everything in her busy day, drove me far off to her dentist—and then waited patiently while I had an abscessed molar pulled, giving me God-sent relief. The Pie Lady's place is a little chunk of paradise. Though she claims not to be a cook—her meals, heavenly! Thank you, Sydney, for your help in my time of need. Your kindness and hospitality will remain in my memory, dear friend."*

> [N. Nomad]

SATURDAY September 5, 1998
TRAIL DAY 232/138 ✦ TRAIL MILE 3,445/2,043
LOCATION ME 15, Monson, home of Sydney *The Pie Lady* Pratt

DR. NORMAN A. HILL AND STAFF IN DOVER-FOXCROFT are all compassionate and caring folks. Even though I had no appointment, they took me right in and attended to me with obvious, genuine concern. What a blessing to have my condition properly diagnosed and treated. The problem was an abscessed molar, not an impacted wisdom tooth . . .

the solution being simple extraction, which the procedure certainly proved to be! So I did not need surgery on my jaw after all. Ah, so now I understand why I didn't make it to the oral surgeon's office in time! In just 24 hours, the gums at the indenture are already healing and the terrible pain and swelling in my jaw are improving miraculously. Dr. Hill had given me a script for penicillin, which I've filled, and as a precaution, am taking. But as he said, "You probably won't need it." I have paid these fine people for their time and professional services, but there is no way to truly pay them for what they have done for me, and I will remain in their debt. Thank you, Dr. Hill and staff!

PROFILES '98

DEREK STODDARD *Easy Rider* DRESSER IS 29, SINGLE, and from Bethel, Maine. He attended Gould Academy in Bethel and is a graduate of Massachusetts Institute of Technology (MIT), Cambridge, with a BS degree in philosophy (concentration in literature).

For years Derek has had a deep desire to hike the AT. His opportunity finally came in 1998. "I left a position as vice president of Internet services at New England Internet Services, an ISP company in which I had part ownership. This was a very demanding technical/management position. Prior to that I had taught multiple subjects in private high schools including biology, physics, computer science, and math."

Easy Rider will probably be remembered as the little guy with glasses and the big, red beard . . . and also as a result of his ability to hike long distances, consistently, day after day. "People were generally surprised to find where I was on the trail, given my starting date." As may be expected, Derek's interests are hiking, climbing, and in addition, blues/jazz guitar (at which he is very, very good!), and, of course, motorcycling.

"There were a number of things that contributed to my deciding to hike the AT. The first and most important was that I have always considered doing it. I grew up near the AT and it was sort of in the back of my mind. I always did a lot of hiking. I would run into thru-hikers in the fall in the Whites or the Mahoosucs and was definitely impressed. The event that really triggered it though was paying off my student loans. I graduated from college with a lot of student debt. Even when I was making next to no money, I would pay extra on my loan payments because it bothered me to have that over my head. I made my final payment in January of 1998. A few days later I was hiking a mountain in the Mahoosucs called Sunday River Whitecap when it dawned on me that I was free to do anything I wanted. A few weeks later I made my final decision and told my boss that I would be starting the trail on May 1. I guess I felt free, and the trail represented an expression of that total freedom."

Derek says, "I've always had a planning deficiency" but it certainly isn't evident from what we've learned about this young man so far! His future plans are "to find work that is less stressful and more physical. I enjoy mental challenges and learning, but I need consistent physical outdoor time as well. In a lot of ways, I think hiking the AT is sort of a 'last hurrah' before settling down and beginning a family. That will probably be my next big adventure."

In conclusion, Derek says, "I'm a firm believer that action and experience are what are valuable in this world. Mistakes are more productive than successes, and anything that can be broken can be fixed. Doing the AT is a wonderful example of how a person, given enough time and gumption, can accomplish anything. It has also been a great demonstration of the less-is-more philosophy. I get more true enjoyment and satisfaction out of my first sip of an occasional cup of coffee here on the trail than I got from most things before. It makes me appreciate the small pleasures. I hope I can carry that with me after the trail."

Meeting and hiking with you, Derek, has been a blessing. The times that we've shared just enjoying nature and hiking together, then the challenge of tackling the Whites and Mahoosucs, have been special, memorable times. Just sitting, talking and laughing in the evenings, these times have added immeasurably to the wonders of my adventure. Thanks, *Easy Rider*, for your friendship and for sharing the joy of being with your wonderful family! These times will forever remain in my memory.

> *"The world puts on its robes of glory now;*
> *The very flowers are tinged with deeper dyes;*

The waves are bluer, and the angles pitch
Their shining tents along the sunset skies."

[Albert Laighton, *Autumn*]

SUNDAY September 6, 1998
TRAIL DAY 233/139 ✦ TRAIL MILE 3,458/2,056
LOCATION Wilson Valley Lean-to

WHAT A GREAT TIME HERE IN MONSON! This is a beautiful little trail town. Sydney *The Pie Lady* Pratt has made my stay a memorable one. It's late morning before I'm ready to head back to the trail, but Sydney again drops what she's doing to drive me back to the trailhead on Pleasant Road. *Desperado, Stickman, Mousetrap, Ted, Ol' Crawdad,* and Ryan and Kierstie have all gone out way ahead of me.

The day remains cool, a most pleasant day for hiking. I am so thankful to have my strength returning. The time at Sydney's has also given my feet a much-needed rest. The big climbs, save for Katahdin, are behind me. I arrive at Wilson Valley Lean-to in good stead and quickly build a warming and cooking fire for the evening. The remainder of the day is then enjoyed, relaxing and talking with good friends *Desperado,* Ryan, and Kierstie.

'Tis less a journey out the land, . . .
and more in the heart of friend.
'Tis more the joy from loving hand.
That lifts me till the end.

[N. Nomad]

MONDAY September 7, 1998
TRAIL DAY 234/140 ✦ TRAIL MILE 3,474/2,072
LOCATION Chairback Gap Lean-to

THE BROOKS AND STREAMS IN THE "100 Mile Wilderness" are like no others. The falls, cascades, and rapids seem constant, near endless, giving them rollicking and joyful personalities. The deep, crystal-clear pools are so inviting, but I certainly know better than to venture there! I hike along one of these glad, playful brooks for a great distance today. There is also much climbing and scampering over rocks and through bogs and tree roots. Today I see my first moose and get my first glimpse of Mt. Katahdin. The Barren-Chairbacks are certainly not formidable mountains, but they have their own charm and beauty nonetheless.

An evening fire is a very pleasant thing. I never tire of a good campfire, a necessity for cooking and now for warming if one is interested in lingering about, not wanting to get into the sleeping bag as soon as the sun goes down.

> *"The moose will perhaps one day become extinct, but how naturally then, when it exists only as a fossil relic, and unseen at that, may the poet/sculptor invent a fabulous animal with similar branching and leafy horns—a sort of fucus of lichen and bone—to be the inhabitant of such a forest as this!"*
>
> [Henry David Thoreau]

TUESDAY September 8, 1998
TRAIL DAY 235/141 ✦ TRAIL MILE 3,491/2,089
LOCATION Logan Brook Lean-to

IT'S A COLD, DRIZZLY KIND OF DAY, and we're off in the swirling mist. The rocks and roots prevent any fair rate of forward progress. When the trail is wet, like today, the difficulty is manifold. I must avoid off-camber rocks at all cost, and hitting a root at anything less than a 90 is inviting close inspection of the ne'er distant mud. I really don't believe ice is any slicker!

Today I'm hiking with *Desperado* and he is dearly suffering. He slipped on a large rock a number of days ago, raking and cutting his shin clear to the bone in the process. The wound is not healing well, and struggling now through the mud and rocks, I fear he has gotten it infected, for the wound looks both proud and very sore. I am relieved when he opts to leave the trail and head for Katahdin Iron Works, a small community several miles out a dirt road. Tears well in my eyes as he hails a logging truck, climbs in, and is gone. We have known each other for months now and have hiked together for so many, many days. We had planned to climb Katahdin together—but in just moments, and just like that—he's gone.

Pleasant River is crossed by fording. It's a deep, wide river with rushing water in great volume. Here is hydraulic force to be reckoned with. I take my boots off and change to my off-road running shoes. The river appears the shallowest at the rapids, which I assume to be the crossing point. Reluctantly I plunge in. The water is ice-cold and the force immediately evident, even at ankle depth. I use my poles for stability, one splayed upstream, one down. Progress is dreadfully slow as I inch my way across, moving neither pole nor foot until I again have four points firmly planted. Each step is utter frustration as the riverbed consists totally of what feels like greased bowling balls. As I near the far shore, and celebrating with great relief, suddenly I cannot find the bottom. I thrust my hiking poles down, down, down, and finally there it is. This is scary. There appears no way around—upstream and down look even less inviting. I'm committed now, so forward I go as I pitch into the drop-off. The force of the current is all but overpowering and the greased bowling balls are still here. My legs are as numb as rubber and are becoming uncontrollable . . . a result of the combined ice water and spent adrenaline. I've been in this freezer almost ten minutes now. I can no longer rely on stability and bracing from my poles; they simply quiver and are flushed aside. I'm up to my hips in rushing water, which is pounding against me with powerful force. I have got to get out of here, but fast. Luckily with two more staggering, stumbling lunges, I'm out of it and quickly ashore. Oh my, there's certainly no lack of excitement this day! I rest long, thanking the Lord, drying my feet, and putting my dry socks and boots back on. I'm later told that the place I should have forded was further upstream!

Though only a short distance down a blue-blaze, I trudge right on by Gulf Hagas. I know I will later regret this decision, as I have been told by many friends to take the time and see the Gulf. But, the rain is falling in a dreary, increasingly angry rage. It is becoming dreadfully dark and I am tired, wet, and cold, a bad combination. I choose to push on, as it is still over 10 miles to Logan Brook Lean-to. I finally make it, arriving late, still in the cold storm that has firmly established its presence. I'll close this entry with a little ditty—if you read this, *Desperado*, here's to you, wherever you are this day, my dear friend.

> *A trail through Maine's north wilderness,*
> *Past bogs and ponds of blue.*
> *Beckons the restless wanderlust,*
> *Down deep in me and you.*
> *So, off in the swirling mist we go,*
> *With our boots and raingear on.*
> *While friends at home and folks we love,*
> *Try figurin' what went wrong.*
> *But we'll rove these woods and mountainsides,*
> *Awaitin' that by-and-by.*
> *A perfect dawn, when packs take wing,*
> *And the treadway climbs the sky.*

[N. Nomad]

WEDNESDAY September 9, 1998
TRAIL DAY 236/142 ✦ TRAIL MILE 3,503/2,101
LOCATION Cooper Brook Falls Lean-to

TODAY IS A SHORT DAY. It dawns cold and dreary, the rain falling in steady drizzle. Comes to mind now an expression that I had heard way back in the Smokies: "No rain, no pain, no Maine." How true! I see numerous moose again today, but they're no happier than am I, not wanting to move very far or very fast either. The steady drizzle is incessant and slowly changes to cold rain. The storm continues to build, and as it does the wind comes up, driving the rain directly at me in pelting waves. In the middle of this I'm now faced with another ford, the east branch of Pleasant River, this one mostly a rock-hopper. I slip on the greased rocks and plunge in to my knees, but no matter, I am already soaked from the driving rain.

As the storm persists and the torrent increases I feel the ever-tightening grips of hypothermia descending. It is less than 2 miles to Cooper Brook Falls Lean-to, not my planned destination, but plans have changed. I reach the shelter greatly relieved and waste no time getting into dry clothes, then into my sleeping bag. A dry shelter has never been so welcome, a warm sleeping bag never such a luxurious place of rest. Shortly come in Ryan, Kierstie, and their dog, Sage. Upon my insistence they enter the shelter with me. I am so relieved to see that they have made it here, that they are safe and will stay. As the storm continues to intensify and the day turns even colder and more forbidding, we are all very thankful to have shelter.

"Sometimes I feel discouraged,
And think my work's in vain.
But then the Holy Spirit
Revives my soul again."

[African-American Spiritual]

THURSDAY September 10, 1998
TRAIL DAY 237/143 ✦ TRAIL MILE 3,524/2,122
LOCATION Wadleigh Stream Lean-to

THE POUNDING RAIN FINALLY STOPS during the night, and dawn arrives bringing a promise of better weather. The continuing tat on the shelter roof proves to be the remaining burden from the soaked over-canopy . . . and it seems that it has even warmed a bit. The kids are up and gone as I try to roust myself out.

There are numerous road crossings today as I near the end of the "wilderness." The trail continues over mountains, across streams, around many lovely ponds and past numerous springs, all with strange, seemingly unpronounceable names, like Nesuntabunt Mountain,

Pemadumcook Lake, Potaywadjo Spring, Nahmakanta Stream. The loons, once so elusive, are now oft seen and heard, their urgent call breaking the solitude across the still mountain mirrors.

I again see familiar faces, hikers approaching from the north. First, what a joy it is to see Kevin, who has just completed his third consecutive thru-hike and has yo-yoed, heading back south through the "wilderness," on his way to Gorham, where he plans to hike the Long Trail. And then comes along *Mother Nature* and *Father Time*, who have flip-flopped and will complete their thru-hike to the south.

There are countless, delightfully inviting campsites all along and around the many lakes and ponds today, but I push on to my planned destination at Wadleigh Stream Lean-to. This day has proven a blessed relief from the misery and engulfing drear of yesterday, and I am taking much pleasure in experiencing the beauty and the calming presence of these north Maine woods.

PROFILES '98

KEVIN ROWE IS FROM SHIPMAN, VIRGINIA, a high school graduate. He is 42 and divorced. When he isn't hiking the AT he's earning his way as a timber-frame log cabin builder. Kevin's interests are natural history and sports. None of us will have difficulty remembering Kevin, for he is one of the strongest backpackers on the trail, covering incredibly long distances day after day. He is hiking in true Jardine* fashion—ultralight gear, shod only in running shoes. He has just completed his third consecutive AT thru-hike.

Says Kevin, "Anyone can do the trail once and then say 'Been there, done that, got that tee-shirt.' There's a difference however, between hiking the trail and knowing the trail." Kevin's future plans are to head west to take on the Pacific Crest Trail—and then after all is done, perhaps after just one more AT thru-hike, to finally kick back—at home.

"Northward, Katahdins chasm'd pile,
Looms through the low, long, leafy aisle."

[Anna Boynton Averill]

---

*Ray Jardine, author of *Beyond Backpacking*

FRIDAY September 11, 1998
TRAIL DAY 238/144 ✦ TRAIL MILE 3,544/2,142
LOCATION Hurd Brook Lean-to

PATCHES OF BLUE ARE POPPING THROUGH and it's really "fairin' up" this morning. Seems I've got the makings for another dandy.

There are a couple of small pulls today as I continue to pass many lovely streams, springs, ponds, and campsites. The last pop is up and over Rainbow Ledges, the summit of which provides a breathtaking view of Mt. Katahdin. It seems that as Katahdin looms before me, more mighty and majestic with each passing day, do the words of Irvin "Buzz" Caverly, superintendent of Baxter State Park for nearly 30 years, ring so true. For he has said, "Having Katahdin at the end of the trail is almost like it was a plan by the Creator of the universe."

We have all dreamed about, thought about, and talked about this mountain for so long. The reality that it is so near and that I'll climb it soon is ever-so-slowly sinking in. It will be the end of the quest for all my dear friends, but for me it will be but yet another mountain to get up and over.

> " 'Maine is where it's at,' I was told by a hiker famil-
> iar with the northern sections of the trail. It is difficult
> to imagine a more fitting climax to a long exhausting
> journey than this rocky monolith . . . Katahdin, visible
> days in advance. The mountain becomes a bittersweet
> goal to hikers who have accepted the trail as home. 'I
> looked forward to finishing,' said Albie Pokrob, 'But,
> the closer I got the more reluctant I was to end the
> experience.' "

[Noel Grove, *National Geographic*]

THE RAIN IS BACK, AND THOUGH IT'S ONLY A SHORT DISTANCE to West Penobscot River it takes near the full morning. The view of Mt. Katahdin from the river here at Abol Bridge is supposed to be one of the finest. But today the mountain is shrouded in gray, rain-draped clouds, and only its flanks are visible. I am not discouraged however, as the forecast is for this storm to move on through, providing a clear day to summit tomorrow.

Just across the river is Abol Bridge Store and Campground. As I turn to enter the parking lot, here huddled under umbrellas are Ryan and Kierstie and their folks, Bill and Linda Kanteres, and Bill and Eve Clark. I no more pull up than an apple and a bag of cookies are handed to me. The rain is showing no sign of letting up, so I soon head for the store. Once inside I meet the owners, Art and Linda Belmont. With Linda's help I get right to ridding the store of most everything they have to eat. First order is a double cheeseburger, followed by a blueberry-filled Danish, then microwave soup, numerous candy bars, and lots of coffee. As the storm intensifies, I linger and enjoy talking with the kids' parents. In just a while, in come *Ranger Bob* and *Moptop*, friends I haven't seen since the Greens. With the day trying to fair a little, Ryan and Kierstie head out for Daicey Pond Campground, but I continue to linger as I haven't consumed quite all of Linda's coffee yet. While waiting I put together provisions for three days to get me on over Katahdin and north out of Baxter State Park—kippered herring, elbow macaroni, gravy mix, bread, peanut butter, cheese, Pop-Tarts, and of course more Snickers bars!

The rain finally relents and I head for Daicey Pond Campground. It really is trying to "fair up." Along the way, my mind is consumed with the events of the past five months, for tomorrow I will climb Mt. Katahdin, "the greatest mountain." At Daicey Pond Ranger Station I meet Gabriel Williamson and his wife, Marcia. Here also today is Brendan Curran. Brendan has hiked the AT extensively and is now a ranger here at Baxter State Park. After registering and talking with these kind folks I head for the lean-to. Here I see Ted again, but only for a moment as he is heading on to Katahdin Stream Campground, at the very base of Katahdin. Ryan and Kierstie have already checked in and shortly comes *Ranger Bob* and *Moptop*. Oh, and what a wonderful way to wind down a great day when also comes *Selky* and *Bush Baby*, great friends I haven't seen since Hanover. Tomorrow is shaping to be a grand day, my final day on the Appalachian Trail.

But this exciting day is far from over. Just as twilight descends and we finally get a good warming fire going, the kids' folks arrive, loaded down with boxes and boxes of pizzas and calzones, along with a cooler chock-full of cold refreshments! I absolutely cannot remember pizza or calzone tasting so good or the company being any better. What a great day! Thank you, Ryan, Kierstie, Bill and Linda, Bill and Eve. Even with all the excitement and anticipation for the morrow I'm going to sleep just fine tonight. I've a full tummy and I'm a contented and happy camper!

> *We all left Springer 'long 'bout spring to hike this famous trail.*
> *Now here we are, what's left of us, the few that didn't fail.*
> *The end's in sight, our final quest, we'll all soon graduate.*
> *'Tis bittersweet, goodbye dear friends, the "Class of '98."*
>
> [N. Nomad]

SUNDAY   September 13, 1998
TRAIL DAY   240/146   ✦   TRAIL MILE   3,562/2,160
LOCATION   Roaring Brook Campground, Baxter State Park

THE DAY DAWNS CRISP AND CLEAR JUST AS FORECAST, a Class I day on Mt. Katahdin, the very best! From the little shelter at Daicey Pond I hurry up the road to the Ranger Station, hoping for an unobstructed view of the sunrise over Baxter Peak. I could not have prepared myself for what I was about to see. At the clearing, in the meadow by the little log library, I tried to maintain my fix on the pond before me but it was impossible. My gaze was uncontrollably drawn up, up, up—to the very summit of Katahdin. My God, what a massive mountain! It dominates my entire field of vision. There is no horizon, only this mighty Goliath—and a little bit of sky. The enormity is overwhelming. The mountain's presence looms with such incredible might as to create a feeling of helplessness—a very real sensation that the pond, the little log building, and the meadow where I'm standing are being drawn uncontrollably toward the giant . . . ultimately to be consumed by it. Then it dawns on me, much as the sun now dawns over Baxter Peak—Lord help me, I'm climbing up there today!

And so begins my final day on the Appalachian Trail. All my dear friends are up and out, headed for Katahdin Stream Campground, the very base of Katahdin. At Katahdin Stream we meet Rangers Bruce White and Christian McGinn, who permit us to store our pack gear on their porch. Ryan and Kierstie lighten their packs for the climb, as do I, by placing belongings and provisions in garbage bags. They will be coming back down to the Ranger Station here at Katahdin Stream, but I will be going on north over the summit, across the Knife Edge to Pamola and on down into Roaring Brook. So Ryan's folks have offered to slack some of my belongings and provisions around on their way out this evening, thus allowing me to reduce my pack weight, which should make for an easier and much more enjoyable climb. Ryan and Kierstie, *Selky* and *Bush Baby,* and I begin our climb together. But at the edge of the campground, near where the trail enters the woods, I linger to read the bronze plaque mounted on a boulder:

Mt. Katahdin

"Man is born to die. His works are short-lived.
Buildings crumble, monuments decay, wealth vanishes.
But Katahdin, in all its glory, forever shall remain the
mountain of the people of Maine."

[Percival Proctor Baxter]

The climb comes easy, as I have prepared for this for months. We are soon above treeline and the ascent slows considerably. Huge boulders, sheer rock ledges, and vertical faces present obstacles to climbing not encountered before. My poles dangle from my wrists as I go hand over hand through the jumble of near-vertical rock. I thought that I would be scared, if not terrified, by the height—but I am not. My concentration is totally fixed on the climb, with no thought given to looking down . . . just where to get the next handhold or foothold to continue upward. Steel rod is driven into the rock face at strategic points, to clutch or to provide a toehold. Quickly, the ascent through the boulders and ledges becomes natural and the climb turns into a scamper. I am pleased with myself, with my confidence, agility, and strength. A man near 60 shouldn't be able to do this with such ease and enjoyment. I pass Ted in the boulders, and the kids are all somewhere down below—this is now proving to be a high in more ways than one.

But now a transition occurs. The boulders and ledges give way to a rocky incline, more like the rock scrambles over countless other mountains to the south. Soon I come to Thoreau Spring, the highest point, it is believed, that Thoreau ascended, having turned back in the face of a storm. The water is sweet and cold. I drink my fill and then top off for the remainder of the climb and the descent on over the Knife Edge and down into Roaring Brook.

The old weather-beaten sawhorse marking the end of the Appalachian Trail, seen in countless photos and videos, is soon in sight. I've read so many accounts written about the emotional flood experienced at this point—the point of realizing that after months of surviving the seemingly insurmountable odds of enduring the rigors of hiking the mountains and valleys of 14 states—that in a short, fleeting moment it will all be history. I was confident I would not experience these emotions, as the climb up Katahdin should certainly be just another day on the trail for me as I continue my odyssey onward into Canada. But was I ever wrong! The AT, indeed, winds an emotion-filled and spiritual path, through enchanted and magic lands. To hike it is an experience that can be talked about . . . but the story, ah, the story cannot really be told! And that experience, that journey, in a moment will also be over for me.

Ranger Bob and *Moptop* are at the summit and I hear their shouts of excited encouragement. I soon reach them. We hug and tears flow freely. The scene is repeated over and over as Ryan and Kierstie arrive, then *Selky* and *Bush Baby*, and finally, Ted. Day hikers mull nearby with puzzled expressions as we cry and hoot and hug.

So, on this 30th day of September 1998, on a beautiful Sunday morning, eight of us finish this incredible odyssey together. We pose together . . . by the old rugged AT sign in traditional fashion, each with a peaceful contentment now of knowing what being here truly means, as a stranger picks up our cameras one by one, and snaps our picture.

GIVEN NAME/ HOMETOWN	TRAIL NAME	AGE	DEPARTED SPRINGER	EDUCATION/ CAREER
Keith David Krejci *Baltimore, MD*	*Bush Baby*	23	April 14th	Environmental chemist
Melissa Mae Sumpter *Santa Cruz, CA*	*Selky*	21	April 12th	Junior at Santa Cruz
Ryan Kanteres *Manchester, NH*	—	24	April 2nd	Philosophy Degree
Kierstie Clark *Newport, RI*	—	23	April 2nd	Theology Degree
Bob Martin *Palmyra, PA*	*Ranger Rob*	25	April 14th	Social Studies Degree
Kristen MacRay *Dryden, NY*	*Moptop*	25	April 14th	Elementary Teacher
Ted Flach *Walton, KY*	—	65	January 24th	Retired from GE
Meredith Eberhart *Dahlonega, GA*	*Nimblewill Nomad*	59	April 20th	Retired Optometrist

Joy on the Mountain

With tears in my eyes,
And lingering goodbyes,
And a slap on the back . . . or two.
In my journal I wrote
This short entry note,
My hike o'er the AT is thru.

[N. Nomad]

My friends turn to go back down the AT to Katahdin Stream Campground and I continue on, alone, over the Knife Edge. On the descent, a young man from Maine, Eric Jones, catches me and asks if I would mind his company. As we descend through the rocks we talk about many things. He was taken by the show of emotion at the summit and asks many questions about my odyssey. He is staying in a lean-to and invites me to share the space with him for the evening, as I have been able to reserve only a tent site.

At Roaring Brook I meet Ranger Kevin Donnell. Turns out, he has guided north and east of Baxter State Park where I'll be hiking, and he takes time from his busy schedule to review the maps prepared for me by Dick Anderson, president of the International Appalachian Trail (IAT), which proves very helpful.

This day I will remember . . . this day I will remember!

"I could list a thousand things I saw that I'll never
forget, a thousand marvels and miracles that pulled at
something in my heart which I could not understand."

[Edward Abbey]

Chapter 4
Le Sentier International des Appalaches/
International Appalachian Trail

MONDAY September 14, 1998
TRAIL DAY 241/1 ✦ TRAIL MILE 3,579/17
LOCATION South Branch Pond Campground, Baxter State Park

STARING INTO THE SOFT, FLICKERING GLOW of the campfire last evening, relaxing once more in the comforting warmth of that kind and familiar old friend, I retreated to delve the depths of thought, indeed to fathom most-near my subconscious as I turned to the days just past and to the unknown days that lie ahead. My emotions became a whirl, a stir of both melancholy and fond memories along with the excitement and exhilaration of preparing for my lone trek into the wilds of the northern Appalachians, into the cold, early grips of winter in the stark tundra and the far off reaches of Canada. My trek on that famous old trail, the Appalachian Trail, is now history and just as it quickly ended, so now just as quickly begins another exciting adventure, a journey of near 700 miles o'er *Le Sentier International des Appalaches/*International Appalachian Trail (SIA/IAT).

I awake to a bright clear day. Eric, who is touring Maine by bicycle, gets out and on his way. Thanks, Eric, for sharing your lean-to with me! As I prepare to head on north I linger to reflect again, as during the

CAP GASPE
10 · 24 · 98
NIMBLEWILL NOMAD
ODYSSEY '98

evening last. I am thinking now about the three unmarked trails that inter-mix with the AT on the summit of Mt. Katahdin by the old weather-beaten sign, the last of the old familiar white AT blazes. For it is there that another trail begins and two other trails pass. Within this park and on that summit these trails may never be marked, their physical presence may never be seen, but they exist all the same and their presence will remain forever. For you see, there are things that man, vain man, with all his influ-ence, wealth, and power cannot change. I speak now of a timeless and unshakable domain beyond the power of man. Man can end the white paint marks of the Appalachian Trail on Baxter Peak, and at his whim, he can also end that venerable old trail there too, but man cannot end these majestic and grand Appalachian Mountains on that summit, nor can he end there this vast and spectacular continent we know as North America.

The first of these trails of which I speak begins on Mt. Katahdin, just as sure as does another trail there end. This trail was the dream and will soon be the reality of another Benton MacKaye. For, just as MacKaye dreamed of such a grand trail along the central Appalachian Range years ago, so has the MacKaye of our time dreamed of another grand trail along the northern Appalachian Range. This dreamer is also the Myron Avery of our time, for he is not only "The Dreamer" but also "The Doer!" His name is Richard Anderson and his new dream trail is called *Le Sentier International des Appalaches*/International Appalachian Trail. It is on this trail that I now depart.

The first of the unmarked trails that passes over Mt. Katahdin begins its journey in the southernmost reaches of the Appalachian Range in south-central Alabama on Flagg Mountain near Porter Gap and con-tinues on to the Cliffs of Forillon where the Appalachian Mountains make their spectacular plunge to the sea at the Gulf of St. Lawrence, Cap Gaspé, Québec. Life is breathed into this trail as a result of an amalgam of wonderful, existing trails all up and down the Appalachian Mountains chain. This trail, which has the AT as its grand section, encompasses the entire range of the majestic Appalachians. It is called the Appalachian Mountains Trail (AMT). It is on this trail that I now continue.

The second of the unmarked trails that passes over Mt. Katahdin is indeed a most grand affair, for its beginning arises from the waters of the Caribbean Sea at the Gulf of Mexico in Key West, Florida, the southernmost point of eastern North America. From there it winds its way north through three time zones and across what is, for all intents and purposes, the entire breadth of the Eastern continent to also end at the spectacular Cliffs of Forillon at the Gulf of St. Lawrence, Cap Gaspé, Québec. This trail, too, is an amalgam of existing trails, with the grand old AT as its backbone. And it includes numerous other trails and roadwalks all up and down the East Coast and Maritime provinces. This trail is called the Eastern Continental Trail (ECT). On this trail I also now continue. And as you read and journey on with me it is about the adventures along this trail that this book is written.

I stop to say goodbye to Ranger Donnell and I'm off to Russell Pond. The trail is mostly a valley walk with very good treadway compared to the heavily used trail south of here. I stop to meet and talk with Tom Lohnes, ranger at Russell Pond Campground. He seems intrigued and taken as I once again relate the story of where I've hiked and where I'm headed. The day into South Branch Pond Campground goes quickly and I'm in early. Here I meet Ed Cunningham, ranger at South Branch, and he puts me up in the bunkhouse. I have it all to myself! These are great accommodations — a well-thought-out design, all fresh and new. In moments I've got a fine warming fire going in the woodstove. This is very comfy. I sleep very soundly, for I am still emotionally drained from bidding farewell to so many dear friends on the AT.

"The happiest heart that beat,
Was in some quiet breast.
That found the common daylight sweet,
And left to heaven the rest."

[John Vance Cheney]

TUESDAY September 15, 1998
TRAIL DAY 242/2 ✦ TRAIL MILE 3,604/42
LOCATION Shin Pond Village

THE HIKE ON OUT OF THE UNITED STATES and into Canada is mostly a roadwalk from here to the international border at Ft. Fairfield, Maine.

At Matagamon Gate, the north entrance to Baxter State Park, I check out with gatekeeper Dana Miller and head on east to Matagamon Store and Campground, managed by proud owners Don and Dianne Dudley. Here I relax with hot coffee and a great sub. There is no electricity way out here in the North Maine woods, so a generator powers the whole operation. The freezer is working fine though, thank you very much, and the ice cream is hard as a brick!

I manage to make it into Shin Pond by late evening, a 25-mile day. I am very tired, but even with my bedraggled appearance I'm greeted with a smile from Craig, and I'm soon the grand recipient of more hot coffee and a great pizza! Craig puts me up in his fine motel — very clean, neat, and comfortable. There's hot water and even good water pressure for my shower. Another good night's sleep . . . in a bed with sheets and a pillow, no less. Isn't it interesting the things we take for granted!

> *"Not to the strong is the battle,*
> *Not to the swift is the race;*
> *Yet to the true and the faithful*
> *Victory is promised through grace."*

[Frances Jane Crosby]

WEDNESDAY September 16, 1998
TRAIL DAY 243/3   ✦   TRAIL MILE 3,627/65
LOCATION Abandoned hunter's cabin, East of Smyrna Mills

THE ROADWALK CONTINUES, A WELCOME CHANGE of pace from the rocks and roots. Most folks can't understand how I could possibly enjoy hiking gravel roads, secondary highways, and even U.S. highways. Granted and I will concede, you wouldn't want to load your gear and your kids in the car and head for northern Maine to hike the shoulders of US 1! But for a thru-hiker the roadwalks are a welcome diversion, offering the opportunity to meet the local folks while allowing some longer mileage days to boot. Up here there are many logging trucks on the road, as timbering is the mainstay; however, the drivers are most courteous and to-the-man have all moved as far as they can into the other lane, thus giving me plenty of space.

While we're on this roadwalk subject please permit this old codger a moment's digression. I consider myself fortunate to be counted among those who had the opportunity to hike the AT on the roads through the Cumberland Valley years ago . . . a section of the trail traditionally, and now historically, known as "The Cumberland Valley Roadwalk." The Cumberland Valley is an idyllic, pastoral place, "settled in" with beautiful rolling hills and peaceful, bountiful farms, like the Messer farm, hard-working folks who permitted hikers to pitch in their clover-blanketed backyard . . . and Bonnie *The Ice Cream Lady* Shipe. That's all gone now, thanks to the "vision" of certain of those in the ATC who have found it impossible to rest until every inch of the trail is off the road. So now, after spending millions and millions of dollars and pi--ing off a lot of folks in the Cumberland Valley, the AT zigzags through the fields. You'll see a few of the neat old farms, and Boiling Springs is a classic trail town, but the true stature of this proud, old valley, the beauty and magic of its lands and people so enjoyed by all who did the roadwalk—ah, that joy, that experience, is gone forever. (Easy, easy, just my opinion!)

As I near Smyrna Mills I pass more homes and the traffic picks up a little. It is late afternoon and the local school bus goes by heading west, dropping kids off. The driver waves in passing and I think to myself, "Bet I'll see her again soon," as there isn't much out there where I've just come from. Sure enough, in just a while I hear the bus approaching from behind. It slows and the driver offers me a lift. She says she can take me up the road a couple of miles to where she lives. I decline the offer but thank her just the same. As I continue on, I can see the bright yellow school bus parked in a yard. As I near I see the young lady, along with her husband and children, out on their porch and they beckon me to come over. Here I meet Cheryl and Roger Stevens. After answering the usual questions of who I am, where I've come from, and where I'm headed, Cherri asks if they might help in any way. Without hesitation, I pull out my water bottle to have it filled, for on roadwalks, unless you're willing to drink from the ditches or knock on people's doors, you'll pretty much do without . . . and I was running on empty! I'm invited into their home and the children seat me at their table. As I eat my fill from a plate of confections placed before me Cherri puts together a bag of food for me and then goes back to her commercial sewing machine where she's making camo totes and packs for the local hunters. As I watch her work, the thought occurs that I could sure use a new water bottle belt pouch. My threadbare bag is full of holes and the elastic cinch gave up months ago. As I prepare to head on up the road, Cherri asks if there is anything else they could do. Sooo, I show her my beat-up old water bottle belt pouch. After Cherri takes one look and spends no more than a couple of minutes at her machine, I become the proud new owner of one of Cherri's custom (water bottle) totes!

I stop in Smyrna Mills for another great pizza then head on east to find a place to spend the evening—an old abandoned hunter's cabin. The lock was broken years ago and never mended, so I push the door open and enter the dark old cabin. The floor is clean but sloping noticeably to the northeast. Here I will roll out my sleeping bag. My tummy is full and I am content. In this quiet little place I will be warm, dry, and comfortable. As I open my pack to prepare my bed for the night I find the small outer compartment stuffed with money! I wonder now, as I light my candle to write this journal entry for today, how many of us have been blessed during our life with such human kindness and generosity. Folks, this is the stuff miracles are made of—bringing us riches and blessings that a winning lottery ticket could never deliver. The Stevens family would not have a clue to the meaning of the term "trail magic," nor what a "trail angel" might be. But then again, it's probably just as well.

> *Great miracles abound,*
> *In this world of toil and sin.*
> *But we must have an open heart,*
> *To take the blessings in.*

> [N. Nomad]

THURSDAY September 17, 1998
TRAIL DAY 244/4 ✦ TRAIL MILE 3,650/88
LOCATION Abandoned weight-scales house north of Littleton

IN JUST A SHORT DISTANCE THIS MORNING, the secondary road I'm hiking passes under I-95. Near this interchange I am served a great breakfast at the Brookside Restaurant, a neat little mom 'n' pop stop. What a great way to start the day, stoking my tank with energy for the morning walk. By lunchtime I'm in Houlton.

For quite a while I relied on the pawn shop watch I bought for a buck while at Ronnie and Judy's in Live Oak. It worked fine until I dunked it once too often. After that I simply relied on my friends on the AT for the time of day. But now, hiking by myself, I need to be able to determine my location accurately using the time/speed/distance triad. Of course, to figure any one of the three variables, I need two of the others in the equation. I can estimate my rate of progress very well under most circumstances and over most terrain. So if I keep track of how long I've been hiking since the last known landmark, I can calculate with remarkable accuracy the distance I've traveled. This is particularly useful when relying on road and topo maps. So, while here in Houlton, I head for the Wal-Mart for a new watch.

Then it's over to the truck stop on US 1 for a bowl of soup before heading north. I'll be hiking US 1 now, into Mars Hill. I had been concerned about the traffic on this busy highway, but there's a fully paved emergency lane, which makes the going most pleasant. So, as I hike into the evening and as my new watch says the sun will soon be setting, I'm able to find another clean floor on which to rest my head—a small unused and unlocked weight-scales building. I roll out my sleeping bag just as the sun and the mercury are dipping. Here I am warm and comfortable. My worry about the possible consequences of hiking this busy U.S. highway have been just that—worry, for this has proven to be a most pleasant hiking day!

> *"A fool beholdeth only the beginning of his works,*
> *but a wise man taketh heed to the end."*
> [Unknown, *Dialogues of Creatures,* 1535]

TODAY IS A SHORT HIKE, ONLY 17 MILES into Mars Hill. I arrive early at the Blue Moose Restaurant and am served a fine breakfast to get me cranking and on my way. On this blustery fall day I pass many nice old homes and farms along US 1. Most of these folks raise potatoes, and with the season in, just about everyone has a produce stand out by the road, with potatoes for sale.

Arriving at Blaine, I stop for a bowl of soup at the local truck-stop. As I'm finishing my lunch, the pastor of Mars Hill Methodist Church stops to chat—and to buy my lunch! Here I meet Rev. Elizabeth Vernon, a very nice lady, and after a most pleasant welcome to Mars Hill, she invites me to church this coming Sunday. I arrive at the little village of Mars Hill by mid-afternoon. I head right for Midtown Motel where I meet Rachel Burtt, the motel owner. After a little Yogi magic from the old *Nomad*, Rachel relents to talking to her husband about the room rate for me. I soon meet Dave Smith, the motel manager, who shows me to one of their vacant apartments upstairs in the back—that they can let me have for a very, very reasonable price for a couple of days! The accommodations are fine, with refrigerator, stove, and plenty of hot water for a soothing shower!

Just up the street is the local A&P where I quickly head to buy food to stock the refrigerator for the weekend . . . and a frozen pizza to fix right away in the oven. I hit the jackpot on my mail drop, receiving many letters and cards from family and friends.

Later in the afternoon and stopping by the motel office to chat with Dave, what a great surprise and coincidence to find that Dick Anderson, president of the SIA/IAT will be checking in later this evening! He's coming up from Portland for a trail construction workday on Mars Hill Mountain. Later in the evening I get to meet him, along with SIA/IAT Board Member Tom Rumpf, and we have a great time. They invite me to breakfast in the morning and I decide to spend the day with them working on the mountain.

"Boughs are daily rifled by the gusty thieves,
and the book on Nature getteth short of leaves."

[Thomas Hood, *The Seasons*]

SATURDAY September 19, 1998
TRAIL DAY 246/6 ✦ TRAIL MILE 3,665/103
LOCATION Midtown Motel, Mars Hill

I'M UP AND OUT BY 7:00 A.M., HEADED FOR AL'S DINER across the
street. Here I'm greeted by Dick and Tom who introduce me to David
Jones, another SIA/IAT board member.

After breakfast we head for Mars Hill Mountain where a group
of David's students are waiting to go to work. This should be a great
trail-building workday. Dick has all the right tools and Dave has the
strong, young workers. The job at hand involves chopping out switchbacks as we crisscross one of the steep ski runs. We get right at it. By
noon we're most of the way up the mountain with the treadway cut and
bright blue and white IAT trail markers up. By 2:30 the job is done.
Back down the mountain, and returning to the vehicles, we find that
Dick has cool refreshments waiting for us in a cooler. He sure knows
how to start, run, and top off a work party. This guy is truly the Benton
MacKaye and the Myron Avery of the SIA/IAT!

On the way out we stop at the ski lift where I have the pleasure of
meeting Wendell Pierce, owner of Mars Hill Mountain. Mr. Pierce has
graciously given the SIA/IAT use of his mountain for this grand new
trail. We have a great time together and I thank him for permitting me to
hike over his mountain!

"Why do men climb mountains . . . tread deep forests, seek solitude?
. . . when we break away into the wilds, we make the decisions
. . . there we may recoup some control over our destiny."

[Bill Riviere, *Backcountry Camping*]

SUNDAY September 20, 1998
TRAIL DAY 247/7 ✦ TRAIL MILE 3,665/103
LOCATION Midtown Motel, Mars Hill

THEY ROLL UP THE SIDEWALKS PRETTY EARLY HERE in Mars Hill, just the occasional logging truck or potato truck to break the nighttime silence. My room at Midtown Motel is upstairs in the old house connected to the rear of the motel, back from the main drag, so the street noise, what little there is of it, doesn't keep me from a long, sound sleep, and I don't stir until 8:30 a.m.

After rolling out I fix myself a little instant coffee on the apartment range and then decide to go for some more homemade toast at Al's, so I head over for that delight and more coffee. As the waitress fills my cup for the third time, I'm thinking about the trouble I had in January and February in northern Florida and southern Alabama with my hands getting cold and my fingers going numb. So I know I must come up with something besides the thin cotton gloves given me by *Mountain Man* at Hatchet Creek Tradin' Post. Folks here in town have told me my best bet would be Poppa's Discount about 2 miles north toward Presque Isle. There is no clothing or department store here in Mars Hill, so I head to the intersection to thumb a ride out to Poppa's. I soon arrive to find that they're not only open, but that they have a grand selection of gloves and mittens to choose from. I've been thinking that I really want some soft lined mittens, but on trying a number of different options, I finally choose a pair of wool gloves to go inside a pair of unlined leather mittens. On trying the lined mittens I found it impossible to do much of anything with them on. However, with the layer combination of gloves and mittens I'll be able to do chores such as making and breaking camp while wearing the wool gloves, which should help keep my fingers from becoming useless nubs. And when the chores are finished, on can go the leather mittens to let the wool do its job. So I go for the glove/mitten combo.

It takes a little longer to hitch back to town but I'm finally able to get a ride directly to the front door at Mars Hill Methodist Church. Reverend Vernon had invited me to attend Sunday service and I decided right away after talking with her last Friday that her suggestion was a good idea. I arrive just as the congregation is finishing the first hymn. Well, Rev. Vernon sees me, though I enter quietly and sit in the last pew. And at the first opportunity, she introduces me to her congregation. So, when "get acquainted time" rolls around, just about everybody makes it by to meet me and to shake my hand. Rev. Vernon, I'm sure glad I came. I've had the enjoyment of meeting a group of warm, caring folks, and I thoroughly enjoyed your inspiring service!

After church, I head for the other little mom-and-pop restaurant just down the street to enjoy their AYCE Sunday buffet. I manage to stuff myself with good home-cooked food, then to top off the feast with some of the best bread pudding I've had in a coon's age. Upon asking for my check, I'm told by the waitress that "it's already taken care of." I know this is Rev. Vernon's generosity because she's the only person I'd told of my dinner plans. Thank you, Elizabeth! There are some really fine people in the little community of Mars Hill. You have obviously set a fine example.

After dinner (in the South, lunch is dinner and dinner is supper) I return to my room and settle down to work on my journal entries, the final few to complete the AT portion of this odyssey. I soon realize that I am further behind than I thought and that I have much more to write about each day than I thought, so I find myself writing all through the afternoon, into the evening . . . and all night! I don't get caught up until 5:00 a.m. Monday morning.

> *"The tints of autumn — a mighty flower garden*
> *blossoming under the spell of the enchanter, frost."*
>
> [Whittier, *Patucket Falls*]

MONDAY September 21, 1998
TRAIL DAY 248/8 ✦ TRAIL MILE 3,686/124
LOCATION Abandoned building across from Customs, Fort Fairfield

---

SO, HERE IT IS, 5:00 A.M., AND TIME TO STRAIGHTEN UP the room and get things in my pack and go. Sleep will have to wait. I head for Al's for some more of that great homemade toast and fresh-brewed coffee.

Then it's back to the post office to mail some things home and get my bounce box off to my next mail drop in Matapédia. I figured I'd need some additional provisions, but I have enough food in my pack for at least a day, maybe two, so I decide to head on out.

I depart this delightful little trail town at 9:00 a.m. to head for Mars Hill Mountain. It's a chilly, overcast morning and Mars Hill Mountain is shrouded in mist and clouds. Big Rock Ski Area is at the base of the mountain and I hear the diesel engine that operates the lift, so I head over. As it turns out, I get to talk again with Wendell Pierce, the owner of Big Rock and Mars Hill Mountain. I take my camera out for a picture of Wendell and he says he'd like a picture of me, so I oblige. I hand him the camera and promise to send him a print.

I make the climb up Mars Hill Mountain in short order, reaching the ridge where the trail heads north on a quad-track/snowmobile road along the ridge and past the ski lift. At the ski lift, a worker is on one of the very top towers installing new cable rollers. Up here the mist and clouds are swirling, as if vapors from a witch's cauldron, creating an eerie sight as I hail the worker. He is not startled to see me, as he is in two-way communication with Wendell at the base of the mountain. "Working in the clouds today!" I shout. "I'm used to it. If you don't work in the clouds, you don't work," was the reply. I am thinking how blessed I've been to have had such incredibly good fortune with weather conditions at the really critical and important times. The view before me now is like the memory of an old black and white movie that fades in and out, blurred by time. But, at the shelter atop the summit with Dick Anderson here Saturday, I could see to the horizon in all directions! Standing near the flagpole from where the 50-star United States flag was first flown and where the sun first strikes the North American continent for most of the year, looking south, I could see Mt. Katahdin dancing on a sea of illusion. And to the north, it seemed, stretched all of Canada.

From the ski lift the trail follows fresh-cut treadway to the northeast and down the mountain, along a secondary road and on to the barricade at the international boundary. The boundary, a 40-foot clear cut, runs directly north over the ridges, down through the bogs and beaver ponds — straight through whatever is there, on a beeline. The swath is overgrown in many places with alder, making the going difficult. The RCMP patrol the accessible sections of the boundary with quad-tracks, so hiking through those sections is easy. However, getting through the bogs and around the beaver ponds is another matter. I've been on this boundary line for many miles and many hours today. There's a shelter on the north end, near Fort Fairfield, but somehow I miss it. I've felt a fair degree of urgency for the past hour as the boundary follows an exposed ridgeline and a bad thunderstorm is intensifying nearby. I move on north with haste and reach the U.S. Customs office at Fort Fairfield just as the skies open. What a blessing to be inside as the rain comes in sheets and the show is right on top of us.

I had noticed an abandoned building, what appeared to have been an old restaurant, across the road from the customs office. It wasn't posted, so as the rain relents, and at first opportunity I beat a path to it. As luck would have it, the front door has been removed and a piece of plywood is propped up to cover it, so I'm able to move it aside and enter a nearly dry (and fairly warm) room. By pushing a couple of old display cases together and laying a piece of pegboard over them I have a fine place to roll out my sleeping bag. I have not had sleep in two days, so as the rain comes again, pounding in waves against the old building, with puddles forming all around me, I tumble into a deep trance-like sleep.

> *"If solid happiness we prize,*
> *Within our breast this jewel lies,*
> *And they are fools that roam."*

[Nathaniel Cotton, *The Fireside*]

TUESDAY September 22, 1998
TRAIL DAY 249/9 ✦ TRAIL MILE 3,698/136
LOCATION Boarding house above Pit Stop Pizza, Perth,
New Brunswick, Canada

SKIPPING A NIGHT'S SLEEP THEN HIKING 21 MILES is not a real smart idea! The pounding rain lets up sometime during the night . . . I know not when, for I sleep soundly and do not awake until the bright sunshiny day finally rousts me out at 8:30.

So, here I am at the international border. In a few moments I will leave the United States and enter Canada. After 248 days and nearly 3,700 miles I have hiked the trails and roads of most-near the breadth of the entire Eastern United States . . . through 16 states, from the Florida Everglades to the near-northernmost reaches of Maine. Two Canadian Provinces and some 525 miles yet remain to complete the "Odyssey of '98."

I head for Canadian Customs with some trepidation. I don't know what there is to fear — I guess it's just natural when you must deal with the authorities. Well now, was my uneasiness ever unfounded. No finer nor friendlier folks will you meet anywhere. They had heard yesterday about my plans to come through from Mel Fitton, an SIA/IAT member from New Brunswick who had prepared maps for me and left them here at the customs office. So, it seems, they were primarily interested in getting my picture! They had failed to get John Brinda's picture last year. John, too, has hiked the Eastern Continental Trail all the way from Florida to Canada. He later sent them a very fine professionally prepared and framed map of his "long hike" . . . but they had no picture of John, so they wanted to make sure that didn't happen again. John, they would really like to have a picture of you! So I am greeted with big smiles and hellos from Sharon Dunbar, Herrick Hansen, and Dirk Bishop. Herrick then gets out his Polaroid camera for an on-the-spot autographed shot. I guess they'll hang it on the wall somewhere or stand it on the counter next to John's map!

Sharon is interested in the route I will be taking now that I'm in Canada. I explain that to follow the designated SIA/IAT route, which I prefer to do, I will have to continue hiking north on the international boundary until I reach the old railroad grade at the Aroostook River. She says, "Now, you know that since you're in Canada, you're supposed to stay in Canada until you cross back at one of the designated border crossings." Dirk tells me that just a short ways north of here, right on the border, I will encounter a very large beaver pond and just after that, a long, wide bog. He explains that, more than likely, I will have to work my way around, which means some necessary straying back on the American side of the border. He invites me upstairs where we can view the border to the north where these difficult spots are located.

A road in the U.S., the Aroostook Falls Road, leads directly to the old railroad grade at the Aroostook River, which would get me there much easier and much faster. However, I explain to Dirk that I have done my best to this point to follow the designated SIA/IAT route and that I would prefer to continue in that manner. They are all sympathetic to my plans to stay on the SIA/IAT. In fact, a call is made to the Mounties alerting them that should any of their border sensors come alive or should they receive reports from local folks that someone was crossing the border at an undesignated location, that it would probably be me. Thus, they have cleared a way for my passage!

I am receiving great assistance from the SIA/IAT folks. Dick Anderson had prepared, with considerable time and much detail, crisp, clear maps of the northern Maine section. And now, waiting for me here at Fort Fairfield customs, is a large detailed bundle of maps and information to get me through New Brunswick, just as promised, by Mel Fitton. Thanks, Dick and Mel. It is apparent that much thought, time, and effort have gone into the preparation of all this information for me. Indeed, I am in your debt!

Dirk also mentions that he had received a phone call earlier from Madeleine Theriault in Madawaska, the president of the New Brunswick SIA/IAT Chapter. She wanted to know when I reached the border, so Dirk offers to make the call. In a moment I'm talking to Madeleine, who has taken a day off to drive to Fort Fairfield to greet me! She answers on her cell phone and is now only a few minutes from the border.

The old saying "one good turn deserves another" must apply here, as, just moments ago, I received a cheerful and enthusiastic "Welcome to Canada" from Sharon, Herrick, and Dirk; and now, as I am greeted by Madeleine and her son Sebastien, another very warm and sincere "Welcome to New Brunswick, we're glad you're here!" Without a skip, I am invited to breakfast, the invitation to which I just as quickly accept. In a moment we are loaded up and headed for Andover Perth. Madeleine says she has a favorite spot for breakfast so we're soon at Mary's Bake Shop and Luncheonette, run by sisters Mary and Greta.

We have a fine breakfast indeed, with more great homemade bread for toast—this Southern boy really isn't missing his biscuits and grits! Madeleine reviews the maps and information that Mel has provided and gives me the name and phone number of a good friend in the Kedgwick area that I should contact for assistance up that way. Behind the counter at Mary's hangs some of the most beautiful hand-knitted wool socks that I have seen since ones made for me by my grandmother. Madeleine sees me admiring them and before we leave Mary's she insists on buying me a pair. I dearly want a pair, give a half-hearted "you really shouldn't," and when she insists again, I choose the white ones!

Back at the customs office parking lot we linger and talk some more. To me, it really is something that she has taken off from her work to drive such a distance to meet and befriend me. The time spent with Madeleine and Sebastien will be a most memorable part of my journey through New Brunswick. Thanks, dear friends!

While on the second floor at Canadian customs, and looking out of the window and down on the houses below, I asked Dirk about the house between the two customs buildings: "Is it in the U.S. or Canada?" And he said, "Yes!" He pointed out, and then I could see the boundary monument right in the yard! So, as I shoulder my pack and head for the border clearing I must walk right through these folks' side yard, between their fence and their house, under their clothesline and on out their backyard! I've told you before, but it stands repeating here again for all you doubters . . . folks, I'm not making this stuff up!

Traveling north on the border, and within just a short distance, I come upon a HUGE beaver pond. These fellows can really back up some water! This pond engulfs the entire border clearing and then some, on both sides of the border. The only way, so it appears, to get around this flood is to follow a two-track trail below the dam on the American side, so over I go. Just below the beaver dam the trail ends and from here on it's bushwhacking and mudboggin'. I spend the better part of 15 minutes going the next 50 yards working my way through brush, tangle, mud bogs, and part of the dam itself. Once around I'm back in Canada, only to meander a number of times onto the American side again as I fight my way through and around numerous bogs. I am glad to get this part of the hike behind me as I reach the old railroad grade at the Aroostook River.

On the old railroad bed, for the first mile or so, is superimposed a paved road. As I'm hiking this roadway, a motor home approaches from the other direction. It slows and comes to a stop, and the old fellow inquires as to where the road might lead. I explain that it goes to the international boundary between Canada and the U.S. and that it stops at a barricade. I suggest they drive on down, for it would certainly be worthwhile as the narrow valley opens into an impressive wide expanse with beautiful mountains in full fall regalia, on either side of the grand Aroostook. After I answer the typical questions, these folks also want my picture. The old fellow is obviously anxious about getting his large rig (with auto in tow) turned around, so I send them along with the assurance that there is plenty of room to turn around at the barricade and tell them to stop on the way back and I would spend some time with them.

I hadn't gone another 100 yards and just past this lovely house, when out in the road runs this fellow after me! He says, "Mister, stop a minute. Please tell me where you're going." So it is that I meet David Brown, the self-proclaimed mayor of Tinker Ridge, just below Tinker's Dam! (Folks, this is true.) After I answer the typical questions, he says, "I've done some hiking and I would sure like to take your picture." I tell him that I don't give a tinker's damn and to get his camera and come on up the road and get in line behind the motor home! In a few minutes, here comes the motor home again, and I stop as the old gent pulls to the shoulder . . . and right behind comes Dave who pulls off and stops behind them. Jeez, you'd think I'd just won the Boston Marathon! Here I meet Barry Unicume and his friend Yvonne Roblin. They're from British Columbia. After the photo op Yvonne invites Dave and me into their motor home for sandwiches, coffee, and dessert. Hot dang, can't refuse this kind of hospitality!

Well, it seems pretty certain I won't get far today. I didn't get out of Fort Fairfield until noon; however, the morning spent at Canadian customs and with Madeleine and Sebastien was a delightful time. Coming up the border was slow going and now I will tarry some more as I accept Yvonne's invitation for late lunch. So into the motor home we go. Yvonne fixes sandwiches for all of us along with hot coffee and lots of donuts. By now the occasion presents where I have to recite a couple of my ditties and Dave insists on getting them on tape. He's a teacher and wants to share them with his students. So I send him home for his pocket recorder. Shortly he's back with his recorder and some goodies for my pack.

I've tarried long with these kind folks and must get back on the trail, so I bid farewell to Dave, Yvonne, and Barry, and I'm on my way. I hope now I can just get as far as Andover-Perth, only 12 miles for the day. As I continue on the old railroad grade along the Aroostook it is definitely "darkin' over" and before long a light, steady rain begins. I garbage-bag my pack and don my rain jacket as the rain turns to a hammering downpour. On I march through the deluge to finally reach the bridge at Andover-Perth. There are no motels or cafes on the Andover side so across the bridge I go in the howling rage.

It's only 7:00 p.m. as I enter Pit Stop Pizza, but it's already dark outside. Here, as I glance at the clock on the wall, I realize that after starting late and goofing away the morning and half the afternoon, I have also lost an hour due to a time zone change at the border. I'm soaked, tired, and hungry—and it's dark. There's good food right here, a bar in the basement, and rooms for rent upstairs, and the rain is really pounding outside. Looks like this is it for today, a most brilliant decision after very little pondering. I meet Lloyd McLaughlan, proprietor of the establishment, and after some discussion and a little Yogi-ing I am offered a room at a very reasonable rate. Lloyd laments that the room he's giving me has no door lock—"As a matter of fact," says he, "it has no doorknob." I tell him that it makes no difference to me if the room has a door!

After a hot hamburger with fries and gravy and a few with Glenn at the bar, along with an autographed (U.S.) dollar bill for his wall, it's time to do some laundry, hit the shower, and roll in. What a day—gotta hammer the road tomorrow!

> *"This is the time of year when it gets late early."*
>
> [Yogi Berra]

CAME IN LAST NIGHT IN THE NEAR DARK, in the rain and in a rush, so I didn't get much of a look at the town. I'm up and ready to go a little after 7:00 a.m., and I head down to the café for some coffee . . . but the Pit Stop is still closed so I decide to look the old town over and find another spot for breakfast. Lo and behold, right next door is Mary's Bake Shop and Luncheonette, where Madeleine and Sebastien had taken me for breakfast yesterday morning. So in I go for another great breakfast prepared by Mary and served by her sister Greta!

The SIA/IAT continues along the Tobique River on the same old railroad grade I hiked yesterday along the Aroostook River. If you've read some of my earlier journal entries from western Georgia, you know I have a distinct disdain for railroad grade treadway. What's left on most of these old railroad paths is loose, unbedded rock, a very unpleasant base for hiking. This old grade isn't as bad as most since it's also used by ATVs and snowmobiles, which have helped pack things down. But this sort of hiking is also boring, except for all the dogs that want to take your leg off because you're passing through their yard! The road paralleling the trail along the Tobique is higher and offers a better vantage of this scenic area, and the traffic isn't bad, so I switch to the road for some "blue blazing" today.

Sections of the Tobique are almost spellbinding. At Tobique Narrows the river has cut like a knife through the mountains. The rail bed has been literally blasted from the vertical cliff wall, which rises abruptly from the rushing torrent. The view up the Tobique at this point is like no other I've seen on any other river — a stunning, halting kind of grandeur, definitely on the wild side.

The river finally settles itself into a pleasant little valley with many old homes and farms along the way. I arrive late afternoon at Plaster Rock and make my way to Roger's, a very modest but clean and well-kept little row of rooms run by a kind old gentleman named Wilfred Lagace, who, after showing much interest in my adventure, offers me a room at a very reasonable rate. Wilfred says, "You pay me what you think it's worth." Turns out, we're both happy!

> *"Have you ever stood where the silences brood,*
> *And the vast horizons begin,*
> *At the dawn of the day to behold far away*
> *The goal you would strive for and win?"*

[Robert W. Service, *The Land of Beyond*]

THURSDAY September 24, 1998
TRAIL DAY 251/11   ✦   TRAIL MILE 3,742/180
LOCATION Bear's Lair, Riley Brook

THE RAILBED AND ROAD CONTINUE BY THE TOBIQUE RIVER for this entire day's hike into Riley Brook. This is the first day of moose-hunting season and around about 9:00 a.m. I see the first pickup truck loaded full with one of these huge animals headed toward the game-check station in Plaster Rock. This is the first of some 10 to 15 trucks that will pass bearing the remains of these hulks. Some are so enormous that I can see them, head and rack above the cab of the approaching truck. One hunter had loaded his kill hind-end first and tight against the cab, but a goodly part of the head, rack, and most of the animal's front quarters still hung out over the tailgate!

There's a grocery store complete with grill and carryout near the little communities of Everett and Two Brooks. Here I enjoy another hot hamburger, including fries, beans, and coleslaw. I was first introduced to one of these hot hamburgers at the Pit Stop Café in Perth. Seems it's a favorite fast-food item up here. It's an interesting combination of very common ingredients familiar to all Americans: bread, fried hamburger, French fries, and gravy. But get this combination . . . the fried burger patty is placed between the two pieces of white bread and right beside this on the same platter go the fries. "Big deal," you say. Ah, but now for the interesting part; this whole concoction is covered over with brown gravy . . . fries and all! Yes, gravy on the French fries. Makes for a somewhat soggy platter, but to a tired, hungry hiker, it's very tasty indeed.

On up the road toward Riley Brook, and in a fellow's side yard, four hunters have a moose hoisted up in a tree in the process of skinning and dressing it. They greet me, and I ask to have a look, as I've never seen one of these animals up close; they invite me over. Seems that in order to dress one of these mammoths, a pole the size of a small fence post must be run between the Achilles-like tendon and the leg bone just above the hind fetlocks. To this pole is tied a very substantial rope, which runs through a pulley fixed high in the tree, then down to the hitch ball on one of the hunters' 4x4 pickups. As the skinning process progresses, the carcass is hoisted higher in the tree until only the head rests on the ground. A hand saw (looks like a carpenter's saw to me) is then used to cut the animal in half along its spine into what is known in the butchering trade as "sides," like sides of beef, only these are sides of moose.

I comment to one of the hunters that the moose appears as big as a cow, and he says, "That's what it is, a cow—a cow moose." The hunters estimate that this one weighs around 500 pounds, not big by local standards, as some cows can tip the scales at well over 1,000 pounds. But, as I stand gawking up at this thing, it looks huge to me! I mention that I enjoy hunting and when I was a youngster I used to go quail, squirrel, and rabbit hunting with my father. We also went fishing every time the occasion presented. Those times spent together are a treasure of memories . . . my first contact with Mother Nature's great bounty that is her vast, never-ending out-of-doors. My mom was a great cook and she always prepared, in finest fashion, whatever we brought home. But this moose is another matter. It will fill a couple of large freezers and feed a good-sized family for probably the better part of a year! One of the hunters reckoned that moose hunting certainly was a lot of fun, but after the "bang," the fun was all over. There's no way a man, or a number of men for that matter, could drag one of these hulks out of the woods. So, the trick up here is to not only scout the moose but to try and shoot it somewhere near where it's possible to bring in one of the large log skidders. This being a machine of considerable might used in the timber harvesting business to drag logs out of the woods.

As I hike on up the road to Riley Brook, a fellow in a pickup stops and wants my picture. He had seen me passing through Plaster Rock and wants to hear more about my odyssey. And shortly, yet another vehicle stops and a young lady gets out and approaches me. Here I meet Marie-Josée Laforest, interpreter and assistant superintendent of Mt. Carleton Provincial Park. Marie is on her way to a funeral in Plaster Rock. Seems everyone up here knows I'm on my way through. No news seems to be big news around here. She wants to be the first to welcome me to the park. Her eyes light up and her voice absolutely jingles as she speaks about Carleton! She says all the folks at the park are excited about my coming and are anxiously awaiting my arrival. Marie provides me with information about accommodations for the evening in Riley Brook and also welcomes and invites me to stay at her home just north of the little village.

Funeral processions are a somber affair, and in a short while I hear the steady increasing hum of traffic behind. I turn to see the hearse and the long line of headlights approaching. I stand and face the procession, waiting at attention until it passes. I am finding that folks up here are more than just good friends, they're more like family, and it seems they're all out today. It's a joy to be in such a remote community that hasn't been swept into and whirled away by our maybe not-so-great modern times. Places such as this really do exist where family values and bonds are still as I remember from the little backhills village in the Ozarks where I was raised. Guess the old-fashioned in me really comes out at times like this. I don't mean to imply that life as we know it today is necessarily bad or good for that matter—just different. For me, I like the way it used to be a lot better, and so do the folks around here! In the past eight months I have been on many different and varied roadwalks. They have all been interesting, certainly a diversion from hiking o'er the mountains and through the woods, much as was the AT Cumberland Valley roadwalk of many years past. This roadwalk today will remain in my memory. Here I've met kind, gentle folk and have seen fine places.

I arrive at the little village of Riley Brook in a chilling evening breeze. I knock at the door of the Bear's Lair, a rustic and nestled-in log lodge on the banks of the picturesque Tobique. In a moment the door opens and I am greeted by Evelyn McAskill, proprietor and lodge keeper. She invites me in and shows me to warm, comfortable quarters. I no sooner get my shower and settle in than a knock comes on my door.

It is Evelyn. She invites me into the lodge's grand room where she has prepared an evening meal for me! The folks in Canada are indeed kind and generous people.

"All I have seen teaches me to trust the Creator for all I have not seen."

[Ralph Waldo Emerson]

FRIDAY September 25, 1998
TRAIL DAY 252/12 ✦ TRAIL MILE 3,768/206
LOCATION Park Offices, Mt. Carleton Provincial Park

I'M UP AT 7:30 A.M. AND EVELYN SENDS ME on my way with a fine bacon-and-eggs breakfast. In just a short while the road crosses the Tobique River and here at the bridge a lady stops her car, rolls down her window, and hands me a fancy half-pint jar of apple preserves. She says she saw me hiking into Riley Brook yesterday and has been told of my unbelievable adventure. I thank her kindly and put the little treasure in my pack to savor later.

Just a short distance above the bridge is Marie's lovely home. I will not see her again, as she will be away this weekend, so I stop and leave a little note of thanks for the warm hospitality extended me.

In a short while I'm at the little community of Nictau. As I pass this lovely farmhouse I'm greeted by the ambassador of the household . . . the family dog. His barking brings some folks around from behind the house. My wave and greeting is returned by an invitation to stop and come in. So I break my stride, snap my Leki poles together, and cross their large, manicured lawn. Here I meet William V. Miller, III, his sister and her husband, Julie and Marty McCrum, Bill's mother, Wilma, and her two brothers, Lionell and Jim Clark. Bill's brother Jim is also present. I am whisked into their lovingly cared-for and spacious old farm home and urged to sit right down at the dining room table. Then come the questions about who I am, where I'm from, and where I'm headed. Sooo, as briefly as I can I recount my story once more. It's then I mention meeting Marie-Josée yesterday . . . on her way to a funeral in Plaster Rock, and that the folks at Carleton were expecting me, so I must not tarry long. That's when Julie mentions that the funeral Marie-Josée was attending was for her father William V. Miller, II.

I put my head down, blush, and feel ashamed for what I've just said, to be in such a rush. These folks have just buried a dearest family member, and even now during their time of grieving, have opened their home and extended their kindness and hospitality to a passing stranger! Well, I relax, sit back in my chair, and chat while enjoying the hot tea and cookies placed before me. Beyond the picture window beside the dining room table, the sun is setting the mountain ablaze across the valley. As we all marvel at the beautiful fall colors I mention that I could not possibly repay them for the kindness they've extended me, but if they would gather around I would recite the inspirational poem about Ma Nature's Paint Brush. There came a hush and my voice lifted and carried the message about the magic spell of fall. I know now this poem about fall, which will close this day's entry, was inspired and written for this occasion. With tears in most every eye, this wonderful family—none ever having wished to be brought together under such circumstances—shares a poignant, very special moment together. Thank you, Lord, for bringing me here today to be where you have lighted and guided my path, and to share with these kind, most generous people.

Bill Miller, III, is a craftsman, a builder of wooden canoes, a vanishing art passed down from his father and grandfather. He shows me his shop with all the wonderful old tools and some of the projects on which he's currently working. Bill is not content just to build these works of ancient art. He fells the trees from his own wood lot and runs the strips, boards, and planks on his own sawmill. While Bill is showing me around, Julie is putting a little package together for me to take along: apples from their trees, preserves made from berries picked on the farm, and syrup, the purest and sweetest maple syrup I've ever tasted. Yup—boiled down from the sap of their own birdseye maple trees right here on the homestead!

The Tobique Valley is indeed a special place, fixed, it seems, permanently in time, when time with family and friends was the most important thing, when those with skill of hand took pride, bringing joy and satisfaction; when a hard day's work was always expected and

always given and when fierce independence and right judgment was
keen. These folks are of that time and tilt long past. I know they've never
wavered from it—standing tall and proud. What a blessing being here
with them, if for but a brief, brief day! I am sure that as I write this,
plans are underway to take the trail from this valley roadwalk to the
woodlands and ridges all along. Soon, many will thru-hike this grand
SIA/IAT, but a hundred could pass here every day and the kind and gentle folk in this valley would certainly welcome them as they have me and
each intrepid could experience the joy and pleasure in passing through
this grand and proud old valley. But alas, it certainly will not endure.

    I have been overwhelmed by the hospitality, friendship, and
generosity extended me by all the folks I have met since crossing the
border at Fort Fairfield into this beautiful country of Canada. As I
approach Mt. Carleton Provincial Park a vehicle passes, turns about,
and then pulls alongside. Here I meet Bertin Allard and Jean François
Paulin. Bertin is the superintendent of Mt. Carleton and Jean
François is one of the park wardens. With warm, friendly smiles I am
again welcomed to Mt. Carleton Provincial Park. I am offered a ride
on into the park, the kind offer to which I politely decline and as I hike
on I am at the park entrance reception building within the hour. As I
approach the visitor's center I am overwhelmed again. Out on the deck
come all the folks working at the park. While Jean François has his
camcorder running, Bertin introduces me to Guy Belanger and Larry
Dyer, who work in maintenance, and Nadine Perron, Steven
Theriault, and Rhonda Pelletier, gate attendants. I am then invited to
continue on to the park office where Larry will prepare an evening
meal for Bertin and me! I hike this final distance quickly and am
greeted again by Bertin in the office parking lot. Not only am I treated
to a great supper of pork chops and fried onions, but I am told that I
will be staying in their warm, private bunkroom while here. Bert famil-
iarizes me with the park and the trail system before departing for
home, and I'm able to take a luxurious hot shower before settling in for
the night. What an amazing, amazing day!

Ma Nature's Paintbrush

Ma Nature's got her paintbrush out,
Brushin' o'er the green.
From her palette, every hue,
To brighten up the scene.
In red and orange and yellow,
She paints so brilliantly.
And there, a touch of umber,
She threw that in for me.
Now what's all this excitement?
It happens every fall.
It's nothing but a rerun,
In case you don't recall.
Well, we've seen the work of masters,
Hanging in our galleries.
But none can match Ma Nature's hand,
When she paints autumn's trees.
Ahh, 'tis a magic time of year,
A spell cast over all.
For all the seasons we hold dear,
The best, by far . . . is fall.

[N. Nomad]

SATURDAY September 26, 1998
TRAIL DAY 253/13 ✦ TRAIL MILE 3,783/221
LOCATION Park Offices, Mt. Carleton Provincial Park

I'M UP AT 8:00 A.M. AND PREPARE TOAST AND COFFEE in the head-quarters' kitchen. At 9:00 a.m. I meet Park Warden Gerard Magualle, who will be spending the day here at the park office. He gets the generator going and the office up and running. Shortly after 9:00 a.m. on a cool, clear morning, I'm off on my hike to Mt. Carleton and Sagamook.

The trails here in the park are professionally designed and constructed and are well blazed and maintained. When I first see the blazing technique, a blue 3x3 metal plate with a narrow white hash mark, I have my doubts about its effectiveness, but as I quickly find, these markers stand out clearly (but not offensively) and are easy to follow.

On the approach to Mt. Carleton the trail ascends the Bald Mountain Brook Ravine. The brook entertains me with joyful song as it cascades over the many falls and rapids on its way to Lake Nictau below. Once the ridgeline is gained I turn south, past Mt. Head. The final ascent to the summit of Mt. Carleton involves a short, steep rock scramble. To this point, I have had the trail to myself this morning, but this being a beautiful Saturday, and the summit being within easy reach from a nearby parking lot on the other side, many families with youngsters are already enjoying the warming sun and the grand panorama. The summit is crowded and the kids are a little too raucous for my comfort, so I quickly move on.

To reach Sagamook, I retrace my path back along the ridge, past the point where I turned from the ascent, and continue on north to Sagamook. The final climb is again a short, steep rock scramble. But, here, as I ascend, I find an abrupt transition, not in the path beneath my feet, but in the atmosphere all around me, as if I am passing through an invisible veil. Below this, the earthly sky, and above . . . a heavenly sight! For it seems, I am entering a mystic, spiritual place. I arrive at the summit to find that I have it to myself. Mt. Carleton, the highest point in New Brunswick, has been popularized and is the destination for most all the folks that come to the park. But lesser-known Sagamook is certainly a much more remarkable place. As I sit here, gazing in wonder at the sights before me, I feel a peace and calm I've never before experienced on any mountaintop. For here there is some form of energy emanating from the very core of this mountain, permeating the ether and creating a quintessence above and all around me, penetrating, it seems, the very depths of my soul; bringing an inner trembling, though I am still! I do not resist but permit flight to my mind and spirit. Then as I linger, and from where I know not, for I am privy to none of it, comes the inspiration for the unusual and mysterious verse that will close my journal today.

The descent from Sagamook is steep and follows many switchbacks, with the trail emerging at the shores of Lake Nictau. Back at the park office, and in the evening, Warden Fred Everett relieves Gerard of duty. After another soothing shower, and as I relish preparing my evening meal in their modern kitchen, Fred and I strike up what turns out to be an astonishing conversation. For Fred, I find, is native to the area and knows much of the history and mystery that surrounds Sagamook. In the course of conversation I ask Fred to tell me about Sagamook. Hesitating, he says: "What do you want to know?" That's when I explain my experience on Sagamook earlier in the day. "Fred," I exclaim, "There is incredible energy rising from and encircling that mountain, not a form that you or I would know or understand, more mystical, but nonetheless physical in a very real and gripping way! Sagamook, I believe, is a very spiritual place!" As we relax for the evening in the presence of a more familiar peace and calm, and sitting at the kitchen table, I recite the inspiration received on Sagamook. Fred then relates this remarkable story to me: "In the days long past, and perhaps for centuries, the great Nations of the Maliseet and Mic Mac poled their canoes to ascend the rivers from the valleys far beyond Sagamook, to come together from other lands at the shores of Lake Nictau, a long, narrow lake held high and close by Sagamook. And from there the tribal chiefs, together, would ascend to the very summit of Sagamook to hold council."

What a truly unexplainable and humbling day! I knew nothing of this history, this mystery of "Great Nations gone before." But yet, somehow I have been whirled up in this ancient, mystic past! How many have climbed Sagamook over the centuries? Indeed, how many have experienced this peace, this calm, this contentment, and the mysterious presence of:

The Spirits of Sagamook

The summit of ol' Sagamook
Isn't all that high.
But, as I climb I pass right through
The bottom of the sky.
From here to turn and look — and gaze,
Into the wild blue yonder;
And try and try, as best I can,

To comprehend the wonder.
Now from this lofty firmament,
I let my spirit soar.
To mingle with the spirits of—
Great Nations gone before.
And as I part this sanctity,
A bit of me will stay.
To rest in God's eternal peace,
That's present, here . . . today.

[N. Nomad]

SUNDAY　September 27, 1998
TRAIL DAY 254/14　✦　TRAIL MILE 3,810/248
LOCATION　Home of Bertin Allard, St-Quentin

AFTER BREAKFAST OF POP-TARTS, TOAST, AND COFFEE, again prepared in the office kitchen, I'm off for the 27-mile hike into St-Quentin. The forecast today is for rain, and as I bid Fred farewell and step off the porch the rain begins. At the visitor's center near the main gate Steve greets me. He asks me to come in and sign the guest register, for in the excitement on Friday, I had failed to do so.

Shortly after I leave the park, an approaching auto slows and stops. It is Rhonda Pelletier, gate attendant, on her way to the park. Rhonda is a native Canadian, a member of the Madawaska Maliseet First Nation, and a good friend also of Madeleine Theriault, the kind lady who met and befriended me at the Canadian border. Rhonda is bearing gifts for me: a braid of sweet grass and a small, carefully bound and tied bundle of sage. We both understand the symbolic significance of this gesture, a gift from her ancestors, and she listens with astonishment as I recite the poem about Sagamook. I thank her for her kindness. Then, with the rain intensifying, we bid farewell and hastened our separate ways.

I would like to take a moment to tell you about Madeleine Theriault . . . a remarkable person. I know Madeleine through her volunteer work as president of the New Brunswick Chapter of the SIA/

IAT. Rhonda knows her through her work professionally as tourism coordinator and consultant with the Madawaska Maliseet First Nation in Madawaska, New Brunswick. Her effort in this latter capacity is helping restore a presence for the Maliseet as a true Nation among the people of New Brunswick, so their rich, long history and heritage can again be prominent. I am humbled to have had close contact with them . . . both of the present and from the past. Their deep dignity and pride is immediate and readily evident. The Maliseet culture, forever a part of New Brunswick, should be known and respected by all. Madeleine, my dear friend, I wish you success in all you do!

The rain is setting in now with "darkin' over" permanence. I brace and push on into its chilling wall. As I reach NB 180 in the darkening swirl a truck stops and the driver offers me a ride. He pulls away slowly and glances back with a puzzled expression as I decline his kindness. This is the first of countless rides offered me today. I have hiked in the rain over many roads, for many miles, for many days, but I have never been befriended by so many people.

Some 3 miles from St-Quentin, who comes out from his home to again greet me? Oh yes! It is Bertin Allard, superintendent at Mt. Carleton Provincial Park. He has a thermos of hot tea and some delicious cookies for me. Down goes the tailgate, off comes the pack, and I thoroughly enjoy this respite. Here I meet his daughter Julie and they invite me to have dinner with them this evening and to stay the night at their home in St-Quentin. I immediately accept and am very thankful and relieved to know that I will soon be out of this bone-chilling rain.

Following Bert's directions, and shortly after the hour, I arrive at their cozy home. Here I meet and am greeted by Bert's wife, Jeanne-D'arc, their younger daughter, Marie-Eve, and Bert's mother, Blanche. I dine and enjoy an evening of fellowship with this kind and generous family. Bert has already been in contact with Andre Arpin at Echo Restigouche. Echo is a resort with cabins, a campground, and a restaurant on the Restigouche River. Thanks to Bert and Madeleine, I'll be staying there tomorrow evening, for both are very good friends with Andre. Madeleine's older son, Raphael, is an employee at Echo but is now away at college in Pointe Gaspé.

Bert has also been in contact with Maurice Simon. Maurice works for Mel Fitton, the SIA/IAT chief organizer in New Brunswick. Mel provided the maps that got me from Fort Fairfield to St-Quentin. Maurice has been charged with the responsibility of trail layout and construction for the sections I'll be hiking north of St-Quentin, and Bert has made arrangements for Maurice and me to get together here in the morning.

I take a long, warm shower to get the chill out of my bones. I'm in the basement den where Bert has kept a fire going in his old porcelain cookstove. I am warm and dry and with great friends . . . many blessings this memorable day.

> *"My road calls me, lures me*
> *West, east, south and north;*
> *Most roads lead men homeward,*
> *My road leads me forth.*
> *To add more miles to the tally*
> *Of gray miles left behind,*
> *In quest of that one beauty*
> *God put me here to find."*
>
> [John Masefield]

MONDAY September 28, 1998
TRAIL DAY 255/15 ✦ TRAIL MILE 3,833/271
LOCATION Echo Restigouche, Kedgwick

I'M UP AT 7:30 A.M. AND AGAIN AM I THE GUEST of the Allard family as we enjoy breakfast together. Shortly, Maurice Simon arrives with a bundle of maps in his hand. The spacious den in the Allard basement has a large picnic table, and we gather there as Maurice lays out the maps. The trail from Five Fingers to Echo Restigouche is quite complicated, and after Maurice spends about five minutes attempting to explain the route . . . and now sensing his frustration, I say to Maurice, "Why don't you just come with me and show me the way?" Well, that's all it took to have a hiking companion for this day! So, after Bert loans Maurice his fanny pack and water bottle and stocks him up with some goodies, we load up in Bert's truck and head out to the trailhead passed yesterday at Five Fingers Brook.

Why are goodbyes always so tough? I've known Bertin Allard for less than four days . . . but it seems we've been friends for a lifetime. So, with tear-filled eyes and a good solid hug, I bid Bert farewell. Thanks, Bert! There's absolutely no way to ever repay you, your family, and all the great folks at Mt. Carleton Provincial Park for the generosity and kindness extended me.

Shortly, Maurice and I are on our way toward Echo Restigouche, over trail laid out by Maurice. Here the trail follows a multiuse treadway for the first few miles, being shared by ORVs, snowmobiles, horses, and cross-country skiers. We then turn and follow Five Fingers Brook, later fording it. Soon we reach the Outdoor Recreation Center, a fine lodge owned and managed by Gerald and Clemence Belanger. It is a new facility with a large swimming pool and manicured lawns all around. The lodge sits close by a dam and spillway and has a spacious covered porch where Maurice and I are invited to relax for a while and have lunch with the Belangers. I know I will never be able to return to all the memorable and enjoyable places I've seen during this odyssey, but if I could, this peaceful place would be one of them.

As we continue on along Five Fingers Brook it is becoming a formidable stream with many spring-fed tributaries joining from deep-cut ravines, known to the folks here in New Brunswick as gulches. The trail now begins to traverse these gulches, making for a roller-coaster hike from one to the next, over grades in excess of 50 percent. There are no switchbacks. The trail goes straight up and over and straight back down. At some locations where the trail is even more precipitous, Maurice and his crew have cut steps into the gulch walls.

Echo Restigouche is near the confluence of Five Fingers Brook and the Restigouche River, and we arrive here around 6:30 p.m. for a short roadwalk to the resort. In what seems to be the style of greeting here in New Brunswick, who drives up the road to meet us, but Andre Arpin! He welcomes me to Echo Restigouche and says he has a cabin prepared for me for the evening. And in near the same breath I am invited to dinner, as his wife, Francine, has supper waiting! So, Maurice and I hasten on to the Arpin home. Bert has brought Maurice's truck out to Echo and before Maurice departs for home and his family, we arrange to meet in the morning at my cabin to review maps I will rely on to get to Matapédia, Québec.

I meet Andre's wife, Francine Levesque, and their daughters Marie Christine and Aerchee, and I am then treated to a delicious evening meal. After supper Andre and Marie-Christine take me into their little town of Kedgwick to get provisions needed for the next five days. I pick up some ice cream, cookies, and Hershey's chocolate. Then back at the Arpin home we gather again at their dining room table for dessert before Andre drives me to my cabin for the evening. As Andre drops me off he mentions that firewood has been stacked on the porch for my use and invites me to build a fire in the woodstove. Even though baseboard heat has the room cozy and inviting as I enter, I can't resist building a fire, and I have one going in short order. This is the fourth night in a row for a shower and a comfortable bed. I am very tired, but it has been a delightful day hiking with Maurice.

> *"Carefree to be, as a bird that sings;*
> *To go my own sweet way;*
> *To reck not at all what may befall,*
> *But to live and to love each day."*
>
> [Robert W. Service, *A Rolling Stone*]

TUESDAY September 29, 1998
TRAIL DAY 256/16   ✦   TRAIL MILE 3,847/285
LOCATION Small plateau-step in Bologna Gulch

I AM UP AT 8:00 A.M. AND GREETED BY THE SUN as I prepare toast and coffee in the cabin's little kitchenette . . . even Pop-Tarts, toasted for a change! Soon comes Andre to take my picture and bid me farewell. And also shortly, Maurice arrives. Again, Maurice lays out the maps and we study them intently. It appears there are many more gulches to cross as the trail follows the Restigouche River, and the maps given me by Maurice show this section to be incredibly rugged.

I was not aware that there is no bus service from eastern Canada back to the area in Maine where I want to go after completing this odyssey. Maurice explains this to me and offers to come and get me when I return to Matapédia, where the bus from Gaspé will drop me off, and from there to take me to the Maine border! So, again with tears in my eyes and another good, solid hug, I bid another new friend and a great hiking companion goodbye!

Andre had mentioned that John Brinda also stayed here last year, and that John was up and gone by 8:00 a.m. But it is now 10:00 a.m. as I continue to tarry before departing this cozy cabin at Echo Restigouche. The trail leaves Echo on a paved road for the first 7 miles, then to a gravel road, then off into the woods. It isn't long until progress slows as the trail returns to the gulches along Haffords and Stillwater Brooks. These brooks cut right through the mountains with the narrow ridges on either side extending like fingers from a hand to abruptly stop at the next larger brook. It is impossible for the trail to follow along these streams as they have cut so deeply into the mountains, forming in the process near-vertical walls rising straight up to form each mountainous finger. The trail goes up and over each of these, across the narrow knife-edge ridge, down into the next gulch, across the next brook, and straight up the other side . . . on and on for what seems like endless miles!

It is late as I arrive at the first designated campsite. I have covered little distance today. I am totally exhausted. My arms and legs move like mush, as if bound with lead! I am on a little plateau-like step above a small, clear-running brook in Bologna Gulch. I get a cooking and warming fire going with the aid of birch bark, and I spend little time by the fire before rolling in.

"There's a hand that stretches downward,
Makes my feet to walk again.
Tho my journey may be rugged,
He'll be with me 'til the end."

[D. Sue Jones Horton]

LAST EVENING THE SUN SET ON A BEAUTIFUL DAY without a cloud in the sky, but at 4:00 this morning I'm awakened by rain on my tent. It is raining steady when I awake again at 7:30 a.m. As I lie here awaiting the rain to ease I am suffering a dull headache and my sinuses are nearly closed . . . probably the result of the bone-chilling rain that I endured last Sunday during the roadwalk into St-Quentin. The rain relents and I am able to break camp and be on my way by 9:30 a.m. The sky still threatens, so I have donned my rain jacket and garbage-bagged my pack.

Progress today is agonizingly slow, strenuous, and very deliberate, with ascent and descent grades in excess of 70 percent. I must move with absolute, constant focus to avoid falling, especially descending the gulch walls, as the rocks and roots are not only incredibly slick, but are concealed by the wet, slippery leaves of fall. Progress slows even more as I reach the ford at Upper Thorn Point Brook. The brook, at this location, is about 30 feet wide with dark, ominous, fast-rushing water. I stop, drop my pack, remove my boots and socks, and put on my off-road running shoes to make the crossing. As I enter the brook the water is bone-chilling cold and I can feel the force of the fast-rushing stream as it surges against my legs and my knees. At the midway point I am up to my thighs in the hammering force. I move very slowly and cautiously, making sure both feet and both poles are firmly planted before taking another step. As is common with these mountain streams, the streambed is a jumble of rocks as slippery as ice, with footing unstable at best. But, I am able to ford without incident and am very relieved to reach the other side. The water in this brook, running high and hard, is overflowing into secondary channels, which I am able to ford at ease. I get out of the wet running shoes as quickly as I can, dry my feet thoroughly, and get my warm wool socks and boots back on.

It would be incredibly difficult to negotiate this treadway with a full pack, if not for the steps that have been hacked from the gulch walls. Even with the steps, progress remains very slow and very strenuous. As I move from step to step, often must I also move my hands from step to step, for in many places the wall is right before me. I have covered very little distance again today as I arrive late and carry water from a little brook to the campsite above Upper Thorn Point Brook. The rain has continually threatened throughout the day but holds off, and I am able to pitch camp easily. The woods, however, are soaked from the early morning rain and without the aid of much birch bark a cooking and warming fire is impossible. It is getting dark much earlier now so I must prepare my evening meal with the aid of my Petzl headlamp. It is 8:00 p.m. as I climb into my little Slumberjack. Just as last night, I am completely exhausted. My head has pounded all day and I have had much difficulty breathing. Nowhere during this odyssey have I had to endure such a constant physical demand as in these ascents and descents. I've never hiked through terrain anything like these mountains in New Brunswick.

> *"To pitch my tent with no prosy plan,*
> *To range and to change at will;*
> *To mock at the mastership of man,*
> *To seek adventure's thrill."*

[Robert W. Service, *A Rolling Stone*]

THURSDAY October 1, 1998
TRAIL DAY 258/18 ✦ TRAIL MILE 3,855/293
LOCATION Small ridge above Upper Thorn Point Brook

SHORTLY AFTER MIDNIGHT THE RAIN BEGINS AGAIN. Sleep is fretful, as I am kept awake by its incessant tat. As the wind pounds on my tent the sinus headache pounds in my head. The rain is hard and cold and continues through the morning, and I am unable to break camp lest I become drenched and chilled to the bone. So I remain marooned in my little shelter. Just as well as I am weary, sapped of strength . . . bone tired. The rain continues throughout the day and I feast on two cold Pop-Tarts and a peanut-butter sandwich.

Having this head cold, I know I must increase my fluid intake, but along with the water consumed last evening to prepare my supper and with what I have downed today, little of what I brought up from the brook remains. So I put my cook pot outside the tent and hold the tent fly at an angle so the ice-cold rainwater is channeled into the pot. Within a short time I am able to collect a couple more quarts of water.

Around 5:00 p.m. the cold rain relents long enough for me to scurry out for my daily duty. Then my ever-present companion . . . rain, returns. But I am blessed to be reasonably warm and dry in my little Slumberjack. As I have been imprisoned here for the past countless hours, marooned on this not-so-tranquil island in the shroud, I have had much time to ponder life as it has been over the past many years, and I conclude that indeed, through all that I have suffered, all that I have endured, I have been blessed in the balance. Sleep is not fretful this night, though I have been kept long.

Life's Blessings

Don't be dismayed by this world's wealth,
'Haps you've been denied your share.
For the measure used is not always right,
In judging what's just and fair.
So go your way, be content each day,
With the metes that are handed out,
For you'll find in the end, blessings tend,
To banish the sorrow and doubt.

[N. Nomad]

FRIDAY October 2, 1998
TRAIL DAY 259/19 ✦ TRAIL MILE 3,864/302
LOCATION Small ridge above Upper Two Brooks

I HAVE BEEN COOPED UP IN MY TENT FOR 36 HOURS because of the cold, relentless rain, but I'm able to get out this morning as the sky threatens but the rain holds off. Soon I reach a vista at an abrupt turn in the trail near Cross Point Island. Here I am afforded one of the most spectacular views seen on any river that I can recall in my memory, perhaps more so even than the breathtaking view into the Tobique Narrows. Looking back at the sheer, stark wall of stone at Cross Point, steel gray in the cold, swirling gloom of this day, it looms as if a forbidden place. But, I must forgive this unkindly presence, for I am sure that it would take on a totally different character in the soft, warm glow of an early morning sun.

As I proceed, the skies clear, and there are many view points all along the beautiful, winding Restigouche River Canyon today, especially above Marshall Island and Pine Island . . . but progress is very slow as the trail is unbelievably steep and treacherous. To further slow progress I get lost on two different occasions. I am unable to find the trail from Gilmore Brook to Upper Two Brooks. I am finally able to work my way around by taking the worker's access trail and an old logging road that follows the ridge around between the two brooks. I was expecting to have to ford Upper Two Brooks, but a tree has been felled across the brook to bridge the stream, and I am able to cross easily. Dark is descending, so I pitch camp just above Upper Two Brooks.

On my entire journey on the AT, the day of least progress due to difficult treadway was 14 miles. That day was spent traversing a very rugged section through the "Notch" and up Old Speck Arm in the Mahoosucs. By contrast, Wednesday, after a full day of hiking, I had covered only 8 miles . . . and today only 9. These mountains are not formidable by any standard, but they are without question the most rugged that I have ever hiked . . . anywhere!

> *"For far over all that folks hold worth,*
> *There lives and there leaps in me*
> *A love of the lowly things of earth,*
> *And a passion to be free."*

[Robert W. Service, *A Rolling Stone*]

SATURDAY October 3, 1998
TRAIL DAY 260/20 ✦ TRAIL MILE 3,873/311
LOCATION Ledge beside branch to Silas Brook

I DO NOT WAKE THIS MORNING UNTIL 9:00 A.M. There was no energy left last night and I fell into a deep, sound sleep. I was physically exhausted, but additionally, I was also emotionally exhausted due to the anxiety and frustration of getting lost. The anguish of facing the possibility of failure totally sapped me. This morning the sun is striking the upper wall of the gulch beyond the brook, which is encouraging, a great way to begin the day!

I am able to follow the trail much better today and as some of the sog goes out of the treadway I move with less hesitancy . . . more confidence. I am able to cross Upper Grindstone Brook without difficulty, but Lower Grindstone Brook requires fording. So I must go through the ordeal of changing to my running shoes. The ford is not at all wide, but it is very deep and the water is very swift and ice cold. Before I can get my feet dry and my wool socks and boots back on I have lost feeling clear to my upper ankles. As the circulation slowly returns it's as if my feet are being attacked by porcupines! It is late morning now, but the little thermometer attached to my pack zipper pull reads 36 degrees.

Progress comes to a near halt again at Cheulers Brook. At the exact point where the trail drops over the gulch wall there has occurred an incredible rockslide. It has swept trees and everything with it to the bottom of the gulch. Much to my chagrin, and once out on this near-vertical slide, I find that descending through this talus is a nightmarish ordeal! Though I am supine, I am near straight up as I push back against my pack as hard as I can, using it as a skid brake against the loose rock. I also dig and jab my heels and poles in to keep from skidding out of control. Rocks kicked loose careen and rattle to the jumble below. Once out on this skid plate, I dearly wish I were anywhere but here. I try moving back to the side, but I just keep sliding down. Luckily, I am able to get a heel dug in, a pole tip wedged, or my pack snagged on a rock. This is a frighteningly dynamic process, not under my control, which moves me along and quickly down as I dig, jab, and drag for all I'm worth! As I skid into the jumble of rock and trees I am able to get stopped. My heart is pounding in my throat as I heave an anxious sigh and run a quick damage-control check on my bod and my pack.

Leaning forward now and peering down through this maze of rubble and brush, I quickly realize that this ordeal isn't over yet! I am still a great distance above the brook, and the trees are lodged and twisted in what seems an impenetrable jumble. Some are wedged in precarious fashion, while others teeter on boulders. I look for another way out, but the way is blocked on both sides . . . and there is no way back up. I pull my shoulder, hip, and sternum straps as tight as possible to secure my pack from pitching me and I begin shinnying, grappling, and tumbling my way on down. Finally I'm in the brook and I heave another big sigh of relief. Once across and part way up the far gulch wall . . . and looking back, the slide doesn't appear all that big a deal. But I thank the Lord for getting me through. I am relieved to have one more potentially hike-stopping obstacle behind me.

Above Silas Beach the trail turns to off-camber slopes bringing much side-slabbing. After miles of this, my feet and ankles become very sore, but I move on as best I can. So it is with mixed emotion that I pause here at the park bench overlooking the great canyon of the Restigouche, for it seems we have been together for such a long time, not necessarily as friends but hopefully with deep mutual respect as tolerant companions. As I turn, completing another 9-mile day—and with a reluctant glance over my shoulder—I bid farewell to this enchanted, untamed land.

Secrets of the Restigouche

The secrets of the Restigouche,
Are known to only me.
The first to hike this river trail,
Along the IAT.
All through these mountains there is cut,
A canyon long and deep.
And to its flank rush joyful brooks,
From gulches rough and steep.
And o'er this all the trail is laid,

Not for the faint of heart.
Built by a chap they call Maurice,
A classic work of art.
If in you there's some mountain goat,
'Twill serve you well, indeed.
Sure-footedness on mountain walls,
A skill that you will need.
Will take you days to hike this through,
The miles you need not rush.
For it will take the strongest man,
And turn his limbs to mush.
So, if you've got the yearn and bent,
I'd recommend to you —
To come and see what I have seen,
And plan to tough it through.
And now I bid thee, Restigouche,
Enchanted land, farewell.
If you would know its secrets . . . come!
For I will never tell.

[N. Nomad]

SUNDAY October 4, 1998
TRAIL DAY 261/21 ✦ TRAIL MILE 3,893/331
LOCATION Snowmobile-trail warming hut below Squaw Cap

I AM STRONGER THIS MORNING, MY FEET SOMEWHAT BETTER . . . and the sun is bright and warm on my face as I scale the last steep gulch wall above Silas Brook. From here the trail moves over to the ridges and tablelands and settles back to more typical and friendly treadway. One interesting section follows for a short distance as the trail turns onto a wide overgrown roadway, complete with telephone/telegraph poles with many cross-arms having scores of insulator pegs and old glass insulators still intact. It's been many decades since I've lifted my eyes to such a sight. What a flood of memories this produces. As I close my eyes I can hear the beautiful old touring cars passing and even smell the sulfur from the chugging and belching old steam locomotive running along beside!

I didn't know what I'd find at Glenwood Park. I'm glad I didn't expect much. It's a large old abandoned wayside with grass growing through cracks in the asphalt. The vandals/thieves have found the well, pulled up the entire pipe and wire, and have stolen the pump, leaving a scattered mess behind. There's an old plaque by one of the still-standing picnic tables that somehow, miraculously, has avoided being smashed to smithereens. Under the Plexiglas (which is still intact) is a faded news clipping with a picture of some old chap who most likely had something to do with the park. The whole seedy place is blocked off from the road by the typical pipe barricade, which I pass as I head out for a welcome diversion on the highway.

I hike along NB 17 for approximately 3 miles then turn onto Upsalquitch River Road for a quiet roadwalk through this pleasant little valley. After some 5 miles the trail crosses the river on an old restored railroad bridge. I'm now back again on this not-much-fun multiuse old railroad bed. After a couple of miles on this foot bruiser, and with evening nigh, I'm ready to call it quits for the day. Up ahead I see a small building at a snowmobile trail intersection. This is apparently one of a number of warming huts placed at intervals along these trails. The door is unlocked and I enter to find my abode for the night . . . complete with picnic table, airtight wood-burning stove, and firewood stacked against the wall. My pack thermometer reads 46 degrees as I glance at it while dropping my pack to the table bench. It takes me less than five minutes to get a good roarin' fire going. I've forgotten how dry wood burns! Old candle-plugged bottles provide light as I cook supper right on the stove.

To complete my journal entry for today, I'll drop this little eyebrow scruncher. As I drifted off to sleep last evening, most-near dreamland, I envisioned someday finding a little old cabin beside the trail, complete with stove, tight walls, and a door that was left unlocked. This dreamland delight brought a gentle chuckle as the sandman finished me off! Tonight, as I bed down, cozy and warm in this little old cabin beside the trail, comes the realization that these unexplainable occurrences are the makings of this grand miracle I am living . . . the "Odyssey of '98!"

*"Nomad, you must certainly realize that you carry a
lot of other people's dreams with you on your odyssey."*
[Tom Wright, BMTA]

MONDAY October 5, 1998
TRAIL DAY 262/22 ✦ TRAIL MILE 3,915/353
LOCATION Pete Dube's Restigouche Hotel, Matapédia, Québec

A COOL, CLEAR DAY WEATHER-WISE, but I get off to a bumpy start
trail-wise. Just above the warming hut a new snowmobile trail crosses
Meadow Brook. The sign says "Squaw Cap Mountain, elev. 1,585 feet."
This trail does lead to Squaw Cap . . . eventually, but it isn't the trail I
should have been on. The climb to Squaw Cap is a steady, easy pull
along an old woodsroad-turned-snowmobile trail. Only the last half mile
requires much exertion. There's another warming hut on the summit
along with numerous towers, buildings, and fences. Not much to brag
about up here. The views are so-so, but most are blocked by some sort of
summit ornament. Squaw Cap is the third highest peak in New
Brunswick, but if you're out climbing mountains in this province I'd say
save your time and head for the second highest in Mt. Carleton
Provincial Park . . . that's Sagamook!

I get into trouble again coming off Squaw Cap. Recent and current
timbering operations north of the mountain have created a maze of logging roads. Most are rutted and choked with mud. More not-much-fun
treadway. I run into many dead ends and go through a "bushwhack from
hell" thinking I know where I'm going, eventually putting in double the
miles and time to get back down to NB 17. The hike along NB 17, until I
reach Rafting Ground Road, is dangerous. The shoulders are narrow to
nonexistent and the 18-wheelers are coming through steady and hard.

In just a while I meet up again with an old friend . . . the
Restigouche River. But here I am treated much more kindly! The 7
miles into Matapédia, Québec, make for a pleasant roadwalk and takes
only two hours. South of here, covering this distance took all day! I see
the town of Matapédia long before I arrive. In fact, I walk right by. It's
across the river in Québec, and the bridge is still a mile northeast as I

pull abreast of the town on the New Brunswick side, but I really don't mind the 2 more miles of walking. Sixteen states and one of the two Canadian provinces are behind me. Only Québec to go.

I'm so glad to be at Pete Dube's Restigouche Hotel in Matapédia! I arrive, totally bushed, at about 6:00 p.m. to be greeted by Pete. He welcomes me with an expression of amusement as he looks at the bedraggled old *Nomad*, but I receive a warm handshake and he shows me to a fine room. The Restigouche is a great place with large, clean rooms and a fine restaurant. I am having much trouble with my feet and need to get them up for a long rest. There just couldn't be a better place. Dang, Pete, I'm so glad to be here!

"Time, distance, terrain, weather and the trail itself cannot be changed.
You have to change."

[Warren Doyle, Jr.]

TUESDAY October 6, 1998
TRAIL DAY 263/23 ✦ TRAIL MILE 3,915/353
LOCATION Pete Dube's Restigouche Hotel, Matapédia

AFTER A VERY RESTFUL NIGHT'S SLEEP, I am already feeling somewhat renewed and rejuvenated. I remember seeing this little café on the way in last evening, so I head there for breakfast and some fresh-brewed coffee. It's only a couple of minutes to the café, Resto Le Temps Perdu, where I meet Marie Letourneau and Jerome Boldue. Good food, great folks.

I head on over to the post office at 9:00 a.m. to find that my bounce box hasn't arrived. I am distraught and get upset, but it's my own fault. When I looked at the New Brunswick map months ago, there in big bold print, was Matapédia. So I assumed Matapédia was in New Brunswick. It is in fact, however, in Québec, just across the border! So, not only did I show the wrong province on my bounce box, but I also failed to list a zip code or provide a return address. So, should there be any surprise my bounce box hasn't made it? Solange and Henry at the Matapédia Post Office are doing all they can to track it down.

David LeBlanc, who has been charged with SIA/IAT trail construction north of Matapédia, comes by in the evening with maps of this area. We talk strategy about how I should proceed to complete the remaining 250 miles to Cap Gaspé.

We calculated that even with the most optimistic estimate for my rate of progress, I wouldn't be scaling Mt. Jacques Cartier until around October 25. This is getting late to be above tree line in the Chic Chocs, so the decision is made to skip the section of trail between Matapédia and the Matane River for now and go up and get the Chic Chocs done.

> *"For most of us, I suppose, the Appalachian Mountains are in the United States and in the English language. Our books encourage us in this; they take us to New England borders, and stop there, just as though plants and animals were also controlled by artificial boundaries. Neither the mountains nor the living things are so controlled."*

[Maurice Brooks, *The Appalachians*]

WEDNESDAY October 7, 1998
TRAIL DAY 264/24 ✦ TRAIL MILE 3,915/353
LOCATION Pete Dube's Restigouche Hotel, Matapédia

STILL NO LUCK ON MY BOUNCE BOX, but a box of goodies sent to me by *Easy Rider*, with the same incorrect and incomplete address, has come in, so I have been encouraged to be patient. I am optimistic now that my bounce box will soon arrive. Another great day of rest at Pete's place!

> *"By walking out alone into wilderness I can . . . after a while begin to see and hear and to think and in the end to feel with a new and exciting accuracy."*

[Colin Fletcher, *The Complete Walker*]

THURSDAY October 8, 1998
TRAIL DAY 265/25 ✦ TRAIL MILE 3,915/353
LOCATION Pete Dube's Restigouche Hotel, Matapédia

I HAVE HAD AN OFFER FOR A RIDE FROM MATAPÉDIA to the Matane River north of here for Friday afternoon by Bruno, one of the members of David's trail construction crew, so I decide to rest another day. Pete encourages me to remain his guest here at the hotel, so here I stay for another much-needed day of rest!

> *"It was so exciting to find out what was around the next corner, or across the rushing river ahead, or to see who we might meet in the next town or café."*

[Peter Jenkins, *A Walk Across America*]

FRIDAY October 9, 1998
TRAIL DAY 266/26 ✦ TRAIL MILE 3,928/366
LOCATION Fir Stand, Hunting Zone 13A, Matane Reserve

ANOTHER GREAT NIGHT OF REST at the Restigouche Hotel. I open one eye to glint out the window into the fog and haze. The forecast is for this sludge to burn off, opening up a warm, sunny day. I finally roll out at 9:00 a.m., dress, and trundle over to Resto Le Temps Perdu. Loading up is always the order of the day before heading back up the trail, so this morning it's a three-egg mushroom omelet and a double order of home fries. Ditto on the toast, and Marie has to put on another pot of coffee before I'm done. Then it's across the Matapédia River bridge to the little grocery store for provisions. I figure to pack an eight-day supply of food to get into the Chic Chocs. Then it's to the other end of town for a stop at the pharmacy for more enteric-coated aspirin and a bottle of Osteo Bi-Flex, the chondroitin/glucosamine tabs the pharmacist had kindly ordered for me. I also pick up some rub-on salicylate to help relieve the near-constant foot pain I've been suffering since Maine. A final trip to the post office pays off. Henry has a smile for me and more mail that has trickled in under the wrong/incomplete address, including my bounce box!

Back at the Restigouche Hotel things are shutting down for the season. The restaurant closed last night after supper and this morning the rear section of the hotel is being secured. It's quite an ordeal. The rooms are all stripped for a final cleaning, then the mechanical systems are shut down and the entire water system is drained and purged.

In my room I set to getting my pack in order and the room straightened up. I find I have a little time before Bruno is due, so I clean and grease my boots. They really took a beating on the Restigouche River Trail (along with my poor doggies) and they sure look neglected. It's amazing what a little lanolin will do—just like new again! I finish my boots and am rubbing the last of the grease into my dry, chapped hands when comes a knock on my door. Bruno has wrapped up the week just as planned and is here right on cue. He still needs to run by the house and pick up his girlfriend, Carole. So I have time to get my backpack in order and head on down to the lobby. What a great stay I've had here. Thanks to all at the Restigouche, especially to you Pete! You have put me up (and put up with me) for four nights, stoked me with five-star food, and in addition to being a great host, you've become a dear friend. I will remain in your debt.

Bruno and Carole arrive, I load my pack, and we're off on a clear, sunny day to the Reserve Faunique de Matane, some 70 miles to the north. Bypassing this lower woodland section (to be hiked in a couple of weeks) should enable me to complete the Grand Traverse, the extensive, above-tree-line alpine section of the Chic Chocs, before the snow closes this tundra down. At least that's the plan! John Brinda traversed the Chic Chocs in late September/early October last year and hit snow then. Looks like I've still got "Indian Summer" with me. Anyway, I'm confident I'll have safe and successful passage. At the end of this two-hour ride, I have made another great friend in Bruno Robert. Just across the Matane River bridge is the entrance road to the Matane Reserve, and Bruno and Carole drop me off here before continuing on to visit friends in Matane, Québec. Thanks, Bruno! See you again when I return to Matapédia.

At the reserve entrance I meet Georgette Levesque. Bless her heart. I get a great big smile as I come through the door, which quickly turns to a full-faced frown as she discovers I speak no French! During the next half hour we progress from "No hike, closed, moose hunting" to "only hike ten to three, mandatory!" This progress, a transitional process, results from a telephone conversation with her supervisor. After explaining to him that I have a regulation orange vest (which Bruno had the foresight to suggest I use, and then loaned to me) things start to loosen up. First he says the reserve is closed to hiking during moose hunting season. "It's for your own safety" was the reasoning. Trying not to sound facetious, I ask, "Are you not concerned about the hunters' safety during moose hunting season?" His reply: "Of course we are." Sooo, for the coup de grace, I ask, "Then why isn't the reserve closed to hunters during moose hunting season?" After a very long pause he says, "Put the lady back on the phone." So out from under the counter come the reserve permit and a map, but I'm still stuck with "only hike ten to three, mandatory!" There is no resistance, however, and not a word is said as I head out the door and on up the reserve road . . . at 4:30!

The hiking days are really getting short now and I must strap on my little Petzl headlamp as I pull off the reserve road to pitch camp under a fir canopy in "Zone 13A." Hunters are still bouncing and rattling by with their rigs loaded with ORVs and camping gear as I enter slumberland in my cozy little Slumberjack.

"Half the confusion in the world comes from not knowing how little we need."

[Richard E. Byrd, *Alone*]

SATURDAY October 10, 1998
TRAIL DAY 267/27 ✦ TRAIL MILE 3,946/384
LOCATION Etang à la Truite, Hunting Zone 19, Matane Reserve

THE BOUNCING AND RATTLING STARTS AGAIN at daybreak as the procession of hunters entering the reserve continues. Complying with the "mandatory" isn't difficult as I catch a few more winks and then lounge in my bag with some Pop-Tarts for breakfast. I break camp in the cool, clear of this morning and fudge a little as I pull back on the road at 9:30 a.m.

The sun is warm on my face, but for only a brief time as a stiff wind starts kicking out of the east and the sky "darks over." I stop in the lee just over a little pop on the ridge to garbage-bag my pack, zip my rain jacket, and cinch the hood; then I'm back out to brace the day. My head cold is pretty much cleared up, but my nose still wants to drip on the map every time I look down at it. Not to worry, though, as it'll fit fine in my stack of smudgy, spotty maps! I'm into a steady pull, which started at the reserve entrance and continues throughout the morning. The rain holds off but the wind persists, and it's turning cutting cold as I detour over to a hunter's lodge at Lac Matane.

I tap on the window to get the attention of a hunter sitting comfortably by the woodstove. As he looks out I rub my hands together and blow on them as if to say, — "I'm cold. Can I come in by the fire?" The mime works and he motions me to come around to the door. As I enter, a young lady clearing dishes from the lodge table greets me. I say, "Hello, how are you?" And she replies, "Fine, how are you?" Hey! The gal speaks English! She continues, "Take off your pack and have a seat . . . would you like a warm bowl of soup?" From what I've written the past few days, it's evident the great Canadian hospitality didn't end at the New Brunswick/Québec border. The delicious, hot bowl of soup is followed by another and then a tall cup of steaming coffee, accompanied by a plate of brownies topped with an absolutely heavenly white fudge sauce . . . and then more coffee!

The conversation with the hunter who motioned me in amounts to little more than a nod as he speaks very little English. But soon another hunter enters the lodge, and when I say "Hi!" he replies, "Hi, how ya doin'?" Bingo! Turns out the chap's from New Hampshire. Over the course of the next few minutes I find out how the Matane hunting operation works. Turns out the moose hunting season here in Québec is a lot longer than in New Brunswick. Down there it's only three days, and if you're a resident and you're lucky you'll get your name drawn from a lottery. But here in Québec, most anybody can purchase a hunting license and pick up their gun and go. Here in the reserve, however, the Crown owns the land, and they've built these beautiful lodges. They pretty much handle the entire setup for you also, including guides. It's such a jam-up operation and there's such a demand to hunt here (there are also a lot of moose) that a lottery must be held. I didn't have the heart to ask the fellow how much he was plunking down for the four-day hunt, the Ritz lodge and meals, the guide service, and all the haulin' around, plus, hopefully, his moose!

No problem lingering in this warm, comfortable place, but I manage to get back out within the hour. As soon as I step off the porch the rain begins. The road continues climbing, and as it pulls, I push on against the wind and rain. I've become very chilled, but by late afternoon the wind slacks off, the rain slows, and it seems to warm a little as I hike on to the offices at Etang à la Truite.

As soon as I reach the office, the door opens and out steps a lady with that grand Canadian ear-to-ear grin, and a big "Hi!" Before I can return the greeting she says, "Follow me, we'll get the bunkhouse open for you." And then she hesitates, saying: "You are staying for the night, aren't you?" I manage an awkward blurt, "Yes, I mean yes ma'am, I'd like to stay. It seems you knew I was coming!" She smiles again, "Yes. Georgette at John (that's the name of the reserve entrance) called me yesterday and told me to watch for you!" As we enter the bunkhouse I tell her I'll not be able to pay very much for the room. With that she whirls around and with her eyebrows up and her dander up exclaims, "You pay nothing here; you pay nothing. It is for you!" With that I finally manage, "Hello, I'm Eb, friends just call me *Nomad.*" So, here I meet Marlene Simard from Matane, Québec. She tells me about her great job—lots of responsibility, but she likes it very much. Come to find out, she caretakes the facilities from Lac Matane all the way to the reserve's eastern boundary.

The building warms quickly. There's a gas heater and an airtight wood-burning stove to help it along. The bunkrooms are complete with mattresses and pillows. And I've got electric lights (the generator runs all night), a full kitchen, including table and chairs . . . and the shower is steaming hot with shove-me-back pressure. And I was just gonna ask if they'd mind me pitching my tent in their yard! Hot coffee, a warm meal quickly and easily prepared on the kitchen range, and a table to sit comfortably and enjoy my supper. What else could a weary, cold hiker possibly want?

Well, why not a little friendly conversation? Marlene had said to come over for a while this evening after I got settled in, so over I go. I'm greeted at the door by Arthur Bernier, and at his invitation and even before I can reach the kitchen table I've got a cold one shoved in my hand! After some conversation and a downed brew, attention turns to the maps I've laid out on the table. I tell Arthur I have a few questions. "Let's have a look," he says, as he brings another round from the refrigerator. I explain that my concern, and the problem I'm having, is figuring how to get from the route Georgette told me to follow through the Matane Reserve, to the trail in Parc de la Gaspésie. The maps for both the reserve and the *parc* show Mont Logan—the reserve map near its eastern extreme, and the *parc* map close by its western boundary. But neither shows a connector trail. Georgette at John couldn't help me, and none of the folks at Lac Matane Lodge were familiar with that area. Arthur, however, is able to give me very detailed instructions and directions . . . right to the familiar bright SIA/IAT metal blazes! After the map review, it is getting late and as I bid goodbye and turn to the door, both Arthur and Marlene press Canadian bills into my hand. As I depart I'm wished farewell with that great Canadian smile and a "When you reach Gaspé, celebrate and have a good meal on us!" Thank you, dear friends, for your genuine kindness and warm hospitality. I will long remember this day and the miracle of it!

I could get up early tomorrow and do the 24 miles into the *parc* . . . but I'll probably be a good fellow, sleep in, and comply with the "mandatory!"

> *"Miracles can . . . be identified in hindsight by the*
> *positive, often profound changes they make in our lives."*
> [Joan Wester Anderson, Where Miracles Happen]

SUNDAY October 11, 1998
TRAIL DAY 268/28 ✦ TRAIL MILE 3,946/384
LOCATION Etang à la Truite, Hunting Zone 19, Matane Reserve

BEFORE MIDNIGHT THE RAIN PICKS UP STEADY AGAIN and continues all night. I awake around 8:30 a.m., stumble to the door, and stick my head out. The rain is not only hard and steady . . . it's hard, steady, and very cold—a bad combination. So I throw another log on the fire to get it stoked up, have a bowl of cereal, and go back to bed.

The rain doesn't let up all day so I stay in the sack to keep my feet up. I have no problem with a few extra Zzzzs. I hand-wash all my socks and pants and get some writing done. Marlene stops by for a minute to say she's glad I've stayed over and to tell me this rain should clear out tonight. I'm in the sack by 9:00 p.m., countin' my blessings!

> *"Knowing God's own time is best, in patient hope I rest."*
>
> [John Greenleaf Whittier]

MONDAY October 12, 1998
TRAIL DAY 269/29 ✦ TRAIL MILE 3,970/408
LOCATION Heated shelter, Mont Louis-Marie-La Londe,
Parc de la Gaspésie

I AWAKE TO A GLORIOUS, CLEAR MORNING! After fixing a grand breakfast of hot Pop-Tarts from the toaster, coffee, and a big bowl of cereal, I get my pack organized, straighten the place up, and I'm out the door at 8:00 a.m. I bid farewell to Arthur and I'm headed for Parc de la Gaspésie. The road follows the shore of the lake for about 3 miles, a very pretty setting. I see lots of moose tracks all along and two of the track makers, a cow with a young one. Would that be a calf?

At 9:45 a.m. a vehicle pulls alongside and stops. Out hops a fellow in a very impressive, dark . . . uniform! It's one of the wardens. I'm thinking I'm in the deep doo now, for sure, but he has that ever-familiar big smile for me as he exclaims: "You must be faraway hiker." He follows that up with "You know you shouldn't be in this reserve, it's moose hunting season . . . but we make exception for you!" I promptly thank him and introduce myself. His name is Luc Forest (honest)! I have to answer the usual questions, after which he wishes me a good hike and I'm on my way again.

The road is rising steadily, and before I reach the *parc* boundary I'm pulling about a 30 percent grade. At the ridgeline and following Arthur's directions I pick up the familiar SIA/IAT blazes, and just to the left of this first blaze, in a jumble of rocks, is a blanket of snow. Even at this below-summit elevation I'm already in the alpine zone where the few trees that are around are stunted and definitely in a struggle to survive. From this lower ridge vantage, to the west, I can see the stark shoulders of Mont Logan reaching to the clouds and on up (down) the trail to the east, the turquoise roofs of two magnificent shelters. It is only 4:00 p.m., but I have made very good time for the 24 miles, so this will be it for today.

I don't know how anyone could pass up one of these beautiful dwellings . . . yes indeed, dwellings! They are like small live-in cabins, complete with porch (enclosed with doors and windows), woodstove with attached wood shed and internal door thereto, a main room with a thermal picture window (looking back toward Mont Logan), and two separate bunkrooms to accommodate a total of eight people. The bunkrooms are complete with two bunk beds each . . . with mattresses. Interior walls are knotty pine, tongue and groove. These things are downtown! I quickly get a fire going with the supply of birch bark, kindling, and matches provided. Chairs (plenty of them) are the plastic outdoor type with backs and arms. The privy is just out the door and water is right down the road. Cooking supper is easy; I just set my pot on the woodstove. Hot coffee right away! With all my chores wrapped up by 5:30 p.m., I am able to relax on the heated porch and watch the sunset over Mont Logan. I gaze in awe, as this breathtaking setting is slowly transformed into purple mountain majesty. The Chic Chocs are gonna be magic. I can see it already; they're just gonna be magic!

The room is warm, the bunk very comfortable. Wonderful, restful sleep, here I come!

> *"Have you ever heard of the Land of Beyond,*
> *That dreams at the gates of the day?*
> *Alluring it lies at the skirts of the skies,*
> *And ever so far away."*

[Robert W. Service, *The Land of Beyond*]

TUESDAY October 13, 1998
TRAIL DAY 270/30 ✦ TRAIL MILE 3,992/430
LOCATION Old cabin (Le Pluvier), Lac Cascapédia, Parc de la Gaspésie

I BANKED AND DAMPED THE FIRE JUST RIGHT LAST NIGHT. My little pack thermometer read 72 degrees when I awoke this morning at 7:00 a.m. I take it with me to the privy to check the temperature outside, as there is frost all around. The mercury keeps dropping, finally to steady at 26 degrees. My poor little skin-and-bone hiney records a temperature more in the zero-degree range as it contacts the privy seat! Plenty of reading material, all in French . . . just as well, as the cold creates a definite urgency to get a move on (no pun intended). Back in the warm shelter, there are just enough coals to boil some water for coffee and to toast a couple of Pop-Tarts. I have used little of the resources here, but I must try to find the caretakers of this delightful place and thank them for leaving the door unlatched. This luxury in the Chic Chocs I won't soon forget!

I bundle up and am on my way by 8:00 a.m. My hands and feet stay warm as the old jitney gets up to normal operating temperature. The trail ascends a little pop on the ridge and as I crest the rise I stop with mouth agape and in total amazement and disbelief at what I see below! To set this stage, and as a reminder . . . Do we not appreciate the fact that we are prisoners of the medium TIME? We are enslaved by it, moving only as it moves and at its whim, to be kept constantly within its grip. But this morning for a brief moment, I break away from the bonds of captor time to move freely back through the ages and to a far-off land. For, as I peer at the mountains below me and to the horizon, I see scores and scores of sharp-peaked summits marooned on a perfect sea of white. Formed as if from mirrored glass float these vapors in near-blinding brilliance, likened to the sun playing its intense narrow band of light across a still, calm lake. But here, visualizing such a likeness, imagine this incredible brilliance to be omnipresent, with light emerging from every angle, merging in every direction. As my time machine whirrs and clanks to a halt, I find myself atop a south-sea island peak . . . possibly Tahiti's

Mt. Orohena, circa the mid-18th century. And from this vantage, likely due to the illusion optics can play with angular light, I see two small cloud tufts transformed into perfect, three-masted tall ships, their pure white sails billowing, set full sail on this mystic, shimmering, mirage of sea. Could this perhaps be John Byron leading Her Majesty's ships the Dolphin and the Tamer? Or, perchance might one of them be Fletcher Christian and his mutineers aboard *HMS Bounty*? Ahh! But the clutch of time is infinitely strong, and as the sun works its magic to quickly lift and consume this cloud sea in just a finger snap of time, I am once again earthbound on this grand, high ridge near the sky, in Parc de la Gaspésie.

I must admit to some blue-blazing today. There is no other choice. Recent heavy rains have made a quagmire of the treadway here on the west end of the *parc*. Progress is brought to near a halt, more a churning action than forward motion. It's January déjà vu. I churned in mud for days in Florida at the start of this odyssey. Reluctantly, I move to the woodsroad, which makes for a 23-mile day, instead of an 18-mile one. The road follows some very happy streams and brooks and I am entertained most of the afternoon by their joyful songs. I try to concentrate on the scenic wildness of the *parc* and listen to the brooks' glad melodies as they rush to the lakes below, but in spite of my very best effort I think almost constantly about . . . my pitiful feet! The pain is unending and unnerving. So I stop, take off my boots, and slather on some more aspirin cream. This brings some relief as I switch to my running shoes for the afternoon. The miles are taking their toll — 270 days and nearly 4,000 miles — a long way and a long time to be on your feet through indescribable terrain, carrying a 30-pound pack. Not only is this odyssey near its end, but I am near ready for the end. Oh, but do I have some exciting days ahead of me, for tomorrow I will gain the tundra over Mont Albert and soon after that, Jacques Cartier, the highest peak in southern Québec. Then next week it's on to the Cliffs of Forillon at Cap Gaspé, the end of the SIA/IAT and the Appalachian Mountains.

As I am walking the road along Lac Cascapédia and as I near my destination for today, a pickup coming toward me slows and stops. Here I meet Adrien Pelletier, concessionaire for Club Grand Yetis (French for "Bigfoot"), a lakeside resort of old but modernized, well-maintained log cabins. This old camp is now on Crown land as are all the beautiful cottages and heated shelters in the *parc*. After responding to the usual questions, Adrien asks where I stayed last night and where I'm headed today. Come to find out he is also the concessionaire for the shelters at Mont Louis-Marie-La Londe where I spent the evening last. He says, "You know you need reservation and must pay to stay in shelter?" I reply that I could not pay much, but that I did burn some of his firewood and that I could pay for that. Then, with the customary broad-beaming Canadian smile he says: "Someone who has walked so far we do not see; you are my guest, and tonight you stay at Le Pluvier, the end cabin on the lake. There is firewood there for you." He is obviously very pleased as I accept his hospitality. I thank him, am on my way again, and within just a few moments I arrive at the old camp on Lac Cascapédia.

Here is the artist's perfect setting, an old log cabin on the lake. How many of these landscapes have we all seen . . . how many can there be? Seeing those faded old paintings always brings a feeling of peace and calm, a trip back in time to a warm, snug place, a time when the pace was slower and the basics were a way of life. Here is that old cabin, nestled snugly on the tranquil shores of this alpine lake, with its meandering shoreline edged with slender, spire-shaped evergreen. And reflected on the lake from across, and all around, the grand, sharp-peaked mountains that are the Chic Chocs. This is indeed a picture-book setting. The old cabin has such a proud character—patina o'er the log walls, the windows and floors that only time could possibly have created. From the old lean-to porch stacked high with split birch firewood, there is an unobstructed view across the calm, peaceful lake, clear to the far shore. Give me a minute or two while you set up your easel and prepare your canvas and I'll get a fire going so you can paint the swirl of smoke from the old stone chimney! And in just a few moments I have that warming and cooking fire going and I settle in, snug and warm in this little old log cabin on the lake . . . the artist's perfect setting from a far-off time and a faraway place.

> *"I shall be telling this with a sigh*
> *Somewhere ages and ages hence:*
> *Two roads diverged in a wood, and I —*

I took the one less traveled by,
And that has made all the difference."

[Robert Frost, *The Road Not Taken*]

WEDNESDAY October 14, 1998
TRAIL DAY 271/31 ✦ TRAIL MILE 4,005/443
LOCATION Heated shelter, Mont Albert Campground

THE TOPOGRAPHIC MAP OVER WHICH THE *parc* trail system is printed
and the trail profile map both seem tame in comparison to what I'm
used to studying. Neither gives a clue to the ruggedness of the terrain
and the extreme of the elevation changes experienced today . . . then it
dawns on me. The contour lines on these maps are in meters, not feet!
The climb up and over Mont Ells is long and very steep. Ditto for
Mont Albert. The hike today is like no other trail I've ever traveled.
The alpine tundra is a rugged yet fragile place. The few plants and trees
that are here are stunted and cling to the rock in what seems such an
anxious way, their life constantly in the balance. I thought I'd seen rock
on Mt. Washington, through the Presidents, on Mt. Katahdin, and
along the Knife-Edge to Pamola, but they pale in comparison to the
rock flanks and ravines of Mont Albert. Here the entire mountainside is
rock, the likes of which I've never seen before, almost volcanic in
nature; not gray, but light tan to dark brown, colors like a hunter's fall
camo, or like the paint of desert warfare. Even in the sunlight these
walls of rock and the endless jumble of boulders cast cold, ominous, and
forbidding shadows. I feel unwelcome, for here I am certainly not "at
one with nature!" I hasten along and feel much better hiking back
down among the trees again.

The descent from Mont Albert goes down, down, and down some
more to eventually emerge by the beautiful lodge Le Gite du Mont
Albert. I have been told that Gilbert Rioux, the concessionaire for the
lodge and campground, is an avid outdoorsman and hiker. It was suggested that I contact him for lodging once here. So with a call to Mr.
Rioux by Pam, the lodge receptionist, I'm a guest at the heated (and
lighted) campground bunkhouse. After I get a shower, do some laundry,

and have a great evening meal, I head for the bunkhouse to find I have it all to myself. In fact there are three bunkhouses, and I have the entire compound to myself! Here are top-flight accommodations: electric lights, large tables and benches, a woodstove right in the center of the room (with wood box full of birch firewood already split), bunks for eight, and "his and her" heated bathrooms right nearby. With birch bark and birch firewood, I quickly get a comfortable warming fire going and settle in for a very pleasant evening. I can even get around after dark without my headlight. Thanks, Gilbert, for your hospitality!

> *"If it's blessings you're a'countin'*
> *Try a morning in the mountains."*
>
> [Jim *Walkin' Jim* Stoltz]

THURSDAY October 15, 1998
TRAIL DAY 272/32 ✦ TRAIL MILE 4,009/447
LOCATION Heated shelter, Lac aux Américains, Parc de la Gaspésie

---

I AM UP AND BACK DOWN TO THE RESTAURANT at Le Gite du Mont Albert when they open at 7:30 a.m. The lodge is a very fine facility and the restaurant, exceptionally so. The roofs on the lodge, restaurant, and adjacent buildings have a very steep 14/12 or perhaps even a 16/12 pitch, characteristic of alpine construction. In the restaurant, the ceiling is cathedral with large timber-peg beams. The stone fireplace rises the full height, which draws your gaze to the high-angled beams above. But enough of this . . . here comes breakfast! This morning I have a four-egg bacon, onion, and mushroom omelet, a double order of toast and home fries, and perhaps half a gallon of coffee!

Descending Mont Albert yesterday and nearing the parking area, I noticed the trail was roped off with a sign attached indicating that Mont Albert was closed for the season. When I inquire this morning at the lodge desk, receptionist Chantal tells me that Mont Jacques Cartier is also closed. Aww! Now wait a minute here! I've come the entire Appalachian chain, am in the shadow of the last great mountain . . . and it's closed! This just can't be happening! The *parc* has an information office just adjacent to the lodge and I had gone by there yesterday evening a bit after 5:00 to find it closed. I thought I'd just gotten there late, but Chantal says that the information office is also closed for the season. In a recent issue of *Backpacker* magazine there's a great article about the SIA/IAT titled *The Province of Dreamers*, written by Paul Mann. In this article, Paul mentions getting a special permit to enter the *parc*'s higher elevations after they had closed. Chantal says the main offices for the *parc* are in Ste-Anne-des-Monts, a local call away, and that she would be glad to call them for me and explain my circumstances. As I watch her talking with the *parc* official, not understanding a word she is saying, I am hoping her expression, which remains very pleasant, is a good sign—and indeed it is. After providing them my name, address, etc., a faxed permit appears right there on the counter! Thanks, Chantal, for this great help. And thank you, François Boulanger, minister of Parc de la Gaspésie!

Back at the bunkhouse I get my pack in order, sweep the room out, and am on my way—in a drizzle—toward Mont Jacques Cartier. The climb begins immediately as I head to Lac aux Américains. The drizzle increases steadily, changing to a constant wind-driven rain and it's also turning cold. There is a heated shelter near the lake and I head for it. When I arrive, the rain is pounding and my little Campmor pack thermometer reads 38 degrees. Wet and cold is a very bad combination and I'm definitely feeling the initial stages of hypothermia as I enter the cabin. With the aid of birch bark and dry wood chips from the woodshed I'm able to get a much-welcome warming fire going. I look at my watch. It's only 11:00 a.m., but it looks like this hiking day is already at an end. Here at the cabin I am at an elevation of 600 meters above sea level. The traverse from Mont Xalibu to Mont Jacques Cartier, a distance of some 2 miles, is all above 1,000 meters and at times reaching 1,200 meters, twice the elevation here at the cabin, most of it above tree line. So I can pretty much figure what's going on up there right now— driving snow, and plenty of it!

In my last phone conversation with my older son, Jay—after explaining that this hike wasn't over yet, having the Chic Chocs ahead and probably some severe weather to boot—he said, "Dad, don't try pushing on when you know you should stop. Wait for another day."

Time to apply that logic, so it appears! The cabin warms quickly as I roll
out my sleeping bag and climb in to stop the shivers and wait it out. This
day has been a serious "darkin' over" day. The rain does not relent, continuing past dusk and into the night. As I prepare my hot evening meal
of rice and gravy, I think of how fortunate I am to be warm and dry in
this little cabin . . . and I thank the Lord for these blessings.

> *"Thro' many dangers, toils, and snares,*
> *I have already come;*
> *'Tis grace has brought me safe thus far,*
> *And grace will lead me home."*

[John Newton, "Amazing Grace"]

FRIDAY October 16, 1998
TRAIL DAY 273/33 ✦ TRAIL MILE 4,009/447
LOCATION Heated shelter, Lac aux Américains, Parc de la Gaspésie

I AWAKE TO THE DIM LIGHT OF DAWN AROUND 7:00 A.M. The cabin
is completely engulfed in the wind-laden swirl. It rushes against the east
cabin wall only to turn and hasten back against the other side. The little
cabin shudders, not knowing which way to brace. If storms could be
angry or happy, this one would certainly be happy in knowing the anxiety
it is causing me. For, though this storm shows no signs of leaving soon, it
occasionally lifts its darkened shroud to reveal the forbidding starkness
above, and I can see the rock fortifications, the sheer walls and crags
above tree line slowly being transformed from steel-cold gray to pure-ice
white, as the storm hurls its force and fury against the escarpment.

Since entering the Appalachians in central Alabama in late
February, I have scaled the summits of countless hundreds of mountains
all along this ancient and timeless range. And now here I sit, stormbound
all this day, pondering the not unlikely possibility of being turned back at
the base of the very last peak. And as I think these thoughts, a feeling of
sadness and sorrow descends over me and I sigh in despair: "Dear Lord,
why have you forsaken me?" I have believed and have said repeatedly that
a path will be provided and that I will have safe and successful passage to

the completion of this odyssey, but now I am consumed with doubt. This mountain before me is tall and rugged and the ice and drifting snow that cap its crown are not my friends.

I get out briefly in the evening and make a dash to the privy. I also hasten to the little brook below the cabin. Here I am greeted and comforted by this playful friend as it sings its song and fills the cabin bucket. I am also comforted as I return to the snug little cabin to prepare my evening meal. For it is at this moment that a still, calm voice softly reverberates within me. "Be not of despair, for I am with you; we will climb this mountain together." Now with this contentment I sit alone at the cabin table, and during the next 45 minutes the remarkable "Ballad of the IAT," which will complete the last journal entry for this chapter, rolls from the end of my pencil.

Earlier, I was certain a dreadfully long, lonely, and restless night awaited me, but I know now that I will sleep peacefully to prepare for the journey on the morrow.

"Standing on the promises that cannot fail,
When the howling storms of doubt and fear assail.
By the living Word of God I shall prevail,
Standing on the promises of God."

[R. Kelso Carter]

SATURDAY October 17, 1998
TRAIL DAY 274/34 ✦ TRAIL MILE 4,016/454
LOCATION Heated shelter, Le Galene, Parc de la Gaspésie

I AWAKE JUST BEFORE DAWN AND TRY SQUINTING AWAY the sleep as I peer out the cabin window. And there they are! A momentary twinkle here, then there, as the stars work to recapture the sky. I feel a rush of excitement as I rise to prepare my first cup of coffee. But the exhilaration is short-lived as the morning dawns to a totally overcast sky. However, as the morning brightens I take yet a closer look to see momentary patches of blue here, then there. 'Tis now I quickly realize that the high altitude mush that had the entire area in its grip for the past two days is gone and the present cloud cover is no more than locally generated mountain weather, which usually burns off, in the absence of other clutter, by late morning.

By 9:00 a.m. the sky is clearing nicely to reveal the ice-covered mountain looming above me. In the past nine months I have climbed many mountains higher than this one, but as I gaze at its enormity—the ice and the rocks—it is a truly ominous sight. But I must go now and climb this mountain, for it stands as the final obstacle. I have prepared long and diligently for this test. I am confident now that, with the Lord's help, I will succeed.

So I sweep out the cabin, shoulder my pack, and head up the trail. The last two days of rain have made a quagmire of what was an already mushy treadway and progress is slow and difficult up to tree line. Here the ground is frozen. Footing is surprisingly good and progress improves considerably. As I continue to ascend, the rocks and frozen earth give way to snow and ice-covered boulders. I am able to avoid the worst ice by seeking footing in the lower, snow-covered rocks. Progress is very deliberate and very slow . . . but I have planned only a little over 7 miles today and I'm getting through! I am in snow and ice for the entire tableland traverse, some 4 miles, but the snow is never deeper than my knees and I never go down once in the ice-covered boulders. As it turns out, one of the unexpected problems, for which there is a quick fix, is the sun glare on the snow. I simply drop my pack, don my sunglasses, and off I go again!

At 2:00 p.m. I am standing on top of Mont Jacques Cartier! Such a strange thing, as I gaze over this wintry scene. The incredible show that is the snow and ice has not changed . . . just my perception of it. For now I look down totally mystified by its pure beauty. This morning I looked up totally mortified by its forbidding presence! The sky is wide and clear, not a wisp of haze as far as the horizon. The summit is pure white with ice and snow. As I sit and rest in the warming sun I feel the warm presence of a forgiving God. Forty-six hours—the time I was stormbound in the little cabin below—is such a short time . . . yet long enough for me to have felt forsaken. How slow and hesitant we are to believe, but how quickly we doubt. Sitting here now, doubt dispelled, faith restored, I am at peace. I will climb on over this mountain and I will successfully complete this odyssey. How, after all the Lord has carried me through, could I have doubted!

As I prepare to depart this place, and as I stop to really look (as Benton MacKaye would say, "Let us tarry awhile —till we see the things we look upon.") I realize that what I am looking upon I wrote about at the table in the little cabin last night! "You'll stand spellbound, while 'round you'll see, Mont Albert's skyland tundra. And to the north, clear to the sea, more of God's boundless wonder." So it must be that my spirit had already made this journey. And perhaps that is why I did not even slip once today in the treacherous ice-covered boulders . . . my spirit had already passed this way. I pause and turn for one more look at this wonderland and as I proceed, the sun-crusted snow crunches beneath my feet. And so I descend this last great mountain. There will be other obstacles in these remaining few days as I complete the northern part of this odyssey . . . But it is literally all down hill from here.

I arrive at the cluster of warming shelters at La Galene before 4:00 p.m. to find one of the shelters left unbattened and open for the winter. I quickly get a warming and cooking fire going, find some water in a nearby drainage, and settle in for the evening. Thank you, Lord, for this incredibly successful day!

> *"Oh mountaineer of time, upon your dizzy height*
> *What lies beyond the day? Beyond the night?*
> *You need not answer, for we're climbing too*
> *And soon enough —will come to share the view."*

[Edward Abbey]

SUNDAY October 18, 1998
TRAIL DAY 275/35 ✦ TRAIL MILE 4,031/469
LOCATION Mont-St-Pierre Motel, Mont-St-Pierre

WITH DAWN COMES A CRISP, CLEAR MORNING. The hike today is a roadwalk to the sea at Mont-St-Pierre, all downhill. As I descend I pass from the first clutches of winter back into the last throes of fall. Leaves scurry, carried along by the vagabond wind as it passes through. The unmistakable pungency of fall is still in the air. My senses know not what to believe as they are jolted from one season to the other.

I now pass by sugar maple groves with their kin all bound, as if fugitives, by the vascular-like tubing of the sap collectors. Workers are busy scurrying about as they secure for winter and prepare for spring, as countless cords of birch firewood are being stacked, the fuel to fire the boilers.

I now catch the first familiar odor of the sea and soon I get my first glimpse of its graceful lenticular arc as I crest a small hill. Soon I am at the small seaside village of Mont-St-Pierre. Turning the corner onto PQ 132 I enter the parking lot at the Mont-St-Pierre Motel. One of the motel room doors is open and as I pass, a woman comes out to greet me. It is the proprietor, Charlotte Auclair. The greetings up here are humorous yet wonderful—a great big smile, followed by a bubbly barrage of French. My response? An expression of dumbfounded befuddlement as I say, "I do not speak French." She responds, "I get my husband Raymond." As Raymond rounds the corner he stops to look at me. "You're a hiker; you come a long way?" After a brief explanation, he says, "You're the second one. John Brinda was here last year. You will stay, too. Are you hungry?" Not awaiting my response, he says, "Come with me, we'll have lunch."

Raymond is very knowledgeable about the SIA/IAT and speaks enthusiastically about it. He knows and has talked with Dick Anderson, SIA/IAT president. He also knows my good friends Pete Dube and David LeBlanc in Matapédia. After lunch, complete with dessert and more hot coffee prepared and served by Charlotte, I get to meet Raymond's folk who have come by. Lucette and Gerard Boily both speak fluent English and we have a grand time together. I recite a poem for them, "The Ballad of the IAT." They are both taken by it and I promise to give a copy to Raymond.

I spend a very relaxing evening with my feet up, working on my journal entries.

> *"Canada is populated by people who will live nowhere else. They are held in good part by the land . . . [They] share a rapture about the beauty of their country . . . Attached . . . by private ecstasies: Small, religious experiences that dissolve the senses, as when a loon cries across a still northern lake, or the ocean thunders against the rocks . . . or the eerie flickering of the Aurora Borealis above the ice."*

[June Callwood, *Portrait of Canada*]

MONDAY October 19, 1998
TRAIL DAY 276/36   ✦   TRAIL MILE 4,055/493
LOCATION Motel Du Rocher, Madeleine-Centre

CHARLOTTE OPENS THE RESTAURANT AT 7:00 A.M. and I am right there. She prepares a fuel-tank-filler breakfast of eggs, bacon, potatoes, toast, oatmeal (with maple syrup), and lots of coffee. Raymond joins me shortly to bring a dreary forecast of wind and rain for the day. I exclaim, "How can that be?" From this splendid breakfast table, front-row-seat vantage point we are enjoying the view of a clear sky and a calm sea as the warm morning sun bathes the towering rock walls which form the western end of the bay.

Raymond explains that the weather can change quickly here, and indeed it does! In a few short moments a full rainbow forms across the western wall and the sky and the now-gray precipice below "dark over" as a storm in total fury drives through hammering the building, whipping the sea to a rage. I sit in disbelief as this storm roars across. Not in any hurry to shoulder my pack and head along with this torrential train, I linger. Raymond talks about life in Mont-St-Pierre and I talk about life on the trail. As I finally head back to my room to prepare to leave, Raymond points to the beach. "Be sure to walk the paved sidewalk along the beach; that's the trail."

In a while, and as I depart, I pass in front of the restaurant. Raymond and Charlotte come to the front door and bid me farewell and a safe journey. As I turn to wave goodbye for the last time, Raymond motions, arms and voice high, "Go across to the sidewalk; that's the trail." and so I do! What a memorable time spent with these folks. They would accept no payment from me other than the pure excitement it seemed they enjoyed just having me as their guest. Thanks, dear friends! You are Canada to the core, the very best example of your country's generous and friendly people.

This will be a long day on the road, eight to nine hours, as I try to make the 25 miles into Madeleine. The rain decreases to drizzle and soon ends, but the wind continues all day. Fortunately it is at my back, to lift and propel me along. An enormous seawall, which the road follows right on top, leads the way along the shore. The wind keeps the sea whipped in a rage, causing it to constantly lunge and crash against the wall and onto the roadway. All along the walk today the mountains come to the sea, often ending abruptly in sheer granite walls and cliffs. As the road weaves its way along, grand vistas open and close to the fore and aft, much like slides projected on a screen as they pass one to the next. This helps make for an event-filled and seemingly short day.

Having arrived at the small seaside village, Rivière Madeleine, my destination for today, I stop at Restaurant Chez Mamie for supper. Annie Langlois, Mamie's daughter, is the proprietor, and her 16-year-old son, Gilbert Lemieux, greets me. Gilbert speaks fluent English and after a brief exchange I find that there is good news and bad news. The good news—I will be able to get a very fine spaghetti dinner. The bad news—the motel where I was planning to stay the night has just closed for the season. Gilbert says he will help me find a place to stay, so the urgency for me now turns to getting on with the spaghetti dinner! I am able to relax and enjoy my evening meal, for as I am being served, Gilbert tells me that the little motel I passed, by the church back in Madeleine-Centre, is open. The owner will not only drive the 5 miles to pick me up when I've completed my meal, but he will bring me back here for breakfast. Thanks, Gilbert, for your kindness and your help!

After supper, Leopold Du Rocher, the owner of Motel Du Rocher, is here to pick me up. He speaks good English, and on the ride back I must explain my odyssey. This brings a baffled expression to Leopold's face, which doesn't change until we reach Madeleine-Centre. The motel is right on the sea. It is very basic but also very clean and well kept. A hot tub of water feels luxurious to my tired, creaking old bones, and I'm able to get a very restful night's sleep.

> *"Canadians are not Americans who live in a colder cli-*
> *mate: They are different people. While they resemble*
> *Americans — wear the same jeans, use the same exple-*
> *tives, drink the same booze . . . goggle at the same cen-*
> *terfolds — they are not the same."*
>
> [June Callwood, *Portrait of Canada*]

TUESDAY October 20, 1998
TRAIL DAY 277/37 ✦ TRAIL MILE 4,069/507
LOCATION Motel Richard, Grande-Vallée

I HAVE MY PACK ORGANIZED AND AM OUT THE DOOR a little before 8:30 a.m. Leopold has offered to drive me back to Mamie's to resume my hike. As I wait by his office I am startled to hear his truck engine start. I'm right by the truck but didn't hear him come out. As I hoist my pack and head around to load up I realize there's no one in the truck! I guess up in this country, it's more a necessity than a luxury to have a remote-start feature on your vehicle. Scraping frost and climbing into an icebox every morning for months on end, I am sure, can get very old very fast. In moments Leopold emerges, I load up, and we're on our way to Mamie's. Thanks, Leopold!

Mamie's is open. I had a fine meal here last evening so I decide to head back in for breakfast. This is definitely a family operation as this morning I meet Mamie's other daughter, Rachele. A lovely place, great food, grand hospitality. Thanks, folks!

The roadwalk today changes dramatically from the cliffside meander of yesterday. The mountains are becoming more rugged and more persistent as they meet the sea, ending in vertical walls and under-cut cliffs, dropping directly to meet the eternal crashing waves of the sea. The road must now climb inland and take to the mountains, making for many long, hard ascents and descents. But PQ 132 is one of the most beautiful and enjoyable of all the roadwalks so far as each new valley, each new cove and inlet, reveals another delightful little Canadian village. The people of Québec take pride in ownership, and even though the dwellings in these small hamlets are all very modest, they are clean, freshly painted, and have well-kept yards. Here live some of the most friendly and happy people I've ever met, full of joyful enthusiasm and vitality. The riotous colors they've chosen to paint their little homes and cottages are just as bright and cheerful. Pure white with fire engine red trim is the most common combination, but it isn't unusual at all to see, for example, a caution-light yellow house with a purple roof and chartreuse trim! You absolutely cannot be sad or glum around these folks. You're just gonna smile and feel warm all over when you are greeted by these people and see these storybook places.

By early afternoon I am nearing Grande-Vallée and see a billboard advertising Dixie Lee Restaurant, so I make a beeline for the place as I polish up on my "Howdy, y'all." The place turns out to be a chain operation with headquarters I don't remember where. The food is so-so, served up in cardboard boxes with plastic utensils, and to my way, a little too expensive. Dixie Lee would be in trouble in Dixie. No self-respecting Southern boy would put up with the coleslaw for very long. But, like my Momma told me years ago, "If you can't say something nice . . ." well, okay folks, the fried chicken was okay. 'Nuff said!

I pulled the same stunt again today as yesterday. I hiked right by one of the very few motels still open this late in the season on my way to Petite Vallée, where the only lodging I can find is a pricey bed and breakfast. And it's turning cold and starting to rain. I hike on east to a small convenience/grocery store and finally get in out of it. After buying a few provisions and exhausting all possible local overnight alternatives (including pitching on the cold, wet ground in the rain), the owner's son, Jean François LeBreux, who speaks reasonably good English, offers to drive me back to the motel in Grande-Vallée. Here I am able to get a very nice room for a reasonable rate.

*"Few Canadians live more than an afternoon's drive
from wilderness. Beyond the towns are woods and lakes,*

and then rock, tundra, and ice that stretches to the top of the world."

[June Callwood, *Portrait of Canada*]

WEDNESDAY October 21, 1998
TRAIL DAY 278/38 ✦ TRAIL MILE 4,093/531
LOCATION Abutment ledge under roadway bridge near St-Yvon

AFTER A GOOD BREAKFAST AT A MOM 'N' POP just past Grande-Vallée, and sticking my thumb out along the same roadway I hiked yesterday, I manage a ride back to Jean François's little store. As I stop in to thank them and say farewell I am greeted with a steaming hot cup of coffee — yet another fine example of the wonderful Canadian hospitality. Thanks, folks!

As I hike on toward Cap Gaspé today, the mountains have their way with PQ 132, first forcing it up, then down, then thither, then yon. The wind keeps pushing as it drives a steady, cold rain against my back. It is late afternoon as I enter the restaurant La Maisonnée in the little seaside village of Cloridorme. Here Lena Richard, the waitress, greets me. She speaks very good English and I soon learn that the only motel in the area just closed for the season. I now know without question where the old phrase "A day late and a dollar short" comes from and I become quickly resigned to the fact that I will be pitching in the cold rain tonight. Lena and owner Denise Minville take obvious pity on my plight as I am served a generous and delicious evening meal, their compliments!

The rain has eased some and with a couple of hours of daylight remaining I decide to hike on. As I leave the little village of Cloridorme the road winds deeper into the mountains. In a while I descend to a narrow inlet cut deep into the hills. There are three very lovely lakes and a small, very picturesque waterfall. Between two of the lakes and just above the falls there is a bridge. Dusk is rapidly descending and the cold rain has returned to be the host for the evening. I decide to explore the bridge and to my delight I find a two-foot-wide ledge under the bridge, high and dry on the main abutment. Here I am not only out of the wind and the rain but have the comfort of the retained warmth of the day.

This is certainly not the Hilton but way up the scale from the blowing rain and the cold, wet ground. I lay my tent down for a ground cloth, roll out my sleeping pad and bag and roll in for a very comfortable, dry, and warm night's sleep. Few vehicles pass, their muffled sounds and gentle vibrations not the least bit disturbing.

> *"All men should strive,*
> *To learn before they die.*
> *What they are running from,*
> *And to, and why!"*
>
> [James Thurber]

THURSDAY October 22, 1998
TRAIL DAY 279/39 ✦ TRAIL MILE 4,105/543
LOCATION Flodo Motel, Rivière-au-Renard

AS DAWN REVEALS THE DAY, I OPEN ONE EYE to peer out across the lake being glazed by the still-present rain. I decide to snooze and give it another hour. Easy decision! Another hour makes all the difference, and it appears the sun may even show this morning. As I hoist my pack and head on east toward Gaspé (Micmac for "Land's End"), the realization comes that this will be my last day on this most enjoyable roadwalk by the St. Lawrence Sea. I had dreaded PQ 132 as I descended the Chic Chocs. But was I ever wrong! For already, though it has been just a short few days, I recall with a most-warm feeling of nostalgia my entrance into the little seaside village of Mont-St-Pierre, where I became immediate friends with Charlotte and Raymond at Motel Mont-St-Pierre. I fell instant captive to the spell of this little world by the sea, to the beauty, the wonder, and the mystique of this enchanted land. Today that trip through this spellbinding little isolated storybook corner of the world will end, and soon, too, will this entire journey.

The road quickly leads back to civilization as I again pass power poles and neat, well-kept cottages. The hike today leads through many lovely villages and again along the sea. The wind is much less troublesome and the day has turned most pleasant.

It is very easy to tell that it's moose hunting season up here. The successful hunters are all driving around with moose head hood ornaments. Yes, moose heads, antlers and all, strapped and lashed to their car hoods! Even the little Hondas. You can't even see the car coming down the road, just this huge moose head! The more ingenious have propped up the entire moose carcass on a specially built outdoor freezer rack/sawhorse right in their truck bed. These fellows are driving around with the meeses standing up in the back of their trucks! Folks, ya just gotta see this. It's a pure hoot!

I complete the roadwalk along the sea a little after 3:00 p.m. and check into the Flodo Motel in Rivière-au-Renard. I had been instructed to contact Raynald Bujold, superintendent of Parc National Forillon upon reaching Fox River ("Rivière-au-Renard" in French). I soon reach Raynald by phone at his home as he is preparing for a flight to Montreal. The folks at the *parc* were anticipating my arrival and Raynald greets me enthusiastically. He explains that the trail through the *parc* to the Cliffs of Forillon has just been completed and that maps and information about the *parc* would be brought to me at the motel.

Soon comes a knock on my door and here, in typical Canadian fashion (the warm smile and grand handshake), I meet Jacques Fournier, chief of Visitor's Services for Forillon. The people in Canada, it seems without exception, take great pleasure and enjoyment in their work, and Jacques speaks with contagious excitement as we pore over the maps, brochures, and booklets he has brought for me.

> *"Does the road wind up-hill all the way?*
> *Yes, to the very end.*
> *Will the day's journey take the whole long day? . . .*
> *From morn to night, my friend."*

[Christina Georgina Rossetti, *Up-Hill*]

FRIDAY October 23, 1998
TRAIL DAY 280/40 ✦ TRAIL MILE 4,125/563
LOCATION Auberge de Cap-aux-Os, Grande-Grève

THE EXCITEMENT ABOUT CAP GASPÉ and Forillon is indeed contagious as I find that I am filled with anticipation this morning, anxious to get going and into Parc Forillon. Out of Rivière-au-Renard the trail is a roadwalk of approximately 8 kilometers to the new treadway on the west end of the *parc*. As I hasten along, a vehicle stops and a young man walks back to greet me. It is Luc Tremblay, a reporter with *Le Journal de Québec*. He wants to interview me and take pictures, but I discourage him as I explain that I have far to go today and must not tarry. We do, however, make arrangements to get together early in the morning at the youth hostel at Cap-aux-Os where I'll be staying the night.

I am soon on the fresh-cut trail and begin the ascent into the mountains of Cap Gaspé. Jacques had mentioned last evening that I would be the first to thru-hike the SIA/IAT in Parc Forillon, and this adds all the more excitement to the day. The morning is cool and clear and the views from the ridge down into the Fox River Valley are panoramic. As I scan to the horizon I see the winding river, the lovely, neatly kept homes along the valley road, and at the horizon, sitting on the sea, the quiet and peaceful village of Rivière-au-Renard. It humbles me to know that I am the first to experience what will bring pleasure and joy to all who follow on this adventure-filled path.

The trail, although long today, is very enjoyable, passing many fine ponds, each with its resident moose. As evening draws nigh and as the sun begins its exit in a blaze, the ridgeline and far-reaching summits are set afire. I linger at the last overlook for the day, a beautiful deck complete with railing and benches, and gaze with repose at the wonder before me, the timeless and magnificent Appalachian Mountains that are Cap Gaspé. I then hurry off the mountain to the road below in the last fading shadows of the evening.

The youth hostel, Auberge de Cap-aux-Os, is a clean, well-kept facility. I am greeted by Alain Fortin, my host, and he shows me all around. After settling in and preparing supper in the very fine kitchen, I make arrangements with Alain's good friend Maryline Smith to pick me up at the *parc*'s east parking lot at 3:00 p.m. tomorrow. For tomorrow, at Cap Gaspé, the Gulf of St. Lawrence, I will reach the end of the Appalachian Mountains, where they plunge to the sea at the spectacular Cliffs of Forillon.

I have the pleasure of sharing a room this evening with Patrice Lasserre, a young lad from Toulouse, France. He speaks very good English as we talk about our respective countries and our mutual interest in the sport of motorcycling. He gets a faraway and longing glint in his eye as he speaks about Muriel, the lovely lass he hopes to marry.

> *"My first approach to the Gaspé was anything but . . . dispassionate. I wasn't prepared for the beauty of the region. . . . Blessed is the land whose fulfillment is greater than its promise."*
>
> [Maurice Brooks, *The Appalachians*]

SATURDAY October 24, 1998
TRAIL DAY 281/41 ✦ TRAIL MILE 4,136/574
LOCATION Church boarding house, Gaspé

I AM AWAKE AT FIRST LIGHT. Even though there will be five full days of hiking north from Matapédia, I am excited about arriving this day at the Cliffs of Forillon, the Gulf of St. Lawrence and the Atlantic Ocean, for today I reach the northernmost section of this odyssey.

I get my pack together and hurry to the kitchen for a quick breakfast of Pop-Tarts, bananas, and coffee. Luc Tremblay is Johnny-on-the-spot at 6:30 a.m., and we spend some time together for the interview. The deal that I had cut with Luc yesterday was that if I promised to take some time with him first thing in the morning, he would drive me back up the mountain to where the trail crosses the road. That arrangement works well, as he wants to hike some with me this morning, so we're off to the trail. We arrive in good order at 7:00 a.m. Luc hikes along and we enjoy each other's company for a while as the trail again ascends to the ridgeline. Luc gets the answers to his questions and takes a few more pictures before departing to spend the day with his family. (A fine article complete with a photo appeared on page two of *Le Journal de Québec* the following Monday.)

The treadway now is some of the finest and the scenery some of the most spectacular I've seen o'er this entire odyssey. The vista, provided by a tower on the north shore, offers a sweeping 360-degree view. This morning Cap Bon Ami is blocked sharply against the sun, which casts its narrow shimmering highway of pure brilliance from the sea's crescent horizon past the looming granite walls of Bon Ami. Here, where the cliffs meet the sea, is a scene paradoxical, the granite walls quiet, unmoving, serene, and steadfast; the sea raging, hammering, a symphony of sound, relentless . . . a cacophonous calm! From the west and the south come the Appalachians from Alabama—to the east and the north, descending, at the sea!

The day passes quickly and I soon find myself standing before the old lighthouse overlooking the Cliffs of Forillon. Near the lighthouse a foundation is being prepared where a monument will soon be placed marking the terminus of the SIA/ IAT. Here I prop up my pack with my Leki poles to create my own monument to commemorate my hike and also to commemorate this magnificent SIA/IAT. I get out a homemade sign that reads "Cap Gaspé, 10-24-98, *Nimblewill Nomad*, Odyssey '98," prop it against my pack, and take a few pictures.

I follow the trail beside the cliffs to the waters of the Atlantic where the mountains disappear below the waves to the ocean floor. Standing here at the water's edge and looking at the cliffs and the end of this—a mysterious, grand, and glorious scheme of things that are these ancient and near-timeless Appalachian Mountains—I realize that for these mountains there is an end, not perhaps in time, but certainly in space. In terms of the presence of man on this planet and that span of time, these mountains are truly immortal . . . and I consider the frailty of man and my own mortality. Soon the last chapter in my life will be written not only in time but also in space as my remaining days flow to their end, much as these mountains flow to their end here at the sea.

Once back at the lighthouse I linger in its shadow. A flood of emotions descends as I turn to leave. I am an old man now and I must face the reality of it. But I'll live out these remaining days with a deep inner contentment in knowing that few have lived any part of their lives with the intensity that I have lived during the miracle of this incredible odyssey.

Mary meets me at the parking lot and we are off to Gaspé on what seems like a long, long ride.

> *"Though here at journey's end I lie*
> *In darkness buried deep,*
> *Above all towers strong and high,*
> *Beyond all mountains steep,*
> *Above the shadows rides the Sun*
> *And Stars forever dwell:*
> *I will not say the day is done,*
> *Nor bid the stars farewell."*
>
> [J. R. R. Tolkien]

SUNDAY October 25, 1998
TRAIL DAY 282/42 ✦ TRAIL MILE 4,136/574
LOCATION Pete Dube's Restigouche Hotel, Matapédia

I'M UP AT 4:00 A.M. TO CATCH THE BUS TO MATAPÉDIA. The ride from the sea around Gaspé is very enjoyable. The coast is dotted with small seaside villages and the rising sun plays a fascinating light show along the islands and cliffs. I shall never forget Perce Rock, an amazing monolith resting on the beach at Perce, the sun lifting its dark, bold silhouette, creating an enormous sunrise shadow across the land. The trip passes quickly and I am soon stepping off the bus and heading for the Restigouche Hotel. I am greeted by Pete, who has that grand Canadian smile and in his customary kindness to me, also a fine room! Pete invites me to remain as his guest and to take an extended rest before heading north again, as he can see that the trail is wearing on the old *Nomad* and that I am very tired. I have been on the trail now for 281 days and over 4,100 miles. But I explain my plans to go back on the trail in the morning, for it seems with just a little luck I should complete this last 80-plus miles by Friday evening, October 30, my 60th birthday.

I have become good friends with Pete and also with Pete's friend Richard Adams. Richard is a legend in his time . . . known far and about as "The Old Man of the River." Richard is 88 now, yet he remains vital and very active. Matapédia is the salmon sports-fishing capital of the world and Richard Adams, for near 75 years, has been the river guide! Both Pete and Richard have expressed an interest in doing some hiking with me, which I consider an honor, and I invite them to go out with me in the morning.

> *"Between the mountain and the sea*
> *I've made a happy landing;*
> *And here a peace has come to me*
> *That passeth understanding."*
>
> [Robert W. Service, *Eyrie*]

MONDAY October 26, 1998
TRAIL DAY 283/43 ◆ TRAIL MILE 4,148/586
LOCATION Hunter's Homemade Camper near St-Andre

ANOTHER GREAT NIGHT'S REST AT PETE'S FINE Restigouche Hotel. He and Richard are both ready and eager to get started as I am greeted at Pete's door. I make a quick dash to the post office and we're headed for the trail by 9:00 a.m. The plan is for Pete and Richard to hike with me into the village of St-Andre, a distance of some 15 kilometers. My determination to reach the Matane River Bridge in five days, a distance over 80 miles to the north, is very ambitious and I am concerned about being held back this very first day by my two hiking companions. My fears are quickly dispelled, however, as we begin our climb to the ridgeline above the picturesque village of Matapédia. Both of these gentlemen maintain themselves in peak physical condition year-round. They love the out-of-doors and I suspect neither has ever suffered a failed opportunity to be there! Pete, at age 57, has guided on the river for Atlantic salmon and in the surrounding mountains for black bear for years. Richard recently added another notch in building his incredible legend by polling a 26-foot-long canoe loaded to the gunwales with 500 pounds of man and gear just after recovering from surgery. So here I am, huffing along behind these true mountain men, in brisk fashion as we claim the first open crest. The SIA/IAT north from Matapédia I find to be a most memorable section. And the first viewpoint above this little village, looking down on the confluence of the Matapédia and Restigouche rivers, is breathtaking!

The morning passes quickly as the trail traverses open hardwood coves and gentle undulating ridges. By noon the trail becomes more rugged as we descend Gilmore Brook, the site of Pico Falls. Here an intricate stairway system has been devised adjoining the falls and along the happily cascading brook. Near the pool below the falls where the forest canopy opens, we enjoy and share lunch in the welcome warming rays of the sun. It seems the picnic table has been placed here just for us! I thoroughly enjoy the company of these dear friends and I become totally captivated as Richard spins his stories and tales of bygone times and of places long ago. As he speaks in soft tones, characteristic of these rugged mountain men, I notice that he has opened his old wool coat to take in the sun's warmth. And it is only after my second take that I realize this kind old gent is wearing a shirt and tie! I am immediately taken by this as being pretty darn strange. But I quickly get it in proper perspective as I realize that this old man is, in the truest sense and in every way, a professional, — the rivers and mountains his office. So it makes perfect sense, for in the traditional fashion, professionals, when in their offices, wear . . . yup, a shirt and tie!

The trail continues on through more open hardwood and along pleasant old grassy woodsroads. Too soon we arrive at the little village of St-Andre. All of these small, remote Québec villages, almost without exception, cluster themselves closely around grand, high-spired churches. The beautiful old church at St-Andre, being situated on a gentle ridge crown, is particularly striking, reminiscent of the church I attended as a child. Here the trail enters the village by the church side yard. Pete's girlfriend, Gaby, has come for him and Richard. The wind has come up and is driving with an increasingly uncomfortable chill. As I bid farewell to these kind friends, and as they climb into Pete's warm pickup, I turn onto the road and into the cold, harsh wind to continue on alone. I have been long on this trail. And my heart is tugging at me to turn and go back with them to their warm homes. But I have come too far and journeyed too long to turn back now. I know it not wise to pause for a final wave goodbye, so I press on, into the biting chill.

The hiking days are so short now. By 4:00 p.m. dusk is descending and I must begin looking for a suitable place to pitch for the night. The wind has not relented and is bitter cold. As I crest a ridge I see a small building in the distance. As I near I find a homemade camper propped up on crossbeams. Through the side window I can see a small table and a bunk complete with mattress. But alas, the door is padlocked and the windows are all secure. As I leave, a little voice tells me "These fellows always hide a key nearby within easy reach." So I turn and take another look. Where could it be? I feel under the camper just below the padlocked door. Oh yes! There, hanging on a nail, is the key! In a moment I'm inside and have my pack off. It is cold, but I'm out of the wind and I won't have to pitch on the hard, frozen ground. Thank you, Lord! Now I'm not feeling quite so sorry for myself. On the little table I prepare a meal of sardines and a cheese sandwich, and for dessert I eat the last Snickers bar from *Easy Rider*'s "care package." I roll out my sleeping bag on the plush mattress and roll in for the night. My water bottle freezes almost solid on the table beside my bed, but I am warm and I sleep soundly.

> *"Sharing mountain time is the glue of great and lasting friendships."*
> [Kim van den Eerenbeemt, *Yamnuska Guide*]

TUESDAY October 27, 1998
TRAIL DAY 284/44 ✦ TRAIL MILE 4,164/602
LOCATION Campsite south of Ste-Marguerite

THE MORNING DAWNS COLD AND CLEAR. Little water remains in my water bottle, mostly ice. I down a couple of Pop-Tarts and am able to stuff my sleeping bag and organize my pack before my fingers turn numb. I tidy up the hunter's little camper, leaving it neat and clean, just as I found it (Thank you, kind sir!) and after padlocking the door, I'm on my way.

It is very cold, but there is no wind. My little pack thermometer reads 20 degrees this morning. The early rays of the sun feel very good as I pass to the sunny side of the ridge. As I cross the ridge into the morning shadows, the sod and earth crunch beneath my feet. The crystalline beauty of hoar ice is all around. I can hear the happy song of a little brook below, and upon reaching the stream I see a challenge before me. The brook is of respectable width and flowing considerable volume. I size up the situation and decide that rock hopping is the way to go. There is a large boulder in the center and to get there I must take a good jump. After the first hop and skip I am committed to this, but I realize I should have stopped and switched from my boots to my running shoes and waded across, for the leap to the boulder is further than I had judged and it is covered with ice. As I make the impossible lunge my foot flies off the ice-covered boulder and in I go! I manage to stay upright, but both my legs become submerged to my knees and my gloves are full of the bitter cold water. I know I must act fast before my boots and laces freeze solid and my fingers quit working. I can see the sun striking the trail 100 yards above and I set a beeline for it. My feet are totally numb and feel like stumps. My boots are already frozen and before I can drop my pack and begin working at getting my boots off, my fingers quit working. Getting my frozen boots and wet socks off becomes an almost impossible task.

One luxury with which I have lavished myself on this odyssey is a (almost) full-size towel. I am very thankful that I have it this morning as I dry my feet and legs and try to mop out my boots. The towel is turning "crisp" as I hurry. Dry wool socks on dry feet begin the immediate process of relief. Even the needle-jabs of returning circulation feel wonderful! I must ford two more streams today—the wide but shallow Assemetquagan River and the narrow but deep Creux Brook—but the plan for these crossings is to hit them this afternoon when, hopefully, things have warmed up a bit.

Later in the morning I reach another fair-size brook, but here is a log bridge, and even though it is broken down on one side I am able to cross easily. In a short distance I hear hammering and I soon arrive at a trail shelter construction site. Here I meet Jean Pierre, another of David LeBlanc's crew members, and momentarily, out of the woods comes

Bruno—always happy, always smiling Bruno, with that warm ear-to-ear French Canadian grin. And after a grand handshake, Bruno exclaims, "The shitter is done; ya wanna try it out?" You just can't help but be happy around these folks! I linger long for much pleasant conversation before bidding Bruno and Jean Pierre goodbye and heading on up the trail.

I soon am on a long, steady ascent, dodging under and over a fine filament of twine played out before me. As I reach the ridgeline, the trail moves over to the bluff and a spectacular view site opens up, overlooking the canyon of the Assemetquagan River. Here I find David LeBlanc and Steve, another of David's crew members, enjoying the overlook and their lunch. It takes little encouragement to join them as I drop my pack and whip a couple of cheese sandwiches together. David shows me the little gadget that plays out the measuring line I had been dodging. It is an ingenious and interesting contraption. Strapped to your belt it simply plays out string, measuring the exact distance as you move along the trail. You can take a reading from the dial anytime, just like from an odometer, and the twine is biodegradable.

The folks here in Québec, as throughout New Brunswick and northern Maine, are highly dedicated to having this SIA/IAT completed and officially open by Earth Day 2000! Even though there has been much contrived controversy, naysaying, and wringing of hands against this joint nation SIA/IAT effort, the trail is becoming and will continue to be a great asset to the people of the United States and Canada. I am finding it to be an incredible trail. This cooperation between our two countries is working just fine! We all know that the last blaze ends on Katahdin. And although the blazes stop there we also know that these grand and glorious Appalachian mountains go on, and indeed I am finding that out firsthand. In the United States, on the granddaddy AT, I continually trekked along with folks hiking and enjoying the trail. But here in Canada, I have been the sole, solitary hiker. Yet I have not been alone, for out here I have met many folks and have made dear friends of most all of them, from Maine to Cap Gaspé . . . all trail builders, all working tirelessly to create and breathe life into this remarkable SIA/IAT.

David tells me that I should have little problem fording the river. This heightens my spirit, as does the pleasure of accepting an invitation to have dinner with him and Bruno upon completing the northern end of this odyssey. So I head on north now with a little more bounce in my step. I soon reach the Assemetquagan, switch to my running shoes to make the ford, and I cross easily without incident. The water is ice cold and my feet again turn numb, but I quickly dry them and get my warm wool socks and boots back on. Upon crossing the river the trail quickly ascends to again regain the ridge with viewpoints back into the canyon of the Assemetquagan and, as the trail turns, down into the narrower but no-less-impressive canyon of Creux Brook. From here the trail descends a stunning and scenic razorback to ford Creux Brook. The crossing here is deceptive as the brook is relatively narrow, but even at the rapids where I decide to ford, the water is deep and running with considerable energy and hydraulic force.

I switch again to my running shoes and take particular deliberation in lashing my boots to my pack, good and secure. I then shoulder my pack, cinching my hip, ladder, and sternum straps as tight as I can stand. Oh yes! I know that all we've been taught, and indeed all I've ever read about fording with a pack, would have us be almost free of it and be ready to instantly bail out. That may be good advice for folks carrying a beggar's load and not accustomed to shouldering a pack. I've carried mine 284 days now and it's part of me. Out here in the remote wilds of Canada where continuation of life and the presence of your pack are synonymous I want my pack to remain a *stable* part of me, especially in situations where, if I lose my balance for a moment, it could pitch me around. I feel that my pack and I have a much better chance of negotiating a difficult ford as a unit, and not loosely engaged as is customarily recommended. I learned this lesson the hard way the first day on the trail in the Everglades where, but for the grace of God, my journey would have abruptly ended. So, in I go, first to my ankles and then below my knees. The rocks are very large and rounded, and stable footing is difficult. My hiking poles quiver and vibrate in the turbulence. I concentrate with total deliberation and focus, taking time to get my poles and feet firmly planted before moving forward. I am tempted to hasten as the water is bone-numbing cold, but I know that I must move slowly and with patience. This pays off, as I am able to cross without a hitch or a slip! I then go into pit crew mode, changing back to warm socks and boots.

    The climb out of the canyon is gradual with the walls diverging to open into a pleasant valley. The trail leads to a woodsroad, which I follow until dusk. I am able to break the ice to get water from the road ruts to boil for supper. I pitch in a small clearing along the roadway. With a little birch bark and some spruce twigs I have a fine cooking and warming fire going. I lean my boots forward toward the fire and lay my wool gloves on them to dry. The wind has subsided, and the drizzle, which began earlier, has stopped. The hot meal and the glow of the fire warm me. If I can make Causapscal tomorrow, this will be the last night I will spend on this frozen anvil-hard ground.

> *"My words are tied in one with the great mountain,*
> *with the great rocks, with the great trees,*
> *in one with my body and my heart.*
> *All of you see me, one with the world."*

[Yokuts Prayer]

WEDNESDAY October 28, 1998
TRAIL DAY 285/45 ✦ TRAIL MILE 4,178/616
LOCATION Home of Andre Fournier, Causapscal

I SLEPT WELL BUT AM GREETED BY FIRST LIGHT through the chilling gloom and swirl of a drifting crystal mist. I banked the fire late last eve in hopes there would be a few warming embers this morning to cut the edge from the biting cold that has come to be my companion, but alas, the fire has burned hollow and the ashes have gone as cold as stone. Breaking camp is a very vulnerable time. I work as quickly as I can with numbing and fumbling fingers as I feel my core temperature dropping. I forgo breakfast to get my pack on and get moving. With age has come a definite reduction in circulation to my extremities. I have little difficulty with my feet, but my fingers and hands are a real problem. I can tolerate the arthritis, the slow-healing dislocated knuckles, and the blue-numbing cold, but what is frustrating and scary is the loss of control, the weakening, molasses-slow movement that even with intense, forceful *will* cannot be overcome. Simple tasks such as zipping up my jacket or tying my laces become demoralizing ordeals. I give up on the jacket zipper to get out and going, crunching the frozen trail. With my wool gloves and leather mitts on now I can feel the faint but welcome shock of the electric quills that signal the return of circulation to my hands and fingers.

The trail to the little village of Ste-Marguerite follows along two-track and logging roads. As I reach an area of active timber harvesting my way becomes confused by fresh trail in all directions. I get my compass out and try to "reckon" most directly toward the village. When I pitched camp last eve I estimated that I was within a couple of miles of Ste-Marguerite. But this morning I have already gone much further than that. I fear that I have already passed the village and am going the wrong direction, for at the village the trail turns sharply southwest. Odds are that I have made a wrong turn at one of the countless intersecting skidder trails.

It is now mid-morning and the day is warming. But the drear continues to hover in a moisture-laden blanket, and through this shroud comes the muffled sound of a distant chainsaw. The trail I have chosen leads me in that general direction, and down yet another intersecting two-track, I see the dark silhouette of a pickup truck suspended in the soupy haze. Two hundred yards back a narrow trail I am at the source of this woods alarm and am greeted by a kind, old, smiling red-faced French Canadian. It becomes quickly apparent that neither of us understands a word the other is saying. French for International Appalachian Trail is *Le Sentier International des Appalaches*. I manage to get that out . . . plus, "Ste-Marguerite." He now understands I am lost and am trying to find the trail to the village. The response is near a minute of the softest, most delightful French dialogue I've yet heard. With his arms akimbo, he occasionally motions in every direction. Facial expressions being fairly universal, I screw my face into the most convincing question mark I can muster. The old woodsman then throws up his hands and motions me to follow him. We load in his truck and he drives me to the skidder intersection from whence I came. Turns out I was doing okay and would have soon been to the village. Over the course of this odyssey I've come to find that I'm almost never as far along the trail as I think. Case in point! As I head up the trail I manage a *"merci,"* and in perfect English the kind old gentleman responds: "Good luck!"

The wind picks up but is not chilling as the afternoon warms. The hike on into Causapscal is pleasant and uneventful. I have been instructed by Pete Dube in Matapédia to call Andrew Fournier upon reaching the convenience store at the outskirts of Causapscal. Andre is the principal at Cegep School (equivalent to our high schools) and is the section leader for the trail I'll be hiking to the Matane River. As I near the store the sky performs a serious "darkin' over" and a steady rain begins. The shelter and warmth of the store is most welcome. As I make the call a woman overhears my conversation and offers me a ride up the hill to Andre's school. Upon arriving I am greeted at the door by a group of students who usher me along to meet Andre. I receive a most enthusiastic welcome, and Andre immediately interrupts his activities to drive me to his lovely home where he patiently reviews all his maps with me.

There is just no getting used to the kindness and generosity of the people of Canada and I am overwhelmed again as Andre invites me to have supper with him and his family and to spend the night at their warm, cozy home. Andre chuckles as the ear-to-ear grin on my face says "yes" before my mouth can manage to!

The hiking hours become more precious as the days grow shorter and there are still two full hours of daylight remaining. The rain has ended and when I mention that I would like to get in a few more miles today, Andre offers not only to pick me up this evening at a point about 5 miles north of town but to drop me off there again in the morning. So, armed with maps to take me to the conclusion of the Canadian portion of this odyssey, I'm off through the lovely village of Causapscal, Québec. On the north edge of town the trail turns through a park and then ascends beside a glad brook to open into upper meadows and lush, rolling farmland. Rain continues to threaten but holds off and the evening is mild. The trail turns onto a quiet country road and just at dusk I hear the gravel crunching behind me as a vehicle approaches. I turn as Andre rolls his window down and I am greeted by that happy, contagious Canadian smile!

Back again at the Fournier home, Andre introduces me to his wife, Helene D'Aoust, and their son, Christophe (same Canadian smiles). Helene prepares a delightful meal and I spend a joyful evening with the Fournier family. A hot tub never felt so good! What a blessing not to have to break ice from two track ruts for water, or sleep on the hard, steel-cold ground!

"The road goes ever on and on
Down from the door where it began.
Now far ahead the road has gone,
And I must follow it if I can."

[J. R. R. Tolkien]

THURSDAY October 29, 1998
TRAIL DAY 286/46 ✦ TRAIL MILE 4,201/639
LOCATION Home of Andre Fournier, Causapscal

A GREAT NIGHT'S SLEEP IN A WARM, SOFT BED! Andre has prepared breakfast for me. As I collect my things and arrange my pack I linger with Andre and Helene, for I want to sort a place in my memory for these kind, generous folks and their comfortable, charming home.

Back to the place along the country road where Andre picked me up last evening, we tarry and talk some more. I know he would like to play hooky and hike with me today, but we bid each other farewell. He must return to his students and his school and I to my solitude and the trail.

The trail soon leaves the country road to ascend the gorge cut by the Causapscal River. Where the trail joins the river I am greeted by gentle waters with quiet dignity. But as the canyon walls close and as I climb, the true nature of this river is revealed. For, rushing at me down through these granite walls, passes a reckless, runaway traveler. Over the boulders and ever-heightening cataracts comes this rollicking, cascading tumult, shouting in ever-increasing crescendos of pure sound! I am taken by this mystifying blend: the purity of sound mixed with the raw, raging torrent. I can feel the shuddering vibration deep in my chest and I am swept up with the rush of it to become dizzy from the excitement all around. I must sit to level my head as I try to comprehend this incredible show.

But I must not linger, as many miles lie before me if I am to reach the city of Amqui by nightfall. I have grown weary from the countless days on the trail. The loneliness, the wet and the cold, the pain, and the never-ending daily strenuous task—all are slowly but surely taking their toll. If I can reach Amqui tonight, I won't have to sleep on the hard, frozen ground again. Tomorrow I will be 60 years old. My bones are tired. Twenty-six miles today and 26 miles tomorrow and I will finish the northern segment of this incredible journey. That's what I want to do. I want to finish tomorrow on my 60th birthday. I'll make it to Amqui tonight and tomorrow night I'll be at the Matane River; from there I will be taken to the De Champlain home in Matane where I can be warm and dry again. I'll do the 52 miles. I don't want to be out on this hard, frozen ground anymore!

After scrambling the canyon walls to sky-high vistas that open across and down into the gorge, the trail leaves the Causapscal and I turn for one last look at this wild, untamed place. Back on woodsroads now I fix my concentration with singular intensity on hammering out the miles to reach Amqui before dark. I rush along as the miles click away beneath my feet. As I shake out of the hypnosis brought by the rhythmic shuffle and the clicking hiking sticks, I realize there have been no blazes. As I stop and look I know instinctively that I am lost. I shout "Oh Lord, not now. Please, Lord, not now . . . I can't get lost now!" But I am lost. I have seen no blazes, no flagging for a great distance. Where could I have gone wrong? Where could I have missed a turn? Andre's maps are so good, the trail marked so well. How could this happen now? I'm standing on a main road and there are houses and power lines around me. This is not the right way. There are no blazes, no flags. I look at the map. Where am I? Which way do I go? I am wasting precious time. I must get back on the trail right away. Across the main road, 300 yards down a lane, there's a house. I rush there and pound on the door. Surely someone here can give me directions. I pound on the door again, but no one comes. I must get back to the road. A car approaches and I hail the driver. He speaks no English. I am becoming very anxious. I sit down by the side of the road and cover my face and my eyes with my trembling hands. I must suppress this fear and anxiety. I have got to calm myself.

I finally quit shaking and look up. Along the road to the west is another dwelling and I can see a vehicle turning in. As I walk hastily toward there, the gentleman sees me coming and waits in his yard. Here I meet Marc Bergeron. He speaks English! Marc confirms that the trail does not pass his home. He studies my map but is unable to help. He does, however, give me directions to Amqui. The roadwalk appears to be a much greater distance than the trail, but I can walk the road with assurance that I will reach Amqui by nightfall. If I retrace my steps in the attempt to locate the trail it could take hours. I choose the roadwalk. I know Andre will be disappointed and upset that I missed some of his trail, but this is the right choice, considering the time and the uncertainty. I bid Marc farewell and it is with much anguish and trepidation that I decide to head up the road away from the trail, on another way to Amqui. A little after 2:00 p.m. I reach the paved road leading to Amqui. Once on this road, and in only moments, a car pulls over and stops on the shoulder. As the man crosses the road and approaches me I immediately recognize Andre. I begin to tremble and tears well in my eyes. I remember now that he had a meeting today in Matane. He is returning from that meeting. Oh, he must be so disappointed and upset with me. But as he comes nearer he greets me with a warm and comforting smile, saying, "When I saw you I knew right away that you made a wrong turn." I can't control my trembling as I apologize for getting lost and for not returning to find my way. I tell him what has happened, that precious time was wasted and had I found the trail I could not have made it to Amqui by nightfall. I tell him that I don't want to sleep on the frozen ground anymore. Andre can see that I'm an emotional wreck. He repeatedly urges me to ride into Amqui with him. He stands and talks with me for a very long time as the traffic rushes by, not wanting to leave me on the busy road. I tell him that I must walk to Amqui and that I will be all right. He reluctantly bids me farewell, turning many times as he returns to his car. I stand, as if frozen in my tracks, as he pulls onto the road and is quickly gone.

It seems such a great distance to Amqui. When roadwalking and when it is possible to see for miles ahead, time passes so slowly. Dusk is approaching as I arrive at the city and head for the Ambassador Motel on the far side of town. As I near the motel entrance a vehicle approaches from behind and I hear someone call my name. "Eb! . . . Eb!" I turn and there is Helene. She says, "I have been looking and looking for you. You will come back with me to Causapscal and stay with us again tonight. Wait here while I call to tell Andre I have found you!"

As Helene disappears into the motel to call Andre I try to piece this puzzle together. I know that Andre became very concerned after finding me wandering along the road this afternoon. He could see immediately that I was distraught and very fatigued. He must have gone to where Helene works as soon as he reached Amqui. She also apparently became very concerned and set out right after work to find me. It was obvious that she was very happy and relieved when she did. On the ride back to Causapscal, and as we both are able to calm down and relax a little, I make Helene promise to let me take them all out for pizza tonight. As we pull into the driveway, Andre pulls in right behind. He greets me with relief and enthusiasm as he tells me he'll be hiking out with me in the morning. Once inside and as soon as I've dropped my pack I head straight for the hot tub again. Helene has a short meeting to attend before dinner, so Chris entertains me with some of his music videos followed by a show that involves many "Barney Oldfield" contraptions he has built for his hamster. Andre watches with beaming pride and we all have a happy time . . . including the hamster!

Helene soon returns from her meeting and we're off for a great pizza and a grand evening. On the way home I have Andre stop at the market while I run in for some ice cream, peanuts, and chocolate for sundaes later. Back at the Fournier home, Andre and I settle in to discuss plans for tomorrow. He will hike with me to Lac Matapédia where Helene will pick him up later in the morning. He wants to be back at school for the afternoon Halloween program his students have planned for him. Andre explains that two of his friends and fellow SIA/IAT trail builders are also interested in hiking with me tomorrow . . . for the full day. Without elaborating, Andre assures me they'll be able to keep the pace for the distance. I say, as I try to hide my reluctance, "Let's do it . . . I can sure use the company." Andre calls them immediately and it's all set. He also calls Mona Doucet. Mona is coordinating my pick-up at Matane River Bridge tomorrow evening, and those plans are also firmed up.

It's great to be warm enough to enjoy an ice-cream sundae! And that we all do just before trundling off to bed. What an incredible, event-filled day. It's great to be with these wonderful, caring friends and to spend another night in their warm, comfortable home.

It seems God always finds a way,
To find a way for me.
His guidance comes thru steadfast love,
'Tis there for me to see.
And as I stumble o'er the path,
I need to keep in mind.
That He has cleared a way for me, . . .
That faith will help me find.

[N. Nomad]

FRIDAY October, 30, 1998
TRAIL DAY 287/47 ✦ TRAIL MILE 4,227/665
LOCATION Home of Viateur and Jocelyne De Champlain, Matane

TODAY WILL BE A LONG HIKING DAY, NEAR 26 MILES. Hopefully, I'll be able to make the distance and arrive at the Matane River Bridge before dark. The plan is to get out early and be on the trail by 6:30 a.m., so I'm up a little after 5:00. I can already hear Andre downstairs. I dress quickly and get my pack ready to go. Andre has breakfast prepared, along with plenty of hot coffee. No time is wasted this morning. Helene bids us farewell and we are loaded up and on our way. On the drive to Amqui, Andre is bubbling with energy and the air in the little truck cab is charged with excitement. Today will certainly be an exciting day, but as we roll along and at the first light of day I begin thinking back over the almost countless dawns of this year . . . for now with sadness I realize that this day will be a bittersweet day for me. This will be my last hiking day in Canada, perhaps forever, for today I turn 60 years old. I will not miss the loneliness and the cold that has accompanied me the last part of this trail, but I will miss this vast, rugged, and beautiful land and I will dearly miss all the gracious and kind Canadian people who have befriended me.

Two hundred and eighty-seven days to shoulder my pack, to trudge through swamps and climb over mountains is a very long time. Four thousand two hundred continuous miles is an incredible distance. Even though I've done it, as I say the words under my breath, I can't comprehend it. I have always had a feeling deep down—from the very first day—that the Lord would protect me, that He would provide safe passage. In my mind's eye I could see all the places ahead, the boundless horizons, the countless miles. I somehow prepared for all of that. I prepared for the going of it. But somehow I never prepared for the finish of it, and today is the day for the finish of it. Andre and I will hike together today. I will make new friends and delight in their company and I will savor every minute of this last day north.

Andre pulls into a grassy parking area on a side street near the trail north of Amqui. Our two hiking companions are already here waiting. As I step from the cab I must brace against the wind. We are in for what is shaping to be a long, cold, rainy day. Oh, but I must catch some of this enthusiasm that is all around me! For there is much excitement as Andre introduces me to his good friends Diane Bouchard and Andre BeRuBe. Andre must interpret for me as I speak no French and they no English. But I know that we will do just fine because we are all mountaineers, woodsmen of the highest order, if you will. The mountains are within us and we know and understand that language, and today that common joy and contentment will suffice.

We shoulder our packs and are on the trail shortly after daybreak. We cross the road I hiked to Amqui during the waning hours of yesterday as the trail leads out on a woodsroad and along a ridge above open fields. The wind is harsh and cutting, but we all push into it with great determination. About an hour into the hike it becomes apparent that my three hiking companions are all well conditioned athletes. The wind is not all that is brisk as we move along at a pace in excess of 3 miles per hour. I must dig my trekking poles in and lengthen my stride to stay abreast. The trail this morning follows near the shore of Lac Matapédia with many fine views, first to the north and later to the west as we pass.

We pause at one especially picturesque vantage to rest. Andre has been telling me about his responsibilities with the SIA/IAT and the enjoyment he has had building the trail here near his home. Diane and Andre BeRuBe are just two of the many volunteers working along with him. As we shoulder our packs and head back on the trail, Diane and her friend take off like greyhounds chasing Thumper.

I guess we all suffer occasionally from that familiar malady known as foot-in-mouth disease! Well, I really stuck mine in my mouth last night. When Andre mentioned that two of his friends would like to hike to the Matane River with me I commented that it would be a long distance and a long day and that I didn't want to be held back. Andre's only comment was that they would maintain the pace and do the distance just fine. Now I know why! Last season Diane Bouchard was ranked first in women's competitive cross-country skiing for all of Québec Province, and Andre BeRuBe was third in men's; and I was worried about these folks keeping up with me? Oh boy!

It seems the morning has gone so fast, for soon we reach the rendezvous point where Helene awaits for Andre. There is a picnic area and beach here on Lac Matapédia and we linger, not wanting to say goodbye. How do you keep sadness from the day when you must bid farewell to dear friends . . . friends you may never see again? This day is going to run the gamut of emotions, I can tell. This birthday I'll remember forever!

Diane, Andre, and I hasten along. Their pace is smooth and rhythmic, never slowing, never varying. Great athletes always make their sport look so effortless, so easy. They truly know how to play the game. By mid-afternoon I am confident that the Matane River is within striking distance and that we will arrive there by dark. So now it really hits me. I finally realize that in a little over two hours, after near countless days and thousands of hours, the "Odyssey of '98" will be all but over. I plan to do the 175-mile roadwalk from the Miccosukee Indian Reservation in the Florida Everglades down to Key West but I doubt if I will feel the swell of emotions that are rising within me now. I am thinking of these beautiful people who are with me today. I know this is Andre's design because of his concern for me. He wanted someone with me today to see me through. Andre interpreted for them earlier as they told how proud they were to be hiking with me. The feeling is deeply humbling. Surely they know how proud I am to be in their company.

I think of the remarkable places I've been, all the glorious and boundless treasures nature has revealed to me; the kindness, generosity, friendship and love of so many wonderful people I have met . . . and in tears of sadness and of joy, bade farewell. Now in tears of joy and gladness, I remember. I become overwhelmed with emotion. I am trembling. I cannot stand. As I clutch my hiking poles I sink to my knees. I am consumed by this whole incredible mystery. So many folks have asked me, "Why?" I have tried to answer, but I could not, for the answer is part of this whole mystery that is now here deep within me; a part of my very soul. But I do know this. In two more hours there will be a miracle in this old man's life—and that miracle will be the "Odyssey of '98!" I sob openly in the presence of my new friends. My tears cascade and disappear in the wet soil beneath my knees. But they are not embarrassed, and I am not ashamed. I raise my eyes and smile a smile of great peace and joy. It is a moment for all of us to smile. Finally, I pull myself up, dig in my sticks, and we move on to the Matane River.

Intermittent wind-driven drizzle is the worst we've had to deal with today and even this relents as we turn sharply southeast. After fording a brook and ascending the ridge we can hear the traffic on PQ 175. In a few moments we also hear voices and just as dusk descends we are greeted by the excited contingent of folks who have come from Matane. They cheer us along as we hike the remaining mile to the Matane River. As we cross the bridge I break from the group for a few moments to go to where Bruno and Carole dropped me off two weeks before. Here I take my last remaining steps on this incredible International Appalachian Trail. I lean and rest my arms on the old rail fence and cradle my head as I bow to give thanks. The miracle has happened. I've done it: 287 days, 4,227 miles. It truly is a miracle! An old man, on his 60th birthday, standing with his head bowed in humbleness and humility . . . thank you, Lord, for bringing me into your grace and for keeping me safe in your care all these days, all these miles. And thank you for these 60 years.

As I return to the group Lulu Bourassa has her tripod set up, camera mounted. Everybody has to have their picture taken with me. We start with the whole bunch—Andre and Diane, and from Matane

Eric Chouinard, Jean Claude Bouchard, Eddy Pellerin, Georges Fraser, Jean-Pierre Harrison, and Nelson St. Pierre. It seems as we pose that these folks are more excited about me finishing than am I! All of this fuss and attention is so bewildering. It is such a grand and happy time. We all then load in a large passenger van, and amid the din and chatter we head for St-Vianney where a friend is waiting for Diane and Andre. I try to spend a few more minutes with these great athletes, but there is too much confusion. Thank you, Diane and Andre, for taking this day to be with me. Your company has inspired me and has made this day most memorable! As I bid these friends farewell we turn and head for Matane where I have been invited to be the guest of Viateur and Jocelyne De Champlain. Viateur is the director of Administrative Services at CEGEP de Matane (equivalent to our community college) and is also the SIA/IAT chapter president for Québec Province. We stop first at Jean-Pierre Harrison's home for some refreshments and a little celebrating. Jean-Pierre, thanks for inviting me to your beautiful home (the hot tub was great!) Eric, trail name *Grand Manie-Tout,* then whisks me away to the De Champlain home.

I am greeted enthusiastically by both Viateur and Jocelyne. I am able to relax and have a most pleasant evening dining and enjoying the company of these very kind people. The De Champlain home is a grand two-story affair with a striking spiral staircase in the center. I have the whole first floor to myself where Viateur has a wonderful warming fire going in the wood-burning stove. After this very enjoyable evening with Viateur and Jocelyne I retire to my room to rest and reflect on this miraculous day. As I drift off to the most contented sleep I keep softly repeating, for I cannot convince myself, "*Nomad,* you did it, *Nomad,* you did it, *Nomad,* you . . . ZZZZZ"

Ballad of the IAT

The Appalachian Mountains,
Don't end in northern Maine.
For as you tack a northeast course,
They reemerge again.
They climb to stand triumphant,

Through New Brunswick and Québec.
And o'er them wends the IAT,
A dreamer's perfect trek.
No mountains stand the likes of these,
Down in the forty-eight.
A wild, yet stately majesty
You'll find they radiate.
Here rugged mountain men do speak,
Strange words in softest tones.
While in them born a hard, tough style,
No meanness in their bones.
Bring me a man who makes friends fast,
And I will bet you this:
Give me a day in Canada,
'N I'll have a longer list!
Down in the States' vast wilderness,
You thought you'd seen it all.
In Canada . . . it doesn't end,
'Til past horizon's wall.
You've hiked past ponds and lakes and brooks,
Fell captive to their spell.
But here, somehow, your heart turns warm,
In their forbidding chill.
Up through the Whites and Presidents,
You touched the alpine zone.
But in the Chic Chocs,
You're above the trees for miles . . . alone.
On earth we search for perfect peace,
It is our lifelong quest.
Up here you'll feel God's presence 'round,
And in you as you rest.
For God's hands hold these mountains up,
His tabernacles high.
You'll never feel more close to him,
Until you cross the sky.

So, come see the rivers Restigouche,
The lovely Madeleine,
The Tobique and the Upsalquitch,
And all 'em in-between.
They'll fill your heart with playful glee,
Their happy songs you'll hear.
Come seek their gladness in the fall,
That magic time of year.
You've seen the bear, the moose, the deer;
And if that pleases you.
Come climb Mont Albert's tundra high,
And see the Caribou.
For here you're nearing Santa's land
With reindeer roaming free.
You'll hike a wonderland of snow,
A Christmas fantasy.
And, if scaling mountains to the blue,
You'd rate a perfect day.
Then come traverse the Chic Choc Range,
And climb Jacques Cartier.
You'll stand spellbound while 'round you'll see,
Mont Albert's skyland tundra.
And to the north, clear to the sea,
More of God's boundless wonder.
Katahdin is the grand finale,
On the old A.T.
But you've not seen the final act,
Until you're at the sea.
For at the cliff of Cap Gaspé,
The Appalachians end.
And here you've scaled the final mount,
Passed round the final bend.
And so, your trek's not over;
You'll need to follow me.
And hike these northern, far-off lands, . . .
Along the IAT.

[N. Nomad]

Chapter 5
Keys/Everglades Roadwalk

SUNDAY November 29, 1998
TRAIL DAY 288/1 ✦ TRAIL MILE 4,227/13
LOCATION Game-check station, Miccosukee Indian Reservation,
Loop Road and Tamiami Trail, Florida

AS YOU CAN SEE BY THE DATE, I have taken a break for much-needed time to be with family and friends after returning from Canada. Ah, and in that journey there's another whole adventure, one that I'll tell you a little about as we hike along, completing these last 175 miles of roadwalk down into and through the beautiful Florida Keys. For it had dawned on me early on in Canada that upon reaching the Cliffs of Forillon at Cap Gaspé, Québec—that at that point, I would have indeed hiked most-near the entire eastern North American continent, save this short stretch from where the Florida National Scenic Trail (FT) begins near the lands of the Miccosukee Nation west of Miami, down to Key West. So, I'd already set in my mind to return to Loop Road, thence to complete this incredible odyssey by hiking to the monument marking the southernmost point of the eastern North American continent in Key West.

I have spent the better part of this day leaning back against my pack, which is strapped to the rear fender of Erv Daley's motorcycle. Erv, a great motorcycle racing buddy of many years, just so happened to be heading this way to visit friends, so he offered me a ride on his BMW and he now drops me off at the old familiar FT trail marker here on Loop Road. Thanks, Erv!

As we get older, I suppose we tend to get more sentimental and more emotional about things. I remember watching that happen to my folks, to many dear friends . . . and now, so it seems, to myself. For here I stand, hearkened back to the last time I stood at this very spot. That seems like a long, long time ago now, a totally different lifetime. So many things have happened to me since then, things that have changed my life forever. But as I reflect back, I realize that it has been only 11 short months since I was last here with Jon. The pickup tailgate was down, and after we had lingered and talked for quite a while, I dragged my pack out, shouldered it, and snapped the buckle. Then, after a good hug from Jon and after much hesitancy and reluctance, I stepped down into the submerged treadway to head north into the unknown. By trail, that was over 4,000 miles ago, 287 days ago — and the Lord only knows how many buckle snaps ago. It is so bewildering how the pathway of life winds, how we weave our way as God guides us along. Today I will not be stepping down into it, but I can see as the trail heads north where I turned for one last glimpse back at my dear son Jon as he stood by his truck with the most forlorn and puzzled expression of sadness on his face.

I hear the last fading "thrump, thrump" from Erv's cycle as he heads on west, just as did Jon on that day long ago, leaving me to the silence and to this trail. As I stand here trembling, I must go down on one knee to steady myself, and finally to all fours. I crawl to the edge of the road by the old FT sign. Here I peer down into the water where the treadway begins and where this unbelievable odyssey began. As I look, I do not recognize the strange face staring back at me from this watery mirror, such a different face, one that should be familiar but is not. The image fades in and out and floats in a ghostly veil as my tears cascade to break the surface. Ah, but do I finally recognize the face, after being locked in a gaze of disbelief for such a long time. For it is now I see Jon's face formed and transformed into mine — looking back at me with that forlorn yet familiar puzzled expression of sadness. Finally I sigh, for just a brief moment does the broken mirror reflect a soft, loving smile. Dear Lord, I pray that someday I will understand.

I stumble along Loop Road in a daze, trying to get back into stride after being away from the trail for nearly a month. I manage to make the

13 miles to the game check station at the intersection of Loop Road and Tamiami Trail, where I arrive in the dark and am invited to spend the evening with attendants Dave and Carol Balman from Miami.

> *"For the test of the heart is trouble,*
> *And it always comes with the years,*
> *And the smile that is worth the praises of earth*
> *Is the smile that shines through tears."*

[Ella Wheeler Wilcox]

MONDAY November 30, 1998
TRAIL DAY 289/2 ✦ TRAIL MILE 4,260/33
LOCATION Behind truckstop, US 41 and Krome Avenue

I ENJOYED A GREAT EVENING LAST TALKING with the Balmans, their friends, and many hunters, all the while being fed great quantities of food by the Balmans. The Miccosukee people are proud and gentle folk. Through the kindness of the Balmans, I was able to roll out my pad and sleeping bag in the game check's screened enclosure. What a blessing to be provided shelter from the mosquitoes this very first night.

I have been dreading this hike today. Before me awaits a 20-mile roadwalk along busy US 41 all the way to Krome Avenue, the very out-skirts of Miami. But I find as I hike along the fully-paved emergency lane that I am provided fair distance from the traffic, and the cars and commercial vehicles are moving at a reasonable pace, so I'm not taking the buffeting and pounding I had feared. On my journey east this morn-ing I pass many airboat concessions, all managed and run by the Miccosukee people. As I hike along, a particularly interesting and color-ful little roadside stand catches my eye. Since I need water and a break from the sweltering sun, I pull off to take a look. As I enter, a young lady and an old Indian gentleman greet me. They are talking with a fellow who appears to be a tourist, so I lounge and look around.

At first glance, the place appears much like any other touristy knickknack place, but as I look closer, I realize that none of this stuff is for sale. In reality it is more a museum, with stuffed critters on the high shelves all around, with faded old newspaper clippings and articles tacked to the wall. One particular clipping catches my eye. It is about the Miccosukee Nation and their people. Beside the story is this picture of a young Miccosukee chief. As I read the article, continuing to glance back up at the faded yellow picture, does it seem that I should know this man, as if we have actually met somewhere long ago. In a moment the young lady comes over and with a full-beaming smile says, "That's a great article about Chief Buffalo Tiger, isn't it?" Smiling back — you cannot help but smile back — I say, "Yes ma'am, but who is Buffalo Tiger?" She replies, "Why that's the chief right over there!" Ah, so now I know where I've seen the young man in the picture. But that picture was taken many years ago of a man who is now very old! As she tells the story about Buffalo Tiger, I become intrigued with the delightful history of it and I ask if I might meet and talk with the chief when he and the young man have concluded their conversation.

To my surprise, the Indian girl turns and goes straightaway to the chief; she interrupts him and brings him directly to me. The young man follows along behind. After the introduction I manage to apologize to both for the interruption. It is such an honor to meet this man, but the chief seems much more taken by meeting me and asks many questions. To my amazement, he is really the first during this entire odyssey, the first to look directly at my feet and inquire as to their well-being! "You have traveled a great distance, do your feet not suffer?" says the chief. As I reply, I am thinking, "Ah, here is a man who understands . . . who truly understands!"

The highway before me is straight as an arrow, with the utility poles continuing to march ever ahead, tapering and merging to a blurred point as the sweltering mirage of heat lifts the road to dance and bounce to the horizon. The hypnotic-like trance caused by the rhythm of my poles clicking the pavement and the constant whoosh of passing traffic is finally interrupted by an eastbound vehicle that catches my eye. It passes but then slows abruptly to turn full around and return along the guardrail. The passenger window goes down as I stoop to look across at the driver. Oh my, it is the young man who had been talking to Buffalo Tiger. He says, "I really enjoyed the account of your story as you talked with the chief today. My name is Mark Baker and I am the producer for

WPBT public television in Miami." I quickly find that Mark has many questions to ask, but since it is getting toward late afternoon I explain that I must keep moving, for I have many more miles yet to cover before dark. Mark then inquires as to my planned route to Key West and asks if it would be okay to return and look for me tomorrow. These most tentative arrangements being made, we bid farewell and I head on east as my lengthening shadow travels and leaps far ahead . . . toward the shimmering and shadowy horizon.

> *"What God is doing you may not know now;*
> *But someday you'll understand why.*
> *Questions that taunt you and trouble your mind*
> *Will one day have heavens reply."*

[Clair Hess]

TUESDAY December 1, 1998
TRAIL DAY 290/3 ✦ TRAIL MILE 4,278/51
LOCATION Bel Air Motel, Homestead, FL 997

THE MICCOSUKEE NATION HAS AN ABSOLUTE GAMBLING EMPIRE going at the northwest corner of Krome Avenue and Tamiami Trail. The searchlights illuminated the entire sky. I guess that corner is the international boundary between their country and the good old U.S. of A. Anyway, I had a devil of a time getting through the traffic at the intersection. Everybody was heading for the casino. I finally managed to get across to the southeast corner, where I settled in behind the truck stop. After setting up camp in some bushes on a little mound of coquina fill, I gave Nina Dupuy a call; she's the Southern Everglades FT Section Leader. I had talked to Nina many times by phone while planning this odyssey over a year ago, but I had never met her. She made it out later, and we had a grand evening talking trail. Back then to my little hideaway behind the truck stop, I was quickly lulled to sleep by the steady, monotonous drone of the idling diesel engines.

Back at Krome Avenue this morning, I turn south, heading straight for Key West. I manage to get out early, but as soon as the sun catches hold and the humidity gets pumping, the road quickly turns into a frying pan. The trucks are out early, too, and the road shoulder is dreadfully narrow, with guardrails that keep vehicles from plunging into the ever-present drainage canals scant feet from the busy roadway. I haven't gone 2 miles when I start picking up change lying along the road. One dollar and fifty cents in all is scattered for the better part of a mile. It starts with quarters, then nickels and dimes, finally trickling off with a bunch of pennies. On the roadwalk today, I pass miles and miles of truckfarms and little makeshift roadside stands. I know I'm still in the United States, but I don't understand the language.

About halfway to Homestead and clicking along in a total daze, I am hailed by a couple of fellows in a little white van. There's some writing on the side, WPBT Channel 2, and I recognize Mark. Dang, I can't believe this. He has actually come all the way back out here to track me down, and he's got a cameraman and a van full of television gear with him! They pull off by a convenience store and I cross over to be greeted immediately by two beaming smiles as Mark introduces me to Allan Farrell. Well, I'm in good shape now and on schedule to get on down to Homestead by early evening . . . and I did promise Mark that I would talk with him today. So we find a little shade and I drop my pack. Allan gets right to setting up the camera and Mark starts off quite gently with the questions. Oh, and these are new questions besides the usual "where'ya been and where'ya going?" I had misgivings yesterday evening when I consented to talk with Mark today. I got to thinking how I didn't need a bunch of hype and confusion on top of all the clatter I'm already having to deal with, especially this late in the trek. I really want to be by myself now, to try and digest all that has occurred over these last remarkable 11 months. But am I ever surprised, for I find Mark and Allan to be two of the most laid-back fellows I've met since leaving the AT! We have a most quiet and enjoyable time together. They get a mile of footage . . . plus what seems a mile of me hiking alongside the road. Before parting, I agree to call Mark the day before I arrive in Key West. Seems they want to come all the way to Key West—that round-trip requiring an entire day—to film me completing this incredible odyssey at the southernmost point monument.

As I near Homestead, the playful ribbing from passing motorists begins . . . "Hey old man, there ain't no snow down here!" These folks are obviously not used to seeing a backpacker popping along with trekking poles!

> *"And if; through patient toil, we reach the land*
> *Where tired feet, with sandals loosed, may rest,*
> *When we shall clearly see and understand,*
> *I think that we will say, 'God knew the best.' "*

[May Riley Smith]

WEDNESDAY December 2, 1998
TRAIL DAY 291/4 ✦ TRAIL MILE 4,301/74
LOCATION Beach at Neptune's Hideaway,
by Hobo Bar and Grill, Key Largo, MM 103

THE FOLKS AT BEL AIR MOTEL TREATED ME MOST KINDLY last evening with a very special rate for the ol' *Nomad*. I'm out early, over to Sam's Restaurant for a fine breakfast, then I'm on my way south again. I am excited yet very anxious about this day, for I will be hiking the shoulders of busy US 1, which will lead me across a scary 23-mile desolate expanse, a literal no-man's-land by foot—all the way to the first Florida Key, Key Largo. It is interesting that I'm back on US 1 again. This will be my second trek o'er this famous byway, having hiked its path on the extreme northern end, clear up in the far reaches of Maine. In between, this odyssey has led me west into the Central time zone, then all the way back east into the Atlantic time zone, to finally return and settle me now, back into good old Eastern time.

Today I'm hiking across the easternmost reaches of the rivers of grass as described in the delightful book *The Everglades: Rivers of Grass*, written by Marjory *The Lady of the Glades* Stoneman Douglas. Here is a vast, mostly untamed area of South Florida's subtropics known to the Indians as Pahayokee, or "the grassy waters." This remarkable place is still home to nearly 300 varieties of birds, 600 kinds of fish, and more than 40 indigenous species of plants. But today, for the entire day, I will primarily see man's invasive presence in this grand scheme — hypnotically gazing at the highway before me as it merges to a quivering and seemingly endless point on the horizon.

As I hike along, stooping to pick up more change from time to time, I keep reminding myself that I will soon be in America's winter playground, the beautiful Florida Keys. Just before turning the bend and heading southwest onto Key Largo I'm jolted from my dreamy little bubble as my attention is drawn to an old pickup as it comes screeching and grinding to a most ungraceful halt on the shoulder behind me. I stop and turn to see a grizzly-looking chap emerge from the whirl of dust. He greets me with, "Did you hike the AT this summer?" I reply, "Why yes, I did, and I'm still going." With a broad beaming smile, now he says, "Well, so did I. You must be the *Nomad.* I've heard about you." Well, dang, here we go again — so now bracing the blast from the trucks and busses whizzing by I shake hands with *Gecko Goat,* one of the most notorious members of all the Hiker Trash Fratority! We laugh as we shake hands, only to shake our heads — and reminisce for the longest time. Thanks for stopping, *Gecko.* What a joy, finally seeing someone who hasn't felt compelled to ask me about my ski poles! I'm sure we'll meet again on up the trail. Take care, *Gecko!*

I am rewarded for my hike today in such a noble way. I'm 41 cents richer, the change in my pocket to show, and now before me is this wide and expansive walkway to hike on through Key Largo. I pull in for the evening right next to the Hobo Bar and Grill (how appropriate), here to be greeted by Angie at Neptune's Hideaway. I'm immediately blessed as I'm offered my own little hideaway under the coconut palms, right on their beautiful, sandy gulf-side beach, and I quickly pitch my tent for the evening. Then to head over — oh, yes — to the Hobo Bar and Grill! This frolic through the Keys is going to be a hoot, I just know it . . . I can see it all now!

> *There comes a time reward seems due*
> *Those toughing the trials at hand;*
> *'Cause from the lot the Lord's picked few,*
> *To lead the banner and band.*

[N. Nomad]

THURSDAY December 3, 1998
TRAIL DAY 292/5 ✦ TRAIL MILE 4318/92
LOCATION Abutment under Hawk Channel Bridge, Islamorada, MM 86

No problem blending in down here, beard, long hair, and all. Conversation is easy and I could just as easily be local. A little more sun (which will certainly be no problem) and I'll be a Parrothead for sure! Aww man, I see now why Jimmy loves and lives this place! Changes in latitude bring changes in attitude . . . ooh, yes! I manage to get up, go for a quick swim, and then get halfway cranking. I'm moving a little slowly, caused by a little too good of a time at the old Hobo Bar and Grill last night. I was sloshin' and healin' to port pretty bad by the time I got back to beachside. Just had a few frosties, that's it—sure glad I stayed away from Margaritaville!

Within the hour this morning I pull alongside the oceanside Holiday Isle Resort. This is a grand old (but just the least bit seedy) highrise hotel. Tourists are all about and there is much activity. I can't resist heading over. On the way I'm thinking, "*Nomad*, you Hiker Trash bum, you're going to get your butt tossed right out of this place." But then I decide, "Aww, what the heck, go ahead, old man, go for it!" And oh my, what a beautiful thing. This has got to be what all the snowbirds up north are dreaming of: white, sandy beaches, two tropical pools, five restaurants, a full-service marina, all kinds of water fun (the personal watercraft are already buzzing about), and the world famous Tiki Bar (which I wisely avoid).

Well, so far so good, so I decide to go for the finest of the fine . . . the penthouse Horizon Restaurant! I still haven't removed my backpack as I enter the classy glass elevator. On the way up I decide not to push my luck, so I drop my pack and remove my sweaty headband. As the elevator stops and the door opens, I'm immediately greeted by the hostess and just as quickly by the cashier. Both give me a beaming smile and warm greetings. Here I meet Karin Wehner and Erica McDonald. I had figured the place would be packed, what with the breakfast crowd and all, but to my surprise only a couple of tables over to one side are occupied. After propping my pack down the way, Karin escorts me in. I can't believe it: she's taking me straight to front and center, right to the table by the plate-glass window, the finest in the whole place! From here, I am afforded the most remarkable view o'er the entire resort and the ocean below. The table before me is set with the finest linen and silver—and the waiter comes directly with a chilled goblet of icewater. The girls continue to smile at me and the waiter is also beaming. You'd think their "ship" had just come in and I was the first mate!

Karin decides to wait on me and she comes to take my order. After rattling off a bunch of fancy menu items, I explain that good old bacon, eggs, and plenty of fried potatoes will work just fine. Of course, by now she's asked to hear my story, and while my breakfast is being prepared, the word quickly gets around to all the help, and definitely to the cook, for Karin soon sets before me a heaping plate of grub, certainly not the style for this kind of fine establishment. Well, folks, okay, certainly you know, and it just goes to show how wacky our take on any given situation can sometimes be, how it seems we have not a clue! These gracious and kind folks were happy to see me and they were obviously more than pleased to have me as their guest. In fact, that's exactly how it all turned out—I was their guest, because they would accept no payment for their service nor for the wonderful breakfast prepared for me. What an amazing time at the Horizon Restaurant! Back on the highway and heading on south, and in a few moments do I turn to look back at the grand old place, to take it all in one last time . . . and wouldn't you know? There they stand at the Horizon Restaurant's penthouse window, waving goodbye. Thanks, dear friends. Thank you for your kindness and your most gracious hospitality!

As I hike along today enjoying the warmth of the sun . . . I see another one lying by the side of the road; I saw two or three yesterday. Oh my, I know there's no way you'll buy this, but please believe me, because it's true. There's positively no way I could ever make this stuff up. And just what is it that I've been seeing lying along the way? Beer cans, folks . . . beer cans. "Big deal," you say. Well, yes, this is a big deal—because these beer cans all have straws sticking out of them—yes, straws! We've all seen people pulling on a can of sody pop with a straw, but sipping beer from a straw! See what I mean? Beats me! The Keys—

ah yes, folks, here's a totally different and most remarkable place. If you haven't been down here you've just gotta get to it—then maybe, just maybe, you'll understand!

What an absolutely blue-perfect day this has been. The Keys are gonna be all I'd hoped for, all I'd dreamed they could be . . . and then some!

The folks in the Keys, quite interestingly, sip their beer through a straw;
They scorch their fish four shades of black, yet eat their shellfish raw.
Indeed they're as kind as any you'll find 'long Main Street U.S. of A.
They'll stop to help a stranger along, even give'm the time a'day.

The weather down here? Hey, fine all year—'cept for the hurricane;
But the locals'll hunker and ride 'er out through the roar and the walls a'rain.
No finer place will you find on the face—of this earth, for your holiday.
The weather's warm and the local charm boasts a paradise for play.

So, come on down . . . jes' lounge 'round, and let ol' Sol kick in;
'Twill warm your heart and your bones'll start to feel like they'll work a'gin.
Yeah, folks done questioned my sanity, but the smartest thing I done,
Was to save the last o' this odyssey for the Keys and the tropical sun.

[N. Nomad]

FRIDAY December 4, 1998
TRAIL DAY 293/6 ✦ TRAIL MILE 4,388/112
LOCATION Beach by Long Key Channel Bridge, Long Key, MM 66

TRAFFIC RUNS ALL NIGHT IN THE KEYS, even the 18 wheelers—especially the 18 wheelers. Most folks down here probably don't notice, but when you're six feet under (not in the ground yet, folks!), on an abutment directly beneath the bridge, as I was last night, the tank battalion rumbling right above, you're inclined to notice! I could hear the heavy artillery coming long before it shook and vibrated my bones. The assault began with a low, sort of harmonic, rumble, hardly perceptible. Then the slow, ever-building crescendo presented. Finally came the grand crashing and eruption of it in a cacophonous, Richter-seven bombardment — the projectile dropping straight in. Oh but gee, isn't it so remarkable, and haven't we all marveled at the incredibly adaptive tolerance that's built into our mental and biological computer systems! For it was that after about the fourth or 20th of those microcosmic earthquakes, all caused by the tractor-trailers rumbling overhead, did I drift into the most pleasant and dream-propelled sleep.

I'm awakened this morning by fishermen passing through Hawk Channel. The morning is dawning cool and clear and I'm out to a diamond-crystal haze-free day in the Florida Keys. As I head ever south I am greeted and then caressed by the soft, warm sun and a most-gentle tropical breeze. Before me now are there such remarkably dazzling jewels of azure and turquoise, a sky so clear and transparent as to make its presence intimately close, so near that I can clutch it, much like a gossamer veil . . . and beside and before me to the horizon is the sea, so remarkably crystalline and pellucid as to appear much as a mirror of the boundless sky.

The hike today crosses the narrow and beautiful keys of the Upper and Lower Matacumbes, and the day has turned perfect, another take-it-for-granted day in the Keys. Soon I reach Islamorada. I can use some coated aspirin, so over to Eckerd's I go. No sooner do I get through the door than the pharmacist comes right away to assist me. "You a hiker?" he says. No rush now, so I give the guy my full pitch; he listens in astonishment. "What's your trail name?" he asks. "I'm the *Nimblewill Nomad*," I respond. He then replies, "Well, I'm *Church Mouse*, Class of '97." Glory be! Turns out he not only hiked with, but became good friends with, *Thunder Chicken*. Okay, okay, I won't say it!

The day passes quickly, and turning onto Fiesta Key, I soon arrive at Long Key State Recreation Area. On the south end and just before the bridge to Conch Key, one of the local conchs shows me a narrow path leading from the highway to the most picturesque and secluded beach. Here is a serene and peaceful paradise . . . just for me for the evening. I pitch right on the beach as the sun sets fire to the sea across the beautiful Straits of Florida. No incoming artillery tonight, just the peaceful lullaby played by the rhythmic waves of the sea gently caressing the sands along the beach at Long Key.

> *As I reflect this day's reward . . .*
> *the good that's come to me.*
> *I bow my head and thank the Lord,*
> *for this grand odyssey.*
>
> [N. Nomad]

SATURDAY December 5, 1998
TRAIL DAY 294/7 ✦ TRAIL MILE 4,355/129
LOCATION Dried-in town house near Seven Mile Bridge,
South Marathon, MM 49

IT IS ANOTHER BLUE-PERFECT DAY IN THE FLORIDA KEYS and as my trekking poles click away at the pavement, the miles click away beneath my feet. The journey south today takes me over Conch Key, Grassy Key, and Crawl Key, all the way to Marathon. I begin to sense now the end of this journey, for today the remaining number of miles will drop below 50 . . . less than 50 miles to go in a total of over 4,400 miles, less than three days in a total of nearly 300. And as the rhythmic motion of hiking this pavement lulls me into a dream-like state, my thoughts drift back and I return to the days spent with all the great friends I have made and all the memorable times I've had . . . like reaching Katahdin. What an emotional time and so, too, for the ending in Canada.

Oh, that final day in Canada, my 60th birthday, what a grand and memorable time. I was whisked away to the beautiful De Champlain home in Matane, there to remain the guest of those kind French Canadians for the whole of the weekend. They devoted their entire time to me; they hosted me, lavished me with gifts, introduced me to their friends, entertained and dined me, escorted me around, acted as my interpreters, and even helped me make the transition back into the real world as I shopped for and tried to find a pair of pants and a shirt, clothing that seemed so out of place to me after the meager trail gear I had become so accustomed to over the past ten months. These dear friends then took another entire day to drive me back to Matapédia, Québec, and to Pete Dube's delightful Restigouche Hotel.

Pete, as usual, was glad to see me and to put me up again as his guest. So I accepted his kind hospitality for the better part of four days as he, Gaby, Richard, and I had a grand time. Bruno and David had invited me to celebrate with them upon the completion of my journey in Canada, so to Bruno and Carole's house I went one evening to enjoy such a grand time with these kind and generous friends. After resting a couple more days and enjoying Pete's company, Maurice came from Kedgwick, New Brunswick, to pick me up and take me to Madeleine's place in Madawasca. Madeleine then drove me back to the border at Fort Fairfield, where yet another dear friend, Rod Newton, greeted me.

After spending the night at Rod's we headed into Presque Isle, Maine, to shop for a junk car to get me back to Georgia. That didn't take long, as Rod helped me come up with a very fine and very cheap clunker . . . good tires, new battery, power everything, the works, for 400 bucks! I could have taken a bus from there back to Georgia, but I wanted to take my time heading back south, stopping to see friends and family along the way, and to share the joy that's come to me, the result of this incredible odyssey . . . and that's just what I did, and it worked so well. I stopped first in Portland, where Dick Anderson had a huge reception for me at his office. Here I got to meet many of the great folks who are building the International Appalachian Trail in Maine. And there at the reception, what a joy it was seeing my dear friend *Easy Rider* again! He invited me to spend the night at his place and he, Nikki, and I had the finest time . . . and I finally got to hear *Easy Rider* play and sing. What an incredible talent!

From Maine it was on to *Stickman*'s lovely home in Freeport, New Hampshire, and from there back to Graymoor in Garrison, New York, to visit Father Fred. The next day I traveled on to Milton, Pennsylvania, to see Ronnie Spotts, an old teenage buddy, and what a joy getting into Hummelstown, Pennsylvania, to see *100# Stormcloud* again. From there I drove to Maryland to see dear family members, Mary and Margie, who had come all the way to Harpers Ferry to get me for the Fourth of July, a wonderfully planned reunion that was not to be because of my stupidity. In Virginia, I was able to see Larry Amos, an old childhood chum and schoolmate who I hadn't seen in over 40 years, and he, his wife Mary, and I shared a very happy time. I had missed going into Rusty's Hard Time Hollow on my way north, so I wheeled in there to spend some time and to get to know this interesting and friendly man. My final stop was back in Hot Springs, where I was welcomed most enthusiastically again . . . and hosted again by Elmer Hall at Sunnybank Inn.

I am jolted back to the day and away from this nostalgic dreaming by an old buggy full of teenagers. They want to have a little fun with the old hobo walking along with the "ski poles." That's okay, kids, have a good laugh on the old *Nomad*! I'm in North Marathon now and the street markers start clicking away: 125th Street, 110th Street, 83rd Street, 64th Street, and finally I pass mile marker 50. Just ahead is the Seven Mile Bridge. It's too late in the day to tackle this thing and the traffic is running hard and steady, so I hang a left onto a street where new town houses are being built. I find one that's most-near dried in, no doors or windows yet. No one's about, this being Saturday, so I head up to find the perfect place for the evening. I had indulged myself earlier, enjoying a fine meal at a local mom 'n' pop in Marathon, so my tummy's full and I'm snug and content. This has been a delightful and most memorable day hiking the Florida Keys.

> *"Out of the hinterwhere into the yon —*
> *Where all the friends of your youth have gone —*
> *Where the old schoolmate who laughed with you*
> *Will laugh again, as he used to do."*

[James Whitcomb Riley]

SUNDAY December 6, 1998
TRAIL DAY 295/8 ✦ TRAIL MILE 4,376/150
LOCATION Abutment under Torch Channel Bridge, Little Torch Key,
MM 28

THE HIKE SOUTH TODAY TAKES ME ACROSS the Seven Mile Bridge and the keys of Little Duck, Missouri, Ohio, Bahia Honda, Spanish Harbor, West Summerland, and Big Pine. Upon crossing Seven Mile

Bridge, one is considered to be entering the "Lower Keys." These are the largest and least developed of this island chain. This area, and on to Key West, is the locale sought by the true Parrotheads who want to get away from it all. Here lie the most tropic of the subtropics, home to the famed Key deer, the beautiful great white heron, the ubiquitous pelican, the raucous gull, the rare American crocodile, and myriad other unique and exotic marine, amphibious, and earthbound plants and animals.

There are many different ways to see and experience the Keys. From Miami you might choose to fly, which will require less than an hour of your time, or you might come by car, which would consume less than four hours. You could bicycle your way down, which many do, taking a couple of days; or you might choose to travel by boat; this would get you through here in a leisurely fashion in three or four days. And then you could always choose to walk—yes, walk! That would take you well over a week. Now, having made this comparison, let me ask (should you hope to see, experience, then ultimately savor the least of this "paradise playground" thing): Might a week of hiking it rather than a few hours or so of rushing it—in that time spent—might there possibly be greater value, greater reward? Indeed, friends, it is true. You cannot possibly experience the pleasure of meeting all the great folks down here nor gain even the least bit of understanding for what this place is all about, for there is such a vibrant, joyful, and carefree magic that weaves its spell throughout this faraway tropical island paradise. No, folks! You could not experience even the least of it by flying or driving or biking or even by boating through. You've got to walk this remarkable place to really get to know it, to know the people and the magic of this special little corner of the world known as the Florida Keys.

I'm up and out at first light, for I want to get across the Seven Mile Bridge before the crushing traffic of the day begins. I reach the highest point on the bridge's center span a little after 7:30 a.m. Up till now it's been going pretty good . . . but then it happens, one of the most incredible phenomenon that I have ever experienced in all of my 60 years on this earth. At one time or another I've dealt with just about everything Mother Nature could possibly dish out . . . a grand chunk of which has occurred this past 11 months. I've endured all types of conditions, from scorching heat, to floodwater, to driving rain, to sleet, hail, snow, and even a couple of tornadoes. But up until now, and though what's just come to pass is the result of man's design, I've never had anything like this happen to me ever before! Those of you who've lived through an earthquake will surely understand the horrifying fright and the uncontrollable shudder that comes from having the earth literally jump up and down. The ground beneath our feet (and especially a huge thing made out of concrete) is not supposed to move around, let alone jump up and down!

So here I stand, the first really big truck of the day having just passed. As the fully loaded tanker approached I could hear its rumbling and feel the vibration as it made the climb, and just before it reached me I could feel the concrete literally sink beneath my feet! As the tanker passed, the roadway rose abruptly in the most alarming fashion, a sensation most like standing on a trampoline. Well, I'll tell you folks, this scares the holy-h right out of me! I grab the railing and hang on for dear life! It seems as though I'm halfway to the moon up here already, fearful and scared to death by the height. I'm all by myself on this incredible mass of concrete . . . and it's flipping me up and down in the most frightful way! The undulating wave created by the rolling hulk moving south ahead of me seems to take forever to finally settle down.

Oh my, what a nightmarish sensation, what an ordeal! For a brief moment I was sure I was a goner—the whole bridge doomed to collapse, thence to plunge into the Straits of Florida, taking me right along with it in the process. Whew! I suppose you won't be surprised if I tell you that I recall very little about the remainder of this day.

True happiness is seldom found among the polished stone,
For on the path where most have trod, scant faith has ever grown.
But should we journey o'er the way where less the path is worn,
'Tis there the most pure radiant light brings forth that glorious morn.
Whereon we rise to greet the day to find our prayers fulfilled.
Pure joy and peace fill full our cup just like our Father willed.
But oh the faith to pass this way, the path few e'er have known;
For 'til we see God's face have we—gone long and far alone.

[N. Nomad]

MONDAY December 7, 1998
TRAIL DAY 296/9 ✦ TRAIL MILE 4,387/161
LOCATION Home of Phil and Ruth Weston, Sugarloaf Key, MM 17

THERE ARE LOTS OF BRIDGES DOWN HERE IN THE KEYS, and that
makes for lots of bridge abutments. I could have found a place along the
beach to pitch last night, but pulling off and ducking in under Torch
Channel Bridge was just a lot easier. There was the steady hum and vibration from the traffic right overhead to deal with, but after walking all day
in the sun and wind it wasn't long until the next thing I knew it was today.

As I'm out and on my way this morning, hiking into another
absolutely perfect day in the Keys, I am filled with such a grand and glorious feeling. For even though tomorrow will no doubt bring another
very emotional time my way, much as on Katahdin and the last day in
Canada, tomorrow being the last day of this incredible odyssey, my mind
is filled now with such happy thoughts. Thoughts that flood over me in
the most blissful and satisfying way, settling me into a mood of total and
absolute, perfect contentment, most-near nirvana. I am thinking of so
many remarkable things that have happened on this journey, things that
simply lie beyond the realm of coincidence, there being no possible way
the wildest of odds could have figured or played into many of the circumstances.

And just for example and to make my point: How many millions
and millions of people live along the sprawling expanse of this eastern
North American continent? Ah, but yesterday did Ed Williams's path
cross my path again! If you recall, Ed and Mary Ann were the trail
angels who came to Punch Bowl Shelter clear back on the AT in Virginia
to bring their magic to *Joliet Joe* and me. Well, yesterday, this van pulled
off the road into a little wayside. I recognized it right away—and right
away did I see and recognize Ed's smiling face again! Oh, were both of
us ever beset with amazement! Ed said, "*Nomad*, is that you—you still
hiking?" Returning his beaming smile, I said, "Yes, Ed, yes, it's me and
I'm still hiking!" At that point, Ed began rummaging around his van,
trying to find a little bit of trail magic to hand out yet again. Judging
from his anxious manner, he most surely had never been caught in such

a predicament before, not having something to dispense to a weary, hungry hiker. As he continued digging around, I mentioned that it wasn't necessary to hand me something every time he saw me . . . this being the third time! But Ed would hear none of that, and in a while he finally came up with a bottle of Gatorade, a bag of pretzels, and an apple! He then beamed with pride as he handed me the goodies!

My hike today takes me across the keys of Middle Torch, Ramrod, Summerland, and Cudjoe. It's a very short hike, as I'm bound for Sugarloaf Key and the home of Phil and Ruth Weston, friends of my good friend Frank back in Nimblewill Creek. In a conversation recently with the Westons, Frank had mentioned that I was heading their way. That's all it took for them to insist I stop at their home before heading out on my final day to Key West. So turning at Sugarloaf Lodge now, I'm headed for Bonefish Lane and the Weston place. And oh my, am I soon greeted by such a beautiful home and by such beautiful people! I am ushered immediately to my private room, right beside the swimming pool and right next to the bath and shower . . . where I quickly head, having enjoyed only the saltwater baths of the turquoise sea since leaving Homestead. After a grand supper prepared by Ruth and after much welcome and enjoyable conversation with Phil and Ruth, I retire to sleep and dream contentedly about the morrow.

> *"There is a destiny that makes us brothers;*
> *None goes his way alone:*
> *All that we send into the lives of others*
> *Comes back into our own."*

[Edwin Markham]

TUESDAY December 8, 1998
TRAIL DAY 297/10 ✦ TRAIL MILE 4,404/178
LOCATION Monument marking southernmost point of
eastern North American continent, Key West, MM 00

I HAD PROMISED MARK BAKER, producer at WPBT Channel 2 in West Palm Beach, that I would call him before reaching Key West, so upon arriving at the Weston home yesterday afternoon, I got in touch with Mark at the television studio in Miami. He commented with much excitement that he and Allan would both be seeing me again and that they would be there at the southernmost point monument to greet me at the completion of this odyssey. Phil and Ruth both plan to be there too, and I have been invited to return with them again this evening and rest and recuperate for a while here at their beautiful home on Sugarloaf Key before catching a bus back north. After a whopping breakfast and a cheerful sendoff by the Westons, I'm out and on my way to the end of this little corner of the world: the Gulf of Mexico and the Caribbean Sea at Key West.

It's another turquoise, blue-perfect day in the Florida Keys—as if there could be any other kind of day in paradise—and I'm out and on my way with a glad, joy-filled heart and a light, brisk step. It seems the journey takes no time at all as I hike along today, for I have become totally immersed in the thoughts and memories from the past 11 months as they flood over me in a tumultuous and triumphant cascade. The keys of Sugarloaf, Saddlebunch, Shark, Big Coppit, Boca Chica, and Stock Island are already little more than a blur in my memory as I turn onto North Roosevelt Boulevard in Key West. I am at milemarker 4 now, a little over an hour from the end of it. I soon turn onto Whitehead Street as I head toward that very last street—Oh, but is there such a street so named in every borough and every little burg in this grand and glorious land—but here is the name so appropriate, a street called South Street.

I have oft heard and have also often read the short little phrase "The journey is the destination." But not until now did I understand the meaning of those words. They are so true, for as I near and as I see the end of this, I realize that the ending is nothing more than that—the end. But what has come to pass during these past 297 days, over these last 4,400 miles, has brought the joy and true wonder of it. I have been blessed in ways that could not have been imagined, ways that certainly until now could have been but little understood. They are blessings both in the knowledge now of the undeniable and unshakable truth that is this grand existence—that comes to fruition only from the universal love of man—my faith in that glorious brotherhood firmly and forevermore restored, and the indescribable grandeur and majesty of Mother Nature's God-given treasures. Ah, her boundless treasures—the magnificent mountains; mountains of all the ages, the spectacular Appalachians, and the rich and fertile lands that sprawl the eastern grand expanse of this continent, the mystifying and majestic horizons of Canada, and these heaven-blessed United States of America.

It is humbling indeed to have been brought into the light and unto the grace of Almighty God, for we did travel together as constant companions o'er this entire journey, and though I have indeed suffered and been tried by the earthbound miseries and lonely times of which I've written, so it is that in His presence and through His grace have I endured, for His presence here within me was steady each and every day, constant, never once withheld. We have journeyed together and I have experienced the unshakable reassurance and steadfast love of God, and I have been and am now the benefactor of such peace and joy in my life that only comes from within—a gift that is the light of His light that radiates from His eternal presence deep within my soul.

I falter as I approach the end at the Gulf of Mexico, but my dear new friends of most recent days are here to reassure me and to cheer me home—and to share in my triumph and joy. Thanks to Phil and Ruth, and Mark and Allan, and a delightful young couple bicycling from Daytona Beach, Milton and Grace Gonzales. Thank you, Lord. We've done it, we've done it. And thank you, dear family and friends; thank you all in the wonderful legion who have befriended me, uplifted me, and brought your prayers and encouragement unto me throughout this most remarkable and memorable journey—the "Odyssey of '98."

> *"Even his griefs are a joy long after to one*
> *who remembers all that he wrought and endured."*
>
> [Homer, *The Odyssey*]

Credits

ALVAREZ, S. A., Fr. Fred
TRAIL DAYS 189, 191, 192—"The Story of Hikers in Graymoor." Garrison, NY: 1998. Excerpts reprinted by permission of author.

ANDERSON, Joan Wester
TRAIL DAY 267—*Where Miracles Happen: The True Stories of Heavenly Encounters.* Brooklyn: Brett Books, Inc., 1994. Reprinted by permission of publisher.

BARTRAM, William
TRAIL DAYS 39, 102, 110—*The Travels of William Bartram.* New York: Dover Publications, Inc., 1955. Reprinted by permission of publisher.

BRILL, David
TRAIL DAY 174—*As Far as the Eye Can See.* Nashville: Rutledge Hill Press, 1990. Reprinted by permission of publisher and author.

CALLWOOD, June
TRAIL DAYS 275, 276, 277—*Portrait of Canada.* Garden City, NY: Doubleday Direct, Inc., 1981. Reprinted by permission of publisher.

CRANDALL, Hugh
TRAIL DAY 163—*Shenandoah: The Story behind the Scenery.* Las Vegas: KC Publications, 1990. Reprinted by permission of publisher.

CURRAN, Jan D.
TRAIL DAYS 43, 48, 70—*The Appalachian Trail—Journey of Discovery.* Highland City, FL: Rainbow Books, Inc., 1991. Reprinted by permission of publisher.

DAVIS, Hattie C.
TRAIL DAY 110—*Reflections of Cataloochee Valley and Its Vanished People from the Great Smoky Mountains.* Maggie Valley, NC: Hattie C. Davis, 1999. Reprinted by permission of author.

DEEDS, Jean M.
TRAIL DAY 167—*There Are Mountains to Climb.* Indianapolis: Silverwood Press, 1996. Reprinted by permission of author.

DeHAAN, Kurt, Managing Editor
TRAIL DAYS 28, 112, 242, 273, 289—*Our Daily Bread.* Volume 43, Numbers 6,7, 8. Grand Rapids: RBC Ministries, 1998. Excerpts of verse by R. Kelso Carter, Frances Jane Crosby, Clair Hess, Linda Shivers Leech, and David Sper. Reprinted by permission of publisher.

DOYLE, Jr., Warren
TRAIL DAYS 148, 230, 262—"Walking the Entire Appalachian Trail." Waynesboro, PA: By Author, 1999. Reprinted by permission of author.

GATEWOOD, Emma *Grandma*
TRAIL DAY 127—"The Reward of Nature," a poem. Reprinted by permission of the family of Emma *Grandma* Gatewood, Lucy G. Seeds.

HEMPHILL, Paul
TRAIL DAY 225 — *Me and the Boy: Journey of Discovery.* New York: Macmillan Publishing Co., 1986. Reprinted by permission of author.

HORTON, D. Sue Jones
TRAIL DAY 256 — *Tranquil Journey.* New Rochelle, NY: New Hope Books, 1997. Excerpt from the poem "The Road That Leads to Home." Reprinted by permission of author.

JARDINE, Ray
TRAIL DAY 29 — *Beyond Backpacking.* LaPine, OR: AdventureLore Press, 1996. Reprinted by permission of author.

JENKINS, Peter
TRAIL DAY 265 — *Walk Across America.* Farmington Hill, MI: Gale Group. Copyright © 1981 Peter and Barbara Jenkins. Reprinted by permission of publisher.

LEONARD, R. Michael
TRAIL DAY 61 — From the article "The Appalachian Trail Connection." Winter issue *Outdoor Alabama.* Montgomery, 1998. Excerpts reprinted by permission of author.

MARET, Darrell
TRAIL DAY 182 — *The Philosopher's Guide.* Harpers Ferry: Appalachian Trail Conference, 1986. Reprinted by permission of author.

LUXENBERG, Larry
Walking the Appalachian Trail. Mechanicsburg, PA: Stackpole Books, 1994.

TRAIL DAY 18 — Reprinted by permission of author.

TRAIL DAY 26 — Reprint from interviews with Leonard M. Adkins by permission of author and Leonard M. Adkins.

TRAIL DAY 115 — Reprint of interview with Dorothy Hansen by permission of author and Dorothy Hansen.

TRAIL DAY 212 — Reprint of interview with David Horton by permission of author and David Horton.

MERTON, Thomas
TRAIL DAY 151 — *The Seven Storey Mountain.* Orlando: Harcourt, Inc. (HBT), 1948 and renewed 1976 by the Trustees of the Merton Legacy Trust. Reprinted by permission of the publisher.

O'KEEFE, M. Timothy
TRAIL DAY 42 — *Hiking Florida.* Helena, MT: Falcon Publishing, Inc. 1997. Reprinted by permission of publisher.

OLSON, Sigurd F.
TRAIL DAYS 101, 147, 166 — *Open Horizons.* New York: Alfred A. Knopf, Inc., 1969. *Wilderness Days.* New York: Alfred A. Knopf, Inc. 1972. Copyrights reverted to author. Reprinted by permission of author's family, Robert K. Olsen.

ROQUEMORE, Susan/HOBSON, Joan
TRAIL DAYS 37, 42 — **From Here to There on the Florida Trail.** Cedar Key, FL: Hobson's Choice Publications, 1998. Reprinted by permission of authors.

ROSS, Cindy

TRAIL DAYS 92, 202—© 1987 by Cindy Ross. Reprinted by permission from *Journey on the Crest* by Cindy Ross. Published by the Mountaineers.

SHAFFER, Earl V.

TRAIL DAYS 98, 117, 124, 132, 143, 160, 220—*Walking with Spring*. Harpers Ferry: Appalachian Trail Conference, 1983. Reprinted by permission of author.

SMITH, Deborah A. *Twilight*

TRAIL DAY 194—From the song "White Blazes Lead Me On" Copyright © 1998 by Deborah A. Smith. Reprinted by permission of composer and lyricist.

STOLTZ, Jim *Walkin' Jim*

TRAIL DAY 271—Wild Wind Records. From the song "Morning in the Mountains" by "Walkin' Jim Stoltz." Reprinted by permission of composer and lyricist.

STRAIN, Paula M.

TRAIL DAY 172—*The Blue Hills of Maryland*. Vienna, VA: Potomac Appalachian Trail Club, 1993. Reprinted by permission of author.

TARAN, S.A., Fr. Peter

TRAIL DAY 190—As quoted from the *Putnam Reporter Dispatch*. Reprinted by permission of author.

THURBER, James

TRAIL DAY 278—*Further Fables of Our Time*. New York: Simon and Schuster, Copyright © 1956 James Thurber. Copyright © 1984 Rosemary A. Thurber. Excerpt from the fable "The Shore and the Sea" reprinted by permission of Rosemary A. Thurber.

WADDLE, Sam

TRAIL DAY 186—*The Greeneville Sun*. Greeneville, TN: Excerpts from "A Mountain Man Named Sam . . ." 6-26-98. Reprinted by permission of Sam Waddle.

WADNESS, Kenneth

TRAIL DAY 173—*Sojourn in the Wilderness*. Prospect, KY: Harmony House Publishers, Copyright © 1997 Ken Wadness. Reprinted by permission of author.

Trail names of individual AT hikers are shown in *italics* followed by real names (in parentheses) where hikers' real names are cited. The rationale for the creation or assignment of a trail name is explained on pages 327–28.